JUST ONE **CATCH**

ALSO BY TRACY DAUGHERTY

Fiction

One Day the Wind Changed
Late in the Standoff
Axeman's Jazz
It Takes a Worried Man
The Boy Orator
The Woman in the Oil Field
What Falls Away
Desire Provoked

Nonfiction

Hiding Man
Five Shades of Shadow

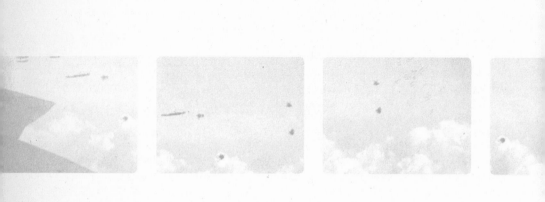

Tracy Daugherty

JUST ONE
CATCH

A BIOGRAPHY OF **Joseph Heller**

The Robson Press

813.54
HEL

First Published in the United States in 2011 by St Martin's Press, LLC, 175 Fifth Avenue,
New York, New York 10010

This edition published in Great Britain in 2011 by
The Robson Press
Biteback Publishing Ltd
Westminster Tower
3 Albert Embankment
London
SE1 7SP

ISBN 978-1-84954-172-5

10 9 8 7 6 5 4 3 2 1

A CIP catalogue record for this book is available from the British Library.

Printed and bound in Great Britain by
TJ International, Padstow, Cornwall

For my family, now and then and to come:

May the generations be blessed

"You can't keep ducking forever."
"I can till I die."

—JOSEPH HELLER,
Something Happened

I am not yet able . . . to know myself; so it
seems to me ridiculous, not yet knowing this,
to investigate alien matters.

—SOCRATES, PLATO, *Phaedrus*

It is impossible to predict or control how you
will be remembered after your death. In that way,
dying is like having children: you never know what
will come out. In Beckett's *Endgame,* he asks his
parents, in effect, "Why did you have me?" and
the father replies, "We didn't know it would be you."

—JOSEPH HELLER, 1975

CONTENTS

W HAT IS MISSING in the moment he will return to, in memory and in writing, for the rest of his life is his sense of himself. The moment is simultaneously brief and prolonged, distorted first by adrenaline, later by the vagaries of memory. And it is dangerous. In his maturity, he will concede that most of us are never more conscious of the pulse in our wrists and the thrumming in our minds than in threatening circumstances. When faced with physical harm or the possibility of sudden extinction, our senses rouse themselves and life becomes both dreamlike (the minutes stretched by an uncanny feeling of moving in slow motion) and wrenchingly vivid (each small gesture an agony of air against skin). But now, in the nose of the thin aluminum plane, as metal, glass, and his teeth rattle to the point of tearing loose, nothing is clear, least of all a fleeting, time-dependent *I*.

Here is what seemed certain just before he crawled into the transparent womb at the front of the B-25. It was August 15, 1944. He was about to fly his second mission of the day. Earlier, he and the rest of his crew had been ordered to attack enemy gun positions at Pointe des Issambres, near Saint-Tropez, France, but heavy cloud formations had prevented them from dropping their bombs. According to military reports, flak cover at the target was "[h]eavy, intense and accurate."

Just one week earlier over Avignon, on the morning of August 8, he had witnessed flak bursts cripple a bomber. "I was in the leading flight," he recalled, "and when I looked back to see how the others were doing, I saw one plane pulling up above and away from the others, a wing on fire beneath a tremendous, soaring plume of orange flame. I saw a parachute billow open, then another, then one more before the plane began spiraling downward, and that was all." Two men died.

Now, on this follow-up mission a week later, the goal was to destroy the Avignon railroad bridges on the Rhône River. It was his thirty-seventh assignment overall, since the end of May, when he had first been stationed at the Alesan Air Field on the island of Corsica, west of Italy.

As he had done thirty-six times before, he took a last pee by the side of the runway (there were no bathrooms aboard the B-25), then slid down the narrow tunnel beneath the cockpit to the bomber's Plexiglas nose cone. The tunnel was too small for a man wearing bulky equipment; he was forced to park his parachute in the navigator's area behind him. Up front, in the glass bowl (the crew called it the "hothouse"), he always felt vulnerable and exposed. He found his chair. He donned his headset intercom so he could talk to comrades he could no longer see in other parts of the plane. The wheels left the ground. Now he was alone, in a blur of blue.

As his squadron began its approach to the Rhône, German antiaircraft guns let loose and flak filled the air. A bomber in another squadron got "holed." A spark, a flash. The plane lost a wing. It dived. No parachutes.

Hurtling through space, the man in the glass cone watched the shining metal fall. A minute later, he was steering his plane. His pilot and the copilot had taken their hands off the flight controls. It was time for him to drop his bombs, and so, to assure a steady approach to the target, he commanded the plane's movements using the automatic bombsight, steering left, steering right. For about sixty seconds, no evasive action would be possible, just a sure zeroing in.

Almost. Almost. There. He squeezed the toggle switch that released the bombs. Immediately, his pilot, Lt. John B. Rome, banked up, away from the target. Rome, twenty, was one of the youngest pilots in the squadron, with little combat experience. The copilot, fearing this green kid was moving too fast and about to stall the engines, seized the controls, and the plane went into a sudden steep dive, back to an altitude where it could be holed by curtains of flak.

In the nose cone, the man who had overseen the bombs slammed into the roof of his compartment. His headset jack pulled loose from its outlet and began whipping about his head. He heard nothing. He couldn't move. I "believed with all my heart and quaking soul that my life was ending and that we were going down, like the plane on fire I had witnessed plummeting only a few minutes before," he remembered. "I had no time for anything but terror."

Just as quickly as it had begun its descent, the plane shot upward, away from the flak, one moment yo-yoing into the next: a vanishing yet interminable instant. Now he was pinned to the floor, looking for a handhold, anything to grasp. The silence was horrifying. Was he the only crewman left alive? *Was* he alive? Would this moment never end, or had everything already ceased?

He noticed the jack to his headset lying free near his chair. He plugged himself back in and a roar of voices pierced his ears. "The bombardier doesn't answer," he heard someone shout. "Help him, help the bombardier." "I'm the bombardier," he said, "and I'm all right," but the very act of asserting what should have been obvious made him wonder if it was true.

TWENTY-TWO YEARS LATER, is it the same self that walks the hills of Corsica, looking for traces of the young man he was, when, as a second lieutenant, he flew sixty bombing missions between May and October 1944—looking, so he can write about his wartime experiences, as he has before and as he will do again?

He is, a taxi driver tells him, the first American from the old Alesan Air Field ever to return here. To celebrate his reverence for the past, the driver arranges a meal for him and his family in a local restaurant with something that resembles pan-broiled veal but is probably goat, with bread and cheese and wine. His wife and children, a ten-year-old boy and a fourteen-year-old girl, tolerate his nostalgia with gentle, mostly indulgent irritation. "Be nice to daddy," the girl tells her brother. "He's trying to recapture his youth." Of course she's right, he thinks, and he feels stupendously foolish. "I [have] come to the wrong place," he tells himself. "My war [is] over and gone."

The only remaining evidence of his bombing missions, at least that he can find as he travels, is a hole in a mountain near Poggibonsi. The mountain was not the target. That day, nervous, his attention drifting— there had been no flak, no danger—he had released his bombs a second or two too late (he remembers this clearly) and blasted the side of the mountain instead of the railroad bridge he was supposed to blow apart. The bridge, hit by other planes that day, has long since been repaired, and looks better than ever.

Time yo-yos back and forth as he crosses green fields with his wife and kids: on the one hand, it's as though certain events never occurred, and then, just as he is wondering if a bombardier with his name and face ever really came to Corsica, he encounters a Frenchman on a Swiss train, a train he has decided to take after giving up touring old battle-fields, where the past has been erased like the bounty of annual harvests. And it is here, where he least expects it, that the ghost of an old self returns, as indistinct yet insistent as a reflection of his features in the window of the train.

The Frenchman—from somewhere near Avignon, perhaps—speaks no English. He smokes cigarette after smelly cigarette. He says he is going to visit his boy in a hospital, where he lies with a terrible head wound from the war in Indochina. He weeps. In French, he tells the American and his befuddled children, "You will find out, you will find out." The future tense seems wrong. Hasn't he *already* found out, already sat among the wounded? But no. He has not witnessed everything. Time still has surprises to spring. Apparently, old fears, and the reasons for them, never disappear. "Why was he crying?" the boy asks once the Frenchman has walked away, clear to the other end of the train car. "What did he say?" the American's daughter asks. Where, now, is the old bombardier? *Who* is he? "Nothing," he says.

SIX MONTHS after peppering the Rhône with explosives, is it the same self that learns about the broken tail of a plane he has occupied before, and that has just barely survived a midair collision with a sister plane? The sister plane, identified in manifests as 8U 43-4064, lost a wing and spun out of control after becoming unbalanced in a strong wind and grazing the other bomber, 8P 43-27657. None of 8U's crew got out alive. 8P limped back to the airfield, its tail as tattered as a piece of paper torn from the rings of a notebook. "How they landed the plane safely is still bewildering our operations officer and the hundreds of men who saw the damaged craft come in," states the group's War Diary for January 21, 1945.

Six months earlier, on August 23, 1944, orders for the 340th Bombardment Group, 488th Squadron, list "2nd Lt. J. Heller" as a crew member on 8P. Among 8U's crew that day is "2nd Lt. F. Yohannan," known affectionately to his buddies as "Yo-Yo." Heller trained with him stateside. If time really could warp, the way it often seemed to when men took to the skies and stress began to alter their perceptions, the fates of 8P and 8U could have intertwined earlier, on the day Heller and Yohannan climbed aboard them. The lives of the two men would have ended differently than they did. History would have been changed. Not for everyone, of course. Or yes—yes, for everyone, whether they knew it or not. Absolutely.

MANY DECADES after concluding his sixty missions, after writing about the war and then writing about it again (including an account of a day in which a B-25 nicknamed the "Schnapps Yo-Yo" disappeared inside a heavy cloud, in the space of only forty-five seconds, never to be seen or heard from again—no flare, no radio message or wreckage), he would be chastised by some literary critics for not writing realistically about individuals in his fiction or plumbing his characters' personalities. "His self-insight comes and goes," one book reviewer would complain. "One might say that [early trauma], never fully faced, led to a certain hollowness, which became part of [his literary] style . . . an unbearable lightness ballasted by melancholy."

Apropos of this charge—that his characters, and perhaps the author, lack a sense of self—he would tell a radio interviewer in 1998, a year before his death, "I . . . don't understand what's meant by . . . time as a dimension. [And] the very words I'm using now to say this are not words I'm choosing to use, my brain is choosing to use them and I can't control my brain. . . . [It's possible] we have no control over what we say or what we do, over what our personalities are like. We can't bring our-selves to believe that. But just because we can't believe it does not mean that it isn't so."

"I'M THE BOMBARDIER," he insisted.

"Then go back and help him, help the gunner," a voice told him through his intercom. "He's hurt."

He crawled back through the narrow passageway toward the rear of the plane and emerged from the tunnel like a baby being born. The side gunner, a young man named Frankel, lay bleeding on the vibrating floor. A hole gaped in the aluminum wall of the plane. An oval wound tore across the gunner's thigh. The bombardier fought a tide of nausea. He barely knew this kid. His squadron had about 100 officers and 350 enlisted men; different crews flew different bombers every mission.

"I'm cold," Frankel said.

In fact, at this altitude—over 49,000 feet, above the flak—temperatures could reach minus twenty degrees Fahrenheit. Gunners were told that their bare hands would stick to the metal surfaces of their machine guns if they were not careful. Exposed liquids, including blood, would freeze instantly.

"We'll be home soon. You'll be all right," the bombardier told the writhing boy. He was chilled, too, and still fighting nausea, from the sight of the gash in the gunner's leg and the smell of his own uniform (most of the men rarely cleaned their flight suits—why wash off your luck?). He held his nose away from his fleece and reached for some sulfa powder. As he poured the powder into Frankel's wound, as he prepared a shot of morphine—all the while, the kid chattering about the cold—2nd Lt. Joseph Heller convinced himself (what self there was) he would not get out of this alive.

PART ONE **Good Fellows**

1. Domestic Engagements

SAN ANGELO, TEXAS, in April 1945 was home to over five million sheep, and considered itself the inland wool capital of the United States. It was among the nation's largest mohair producers, served by the Santa Fe Railroad, which hauled the city's wool products across the country and brought in over one million dollars in annual revenue. Though automobiles were still a luxury for most people, traffic snarled San Angelo's streets. The downtown area—in a city of just under fifty thousand folks—was booming. Men came to buy Prince Albert tobacco—at sixty-seven cents a can, an easy path to personal style and sophistication. Women shopped for Lydia E. Pinkham's Vegetable Compound, whose newspaper ads in the *San Angelo Standard* promised to "help women who on occasion feel nervous, fidgety, irritable, tired, and a bit blue."

If they felt nervous and tired, it may have been because more young men than ever, just back from fighting in Europe, thronged San Angelo's eateries, alleyways, and movie theaters—along with the wool trade, the cause of the city's boom. "There was a 'Western Craze' . . . after the war that was sweeping the nation. We were making decorative spurs and buckles and even had traveling salesmen who went all over Texas wholesaling our goods," Chase Holland III, owner of Holland's down-town, told a local reporter in 2007 when asked about the "good old days." The store was one of eleven jewelry shops that opened to serve returning soldiers eager to surprise their sweethearts with engagement rings, put the war behind them, and move ahead with careers. In their stiff uniforms and spit-shined shoes, the young men would mill around the glass counters, shyly, standing aside when slammed by the smell of wool. Now and then, a "pretty grubby" fellow, someone who looked "like he had just finished shearing a thousand sheep," in Holland's de-scription, would push forward, determined to examine necklaces, ear-rings, and bracelets. Unlike the soldiers, most of whom were starting from scratch, the ranchers were doing just dandy. They knew what they wanted, and they could afford the best baubles.

Many of the servicemen were biding their time in Texas, assigned here while waiting to be discharged under the military's impending point system, whereupon they would join their families or fiancées in other parts of the country. Goodfellow Field, occupying over a thou-sand acres four miles southeast of downtown, and consisting of a pilot-training school with three paved runways, seven auxiliary landing fields, extensive housing facilities, and a circular concrete swimming pool, was their home. The field had been named for a local pilot who had died in turbulent skies over France in World War I.

For those who had never previously visited West Texas, the dry, flat landscape came as a shock. Often in the late afternoon, mournful thun-der rolled south across the plains, accompanied by heavy winds. With-out warning, sand could kick up, whip about the treeless terrain, and make the day go dark. Flying particles swelled the air. (Within a few years, a sudden swift tornado would kill thousands of sheep and se-verely damage several planes at Goodfellow.) Still, most of the boys were happy to stroll at leisure across the solid ground, stretch their arms, and breathe, even if occasionally it meant filling their mouths with grit.

Just a few months before, the boys had had more reason to appreci-ate Goodfellow Field: Its Instrument School and Post Operations arm employed seventeen Women Airforce Service Pilots. They served as flight trainers and inspected aircraft that had been repaired after being red-lined for serious malfunctions, to see if they were fit once more for students. Some of the male pilots "were quite dubious whether or not we were capable of flying anything larger than a kite," said Jimmie Parker, one of the WASPs. But Maj. John Hardy, the base's director of flying, said the girls always compared favorably to the boys. The WASP program was disbanded at Goodfellow in December 1944 because the attrition rate among combat pilots had proven to be lower than expected, leading to a surplus of male pilots. Nevertheless, under the command of Col. Harold A. Gunn, Goodfellow maintained an easygoing, cordial atmosphere; on the base, the worst behavior was likely to come from the weather.

Joseph Heller arrived in San Angelo in early March. The base no longer has a file on him, but his personal flight records clarify the chronology. His last combat mission was on October 15, 1944, a bombing raid on railroad bridges at Ronco Scrivia, Italy, amid "scant, inacc[urate]" flak, according to the military report. Heller left Corsica for Naples on January 3, 1945. From there, he was shipped to the States, arriving in Atlantic City on January 28. From October to January, he'd had a lot of time to fill in a wet, muddy tent. Transportation home could be delayed for many reasons, including incomplete paperwork, bad weather, difficulties arranging passage back to the States, and the military's insistence that men in line for awards, including the Air Medal for number of missions flown, with clusters for additional missions, hang around to receive them.

"I pretty much enjoyed [Texas]," Heller recalled. Those spring months were far better than the "deeply depressing, incapacitating winter . . . into which I was harshly plunged on my furlough after I'd returned by steamship to the States from Corsica in January and found myself back in Coney Island," where he'd grown up, he said.

Nearly twenty-two, he was a slender, big-boned man just under six feet tall, with a dimpled chin and dark hair, whose short military cut could not hide its tendency to curl. Years later, a journalist, describing a photograph of him taken at about this time, said "his large nose and his eyes sit uneasily on a dark, skinny face. He looks scared and underfed . . . the eyes seem to stare directly outward and directly inward at the same time." Easy in his body, self-contained yet friendly, he was well liked in spite of feeling, later on, that he did not make much of an impression on anyone with whom he served in the military (his speech alone, swift and plentiful, peppered with personal tics and a Brooklyn accent, would have left its impress on boys from other parts of the country, with hard *t*'s at the ends of words, *r*'s slipping almost into *w*'s, and swallowed final phrases). His perception that few people noticed him says more about the intensity of his inner life, and his focus, than it does about his capacity to socialize and accommodate himself to just about any situation.

He had "almost nothing to do" at Goodfellow, he wrote in his memoir *Now and Then,* but that was okay because "I am generally not a hard person to please." It would have been just fine with him if Jimmie Parker and her fellow WASPs returned to oversee flight training and airplane inspections on base. After completing sixty missions in Europe, and especially after believing he was doomed on his thirty-seventh mission, he wanted nothing more to do with flying craft. Hence, the steamship home from Italy. "I was so terrified on my last few missions, I made a vow that if I ever got out of [the] war alive, I would never go up in an airplane again," he said.

His base pay at Goodfellow would have been half again as high if he had agreed to the required four hours of flight time a month, but upon first returning to the States and undergoing a medical exam in Atlantic City, he told the military doctor that the memory of gasoline fumes inside a plane was sickening to him. At the time, Heller believed he was merely lying to the doctor, just looking for a way to dillydally until he had earned enough points for a discharge, but the more he talked to the medic, he said, the more he realized the lie "turned out to be true."

His nerves weren't helped by the number of training accidents that occurred at Goodfellow while he was stationed there—as many as twenty-two per month, owing to "wing tip[s] [being] dragged; faulty technique; hard landings; [and] collision with parked aircraft," according to reports. (BT-13s, known as Valiants, were used in training; they had a ceiling of 16,500 feet, and were called, by wary pilots, "Vibrators.")

None of the accidents was fatal, but they were all noisy and frightening. Heller kept his head down, writing PR for the base in a low-slung wooden room clacking with typewriters. He was a pretty fair typist. One of his tent mates, during his last weeks on Corsica, freshly arrived to replace a man who had finished his tour of duty, had brought with him a portable typewriter. The kid harbored literary ambitions, but he was too busy getting in his flight time to do any work; meanwhile, in the afternoons, Heller, who had completed his missions and was waiting to leave, hunkered down alone in the tent and made use of the kid's machine. Heller, who had been keeping a diary of his missions, typed up a chronology of his experiences. He toyed with the idea of writing short stories about war in the bare-bones, dialogue-heavy manner of Hemingway. He had also been reading William Saroyan and John O'Hara, writers who, like Papa, appealed to him because of their colloquial dialogue and lean descriptive passages. The U.S. government published a series of books for servicemen, the Armed Forces Editions, paperbound collections, which made available to Heller, among other classics, Stephen Crane's "The Open Boat," a story of shipwrecked sailors, written with a powerful, hypnotic rhythm and lulling, repetitive dialogue. Impressed by the story's rocking, wavelike style, he imagined a similar tale, updated to the present time: a terse back-and-forth conversation between a bomber crew in trouble and a Corsican air base. He thought of calling the story "Hello, Genoa, Hello, Genoa," after the title of a one-act play by Saroyan, *Hello Out There*. Finally, instead of attempting this story, so close to his undigested experiences, and therefore hard to articulate, he began to draft a piece about a married ex-serviceman adjusting poorly to life at home—a projection, perhaps, of his fears about settling down once he returned to the States. Emotionally, he distanced himself from the subject by using a spare, slick-magazine style reminiscent of O'Hara, who, like similar writers (Saroyan, Irwin Shaw), expressed what Heller later admitted were "hard-nosed, sexist attitudes . . . embodying . . . implicit assessments of materialism, wealth, Babbitry, and ideals of masculinity and male decency that I . . . accepted as irreducibly pure."

"HE TURNED OVER on his back and stared at the ceiling, feeling unhappy, wanting something and not knowing just what it was," Heller wrote, fiddling with the piece he'd begun on Corsica. He returned to it, now and then, between banging out memos and press releases for Goodfellow Field. At night, in his bunk, he'd lie awake, listening to music on the local radio station, KGKL, wishing instead to catch a one-act drama, the kind he'd loved in the evenings as a kid in Coney Island.

Sometimes, on a day pass, he'd ride up a wide, dusty street into downtown San Angelo with some of his comrades, going to the Texas Theater for a Frank Sinatra or Dorothy Lamour movie, or to watch the town's fidgety women shop for Vegetable Compound. Heller recalled himself as a "boyish and ravenous satyr" at this time in his life, but "in depth of experience still almost a virgin."

Teenaged girls and boys milled in front of the Cactus Hotel. Inside the hotel's glamorous Crystal Ballroom, an armed forces recruiting film, *Baptism of Fire,* played regularly. As Heller passed the unsure youngsters, excited and confused about their futures, and as he observed servicemen, home from their tours, hoping to shut their pasts behind them with the purchase of an engagement ring, he considered how far he had come in a short time: Just a few years ago, he'd been as aimless, but as gung ho for a fight, as these boys in front of the Cactus, and now he was a man about to be married, maybe, and embarked upon a career just as soon as he received his discharge.

In the short story he'd been working on, he had the young husband say to his wife, "I married you because it was part of the dream . . . [t]he sugar and tinsel dream of life." It was, he says, "the thing to do." On some level, Heller may have been as skeptical of the "*Reader's Digest* beautiful panorama of a beautiful life" as his fictional husband, but in another sense, he *did* believe it was the thing to do (if nothing else, as a way of channeling his sexual urges), just as he both pitied and understood the naïveté of the teens in front of the Cactus, who dreamed the glory but could not imagine the reality of a baptism of fire.

In January 1945, when he'd received his orders to vacate Corsica, he was flown to Naples along with Tom Sloan, another bombardier from his group, who was also scheduled to return to the States (throughout the flight, Heller kept his fingers crossed, on both hands, for safety and luck). Sloan was married, with a one-year-old at home, and had never been tempted, like his buddy here, to sleep with prostitutes or other available women on R & R trips to Cairo and Rome. On the flight to Naples, Heller was impressed with Sloan's eagerness to return to wedded bliss.

When offered transport home by air or sea, Heller chose to sail back with several thousand other boys on a troopship, the former SS *America.* The ship sailed alone, without naval escort. Heller spent most of the ten days at sea trying to sleep in the cabin—outfitted with two tiers of bunk beds—he shared with six others. The ship docked at Boston; from there, he took a train to Atlantic City for his medical exam, routine processing, and reassignment.

On furlough, he returned to his family apartment in Coney Island as something of a glamorous war hero. The role—for it did feel like an act—embarrassed him. "I don't want to sit in a room filled with people who are all beaming at me as if I were some marvelous mechanical toy, and play the modest hero. I don't want to tell anybody what it was like and smile shyly as they tell me how wonderful I am," the husband informs his wife in the story he'd been writing. He was thinking of calling it "I Don't Love You Any More."

The weather in Coney Island was gray and oppressive. Not even a hot dog from Nathan's could cheer him up. While he had been overseas, Luna Park, one of the area's great amusement centers, had burned down, leaving smoke and char. Few of his old friends were around. Some were still overseas; in the last couple of years, many had gotten married, and most of the others were planning to marry. It was the thing to do.

Heller went to movies by himself, walked around town (he had not yet learned to drive), and generally moped, realizing with a shock that he missed the military, where he had been kept plenty busy. His brother Lee, fourteen years his senior, told him to get off his rear and take a vacation: Why not go to Grossinger's, a famous resort hotel in the Catskills, well known not only as a place of fun and relaxation but as a place for men to meet women? Heller had never heard of it. Lee kept insisting, telling him he could afford it. The family had been saving the allotments from his Air Corps pay, which he'd sent home every month. When his kid brother stalled some more, Lee made the arrangements, reserving him a spot on a van that would leave from Brooklyn and eventually twist along mountain roads on the old Route 17, up the Wurtsboro Hills, to the city of Liberty. It'll be great, Lee said. As a war hero, you'll be fawned over. Look at you, look how tan you are from all that Mediterranean sun.

Heller put on his green winter flight jacket, with its thick fur collar and his silver first lieutenant's bar, and boarded the van. His fellow passengers stared at him admiringly.

Grossinger's had begun as a private seven-room farmhouse in 1914 and developed over the years, along with hundreds of other hotels in the area, into a Jewish resort catering to thousands of guests at any given time. Acreage in the Catskill Mountains, just under a hundred miles northwest of New York City, had been cultivated by Eastern European immigrants, beginning in the late nineteenth century. Jews had not been allowed to own land in Russia; for those who came to the United States, buying property was an assertion of identity and freedom. Many of the families who settled in the Catskills knew the basics of raising livestock from the work they had done in Russia. Other families came from European ghettos. The area was remote enough that it provided an enclave for preserving culture: The music, food, and language of old-world shtetls flourished here, along with urban rhythms underpinning rural necessities.

In time, financial need forced many of the farmers to use their land for alternative businesses. Opening up their kitchens, barns, and small lakes to travelers proved lucrative and increasingly popular. Jewish laborers on the Lower East Side of Manhattan, discovering the novelty of having a little spending money in their pockets for the first time in their lives, and looking for a pleasant escape during the hottest days of summer, took to the mountains in bigger and bigger numbers. This was a new phenomenon: vacations for the working class. An individual earning, say, thirty dollars a week could stay at Grossinger's for five days, sharing a "country" cabin with two others, for around $39.50. By the mid-1940s, the Catskills were known as "the Jewish Alps," and the hotel resorts had become destination points for people of all classes—lower, middle, and upper, with more and more celebrities to boot—looking to play.

The "mountains had everything," said Sam Levenson, a resort entertainer, "girls, bedbugs, handball, chicken . . . milk hot from the hot cow, swimming in a pool about the same size as in the picture postcard, and nature—manure at [your] window." Joyce Wadler, an essayist who called herself a "survivor" of Catskill retreats, wrote, "This is what it was like, in the Borscht Belt [so called because of the endless servings of the beet soup, topped with sour cream, in resort kitchens]: full of noise, full of Jews, and the jokes grew on trees."

Heller had never given much conscious thought to Judaism, but his family *was* Jewish. This was another role he could play with confidence. It was the off-season when he arrived at Grossinger's. Skiing, ice-skating, basketball, and dancing were the popular weekly activities. He had never skated, but he was blessed with strength and good physical coordination, and he learned quickly. Besides, he knew he cut a striking figure in his flight jacket. He was also a novice dancer, but buoyed by the attention his evening attire brought him—his officer's dress with wings and the silver oak-leaf clusters he had earned for completing his missions—he moved smoothly across the ballroom's wooden floor as the "orchestra" (consisting of no more than five or six musicians) blatted out rumbas.

Lee had been right. Heller was enjoying himself, but he was sorry there were not dances on Friday nights also. As an observant Jewish business, Grossinger's staged no entertainment on the Sabbath. Within a few years, to stay competitive with non-Jewish resorts, the hotel owners would begin to conduct a weekly *shtar m'chirah,* a sale to a "Shabbos goy" for twenty-four hours, for the sum of one dollar. If the *goy* put on a show, no religious rules would be broken. At sundown every Saturday, he sold the hotel and its eight hundred acres back to its Jewish owners.

But this deal was not in place in 1945. Instead, there was a Friday-night lecture by a rabbi. Heller sneaked into the woods to smoke a cigarette—also forbidden on the Sabbath.

Heller gorged himself with food. He had never eaten like this, with such a flavorful array set before him, and he didn't know when he'd have the opportunity to eat this way again. Where would he be assigned? How long would he have to wait for his discharge? Pot cheese, jumbo potatoes, cold fish, boiled chicken, chow mein, challah rolls, eggs and onions, the plentiful borscht, and blintzes folded as carefully as an American flag at twilight.

What had seemed awkward at home—playing up his soldier-boy status—was pleasant and rewarding here. No one knew him. He didn't have to explain himself, or worry that someone would accuse him of puffing himself up ("Nah, he ain't really nobody; that's just Joey"). He liked receiving the frank admiration of strangers, especially attractive young women, many of whom were here with their parents for the clear purpose of sussing out promising male prospects. Lee had told him everyone knew girls went to Grossinger's looking for marriage material.

Their eyes followed him as he strolled through the woods, or passed through the Main House, where the social director led guests through a game of Simon Says ("Simon says turn and hug the person next to you"), or as he stepped out on the ice in his skates while Irving Jaffe, a former three-time Olympic skating champion, now Grossinger's house pro, gave lessons in another part of the rink. Heller smiled as he watched the girls watch him. He'd circle the rink slowly; in the middle of the ice, some young lady or another would spin as swiftly as a storm, whipping up white vapor.

When a girl's mother or father thanked him for his service in the cause of freedom, he'd grin modestly and thank them in return. He felt as pleased—and amazed at the ease of it all—as he'd felt in school, as a kid, whenever teachers praised his writing ability. He was just doing what he'd been told, fulfilling his assignments. But it seemed that sometimes he was able to fulfill them a little better than others.

Every night at dinner, the hotel's mimeographed daily bulletin, the *Tattler* (the name suggesting childishness and indulgence, as well as titillation), announced special events or gala balls, which, all the guests knew, were occasions for singles to get together. There was, for example, the Champagne Hour, where wives could show off to their husbands the dance steps they'd learned in classes all week, or, more to the point, where those on their own might find a partner, on and off the dance floor. In the Catskills, the "air was redolent of grass, flowers, ozone, and sex," wrote Abraham Cahan in his novel *The Rise of David Levinsky*. If, in the off-season, the smell of grass and flowers was replaced by the odor of burning pine and the sharp, moist no-scent of snow, the deeper trace of physical need and longing remained. Unmarried men and women in their thirties and forties did their best not to schlump around in despair and defeat. "I learned to spot a single woman," Tania Grossinger wrote in her memoir about growing up at the hotel. A single woman "brought four or five suitcases up with her for a three-day weekend. . . . She borrowed her married sister['s] . . . mink stole and her girlfriend['s] . . . rhinestone earring, necklace, and bracelet set. . . . She hoped to find a man who would drive her back to the city and would not find the fact that she lived in the Bronx or Brooklyn GU (Geographically Undesirable). She changed her outfit a minimum of four times daily. . . . She really wasn't looking for someone to sleep with in the country. What she *was* looking for was someone to marry in the city."

Then there were the parents of young women seeking to secure their daughters' futures. Men who went to Grossinger's were "good people"— not necessarily because they were financially secure, but because by going there they exhibited a desire for betterment and assimilation in the broadest, most flexible sense of the word—not turning away from Judaism, but integrating more fully into American culture. As Phil Brown, who also grew up in a Catskills resort, puts it, "[G]oods and entertainment that were previously unavailable to these largely immigrant people were now accessible" in places like Grossinger's. To partake of these luxuries "represented an acculturation to American life—the immigrant was no longer a greenhorn but a citizen of the New World."

To *take a vacation* suggested it was normal for a Jew to be a regular wage earner, an American. At the same time, the insular Jewish character of these resorts reinforced tribal solidarity. Simultaneously, one could wear and drop the mask of mainstream acceptability, or, perhaps more accurately, wear a mask of utter transparency.

Similarly, Heller's military uniform proclaimed his solid character. Is it any wonder he didn't have to ask anyone to dance? At Grossinger's, the girls weren't shy. "There was no time for subtle flirtations," wrote Tania Grossinger. "The emphasis was on 'now.' And if not 'now,' at least 'tomorrow.'" This was an attitude made even sharper, in the winter of 1945, by stories of mass killings that had leaked out of Europe during the course of the war, rumors recalled for everyone by Heller's dress. Don't stop moving, don't let go of each other, don't think about what lies beyond the trees, the mountains, and the cold, clear moonlight above us.

One night at Grossinger's, "I met the girl," Heller wrote in his memoir. Actually, he met the girl's mother, who then introduced him to the girl. "At a dance contest one night, my grandmother asked my father to be her partner," says Heller's daughter, Erica. "They won the contest and a bottle of champagne and went back to my grandmother's table and met my mother, who was initially underwhelmed. My grandmother had [first] met him while they were checking in, and sensed something special" that might appeal to her daughter.

Shirley Held was a twenty-one-year-old redhead who loved to laugh and joke dryly, a quick, subtle wit. She was svelte, relaxed, and gorgeous. A product of Brooklyn, she now lived on Manhattan's Upper West Side with her parents, both of whom took to Heller immediately. Like everyone else, they were impressed with his officer's uniform. "They had each grown up very poor so they had no snobbery," says Erica. "Dad was ambitious and had a plan." The Helds liked the sound of that. Heller's plan was to pursue the writing for which his teachers had always praised him (he'd been considering this more and more seriously ever since co-opting his tent mate's typewriter in Corsica) and to begin by going to college to study literature, now that the G.I. Bill had put college within reach. To be a literary man was to be something quite respectable in the America of the 1940s, especially among well-read Jewish families, for whom the tradition of biblical study had instilled a reverence for language, and for whom achievement in the arts was a sign of intellectual accomplishment as well as successful assimilation into the culture. (Just a few miles from Grossinger's, at Grine Felder, a bungalow resort colony, Isaac Bashevis Singer had recently worked with his older brother, Israel, and a man named Zygmunt Salkin to re-invigorate Yiddish theater on American soil by staging plays and form-ing a conducive atmosphere for literary activity.)

Shirley's father, Bernard, whom everyone called Barney, was partner in a garment company on Seventh Avenue, specializing in ladies' sports-wear. "He was very handsome, elegant, soft-spoken, a mensch," says Erica Heller. Right away, he "loved my father." So did his wife, Dottie, who wasted no time in pushing him toward her daughter. In the heady, urgent atmosphere of this Jewish retreat, with relief in the air after many years of war, but with Hitler still running loose in Europe, plans were made quickly, surely, and without fuss. For the Held family and Joseph Heller, it was love at first sight.

Dottie seized every opportunity to bring the young couple together, with help from the social director, also called the "tummler." The word *tummler* is "derived from tumult-maker," according to comedian Joey Adams, who once worked as a social director in the Catskills. It is "Cas-tilian Yiddish for a fool or noisemaker who does anything and every-thing to entertain customers so that they won't squawk about their rooms or food." Tummlers often worked as waiters. Between meals, they sang and danced, told jokes, mingled with the guests, and worked infor-mally as *shadchans,* or marriage brokers.

Saturday nights gave tummlers—and, in this case, Dottie Held—plenty of chances to squeeze a girl and boy together in an air of carefree gaiety. At Grossinger's, Saturday nights were star-studded extravagan-zas, featuring big-name entertainers like Milton Berle, Buddy Hackett, Alan King, or Eddie Cantor. Often, the hotel would engage a vaude-ville troupe, and audience members would laugh at their own eating habits, speech patterns, professional anxieties, and sexual attitudes as parodied by the actors in skits that turned self-recognition into self-hatred, self-deprecation, and finally into gentle self-acceptance: the process, itself, a parody of the stages of assimilation, an acknowledg-ment of the confusion sparked by a desire to remain individualistic yet fit into something larger. This desire was, again, like donning and shed-ding a mask at the same time. Yiddish theater scholar Ellen Schiff wrote that vaudeville acts in the first half of the twentieth century al-ways "included a whole variety of ethnic caricatures which exploited the traits familiarly associated with . . . the Irish, Germans, French, Swedes, and . . . [that] burlesque concoction, the stage Negro. The Jew figured as an ethnic among ethnics," and was therefore seen by audiences (including Jews) as not quite "white." In fact, Jewish entertainers performed, with remarkable frequency, in blackface, a mask that let them be in on the jokes along with mainstream America but also marked them as the *butt* of the jokes.

Heller laughed as loudly as anyone on Saturday nights—tickled by Shirley Held's charming presence—but he couldn't help but be aware that he was living a vaudeville skit: Back in Coney, his military costume made him terribly self-conscious, fearful of casting himself as someone he was not, a war hero; here at Grossinger's, the smart dress gave him freedom to play the hero to the hilt among happy strangers, and to win the heart of a girl (after all, this *particular* skit was a comedy).

And he was determined for it to reach its happy ending. In his spare moments, he worked hard on understanding story conventions, and getting them right. By the time "I returned to the city [Shirley and I] were already going steady," he wrote. "I had great expectations."

Shirley's family occupied a multiroom apartment at 50 Riverside Drive, an elegant sixteen-story structure built in 1930 of light beige brick, overlooking the Hudson. The apartment had wooden floors and French doors. Dottie's taste was spare and immaculate, and she would pass her flair for interior decorating on to Shirley.

For the next several days, Heller spent more time in the city, courting Shirley, meeting her friends, and enjoying meals at her family's home, than he did in Coney Island. And then he was assigned to go to Texas.

SIGNS IN THE WINDOWS of the jewelry stores in downtown San Angelo advertised specials on engagement rings. Heller passed by them, fear and skepticism bumping up against his great expectations. Just what *was* this "sugar and tinsel dream of life" he seemed to be rushing toward with all these other boys? It had been easier to imagine the dream, weeks earlier, at Grossinger's, surrounded by laughter, food, and pretty girls. Here on a military base, amid dust and howling wind, with planes lurching unsafely all around him, the dream appeared to be so much hoopla, nothing more than a stage performance.

What do you want? the wife asked the husband in the short story he kept tinkering with. "A pitcher of beer," the husband replied flatly. Beyond that, he didn't want to think.

In his memoir, Heller says he corresponded regularly with Shirley while stationed in Texas. These letters seem to be lost.

One afternoon, almost as a lark, he slipped the pages of the latest draft of "I Don't Love You Any More" into an envelope, which he addressed to Whit Burnett at *Story* magazine. He had read in some newspaper or army publication that *Story* was looking for fiction by returning servicemen for a special issue. Heller had never seen a copy of *Story,* but he thought he remembered an old pal from Coney Island, Danny Rosoff, talking about the magazine. At school, Rosoff used to drop the names of Faulkner, Hemingway, and Fitzgerald, though Heller suspected his buddy had only heard of these writers but not read them.

Story had a circulation of about twenty thousand and boasted work by William Faulkner, Sherwood Anderson, Thomas Mann, and one of Heller's favorites, William Saroyan. Burnett had started the magazine in the early 1930s with his then wife, Martha Foley, who went on to edit the annual series *Best American Short Stories.* In March 1940, the magazine published the first piece by an unknown author named J. D. Salinger, who had taken a writing course at Columbia with Burnett (showing very little promise in the beginning, according to the teacher).

Heller had no idea how long it would take to hear back from the editor. He tried to forget about the story, but on his rides into town, his eyes would stray to the magazine racks in the drugstores. *Story* was never among the colorful publications—instead, there were *Time, Look,* and *Life,* exhibiting in their full-page ads a schizophrenia similar to what he had witnessed in vaudeville shows at Grossinger's. Everyone knew money was tight and that many products had been rationed during the war, such as tires, bicycles, gasoline, fuel oil, stoves, sugar, coffee, and shoes. And yet the magazines displayed an endless bounty of goods, a frenzy of consumer pleasure. What was being masked here? (In 1942, for both economic and patriotic reasons, the IRS issued a ruling that gave companies a business discount on any ad that featured a wartime theme; as a result, magazine advertising increased more than 60 percent during the war years, despite widespread product rationing.)

Heller left the magazines on the racks and returned to the base to read Stephen Crane.

Sometimes in the evenings, the sky grew dark and green over Goodfellow Field as thunderstorms and the threat of tornadoes moved across the plains. Chilly pockets filled the dusky air, floating about unpredictably like invisible flak. Heller listened to big-band music on his radio, wrote letters to Shirley, and thanked his luck that he still had two good feet and his feet were on the ground. Only his words would take flight now, on planes winging their way to Shirley or to Whit Burnett, in streams of wind made heavy with the murmuring of dust, the lowing of sheep.

2. A Coney Island of the Mind

A S HE LAY in his bunk at Goodfellow, listening to sand scratch the window screens and animals stir in rugged fields, Heller recalled, with what he knew was nostalgia (for hadn't he just tasted a bleak eastern winter right before going to Grossinger's?), the breath of surf along the boardwalk. The following afternoon, as his buddies opened their mail, he wondered when, or even if, he would hear about his short story. Then he thought again of Danny Rosoff muttering, "Hemingway . . . Faulkner." Proudly, he remembered the grand ambitions of his motley old pals. Nostalgia, yes. His recent glimpse of Coney Island—deserted, dark—had convinced him he could never live there again. We speak of haunted places, but can a place haunt itself? Heller thought Coney was spooky that way. It was past its prime before it ever came into its own. It was a series of fleeting images unattached to any reality and overlaid on one another year after year.

But was he wrong to remember his childhood as pretty damn wonderful—not just his experiences but the place, too? *Wasn't* everything better then? Already, as a young man, he was beginning to suspect that, on a public scale at least, every change was for the worse.

JOSEPH HELLER had been born into the bright carnival that was Coney Island on May 1, 1923, the same year the Riegelmann Boardwalk went up to handle the larger crowds made possible by laws granting greater public access to the beach, and by the completion of the subway line from Manhattan (in forty-five minutes, and for just five cents, a passenger could get from Times Square to the Stillman Avenue stop). The boardwalk was also intended to halt what some saw as Coney's decline. Many of the old Victorian-style hotels that had once drawn to the shore an opulent clientele had fallen to ruin, failures brought about by antibetting laws and Prohibition or devastating fires. Dreamland, where tourists could visit Africa, Asia, or Hell (garishly painted and elaborately staged) had, perhaps fittingly, burned. Tides had eroded the beach, turning it into a poorly tended narrow strip of sand. But entrepreneurs such as Edward Riegelmann saw opportunities, with inexpensive transportation and new land-use ordinances, to lure different kinds of crowds, poorer but eager for excitement, to the oceanside playground. "At Coney Island . . . the abiding talent is for the exaggerated and the superlative," wrote Edo McCullough, nephew of the man who had founded the Pavilion of Fun. Each time crisis spawns a change, the alterations have been "so violent as to obliterate . . . the memory of what was there before."

Riegelmann's boardwalk, eighty feet wide and running half the length of Coney Island, quickly became the area's new icon. New and cheaper amusement rides cropped up beside it. Contractors were hired to pump in sand, adding 2,500,000 square feet of new beach open free to the public (in the entrepreneurial spirit of the place, the contractors skimped on expenses by sluicing sand from the wrong source, and the "improved" beach looked slightly jaundiced).

"One must go to Coney Island," remarked Édouard Herriot, France's prime minister, thrilled after a visit to Riegelmann's promenade. There, one sees an "inexhaustible human river flow[ing] . . . past . . . Italian or Greek rotisseries, which turn out an uninterrupted sausage called hot dogs, past the naïvely pretentious astrologers' booths, the tattoo artists and hideous four-legged woman. One is carried along into the torrent with all the languages and all the races of the globe." Coney's excitement could also be chaos, its marvels mere decadence: the Spanish poet,

Federico García Lorca, visiting not long after the French prime minister, noted the boardwalk's "vomiting multitudes."

In 1923, 40 percent of Coney Island's year-round residents were foreign-born. In addition to the Italians and Greeks, thousands of refugees from Scandinavia, Poland, and Russia had settled there. On any given day, along the boardwalk, one witnessed Hasidic Jews strolling in serious conversation, young girls chomping gyros, and old men arguing the merits of socialism. Before the turn of the century, when large sections of Coney Island were given over to gambling, drinking, and other vices, the place was known as "Sodom by the Sea." Nowadays, as the amusement park king, George C. Tilyou, had once proclaimed, "If France is Paris, then Coney Island . . . is the world."

Its identity had always been mired in ambiguity and instability. For instance, it was not really an island. Once a series of small sand spits, constantly reconfigured by the tides, it eventually coalesced and joined the rest of Brooklyn when a creek that separated it from the larger landmass filled in. The Dutch claimed it but seemed to want little to do with it (they gave it the name it goes by now, Conyne, meaning "rabbit"—the creatures were plentiful there). In the early nineteenth century, businessmen began to exploit the beach area for use as a summer resort; the seduce and entertain mentality that would govern subsequent development, at least for the next 140 years or so, locked in. Eventually, sea bathing, horse racing, and the delicacies of clams lured bigger and bigger crowds (among them, the young poet Walt Whitman, who came for the clams, and who said he loved to "race up and down the hard sand and declaim Homer or Shakespeare to the surf and seagulls").

As early as 1876, George Tilyou, then fourteen years old, embodied Coney Island hucksterism, and was convinced that people were gullible enough to pay good money for worthless items as long as these items displayed price tags touting their value. People proved him right. He sold cigar boxes of "authentic beach sand" to tourists, as well as medicine bottles of "authentic salt water" for a quarter apiece. He earned $13.45 his first day out. Twenty-two years later, with that same boldness, he would lease a plot of land at Coney's Bowery and West Eighth Street, put up a sign that said, falsely, ON THIS SITE WILL BE ERECTED THE WORLD'S LARGEST FERRIS WHEEL, and open an amusement park. The wheel measured 100 feet in diameter, and his pretty sister Kathryn sat in the ticket booth. She wore their mother's diamond necklace and was surrounded by two large men, whom Tilyou had hired to pose as body-guards, protecting the necklace. This effective bit of showmanship was the beginning of Steeplechase Park.

By the time Joseph Heller was born, the area's self-image had spun up and down like a bumptious Ferris wheel car. It is a "glorified city of flame," wrote the esteemed critic James Gibbons Huneker, where "every angle reveals some new horror." On the other hand, the painter Reginald Marsh lovingly described the beach crowds as "moving like [the] compositions of Michelangelo and Rubens."

Once, after a visit to Dreamland, Sigmund Freud reportedly remarked, "The only thing about America that interests me is Coney Island." If so, it's not hard to see why: In the space of a few feet, one could fly to the moon, witness cities burn or see the destruction of Pompeii, watch automated blowholes spread women's skirts, study premature human babies displayed in an incubator, and laugh at a pin-headed man or "the" Wild Man from Borneo. People lined up for rides that would slam them against walls or turn them upside down ("Centrifugal force never fails," boasted a boardwalk carney). Hero-pilot Charles Lindbergh remarked that a Coney Island roller coaster was "scarier than flying." Most of the rides "succeeded because they combined socially acceptable thrills with undertones of sexual intimacy," a Landmarks Preservation Commission report once said. And if, full of surging life, you felt like completing the journey, you could be buried alive in a coffin-shaped room with a glass ceiling, or you could descend into the Inferno to see demons drag away the wicked (Hell, it turned out, was adorned by statuary made by French sculptor Maurice Goudard—Americans always *suspected* the French had something to do with eternal torment).

Time seemed to have no meaning in Coney Island, or only as much meaning as delirium might have. Year after year, the place died and was reborn. It was resplendent; it was doomed. It was Now; it was Then. And something of the otherworldly, if not the Divine, appeared to govern its cycles. Again and again, sections of the city were destroyed by fire, most recently, in the years before Heller was born, in 1907, when the Cave of the Winds suddenly ignited, and in 1911.

Fires, mostly pleasant ones, were among Heller's earliest memories: the "barnfires" fueled by broken fruit crates, over which his family ate charred marshmallows and smoky, sandy "mickeys"—roasted potatoes—on the shore, along with hundreds of other summertime revelers; and

fireworks, every Tuesday night during summer, shot from a boat an-
chored at the Steeplechase pier. "It *brent* a fire in street," his mother,
Lena, warned him gutturally whenever he ran barefoot from the apartment onto scalding pavement. Lena could barely speak English. Her
uneasiness with the language often embarrassed the family. Early on,
her insistence on speaking Yiddish and sometimes a little Russian struck
young Joey as a refusal—of anything, everything—and the bitter humor
of the Yiddish was unmistakable even to a child: If not the sentiments,
he understood the weary, mocking tone. It was a language of longing
and displacement, qualities made even more palpable by his mother's
stubborn use of it, even though it clearly isolated her from her greater
surroundings. "I was not aware of coldness *or* warmth [from my
mother]," Heller told an interviewer years later. Just intransigence and
nay-saying—as well as noisy silence, for though she talked often, she
generally did not attempt to communicate, at least not directly.

Isaac Daniel Heller, Joey's father, emigrated from Russia to New York
in 1913. His four-year-old boy, Hillel Elias, known as Lee in America,
arrived with his mother shortly before or after Isaac. Briefly, the family
lived in Manhattan, then in Spring Valley, New York. After that, they
moved to Coney Island. As an adult, Joseph admitted his father's past
had always been murky to him. "I . . . never grappled much with the
idea of trying to find out more about him," he wrote in *Now and Then*.
He understood only that his father had come to America "from somewhere in western Russia." He wrote, "I prefer not to [know more]."
[K]nowing more would make no difference. . . . I know him by his absence." That the figurative lack of a father would soon enough become
literal only added to the older man's mystery.

Ambiguity clouds the family name. The German word *heller* means
"lighter" or "brighter." Ashkenazi Jews were said to apply the word to
someone with a light complexion. Some historians trace the name to
the sixteenth century and the city of Halle, Germany, where it was
linked to a coin, the *Heller,* in use there; others say a rabbi and scholar
named Yom-Tov Lipmann is the source of the family's lineage. At one
point, he lived in Halle, and a bastardized form of the city's name came
to be associated with him. From the sixteenth to the early twentieth
century, thousands of families called Heller migrated east from Austria
and Germany. Records indicate that many Hellers arriving in the United
States at around the time Isaac did came from the old Lithuanian fron-

tier, once part of Poland, now belonging to the Ukraine. A sheet from the fourteenth census of the United States, dated January 8, 1920, lists Isaac Heller's place of origin as Russia and his native language as Yiddish. No further details. However, a ship manifest dated September 29, 1913, indicates that Elias Heller, age four, traveled on the *Lapland*, a nearly nineteen-ton steamship sailing from Antwerp. Elias came from Tschschonovitz, Russia (his last residence). He was born in Gulanowie, Russia. These towns are difficult to pinpoint: Linguistic, cultural, and political barriers led to many mistakes and alternate spellings on ship manifests and immigration records; names and national borders were exceptionally fluid in that part of the world. The likely possibilities suggest Elias was born west of Moscow, within a couple hundred miles of the city, and that just before coming to the United States, the Hellers were living in the Lithuanian/Polish/Russian frontier. If so, they came from an area with a centuries-long Jewish history, and with many Hasidic sects. At the beginning of the twentieth century, oppression from the Russian czar, as well as violence perpetrated by Cossack soldiers and Polish gangs, forced many Jewish families to leave. In the United States, Isaac declared himself a Jewish agnostic, in flight from Czar Nicholas II, and a strong supporter of socialism.

The 1920 census lists him as a "chandler" (though his primary occupation was driving a delivery truck for Messinger's Bakery), and it gave his age as thirty-five.

In 1913, the year he arrived in Coney Island, socialism was a topic du jour in New York's Jewish communities (and a subject of fear in America's mainstream press; in September of that year, the *New York Times* charged Teddy Roosevelt with "redistributing [America's] wealth," under the headline ROOSEVELT'S SUPER-SOCIALISM). Abraham Cahan's popular newspaper, the *Jewish Daily Forward,* undoubtedly a staple in the Heller household, as it was in every Jewish neighborhood, spread the socialist gospel, as well as labor unionism, in straightforward Yiddish accessible to working-class readers ("Not to take [the] paper was to confess you were [a] barbarian," Irving Howe once wrote).

That same year in Coney Island, a prime example of American capitalism came to pass. Nathan Handwerker, a dishwasher at Charles Feltman's hot dog stand, decided to undercut his boss by selling the morsel Feltman claimed to have invented—the charcoal-cooked frankfurter—for five cents instead of the usual ten. Initially, the plan backfired. The public, long accustomed to rumors that hot dogs were made of horse meat or some other unsavory material, distrusted the inexpensive dog. To counter these fears, and lure more eaters, Handwerker hired transients from the beach to crowd the tables in front of his stand. The men's disheveled appearance did not encourage anyone to approach. According to some stories, Handwerker then dressed the transients in rented lab coats; other accounts say he offered free hot dogs to interns from Coney Island Hospital. In any case, he advertised his stand as a place "where the doctors eat"—what could be safer than that? From then on, Nathan's hot dogs became a famous Coney Island product (and a favorite food of Joseph Heller, in childhood and beyond).

Coney was a confusing place for an immigrant to land, its basic nature as hard to grasp as one's image in a house of tilted mirrors. The clearest picture we have of the perplexities facing the generation that shaped Joseph Heller is found in the *Jewish Daily Forward*'s "Bintel Brief" (literally, a "Bundle of Letters"), an advice column for immigrants befuddled by modern America. "People often need the opportunity to pour out their heavy-laden hearts. Among our immigrant masses this need was very marked," Abraham Cahan wrote in his memoirs. Problems between parents and children (kids quickly becoming accustomed to New World freedoms and abandoning old values), ambivalence about integration, ethnic tensions ("I am a girl from Galicia and in the shop where I work I sit near a Russian Jew. . . . [Once] he stated that all Galicians were no good. . . . Why should one worker resent another?"), and fears and temptations about intermarriage filled the daily column. Many letters addressed domestic tensions caused by new opportunities discovered in the United States.

More striking than the confusions battering these uprooted souls was the series of mixed signals offered by the column's wise men (sometimes Cahan himself, but more often S. Kornbluth, one of the paper's editors). For example, some replies encouraged intermarriage as a way of becoming more Americanized; on different occasions, the editors suggested intermarriage was a curse, certain to cause isolation.

The immigrant self was perpetually unsettled. As "The Bintel Brief" made clear, many people preferred to air their emotional struggles anonymously, not only because the pain was so great but also because the very nature of their problems, not to say the solutions, were hard to identify, and always shifting. The strongest impression one gets from these columns is that the wave of immigrants that included Joseph Heller's father led double lives. They were never fully comfortable in their adopted world, but they were unable to return to their pasts (you will be "strangers to [your] own neighbors" in your old homelands, the editors warned). Of necessity, men and women of this generation were largely reserved, for their old languages lacked the vocabularies to define the conundrums they encountered.

IT WAS A WORLD of silence, but not a silent world. On summer mornings, the cries of Italian fruit peddlers drifted up from the streets through the open windows of the Hellers' four-room apartment: "If you got money, come down and buy. If you got no money, stay home and cry." Gull calls and the distant screams of roller-coaster riders droned just beneath soaring Puccini arias from the Kent radio in the living room, which Heller's mother kept on all day while she hunched above her Singer sewing machine, its whirring and tapping an accompaniment to the music. Though the 1920 census indicates she was unemployed, she worked as a seamstress, making and mending clothes for many of her neighbors, as well as converting old bedsheets into curtains. At night, she withdrew into her bedroom to read Tolstoy in Yiddish, especially *Anna Karenina* over and over. She had always loved to read. In Russia, members of her family worked as bookbinders (many years later, her brother Sam would land a job repairing books for the Brandeis University library).

The Hellers occupied an upper floor in a small yellow-brick building on West Thirty-first Street, between Mermaid and Surf avenues. Lee was fourteen now. A daughter, Sylvia, had been born in 1914. Everyone in the family called the youngest boy Joey. They shared the building with a family named Winkler, and little Joey shared a baby carriage with the Winkler infant, Marvin. "He used to wet my carriage, and he was ten months older," Marvin told Barbara Gelb for a *New York Times Magazine* profile of Heller in 1979. When Heller was older, his mother swore to him that whenever he'd nursed, she'd have to snatch him away from her breast, for he would never stop. Among the first smells he recalled were the duskiness of walnuts, the sweet softness of old apples, saved from going to waste by his mother, who would fold them into noodle puddings, and the floury flatness of day-old cakes, rescued from the bakery by his father. His father sat at the kitchen table at night, eating slice after slice of dry, hard cake.

Joey's first memory of his father's voice was a sharp command: One day, Joey wandered close to an open window, curious about the fire escape, and his father called him back. Sometimes at night, strange noises from the street or from the beach a few blocks away woke Joey in fright, and he'd crawl into bed with his parents, warm and content in the space between their bodies. On some afternoons, his father took him riding in the delivery van, letting him press the automatic starter and pretend he was driving. Slowly, they passed through a bewildering mélange of voices—the census reveals an immediate neighborhood teeming with Russians, Germans, Armenians, and Italians. Though Joey's parents rarely took him to synagogue (occasionally, they made exceptions for High Holiday services), he was surrounded by Jews and Jewish culture. Lists of the area's religious institutions at the time (the Young Men's Hebrew Association of Coney Island, Adath Israel, the Jewish Communal Center, and the Coney Island Talmud Torah) indicate large and active memberships.

Sometime before his fourth birthday, Joey had to have his tonsils removed. As he remembered the experience, his father drove him to Coney Island Hospital and left him alone, with a parched throat and little understanding of what was happening. Figures in white moved along the corridors, silent and remote. Where was his father? Why had he gone? How *could* he have gone?

Lee distrusted Isaac even more than Joey did. He recalled riding with the older man in a horse-drawn delivery wagon in Manhattan upon first arriving in the United States. On steep, icy streets, Isaac whipped the horse so brutally, passersby berated him for cruelty. Though Lee claimed his father was never mean to him, he would grudgingly admit, in later years, with tears in his eyes, that the two of them did not have an easy relationship. "There were lots of Jewish criminals around and he didn't want me to turn out bad," he once explained to his little brother. Isaac's pressure on Lee to work hard and obey him was so intense that, one summer soon after Joey's birth, Lee ran away from home. One morning, he traveled to New Jersey to apply for a job, realized he wouldn't get hired, and, rather than go back to face his father's disappointment, decided on the spur of the moment to board a train west. He was gone for nearly three months, traveling with hoboes, working odd jobs with farmers and ranchers in Arizona and California, sending postcards to Lena to assure her he was all right. Joey remembered the day Lee returned. Isaac was playing with Joey in the street, showing him how to wind the rubber-band propeller on a model plane, when Lee sauntered up to them from a nearby trolley stop. As soon as Lena saw him, she said something like "When you come from California, you've got to take a bath," and took him inside the apartment. Joey glanced up at his father, who was gripping the model high in his hand: a trembling airplane silhouetted against the sun.

FOR SOME TIME, Isaac had complained of stomach pains, and Lena noticed his stools were black as coal. Later, she believed the prodigious amount of cake he ate every night led to his bleeding ulcers.

One day, not long after Joey turned four, his family held a party. He hadn't seen his father for days, and Isaac was not around that afternoon. Joey's mother dressed him in a nice suit and pointed to a line of cars parked outside the apartment. The cars' interiors were hot. He didn't want to take a ride. Older boys from the neighborhood, also wearing suits, approached him to try to nudge him into a backseat, but he ran from them, thinking it was a game. Finally, he was forced to make the trip. Everyone got out of the cars in a large garden that had a stone bench and a rail fence. The day was brilliantly sunny. Adults, many of them strangers, fussed over Joey. An aunt he barely knew gave him a dollar. If he heard the word *funeral,* he didn't know what it meant.

Years later, he would learn from his sister that their father had gone into Columbia-Presbyterian Hospital in Manhattan for an operation on a stomach ulcer. Apparently, the surgeons stitched him poorly and he died of internal bleeding. He was forty-two years old. Sylvia, not quite thirteen, accompanied Lena on the subway into Manhattan when they received news of Isaac's death; Lena could not read the subway maps. Sylvia got them to Times Square, but she became confused at that point, misidentified a train, and led them astray, deep into the Bronx. The day, and their grief, seemed endless.

Possibly, Lena sent Joey to relatives the week before the burial so he would not be upset by the mourning and the ritual of sitting shivah. Later, he could never recover any memory of this period. In the week following the funeral, Sylvia wore heavy black dresses every day, though the late afternoons were broiling. Finally, one evening, Lena told her, in a gentler tone than usual, to put on something lighter and go down in the street to cool off.

The 1930 census lists Lena as "head" of the household, still without outside employment. Lee (Elias) is recorded as a "bookkeeper." Lena and the children moved across the street to a slightly cheaper, though similarly sized, apartment (with the first month's rent included free), next to a sandy trench dug for a trolley line, that all the neighbors called Railroad Avenue. The building was owned by an Italian family named Provenzano. Once the Hellers' belongings were out of the old place, Lee handed Joey a broom, picked up another broom, and told his little brother they were going to sweep out the empty rooms they had left behind. When Joey asked why, Lee replied he didn't want the new tenants to think the Hellers were slobs. Shortly after settling into the new place, Lee saved some money and bought Lena a brand-new radio.

What followed was a period of relative calm, at least on the surface; for Joey, it was a cozy, peaceful time. Lee was out of the house, working most days, returning in the early evenings. Lena shopped for, and cooked, dinner every night: smoked whitefish, kasha, and potato knishes deep-fried in vegetable oil. Lena bought these from a neighbor woman who sold homemade foods on the street—the knishes were a nickel apiece. The woman carried them from block to block in a kettle covered with black oilcloth. Sometimes, while cooking, Lena had to pause to break up a spat between Sylvia and Lee; the apartment was small and hot, especially in summer, and tempers grew short. Lena refused to let brother and sister go to bed angry with each other. After dinner, she would often say, half in Yiddish, half in English, that she could use a little ice cream. She'd give Joey a dime and send him off to a nearby soda fountain, with instructions to return with a pint of Golden Glow. The family gathered around the carton and ate all the ice cream on the spot, because they had no refrigerator. These moments were immensely satisfying to Joey. As an adult, he would look back and realize that, on some level, he had already learned not to want more than he could reasonably hope to have. What he had was blessing enough: the Jewish concept of *dayenu*. A pint of ice cream was plenty.

When fall came, Sylvia would sit near an open window in the evenings and do her homework by the light of a streetlamp outside, to save electricity. In the spring and summer, the family rented space to a succession of boarders. The children had to squeeze together in a single room; sometimes, one of them slept in the kitchen. One summer, one of these boarders played classical music every night on the family radio. Joey discerned familiar melodies in some of the performances. With a shock, he understood that playful echoes of Tchaikovsky popped up in big-band tunes such as "My Blue Heaven" and "April Showers"—songs he had heard in the afternoons on "Your Hit Parade." Without his full awareness, his keen ear had revealed to him some of the secrets of art: the richness of tradition and the impulse to play against it—variation, improvisation, and parody.

He was a precocious reader. Often, after dinner, every member of the family opened a book. Early on, Joey read the Rover Boy series and the tales of Tom Swift. An older cousin on his father's side, a man named Nat Siegel, who worked as an accountant in the city, brought him books.

For a while after Isaac's death, family drop-ins were regular. Many of Isaac's relatives lived in the city, and Lena remained close to them. She welcomed their care and concern, and Sylvia seemed to enjoy their visits, but Lee usually withdrew whenever his father's people came around. His aloofness embarrassed Lena. Though normally courteous and polite, he had inherited his father's reserve. His transition to his new country had been difficult. Years later, in a letter to his little brother, he would recall how the "goyim-Irish" in Coney Island used to call him "Jew-boy." "I was told [by my playmates] to lie on the ground, open my fly[,] and reveal [my] penis and then all the goyim kids would spit on it," he wrote. "I raised no objection—that said I was a good kid and then I would be allowed to play with them."

These experiences, as well as his naturally gentle temperament, pushed Lee beyond self-effacement, toward self-contradiction. At the end of a long day, he would simultaneously affirm and deny he was beat. He would complain about his tasks yet insist they weren't so bad. In these small ways, he implied nothing was what it seemed, and no one really knew him.

His behavior intrigued Joey as much as the laughter and speech of the big, loud people (strangers, though family) who came to see his mother. He would linger in the living room doorway, listening to the group tell affectionate stories about someone called "Itchy." It didn't occur to him until he was an adult that Itchy was a nickname for his father—a variation of Yitzak, Yiddish for Isaac (the name means "he who laughs").

Did he miss his father? He wasn't sure. Had he *known* the man? No one asked him what he felt. Lee was now largely in charge of him, correcting his behavior in company, seeking his help with errands, but Lee was not someone he could talk to, even if he knew what to say. Though Lee had assumed a mantle of responsibility, he was still a boy. One day, flirting with a group of girls, he abandoned Joey near Steeplechase ("the Funny Place"). A policeman found the child wandering alone and took him to the station, where Sylvia picked him up.

In *Now and Then,* Heller observed that around this time, he began to bite his nails, a nervous habit, which he implied was associated with the effect his father's absence, or his silence about it, had on him.

During summers, Lena, busy with her sewing, lost track of Joey as he ran to play on the beach with neighborhood friends: his old pal Marvin Winkler, whom everyone called "Beansy," for reasons no one could later remember; a boy named Murray Rabinowitz, known as "Rup"; Tony Provenzano, son of the Hellers' landlord; Lou Berkman; and Danny Rosoff, called the "Count," perhaps because of his fondness for swashbuckling tales in adventure books. The kids would fly past Moses' Candy Store (Mr. Moses, always scowling and hitching up his trousers), skitter by a Catholic orphanage located between Surf Avenue and the boardwalk, and stare at the pale, freckled boys behind the gate. Joey and his gang spent afternoons playing punchball or throwing confetti in the faces of girls, hearing them scream in delight and irritation (the boys especially liked to torment two neighborhood gals known to some of the older guys as "Squeezy" and "Frenchy"), or pooling the nickels their parents gave them for chocolates, jelly doughnuts, potato chips, or pretzels. Then they'd sprint, shouting and laughing, toward crowds sunbathing on the sand or lining up like obedient soldiers, wearing backpacks and carrying provisions, waiting to ride the Wonder Wheel, Shoot-the-Chutes, the Mile Sky Chaser, the Tornado, the Thunderbolt, or the brand-new Cyclone. Ride by ride, Joey built his courage for the next teeth-rattling challenge. He once said, "I approached [the Chaser] . . . in the same frame of mind with which I suppose I will eventually face death itself—with the conviction that if other people could go through it . . . I could too." (The Mile Sky Chaser featured a sudden eighty-foot drop.)

The boys discovered that elderly visitors to Luna Park or Steeple-chase, becoming fatigued, did not use all their ride tickets. Joey and his friends would sneak inside the parks and ask the oldsters if they could take the unused tickets. Joey gathered enough passes to go many times on any ride he wanted—to the point that soon he was so blasé, he never wanted to ride anything again. Thrills! Spills! Excitement! Nothing lived up to its billing for long. "[Eventually,] I could anticipate accurately every dive and turn of the Mile Sky Chaser with my eyes closed better than, years later, I was ever able to read an aerial map in the air corps," he wrote in his memoir.

Walking home each dusk, passing fashionably dressed couples being pushed along the boardwalk in rolling wicker chairs, Joey loved the raucous patter of Yiddish rising from porch stoops as women, fresh from doing the day's laundry or washing dishes, sought company and cool air. His mother was not so enamored of the neighborhood. The crowds were growing bigger on the boardwalk—louder, more vulgar, she thought. This was no place for a kid. Coney was a "*chozzer* mart," she hissed: a pig market.

Since the completion of the subway line from Manhattan, the number of daily visitors to Coney Island at summer's peak had almost doubled from half a million just a few years before. There *was* more noise and trash. Known as "the Nickel Empire" now, because of the five-cent train fares and the cheaper entertainments on display to draw bigger and bigger throngs, the place was pure frenzy. Sometimes there wasn't enough space on the beach for a person to drop a towel. At the Municipal Bath House, where families changed from street clothes into beach wear or bathing suits, only twelve thousand lockers were available. Some Coney Island residents, seizing a chance to make a dime, erected changing tents out of bedsheets and lured people to the sidewalks in front of their apartment buildings or bungalows. Families took to undressing in the open or under the boardwalk. It disgusted Lena to catch from her window flashes of naked bodies, skinny, fat, disintegrating. On side streets, people ate pungent fried foods from sloppy tubs brought from home. Lena hated the way Joey and his pals hung around beach gymnasts, loudmouthed oafs, barely dressed, flexing their muscles, standing on their heads or balancing awkwardly on the exposed torsos of their girl-friends. Food wrappers and paper cups amassed like sediment in the Railroad Avenue trench, and on windy afternoons they blew up into the street against your legs.

Lena was immensely relieved when Joey became old enough for kindergarten and sleepaway camp in the summers. Anything to keep him off the beach. She sent him once to Surprise Lake in Cold Spring, sixty miles north of New York City. Surprise Lake was a Jewish camp catering mostly to underprivileged families from Manhattan's Lower East Side (in time, alumni from the camp would include Eddie Cantor, Walter Matthau, Neil Simon, Larry King, and Neil Diamond). Proba-bly, Lena learned about the camp from Lee, who was more conscious than she was of the world beyond Coney Island. Lee filled out the pa-perwork, making sure Joey qualified for financial aid. Lena helped Joey pack his suitcase. Two weeks later, when he returned, she discovered that none of the clothes had been touched. He had used his toothbrush and comb but never once changed his shirt or pants. When Lena asked him why, he replied that no one had told him to unpack. Plus, he'd found it easier just to leave the bag alone.

In 1930, he entered first grade at Coney Island's PS 188. He was a bundle of anxiety. Family members had always told him he was hand-some, and now he studied his face obsessively in the bathroom mirror to make sure none of his features had deteriorated overnight. He feared he was already going bald because his forehead was so much higher than his ears. He tried different parts in his hair, worried about his height. Mostly, he checked the mirror each morning just to make sure he was still Joey Heller.

He fantasized constantly. His imagination, along with his already well-developed reading skills, distinguished him from his classmates during his early school years. Teachers praised his writing and read it aloud in class. At one point, his cousin Nat Siegel gave him a prose translation of the *Iliad*: the first work of literature to make a "real im-pression" on him, he said. "I read that and reread it almost without stop." Afterward, he loved doing book reports. In one paper, he as-sumed the persona of Tom Sawyer. For another assignment, much later, he wrote from the point of view of the metal in the gun that killed Abraham Lincoln. It pleased him to get good grades, and to hear his works read aloud as models of excellent writing. Some of his classmates began to resent the favor he earned from teachers, and his nervous maladies worsened. Warts sprouted on his hands and arms, as many as seventeen during one stretch.

Like the amusement park rides, whose thrills paled quickly, the teachers' praise came to be routine, and Joey grew restless in class. Many years later, Sylvia recalled an incident. "Joe brought home a note from his teacher, asking my mother to come to school and talk to her," she said. "We were all terrified. My mother didn't trust her English, so I went. . . . The teacher told me Joe never listened in class and always looked bored. She said she kept trying to catch him, but he always knew the answer. She admitted he was too bright for the class, but he was demoralizing the other kids and frustrating her. All we could do was tell Joe to try to look as though he was paying attention."

So he masked himself: sometimes studious and polite, at other times, to hide his uncertainties and fears of physical afflictions, preening and loud. "He was brighter than all of us. He was a needler, a big mouth," Beansy Winkler told Barbara Gelb. "Joe," he said, became a "pain in the neck."

JOSEPH HELLER was bright enough as a child to absorb the knowledge that he inhabited a wildly contradictory world; the way to negotiate its seams was to split himself—on the one hand, acting boldly, and on the other, withdrawing to replenish and nourish his imagination. Force and avoidance: modes of existence oddly consistent with the surge and lull of Coney Island. At summer's peak, the force of bodies yearning for physical release overwhelmed the boardwalk, the beach, and the residential neighborhoods. In the off-season, during the gray winter months, visitors' avoidance of the area was so total, the silence was eerie. The surf, with its hidden undertow, appeared to reclaim what primitive appetites had chewed up and distorted only weeks before.

The question remained: What *was* Coney Island? A big top or a family enclave? For that matter, was it America or Russia—or Italy, Armenia, or Germany? A petri dish for socialism, as Isaac Heller believed—where the working class could bask in leisure and freedom—or a fountain of capitalism, as George Tilyou, Edward Riegelmann, and Nathan Handwerker set out to prove?

More to the point, perhaps, Morris Lapidus, a Russian immigrant, and an architect both revered and derided for his dramatic decorative styles, once wrote that his first "emotional surge" about architecture came from a visit he made as a child to Luna Park. "I was standing on [an] elevated platform just as dusk was falling [over Coney Island,]" he wrote, "and the lights went on. To me it was the most beautiful sight I'd [ever] seen. Of course, I knew it was hanky-pank, a circus and showmanship. But to a child of six it was all the wonders of the world. I never outgrew it."

In the 1930s, little Joey Heller could articulate none of these perspectives, but he had taken them all in, including Lapidus's secret for grasping Coney Island's wooly mix, which was that no secret existed. Coney contained multitudes, to paraphrase an old visitor to its shores. To judge it one way or the other was to miss too many things of importance. Its beauty lay in its wastes, its wholeness in fragments plucked from ruin. These things, Joey knew instinctively.

Six decades later, reflecting on his literary career, he told an audience at Michigan State University that he didn't know if the combination of "morbid[ity]" and "comedy" in his writing had come from the "garishness [and] . . . gaudiness" of his Coney Island childhood, but once, when a critic suggested this possibility, he "like[d] the thought"—that is, it felt right to him.

In his memoir, he recalled his youth with fondness and nostalgia. It is striking, though, that one of the most visceral passages in the book concerned the end of each day, "when the ticket booths close[d] and the lights [went] out." Then, he wrote, "Coney Island [was] . . . rather unclean":

> The aromatic foods that had been fried and grilled turned greasy.
> In the early hours of the next day the odors in the street already
> signaled decay. Even the fresh breezes from the sea, which had
> awakened keen appetites earlier and stimulated the other senses,
> could no longer bear away those repellent effluvia of garbage. [I]
> had already realized that in winter Coney Island was in the main
> a lonely, dark and windy place for people grown too old for
> homework, roller-skating, or playing tag.

In detail and tone, the passage resembles Isaac Babel's descriptions of a Russian city street following a pogrom ("My world was small and horrible . . . the earth smelt of . . . the grave and of flowers . . . [and I] wept more bitterly, completely and happily than I ever wept again in all my life," Babel wrote in "The Story of My Dovecot"). As a child, Heller did not know about the world his father had fled, but he may have sensed in his mother's bitterness, in the mockery and mourning of her Yiddish, that the world his father found was, in fundamental, spirit-crushing ways, not awfully different from the one he'd sought to escape. What *was* clear to the child was that he could not make his way in the world without a hustle or a scam, or at least the knowledge that what people *said* was going on really wasn't going on.

"I DIDN'T REALIZE then how traumatized I was. As a boy in school I used to say my father was 'deceased.' I was aware without being aware," Heller told Barbara Gelb in 1979. ("As always, when talking of his parents, he stutters very slightly," Gelb noted.)

"Joe was a nervous wreck," George Mandel told Gelb for her magazine profile. Years later, when reminded of this comment, Mandel expressed surprise he'd ever said such a thing, but he added, "I do recall . . . [his friends] were careful not to shout his name from behind for fear he might jump off the sidewalk in traffic." Heller had met Mandel around the neighborhood and they became pals, sharing quick wits and rich imaginations.

In his memoir, Heller recalled "suffering headaches" as he grew into his teens. He continued to bite his nails and study his image in the mirror. He tended to avoid the amusement parks now. Instead, he and his friends transferred to the beach lessons they had learned in the parks—that *everything* is a game designed to sucker somebody, and most people can be conned into wanting what they don't really want. The boys bought ice cream and soda pop, then turned around and sold them at a higher price to younger kids. Or they'd resell the jelly apples they'd bought from a neighbor woman, Mrs. Gelber; some of the apples were rotten and had worms in the center. Sometimes, a member of the group would steal costume jewelry from his parents' bedroom and peddle it. The gang could always spot plainclothes cops: The men wore shirts outside their trousers to conceal weapons and badges. Besides, they were all Gentiles.

Seeking more gainful employment, Heller—still Joey to his friends—took an evening newspaper route, delivering the reactionary Hearst paper, the *New York American,* which attracted few readers among the Jewish and Italian families in his neighborhood. After school each day, he walked down to the Stillwell Avenue subway station, grabbed a Nathan's dog, and picked up his bundle of papers, paying a penny and a half for each. Then he hawked the things for two cents. One night, at an Irish bar along the boardwalk, a man seated at a table just inside the doorway called Joey in, snatched a paper, read the racing results on the back page, and returned the paper. Then he gave Joey a dime. "I was in heaven, strolling on air as I went back outside," he wrote in his memoir. "I was in love with a world that had such humans in it."

The incident cemented a certainty in him that would drive him all his life: "[F]ew pleasures are so thoroughly reinforcing to the spirit as the arrival of unexpected money," he decided. Years later, recalling the aunt who had given him a dollar at his father's funeral, he wrote, "I associate money with life, and an absence of money with death. I can't help it."

Because the newspapers didn't move well in his area, he riffed on the headlines, or tried to spice them up, to attract more readers. "Extra! Hitler dies . . . his mustache!" he would shout. He had only the vaguest idea who Hitler was. After finishing his route, giving away the remaining papers to his favorite families, he ran home, did his homework, and challenged his imagination more thoroughly than when falsifying the news. Inspired in part by Danny the Count's talk of Hemingway, Fitzgerald, and Faulkner, he tried penciling a few short stories, using as models the "short shorts" he found in the copies of *Collier's* or *Liberty* that Lee or Sylvia brought home occasionally (the short shorts were a thousand words or less, and usually ended with a big surprise). Many of his efforts echoed the *Iliad,* with facts and details smuggled in from whatever he was studying in school.

Walking to his classes in the mornings wasn't the cinch it used to be. As the neighborhood boys got older, they split into factions, divided by personalities, interests, and cultural backgrounds. The Italian boys threatened to beat up the Jews, and vice versa. Occasionally, gangs of boys threw small rocks at one another. Joey never encountered serious trouble, but he had to be more careful now. The place was rougher than before, money was scarcer (the Depression was deepening), and local neighborhoods were constantly unsettled by rumblings of change. A familiar joke was, "First this was Coney Island, now it's Cohen's Island, soon it will be Coon's Island."

In the afternoons, after school, some of Joey's friends gathered outside Sammy the Pig's pool room, near Happy's Luncheonette on Mermaid Avenue, to smoke marijuana and listen to the older boys talk about gambling and girls. Generally, Joey craved food more than weed, and he'd spend all his newspaper money on Happy's pork chops.

Lena worried about the coarsening effects of the Depression on her family, but her hopes that politicians or community leaders could clean things up weakened by the year. Joey recalled the last surge of political excitement in his neighborhood—it erupted the year he turned nine. Norman Thomas brought his socialist message to Coney Island; standing next to hot dog stands and merry-go-rounds, he promised to "repeal unemployment," while crowds cheered and munched on pickle sandwiches. Joey, Sylvia, and Lee taught Lena enough English to qualify her to vote. On the eve of the 1932 election, Joey joined a torchlight parade, chanting with a group, "Hoover, Hoover, rah, rah rah! Put him in the trash can, ha, ha, ha!"

In truth, he had already understood—and learned to distrust—the dynamic behind most American politics. By watching the shill games along the boardwalk, he grasped that the barker, the person with power, always offered more than he could deliver (therefore, he could never really lose), but his constituency walked away generally satisfied at having participated in something, with the occasional illusion of winning.

Nineteen thirty-two came and went. Coney's trash cans overflowed. Lena felt it was too late in life to convince her family to turn to religion for steadiness and solace; she herself had never been so inclined, but some part of her suffered guilt at being nonobservant. She worried that if the kids didn't dress nicely on High Holidays and appear to be off to services, other families would suspect they were Communists. One by one, many of Joey's friends celebrated bar mitzvahs. He did not.

He was more likely to grapple with spiritual matters—thoughts of mortality or the meaning of existence—on the beach or in the sea. He and his friends liked to do the dead man's float in the ocean, letting the tide carry them far from shore, then beelining to a bell buoy about a quarter of a mile out. It was an exhausting adventure, and they alternated dog-paddling with intensive arm strokes, or they gave in to the tide as it carried them toward their goal. One day, one of the boys announced he was too tired to make it back to land. Joey and the others gathered around and got him safely to shore. Only afterward did it occur to Joey how powerful the tide was, and how close they had come to being washed away by it.

What struck him most, out by the buoy, was the roaring quiet, the way it swamped Coney's clamor. Everything that loomed so large on the beach—the roller coasters, carousels, and Ferris wheels—became, at this distance, thimbles, needles, pins. In these moments, bobbing on the waves, tugged by the tide, Joey began to think he had a "haunted imagination," a contemplative streak with an undertow of sadness and resignation.

On another "haunted" occasion, he observed a batch of kites break loose from its anchor on the beach. He ran up alleys and streets, keeping the kites in view; eventually, the string binding them snagged on a radio aerial on a rooftop next to his apartment. He scurried up the stairs to the top of his building, crawled onto the brick parapet, and reached for the nearest kite, which flopped just out of reach. He swayed, straightened, then leaned forward a little over a row of trash cans far below, until it occurred to him that any moment now he might plunge from the sky.

He discovered a different kind of spiritual mystery—the aesthetic—in the early evenings, in the apartments of the families with whom the Hellers shared the building. The Provenzanos had a player piano, whose mechanical proficiency fascinated Joey. Tony Provenzano owned a collection of finely painted lead soldiers, less engaging for the fantasies of war they provoked than for their beauty when lined up symmetrically. The Kaisers, on the second floor, across the hall from the Provenzanos, owned a phonograph. They played Enrico Caruso over and over, as well as a comedy record called *Cohen on the Telephone,* delivered by a man with a thick Yiddish accent, and detailing, with painful hilarity, an immigrant's inability to properly place a call. The Kaisers also owned a complete set of *The Book of Knowledge,* and Joey sat for hours in the apartment with his friend Irving, reading through entries on insects, ancient lands, and do-it-yourself projects.

Also in the evenings, groups of boys, filthy with beach sand, went to the movies, walking to the RKO Tilyou or the Loew's Coney Island. The Marx Brothers were Joey's favorites. Harpo had first teamed up with Groucho and Gummo in 1907, at Henderson's Music Hall in Coney Island. In their physical antics and verbal swiftness, the brothers seemed to embody the chaos of the place, and Coney Island served as a backdrop in several early film comedies, including those of Fatty

Arbuckle, Harold Lloyd, and Buster Keaton. One evening, a new movie theater opened up, the Surf, just a block away from the Hellers' apartment, and Joey took his mother. The film was *One Night of Love,* which featured a Puccini aria and melodies that echoed his music. Joey fell for the lead actress, an opera singer named Grace Moore, who would die in a plane crash some years later.

The movie was a pleasant shared moment with his mother. He didn't have many like it. He fought with her as he got a little older, more independent, less inclined to stay home—though usually these were struggles of silence or tense avoidance. "You've got a twisted brain," she told him one day when he frightened her by climbing a telephone pole just outside the kitchen window and asking nonchalantly as he peered at her, "Ma, can I have a glass of milk?"

Another time, angry at her demands on him, he called her a bastard, believing she wouldn't know the meaning of the word. "At once I saw with terror that I was mistaken," he wrote in *Now and Then.* "She gasped with incredulity, and staggered back a step. And I knew in an instant . . . that I never wanted to see her again with such an expression of deep hurt. I prayed she would never tell anyone."

More than his mother, he turned to Lee for guidance and support, which is not to say he obeyed his brother unconditionally. One night when Joey was down on the street, Lee called to him, saying it was late. Time for him to come up, take a bath, go to bed. Joey refused. Lee came after him. Joey ran. Suddenly, a car turned a corner, blinded Joey with its headlights, and screeched to a stop just as it nudged the boy and sent him sprawling against its bumper. Shaken, he let Lee lead him upstairs.

On another night, Lee caught him smoking a cigarette in a storefront on Surf Avenue, about a block away from home. "How long have you been doing that?" he asked. Joey didn't answer. He crushed the butt with his foot. "As long as you're doing it, you might as well do it at home," Lee told him. "You should try not to do anything outside the house that you wouldn't want us to know about." He pulled a pack of smokes from his pocket. "Here, have one of mine," he said.

After their father's death, Lee had abandoned his dreams of going to college. He knew his family depended on him, and he took seriously his role as Joey's mentor. He wouldn't talk about Isaac. The closest he'd come was to recall the wonder of discovering oranges in the galley of the ship when he was four years old, sailing from Russia.

When Lee was twenty-nine, he married a sweet woman named Perle, and prepared to move to Crown Heights, where he hoped work would be more plentiful. On the day of the wedding, Joey was fifteen. He sat in the synagogue, hot in his suit, his attention drifting until his mother walked up the aisle as part of the procession. The rabbi praised her for the love and generosity she had shown the groom as she raised him, though he was not her biological son. Joey sat up straight. The rabbi went on, honoring Lee's and Sylvia's "stepmom." All around the room, guests smiled and wept with happiness. Joey could not speak.

3. Fear of Filing

EACH TIME, the dream followed the same course, but its predictability was not consoling. To the contrary, its fixed sequence intensified Joey's terror. First, a man with a shadowed face approached the apartment and walked through the front door. In his bed (in the dream), Joey came awake. He knew the man was there. Next, he visualized the blackened figure stride from room to room, on his way to find Joey. The steps grew louder; the boy sat up in bed, the sheets as resistant as wet sand. Time stretched like a roll of taffy. Now he pictured the man just outside his door, the face still a dark wedge, his hands reaching toward the room, toward Joey . . . and then the boy *really* woke, with a half moan in his throat. He was as parched as the day he'd lost his tonsils.

The confusion did not dissipate during his waking hours. In the mornings, he studied his mother's face as carefully as he watched his reflection in the mirror. Certainly, he resembled her: the same high forehead, big cheekbones, curling mouth, brown eyes. Lee and Sylvia had bright blue eyes. Now he could see it: They looked like each other, but not much like him. Or perhaps his perceptions had been distorted by his second glance at the family. Joey stoked the fury he'd felt ever since the rabbi had referred to Lena as Lee's stepmother at the wedding. "I felt victimized, disgraced," he wrote years later. "I [fell] silent." He trained himself "to stifle painful emotion," becoming the "walking proof of . . . Freud's theories of repression."

The humiliation caused by his family's foggy past deepened when his friend Beansy Winkler reacted to the news with a shrug. Beansy said his mother had told him about the Heller family ages ago. She had cautioned him not to hurt Joey's feelings by bringing the matter up. Lena, Lee, and Sylvia insisted they had never attempted to hide anything. They all assumed he knew the truth (How *could* I have known? he screamed in his head), and so there was no reason to talk about it. No secret, no scandal. "Our stepmother raised us as though all three of us were her own children," Sylvia told Barbara Gelb. "It never occurred to any of us to discuss it with Joe."

Sullenly, Joey prodded Sylvia with questions: Who *was* her real mother? What had happened to her? What was their dad like, really? Sylvia answered that her mother was ill and had died. Soon afterward, their father grew ill and died. That's all he needed to know. The family moved on and looked after itself. (The *Lapland*'s manifest, which records Elias Heller as a four-year-old passenger on the ship that arrived in New York in 1913, shows him traveling with someone named Pauline, identified as a "housewife" who could read and write. Years later, in a letter to his brother, Lee wrote that, of the family, it was "just mom and me" on the boat, and that's all he would ever say.)

A curtain of silence drew around the Heller apartment. Joey brooded, lashing out at Sylvia when she bleached her hair one day, or came home smelling of cigarettes, though he didn't really care about these things. In his head, he mocked his mother's insistence that all she did was work for her family; she never did anyone harm, she said, and what thanks did she get in return? Petulance, prickliness.

No harm? Just listen to her curse! Torrents of miserable Yiddish! In the background, on the radio, the hateful chants of Father Coughlin. He would drone, angrily, throatily, until someone in the household realized the terrible things he was saying—against Negroes, Jews—and turn him off.

In calmer moments, in the evenings, after homework and ice cream, Joey would set aside his bruised feelings and reflect briefly on the others' hardships: Lee and Sylvia, orphaned, taken in by this woman; Lena, in a strange country, raising two children not her own.

She urged Joey to go to synagogue and say Kaddish for his dead father. He suspected she was less concerned about his desire for family connections than about cultivating appearances for the neighbors.

And appearances were the problem. They couldn't be counted on. One Father's Day, Joey noticed neighborhood boys giving their daddies presents. He bought a carton of Camels for Lee. Brother, father figure, now husband—Lee's guises were hard to penetrate. He owned a tennis racket—probably obtained one summer when he worked as a camp counselor—but he never took it out of the closet. It sat there in its strange wooden frame, collecting dust, yet he wouldn't get rid of it. On Joey's behalf, he'd send away for college catalogs (never too early to start thinking about it, he'd say)—Harvard, Yale, MIT, Oberlin—and then remind Joey the family would never be able to afford to send him to school. And if Lee was hard to locate beneath these shadowy layers, what about Joey himself? Of his Father's Day gift to his brother, he wrote in his memoir, "I still am unable to decide . . . whether the deed was one of sincere gratitude and affection or merely a stunt contrived to excite comment and win me some complimentary attention."

By 1938, Lee was living with his wife in Crown Heights and working in a brokerage firm on Wall Street. In his absence, some of the air seemed to leak out of the apartment. Joey, Sylvia, and Lena pantomimed nitwit routines of courtesy, hoping to banish the tension in the home by pretending it didn't exist. Each evening, on the radio, the WNYC announcer would chirp that he was "coming to [his listeners] from the city of New York, where seven million people live in peace and harmony and enjoy the benefits of democracy." Nitwits, everywhere.

Then came night, and a dark face rising from sleep.

Discomfort followed him out the door in the mornings, into the streets, coloring everything he saw. In its off-season dreariness, Coney seemed to him more desiccated than ever. Gray light, like gauze, hovered over the West End Villa nearby, a row of single-family bungalows where Lee had met Perle (her family used to rent a place there every summer); deserted now, the buildings seemed squat and ugly. Joey watched elderly men and women struggle with steep, uneven stairs along the sides of multistory apartment houses, watched for signs of movement in the dark, gazing at the empty windows of the Half Moon Hotel a couple blocks away. Braving the boardwalk in wind and spitting rain, he'd see condoms washing ashore in the waves (he and his friends called them "Coney

Island whitefish"), newspapers, blown from trash cans, covered with fruit peels, smears of mussels, or sticky bits of crab shell scattered across the headlines like colorful appliqué. The beach, mined with half-buried detritus, smelled like a soggy carpet. Here and there, a merry-go-round or a concession stand remained open. More often than not, their proprietors' breath gave off whiskey. Mechanical laughter from some "Spectacular Show!" down the boardwalk followed him everywhere; whether it was hysterical or bored, he couldn't tell.

Schoolwork, never challenging to him, became less so (though he liked having something to do). *Getting* to school was an ordeal now. He had started high school at Abraham Lincoln on Ocean Parkway, three miles from his neighborhood. To get there, he took the Surf Avenue trolley, through the amusement area and up Neptune. Or he'd ride a bus— rollicking, usually, with big, muscled boys from Sea Gate, a once-exclusive enclave (no Jews or Italians), now fallen on tough times, on the western edge of Brooklyn, where the Coney Island boardwalk ended. Many of the boys on the bus were linemen on the high school football team.

Lincoln, built in 1929, was overcrowded with kids from all over Brooklyn. The entering classes had to occupy an annex on the top floor of a nearby elementary school. The main campus and the annex were located in a predominately Italian neighborhood (though the teachers were mostly second-generation Jewish college graduates). As he always had, Joey negotiated most social situations, including awkward meetings with new kids, by being a fast talker, a wisecracker. Once, an eighth-grade teacher of his, a Miss Lamm, appointed him class monitor while she stepped out. She knew this was the best way to neutralize the most disruptive kid in class. Joey stood, swaggering, and said to the group, "Okay, youse guys, quiet down," and they did. In high school, the students made fun of their teachers; they secretly referred to T. D. Bartells, their algebra instructor, as "Titty Bottles." Frequently, he threw chalk bullets at Joey for misbehaving in class.

For all his bravado, Joey worried about being accepted, doing well, looking good. Some of his classmates called him "Horse Head" because of his large skull. His thick hair drew lots of stares from girls, but he wasn't sure he wanted it to curl so much. Sometimes at night, he'd steal one of his sister's hairnets and sleep in it. The fear of her catching him wearing one of those things was as great as his worry over the prospect of another bad dream.

LIKE LEE, Sylvia was often gone from the apartment now. She had always been a hard worker. As a little girl, she would take the family's empty soda bottles back to Mr. Moses at his corner candy store for a two-cent deposit (that is, *if* she could snatch them away from Lena; before the beach became too "vulgar," Lena liked to bathe her legs in the surf and then fill one of the bottles with seawater to wash the sand from her feet). When Sylvia was older, she worked as a locker girl at Hahn's Roosevelt Baths and then sold frozen custard on the boardwalk. She always hoped to save enough money to buy the kinds of fashionable skirts and sweaters her classmates wore, and discard the dark hand-me-down dresses that came from an older first cousin. As a teenager, she offered to help Mr. Moses in his store. For a long time, his telephone, in a booth just inside the door, was the only one in the neighborhood. Sylvia's first dates were arranged on this phone; she blushed as she flirted and joked with the boys, whispering into the receiver as people milled about her in the aisles. As a kid, Joey sometimes earned a couple of pennies from Mr. Moses for running to get someone who had a call.

By the time Joey reached high school, Sylvia had secured a spot at R. H. Macy's department store in Manhattan, but not before encountering astonishing barriers at various employment agencies. In newspapers, many "Help Wanted" ads stated explicitly that no Jews need apply; the agencies' attitudes were only a bit less obvious. Sylvia learned to put the word *Protestant* on her applications. "I didn't even know what Protestant was but I knew it was good," she said. It cost a dime for the trolley and train into the city, and a quarter or so for lunch. "I would give my pay to Momma each day but most of the time she wouldn't take it all. She'd put some of it in my drawer for me to save," she recalled.

Lee also faced anti-Semitism in the jobs he'd gotten, which included making deliveries for a laundry in a horse-drawn wagon ("Where does a Jew come to a horse?" Lena would say in a worried tone each day. "Watch out for those horses"), working at Woolworth's, and serving as a caterer's assistant. Now, in his Wall Street job, he was miserable; temperamentally, he was not a bully, and he was therefore ill-suited to the brokerage firm.

Joey knew none of the specifics of his brother's and sister's professional lives, but he felt their tensions in the evenings, when Lee would stop by to check on Lena, and when Sylvia returned from the city, her fingers smelling of the corned-beef hash she'd had for lunch ("We all hated [it], but it was the only thing that could be divided" among several people with little spending money, she said). She talked about a "fanny pincher" she had to work with, but in a veiled and jokey way, as though he didn't really bother her. Lena listened silently to the stories, frowning, shaking her head, while turning a frayed collar on a man's shirt or altering a dress. A cousin of hers had opened a clothing shop in Flatbush and threw her some work now and then.

The stress and exhaustion in the apartment drove Joey from it as soon as he finished most of his homework each night. He sought a space of his own (the others had kept from him a secret existence; now, it was *his* turn to forge a separate life). He'd go downstairs to his friend Irving Kaiser's apartment—just above Mr. Kaiser's tailor shop—and listen to records. Also, Irving owned a typewriter. Joey would pound out some of his book reports on it; occasionally, one of them veered into a free-form fantasy or the beginning of a short story, most of which he kept to himself (it pleased him almost as much to hoard his brilliance—a surprise that would one day dazzle everyone—as it did to show it off). In school, he was forced to read Keats and Yeats, but he didn't give a fig for them. Nor did he join the students who worked on the literary magazine or the school paper, *The Lincoln Log*. They liked to run about, à la Walt Whitman, shouting Shakespeare into the wind. Danny the Count ("I taught you how to hustle, so *listen* to me") told Joey he should read Benchley and Wodehouse.

Instead, he preferred the contemporary fiction in the magazines Lee and Sylvia brought from the city, or the books they checked out of the circulating library in Magrill's Drugstore, over on Mermaid: the Studs Lonigan trilogy and the stories of Damon Runyon and John O'Hara. A friend of Sylvia's, on learning that Sylvia's little brother showed an interest in writing, brought him a copy of Irwin Shaw's story collection *Sailor Off the Bremen*. Afterward, Joey began looking for Shaw's fiction in *The New Yorker*. "When I [finally] came in contact with good literature [in college], it was kind of a joke," he recalled in a radio interview in 1984. "It took me many, many years to be able to read novels in which dialogue and melodramatic actions were not the key." At one point, however, a copy of James Joyce's *Ulysses* made it into the Heller apartment, on the strength of its alleged obscenity. It returned to Magrill's unread by any member of the family, though years later Joe recalled the thrill of running across the word *snot* in its pages.

For a while, he was drawn to the Kaisers' apartment for reasons other than records and the typewriter. A young woman boarded with them. Her boyfriend worked at a concession stand in the amusement area. The woman had a habit of walking around in a half slip and bra, with the door to her room partly open, or in the hosiery she'd bought at Baumel's Specialty Shop nearby. Joey kept hoping to catch glimpses of her. More and more, girls had the power to astonish him. One day, he was standing outside Kaiser's Tailor Shop when Dolly Partini, an Italian girl who lived across the street, walked past him carrying a pail full of mussels from the beach. Often, Joey and his friends killed time by plucking mussels from rocks or catching crabs by using cracked mussels as lures, but otherwise, he didn't know what they were good for. Dolly dizzied him by telling him they were wonderful to eat. The smell of the sea rose, brackish, from her pail and unsettled his stomach.

At school, he developed "secret and serious, nonsexual crush[es] on one girl or another," he wrote in *Now and Then*. Usually, his ardor settled on whichever female occupied the sight line between him and the teacher. The joy was less in interacting with a girl, or even watching her, than it was in storing a hidden pleasure.

Food was his other private, sweetly guilty indulgence. He had never forgotten the comfort of sitting around eating ice cream with Lena, Lee, and Sylvia in the days shortly after his father's death. Now, whenever he felt unhappy or tense, he "prowl[ed] about the kitchen" at night, "agitate[d]" by a "rapacious appetite," he wrote. He kept his kitchen raids secret, and yet, from time to time, he appeared to desire an end to the furtiveness. "[Once,] I found in the cupboard a bulb of garlic with several of the cloves already broken loose," he recalled. "I thought surely that if I ate one or two, nobody would know. They soon knew. Everyone knew. For the next few days, people even half a block away knew."

"[ONE EVENING] I learned that once you had a breast in your hand, there wasn't much you could do with it," he said.

The boys and girls of Abraham Lincoln formed social and athletic clubs in the basements of homes or in back rooms provided by local store owners. Adults encouraged these clubs, hoping to keep the kids out of trouble on the streets and (though this went largely unsaid) to prevent too much intermingling of ethnic groups, as well as fraternizing among lower and middle-class kids. With money from his newspaper route, Joey chipped in with several friends to rent a cellar in a two-family house and buy some bare-bones furniture and a phonograph. They called this Club Hilight. The Club Alteo ("All Loyal to Each Other") was another popular gathering spot; it was located in the back of a store on a side street, two blocks from Joey's apartment. The Alteo was a venerable institution, started several years earlier by kids who were now in their twenties. Joey and his pals constituted a second generation.

Kids of roughly the same age, and all known to one another, hung out at the Hilight, listening to records. The Alteo's crowd was decidedly more diverse in age, geography (though limited to Brooklyn), and experience. There, Joey heard Duke Ellington's music for the first time, and that of Count Basie. He realized with mild shock that he preferred these innovative black musicians to the blander, more commercial talents of Tommy Dorsey and Glenn Miller. At the Alteo, he heard older boys brag about sexual derring-do. He saw the "vipers"—the heavy marijuana smokers—sneak out the back door. He watched couples do the lindy hop, and tried to discern the physical signals sent by girls *and* boys, for it amazed him how the sexually precocious always found one another quickly. Clearly, he was not advanced that way, because most nights he was stuck against a wall, gawking, though his body hummed with curiosity.

Fortunately, there were plenty of curious girls, too, including some he'd known since elementary school: Ruth Gerstein (the first girl he ever kissed, in a game of Spin the Bottle at their eighth-grade graduation party), Gladys Simon, and Phyllis Ritterman, who had told him as early as fourth grade that she wanted to be a novelist. Before long, he had managed to explore a female breast, then sat there wondering what to do with it. (A few months prior to joining the clubs, he got his first quick "feel," from a classmate he barely knew, at a well-known gathering spot for teens, Lindbergh Park, named after the famous pilot. The park was in Sea Gate, where Jews were not particularly welcome.)

One night, a girl from Joey's French class, known to him as Gertrude, showed up at the Alteo accompanied by her older sister, who introduced her as Gail. What did this mean? Had she adopted an alias in preparation for indulging in unspeakable behavior? She wore a tight sweater and a high-lift bra, lipstick and mascara. Joey had never seen her like this. She caught his eye, recognized him, and looked away, embarrassed. The older boys, the seniors, circled her. Women's secrets were many, their mysteries manifold and deep.

Sexual maneuverings aside, the clubs provided safe places for like-minded kids to mingle and find support. To his fellow club members, Danny the Count sang his Faulkner refrain. George Mandel rhapsodized about Beethoven and Basie. He and Joey had become quite close, though Mandel was three years older and Joey was a junior member of the club. Joey was "perceptive enough to be wary of [people], even scared," Mandel noticed. But he was also "courageous enough to be . . . daring." The two of them shared an interest in contemporary fiction; already, Mandel had earned the right to call himself a professional writer. He was making three hundred to four hundred dollars a week scripting and illustrating comic books. His drawings of the human figure had an angular clarity, and he possessed an uncanny ability to expose the foibles of vanity. His sly puncturing of social hypocrisy would undergird what the mainstream press later termed the "Beat ethos." At first, some of his friends laughed at the amount of time he spent doodling, but the comic-book industry was beginning to burgeon. An outfit called National Allied Publishing, working out of a tiny office in Manhattan, solicited freelance artists, many of whom were high school kids happy to work at a rate of five dollars per page. In just a few years, ever since Dell Publishing and the Eastern Color Printing Company in Waterbury, Connecticut, had teamed up to present newspaper funnies in a tabloid-style format, the comic book had flourished. When Mandel drove up to the Club Alteo one day in a blue convertible with hydraulic transmission and an automatic top, his friends stopped laughing at his doodles. Over the next couple of years, he earned more and more, working primarily for a company called Funnies Inc., as comics became increasingly popular, riding the caped shoulders of Superman. Two Jewish high school kids in Cleveland had created the Man of Steel. They sincerely believed in America's promise. Superman was the ultimate assimilationist, emigrating from another planet to proclaim the American way. No shadowy evildoer—not even a Nazi—could escape him.

Joey spent hours at the Club Alteo, poring over Mandel's drawings, sharing story ideas with him. Together, they recited absurd variations of well-known passages from the Bible, or conceived jingles that parodied radio ads. Joey's take on a popular Pepsi-Cola commercial went like this: "Pepsi Cola hits the spot / When I drink it, how I fart / Twice as much for a nickel too / Pepsi Cola is the drink for you." Playing off another ad, he'd sing, "If there's a gleam in her eye / Each time she unzips your fly / You know the lady's in love with you." This silliness required little creative effort, but it got Joey listening carefully to the "Lucky Strike Hit Parade" and absorbing the pacing and structure of ads. A successful parody, he learned, gauging the depth of his friends' laughter, depended on crack timing and perfect understanding of the form. He also discovered (consciously—he'd known it all along) that twisting English into the Yiddish syntax he'd heard all his life from his mother usually produced satisfying comic results.

Bleaker and bleaker, Coney seemed, after an evening of music, tall tales, and maybe an intimate grope with a girl. Walking home, or wandering past Feltman's, Hahn's Roosevelt Baths, or Paddy Shea's saloon, the boys passed ash cans stuffed with chewed corncobs or half-eaten hot dogs. Occasionally, they'd go as far as Gravesend Bay, where a dye factory heaped sulfur on its grounds. The boys pulled matchbooks from their pockets and tossed fire into the little yellow hills. The flames flared blue, igniting the night, providing a moment's distraction.

School was distracting, too, for which Joey was quietly grateful. Math gave him a little trouble now and then, but his English classes were a snap. He took a typing class, ostensibly to aid his writing, but mainly to meet new girls. His fondness for their sweaters explained his mediocre progress on the keys.

A few of the girls admired the Boy Scout uniform he sometimes wore to school. Joey had never been much of a joiner, and he probably became a Boy Scout under pressure from Lena or Lee, who extolled the wholesomeness of the group's social activities. He didn't participate much in the organization, but the uniform made him feel like a comic-book superhero. It hid his secret identity—the nail-biting worrier.

At the Alteo, Joey was torn between villain and hero. Sometimes, he'd see three or four older boys latch onto a girl with whom they seemed to have an unspoken arrangement. One by one, they would disappear into a back room with her. He felt titillated, sad, strangely angry—at who, or what, he wasn't sure. He should do something, shouldn't he? What should he do? Stop what was clearly bad for the girl (he had overheard some of the girls whispering about these fast Coney Island boys who'd dance you into a back room and force you to give them what they wanted)? Or join in? Was he just being a coward?

When he turned sixteen—the year was 1939—he got a part-time job as a messenger for Western Union, earning the minimum wage, twenty-five cents an hour. For four hours a day, after school, he delivered telegrams in the city. He spent most of his paychecks on secondhand phonograph records for the Club Hilight. But the clubs were beginning to lose their allure for him. More and more vipers filled the alleys behind the cellars, or congregated in the stores' back doorways to smoke. The older boys stole away the most attractive girls.

IN 1939, Russia invaded Finland. the *Iliad* clashed in Joey's head with Mandel's comic books as well as details snatched from the newspapers. He drafted a short story about a Finnish soldier fighting off Red hordes. After many hours of scribbles, more scribbles, and erasures, he rushed downstairs to Irving Kaiser's typewriter and got the story down on beautiful clean white sheets. Immediately, he mailed it away—first to *Collier's,* then to *Liberty,* and finally to the New York *Daily News,* which published fiction in those days. They all rejected the piece. He didn't tell Mandel. He hid the rejection slips. For a while, he avoided the clubs; he had nothing to talk about to distinguish him, to raise his esteem in the eyes of his friends and the girls. He took solitary walks on the beach. One evening, he saw a woman he knew, the older sister of a girl in his building whose little brother had drowned one summer, not long ago. The woman was kissing a man beneath the boardwalk, letting him run his hands across her breasts. The man's face was hidden in shadow. Joey looked out at the ocean, at the invisibility—the absolute erasure—of the woman's dead brother. Each time the man touched the woman's breasts, the drowned boy's spirit seemed to drift farther and farther out to sea.

Joey returned to his apartment house. He heard someone typing behind the Kaisers' door. He paused on the stairs. His Finnish soldier was a joke. The Red hordes had swept him away. They were sweeping everything away. The world was changing—newspaper headlines had gotten bolder, darker, scarier. The social clubs were changing. Girls were changing. So was he.

Within a few years, he would stand again on these stairs, outside the Kaisers' door, thinking of his friend. Irving Kaiser would experience his last thought in Italy, where he would be blown apart by a German artillery shell.

"THIS IS THE VOICE of . . . miserable men who are buried but not covered over by earth, tied down but not in chains, silent but not mute, whose hearts beat like humans, yet are not like other human beings. . . . [W]hy are we [treated like this]? For the horrible crime of being poor."

These sentiments appeared in the *Jewish Daily Forward*'s "Bintel Brief" in 1910, but nearly thirty years later, they could have served as testimony for many of the men on subways and in train stations whom Joey witnessed on his way to work each day for Western Union. In Coney Island, "[w]e were prudent with money," he wrote, but "I was . . . kept ignorant [of] the threat of true poverty." It was not until he took a job in the city and began to keep track of wages that he registered real desperation. The contrast with certain other commuters, men wearing Rogers Peet suits—some of these fellows could even afford suits from Brooks Brothers—was stark. He noticed that passengers from Coney Island, Bensonhurst, and Borough Park tended to read the *New York Post* and *PM*. At the Bay Ridge stop, where riders from tonier areas caught the train, copies of the *Journal-American* or the *New York World-Telegram* appeared in well-pressed laps. For the first time in his life, as far as he knew, Joey found himself among Republican voters. These people wouldn't be caught dead in Coney Island—not outside the Pavilion of Fun.

He was amazed to be working in the city. The job connection had come through Sylvia or Lee (later, he couldn't remember which); one of them had a friend who managed a Western Union district office in Bensonhurst. This man arranged an interview for Joey with someone named Shorter, in the main headquarters at 60 Hudson Street. Joey assumed he'd be assigned to Brooklyn, but his optimal hours—after school and on Saturdays—best matched the schedules of on-the-go city businesses. He was told to requisition a uniform (brown leather puttees) from the supply office and prepare to learn his way around the West Side.

After school each day, he'd catch a trolley to the train (this took a ten-cent bite out of his pay, and there'd be another ten coming home—

until he learned to take the subway directly from school), ride to Union Square, and then walk to the Flatiron Building, where a central locker room offered space enough for forty or fifty messengers to change into their uniforms. In an office on Seventeenth Street, Teletype machines spit out half-inch paper strands dark with words (the comedies and tragedies of daily commerce, and of ordinary lives); the machine operators pasted these strips onto yellow forms, folded the forms into envelopes, and handed them to the waiting messengers to be delivered to nearby addresses. Businesses in the area included Ohrbach's, Mays, and S. Klein's. Joey amused himself by timing the traffic signals as he hopped from one office complex to another, adjusting his pace so he always caught the WALK command. He dreaded the day (it never came) when he'd have to hand someone a yellow envelope with two red stars stamped on it, meaning sad news.

Many of the offices he saw were nondescript, temporary-looking. Lots of closed doors. What went on in these places? How did these outfits justify the amounts of money (*whatever* amounts they were) spent on lighting, carpeting, rent? He was astounded to see trucks lurching into the city, apparently from all over the country, bringing vegetables and fruits, dumping them at various distribution points, from which they'd be disseminated to the kitchens of the rich and the poor, into the bodies of penthouse dwellers and cellar rats, and finally into sewers and trash mounds. He was appalled to hear the squealing of animals and to smell blood from within what looked to be warehouses near the Hudson. To quell his stomach at the end of a day, he'd bum a Spud or a Kool from one of his older coworkers. Once in a while, he'd saunter into a tavern and bluff his way to an ice-cold beer.

One day, one of the older fellows, a full-timer, twenty-one or twenty-two, returned to the office from a delivery he'd made to an apartment up near Gramercy Park. He swore that a man had let him into the apartment, where a beautiful and provocatively dressed woman languished on a couch. The man offered to pay him to make love to the woman. The messenger's coworkers scoffed at this tale—hesitantly. Certainly nothing like that had ever happened to Joey. Not even close. He wondered if this guy was making up stories to take his mind off rumors they all heard about something called the Selective Service Act, which, if passed by Congress, could mean military conscription for boys his age.

Soon, Joey was transferred uptown to a Western Union office in the

General Motors Building between West Fifty-seventh and West Fifty-eighth streets, near Columbus Circle. Now, the subway ride was a little longer after school, but the job was easier: This office served only those businesses inside the GM complex. It was staffed by a pretty young woman, a Miss McCormack, who mused freely about her man troubles. Joey's fellow messenger here was a friendly twenty-one-year-old named Tom Fitzgerald, who fretted mightily about Selective Service and whiled away his time practicing penmanship.

Joey's favorite office in the complex belonged to the Manhattan Mutual Automobile Casualty Company. The receptionist, a "Miss Peck or Miss Beck," he recalled, smiled at him broadly each time he popped in with a telegram for the company. She was "dark, buxom, married, mature." Each afternoon, he looked forward to her warmth.

In another office nearby, two young men tinkered with the taste of ice cream dispensed by vending machines. When Joey brought the men a telegram, they'd ask him to stay for a moment and try their latest formula for chocolate or banana. He felt like a kid, cozy and safe, and took to dropping by the office even when he didn't have a message for the guys.

Each day, he overheard business chatter: deals, plans, concerns about advertising. He knew that many of the General Motors execs were sending telegrams to potential delegates to the Republican National Convention. Most of the GM men supported Wendell Willkie as the man to beat FDR.

Talk of politics and the draft filled Automats, bakeries, and food stores in the immediate neighborhood. Joey listened closely to arguments, hopes, and fears as he wolfed down buttered rolls, baked beans, and chopped sirloin in Horn & Hardart, or lingered over a cream cheese sandwich in the Chock Full o' Nuts on Fifty-seventh Street.

ARGUMENTS WOULD NOT HELP George Mandel. Or Henny Ehrenman. Or Abie Ehrenreich. Or many other boys from the neighborhood. On September 14, 1940, the United States Congress passed the Selective Training and Service Act, requiring men between the ages of twenty-one and thirty-five to register with local draft boards. It was the country's first peacetime conscription. Draftees would serve for twelve months. Mandel, Ehrenman, and Ehrenreich rode down to Whitehall Street, in lower Manhattan, for the induction ritual, where they were tested, processed, and labeled. Soon, they left for military training. Club regulars mourned the loss of Mandel's swanky car, which many of them had borrowed or ridden in.

For the boys left behind, still awaiting high school graduation, it was hard to know how to plan. College was out of reach for them financially. Good jobs were scarce. The draft was the only certainty. In the evenings, Joey came home from his Western Union job, to find more and more boys smoking dope in the stairwells of his apartment building. No one ran them off.

Western Union reassigned him to Brooklyn. Each day he rode up Kings Highway or Flatbush Avenue, sometimes all the way out to Gerritsen Beach, on his bike, which he had purchased the summer before, on the day Lou Gehrig gave his farewell speech at Yankee Stadium. "[Y]ou have been reading about the bad break I got," Joey heard Gehrig say on the radio. "Yet today I consider myself the luckiest man on . . . this earth. . . . I have an awful lot to live for." Joey couldn't imagine what the man faced. Total paralysis? What would that be like? How could he be so cheerful about it? For the first time, Joey felt keenly grateful for his arms and legs. The bike flew him past Dubrow's Cafeteria and Floyd Bennett Field, with the big silver planes on its runways. He delivered telegrams to Italian families, whose houses were pungent with the "fragrances of olive oil, garlic, and tomatoes . . . ingrained in [the] wallpaper, rugs, plaster, and upholstery," he recalled.

One day, on Bedford Avenue, a desperate young man offered Joey a dollar to run into a house and sing "Happy Birthday" to a girl at a party inside. Before Joey left, the girl's mother, or perhaps it was her aunt, tipped him an extra quarter. This was his biggest single payday as a Western Union boy. The flush times didn't last. Western Union let him go just before his high school graduation. On the advice of some older colleagues, he applied for unemployment benefits; he received six dollars a week for thirteen weeks. This was more than he'd made while working. Clearly, money played by its own wacky rules.

Meanwhile, graduation came and went for the class of '41. To celebrate, Joey went to dinner with his mother, Sylvia, and Lee, then took a subway into the city to hear Billie Holiday perform at a jazz club on Fifty-second Street. The next day, after receiving his diploma, he perused the want ads in the paper. The following Monday morning, he went back to the city to canvass employment agencies.

An outfit on Beaver Street, in Manhattan's Financial District, sent him to the General Motors Building, which he knew so well from his Western Union days, to an interview with the Manhattan Mutual Automobile Casualty Company. He was crushed to discover that the lovely Miss Peck (or Beck) didn't remember him. Another secretary, a Miss Sullivan, followed by her boss, talked to Joey for a few minutes, then offered him a job as a file clerk for sixty dollars a month. The company provided liability insurance to taxis, limousine services, and independent travel operators. Files proliferated whenever an accident occurred; Joey's task was to shuttle them to and from the appropriate desks until they were no longer required, at which point they were banished to the basement storeroom or to the even more morguelike warehouse in midtown Manhattan for the deadest of dead records. Joey dreaded entering these shadowy catacombs, where people's lives were piled up and discarded. On the other hand, he liked seeing how fragmented bits of information could be cataloged, cross-referenced, saved—the abstract made concrete, shuffled and reshuffled into manageable form, or mixed until surprising new information emerged.

On most days, his mother packed him a lunch of seeded rolls, canned salmon and onion, and apples, oranges, or bananas. He discovered he could waste time easily while pretending to search for a file he'd already found. He also learned that stairwell landings between floors, as well as the dead-records storeroom, were trysting places for his slightly older colleagues. A young woman named Virginia, who had been to college, liked to flirt with him, and he developed a major crush on her. He would follow her into the storeroom, excited and a little frightened. Her first intimacies with him were verbal—titillating confessions: troubles with a lawyer and an adjustor in the company, both of whom she was dating, and both of whom wanted her to be more "accommodating." She also said an elderly married man in an office upstairs always asked her out for drinks and dinner after work. He was sweet and polite, and merely enjoyed her attentions, but he seemed sad. Joey was astonished at the subterfuge, desperation, and shenanigans that underlay otherwise-decorous lives. Virginia's amours with others made her all the more desirable—and a bit beyond him.

Joey hated returning to Coney Island in the evenings after work. He delayed the subway ride as long as he could. One night, he asked his friend Lou Berkman to join him in the city for an opera. Joey had become enamored of classical music, listening to the radio, and he had gone to see *Carmen* at the Met one Saturday afternoon. The performance had involved live horses onstage, and he couldn't stop regaling everyone he saw about the spectacle. With Berkman, he seriously miscalculated; his friend had no patience for the dancing or songs; the seats were cheap—high up and uncomfortable—and the score, Wagner's *Tannhäuser,* was hard for the boys to follow. Berkman swore off opera for the rest of his life. Joey found himself between worlds: longing for something more than Coney's dead ends, yet unable to learn enough, fast enough, to run with the sophisticates he witnessed all around him in the city.

At Casualty, two of his colleagues got drafted. One of the boys' mothers threw a large dinner party in her son's honor at her house in the Bronx. The family was Italian. Though Joey had known a lot of Italian kids in Coney Island, he had never been invited to eat in any of their homes. This was his first full Italian meal and he didn't understand the concept of multiple courses. He stuffed himself on spaghetti and meatballs before watching chicken, vegetables, and dessert materialize in all their glory before him.

When a third colleague received his draft notice, Joey began to wonder if a different sort of job might stave off induction. Some of his friends were seeking work in military shipyards, responding to rumors that such labor might exempt them from the draft. Even if the rumors proved untrue, the pay was a dollar an hour for an eight-hour day: scads of money. Joey resigned from the Casualty Company, regretting only his departure from Virginia.

FROM THE FATHER of a friend at one of the social clubs, Marty Kapp, Joey got a letter of reference to work as a blacksmith's helper at the Norfolk Navy Yard at Portsmouth, Virginia. Other boys from Coney Island had secured positions there. Mr. Kapp, an electrician, wrote that Joey had once worked for him (he hadn't) and that he possessed impressive mechanical expertise (he didn't). The man was happy to help Joey because FDR had signed an order, in the summer of 1941, extending draftees' service beyond twelve months. Neighborhood boys were vanishing into the military at an alarming rate—and for good, it seemed. If working in the navy yard meant a possible reprieve from the draft, then Mr. Kapp was all for it. Who was going to remain at home to assist small businessmen? he wondered.

Lee helped Joey with his paperwork and transportation arrangements. One day, in the summer of 1942, Joey boarded a train for Portsmouth. He was glad to be shut of Coney, and yet he had a foreboding he would never return. No one spoke to him on the train. He got off in Cape Charles, Virginia, and hopped a ferryboat across the Chesapeake Bay. On the other side, he checked into a cheap hotel for the night. Except for him, the hotel seemed empty. He ate alone in the restaurant. The desk clerk had a strange red birthmark on one side of his chin. Joey lay awake in his room, fearing sudden intrusion by a stranger who'd slit his throat and steal his suitcase.

The following morning, relieved to be alive, he caught the ferry into Portsmouth. At the dock, a man pointed him toward a bus. Eventually, he arrived at the Norfolk Navy Yard, stowed his stuff in a bungalow, where he'd sleep in a small single room, and reported to the main office. The next day, he clocked in at the shop (above the entrance hung an E FOR EFFICIENCY banner). Joey wore the work shirt, trousers, thick gloves, and metal-lined hard hat Lee had picked out for him. Within minutes, sweat drenched his clothes. In his section of the factory, giant drop forges shaped rivets, bolts, and buckles. A man handed Joey a heavy set of tongs. His job was to carry burning metal rods from small wall furnaces to an anvil or a forge so the blacksmiths could work them however they needed. Sometimes he was asked to cut the rods using a shearing blade, or to roll a barrel of bolts to an electric grinding wheel on a hand truck and file extraneous metal fringes off the heads. On one occasion, the shearing blade nearly sliced his fingers (he had been distracted by a coworker). That night, he lay in his bunk, reliving the horror. He tuned his portable radio to WQXR, all the way from New York City, and soothed himself with the music of Tchaikovsky, Mozart, and Bach.

He ate most of his meals in a nearby boardinghouse run by a middle-aged woman. Lena would have called her zaftig. Her twenty-year-old daughter made eyes at all the boys. Despite heavy bricks of corn bread emerging from the boardinghouse oven, Joey lost several pounds his first few days on the job. Inside the factory, to guard against heat exhaustion, the workers swallowed salt tablets all day long, dispensed from plastic cylinders attached to walls and wooden posts. Whenever government inspectors came through, the blacksmiths increased the levels of the furnace blasts, switched on all the grinding wheels, and got the drop forges pumping. The inspectors, in their well-pressed suits, nodded admiringly (often uncomprehendingly), trying to ignore the fact that their shirt collars were getting soggy and limp. Among the workers, on such occasions, the salt tablets disappeared more quickly than usual.

In the evenings, when a factory whistle blew the end of the shift, a few of the boys claimed they were going to catch a ferry into Norfolk and go to a cathouse over on Bank Street. Joey never considered going with them, figuring the experience would be disappointing, and then he'd feel wretched about wasting his pay. An even more frightening prospect was that the visit would turn out to be glorious, and he'd never be able to resist returning, losing his money again and again.

On the factory floor, the boys could not resist sexual innuendo and jokes at one another's expense. In addition to the trousers, hat, and gloves Lee had bought him, Joey wore a huge pair of shoes his brother had recommended. They were padded, with steel caps on the front to protect the toes. Southerners in the shop insisted the size of a man's feet predicted the length of his cock. Joey suffered constant ribbing until he got rid of the shoes. "Circumcised," he explained the morning he showed up with more modest footwear. His coworkers didn't know what he meant.

JOEY LASTED fifty-six days at the navy yard and then wore out, both physically and spiritually. By now, it was clear the work offered no deferments from the draft, and no chance for further advancements. He gave notice. On his way back to Coney Island, he stopped in Washington, D.C., where his friend Marty Kapp held a civil service job. Kapp had to work, so Joey spent most of the weekend on his own. He attended an outdoor concert, his first live symphonic performance: a Tchaikovsky violin concerto. He toured the usual monuments and felt no inklings of wartime worry.

Back home, he joined a smattering of his old buddies, wandering the streets aimlessly or watching the parachutes drop from the big new ride at Steeplechase Park. Beansy Winkler had a part-time job stringing pearls in a factory. Danny the Count was peddling costume jewelry on the beach and occasionally in Manhattan, at the subway entrances near Union Square. Lou Berkman had joined his father's junk trade, selling scrap metal from neighborhood demolitions and abandoned amusement rides. Joey took temp jobs, working briefly as a shipping clerk at the U.S. Hatband Company, helping Sylvia count inventory at Macy's, following Lee (who'd had enough of Wall Street) to a small factory in Manhattan that did drill-press work for the defense industry. But mostly, he bided his time. Surely the war in Europe would end soon, and the United States would manage to stay out of it. . . .

Then the government announced it was lowering the draft age from twenty-one to nineteen. That settled it. He was going anyway, so he decided he might as well go on *his* terms and choose his branch of the service. Patriotism had nothing to do with it. Patriotism was so much nonsense on the radio. "[At the time,] we did not know about the concentration camps. . . . I don't think most of us knew what the war was about," he said at a literary symposium at the University of South Carolina in 1995. "One thing I do know is, we didn't go to war to save the Jews. . . . If that had ever come up as a goal, Roosevelt never could have gotten a declaration of war." For most boys, the decision to enlist was pragmatic. They had nothing better to do. "[B]y the end of 1942, the beginning of 1943, everybody, everybody, was in uniform," the writer Paul Fussell said at the USC symposium. "The whole culture of the country was benign military."

"The day I enlisted"—October 19, 1942—"was like going off to watch a baseball game. . . . I went with great good spirits, went with a few friends. . . . Had no idea what we were doing except that what we were going to do was more exciting, more romantic, more adventurous than what we were doing at home," Heller told the symposium crowd.

Heller, he was—Heller this, Heller that—to the various doctors and psychiatrists he stood in line to see at the induction center at Grand Central Station. "Somebody said something, and you nodded, and you took a step forward—and you were in the Army," he said. The place was like a palace. When a shrink asked if he liked girls, he took it not as a test of his sexual orientation, but as a promise the gift of a uniform might help him fulfill.

A good American, he spread his butt cheeks, turned his head, and coughed.

IN THE HOURS following the bombing of Pearl Harbor, the editors of *Time* magazine scotched the cover they had planned for that week—a story about Walt Disney's new cartoon fantasy, *Dumbo*. Instead, the magazine focused (with as much detail as it could) on the Japanese assault. Dimouts were ordered for Coney Island, to help protect U.S. coastlines. Only two thousand shrouded lightbulbs burned at Steeple-chase Park each night, instead of the usual ten thousand. "[T]he feeling after Pearl Harbor was nationwide," Heller recalled at USC. "[The] whole country was in support of [military action] after the attack." And then Germany declared war on the United States.

"[S]ociety in America [during that period] was rigidly hierarchical," Fussell recalled. The fact that "almost everybody on the street between the age of eighteen and forty was in uniform made [us] rank conscious, so you knew exactly who everybody was, at least externally, at any time. Everybody was identifiable . . . which made it a very special uni-verse. The result of this . . . was I think to shrivel the interior life a bit. Everybody became his or her public self. . . . Wit was out; irony was out—you were what you pretended to be."

But what *was* the right pretense? Uniform or no, Heller wrote, he and his pals had entered the "'moratorium' that emerges in the lives of most Western young people between the end of adolescence and the onset of maturity, during which the individual doesn't truly know what he or she is or where he wants to go, . . . or what he should de-cide to become. It is a season of baffled uncertainty . . . and can lead to grave mistakes." Because of the timing, the war—for better or worse—"took most powers of decision out of our hands, and swept us into a national endeavor considered admirable and just." In that sense, there was no pretense, no questioning, no thought at all, in fact.

Besides, Henny Ehrenman, home on furlough from Lowry Field in Colorado, said the Air Corps was *good times*: lots of drinking in Den-ver saloons with very loose girls.

Days before Heller left for a military reception center at Camp Up-ton, Long Island, his mother sat in the window of her apartment—the window her little Joey had once nearly fallen out of in his attempt to reach the fire escape—scanning the skies, fearing the sudden appear-ance of enemy dirigibles. She told her neighbors she remembered the excitement she'd felt as a girl when an airplane passed overhead and whole families ran out of the house to see it. She recalled the first songs she had learned to sing in the United States—"Don't Go in the Park

After Dark" and "I Didn't Raise My Boy to Be a Soldier." She hummed them softly, sadly now.

On the morning of her son's departure, she and Sylvia walked him to the trolley stop outside Mr. Moses's candy store at Railroad Avenue. From there, he would ride to Stillwell Avenue and take the Sea Beach subway line into Penn Station. He promised his mother he'd write from Long Island. She smiled gently, gave him an automatic kiss on the cheek, and hugged him stiffly. He got on the trolley, waved. He didn't look back. It was a typical family scene, he thought: his mother distant, buttoned-up, almost indifferent. That woman couldn't be moved. In fact—and he would not learn this until many years later, from Sylvia, once Lena was dead—the moment the trolley pulled away, his mother began to sob. Without Sylvia's support, she would have fallen to her knees in the street.

4. A Cold War

LENA HEARD from her son that he had been sent from Long Island to Miami Beach, Florida, for basic training; from there, he had taken a train to Lowry Field in Denver, Colorado—an eleven- or twelve-day trip—for further testing and technical training. Now he was stationed at the Santa Ana Army Air Base in California for aviation cadet training and preflight classification. Eventually, he would fly in airplanes over disturbed territory. She knew he would die in a crash. In his phone calls and letters, he could not talk her out of this possibility.

Her days in the apartment now, with her family scattered, were quiet and slow. She wanted a change—a turning away from drab reminders of the past, fresh colors to perk her up. She decided to hang new curtains in the kitchen, and so one morning, she pulled a small stool up to the window, gripping the drapes. She stretched, shook, wobbled, and with a sudden crack of wood, the stool gave way. She tumbled to the floor. Pain shot through her hip and thigh. She couldn't tell if she had broken anything. She couldn't stand. She crawled toward the window and lifted herself to the sill. Across the street, in an open window of another apartment building, Jeannie Goldman, a girl Joey's age, stood taking the air. Weakly, Lena said her name.

THE CHAPLAIN'S OFFICE at the Santa Ana Army Air Base called Joseph Heller in. A telegram had arrived at the base, from Heller's sister, informing him that his mother had been taken to a Brooklyn hospital. On the spot, the chaplain arranged an emergency leave for the young man, helping him secure a Red Cross loan to pay for the train ticket.

In the days spent traveling cross-country, Heller recalled the reoccurring dream he used to have of the shadowy man entering his room. Fears for his mother—and anxiety about not being able to help her—reversed the dream, and he worried he wouldn't recognize Lena when he saw her. Like an infant who fears his mother will never return the instant she leaves the room, he felt premonitions of catastrophe in the slightest change. It was not the first time the mother he thought he knew had disappeared.

Gingerly, one afternoon, he entered the women's ward of Coney Island Hospital. The place smelled of Mercurochrome and sterilized metal, odors that brought back to him the uneasy night here when he'd had his tonsils removed, when his father had left him on his own. He felt disoriented. From across the room, he spotted his mother. Her hair had gone shockingly white. As he had feared, her features were not familiar. She didn't seem to know him, either. He kissed her forehead and hugged her. Nothing he said could blow away the fog in her eyes. He slumped in despair. Then, across a row of flat white beds he saw a woman gesticulating wildly. She had a plaster cast on her leg. Lena. Exactly as he remembered her. He glanced back at the woman beside him, a total stranger. From a distance, his mother continued to wave at him in fitful exasperation. He approached her sheepishly, holding his cap in his hand. Lena looked up at him and said, "You have a twisted brain."

HIS MOTHER HAD BROKEN her hip and would probably walk with a cane the rest of her life. Generally, though, she would be fine. Heller returned to California, secure in the knowledge that Lena could summon her downstairs neighbor, Mrs. Kaiser (another widower now) anytime she needed to by whacking her cane on the floor.

Back in Santa Ana, he stared at the open suitcase on his bed, dreading the task of separating dirty clothes from clean, of refolding and putting away his things. He remembered the summer Lena had packed his suitcase and sent him off to camp; how easy it had been just to leave everything in the bag; how nice it would be if Lena (or, more precisely, some mother figure who would then go away whenever he wanted her to) were here to help him unpack. The barracks beds were all the same—low, flat, and springy. Towels were to be folded a certain way—once, vertically—and hung at the foot of one's bed. The men were not allowed to display personal photographs. As at Surprise Lake years ago, it hardly seemed worthwhile to empty his case.

He loved the warm late winter here, but he wasn't sure California was safe. On the base, talk spread rapidly that Japanese-Americans, living in the state, were engaged in domestic spying, and many of them had been removed to detention centers. A Japanese submarine had shelled an oil facility near Santa Barbara. Each night, searchlights scanned the skies over Los Angeles and antiaircraft gunners perched in the hills above the city. Miami Beach and Denver had been much more pleasant. In Florida, sunshine bounced off the surface of the ocean as if the water were tin, and everywhere you walked, you were likely to trip over bunches of oranges—at a dollar a sack, they were plentiful in and out of the messes. Now, *that* was basic training! The Air Corps did it right. They rented nearly every hotel along the beach to house their enlisted men and officers. After a day of drills, the men would lie around half-naked in their rooms, drinking and listening to radios. Even the mess boys—mostly black enlisted men—charged with cleaning the kitchens (sweeping away orange peels, mopping up apple butter and jam) spent much of their time sipping whiskey and playing jazz records on portable phonographs. The military had the run of the city. On weekends, the men slipped away under piers on the beach with a bottle and a girl (locals, known as "camp followers") to lie on dark, damp sand still warm from the day's sun. It almost never rained at night; dawn often saw fellows staggering back to their hotels, emptied of all desires. The air smelled of flowers and fuel. Years later, Heller recalled doing the lindy hop late into the night at a Florida dance hall, and then, in a deserted parking lot, on the fender of a sports car, achieving sexual release (though not intercourse) in the presence of a woman for the first time, a woman he had met that night and whom he had awkwardly taught to dance.

Every so often in the afternoons, cool green thunderstorms scrubbed the beaches and the air.

At Lowry Field in Denver, he'd sat in classrooms, absorbing bomb specs and details about machine guns and other armaments. The mess hall, located in a former sanatorium, was open around the clock to accommodate the cadets' staggered schedules, and Heller would often slip out of bed and head for the mess to get an extra late-night meal or to sneak in a second breakfast. "I loved Denver," he wrote years later. "It was winter, but it was a beautiful winter, the kind of winter you never see in New York." On the base, lists were posted of local families who wished to invite servicemen to their houses for dinner, in appreciation of the boys' sacrifices for their country, and to help the war effort. "They didn't care if you were from Coney Island," Heller wrote in amazement. "They might have cared if you were black." He was stunned by "how courteous and generally . . . warmhearted" westerners were. "There . . . [was an] affection and optimism that New Yorkers are not accustomed to," he said. But he didn't press his luck and reveal he was Jewish. The only trouble he ran into at Lowry came courtesy of fellow Brooklynites, a pair of enlisted men from Norwegian and Irish neighborhoods who had grown up taunting Jews. The westerners and southerners Heller met didn't know the first thing about Judaism, and his relationships with them were friendly and uncomplicated.

Then came another train trip, this time to Santa Ana—an airfield without airplanes. So far, he had spent most of his military service in poorly lighted railway or bus stations, lost among duffel bags and the smell of wet cotton, in lines with other soldiers, with young girls, many of them carrying sick, wailing babies, almost too heavy for them, and with MPs in their sharp white leggings, twirling nightsticks as if they were America's last defense against villains.

In California, he sat in more classrooms, learning the geometry of killing. A plane travels at so many feet per second; a cartridge travels so many yards, so fast. To hit a plane coming at you, aim behind it, because of the forward airspeed of your ammo and the opposing plane's swerving path. . . .

The lessons were sometimes difficult, and often boring, especially those on the Theory of Flight (and he didn't much care for Chemical Warfare, Camouflage, or Code), but he had to admit his standard of living had almost doubled since joining the military. The food was good—

though the army skimped on butter—and, once he made second lieutenant, he stood to earn $150 a month, plus $75 dollars flight pay for a minimum of four hours aloft monthly. Adolf Hitler seemed to have done him a favor.

In addition to technical savvy, his classes tried to instill in him a solid swagger. "They put us in dark rooms . . . and had voice-overs of planes fighting—you know, an American plane gets shot down; he's parachuted out; and the Jap Zeroes start machine-gunning him on voice-over," William Price Fox said at the USC literary symposium in 1995. "And you come out of there just bristling. You could bite a fireplug. Go into combat that minute, anything."

The men who taught the courses demanded more respect than their abilities warranted. As Samuel Hynes, a World War II aviator once wrote, "The most surprising thing about preflight school is that we [all] managed to survive it. . . . I don't think we learned much there, but we did learn . . . to hate our enemies—not the Germans and the Japanese . . . but the nonflying, Attitude-talking martinets who commanded us, and the military system they represented."

Still, the combat-simulation trainers were almost as much fun as gun games in the penny arcades in Coney Island.

On classification day, thirty-five weeks after the beginning of his classes, Heller was told that his aptitudes, mental and physical, suited him best to be a navigator/ bombardier. He was given more physical tests, blood samples were taken from his inner elbow, and he was sent to bombardier school in Victorville, out in the desert, in far southeastern California.

On bombing runs, he learned, the bombardier was always the hero or the goat. The success or failure of each mission depended on his timing and accuracy. He also learned that the average life expectancy of a bombardier in heavy combat was three minutes.

His instructors showed him a Norden bombsight, a supposedly top secret device, though Heller swore he had seen photographs of it in popular magazines before he went into the Air Corps. Many generals believed its accuracy would win the war. Turning the sight mechanism to keep its needle centered over the intended target and guiding the plane through the bombsight's connection to a pilot directional indicator, the bombardier was said to be nearly infallible in locating his target from as high as thirty thousand feet. The sight was controlled by gyroscopes

and "weird, twisted pieces of metal, each one representing possible com-
putations on line graphs and bar graphs, and they were supposed to be
coordinated," Heller explained. "The Norden bombsight, I think, was
theoretically perfect, assuming the right information was put into it,"
but even in training he saw this was "impossible because ... air speed,
ground speed, wind speed changed constantly," so you "couldn't possibly" use the thing. Nevertheless, all bombardiers were forced to take the
following oath: "Mindful of the secret trust about to be placed in me by
my Commander in Chief, the President of the United States ... and
mindful of the fact that I am about to become guardian of one of my
country's most priceless military assets, the American bombsight ... I do
here, in the presence of Almighty God, swear by the Bombardier's Code
of Honor to keep inviolate the secrecy of any and all confidential information revealed to me, and to further uphold the honor and integrity of
the Army Air Forces, if need be, with my life itself."

ON JANUARY 20, 1943, H. H. Arnold, commanding general of the
U.S. Army Air Forces, had announced that President Franklin Roosevelt
and Prime Minister Winston Churchill of Britain agreed with U.S.
Army Air Force's recommendations that round-the-clock bombing be
conducted against German troops in North Africa. Two months later,
American workers in war-related industries were ordered to spend a
minimum of forty-eight hours per week ensuring that production met
military demands.

During this time, while Heller was in training, the U.S. Army Air
Forces grudgingly admitted there was a morale problem. As early as
1942, a Colonel Grow, surgeon of the Eighth Air Force, had officially
noted that the spirit of combat troops in the European theater was "not
all that it should be to obtain the maximum efficiency in operational
missions," and the primary cause of this was the troops' awareness of
survival estimates. These estimates reported an average personnel loss
of 5 percent per mission, which theoretically meant they would all be
dead after twenty flights. Colonel Grow suggested a mission limit of
fifteen, but his recommendations were not acted on. Throughout the
early months of 1943, adequate replacement troops were not being received in the European theater, and uncertainties spread among the men
about the number of sorties they were going to be forced to fly. Morale

plummeted further. A study prepared by group and division surgeons, entitled "Morale in Air Crew Members, Eighth Bomber Command," released on March 9, 1943, strongly urged establishing a fixed combat tour. Finally, Ira Eaker, commanding general of the Eighth Air Force, announced that twenty-five missions would constitute a tour of duty for frontline bomber crews.

Shortly after completing bombardier school on November 13, 1943, Joseph Heller received a letter telling him that the secretary of war wished to inform him that "the President ha[d] appointed and commissioned [him] a Second Lieutenant" and that "this commission [would] continue in force during [sic] the pleasure of the President of the United States for the time being, and for the duration of the war and six months thereafter unless sooner terminated."

In February 1944, Heller was sent to the Columbia Army Air Base, in Columbia, South Carolina, for advanced flight training. By the end of the following month, he had logged thirty-six hours and forty-five minutes of flight time there.

It was hard to know which was worse: the cockroaches in his bed or the battery of shots he had to take to prevent cholera, smallpox, tetanus, and typhoid, in preparation for going overseas. His left arm puffed and throbbed. In addition to flight training, his duties on the base included early-morning bodybuilding, calisthenics, and detail work, such as firing the shower room's boiler, hanging flypaper in the barracks, and cleaning the icebox in the mess hall. Columbia provided few weekend diversions. Quaint shops sold three scoops of ice cream for a nickel and banana splits for twelve cents apiece. An informal history kept by the bomb group to which Heller would be assigned asserts that "entertainment [in Columbia] was limited to a fairly decent meal and a few drinks, but . . . upon presentation of the bill one would think they had paid a first installment on three rooms of furniture."

By the time he left South Carolina in April, Heller had logged over 230 hours in the air. The B-25s on which he trained were medium bombers, with two engines and twin rudders on a tail boom, and a top turret featuring two fifty-caliber machine guns. The planes had a range of approximately fifteen hundred miles, round-trip. On the ground, they looked ungainly and silly, creatures out of their element—not something to which you'd trust your life. Heller discovered he was not a natural flier. Some of the guys took to the aircrafts as smoothly as sexual maestros had gravitated to girls back in the old social clubs at home. Heller was not afraid to fly, but he was not at ease with parachutes, fuselage, screaming blue flames. These were not part of his pulse. Yet eventually he adjusted—if not with talent, then with competence. He learned to roll with the plane as it maneuvered, to think of the plane as sitting still, and to sit still with it, while the world outside lurched and swerved.

The sky was vaster than he had ever dreamed: a glorious nothing, shimmering with emptiness. Far below, the land abstracted itself into green-and-gold patches, triangles of brown and blue, squares of light and dark. Heavy in his flak suit, he felt, with each new burst of speed, as weightless as a kite ripped from its anchor. Up high, heat battled cold on the surface of your skin, in the meat of your head: It was like drinking hot coffee that suddenly went tepid at the back of your mouth.

In the mornings, he and his crews loaded training bombs onto the planes: shells filled with nearly one hundred pounds of sand and about three pounds of black powder, whose patterns, once the powder hit the ground, revealed various degrees of accuracy. On practice runs, two students took turns dropping the shells on triangular shacks or concentric rings set up as targets in South Carolina fields. One student would pull the toggle switch while the other photographed the drop using a movie camera aimed through a four-inch hole in the plane's floor. Later, the students studied the films, looking for mistakes they had made.

Always, as he approached the practice targets, Heller leaned forward, straining against his seat belt as the plane dived. He tried to center the target in his bombsight, called to his pilot, "Level! Level!" and then parted the bomb bay's doors. As the plane pulled up in a steep bank, he looked back, to see little puffs of smoke rising and falling below. The dive was exhilarating—a heedless plunge—the pullout even more so, as it meant a return to safety. Thrust and relax: What could be more appealing to a twenty-year-old boy?

He also flew gunnery missions, the planes winging single file over the ocean and then circling back to base. On the way, instructors told the students to shoot their machine guns in bursts and not hold their fingers on the triggers, as this would cause the gun barrel to heat up and fire rounds on its own. Often, weary at the end of a day, students ignored the rules, hammering the triggers hard, but the instructors let this pass. Planes sometimes landed pinpricked with holes, or with their antennae shot off, courtesy of their companions. Always, on a gunnery flight, one or two men threw up, nauseated by the gunpowder fumes.

Once you were over the ocean, it was tempting just to keep going until you were swallowed by the light or the darkness. Heller thought of the bell buoy off Coney Island, the one he used to swim to as a kid, and how easy it would have been to give himself to the undertow.

Night flying he loved. Cities reduced to halos. The green and red lights on the ends of his wings were like phosphorescent birds dipping down out of the stratosphere. All distances flattened to black. At night, the planes made sounds he was never aware of during the day. In the stillness of the dark, each rattle, hum, and tick became amplified. Perhaps this psychological difference accounted for the rule that crew members flying after sundown had to use oxygen starting at five thousand feet, though this directive didn't apply on day flights until much higher altitudes. Or perhaps there really was less oxygen at night.

Since bombardiers were sometimes asked to navigate, Heller had to practice guiding a bomber in cross-country formations—a skill he never mastered. The cross-country flights could be up to four hundred miles long, round-trip. Once, he lost Georgia. Another time, electrical storms interfered with his radio compass. He didn't know where he was. He pointed to the bank of a river below and told his pilot to turn left—he was sure he'd find a familiar landmark on the river's opposite bank: a small farm, automobile headlights on a backcountry road. It turned out that the river he'd spotted was really the shore of the Atlantic, and he had pointed his crew toward Africa. Clouds yawned ahead. Finally, the pilot took over, patching together various radio signals to get them back to base with just enough fuel to land.

At Anderson Army Air Field in Walterboro, South Carolina, just down the road from Columbia, Heller's group received gas masks, helmets, decontaminators, and weapons. The group's commanders made the men practice safety drills during imaginary air raids, hike through thick pine forests with their gas masks on, and practice falling into ditches as planes strafed them, dropping flour bombs. The men bonded more quickly than ever under these sweaty conditions. Heller particularly liked an easygoing, humble young fellow from Philadelphia named Francis Yohannan. He was training to be a pilot. Together, he and Heller joked about the hikes ("jackassing around," they called it) and the food (as another member of the group wrote, "It is an unwritten law [in the army] that food must not be separated. . . . Army SOP calls for prunes on top of pancakes. Unless you have had baked beans topped with rice pudding, you never before really enjoyed the true flavor of either").

At Walterboro, Heller also liked a thoughtful young medic attached to the 488th Bomb Squadron, a draftee named Benjamin Marino. Like Yohannan, Marino would accompany Heller overseas in the next few weeks.

ON ONE OF HIS LAST training flights, Heller and his crew traveled, along with several other planes, to Brooklyn's Floyd Bennett Field, which he used to pass on his bicycle, delivering telegrams for Western Union. Once on the ground, the crews had time to kill before returning to South Carolina. Heller took two of his comrades, a pair of Chicago boys named Bailey and Bowers, into Manhattan, which they'd never seen, and treated them to a meal at a restaurant called Lindy's. "[T]hey weren't entirely at home with its raucous splendor or mainly Jewish menu," he wrote years later. He ordered a chopped liver and smoked turkey sandwich on rye, a sour pickle, a sour tomato, and strawberry cheesecake for dessert. His buddies bristled at the happy talk of FDR at the tables around them. They told Heller they were strict isolationists and didn't approve of the president's leadership. One of them said everyone in the place looked like Harry the Horse, from the famous Damon Runyon story, "by which he meant, I was aware, that they all looked Jewish," Heller wrote, "and of course [they] did," including him.

On the way back to base, flying low over Brooklyn, Heller sat in the plane's nose cone, seeing Coney Island spread narrowly before him, exposed, vulnerable.

HELLER'S FLIGHT record for April 27, 1944, signed by Maj. Homer B. Howard, lists him as "in transit overseas," with over four hundred hours of flight time under his belt. He had been assigned to the 340th Bombardment Group, 488th Bomb Squadron. He had left from Hunter Field in Georgia. At first, he had no idea where he was headed; he was just thrilled to be escaping the Deep South's kamikaze mosquitoes. They had become peskier as the weather warmed up.

Right before he left, he heard from friends in Coney Island that his old pal Abie Ehrenreich, who had been serving overseas as an aerial gunner, had been shot down over North Africa several months back and was apparently a prisoner of war.

Once airborne over the ocean, the crew opened its sealed orders, as it had been instructed to do. Earl C. Moon, the copilot, read the orders aloud. First stop: Natal, Brazil, about an eight-hour leg. Then Ascension Island, Liberia, Marrakech, Dakar, and Algiers. An auxiliary fuel tank had been installed in the bomb bay for the extended trip. Along the way, the crew was supposed to stay alert for the wreckage of a pair of planes that had taken off days earlier on an identical route. This did not inspire confidence.

Heller didn't want to swallow his Adabian tablets, for the suppression of malaria, fearing they'd give him symptoms of the disease. Nor did he care for the mosquito spray the crew had been ordered to use on the plane so they wouldn't ferry virus-infested insects down to South America. This was the first time he had ever seen an aerosol spray can.

In Natal, he ate seedless oranges and small green bananas. He didn't much like them, or the powerful, bitter coffee. But cigarettes were a nickel a pack, and whiskey was plentiful.

On Ascension Island, he watched a few of his comrades fishing in the sea (using raw meat for bait) and saw a bad movie one night on an open-air screen erected on a hill.

The crew was told about other planes that had failed to complete the journey they were now making, and whose wreckage they were supposed to keep an eye out for.

The Frenchmen Heller observed in Marrakech astonished him, sipping expensive aperitifs in luxury hotels as though the Germans had not overrun their country and people weren't dying each hour, so they— the affluent, lolling about here in Morocco—might one day return to their lavish estates. Somehow, he felt he was witnessing a fundamental truth about the nature of war, if only he could grasp its complexities.

At an American replacement center in Algeria, his group waited to receive word of its final destination. A character in his novel *Closing Time* (1994), clearly based on him, says, "[In Algeria], I shared a tent with a medical assistant, older than I, also [a]waiting assignment, who [like me] wished to write short stories like William Saroyan and was also positive he could. Neither of us understood that there was no need for more than one Saroyan. Today we might conclude from the insignificance of Saroyan that there had not been great need for even one."

Waiting around, the crews were bored, but their superiors had warned them not to wander far from the replacement center in search of booze or women. A GI had been murdered recently, his body found castrated and his scrotum sewn into his mouth. The men didn't really believe this story. Nevertheless, they stuck close to the base.

Finally, the orders came through: Alesan Air Field, Corsica. Heller's official date of assignment there was May 21, 1944. Within a few weeks, several of the men would erect a sign on the outskirts of the field, proclaiming, 340TH BOMBARDMENT GROUP (MEDIUM), THE BEST DAMN GROUP THERE IS (PRODUCT OF U.S.A.).

HELLER LEARNED he'd be sharing his tent with a dead man: an Okie kid, Pinkard, who had been shot down and killed while trying to bomb a railway bridge north of Ferrara, Italy, in the Po Valley. Pinkard's cot had been left untouched since his death, and his presence, in the form of his absence, was loud inside the tent.

The U.S. Army had established seventeen airfields on Corsica, and the men's tents were scattered all around them, on rolling ground at the base of a low hill, beyond which snowcapped mountains glimmered. A single electric generator served each humble shelter; in cold weather, the men had to improvise to keep warm, constructing makeshift stoves, many of which exploded or set canvas walls on fire. Commanders closely monitored electricity use. An entry in the War Diary of the 487th Bomb Squadron, for October 7, 1944, noted that a "Capt. Winebrenner made a lite [sic] inspection of personnel tents this morning and clipped only one wire. Apparently it was the only tent honest enough to leave their high voltage bulb in. Other tents with two lights were smart enough to conceal one." (The War Diaries—daily logs—were army regulation; various men contributed to the record, often anonymously.)

Mud and piles of stinking garbage tossed about the tents attracted mice and rats. The men shot at the creatures with Colt .45s, using the ammunition they'd been issued in their survival kits when they'd first flown overseas. "[T]he sound of a .45 discharging inside of a tent is ear-shattering," corpsman George Underwood recalled in an oral history of the air base. "If [the] shots missed their targets, at least they succeeded in terrifying the rats, as well as folks in the neighboring tents." When heavy rains came, as they often did, washing away tent pegs in swift brown rivulets, the men discovered the downside of indoor target practice, and sat shivering under chilly leaks. The mud became goo; the roads and walking paths, never fine to begin with, deteriorated altogether.

When Heller arrived on base, Alesan personnel were still suffering from two devastating setbacks. First, on March 22, 1944, Mount Vesuvius had erupted, destroying most of the 340th's airplanes, which had been stationed near Pompeii. The group scrambled to relocate. It secured replacement planes for its new spot on Corsica, still technically behind enemy lines, though the island had just been liberated by the French and local partisans known as the Maquis, after a scrub brush common on Corsica that had given the partisans cover. The base was still in a state of chaos from the 340th's move, and the shiny new replacement planes made everyone nervous: They had not yet acquired camouflage paint, and shone like mirrors from the sky.

Second, a week before Heller arrived on Corsica, in the early-morning hours of May 13, eighty JU-88 medium bombers from the German Luftwaffe flew in low, accompanied by several Focke-Wulf Fw-190 fighter planes. They bombed and strafed the base for an hour and a half, killing twenty-four men and wounding over two hundred others, shattering sixty-five planes, and blowing up the gas dump. The raid came in response to the U.S. policy of dropping phosphorus bombs on antiaircraft gunners, a policy that Germany claimed was a breach of the Geneva Conference.

On May 13, right before the German planes dived out of darkness in wave after wave after wave, a single twin-engined British Beaufighter appeared above the base, dropping lighted flares to guide the main force in. Later, U.S. commanders speculated that the Germans had captured this plane and left its British markings intact to trick the Americans. The attack left craters in the roads that were still gaping and smoking when Heller landed on the base. Wrecked airplane parts littered runway edges. The men were jittery. "A few practice shots from the field had everybody in their slit trenches for a while the other night," stated the 487th's War Diary for May 29. "Some weren't aware that it was only practice and others were avoiding falling shrapnel." The diary entry for the next night read: "Two air raid alerts got the boys out of bed twice during the evening." Following the German attack, some men moved their tents into concealed wooded areas. One group kept its tent where it was, out in the open—the men had spent too much time customizing it to take it apart; besides, they figured if the Germans returned, they wouldn't bother with a single isolated tent.

Soon after settling in, Heller was assigned one of his tent mates, a stumpy, taciturn boy from Kentucky named Edward Ritter, "something of a tireless wonder as a handyman, one with unlimited patience who took pleasure in making and fixing things," Heller wrote. Ritter transformed the tent into a cozy home by constructing a fireplace, complete with a mantelpiece made from an old railroad tie, on which the boys placed photographs of buxom Hollywood actresses. Ritter also fashioned a stove that drew fuel from an outside can and dribbled it onto sand inside a metal drum placed near the tent's center pole. His constant tinkering with items irritated Heller, but the Brooklyn boy admired his buddy's ingenuity and soon marveled at his imperturbability in combat: On at least three occasions, Ritter would either crash-land or bring a damaged plane back safely, never showing "symptoms of fear or growing nervousness, even blushing with a chuckle and a smile whenever I gagged around about him as a jinx," Heller wrote.

Next door lived Francis Yohannan, in a space he shared with, among others, a boy named Joe Chrenko. Soon, on R & R trips to Rome, Chrenko would pass himself off as a *Life* photographer so he could smooth-talk girls into posing for him. In Rome one day, Yohannan bought a golden cocker spaniel, which also came to live in his tent.

The men Heller met, hailing from all parts of the United States, were so distinctive, and uniquely different from the Brooklyn lads he'd known, they seemed to him like characters from a novel, and he noted with amusement their features, habits, and personal characteristics: Col. Willis F. Chapman, the group commander, who always walked around with an elaborate cigarette holder in his mouth; Capt. Vincent Myers, a half-Comanche from Cameron, Oklahoma, a square-shouldered Golden Gloves boxer whom everyone called "the Chief"; the pale, bird-thin Doc Marino, whom Heller had met in South Carolina; and Chaplain James H. Cooper, a shy, pimple-faced fellow from Ohio who lived alone in a tent in the woods, slightly separated from the other men, puffing at night on a tiny corncob pipe.

EARLY IN 1944, the U.S. Army Air Corps mounted a massive bombing campaign against German aircraft production centers in Berlin. Combined with the German defeat in North Africa, in May 1943, and the push the Allies were making toward Rome, U.S. commanders hoped the war in Europe had turned in their favor. Troop morale was generally high. It was the task of the 340th Bombardment Group to provide support to frontline divisions, and to the main European air offensive, by disrupting German supply lines and communications, destroying roads, railway tracks, and bridges in Italy, France, Austria, and Yugoslavia. The Germans' main supply route to the Italian front from central Europe was through the Brenner Pass, in the Alps, and many of the group's missions concentrated on that region.

In June, the Allies drove the Germans out of Rome and invaded Normandy. However, what most concerned the men of the 340th was the number of missions they had to fly, and the unnerving accuracy of the German 88-mm cannons, particularly at the marshaling yards of Rimini and Ferrara, as well as at the Bologna supply dump—frequent bombing targets. The cannons, the *Fliegerabwehrkanone* (flak, for short), fired twenty-pound shells to over forty thousand feet; the shells then exploded, spraying the air with hundreds of swarming metal shards. To achieve maximum accuracy on their bombing runs, the American B-25s came in at between seven thousand and twelve thousand feet, making them highly vulnerable to flak. Furthermore, over some targets in the Brenner Pass, in the midst of steep mountain shadows, the planes often banked *beneath* the highest peaks, and the Germans fired at them from above.

Frequently, the B-25 crews flew two missions a day. Since they operated behind the front, they traveled fairly short distances and rarely encountered enemy planes. They called their missions "milk runs," to denote their relative ease. Because of this, the B-25 mission limit was higher than that of the B-17s and B-24s on the front lines. In May 1944, when Heller arrived on Corsica, the limit was fifty for the Mitchell medium bombers. On June 22, the 487th's War Diary reported, "Word is going around that any combat crew member who has not put in one year of overseas duty will fly 70 missions before returning to the Z of I [zone of interior—that is, the United States] which is quite a leap from the prescribed fifty missions to a tour. Quite naturally this isn't going over too big with the boys. . . ."

Soon thereafter, General Knapp at Wing Headquarters confirmed the raised mission limit. There was a flight crew shortage, he said. Daniel Setzer, who has studied the 340th's time on Corsica, believes the limit rose for another reason. "Mussolini was gone [by the summer of 1944] and Italy had joined the Allies," he says. "Rome had fallen. The Germans were being pushed back by the Russians on the Eastern front. The US successfully invaded France . . . it was clear to everyone that, barring a miracle, Germany could not win and its army would soon lose the will to continue fighting what was quickly becoming a futile war. Our army planners must have felt that one more concerted push using experienced flight crews would do more to insure victory than continu[ing] to bring [fresh troops] to the European theater." Besides, Setzer says, "military planners were already turning their thoughts to the defeat of Japan."

At the start of his tour, Heller wasn't troubled by forthcoming assignments. "I wanted to see what was happening. . . . What I'd seen in the movies," he explained. "I wanted to see parachutes. I wanted to see planes going down in flame. And I would say close to half my missions were milk runs. There were no German fighters in Italy by the time I got overseas. So all the opposition came from anti-aircraft fire, and if I went on missions and . . . there was [not] any [flak,] I was disappointed. I was stupid."

The novelist William Styron, a fellow veteran of the European war, put it another way. "[The] smell of romance . . . is what you got for going off . . . and getting your ass shot off," he said. "And that is, to me . . . the metaphor for the strange bargain one makes as a young man, going off to war. The allure was so extraordinary, the allure, the glamour, the gold bars, the tailored uniform—for what? To . . . get your ass shot off."

Yet few of the men questioned the war's rationale. "I saw it as a war of necessity," Heller said. "Everybody did. . . . Pearl Harbor united this country in a strong and wholesome and healthy way." And at first, island life for him was relatively "comfortable," he recalled. "[A]ll decisions were made for me, and I found I liked that . . . because none of the decisions being made seemed to be particularly abusive. I was being treated very well, even by the German anti-aircraft fighters."

IN THE FORMERLY SECRET, now declassified, "History [of the] 488th Bombardment Squadron, 340th Bombardment Group," compiled by

Captains Homer B. Howard and Everett B. Thomas, the primary goal of the group, in Heller's time, was "Medium level bombing of bridges," with the secondary, "low level" aim of "strafing . . . gun positions." Heller flew his first mission on May 24 over Poggibonsi. The night before, he received his assignment and knew he'd be flying with Joe Chrenko. At a briefing with the pilots, he was handed maps and a list of targets. The maps indicated all known antiaircraft gun positions.

He was issued a flak suit—essentially an apron with metal plates sewn inside it—a fleece-lined leather flight suit, and a parachute. After breakfast, the following morning, he and the rest of the crew were driven in a large truck to a plane sitting on a runway. The ground crew, charged with maintaining the plane (often, these men slept on the runways beneath the B-25s), had stocked the bomb bay, loaded the machine guns, fueled the plane, and patched the flak holes it had gotten on previous missions.

Heller, quiet, tense, apprehensive, peed in the field and then slipped inside the "hothouse."

The engines boomed (there were no mufflers, and the exhaust system consisted of just a simple straight pipe). Once in the air, the gunners fired a few rounds into space, a test, and then everyone concentrated on their individual tasks. On the mission to Poggibonsi, thirteen planes coordinated their movements, settling into tight formations known as "boxes," each box consisting of six Mitchells (with one extra bomber, in this case). The box was a vertical and horizontal arrangement of half a dozen planes, configured in such a way that they could protect one another and maintain a precise pattern for the drop.

A Mitchell B-25 could carry up to three tons of explosives.

A fifty-caliber machine gun swung on a ball swivel in front of Heller's face. On this particular flight, he didn't have a Norden bombsight. He had been told to tug his toggle switch the instant he saw the bomb-bay doors open on the lead plane.

The account of the mission in the squadron history recorded "many direct hits" on the railroad tracks leading to the main target—the bridge—with "possible hits on the bridge itself." None of these "possible hits" was Heller's. Nervous and distracted, he had released his bombs too late, and he knew it. Flak activity was "nil."

Later that day, he flew a second mission, this time to Orvieto. "Scant and inaccurate" flak; "complete overcast on target[;] cumulus up to

20,000 [feet]," said the report. The planes returned to base without releasing their bombs.

He had done it: survived his first day. No one had shot at him—either that or they had missed by miles. Maybe this was going to be a cinch.

He flew seven more missions that May, encountering "meager, inaccurate" flak on just two occasions. Over Tivoli, on the morning of May 26, he and his group "failed to spot the target," a railroad junction, and "laid a compact pattern" somewhere west of their goal. Almost as an afterthought, the account concludes, "A hospital along side the primary target received several direct hits." The following day, with "ground haze" obscuring the target, a railroad bridge at Pietrasanta, he wasn't sure what he'd struck, but his group dropped ninety-six five-hundred-pound bombs. On the twenty-ninth, twelve Mitchells, including Heller's, pounded a viaduct at Bucine (about twenty-five miles southeast of Florence) with forty-eight one-thousand-pound bombs. They scored direct hits, but the report noted that, prior to the drop, crewmen observed what "appeared to be a gaping hole in the center of the viaduct from previous bombings."

Missions completed, the crews checked in their flak suits and parachutes, collected ritual shots of whiskey, and returned to their tents to tell stories of the day and mix drinks in their infantry helmets.

ON QUIET NIGHTS, when the air was mildly gusty, and the constant rustle of a tent flap sounded like a man marching determinedly to the ends of the earth, Heller swore he heard the dead Okie snore.

FROM THE AIR, the island's tidy shape resembled a battleship. The men called it the "USS *Corsica*." Sometimes they felt as cramped, living on the island, as if they *were* stuck in the hold of a ship. In sunny weather, the countryside was pretty: silhouetted saw-toothed mountains, cork trees, and groves of bamboo, a gently canted terrain covered with flinty soil, and curling, blue-green waves lapping nearby beaches. But the men grew restless contemplating beauty. Their fishing privileges were severely restricted, so they wouldn't hamper the natives' livelihoods. A movie screen stood on a hillside, but the army's choice of films was rarely inspiring (Deanna Durbin in *Honeymoon Lodge* was shown the night after the attack on the Bucine viaduct). "People think it's a joke when I say that [among soldiers] the most hated man in the world was not Adolf Hitler. He was Frank Sinatra," William Manchester said at the USC symposium. "[W]e would see pictures of Frank Sinatra, who was surrounded by girls our age, trying to kiss him," and the men would yell. Whenever Special Services showed up to screen sex-safety films, the corpsmen hooted and laughed themselves sick.

Sickness often restricted activities, recreational and otherwise. Soldiers "had dysentery all the time," Paul Fussell recalled. "You can imagine how hard it is to believe in the high and noble purpose of the war when you can't control your own bowels, and you come up to the . . . commander to make a snappy report on something and all of the sudden your bowels move, noisily, right there, and perhaps his do as well, only he's a major or lieutenant colonel. This is the atmosphere. Everything is a mess all the time." The misery was compounded by frequent heavy rains. "[H]alf the squadron was inundated" by a particular downpour, stated an entry in the War Diary. "[S]everal inches of water . . . tended to make a rowboat out of [each of our] happy homes." On wet nights, Heller huddled beneath a poncho, next to Ritter's stove, adding up the money orders he planned to send home—sometimes four hundred bucks a pop.

When the sun came out again, some of the men entertained themselves by flying daredevil stunts (squeezing between flagpoles or buzzing the beaches at astonishingly low altitudes, especially if local women happened to be sunbathing). Just before Heller arrived on the base, two pilots had died, crashing into a mountain.

On July 15, Heller encountered his first "accurate" flak of the war. The squadron set off to destroy bridges and a fuel dump four miles north of Ferrara. Eleven days earlier, four planes had been holed over these targets; the men knew the place was hot. As he approached the IP, the initial point of the run, Heller went over in his mind everything he had to consider: What is the rate of closure? How fast are we coming in? What's our elevation? Level, level . . .

That night, the War Diary reported, "Seven planes [were holed] and one man [was] seriously wounded. . . . [Sergeant] Vandermuelen got it through the side."

The next day, the record noted, "Vandermuelen died at 0200 hours. The Ferrara bridges [are] getting to be a jinx for us." Around camp, boys said Vandermuelen's midsection had been severed. Reportedly, he had moaned, "I'm cold, I'm cold," until the moment he died.

Then, on August 15, something happened to Joseph Heller. Over Avignon, flak pierced his plane, tearing apart the gunner's thigh. That day, three other B-25s went down. Among those killed was Earl C. Moon, the copilot on Heller's journey overseas. "Flak: Heavy," the squadron history reported. "Red hanging puffs. . . . 5 chutes seen coming from [a holed] plane, 1 failed to open properly. Left engine [caught] fire and right engine was out."

As his plane veered and bucked, descending, then shooting back up, Heller patched his gunner's leg. Like Sergeant Vandermuelen, the kid, Carl Frankel, kept saying he was cold. Heller responded with "sickly attempts at solicitous and reassuring platitudes," he wrote. "When I went to visit [Frankel] in the hospital the next day, he must have been given blood transfusions, for his Mediterranean color was back, and he was in ebullient spirits. We greeted each other as the closest of pals and never saw each other again."

The war changed for Heller. The 486th's War Diary said the corpsmen hoped to "forget about the [Avignon] mission," but Heller couldn't let it go. "Ferrara . . . had [already] assumed in my memory the character of a . . . nightmare from which I had . . . escaped without harm in my trusting innocence, like an ingenious kid in a Grimm fairy tale," he wrote. Avignon calcified this fear. He understood the situation clearly and unequivocally: "They were trying to kill me. . . . [The fact] that they were trying to kill all of us each time we went up was no consolation. They were trying to kill *me*."

He wanted to go home.

Eight days later, he hurtled into the air again, terrified. The 488th had been ordered to bomb the bridges in Pont-Saint-Martin, over the Settimo River, in northwest Italy. Having received the codes and radio frequencies to use on the mission, Heller settled into 8U. His friend, Francis Yohannan, occupied a sister plane, 8P. Six months later, these two planes would collide in midair.

That day over Pont-Saint-Martin, August 23, 1944, the Americans hit the bridges they were after but also badly damaged the center of town. Roger Juglair, a village resident, has calculated that 130 civilians died during the bombing run, a fact Heller probably never knew for certain. (The 489th's War Diary said, "This period was one of ordinary activity with nothing special to note.") Among the dead were several children who had been attending a sewing class in a kindergarten when the bombs struck. "I'm not aware of any of our consciences ever being bothered [by any of our missions]," Heller once said. "We didn't talk. We didn't sing patriotic songs; we sang risqué versions of other songs. I don't recall anybody being troubled by the bombs we were dropping." The men just wanted to do the job and get the hell out. A possible exception on the mission to Pont-Saint-Martin was 2nd Lt. Clifton C. Grosskopf, the pilot of 8K. He later reported his bombs fell wide of the target because he committed "pilot error" while "executing evasive maneuvers." There had been no flak; Grosskopf's account is odd, says Daniel Setzer: "[O]ne can only conclude that the pilot . . . took it upon himself to wrest control of the aircraft from the bombardier before the bomb run was completed in order to avoid bombing the village."

In *Catch-22,* Heller would describe "bombing a tiny undefended village, reducing the whole community to rubble"—a mission whose "only purpose [was] to delay German reinforcements at a time when we [weren't] even planning an offensive." Perhaps he thought of Grosskopf when he wrote, "Dunbar . . . dropped his bombs hundreds of yards past the village and would face a court-martial if it could ever be shown he had done it deliberately. Without a word [to anyone] Dunbar had washed his hands of the mission."

AT THE END of August, Heller was promoted to first lieutenant.

In mid-September, after flying forty-eight missions, seven of them through "heavy" flak, he felt unusually jumpy about a scheduled run to Bologna, a notorious hot spot. He was not slated to make this run, but he shared his comrades' worries, fears that mounted as nasty weather delayed the offensive. After the second cancellation, the War Diary noted that the "men [were] . . . apprehensive." On September 16, when planes finally left the ground, the log recorded jauntily that "exacerbated nerves" had been "ameliorated." To the crews' surprise, they encountered moderate flak, and the mission was deemed a success. Back in his tent, Heller slipped money orders into envelopes. Whatever his nerves were, they were not "ameliorated."

"THE FIRST AMERICAN SOLDIERS [marched into] Rome on the morning of June 4 [1944], and close on their heels, perhaps even beating them into the city, sped our congenial executive officer, Major Cover, to rent two apartments there for [recreational] use by the officers and enlisted men in our squadron," Heller said in his memoir. With the apartments came "cooks and maids, and . . . female friends of the maids who liked to hang out there."

In a separate account, Heller wrote, "[F]ellow fliers were coming back from Rome with . . . scintillating narratives of high life. . . . They spoke, rhapsodically and disbelievingly, of restaurants, night clubs, dance halls, and girls, girls, girls—girls in their summer dresses and skirts strolling everywhere on wedgie shoes with lofty heels and thong laces winding up . . . to the calves like gladiator boots."

When he finally got to Rome, in urgent need of downtime, his comrades told him the "most valuable phrase" for romance was, "*Quanta costa?*"

Major Cover's apartments overlooked Via Nomentana. "[We] had horse-drawn cabs when[ever] we wished," Heller recalled. In *Closing Time,* he noted—through the eyes of a character he said was based on him—"On the second day of my first leave there I returned from a short stroll alone and came back just as . . . Hungry Joe [whom Heller always claimed was based on Francis Yohannan's tent mate, Joe Chrenko] was getting down from a horse-drawn cab with two girls who looked lively and lighthearted. . . . 'I'll treat you,' [he said to me]." Heller continued:

> He let me start with the pretty one—black hair, plump, round face with dimples, good sized breasts—and it was . . . thrilling, relaxing, fulfilling. When we switched and I was with the wiry one, it was even better. I saw it was true that women could enjoy doing it too. And after that it has always been pretty easy for me, especially after I'd moved [back] to New York . . . and was cheerily at work in the promotion department at *Time* magazine [as Heller would be]. I could talk, I could flirt, I could spend, I could seduce women into seducing me.

One thing he never forgot: Rome was a hell of a lot cleaner than New York.

The Hotel Bernini Bristol, at the bottom of Via Veneto, housed the American Red Cross Officers Club. Heller and Chrenko would drink there after hours and get breakfasts there in the mornings. Occasionally, in the club, Heller ate a hot dog for lunch, but always they were sorry echoes of Nathan's.

"Killing time between meals and other pleasures . . . one sunny afternoon," Heller and Chrenko "chanced upon a small storefront advertising itself as The Funny Face Shop," Heller said. "[W]e went inside to have our faces sketched." The young artist, who had been struggling to make a living during two foreign occupations, first by the Germans, now the Americans, drew caricatures of tourists. His name was Federico Fellini, the same Fellini who would one day make a name for himself as a brilliant filmmaker. "The drawing of me was exceedingly accurate," Heller said. "Not until Fellini drew me did I ever appreciate I had a nose."

He admitted, "We knew next to nothing about the city and its history." Instead, he studied the "sanctioned night spots." In the clubs, "there would be at least one female singer belting out just awful renditions of American hit-parade ballads, along with a small band containing a violin and accordion attempting American swing. Inevitably, some mournful Italian would warble 'O Solo Mio' and a missing-Mom song."

One afternoon, Heller blundered into what he thought was the reception area of a restaurant. He saw "about twenty calm enlisted men waiting patiently on straight-backed chairs . . . calm until, with instantaneous consternation, they [recognized me as] an officer." He suffered "a second or two of shocked embarrassment [and] turned around and fled." He never returned to the brothel.

Other clubs held tea dances in the afternoons, then became rollicking dance halls at night. One evening, in one such club, an older British officer introduced Heller to a "girl named Luciana who wanted to dance more than he did." Heller said, "I was a lousy dancer . . . but she was worse, and so, it seemed, was everyone else." Luciana worked for a French company in a nearby office. "Alone with her in a café later I made passes," Heller wrote. "She declined to come back with me to the apartment because, she said, it was too late." She promised she'd drop by the following morning before work, if he gave her his address. He did, but didn't think he would see her again. The next day, "[t]o my utter amazement . . . I was sleeping soundly when the maid awoke me to announce [Luciana's] arrival. She would accept no present from me when she left, not even a token gift for carfare and such, and I have been in love with her since, and with all women of generous nature."

THE ROMAN PARTIES made it even tougher to abide the USS *Corsica*.

Other R & R spots had their charms. On the island of Capri, Heller was captivated by the legend of the Lucky Little Bell of San Michele. "Once upon a time a little shepherd lived [on Capri] and he was the poorest of the poor children of the place," began one version of the story. One night, in the darkness, the boy lost a small sheep he was tending. Fearing he would be punished for his carelessness, he wondered what to do, when he heard the faint ringing of a bell. Believing this to be the copper object on the missing animal's neck, he ran up a hill, past thistles and pebbles. A burst of light stopped him in his tracks. San Michele appeared to him, riding a white horse. "My boy," said the saint, removing a modest bell that hung against his breast. "Take this and always follow the sound of it and it will keep you from danger." Since then, the boy's life had been filled with sweetness.

Photographs of Heller in his tent, back on Corsica, wearing his flight jacket, reveal a tiny copper bell pinned to his collar, just above a round patch bearing the squadron's insignia, a busty nude female wielding a lightning bolt, straddling a bomb.

On one of his last flights, on the morning of September 23, 1944, Heller was assigned to chaff detail. Instead of bombs, his plane would carry bales of aluminized chaff. The crew would drop them to confuse enemy radar. The assignment came at the last minute. Word reached the squadron that a German division planned to tow the Italian cruiser *Taranto* into a deep channel in the harbor of La Spezia—a large seaport— and scuttle it to create an obstacle for Allied troops. Commanders called on the 340th to destroy the cruiser.

"Because we carried no bombs, we could go zigzagging in at top speed and vary our altitudes," Heller wrote in *Now and Then*. Also, he said, "I shrewdly deduced there was no need for a bombardier [on this flight]."

He perched behind the pilot, wearing one flak suit and wrapping a second suit around his legs and groin. Tightly, he gripped his parachute pack (something he couldn't do when cramped inside the nose cone). The pilot and copilot were new to the squadron and didn't know what to make of him as he sat behind them. "It's okay," he told them with more authority than he felt. "Let me know if the German fighters show up and I'll go back [down below]."

The sky grew thick with flak. The tail gunner broke his thumb while tossing out chaff. When the pilot banked up and away from the harbor, Heller turned his head. He felt, he said, "greatly satisfied with myself and . . . with all the others as well. We were unharmed; the turbulent oceans of dozens and dozens of smutty black clouds from the . . . flak bursts were diffused all over the sky at different heights. The other flights were coming through without apparent damage. And down below I could watch the bombs from one cascade after another exploding directly on the ship that was our target."

For this mission, the 340th Bombardment Group was awarded the Presidential Distinguished Unit Citation. After nine more flights—the last on October 15—Heller was done. Initially, he'd expected to fly fifty missions. Later, he was ordered to complete seventy. He wound up flying sixty. "I have not been able to get an answer as to how he managed to end his tour of combat with 'only' sixty missions. The limit had been set to seventy," Daniel Setzer says. The 487th's War Diary concedes, "The rules governing the disposition of combat crews changes so frequently . . . it's difficult to determine who will and wont [sic] go home." Heller made no bones about the fact that he was terrified. Like several of his comrades, he was "flak happy."

The raised mission limit appears to have caused more consternation in the 488th Bomb Squadron than in any other unit. The War Diary entries for October and November 1944 trace a growing disquiet in the camp: "Many of the crews . . . have reached 60 missions and consider themselves done" (October 3); "Morale is none too high, everyone seems restless" (October 5); "Maj. Cassada told crews that they would have to fly more than 60 missions" (October 24); "Maj. Brussels, Group Flight Surgeon, spoke at noon in the dispensary to the crews who are sweating out rotation. All of them have between 60 and 70 missions" (November 23).

Given Heller's schoolboy reputation as a loudmouth, it's possible he helped lead a mounting opposition to the raised limits, and demanded flexibility in the rules.

In November 1944, bomb squadrons from Corsica flew forty-eight missions over the Brenner Pass. Two hundred and twenty-four planes got holed; five were lost. Heller spent most of that month in his tent. He sent money orders home. By absentee ballot, he voted for FDR.

In December, "two chaste beginners, both lieutenants freshly shipped overseas, moved into" the tent Heller shared with Ritter. "They replaced a pair who had finished their tours and already left." One of them brought a typewriter. The dead Okie remained. A "huge and invisible divide [existed] between me [and the newcomers,]" Heller wrote. "I was through," and they had several more missions to try to survive. A photograph taken inside the tent that month shows a group of men gathered around a Christmas cake. Ritter retires into the shadows, gazing warily at the pastry, as though it might explode; Bob Vortrees, a pilot recently wounded in the hand by flak, cuts the cake awkwardly with a large and serious knife; the newbies, Hy Tribble and Emmit Hughes, whose smiles couldn't be more forced, look on; Heller sits apart from the rest, cupping one hand in the other as he holds a cigarette and leans forward toward the typewriter.

IN EARLY JANUARY, just before shipping home, Heller, along with two of his buddies, Tom Sloan and Hall A. Moody, did R & R in Cairo. No trips out to the pyramids for *these* boys, just nightclub after night-club. Their hotel swarmed with American and British officers, as well as American oil workers on their way to Port Said. Heller didn't know anything about the Mideast petroleum reserves these men spoke about so excitedly. His favorite place in Cairo was a steak and shrimp restau-rant called Pastrudi's. Dominating the center of the dining room was a Reuter's news ticker. You could munch and drink and watch the world come spitting out of this machine. One night, a few blocks from his hotel, Heller was accosted by child beggars with suppurating sores on their faces and limbs. It was a vision of Hell, far worse than the French-ified Inferno along the Coney Island boardwalk. "There were flies in inflamed eyes," Heller said.

A week or so later, he paced the streets of Naples, waiting for the ship that would carry him back to the States. The moment he had got-ten off the plane there—the last time, in many years, he would fly in any kind of aircraft—he felt a young boy tug his sleeve, offering him his sister at a very low price. The "skinny, smiling girl in a thin and ragged coat standing behind him . . . reached out to rub my groin," Heller wrote. He scurried off the runway and lost himself in the city. "It was cold and dreary," he said. "[N]one of that radiant kind of prodigal gai-ety that had practically vibrated in . . . Rome and Cairo, an air of con-tinuous carnival."

On the ship, going home, he ate apple pie in the officers' mess. Most of his cabinmates got seasick, and Heller was one of the few people returning to the dining room each morning and evening. "At breakfast the fourth or fifth day out, after we had passed Gibraltar and were well into the Atlantic, I took my seat at an empty table and was stunned . . . to find myself being waited upon by a lieutenant colonel, with a major working as his helper and a captain doing the tasks of a bus boy," he wrote. As it turned out, a ground-unit commander who had grown impatient in Naples while waiting for transport had volunteered his men for menial duties if they could be squeezed aboard ship. This particular morning, all the lower-grade fellows were vomiting back in their cabins, so the cooking and cleaning fell to the higher-ups. In his mind, Heller commanded the vessel.

5. "I Don't Love You Any More"

[T]HERE WERE[N'T] MANY young men who came out of World War II . . . who did not believe that the world had been saved for democracy and that there was this vast . . . sunny plain of peace that was going to last forever," William Styron said.

Back in Coney Island, the sun wasn't shining, and whatever satisfaction or confidence Heller may have felt aboard ship on his way home clouded over quickly. Aimless and depressed in the days before Lee suggested he go to Grossinger's, he wandered past the ash heap that had once been Luna Park, as shaky on his feet as if he had been battered in a bumper-car frenzy. The Luna Park disaster had been a bonanza for his pal Lou Berkman, who was working now in his family's junk business. Berkman and his father picked scaffolding, pipes, lumber, and asbestos out of the moldering debris and sold it all. The rest of Heller's friends weren't doing so well. Abie Ehrenreich was still missing overseas. And George Mandel, who had gone to Europe with the infantry, had been shot in the leg in Holland. While recuperating in a military hospital, he heard about the Battle of the Bulge, to which his unit had been ordered. He checked himself out, eager to rejoin his comrades. A sniper shot him in the head. He had survived—his condition uncertain.

HELLER STORED his Lucky Little Bell of San Michele on the scuffed wooden floor beneath his bed in the barracks at Goodfellow Field. He thought of it each time the West Texas wind carried the lowing of sheep across dry, brittle plains. The mail had brought him no word about his short story, and he hadn't heard from Shirley.

From outside his window came a burst of unintelligible language. A group of Filipino officers had just arrived on the base for a taste of American flight training. They had not flown since the Japanese invasion of Pearl Harbor, and they were more than a little rusty. Heller felt glad he had nothing to do with training. (His flight record for March 1945, signed by Capt. Ernie E. Groce, confirmed that "No Flying Time [was] Accomplished at This Station.")

Heller was one of a "great number" of combat returnees assigned to San Angelo in the spring of 1945, according to the *History of the 2533rd AAF Base Unit (Pilot School, Prim-Basic) at Goodfellow Field.* "Almost without exception, the . . . returnees . . . required more time to adapt . . . to flying [again], the cause . . . being that all had suffered combat fatigue . . . and apparently had not had sufficient time to recuperate from the rigors of combat flying."

The account went on to say that now that the men had been reassigned, "it is impossible to state how these officers will work out." Most of the men had "no administrative experience. They are in general pilots who flew their missions and returned." The base commanders felt overwhelmed by the heavy "rotation policy" and "rapid turnover" of individuals, many of them traumatized by their time overseas. The returnees' morale was low, "with separation from the service the ultimate goal of the majority of personnel."

ANOTHER MAIL CALL. Another silence from Shirley. Heller lay on his bed with a copy of *Flight Time,* the base newspaper, studying its breakdown of the military's impending point system. Men would be discharged according to points they'd accrued, the tally based on number of dependent children (twelve points each), length of military service and time of service overseas (one point each per month), and number of medals earned (five points a medal). The magic number was eighty-five.

Sixty missions. Surely that, by itself, was enough.

Stan Kenton's Orchestra, featuring the singer Anita O'Day, was scheduled to play a Goodfellow concert—the first time a "name band" had performed on base, according to *Flight Time*. Heller would have rushed to see Duke Ellington, but Stan Kenton he wasn't so thrilled about. Trips into town, these days, were less fun than they used to be because local businessmen had begun to complain about soldiers loitering rowdily in the streets. Colonel Gunn had established "courtesy patrols" in town—more MPs—to improve the "military discipline of personnel at this station." The paper listed upcoming movies at the base theater: *Snow White and the Seven Dwarfs, Dillinger,* featuring Edmund Lowe and Lawrence Tierney, and a frittery Tracy/Hepburn concoction, *Without Love,* also starring Lucille Ball. Apparently, a USO show was in the works. It would highlight Spanish dancers and a local magician. So much to look forward to.

There had been nineteen training accidents in the past four weeks. Communication problems with the newly arrived Filipino officers were not likely to improve *that* number.

Eighty-five points. He didn't have enough. Did he?

Why hadn't he heard from Shirley?

In his lassitude, in the heat and grit and boredom, it was easy to believe that Grossinger's had been a dream, the redhead he had met just another glamour shot in the back pages of *Flight Time*. In the paper, pictures of beautiful women always appeared next to photos of infants labeled "Papa's Pin-Ups." (What was the message here? Unlimited sex *and* family sentiment? The good life—doubled—for which you boys have been fighting so bravely? You can have it all?) He had to concentrate to convince himself he really *had* met the girl in the far-off Jewish Alps, and to remind himself how the moment had occurred, so he could relive it until the memory was embedded in stone.

A dance contest. A bottle of champagne. A smiling young girl.

Now, at Goodfellow, as more days passed without encouragement from Shirley, Heller began to suspect something was wrong, and he phoned her. He was right. "My mother got cold feet," Erica says. "My grandparents [were] convinced . . . she was making a mistake. They were his biggest fans." She recalls, "There was a famous family story about him riding to New York on a milk train from Texas, to get her to change her mind."

"Milk train" could have been a euphemism for any form of cheap travel, but given the time and place, the phrase probably should be taken literally. "Trains that made stops at most every small town and even a few of the larger farms were called 'milk trains' because one thing they did was to pick up the fresh milk," explains David Wood of the Railway Museum of San Angelo. According to Wood, nine milk trains and seven "doddlebugs," or self-contained motorized cars also carrying passengers, left San Angelo daily in 1945. The trains went to Fort Worth, Texas. From there, several routes were available to New York—most likely through Kansas City and Chicago.

Heller's mission to retrieve his girl probably occurred in late April (we know, from some of his statements, that he was back at the base in early May). "Obviously, he was quite persuasive," Erica says.

"It was Shirley's mother who [really] took the initiative when I was alone with her one afternoon in her living room," Heller recalled in his memoir. "'Barney thinks,' said Dottie, with the devious premeditation that was second nature to her and occasionally endearing—it was likely that Barney, the husband, had no inkling of what she was up to—'that it's because you don't have the money that you don't give her a ring.'"

"Give her a ring?" Heller blurted. "What for?"

"To get engaged to be married."

Now, *that's* persuasion. Dottie knew how to get things done—at Grossinger's and now on the Upper West Side.

"I had money enough for the ring," Heller wrote. "[Dottie] made the purchase and billed me just $500. [Immediately,] friends and families on both sides were delighted with the match. I was a young and unformed twenty-two and a half; the bride had just passed twenty-one. Almost every fellow I'd grown up with in Coney Island was getting married at about that time."

Ring on finger, kisses offered, assurances made, he returned to Texas to finish serving his time.

"V-E DAY"—May 8, 1945—"was pretty banal for me," Heller told a *Newsday* reporter. "I was . . . at [the] San Angelo Army Base in Texas. We knew V-E Day was coming, but didn't know what day it was going to be. Finally, we heard the announcement over the radio. The day came and went. I don't remember any great celebration." The mess hall served a cake, but that was all. "[T]he men were mostly concerned about the point system. . . . Everybody was asking, 'How many points do you have?'"

Combat returnees rejoiced that Hitler had apparently killed himself in a bunker somewhere at the end of April; they had known victory in Europe was imminent. On May 8, President Harry Truman celebrated his sixty-first birthday and dedicated the victory to the memory of Franklin Roosevelt, who had passed away on April 12. Nationwide, flags remained at half-mast. At Goodfellow, *Flight Time* made sure the returnees didn't get too giddy. Right after V-E Day, rumors circulated on military bases that the VA had announced plans to release from active duty between 200,000 and 250,000 soldiers. *Flight Time* insisted this story was "without foundation," and quoted Secretary of War Henry L. Stimson to the effect that soldiers would not be released "en masse."

A few days later, the paper cautioned military personnel that "the war is about half over." *Flight Time* ran a piece attributed to the "Camp Newspaper Service" that read, in full: "The State Department has made public evidence of German plans for continuing to fight for world domination even after total military defeat. The evidence was collected by various Allied Governments, and is based on reliable information, according to State Department officials."

Meanwhile, Goodfellow's new swimming pool was now ready for use, and all the men on the base were required to take a swimming test.

Dust storms showered the pool; some afternoons, the air turned so brown, the only things visible, more than a few feet away, were telephone poles staked here and there. Towels, clothing, beds, and food smelled of loam. Whenever someone smashed a Ping-Pong ball in the rec room, puffs of dust rose from the table.

Heller sat on his bed, counting and recounting his points.

Later, he claimed he left Texas in mid-May and was officially discharged at Fort Dix, in New Jersey, on June 10, 1945, one of the first men released under the new point system. Records obtained from the Military Personnel Records Facility of the National Personnel Records Center in St. Louis do not say how many points he had. At rough glance, the total appears to fall short of the required minimum. Chad Dull, currently the base historian at Goodfellow Field, expressed surprise that Heller was released before the end of the hostilities with Japan. This odd timing, combined with the fact that Heller came home without flying his required seventy missions overseas, logging no flying time in Atlantic City or San Angelo, invites speculation that he received medical dispensation for an early release. He told a doctor in Atlantic City he couldn't fly anymore; at San Angelo, he was clearly one of a number of men pegged as suffering from combat fatigue.

On the other hand, Secretary of War Stimson introduced the point system on May 12. Many confusions and exceptions—inadvertent and otherwise—attended its implementation. The rules governing officers were enforced less strictly than those for enlisted men. Sixty missions *was* a lot.

"[One] weekend . . . an order arrived [at Goodfellow] to discharge a certain number of officers," Heller wrote in *Now and Then*. "I had lost most of my pocket money in a dice game or card game . . . and just happened to be on hand"; if so, his escape was simply fortuitous. His individual flight record confirms that on May 14, he was reassigned to a "separation center." His Certificate of Service confirmed that his "service was terminated" by "Honorable Relief from Active Duty," on June 14, 1945.

He packed up his Lucky Little Bell and returned to New York. He and Shirley—probably, more accurately, Dottie—made plans for an autumn wedding in the synagogue Shirley's family attended, Congregation B'nai Jeshurun. It was located on Manhattan's West Eighty-eighth Street, between Broadway and West End Avenue. With Shirley's blessing, Heller applied to the University of Southern California, under the G.I. Bill (California had seemed golden to him during his military training there, despite wartime fears of a coastline invasion).

One day, during "a spell of beautiful weather," he spent a day strolling around Coney Island, "with little idea of what to do with myself," he said. The old social clubs had "passed away of attrition." The rides looked smaller than he remembered. Wasn't liberation supposed to feel more *liberating* than this? On Surf Avenue, he spied an old school chum, Davey Goldsmith, home on furlough. They traded tales of old friends—Abie Ehrenreich, about whom there was still no word; George Mandel, who seemed to be recovering, though he now had a metal plate in his head (the sniper's bullet had penetrated his helmet but only went so far into the brain). Many of their mates had dropped out of school and gone to work at lousy jobs.

Heller treated Goldsmith to a Nathan's dog and french fries, and for a moment they felt like kids once more. "When we went on the Parachute

Jump, I was tense again for just the few seconds of suspense that preceded the unexceptional drop along protective guide wires," he recalled
in his memoir. "But coasting down, I had to wonder why anyone would
want to ride it a second time." To himself, he admitted, "After sixty missions overseas, I was now selective in my adventures." The Coney Island
part of his life was over. He was no longer his mother's little Joey. Nor
was he "Heller this, Heller that," with a military bureaucracy to make
up his mind for him. He was Joe Heller, about to be married. Relief
flooded him—*and* apprehension. As he gazed at the ocean one last time
and looked across the old neighborhoods, he "felt with sadness that
something dear was behind me forever."

MORE THAN THE WAR, the acceptance letter from *Story* magazine
that arrived at his mother's apartment one afternoon in midsummer,
forwarded from Texas, made him feel like a hero. Only his old pal
Danny the Count had heard of *Story,* but the news that "our Joe" was
about to become a published author impressed everyone, including his
fiancée's social enclave on Riverside Drive. "Overnight, I was, or felt
myself [to be], a local celebrity," he wrote. "I became talked about." He
liked the adulation.

The summer brought more good news (maybe the Lucky Little Bell
was working its charms): an acceptance letter from the University of
Southern California; and then, on August 6, word of Hiroshima.

"I cannot recall a single expression of outrage in this country against
Harry Truman for dropping the bomb on Hiroshima. Or Nagasaki,"
Paul Fussell insisted in 1995. "The criticisms . . . came . . . later." Infan-
trymen like William Styron, still on the ground at the time, felt the bomb
had saved their lives. "I really honestly believe [I] would not be here
[otherwise,]" he said. As for Joe Heller: "I was a very happy civilian . . .
when the atom bomb went off," he said. With the defeat of Japan, with
no danger now—under any circumstances—of returning to combat, he
could almost relive his missions with fondness. Dreamily, he recalled,
"[O]nce we were in formation [on the way to a target], I'd put on the
radio, and I'd listen to music, and I'd hear songs—*Carousel, Louisiana
Hayride,* the music of *Oklahoma*—and you'd get these bouncy tunes on
there." In more somber moments now, he'd realize that, despite all he'd

lived through, he "knew nothing about war . . . very little about [his] own combat experience." What he knew—*all* he knew for sure—was that the war was over and Joe Heller was the author of "I Don't Love You Any More."

IF SHIRLEY HAD READ "I Don't Love You Any More" as disguised truth, she would have run screaming from her handsome young intended. The story's view of marriage is pitiless: Cohabitation is an unnatural arrangement that corners men and women into grating and dehumanizing routines. Couples remain committed to one another for reasons unknown. Whether the fundamental flaw rests in individuals or in middle-class morality remains unexplored.

During the course of the story, a war veteran who has just come home discovers he no longer loves his wife. He is "purposely" cruel to her, "not really wanting to be, but nevertheless deriving some perverse pleasure in seeing her unhappy." Her habit of being "considerate" toward him somehow "mak[es] him bitter." He argues with her in repeated banalities, refuses to get dressed to greet another couple who'll arrive any minute, and keeps demanding a pitcher of beer. The wife leaves (for good, the husband fears), the visiting couple arrives, expresses concern for their friends, and then the wife returns with the beer. The husband grins at her "like an erring schoolboy" and the wife smiles "sheepishly."

The piece is dialogue-heavy, choppy. It moves like an awkwardly staged one-act play. There is little evidence of an authorial eye: The wife is described as "well rounded so that she possessed a strong physical attraction."

Shirley was not a naïve reader. Joe appreciated this. She understood what he said of the story years later: "[I]t [was] based on things I knew nothing about except for my sifting around in the works of other writers": Shaw, Saroyan, Hemingway, O'Hara. The story was "malign and histrionic" because these writers were malign and histrionic. The couple's unhappiness meant nothing; it was a "convention" of the kind of short fiction he had been reading.

Shirley admired the young author's attempt at a metaphor: Throughout the piece, the husband plays with a Chinese puzzle, two metal rings he can't prize apart despite his most brutal efforts.

"I Don't Love You Any More" appeared in the September-October issue of *Story,* just as Joe and Shirley were finalizing wedding arrangements. In the contributor's note, Joe said he had been "comfortably rehabilitating" himself since his discharge "under the point system," and that at present he was "busy trying to get a play produced." He had not penned any plays, other than a few stabs in high school at crafting something along the lines of the radio dramas he used to listen to at night, or a comedy in the vein of Moss Hart or George S. Kaufmann.

"I Don't Love You Any More" earned him twenty-five dollars. He was now a professional writer, like his poor, broken friend George Mandel.

AT GROSSINGER'S, and during the brief leave from Texas, when he convinced Shirley to stay with him, he barely had time to pause and contemplate the girl who was going to change his life. From the beginning, Shirley was Joe's "most appreciative audience (and sometimes his crooked straight man)," according to Barbara Gelb. She was fiercely loyal to him (championing his short story to everyone they met), but not without irony, sometimes at his expense. She could "laugh and cry at the same time, and [was], therefore, the perfect Heller heroine," Gelb said: a mixture of "gaiety and rue." Shirley joked with friends that she shared with Joe an admiration for Joe Heller.

Dolores Karl, who would soon become one of Shirley's closest friends, described Shirley as "very elegant, though understated. She knew how to dress on a budget. She knew how to put it all together."

At Grossinger's, Joe had thought her "privileged," though her parents had struggled up from poverty. She carried herself with dignity, confidence, and pride, a manner learned from her mother. "Dottie and Barney were an interesting couple. There was no question she was the boss and everyone knew it," says Jerome Taub, Shirley's cousin. "Dottie made all the important decisions and Barney just went along with everything." His main sportswear factory was in Philadelphia, but he had to commute because Dottie insisted on living on Manhattan's Riverside Drive. She knew the power of appearances.

Together, Dottie and Shirley educated Joe in social taste and etiquette. For example, he was astonished at how well (and deeply) they "knew the difference between sirloin steak and top sirloin, prime rib and top round." He learned from them that "only first-cut brisket was suitable for a good pot roast."

These sorts of distinctions, and belief in their importance, enveloped him during preparations for the wedding. The arrangements had to be perfect. Like Dottie and Shirley, B'nai Jeshurun was modestly sized but graceful. The street, one block west of Broadway, was quiet. The bright orange and rusty-tan of the synagogue's facade nicely complemented the large brown door, appearing to darken the tone of the wood. The door opened wide beneath an elaborately carved stone arch topped by a Star of David. The building had been dedicated in the fall of 1917, in what was then a rapidly growing upper-middle-class Jewish neighborhood. For over twenty-five years, Rabbi Israel Goldstein had served as B'nai Jeshurun's spiritual leader. A well-known Zionist, he traveled frequently to promote his cause; he would also be instrumental in founding Brandeis University.

"There was at all times a degree of competition between the congregational responsibilities of my rabbinate and the broader claims of my public career," he admitted in his memoir. "Nevertheless, to the best of my ability, I [balanced] my duties wholeheartedly." On October 2, 1945, these duties included marrying Joseph Heller and Shirley Held.

It was a busy month for the rabbi. On the day he led the wedding ceremony, he helped draft a telegram to President Truman on behalf of the Interim Committee of the American Jewish Conference. The telegram said that Great Britain should facilitate the immediate entry of 100,000 Jews into Palestine and that this should be seen as an "initial step toward the definitive solution of establishing a Jewish national homeland [there]." It was his firm belief that "sufferance ha[d] been the badge" of the Jewish people, but it was not written that "sufferance [was their] destiny." He said, "Our destiny is to be a people among peoples, standing on our feet upon the hallowed soil of our fathers."

He did not pronounce such sentiments at the wedding, but the gravity of the rabbi's beliefs colored the ceremony. On the marriage certificate, beneath dark blocks of Hebrew, Joe and Shirley signed their names. The signatures were careful: no joyous rush or heedless impatience to get things done; rather, a solemnity and an apparent recognition of the occasion's seriousness.

Later that day, at a reception at Dottie and Barney's apartment, there "was a lot of drinking, especially by Joe's family and friends," says Jerome Taub. His part of the family was in the liquor business, and "the family motto was, 'Liquor is made to be sold, not to be drunk.' So there was no excessive drinking on our side." He didn't know Joe, but his immediate impression was that he lived "in his head." Maybe he was a little shy, perhaps intimidated by the Held and Taub families, who were well off compared to Joe's mother, brother, and sister.

After the reception, Joe and Shirley tossed their bags in Taub's car. He drove them to the train station. Along the way, "one of Joe's relatives"—his brother Lee, Taub thinks—"got very sick" from all the booze he'd consumed "and threw up out the car window."

At the station, Joe and Shirley boarded a Pullman train for Los Angeles and waved good-bye to their families—Sylvia crying; Lee silent; Lena, with her cane, struggling to distinguish Shirley's name from the name of Lee's wife (Shirl/Perle turned out to be a tongue-twister for her).

"The motives for my decision to go to the University of Southern California remain opaque, but they doubtless included the indispensable one that I was accepted there," Joe recalled years later. "I don't doubt that they were also evasive in purpose, intended to delay, to buy time. I didn't want . . . to have to decide right away what I was going to do for the rest of my life. . . . I felt myself much too young. . . . Going to college was easier and more appealing than going to work and certainly . . . more respected."

With a Pullman berth for a honeymoon bed, and his name in print in the magazine sticking out of his coat pocket, he snuggled with his wife. Together, they dreamed aloud about the far West's lovely hills.

PART TWO **Happy Valley**

6. Words in a Box

I T WAS A BLUSTERY New York early-autumn day. Joe walked crisply across Washington Square Park. Rumor had it that Robert Moses, the parks commissioner, planned to remove the park's fountain and construct a turnout in the middle of the block that could accommodate eight to ten buses at a time. He'd been aiming to route traffic through Washington Square since before the war, despite the Villagers' protests. The man was like a desk general: no idea, and no interest in, conditions on the ground. NYU wasn't much better. Over the shouts and picket signs of the neighborhood's Save Washington Square Committee, the school was apparently going to raze the old bohemian row houses and tenements along the park's edges for a big new law school. It was easy to laugh—as many students did, shuffling by the picketers on their way to classes—at the neighbors' futile demonstrations. Still, the people's presence in the streets, yelling slogans, made for plenty of excitement.

Joe headed for the Education Block building, just east of the park. The latest figures he'd heard claimed NYU enrolled more veterans than any other university in the nation—over twelve thousand—and you could spot every last one of them: rumpled, prim—no longer *at attention* as they used to be in the army, but with tattered vestiges of the old discipline. Sleepless and serious. Above all, serious. They took too many classes. They wanted to learn.

On the corner of West Fourth and Washington Square East, Joe pulled from his coat pocket a letter in a familiar cream-colored envelope, which he'd received earlier that day. Again he read the note, dated September 8, 1947: "We feel compelled to say no to it . . . Somehow—and perhaps we're wrong—we find it hard to believe that a gang of boys would smoke marihuana [*sic*] right out in the open, especially in their home neighborhood."

Was this guy kidding? Had he been to Coney Island? Did he ever leave his office?

Joe read further: "One little suggestion, though: are you writing out of your own experience? If you're not, I think it might be interesting for you to try—for a while, at least—to concentrate on people you know and emotions you share." The letter was signed by Donald Berwick, for *The New Yorker*. The joke was that this latest short story, "Murdock, His Son, and a Man Named Flute," was closer to Joe's experience than anything he'd tried up until now. It was straight out of Sammy the Pig's pool hall and Mermaid Avenue. He was proud of the story's symmetry: the way the father, a two-bit bookie, defends his racket by telling his wife if he didn't run the numbers, someone else would, and then hears a similar excuse from the man who sells dope to his son; the way Murdock beats on his boy and then gets manhandled by the doper. Well, maybe *The New Yorker* didn't like Runyonesque characters, though Joe had tried the magazine with everything he had, humor as well as grit. It seemed that every week, the cream-colored envelopes showered down on him. Berwick couldn't have taken the time to read these things, could he?

A gust of wind blew leaves along the curb. Joe pulled his coat collar up. On afternoons like this, he almost wished he'd stayed in California.

"Murdock, His Son, and A Man Named Flute": A blocky title. Maybe it was a blocky *story,* step by telegraphed step. Was it too obvious, lacking evocative power? Still, the practical thing to do was to stick the story in another envelope, send it somewhere else. Don't even think about it. Keep the pages flying.

Early that evening, after classes, he caught the subway to West Seventy-sixth Street, heading to the apartment he shared with Shirley just off Central Park West, near the New York Historical Society and the American Museum of Natural History. Shirley's parents had helped them land this place after they'd returned from Los Angeles. A friend of Dottie and Barney's owned the building, a slim five-story brownstone with a nice new elevator. In their first year back, Joe and Shirley had occupied a small apartment here with a roll-out sofa; then a bigger space opened up, one floor above, with a full kitchen and bedroom. Dottie and Shirley decorated it immaculately, and Dottie often went over to cook for the couple: prime rib, pot roast. Barney helped with the rent, and with extra school expenses. Sometimes, Joe augmented his monthly income by working part-time, after class, in the circulation department of a magazine called *American Home*.

Now, at the kitchen table, Joe spread the pages of his latest rough draft, a piece based on the tale he'd heard years ago, as a Western Union messenger, about the fellow delivering telegrams who meets a couple who wants him to make love to the woman while the man watches. He had in mind a story of lost innocence, the education of an adolescent, along the lines of Sherwood Anderson's "I Want to Know Why," which he'd just read. But he couldn't find the right tone. He'd never been *that* naïve. And what was the point? The rich can be as morose as the poor? Everyone knew that, didn't they?

He wrote, "He had been kept close to home while his father was alive, and it was only recently that he had been allowed the freedom of observation. The world about him was beginning to unfold slowly in a vast and puzzling panorama, delighting him with each new revelation."

He set the pages aside. He asked Shirley if she wanted to invite guests for dinner that weekend. She liked to entertain. What about asking his writing teacher, Buck Baudin? Buck was just six years older than Joe; he was starting to earn good money, selling stories to magazines. He'd had a couple of pieces in *Esquire*. *Good Housekeeping* paid him fifteen hundred dollars for a story.

It was a matter of writing quickly and steadily. Joe remembered he'd kicked out a draft of "I Don't Love You Any More" in about two hours. He'd fiddled with it quite a bit after that, but this wasn't such onerous work. You get an idea, you trust it, and you go with it. Or so he told himself.

In *The Fiction of Joseph Heller: Against the Grain*, David Seed notes the many direct echoes of Hemingway in "I Don't Love You Any More." Like Krebs in Hemingway's "Soldier's Home," Joe's war vet is disillusioned by what he's witnessed: He refuses to play the hero, just as Krebs feels a "distaste for everything that had happened to him in the war." Like the bored couple in Hemingway's "Cat in the Rain," Joe's young newlyweds don't know (or refuse to face) what makes them unhappy. It seems Joe had taken his structure from "Cat in the Rain": The woman in Hemingway's story wants a kitten, just as Joe's veteran craves a pitcher of beer (clearly, kitten and beer are substitutes for *real* solutions to problems). At the end of each piece, the characters get what they asked for. In "I Don't Love You any More," a cruel husband goads his wife into expressing her misery by refusing to state his own, as Nick does with Marjorie in Hemingway's "The End of Something" (love "isn't fun any more," Nick finally admits—though he can't say why).

The truth is, Joe didn't kick out drafts; he labored over them carefully, with fine literary models in mind. Quickly and steadily would never be his method, as he was already beginning to suspect. But quickly was how he wanted success to land—perhaps this accounted for his swift abandonment of California: a restlessness, an impatience with the slightest thing that felt out of whack or appeared to impede what he wanted.

He glanced up from the kitchen table at his busy, pretty wife. It hadn't been a mistake. She, too, was glad to be back in New York. He was sure of it.

FROM THE BEGINNING, Los Angeles had felt like a folly. Early October 1945: The first few days, they'd stayed at the grand old Ambassador Hotel on Wilshire Boulevard. A celebrity palace (Charlie Chaplin, Rudy Valentino, Gloria Swanson, Kate Hepburn, on and on and on), it was the kind of place you could wander around in for days and never find your way out. Joe and Shirley danced—their official honeymoon—in the hotel's Coconut Grove nightclub, along with hundreds of other exservicemen and their gals. Late at night, they ordered room service from the lavish kitchen (in the pantry in which, twenty-three years later, Senator Robert F. Kennedy would be fatally shot). Splashy digs, but they couldn't live like that for long. They were burning through the money from their wedding.

Through the housing office at the University of Southern California, they found a rooming house on South Figueroa Street, near Washington

Boulevard, in the south-central section of the city. Once a leg of Route 66, Figueroa ran north-south between the Pacific Coast Highway and the Ventura Freeway. Washington Boulevard extended nearly to the ocean. USC was close, and so was Watts. Faux-Moroccan and garishly painted Tudor architecture lined the streets. The smell of melted cheese and sizzling chili oil came from all the Mexican and hole-in-the-wall Chinese cafés in the neighborhood. The Hellers' landlords, an elderly couple, Mr. and Mrs. Hunter, belonged to an evangelical Christian sect, to which Mrs. Hunter tried to convert Shirley (apparently, she was afraid to approach Joe on the subject). The old woman also confided to Shirley that her husband had never satisfied her sexually, a calamity that sometimes led her to sit on a cake of ice. Shirley began to avoid the woman, and Joe didn't know what to say to the silent Mr. Hunter, who slipped about the property, wraithlike, always wearing a blue or a gray cardigan sweater.

The Hellers had no kitchen; politely, they declined their landlords' offers to come into the main house to use the stove. The newlyweds ate in a Greek coffee shop nearby, as well as in other cafés. Once, they spotted Rosalind Russell in the Brown Derby. But mostly, they noticed all the mortuary monuments on the sidewalks. Cemetery sculpture was booming in the area.

A few years earlier, in the midst of the Depression, bands of "wild boys," as the locals called them, converged on South Figueroa Street, the site of a large government relief center. It housed itinerants (like John Steinbeck's Joad family) who had headed to California for agricultural work and wound up in L.A., where they scrabbled for jobs in the defense industry. In the mid-thirties, over twelve thousand transients a month descended on the city. These days, nearby Watts still reeled from too many immigrants. "Mud Town," Watts was called; formerly a sandy, treeless area, it had once served as the L.A. water basin. Estimates said about two thousand people a month, most of them black, were moving in now, displacing the area's former residents, a mix of Chinese, Mexican, and Jewish families. An area covering two and a half square miles, it now had the highest population density of any place in Los Angeles County. Recently, the government had withdrawn its federal housing subsidies, leaving scores of people with mortgages they couldn't afford, and police and local officials trying to keep the lid on a pressure cooker. Sometimes, on his way to campus, Joe liked to digress and walk past the odd towers in Watts made of bottles, broken dishes, and seashells, rising ever higher inside a walled garden belonging to a man named Simon Rodia, an Italian immigrant who said he "wanted to do something for the United States because there are nice people in this country." The towers redeemed Watts's ugliness, up to a point, turning waste into beauty, but Joe could feel the desperation and uneasiness in the area. Twenty years later, in August 1965, rioting and looting in Watts would claim the lives of thirty-four people. Simon Rodia left Watts and never returned. He wouldn't talk about the poverty and racism he had seen there. "If your mother dies and you have loved her very much," he said, "maybe you don't speak of her."

This was not the California Joe remembered from his military-training days. He recalled the pleasure of taking a bus down to Newport Beach and over to the Balboa Peninsula, a mini-Coney Island with amusement rides, pretty girls, and an exciting concoction he hadn't tasted before, frozen bananas covered with chocolate and candy sprinkles. By contrast, L.A.—or at least the patch of it Joe and Shirley squatted in—was, in Raymond Chandler's words, a "neon-lighted slum." Here, "the bright gardens had a haunted look," Chandler wrote in his novel *The Big Sleep.* The city offered "the most of everything and the best of nothing"; it was a place where "everything [was] like something else."

Basically, L.A. was a federal garrison. Government money, feeding the production of military aircraft by Lockheed, Northrup, North American, and Douglas, had turned California's economy into the seventh largest in the world. The poverty recorded in Steinbeck's *The Grapes of Wrath* was augmented now by the frenzy of opportunism traced in Nathanael West's *The Day of the Locust* (intriguingly, both novels were published in 1939, when *The Big Sleep,* an elegy for a clean and peaceful urban West, also appeared).

Joe and Shirley took long walks under leafy carob trees, past neat and colorful stucco houses (as much to avoid the Hunters as to try to find beauty and serenity somewhere). In the mornings, they paused to admire willowy fog curling around bushes and cars. They did not make many friends. Joe was too busy studying to socialize with his class-mates, most of whom were younger than he was. For a while, Shirley halfheartedly tried to develop an interest in football, but in the end, she had to admit she didn't give a damn about the Rose Bowl.

They spent their evenings reading (Shirley surrendered to *Wuther-*

ing Heights), sightseeing in Hollywood, or listening to classical music and comedy shows (Fred Allen, Jack Benny) on the radio. They grew fond of shish kebab—it was a cheap meal—with french fries, rice, and salad, all for under two dollars. Shirley couldn't afford new clothes. She didn't want to write her parents for money—they had already been so generous. She wondered whether she would ever have nice hair and nails again. There had been a beauty shop on the train from New York, but she feared she wouldn't see another hair dryer in this lifetime.

During his second semester, Joe arranged his class schedule so he could get away early in the afternoons and meet Shirley at the Santa Anita racetrack in Arcadia. It had just opened again as a horse-racing venue after serving for three years as an internment camp for Japanese-Americans. Before the war, Seabiscuit had become the most famous racehorse in the world by winning the $100,000 Santa Anita Handicap. Betting on the horses, against the sunny purple backdrop of the San Gabriel Mountains, became Joe and Shirley's favorite California pastime.

Joe liked the idea of school better than school itself—at least initially. He had begun as a journalism major but quickly discovered that the kids in journalism classes couldn't write worth a damn. "I wanted to find [things] out [, but] I wasn't sure what I wanted to learn," he wrote years later. His most valuable object of study at USC was his own temperament. He knew he was smart—he had always been good in school—but he learned he didn't really have a scholarly disposition. He seized on facts and figures randomly, if and when they pleased him or served his mental projects. He wasn't about to engage fully in Latin or literary exegesis just because he was supposed to.

Before leaving New York, he had purchased a portable typewriter at Macy's, using Sylvia's employee discount. On this machine, he wrote his English compositions, always trying to tweak them so they would satisfy the class assignment and maybe also be suitable for magazine publication of some sort. On his own time, he continued to read John O'Hara, Irwin Shaw, and William Saroyan, and to dream of publishing short stories in *The New Yorker.* In his classes, he discovered a liking for Aldous Huxley (briefly) and H. L. Mencken. In particular, he appreciated the sarcastic humor of Mencken's *In Defense of Women.* Men were more foolish than women, Mencken wrote, because men are easily hoodwinked into marrying ladies and having to put up with them. "I am embarrassed to confess that more than Mencken's vocabulary found its way into my literary thinking," Joe wrote years later. "It was the fashion, the convention of the time, to present women in a stereotyped way as targets to be . . . derided." He attempted similar humorous pieces and sent them to magazines, without success. Still, he viewed his English assignments as "opportunities to show [his] stuff." In the meantime, he dispatched most of his science and history requirements.

One day, his English teacher told the class to write a short paper defining some kind of method or device—an exercise in the power of description. Joe wrote a fanciful piece called "Beating the Bangtails," later retitled "Bookies, Beware!" It was about a precocious inventor named Marvin B. Winkler (after Joe's old Coney Island friend), who creates a surefire process of handicapping the horses at the Santa Anita racetrack, using various paraphernalia—not very tautly described: "And thus a new weapon, the pure science method, had been added to the age-old onslaught of the bookmakers." When he got the paper back, Joe carefully erased the A the teacher had scrawled at the top of the page, slipped the piece into an envelope, and sent it to *Esquire*.

A few weeks later, an excited Shirley met him at a trolley stop as he was returning to the rooming house one day after classes. She waved an opened letter: an acceptance notice from the magazine, along with a check for two hundred dollars. Promptly, he blew the money at the racetrack.

HE HAD NOW PUBLISHED pieces in two prestigious magazines, *Story* and *Esquire*. He entertained visions of making a living as a writer, cranking out two or three short stories a week—just a job. But already a deeper, slower, more ambitious passion moved him. Years later, he would say that reading *Story*, even more than reading *The New Yorker*, *Esquire*, and other magazines that paid greater sums for work, showed him that "fiction is not merely a diversion, but a vital form of art."

From California, he wrote to Whit Burnett at *Story*, enclosing four rough chapters of a novel he'd begun and asking for the editor's thoughts. Burnett took a while to reply. In August 1946, he finally wrote back, saying he feared Joe had succumbed too much to the influence of Thomas Wolfe (whom Joe had been reading in classes). Burnett added, "I am wondering, too, if the treatment of a flier facing the end of his missions and thinking over the meaning of the war has not been pretty well done to death. . . . If so, this book might have hard sledding."

"I [THEN] HAD THOUGHTS of becoming a playwright. . . . It seemed easier. There were fewer words," Joe recalled. At USC, he enrolled in a course on contemporary theater. He clashed with one of his classmates, an attractive blonde named Mary Alden, every bit his equal in knowledge and creativity. They dominated discussions in class, almost always disagreeing. Alden had done some work in theater, and she felt that by not acknowledging her experience, Joe was failing to show her respect. On the other hand, he had come from New York, and could drop names as well as facts about Broadway. He liked her but could not win her over with jokes. Their sparring he saw as good fun, but she, he reflected, "held as sacred what I took for sport." Over the years, this dynamic—he needling, the other person scowling, unable to accept his humor—would characterize many of his social encounters.

It was not just the isolation he felt in school but also the fear that perhaps he had exiled himself from the people and places that seasoned his best literary material that soured him on California. Here he was, in the land of Chandler and Nathanael West—writers he admired but could not absorb—yet imaginatively, he was living in the East. He had discovered Jerome Weidman, whose novel *I Can Get It for You Wholesale,* set in Manhattan's Garment District, pulsed with the erratic rhythms of Yiddish English and the hammered beat of physical work. To be strolling in Southern California while mentally rubbing elbows with noisy Lower East Side Jews was like trying to swim in a business suit. He was flailing about in the wrong element, and his muscles were getting soggy, slow.

Once more, he appealed to Whit Burnett. A big, voluble former newspaperman, Burnett liked Joe's scrappiness and his apparent dedication to literature. He suggested that Joe apply to New York University, to which he wrote him a letter of recommendation. Joe knew Shirley was willing to sacrifice on his behalf and do whatever he thought he needed. He also knew she was miserable in L.A. Despite the chaos and hardship of another move so soon, he was pretty sure she'd do cartwheels all the way back to Manhattan.

MAURICE "BUCK" BAUDIN, Joe's writing teacher at NYU, was a scholar of seventeenth- and eighteenth-century French drama, but recently he had published short stories in magazines. In his fiction-writing classes, he said talent couldn't be taught. Technique and editing—these could be learned. Good writing, he insisted, depended on careful reading. From the selection of classic stories he asked his students to read as models of literary craft, he published an anthology, *Edgar Allan Poe and Others: Representative Short Stories of the Nineteenth Century.*

Like Whit Burnett, Baudin admired Joe's tenacity and his capacity to exert energy on subjects he decided to master. If *Story* had coaxed the artist in Joe to raise his voice, Baudin's pragmatic approach prompted Joe to develop discipline and a professional, tough-skinned attitude toward his writing. Baudin told students to scour the contents of magazines, learn what editors wanted, and write in a calculated manner.

"I couldn't deny to myself that I really had an imagination and a real appetite for knowledge, for reading, particularly about literature, philosophy, history," Joe told an interviewer, Charles Ruas, in 1985. "[But] I didn't have any concept of what I should write—almost everything I wrote was imitative." Following Baudin's advice, "I would read a story in a magazine like *Good Housekeeping* or *Woman's Home Companion,* and I would then try to write a story for them. I was not very good at it." It was like sizing words to fit into perfect slots in perfect little boxes. "I wasn't even writing out of my own experiences as much as writing out of my experience of reading other people's work." Still, he had mixed and was starting to simmer a potent combination: hardheaded professionalism linked with stirrings of artistic ambition and vision, even if the vision remained, at this stage, a mirage. The rough chapters of the war novel he had sent Whit Burnett appear not to have survived; they would have told us much about Joe's early vision, and its relationship to what came later.

Baudin became friends with Joe and Shirley, and he went to dinner a few times at the apartment on West Seventy-sixth Street. Despite their closeness in age, Joe had trouble calling the man by his nickname. After all, he was a teacher and a successful writer. Joe followed his lessons to the letter. "[He] pointed out my faults to me—he'd say throw away the first three or four pages, and he was right," Joe acknowledged.

In Baudin's courses, Joe absorbed other examples of the writing life.

A fellow student, David Krause, "wrote perfect short stories but couldn't be persuaded to submit them for publication because he didn't think they were worthy," Joe recalled. Another classmate, Alex Austin, "a meager, short fellow who seldom raised his voice above a whisper, even when reading aloud in the classroom," had already published hundreds of poems and stories in literary journals obscure to the other students. "It was an essential part of his daily regimen, like brushing teeth, to write at least one short story every afternoon," Joe said. "[H]e would sit down at his typewriter, devotionally, often without a thought in mind, and simply begin typing. He had novel-length manuscripts, too, and Baudin was reduced to imploring . . . him to limit the number he handed in." All this, too, was part of learning to be a writer: gauging the pros and cons of other people's methods, personalities, and working habits, judging the constraints of perfectionism, the advantages of a certain amount of compulsion, trying to temper and balance creative forces, critical discernment.

Years later, Joe learned that James Jones attended NYU in the late 1940s and took creative-writing courses there, but these two, who would eventually define the beginnings of postwar American writing, never crossed paths at the university. Jones recalled that time as the loneliest in his life. In 1999, at a symposium honoring him on the Southampton campus of Long Island University, Joe said, "[I]t's a pity . . . we [didn't] meet then because I was very much at home in New York, and I possibly could have made the experience more joyful for him." He admitted, on the other hand, that "had we met then, we [probably] would not have gotten along. He was . . . very principled . . . an almost puritanical man from the Midwest and I was a shifty opportunist. I was a smart-ass Jew from Coney Island. . . . In most ways, he had a much better character than I had."

In general, Joe's fellow students at NYU impressed him as more on the ball than the kids he had taken classes with in California. Edward Bloustein, whom Joe met in a philosophy course, went on to become a Rhodes scholar, at a time when such honors came rarely to Jews. Joe became friends with Joan Goodman, who would develop into a celebrated freelance journalist, publishing profiles of newsmakers in the *Los Angeles Times,* the *New York Times Magazine, Cosmopolitan,* and *Playboy.* She kept telling Joe she'd met a fabulous student she knew he would adore, though the men never bumped into each other—a guy

named Mario Puzo. (In a couple of years, George Mandel would introduce Puzo to Joe; Mandel met him in the pulp-magazine world.)

As opposed to the squalor Joe had lived near in south-central L.A.,
New York offered him energy, optimism—and style (it had the advantage of being a financial center rather than an industrial hub). Almost
all the men in Manhattan wore suits, it seemed, and the women flashed
white gloves and shiny high heels. As a kid, visiting from Coney Island,
he'd scoffed at these spectacles, but now the city's stylishness appealed
to him as attractive, desirable, adult. In the windows of certain restaurants, you could watch chefs in dazzling white coats carve mountains of
meat, like sculptors displaying their brilliance, an artistic vision.

In January 1948, Joe published a story called "Lot's Wife" in NYU's
new literary journal, *Apprentice*. It opens with a man lying in a road in
the middle of the night. Another man bends over him. The reader learns
that two cars have crashed, the man in the road has been injured, and the
other man is talking to keep him alert until help arrives. The Samaritan's
wife, apparently responsible for the accident, refuses to get out of the car
to see to the hurt fellow. She sits behind her steering wheel, smoking and
staring off into space. A rather heavy-handed parable about individual
responsibility, the story is notable, in retrospect, for the situation of one
man tending another while the injured one complains he's cold. (In similar fashion, the war vet asserting independence by refusing to put on his
clothes, in "I Don't Love You Any More," remains that story's most interesting aspect, foreshadowing Yossarian's actions in *Catch-22*.)

In the college newspaper, a fellow student, reviewing *Apprentice*,
savaged Joe's story. It was pallid, he said. "That should have steeled me
against unkind critiques in the future," Joe said many years later, "but
nothing does."

He continued to filch ideas and curt, enigmatic dialogue from Papa,
like plucking chocolates out of a box. Joe's piece "Nothing to Be Done,"
written at about this time, was an extension of the slender plot in "The
Killers." Joe's impulse to foreground the events of a story—as opposed
to Hemingway's "iceberg" method of hiding most of what's happening
between characters—reveals why Papa finally proved to be an unsatisfactory model for Joe. For Hemingway, existential ironies emerged out
of whatever remained unsaid; in Joe's best work, they would come from
what's said and said again, until words slip their meanings.

"The Death of the Dying Swan," a story from this period, mined domestic misery yet again. The husband thinks he "long[s] for people who were real, people who lived with honest passions and found vigorous pleasure in the mere event of existing, people for whom death came too soon." By contrast, his wife's notion of ecstasy is a successful cocktail party. "Darling, something terrible has happened," she tells her husband. "I'm all ready to serve cold cuts and there's no mustard." In another piece, "Girl from Greenwich," Joe imagined a literary reception for a novelist (he had never attended one). Again, the ironies fly: no-good novels become bestsellers; to curry favors, reviewers give good notices to hack writers; always, always, men and women lie to one another.

In story after story, Joe labored to refine what he thought magazine editors wanted: terse, witty dialogue; urban nonchalance; minimal, hard-edged descriptions; and social irony bleeding into cynicism, redeemed by a dollop of romance: a desire for upright behavior and principled devotion.

One day, in the margins of a piece Joe turned in for class, Baudin wrote that he should drop the first three pages and start the story at the top of page four. This advice was consistent with Baudin's previous notes to Joe. "I was [always] taking too long to begin, dawdling at the opening, as though hesitant to get going," Joe recalled in *Now and Then*. "It's a quirk of mine, perhaps a psychological flaw, that has lasted."

He did as told and submitted the story, "Castle of Snow," to *The Atlantic Monthly*. Within a few weeks, he received a letter from an editor at the magazine, who suggested revisions and resubmission. Rewrites done, he sent the story back. In March 1948, it appeared as an "Atlantic First" (the appearance, for the first time, of a new writer in the magazine's pages). The byline said Joseph Heller, a junior English major at New York University, was "thinking and writing in terms of peace." "[I]n our judgment," the magazine stated, his short stories "give very real promise."

"Castle of Snow" was conceived and executed from a different emotional/mental plane than anything Joe had written up until now. For whatever reason—perhaps an exercise or suggestion from Baudin, perhaps a vague intuition—for this piece, Joe stopped trying to match magazinespeak and found a voice genuinely his own. In later years, he would claim his best work was generated not by plot, character, or idea, but a fully formed first sentence. Usually, he didn't know where the sentence came from—who was speaking it or what it was about—it was simply the language, the rhythm, persuading him this was a promising beginning. He would go from there. Certainly the narrator, and his retrospective viewpoint, distinguished "Castle of Snow" from Joe's efforts to date.

The story begins, "My Uncle David was a sober man, and my Aunt Sarah, an earthy, practical woman, lived uncomplainingly with him in what seemed to be a perfect and harmonious relationship." Already, complexities bristle. The phrase "lived uncomplainingly" implies reasons for complaint, while harmony merely "seemed" to exist in the home. Clearly, the narrator knows things now he didn't know at the time. The theme of innocence lost, which Joe was unable to limn successfully in his story about the Western Union messenger, exists here in the voice, in the narrator's character and temperament, rather than in a forced or melodramatic predicament.

We learn that Uncle David, a Russian immigrant to the United States, an avid reader and dreamer who mourns the failure of the Russian Revolution, has lost his job, and Aunt Sarah's drive to hold the family together oppresses them all. The narrator was a schoolchild at the time, living in his aunt and uncle's house. What happened to his parents, we never hear. The setting is not identified, but Joe clearly drew on Coney Island. As a boy, the narrator witnesses crushing poverty—including the eviction of a family from its house—but cherishes the coziness of the neighborhood. Eventually, his uncle lands a job at a bakery but refuses to cross a picket line—he realizes he's been hired as a scab. He won't betray other men. Coming home from the bakery, he stops to play in the snow with some neighborhood boys. He loses himself in the joy of remembering the way it snowed in Russia when he and Sarah were young, and the "culmination of all that is beautiful in mankind" still seemed possible, in the giddiness of the revolution.

Sarah is humiliated by her husband's childlike behavior, and she scolds him into submission. The story peters out at this point. Overall, it suffers from Joe's inability to visualize in detail—Sarah's "unforgiving face disclos[es] her anger," we are told in lieu of an arresting *image* of her rage. But the elegiac tone, the gentle sympathy enveloping the characters, including the harsh old aunt, and the vivid neighborhood portrait make "Castle of Snow" honestly moving. Like the best fiction, the piece remains with the reader almost as a living memory, rather than as a memory of a story once read.

Instead of using formulaic conventions, laid like grids over tenuous plotlines, Joe has built into the story metaphors, contrasts, and ironies emerging naturally from the characters. David is soul to Sarah's "earthy" body: We experience this in the way he loves his books but is finally willing to surrender them—sell them to support the family—because, finally, it is the *knowledge* from books, the intangible gifts we carry inside, and which will die with us, that matter most to him. Sarah worries only about the books' physical bulk, and the space they occupy in a trunk.

The narrator is unconsciously disturbed by the neighbors' eviction because the sight of a "pile of furniture stacked desolately in the street near the curb" must remind him that he, too, was forced from his home. His aunt and uncle love him, but he is, essentially, a guest in their house. The passivity in his speech—"There must have been some money saved"; "My cousin was [also] moved into my room"—underscores this fact.

Parent figures replacing parents, a past obscure and unexamined (something to do with Russia), a bakery job: Joe's story draws power from latent emotions surrounding his own experiences.

The Atlantic Monthly paid him $250 for "Castle of Snow." James Jones's short story, "A Temper of Steel," appeared in the same issue as another "Atlantic First." Shortly thereafter, Martha Foley chose "Castle of Snow" for inclusion in the annual *Best American Short Stories* anthology. In her forward to that year's collection, which offered pieces by Elizabeth Bishop, Paul Bowles, Elizabeth Hardwick, Jean Stafford, and Jessamyn West, Foley wrote that these writers were the "vanguard of the much-heralded and long-awaited 'post-war generation' in literature." They are, she said, the "product of travail. Not only did they have to endure the worst world war in history, but their childhood and youth were shadowed by the depression. We may expect from them a different kind of writing from that of the first famous 'post-war generation' of the nineteen-twenties"; these young writers, just coming to maturity, "write with pity and sensitivity."

MORE AND MORE writers were feeding their words into big, noisy boxes appearing in living rooms all across the country. Television was hungry for wordsmiths. Buck Baudin seized the opportunity. He branched out from publishing stories in *Esquire* and women's magazines to penning science fiction and eventually selling a few story ideas to shows such as *Alfred Hitchcock Presents* and *General Electric Theater*.

In class, he encouraged working for various venues; above all, he stressed an objective approach to writing. He did not inspire in Joe the imaginative play that would seed Joe's most important breakthroughs as a writer. Still, his editorial advice was generally sound, and he remained a staunch supporter of the young man's work. One semester, he bundled up four of Joe's stories and sent them to his literary agent. A note came back saying none of the pieces was publishable. In the meantime, Joe sold two of them ("Girl from Greenwich" and "Nothing to Be Done") to George Wiswell, an editor at *Esquire*. He placed the now-titled "A Man Named Flute" with *The Atlantic Monthly,* following the magazine's enthusiastic response to "Castle of Snow."

By the end of the summer of 1948, Joe had published seven short stories in some of the best magazines in the country. He was preparing to graduate Phi Beta Kappa from New York University (having taken summer courses to accelerate his progress). He had his eye on the graduate program at Columbia. Perhaps he was considering a novel—many of his stories concern the same characters, a married couple, Sidney and Louise Cooper. He had the credentials to become a successful author, and he had begun to establish a track record. He was, as Martha Foley said, in the "vanguard."

7. Naked

B Y NEW YEAR'S DAY 1949, in spite of his recent publications, Joe felt "inept and immature," convinced he was "not naturally a fiction writer." Martha Foley may have tapped him as one of the country's most promising young short story writers, but the real literary news of 1948 was the appearance of Norman Mailer's *The Naked and the Dead*. A sprawling combat novel, dissecting an army unit as if it were a microcosm of America, the novel was "[a] tome, [a] masterwork," Joe realized. It was a "book with tremendous breadth and scope."

Suddenly, World War II belonged to Norman Mailer. The author's face adorned the cover of *The Saturday Review*. "We were about the same age . . . and it put me in my place," Joe said. "War novels were coming into vogue. . . . The first war book that made a big sensation, although it was not comparable to Mailer's, was John Horne Burns's *The Gallery*, which came out in 1947." Joe worried about producing run-of-the-mill work that would wind up lost in a publishing trend. Whit Burnett had warned him about this. "I suppose I did have a fear that if I [wrote] a novel it would be based on the war," he said.

In *The Naked and the Dead*, "Mailer was very good as an illusionist,"

Joe thought. "He gave the impression that he had experienced the actions he wrote about." Joe knew *his* prose was weak on detail; an illusionist he was not. Besides, he said, "I felt that my . . . war experiences were very limited." After reading *The Naked and the Dead,* he firmly decided he "had better stay away from [the] subject [of war] until I had something different to write about [it]."

For all his skill in describing physical action, Mailer, at this stage of his career, didn't have much new to say about fighting. His soldiers were not like the warriors in Greek dramas, whose tragic experiences brought them face-to-face with their contradictory natures and the controlling forces of the universe. Mailer's young Americans, lacking any historical sense, and acting without grasping the gist of the conflict, discovered only violence at their cores: a fierce rush of power over others. Ostensibly, their goal, like that of the soldiers in Burns's *The Gallery,* was to recover the pastoral goodness of life at its most primitive—achieved through brave physical feats: storming Eden.

On the surface, Mailer's stark, dispassionate style looked back to the quintessential American war novel, Stephen Crane's *The Red Badge of Courage,* the skeletal sketches of Hemingway (with a touch of Dos Passos's grandeur), and the naturalism of much Depression writing: in this sense, though it was written in the forties, *The Naked and the Dead* was, spiritually, the last great American novel of the 1930s. Modern warfare had yet to find the writer that could illuminate its complexities and contradictions.

Joe saw this. He had started graduate studies in English at Columbia University. The more he read—the greater the variety of literature he was exposed to—the more he recognized that contemporary American writing, hobbled by outmoded conventions, was unable to document the nation's new realities.

He took a course taught by Lionel Trilling, who had just been promoted to full professor (in the mid-thirties, Trilling had become the first Jew to get tenure at the university). At the time, Trilling was preparing to publish his landmark volume, *The Liberal Imagination.* Anticommunism, pessimism about political action, the individual's struggle against dogmatism: These topics were much on his mind and influenced his classroom discussions. Above all, he would teach, as he wrote in the book, that "literature is the human activity that takes the fullest and most precise account of variousness, possibility, complexity, and difficulty." Therefore, it is uniquely primed to make the deepest sense of our imaginations, politics, and humanity.

Trilling did not enjoy teaching and kept his distance from most students. But Joe would have recognized in him a kindred spirit of sorts: a man profoundly ambivalent about institutional life, his Jewish background, and his desire for literary success. In 1947, Trilling had published a novel entitled *The Middle of the Journey*, concerning ideological battles among 1930s progressives (featuring a character based on Whittaker Chambers). In *Commentary*, a journal founded by the American Jewish Committee in 1945, the novel had been panned for not being Jewish enough. The reviewer, Robert Warshow, pointed out that none of the book's major characters were Jewish, though the politics that engaged them, primarily anti-Stalinism, were "in large part . . . Jewish middle-class" issues. Warshow accused Trilling of failing to grapple with the " 'essence' of [our] experience."

To those in the know, the review had a snide personal subtext. Trilling had refused to serve on *Commentary*'s advisory board; he wished to keep his intellectual life separate from Jewish values. Following Warshow's review, he became more and more convinced it was "never possible for a Jew of my generation to 'escape' his Jewish origin," and it vexed his writing. Like Joe at the time, he was a man in search of a literary voice different from the ones previously modeled for him. In years to come, he could not manage a breakthrough. He published no more novels.

Nor would he come to terms with America's larger cultural shifts after the war, of which Joe's fiction would become emblematic. Five years before Joe arrived at Columbia, Trilling had encountered Allen Ginsberg and Jack Kerouac. They had been students at the university (Kerouac briefly). Ginsberg said Columbia was a "horror": "[T]here was just nobody there . . . who had a serious involvement with advanced work in poetry," he complained. "Just a bunch of dilettantes. And *they* have the nerve to set themselves up as guardians of culture? Why it's such a piece of effrontery—enough to make anyone paranoiac, it's a miracle Jack or myself or anybody independent survived."

Despite this attitude, Ginsberg sought Trilling's blessing for his poetry, perhaps recognizing in him a kind of Jewish father figure—a role Trilling refused to accept, for the most part, though he once helped Ginsberg out of a serious legal scrape.

In 1956, when Ginsberg sent his old professor a copy of *Howl,* Trilling pronounced it "dull." His wife, Diana, reflecting her husband's view, regarded the Beats as phony rebels, who harbored no real understanding of individual freedom. They were, she said, "panic-stricken kids in blue jeans, many of them publicly homosexual, talking about or taking drugs, assuring us that they are not out of their minds, not responsible. . . . Is it any wonder, then, that *Time* and *Life* write as they do about the 'beats'—with such a conspicuous show of superiority, and no hint of fear? These periodicals know what genuine, dangerous protest looks like, and it doesn't look like Ginsberg and Kerouac." Give *me* the Scottsboro boys and W. C. Handy's blues, she said: now, *that's* radicalism.

The Trillings' nostalgia for an old "new," and their tone deafness to fresh cultural strains—made messier by the sense that on some level (at least among New York intellectuals) this was all a Jewish family quarrel—were apparent by the time Joe showed up in Professor Trilling's class. The older man's insistence that literature was part of a mighty cultural battle, coupled with his disgust at the forms the skirmishes seemed to be taking, increased Joe's irritation with the story conventions he was trying to copy from the pages of mainstream magazines.

The small and always airless domestic sphere, the oblique, abrupt dialogue, and the romantic cynicism: These tropes seemed more and more limited, even moribund.

The world was bigger than short stories, so fashioned, suggested. Even in the constrained and pleasant world of Morningside Heights, in the stacks of the Low Library on campus, amid the laughter in neighborhood taverns such as the Lion's Den and the West End Bar, among veterans and young husbands just like him, Joe discerned a stunning cultural complexity, about which contemporary literature was largely silent. It dazzled him with possibility. He had left the war and come to college, feeling that, generally, the country spoke with one voice. Yet now, in coffeehouse conversations, he heard different registers of American speech. As a kid, he had distinguished between Republicans and Democrats, but now he became aware of multiple shadings of moderate and extreme, liberal and conservative, isolationists and expansionists, like those who supported the Marshall Plan. He heard the split between those who, even after the fact, felt that defeating Japan, rather than Germany, should have been the war's first priority—for these people, patriotism was paramount; Japan was the country that had attacked us; it was a matter of national pride—and those, on the other hand, who felt it had been correct to halt Germany's ambitions first. For them, human rights had been the main issue.

The self-declared patriots tended to be anti-Roosevelt, coming from rural backgrounds; most of the human rights advocates came from urban professional families espousing liberal politics. In part, this debate had been rekindled on campus by *The Naked and the Dead,* in the dialogues between the characters Hearn and Cummings, heavy rehashings of various strains in the American character. To his credit, Mailer had been *trying* to grasp something essential, but his attempt, for all its boldness, its undeniable greatness, was finally pretty clumsy, Joe felt.

The vets on the Columbia campus, hailing from all across the nation, reaping the benefits of the G.I. Bill, represented the full political spectrum. Conversations in and out of class were heady, if often confused and confusing. David Herbert Donald, then a young history teacher, recalled, "Most of the students were veterans . . . much older than I, and all knew much more of the world than I, who grew up on a farm in Mississippi. I felt lucky if I could keep one day ahead of my students, and I lived in constant fear that I would be exposed as an ignoramus. I tried to compensate by working very hard on my lectures, ransacking the Columbia libraries and staying up night after night till long past midnight."

Joe feared exposure, too. He hadn't read enough. His published pieces were hollow—frankly derivative, as any smart reader could see. Steadily, in classes, in long hours at the library, in conversations over drinks, he began to "acquire . . . standards and learned to be more critical," he said. "I now wanted to be new, in the way that I thought, as I discovered them, Nabokov, Céline, Faulkner, and Waugh were new—not necessarily different, but new. Original." For a while, then, in spite of impressive publications, accolades, and every indication of promise, Joseph Heller stopped writing fiction.

In *Leopards in the Temple: The Transformation of American Fiction, 1945–1970,* the critic Morris Dickstein wrote, "We can scarcely understand postwar fiction without seeing how few writers from the pre-war years actually survived the war itself." His comments are worth quoting at length in order to understand the context into which Joseph Heller tried to launch his literary career:

Some [prewar writers] died literally, and others simply lost their creative edge in the changed conditions of the postwar world. West and Fitzgerald died on successive days in 1940, Sherwood Anderson in 1941 (along with Joyce and Virginia Woolf, whose greatest influence in America was yet to come), Dreiser in 1945, Gertrude Stein in 1946, and Willa Cather in 1947. Most of the proletarian writers disappeared after one or two books, some to Hollywood or *Time* magazine, which both remained sympathetic to social melodrama, others into children's writing, historical fiction, or pulp fiction. . . . Committed social novelists who remained prolific were unable to regain the élan of their best work. Steinbeck would never again write anything to match the urgency of *In Dubious Battle* (1936) and *The Grapes of Wrath* (1939); James T. Farrell and John Dos Passos would never equal the social grasp and personal intensity of their Depression trilogies. . . . Their naturalist methods, which required an immense piling up of realistic details, and a minute verisimilitude, seemed unable to encompass the complexities and absurdities, to say nothing of the social changes, of the postwar world.

Richard Wright drifted into abstraction after *Black Boy* (1945). Novelists of manners—J. P. Marquand, James Gould Cozzens, John O'Hara—"were the diminished heirs of . . . writers from New England and the Northeast who closely documented the lives of the upper and professional classes," Dickstein argued. Their work "devolved into a mere social record of . . . the status anxieties and sexual or professional problems of a declining elite." Finally, Dickstein said, only "the ravages of age or alcoholism and the fragility of genius could begin to explain the decline of the greatest writers of the interwar years, Hemingway and Faulkner, which set in just as their earlier work was gaining them readers, fame, and increasing literary influence."

The vogue for war novels in the late 1940s signaled a need for new subjects, new treatments of old themes, new means of expression, but Mailer and others were mired in received notions of craft. The attempt in *The Naked and the Dead* to make individual soldiers representative of broad social types was an extension of the proletarian writing of the 1930s. In his introduction to the massive anthology *Proletarian Literature in the United States* (1935), Joseph Freeman had written, "[F]rom the fate of a people [proletarian writers] derive their stirring themes. . . . Rural life, the factory, New York's streets, the office, the mill town, the south, the west, Jews, Yanks, Irish—these are the locales and characters which enliven proletarian fiction." And they were present on Mailer's battlefields, there (as Freeman would have said) to achieve the familiar goal of baring a "civilization rent asunder by a class war": thus, the inability of such fiction, however well-intentioned, to embrace the diversity it strove for and transcend its bullhorn monotone.

If the approach to subject—even in a combat setting—came from the previous decade's political writing, the dominant tone of Mailer's book, and of many 1940s war novels, bled through from pulp fiction and men's adventure magazines. These were offshoots of nineteenth-century dime novels about western heroes such as Billy the Kid, and Frank Munsey's *Argosy,* which printed adventure fiction on cheap pulpwood paper, giving the genre its name.

At their peak, in the 1930s, the ten-cent pulps had a circulation of more than ten million. From the beginning, Westerns drew avid readers. Titles such as *True Detective* and Hugo Gernsback's *Amazing Stories* became increasingly popular. In his inaugural issue in 1926, Gernsback promised "something that has never been done before in this country . . . scientifiction . . . a charming romance intermingled with scientific fact and prophetic vision." Stylistically, pulp tales shared a preponderance of informational dialogue, explaining plot details; spare description, so as not to impede the action; and clichés, to quickly encapsulate personalities, settings, and meanings.

During the war, paper shortages impaired printing and distributing pulps, but afterward, pulp fiction found new life in the form of mass-market paperback books. "Running parallel to many combat/war novels [of the 1940s] was the gangster/detective fiction of Mickey Spillane," said the critic Frederick Karl (soon to become Joe's pal). "His [character] Mike Hammer is the ultimate, in popular culture, of the masculine military type. Hateful of Communists, patriotic, associated with the right, a male chauvinist, a defender of a reductive form of democracy, Hammer represents a kind of caricatured military. As in the novel of combat, Spillane's work simplified and reduced to violent endings all social, political, and ideological conflicts—hammered them down, as if in a gigantic air raid." (Fittingly, perhaps, Mickey Spillane, like Joe, had been a World War II flier.)

The smuggling of pulp material into book form gave it a smidgen of literary respectability. And, as Spillane reminded readers at the University of South Carolina's World War II Writers Symposium in 1995, "[I]n the 1930s . . . the pulp fiction world was filled with magazines whose jade was battle aces . . . battle birds of the air that dealt with World War I. . . . But there wasn't much of an outlet for war stories at that time except for the pulps. The publishing industry hadn't reached out that far yet." Following World War II, he said, the "paperback . . . opened up a vast field [for] writers."

This was especially true when the "Fawcett [company] first came out with [its] Gold Medal concept. . . . I was sitting with [the publisher] Roscoe Fawcett, [and] we developed this thing together, of having original paperback stories," Spillane said. With so many veterans swelling contemporary readership, combat tales were a natural, along with other pulp standbys.

In this sense, then, the real innovation of *The Naked and the Dead* lies in its introduction of a previously underground phenomenon into mainstream literature: not the war story, which Crane and Hemingway had taken up in important and serious ways, but the *pulp* war story, with its emphasis on physical action rather than the psychology of violence, sprinkled with touches from Stephen Crane and the overlay of political (that is, proletarian) concerns.

None of this addressed Joe's suspicions that the heralded conventions failed to *read* the current moment. *The Naked and the Dead* declared itself a novel of *now,* but it looked firmly backward, as did most contemporary short stories. However much he admired Mailer's book, Joe knew "that type of writing was going to go out of style."

Perhaps nothing illustrated the paucity of conventions better than the magazines Joe had been poaching. Critic Bergen Evans, writing in *The Atlantic Monthly* in February 1948 (just one month before Joe's appearance in its pages), said changing attitudes, rooted in harsher realities and smaller stomachs for sentimentality, postwar, were wreaking havoc on fiction, which had yet to find appropriate expressions for the country's new outlook.

For example, the "popular novelist of today," and the writer of women's magazine fiction, "has to limn daydreams for a different group of women living under different circumstances," Evans wrote. Readers of fiction still believed, or wanted to believe, "in true love," but shifting cultural conditions—not the least of which was the "appalling increase [in the number of] marriageable women over marriageable men"—led to a conviction that "moral values" have been "revers[ed]." Women didn't want to hear about devotion and domestic security. "[They] long to be told that escape from dullness is possible and one of the main avenues of escape . . . is *un*true love," said Evans.

Thus, women no longer hankered for a virtuous man, but a specimen with "the face of a god and the loins of a stag." If fiction offering such love "reflects the psyches of [its] readers, as to a considerable extent [it] must, [its] most disturbing feature is [its] aggressiveness," Evans wrote. "Love . . . exists to give the woman a chance to 'get her own back,'" after a taste of independence during the war years, when many women joined the workforce, followed by the bitterness of losing freedom in the postwar rush toward married conformity. "[Love] is, apparently, the one means thought to be at her disposal for humiliating men and 'putting them in their place.'" The uneasy fit of old beliefs with new social predicaments had antiquated the once trusted tropes of fiction, and led to absurdities of style and story. "[T]he authors . . . seem bewildered at times by the impetuosity of their creations," Evans wrote. "'How did they get into bed so quickly?'" asks a narrator in one of the books he cited.

"Must We Change Our Sex Standards?" asked the lead article in the June 1948 *Reader's Digest*. The article examined the just-released Kinsey Report. "[Americans] have [now] been told that practices long held in abhorrence must . . . be regarded as acceptable," the article explained. "Science, so it is said, does not recognize any expression of sex as 'abnormal' . . . [and] pretty much anything is all right." How were the conventions of women's fiction—*any* fiction, for that matter—supposed to tackle *this* monster? Just three years earlier, in his story "I Don't Love You Any More," Joe had mentioned *Reader's Digest* as an arbiter of the "sugar and tinsel dream of life." Who could have predicted that in so short a time the magazine would describe "abhorrent" sexual practices (even if it *was* to denounce them)?

The changing subjects in Norman Rockwell's cover paintings for *The Saturday Evening Post* established as firmly as anything that America had swerved from the past, with no going back. The magazine's publisher, George Horace Lorimer, was a staunch, anti-Roosevelt Republican who wanted every aspect of his magazine to reflect his faith in hard work, self-reliance, and optimism about the nation. Rockwell's covers, featuring idealized main streets and happy folk in commonplace, often humorous situations, mirrored the ways the magazine's middle-class sub-scribers viewed themselves. "[I]f Rockwell drew cliché situations, then America itself was a cliché," the artist Milton Glaser once said. "Not one of his drawings depicted something that did not exist."

This made it all the more troubling to conventional sensibilities when Rockwell showed women in the workplace—Rosie the Riveter on the cover of the May 29, 1943, issue—or men in uniform who were obviously hampered mentally, physically, and emotionally. Lorimer had died in 1937. "It was fortunate . . . [he] did not live to see Rockwell's contributions to the covers of the Second World War period," wrote John Tebbel and Mary Ellen Zuckerman in their study *The Magazine in America, 1741–1990*.

The immediate postwar years were even more turbulent. Weekly, monthly, magazines reported on the disarray in America's foreign pol-icy and belligerent talk from Russia (we should "transact our necessary business with Russia at arm's length," declared *The Atlantic Monthly* in February 1948). Again and again, articles appeared on the establish-ment of the state of Israel and the resultant rise in Arab militancy, on the Berlin blockade and airlift, on fears of nuclear proliferation.

What place did the fiction of "happily ever after" have in a world like this, except as escapist fare? This question dogged the literary jour-nals, but Joe knew it was the wrong one. Some fiction had *always* been escapist—honorably so, in fact. But what of the fiction that—to para-phrase Lionel Trilling—sought to take full account of human complex-ity? How did it move forward in such volatile terrain?

Attempts at answers came from Saul Bellow (*The Victim,* 1947) and Truman Capote (*Other Voices, Other Rooms,* 1948), but the former was schematic, whereas the latter seemed merely confectionary. Both men had yet to find their literary footing. Nelson Algren's *The Man with the Golden Arm* (1949) recycled naturalism even more gleefully than Mailer had, and Carson McCullers's novels from earlier in the decade (*The Heart Is a Lonely Hunter,* 1940, and *Reflections in a Golden Eye,* 1941) fo-cused so thoroughly on southern grotesques, they had little to say about the world beyond their narrow confines. Compelling writers, all; but it was hard not to feel that the American novel was fraying a bit, unable to store—in the boxes it had built for itself—all it was asked to hold.

As for the short story: "Not for one hundred years, not since the writing of Edgar Allan Poe, has the short story in America displayed the tendencies it has shown during the past year," said Martha Foley in her foreword to the 1948 edition of *Best American Short Stories*. "The overwhelming tension, the terror, the specter of undefined guilt which permeated Poe's work are the most obvious attributes of today's short story writing." The "re-emergence of the old-fashioned ghost story," the "breathless awaiting of the unknown," was, Foley wrote, the short story writer's response to the "atom-bomb-inventing, airplane traveling, electronically powered United States of America." Furthermore, the stories' preoccupation with ill-seen fears could be "linked to the war" and its aftermath. Yet here again (if Foley's generalizations held up), writers were responding to the new with well-worn gestures. Ghosts were creepy. They were not—in this flashpoint moment—particularly informative.

IN A PASSAGE he ultimately cut from his first novel, Joe mocked the writing of an academic thesis. It was, he wrote, a process whose primary requirement was to make "an original contribution of nothing new to a subject of no importance." For his M.A. thesis at Columbia, he chose as his subject "The Pulitzer Prize Plays, 1917–1935." He didn't much care about the topic, nor did he know, exactly, what a thesis should entail. "I'm surprised [it] was approved," he wrote later. It was a "trivial, unfruitful subject." Nevertheless, it indicated both his practical ambitions and his growing dissatisfaction with the fiction he had written. Perhaps by studying the prizewinning plays of his lifetime, he could learn to be a successful dramatist. "I'm not sure that my motivations then . . . were worthy ones," he said. He was soon to graduate. "I really wanted to make money and have some kind of status. . . . I write dialogue rapidly, so I thought I [might be] in playwriting or radio."

At night, in the apartment on West Seventy-sixth Street, he worked on his thesis. Occasionally, he and Shirley invited someone to dinner— Buck Baudin was still a frequent guest—or Shirley's mother dropped in to cook for them and her husband. "[H]er parents found delight in watching me eat—always a second helping, often a third," he recalled. Dottie was particularly proud of her prime rib crusted with garlic, salt, and paprika.

Joe had trouble convincing his brother and sister to visit. They worked hard, and subway travel, on a weekend or at the end of a day, was an extra ordeal for them. When they did come, Lee's wife, Perle, "gushed in praise at the [apartment's] sensible arrangement and the authentic look of several of the almost-genuine antique pieces" Shirley and Dottie had found to decorate the place, Joe said. Lee told Joe how proud he was of his achievements in school. He tried to ignore the splinters of jealousy he felt over his little brother's opportunities.

Few of Joe's old Coney Island pals had gotten out—or gotten far. Beansy Winkler had joined a photographic firm, converting Air Corps footage into color film for commercial use. Lou Berkman had left his father's junk shop to start a plumbing-supply business. Davey Gold-smith went to work for a hatband company.

George Mandel was the happiest success story Joe knew. He had recovered from his head wound and moved into a Greenwich Village loft to paint and write. He still illustrated comic books and lived, as well, on disability payments from the army. The comic-book industry had expanded during the war years, as superheroes—many of them fighting Nazis—embodied America's hopes and fears. "Superheroes al-lowed adolescents and adults to slip back to the confidence and inviola-bility of that last moment of childhood," wrote Gerard Jones in *Men of Tomorrow: Geeks, Gangsters and the Birth of the Comic Book*. "It had been a long, nerve-wearing run for twenty years, through Prohibition and sexual revolution and economic transformation and urbanization and Depression and the rumors of war, when a naïve nation had to pre-tend to be adult and sophisticated."

Most importantly, while serious fiction struggled to make sense of the war's consequences, comic-book heroes could serve unabashedly as "slap-stick comedians in a vaudeville of holocaust," Jones said. If given free rein, a talented and ambitious artist like George Mandel was well positioned to help the comics move from the straightforward heroism required in com-bat to the superhuman challenges awaiting peacetime America.

Often, Joe visited Mandel in the Village, sometimes in the company of Danny the Count. Mandel entertained them with stories of his recov-ery in the ward of a military hospital. Everybody in his sector had suf-fered a head wound, he said. Each man wore a turban of bandages. One day, a fellow patient dreamed up a money scheme: He was sure it would make him a millionaire once he got back to the States. He walked around the ward, asking everybody what they thought of his idea. The men told him he was brilliant. When he got to Mandel, he said, "All the guys think I'll make a million dollars. What do you think?" "Yeah, sure," Mandel told him. "But maybe you better ask somebody who ain't been shot in the head."

"YOU'RE NOT GOING to England!" Dottie said.

Shirley had just informed her mother that Joe had received a Fulbright Scholarship. President Truman had signed the program into law a few years before, by which war-surplus money could be used to facilitate student exchanges. What it meant for Joe was a year of study at St. Catherine's College, Oxford University.

"I didn't even wait to see if my master's thesis had been accepted," Joe recalled. "There was a ship sailing with two or three hundred Fulbright and Rhodes scholars."

He also seems to have "cut corners" on his foreign-language requirement, confessing in his memoir that a "charitable young lady from California," presumably a fellow student, "surreptitiously helped me meet the . . . requirement." He added, "I'm sorry now I did that."

As when he had crossed the ocean after the war, he was one of the few people who didn't get seasick. He retained a healthy appetite. Days later, Shirley was grateful to be on solid ground.

St. Catherine's College, whose roots went back to 1868, sat on the bank of the Cherwell River, on the east side of Oxford. It had a glass and concrete facade, with a prominent bell tower and a large dining hall inside, noteworthy for its striking Cumberland-slate floor. If Shirley had visions of spending a year touring the romantic old capitals of Europe, she was soon crestfallen. At one point, she and Joe did catch a ferry from England to France, and passed a few days in Paris, enjoying the restaurants (which seemed to have recovered from the German occupation more quickly than anything else). They also made a halfhearted, but failed, attempt to find a synagogue there in which to observe Yom Kippur; Lena had warned them before they left the States that Europeans would think badly of American Jews if they didn't attend services.

For the most part, Joe hunkered down at Oxford and immersed himself in books. "When I had the Fulbright, I spent one term on Milton and one on Chaucer and one on Shakespeare and I came to the conclusion that Milton is pretty much of a waste," he told a journalist in 1969. "There's almost nothing he says that's pertinent or of any importance to us today, not only in terms of philosophy or attitude but even aesthetically." The remark shows he was continuing to read for his writing, not for any scholarly pursuit. Nevertheless, he also read a "massive amount of Shakespeare criticism from Samuel Johnson to Jan Kott." He read Swift and Voltaire. Aristophanes fascinated him, he said, because of his interest in "war mentality and . . . wartime society."

College reports indicate he made "very good progress" while at St. Catherine's. An old friend from NYU, Edward Bloustein, who went to Oxford as a Rhodes scholar, remembered Joe "was impressed by the place more than his studies and spent a considerable proportion of the year working hard on a short story." The story does not seem to have survived, or to have stirred a desire in Joe to return to fiction full-time.

Bloustein, who later became president of Rutgers University, spent much of his time at Oxford trying to repair international relations after Joe had swept through a room. "I [always] had a distinct sense of the strength of this guy," Bloustein told Barbara Gelb. "But he had . . . a very biting humor that sometimes distress[ed] me. His humor [was] delivered so deadpan, people misinterpret[ed] it and [could] feel insulted. This happened often when I was with him in England. I would take the people aside and explain Joe to them, and then they would find him the attractive man he [was]."

Before Joe sailed overseas, he left a dossier with the Columbia University Placement Bureau, to be mailed out whenever a job opportunity arose. Journalism, teaching—he wasn't sure what he wanted, but on January 31, 1950, he wrote Professor Theodore J. Gates at Pennsylvania State College to apply formally for a teaching position in the Department of English Composition. The Placement Bureau had notified Joe of the opening. "I have had no previous teaching experience," he admitted, "but my scholastic record is a good one." He said he planned to return to the United States at the end of June. As his residence, he gave Dottie and Barney's address.

Gates replied that, despite the department's need for instructors, "I believe I should not encourage you to apply." The college would insist on a personal interview, he said, and Joe's long-distance circumstances did not make this possible. Joe did not give up. "Although I should prefer to finish the year at Oxford, I could manage to leave several weeks before the end of June if the interview is necessary before then," he wrote back.

Gates recognized that no other applicant matched Joe. Already, his credentials—publications in *Story, Esquire, The Atlantic Monthly,* and *Best American Short Stories,* all within a five-year span—surpassed those of most tenured members of the department. Gates wrote to the director of placement at Columbia, professing his interest in Joe and requesting a photograph as well as "detailed information on his personality." On March 24, 1950, Margaret Morgan of Columbia's Division of Teaching Placement replied that New York State's antidiscrimination law precluded sending a photograph; however, she recalled Mr. Heller as "a very fine appearing young man." She said she had phoned Mr. Paul S. Wood, with whom Mr. Heller had studied in Columbia's English Department. Mr. Wood reported that Mr. Heller was a "fine looking, clean-cut lad; [he] makes friends and holds them. He is a little shy, but this should not provide a serious difficulty, since he improves upon acquaintance and his shyness would not prove to be an obstacle in his classroom teaching."

Follow-up letters of recommendation asserted that Joseph Heller was a "young man of serious interests, creative gifts, and high intelligence" (Sidney Hook, Department of Philosophy, NYU); a "poised and mature" person, with "excellent powers of expressing his thought both orally and on paper . . . clearly the best in [his] class" (Lionel Casson, assistant professor of classics, NYU); a man who "does well at anything he puts his mind to" (Maurice Baudin); and an "extremely personable gentleman" (Lillian Hornstein, assistant professor of English, NYU). Joe's thesis director, Paul Wood, said again that Joe was "somewhat retiring" (special deference toward a man with so much authority over him? dreaminess? impatience?). But Joe, Wood concluded, was "unusually likeable."

His college transcripts list a wide range of courses, including Latin and Greek, Economic Behavior, Shakespeare, the English Bible, Modern Art, Modern Music and Its Backgrounds, Writing for Radio, and Theories of the Universe.

"I am twenty-seven years old and married," Joe informed Professor Gates.

By May 3, the Department of English Composition at Penn State had narrowed its field of applicants from eighty to ten. Professor Gates urged Joe to return to the States and set up an interview as soon as possible. The job paid three thousand dollars for the academic year, he said. Joe replied he was "scheduled to arrive in New York on July 1, but I could attempt to secure earlier passage if that is longer than you are pre- pared to wait." Gates said July 1 was "satisfactory." "In other words," he added, "we are holding the place open for you."

On July 5, Gates wrote Joe, in New York, that he should take the Pennsylvania Railroad to Lewiston, then catch the Boalsburg bus to State College. The next letter in the men's exchange came from Joe in New York. It is dated July 31. He had been offered the job, and he wanted to assure Professor Gates that "I am not in the reserves, orga- nized or inactive, and I would venture the opinion that only under a program of total mobilization would I be considered for conscription." He asked Gates for help securing housing. He said he and his wife would be willing to share an apartment or a house. "My efforts to find a place to live [there] have met with failure till now," he wrote. "As you stated, vacancies are few, and those units which have been offered to me are miles beyond the bounds of economy."

Like most college towns in the country, State College, Pennsylva- nia, was still overrun with veterans taking advantage of the G.I. Bill. Trailers and prefab structures lined the town's dirt streets, and many faculty members lived in semipermanent buildings on campus, amid constant, noisy construction of new academic halls. The land felt raw, cold, and exposed. Locals referred to the area and its surroundings as "Happy Valley."

8. Tea and Sympathy

FROM THE MAIN campus gate, South Allen Street appeared to be made of sky more than asphalt; a mild curve of earth led the eye gently upward until the road petered out into late-afternoon clouds or early-evening starshine. Together, the buildings on either side of the street—nothing over three stories high—resembled a failed movie set, ready to be torn down and stored away. Automobiles, wide-grilled, big-bumpered, shiny, and black, lined up like insects having shed their carapaces in a ritual of mating or dying. They crowded out all other moving things. Local business owners complained of ex-servicemen marauding about town, intoxicated, but the street often seemed deserted to Joe from his campus perspective. Evergreens waved in chilly breezes. In their bending and swaying, they seemed to convey the odor of manure (from nearby farms), which sometimes pervaded the town, especially when the air hung heavy and still.

The Department of English Composition occupied the Sparks Building, a large rectangular structure of light brick and simple concrete ornamentation, surrounded by thin young trees. The lecture theaters were spacious and steep, tier after tier of hard wooden seats whose straight backs and skinny armrests clashed with the necessities of human anatomy.

In the front of the rooms, small tables with flimsy lecterns gave the teachers some modicum of authority. Blackboards, built into the walls and attached to rollers, like windows in frames, moved up and down. To a jittery young instructor, they could seem like sets of teeth ready to chomp one's back.

Joe's new colleagues in the liberal arts did not try to hide their poor morale. The college administration—in flux since the recent death of the school's long-term president—aggressively courted federal dollars for scientific research related to national defense. In particular, administrators were excited about developing an underwater sound laboratory, whose purpose would be to explore technological innovations in submarine warfare. Little attention, and even less money, filtered down to the humanities. Until very recently, the largest program in the School of Liberal Arts had been Commerce and Finance, which most humanities teachers argued belonged in a School of Business. Besides, they said, the program—like most programs in the liberal arts—had been stagnant for twenty years.

"In those days, [Penn State] was more of an agricultural school than anything else. Our classes were filled with kids from the coal mines who were brought in to play football, box, wrestle, and then kicked out for poor grades," Frederick Karl recalled. Like Joe, he was a first-year composition instructor. He was working, long-distance, on finishing his Ph.D. requirements at Columbia. "Penn State was, for us New Yorkers, the heart of the boondocks," he said.

He remembered that "Joe's office was across the corridor from mine, and boy, was he bored." Joe had no interest in the essentially remedial-level writing classes he taught. The students, he said, showed even less enthusiasm. "He would come over to my office, put his feet up on my desk, and insist on talking," Karl said.

"Come have lunch," Joe would say.

"I have work to do. Don't you have work to do?" Karl replied.

This casual banter would characterize the men's relationship for the rest of Joe's life. Karl, tall and bearded, deliberate in his movements and speech, was a disciplined, methodical scholar whose interests ranged from Joseph Conrad to Franz Kafka to the contemporary American novel. He didn't enjoy teaching composition any more than Joe did, but he took the work seriously and dispatched it without complaining. Joe figured it was his duty to save his new friend from the burdens of his responsible nature.

Joe and Shirley had still not found good living quarters and occupied a cramped, spare space near campus. As a result, "Shirley was often back in New York," Karl said. "I was planning to get married, and Joe's desperation for company was such that he asked me and my wife-to-be to move in with him [somewhere]. Nothing came of that, perhaps fortunately, since close proximity then might have destroyed what would prove to be a fifty-year friendship."

When Shirley was away, staying with her parents, Joe fell into a routine of teaching classes during the week and then catching a train to Manhattan on the weekends. He considered buying a car, but the Pennsylvania road system was so bad at the time, the trip to New York took nearly eleven hours.

According to Erica Heller, Joe and Shirley were together in Manhattan one weekend, "walking on the street, carrying groceries, when my mother stepped in a pothole and tripped. A piece of the wine bottle they'd been carrying went through her left hand, severing an artery. She needed several operations. I know they sued the city and won, but she had to see a doctor for quite some time [after that]."

Karl confirmed that at a certain point, early in Joe's first year at Penn State, Shirley stayed in New York more or less permanently to receive the medical attention she needed.

Miserably, Joe sat in his squat, stale-smelling bedroom, recalling balmy nights back in the city, when he and Shirley entertained friends with drinks on the rooftop of the building on West Seventy-sixth (though perhaps not all of his memories were pleasant—Erica remembers hearing as a child that her parents were once robbed in that apartment, though she can't recall details). In the summers, Dottie and Barney usually took a country house or went off on vacation to some luxury hotel somewhere. They would invite Shirley and Joe along.

Now, Joe was breathing cow-shit fumes, going to lunch with a friend who'd rather be working, and trying to decide what to do with cheating students. One day, when he caught a pair of boys copying each other's assignments in class, he remembered his own "malfeasance" with the foreign-language requirement at Columbia, and was "compelled . . . to show mercy," he said.

AS HE DID with Frederick Karl, Joe got along well with most of his colleagues. Gordon Smith was an exception. He was one of those people who interpreted Joe's sarcasm as mean-spiritedness. One weekend, the men and their wives visited the Gettysburg battlefield and cemetery. Joe made jokes about war, heroism, and the realities of combat versus mythic representations of it. He hopped around the field like a rabbit and said to Smith, who considered himself a Civil War expert, "What happened on *this* spot?" and "Who got shot *here?*" Smith thought him disrespectful. The budding friendship sputtered; Smith refused to speak to him again.

With another colleague, Joseph Rubin (a fellow veteran), Joe felt comfortable enough to confess his homesickness for New York. In Bernard Oldsey, whose keen interest in contemporary fiction matched Joe's, he found another confidant. They kicked around ideas for a movie script together, a World War II drama that never went anywhere. And Bob Mason and his wife, Abby, were especially sweet. They forgave Joe's rough edge because they understood he rarely meant his sarcasm to be taken personally. Bob appreciated the fact that Joe always "wanted to be honest, in a way, and literal." "When you needed him, he came through," Abby says—as when she had her first child at three in the morning, one terribly cold day, and they called Joe to stay with them at the hospital.

Joe also got to know Dr. John Campbell Major, a specialist in British literature, who had gone to school in Nebraska and Pennsylvania, taught for a while at Oregon Agricultural College, and served as a major in the army. The students called him Doctor, but it amused Joe to think of him as Major Major.

Another veteran on the staff whose name caught Joe's attention—though apparently the men never met—was Robert Oliver Shipman. A married father of three, Shipman held a reserve commission in the army, at the rank of captain, and served on campus as a chaplain and spiritual adviser to student groups. Consciously or not, Joe filed these details in his head.

For many in the campus community, athletics filled aimless hours. Over the years, Penn State's athletic teams had achieved mixed results; perhaps this accounted for the fact that a scrappy student boxer named Charles Allan Tapman remained a campus legend over a decade after his departure. He was a 127-pound featherweight who received a trophy as the "Top [Nittany] Lion Boxer" in 1939. Often overmatched, in terms of strength and skill, he nevertheless managed to compile an impressive win-loss record by being—according to college newspapers—"plucky," "gentlemanly," and in "magnificent physical condition." The "old lion in [him]" always gave him "raw, red courage," according to a letter in the March 17, 1939, *Penn State Collegian.*

Joe found it both touching and sad that people still spoke of Tapman reverentially, as though his spirit conferred blessings on the campus. Obviously, he had been a lovable underdog of a man, cheated—by many accounts—out of a collegiate title in 1937 by a Jewish boxer from Cornell named Moses Goldbas. Reports of the title fight concurred that at one point the referee had separated Tapman and Goldbas from a clench. Tapman stepped back, but Golbas rushed in and slugged him, unawares, with a left hook, which floored him. Tapman recovered, but he was not the same, and lost the bout on points. Officials failed to penalize Goldbas for violating the rules: an injustice that lived on in the hearts of the Lions. For his part, Joe told Joseph Rubin he was charmed by the thought of a boxer named Tapman.

For single faculty members not thrilled by sports, and those, like Joe, often left on their own, "the box" was the cure for loneliness. Ever since the 1936 Olympic Games had been broadcast over television stations in Berlin and Leipzig, the enthusiasm for live programming beamed into one's home had spread around the globe. Joe found it ironic, given television's commercial breakthrough in Hitler's Germany, how, in the United States, the box was essentially Jewish. That is, the variety shows he watched on friends' bulky, flickering TVs—*The Jack Benny Program, The Burns and Allen Show,* Milton Berle's *Texaco Star Theater*—were nothing more than the old Borscht Belt vaudeville shtick he had enjoyed at Grossinger's the week he met Shirley. In particular, Sid Caesar's *Your Show of Shows* had the flavor of the Catskills on a Saturday night—now quickly becoming part of mainstream entertainment in America.

In little over a decade, Joe would know all the writers in Caesar's stable: Larry Gelbart, Mel Tolkin, Neil Simon, Woody Allen, Carl Reiner, and—in an especially close friendship—Mel Brooks, who cut his teeth in the Jewish Alps. Norman Barasch, another television scriptwriter friendly with Joe, explained, "You look at the number of Jewish comedy writers of that generation—Simon, Gelbart, Brooks—and it's more than a coincidence. Their humor came about as the result of the social situation they found themselves in growing up. There was no money. It was very anti-Semitic. When your childhood is not very pleasant, you turn to whatever you can, which in our cases was comedy. Joe was in the same position. Plus, he had an iconoclastic, antiauthoritarian makeup to his character anyway."

Joe was amazed to see mocking, self-deprecatory, antiauthoritarian Yiddish humor slipping into the consciousness of millions of Americans far removed from the urban East Coast. And he appreciated the way Caesar's writers based most of their comedy on banal situations, following the logistics of the circumstances to absurd extremes. This fidelity to logic kept the skits truthful, even at their wildest. Frederick Karl praised a similar principle in the works of his beloved Franz Kafka. Once you accepted *The Metamorphosis*'s premise—that a man could be turned into a giant vermin—the story unfolded with rigorous plausibility, he said: All events were the inevitable consequences of what had come before.

Joe was too restless to sit and watch television for long periods. The medium interested him sociologically but didn't stimulate his intellect. He preferred to read. Of the Kafka books Karl recommended to him, Joe seized most fervently on *The Trial*. He recognized, in a hapless man's conflict with a self-perpetuating bureaucracy, a bit of his military experience—the continual upping of the mission count as a flier was about to complete his duty.

Furthermore, "the idea of being charged with something and not knowing what it is, and being judged guilty . . . [the authorities acting] sure [you] must have committed some crime because everybody's committed some crime," reminded him, he said, of something else he had seen on television, though logical and humorous it most certainly was not: a report on the hearings of the Special Committee on Un-American Activities, as well as the Tydings Committee's investigation of Joe McCarthy's charges that "persons who are disloyal to the United States are . . . employed by the Department of State."

The more Joe thought about Kafka, the more he thought Kafka's attitude, his use of anxiety and mystification, was appropriate to America now.

Joe took other books from Karl, and read randomly, but with increasing discrimination, on his own. Faulkner's *Absalom, Absalom!* had a "structure" he admired, an "epic feeling," he said. He reread Nathan-ael West, more appreciative from a distance of the way West trans-formed California's grimness into truthful absurdity (à la Kafka). In the same week, he read Louis-Ferdinand Céline's *Journey to the End of the Night* and Vladimir Nabokov's *Laughter in the Dark.* He was bowled over by Céline's "slangy use of prose and the continuity that is relaxed and vague rather than precise and motivated," he said. In Nabokov, he admired the "flippant approach to situations which were filled with anguish and grief and tragedy," the "blending of the comic and tragic."

He no longer wanted to think about the short stories he had pub-lished. He was learning new ways of approaching fiction. He wanted to manipulate time, structure, and colloquial speech the way Céline did, but he wasn't sure he could. Besides, what did he want to say? And about what?

A BRIEF NOTICE in Leonard Lyons's syndicated gossip column, "The Lyons Den," on November 16, 1954, revealed that Joe's typewriter was not entirely idle while he taught at Penn State. Lyons reported, "Robert Anderson, author of 'Tea and Sympathy,' and his agent-wife, are being sued over the play by Bob Mason and Joe Heller, former teachers at the Univ. of Pa [*sic*]. They don't claim plagiarism, but a breach of 'fiduciary relationship.'"

This was the first, but certainly not the last, time Joe Heller's name popped up in a newspaper gossip column.

Robert Anderson, who would write several plays, including *I Never Sang for My Father,* as well as the screenplays for *The Sand Pebbles* and *The Nun's Story,* got a glorious start on Broadway with *Tea and Sym-pathy,* the story of an artistic boy shunned by his prep school classmates on suspicion of being homosexual. Reviewing the production in the *New York Times,* the esteemed critic Brooks Atkinson said that *Tea and Sympathy* "restores our theater to an art again with a fine play . . . [of] great skill and beauty."

Anderson's wife, Phyllis Stohl, was a director and literary agent. Bob Mason, who lives now in Washington, D.C., maintains that Anderson swiped the screenplay he and Joe wrote in Pennsylvania. "Joe said that, in New York [while on a holiday break from teaching], he'd met someone from Hollywood who was trying to find a role for an adolescent boy struggling to come into manhood. So Joe concluded that maybe we had a chance at something if we worked on this play. We'd meet in my apartment or his house," Mason says. They submitted the script to Stohl, who pitched it to Otto Preminger. "He invited us to the St. Regis Hotel in New York, where he was staying," Mason says. "We met for four hours. Preminger was really taken with the play. This was on a Friday. He said, 'Okay, Phyllis, send me the contracts on Monday. When Joe and I left, we were just walking on air. But nothing happened."

Next thing Mason knew, Stohl's husband was being praised for having written what was essentially *their* play. "We hired an eminent lawyer, Rudolph Halley, on a contingency basis," he says. "None of us had any dough. He did everything he could. Interviewed everyone. Preminger said he didn't remember the meeting with us, because he had so many meetings, but he said, 'The way Heller and Mason describe things sounds like the way I work.' We finally gave up because we heard Phyllis was dying of cancer, and the Andersons had moved the money around, somehow, so the best person to sue wouldn't really have access to it." Stohl died in 1956, and Anderson passed away in 2009.

Curiously, when asked by the *New York Times* about *Tea and Sympathy* in a wide-ranging interview in 2004, the playwright and director Arthur Laurents would only mutter, "That play is a fraud."

The most famous line in the drama occurs at the end. The wife of the housemaster at the prep school—played by Deborah Kerr, in 1953, in her Broadway debut (the same year as her appearance in the film version of *From Here to Eternity*)—befriends the ostracized boy, to the ultimate ruin of her marriage. Pulling the boy into her arms, she says, "Years from now when you talk about this, and you will, be kind."

SENATOR JOSEPH R. MCCARTHY resembled a praying mantis whenever he opened his mouth (especially on a washed-out, jumpy television screen): a mandibled creature, eating its own. In the marines, during the war, he had flown twelve combat missions as a gunner-observer—hence, his self-given nickname, "Tail-Gunner Joe," and his campaign slogan, "Congress needs a tail-gunner." It turned out that he had falsely inflated his combat record, claiming thirty-two missions instead of twelve, in order to qualify for a Distinguished Flying Cross.

His unremarkable Senate career got a boost on February 9, 1950, when he told a Republican Women's Club in Wheeling, West Virginia, that the "State Department is infested with Communists." Over the next four years, his reckless (and never-substantiated) charges against Jewish professionals in show business, and against hundreds of government employees, including Harry Truman's secretary of defense, George Marshall, architect of the Marshall Plan (and, McCarthy said, part of a "conspiracy so immense and an infamy so black as to dwarf any previous venture in the history of man"), spawned Senate hearings, vigorous debates in the media, and considerable domestic turmoil.

Joe was disgusted by the senator's antics, but he recognized that McCarthy was merely exploiting a national mood. If there had been no Joe McCarthy, the period would still be known for its "Red scares."

One night on the Penn State campus, a faculty member gave a speech denouncing McCarthy for his "career destruction of mere Communist suspects." He was preaching to the choir. The audience nodded agreeably.

George Mandel happened to be visiting Joe at the time, and they had gone to hear the speech together. "With reflexes attuned to Joe since high school days . . . I sank down [in my chair] as soon as he raised his hand," Mandel recalled. Joe "called across the auditorium to ask if *actual* Communists could justifiably be ruined." The speaker, flustered, "pharumph-phumped," Mandel said, and "side-stepped into the wings." Audience members turned to Joe, wide-eyed. After all, the speech maker was a well-respected, tenured member of the college community. Joe was just a neophyte English lecturer.

Mandel told Joe he had been working on a novel, all about the jazz scene in Greenwich Village. This news unsettled Joe, and intensified his feeling that he was wasting his days here in the "boondocks," cut off from the sources of his creative energy. Clearly, New York was feeding his old friend, who seemed to be faring well after his war wound, though occasionally he suffered a mild seizure. He and Joe reminisced about Coney Island—theirs had been a Jewish neighborhood without any "Jewish hang-ups," Mandel said wistfully—and Joe felt even more homesick.

He decided he was falling farther off the planet when James Jones's *From Here to Eternity* appeared just as Joe was beginning his second year as a composition instructor. Jones and Joe had come out of the literary starting gate at about the same time, three years ago, with stories in the same issue of *The Atlantic Monthly*. With this immense new war novel, Jones had pulled ahead. He had even outdone Norman Mailer (Mailer said Jones was the "only one of my contemporaries who I felt had more talent than myself.").

Okay, Joe thought. This was not Santa Anita, after all. Writing was not horse racing. But it was hard not to feel a *little* jealous while admiring Jones's achievement. "[At the time,] I could not see myself spending more than two years writing a novel. If I wrote a novel, I wanted to finish it quickly and have it published quickly," Joe recalled. "So I had written thirty, forty, fifty pages of [a] novel, and then I read *From Here to Eternity*. . . . I said, 'No chance of that.' . . . I did not have the vocabulary. I didn't have the patience. I didn't have the knowledge. I didn't have the talent. I didn't have the intensity or the interest that any respectable novelist would have in order to go to work [, so] I threw those pages away. . . . [I figured] there was nothing I could add to war literature that was not in *From Here to Eternity* and had not been produced before by Norman Mailer and . . . John Horne Burns."

From Here to Eternity followed a reluctant hero, Robert E. Lee Prewitt, as he tried to establish an individual code of honor in a world gone awry, moving through a devotion to art (playing the bugle), fidelity to war (boxing), and attempts to escape mass organization. Like *The Naked and the Dead,* Jones's novel was faithful to naturalism (that is, the triumph of fate over character). It proclaimed a proletarian social outlook (Prewitt was the son of a coal miner, at the mercy of one financially based injustice after another). But what distinguished it from Popular Front screeds and Mailer's book was Jones's refusal to indulge in either unearned optimism or easy cynicism. If, spiritually, *The Naked and the Dead* was the last great American novel of the 1930s, *From Here to Eternity* was the postwar era's most eloquent elegy for the world it would bury.

Joe found some consolation in the fact that his recent reading of Céline, Nabokov, and Kafka had kindled his interest in styles and techniques other than realism. More than that, he had come to believe *he* was not a literary realist. This was akin to admitting to Joe McCarthy he was not a true American.

He may have fallen behind his contemporaries, but if he ever managed to pull something together, it was going to look different from anything that had ever been published in the United States.

Adding to Joe's present discomfort was the fact that his Kafka pipeline had disappeared: Frederick Karl, and his young bride, Dolores, had left State College and moved to Manhattan, where Karl had gotten a job in the English Department at the City College of New York.

Joe slogged through another year of boring courses with bored students, taking the train to see Shirley in New York on the weekends. At around this time, according to Barbara Gelb, Joe "calculated that his life was half over, and began to fear he had no future." The current arrangement could not continue—especially once Shirley learned she was pregnant.

In the spring of 1952, Joe began to apply for jobs in New York. Since he did not hold a Ph.D. degree, a plum academic job in Manhattan was probably not feasible. Besides, for now, he had had enough of teaching. On May 27, he wrote to Professor Gates, requesting a leave of absence for the academic year 1952–1953. "I have the opportunity at this time to secure a position in the publishing field, and it is my intention to spend the year acquiring professional experience in editorial work." Nothing suggests he had any editorial opportunities; he used this as an excuse to secure a leave. He had no thought of returning, under any circumstances.

To the dean of the School of Liberal Arts, Professor Gates wrote that "Mr. Heller is an accomplished writer, particularly of fiction, and he believes that editorial experience will be of benefit to him." He recommended the leave, and it was approved.

Joe's colleague Joseph Rubin sensed that Joe would not come back. Joe assured him, "I don't hate anybody here."

On March 20, 1953, Joe wrote to Professor Gates, "It is now certain that Mrs. Heller and I will not return to State College and that I will therefore not resume my teaching duties when my present leave of absence expires." He offered his formal resignation, and asked Professor Gates to "convey my respects to the other members of the department and express my appreciation for all that was done to make my two years with them as pleasant as they were."

The following fall, the Army Air Force and Exchange Service, located on West Forty-third Street in Manhattan, wrote to Gates, asking for details about Mr. Joseph Heller's "ability to get along with others, his general stability, his initiative and his ability to think for himself." The Exchange Service was considering Mr. Heller for a job. Gates responded, in a handwritten note rushed to New York via Western Union, that Mr.

Heller had always performed his job well, that he was well liked and talented. He was sorry Mr. Heller had left. In a follow-up note (perhaps with Joseph McCarthy's TV chatter ringing in his head), Professor Gates said Mr. Heller was "honest, dependable, and loyal."

Many years later, a teacher in the Penn State English Department, Stanley Weintraub, invited Joe back to campus to give a reading of his fiction. "He declined," Weintraub recalled, "writing on a postcard that he never wanted to set foot in Happy Valley again."

PART THREE Live Forever

9. Caught Inside

SN'T THIS THE BUILDING where they found dead people on the roof?"

This anonymous 2009 posting on a Web site devoted to discussions of New York City real estate rumors captures one of the chief characteristics of the Apthorp Building, located between Broadway and West End Avenue and stretching from Seventy-eighth to Seventy-ninth streets: Once inside, you either dream or fear you'll never escape it, depending on your temperament. Joe and Shirley Heller moved into the Apthorp in the summer of 1952, while Joe was on leave from Penn State.

The building, completed in 1908, has a history to enflame the most overheated gothic imagination. "This is like the House of Usher," a longtime tenant once said. "Beautiful on the outside, but on the inside it's a corpse, and its guts are rotting away." Another tenant swore that he once turned on his kitchen faucet and "pigeon feathers . . . [came] out." Chandeliers in the old elevators used to chime with the creaky movements up and down: a whispery music conjuring visions of long-gone visitors in diaphanous gowns and suits as white as light. It was a place entirely worthy of the oddities that would distinguish Joe Heller's mature fiction, which began to take shape in Apartment 2K South, situated, strangely enough, on the north side of the Apthorp's interior courtyard.

From around the time of the nation's founding, no plot of ground spoke more volubly of America—and money—than Charles Ward Apthorpe's combined land holdings along what is now known as upper Broadway in Manhattan. The history of this particular sod was irony-soaked, in ways Joe richly appreciated.

Apthorpe was a British Loyalist who built one of the grandest pre-Revolutionary houses on the continent. The house, finished in 1764, known as Elmwood after the stately elms that surrounded it, faced the Hudson. Here, George Washington rested with some of his troops following the Battle of Long Island during the Revolutionary War. After the war, Apthorpe was indicted for high treason, but—in a foretaste of the American way—his wealth enabled him to escape the charges.

His mansion fell in 1891 to make way for Ninetieth and Ninety-first streets. Litigation among his heirs and several other families who claimed parcels of the land, including some of the most famous names in New York history—Astor, McEvers, Van den Heuvel, and Burnham—befogged the courts for years, in grim Dickensian fashion, and was finally settled in the first decade of the twentieth century. One can almost hear the sigh of relief in a *New York Times* article, dated July 24, 1910, celebrating the laying to rest of the "doughty royalist Charles Ward Apthorp."

William Astor commissioned the prominent architects Charles William Clinton and William Hamilton Russell to design the Apthorp Apartments, a twelve-story limestone structure modeled on the Pitti Palace in Florence. Its presence transformed the atmosphere of quaint colonialism that had characterized the area for over a century, and signaled the move toward apartment living that would shape Manhattan's crowded and frenetic future.

The Apthorp's High Renaissance exterior, carved and rusticated, featuring large cornices and a three-story porte cochere leading to a formal courtyard with a garden and two fountains, was elegantly tasteful. There were two arched entrances endowed with bas reliefs of garland-bearing female figures and delicate ironwork in and around the gates. Putti were tucked modestly beneath the rooftop cornice, which overlooked the Italian Romanesque First Baptist Church, built in 1894, just across Seventy-ninth Street.

Originally, the building sheltered ten apartments per floor, each with glass-paneled French doors, room-size foyers with mosaic tiled floors, and Wedgwood friezes. In the late 1930s and throughout the 1940s, many of the apartments were divided into smaller units. Because they overlooked an interior courtyard, several of the rooms received poor, indirect lighting: a trade-off for the cozy, private, secure atmosphere created by the design.

When it opened, the courtyard measured 95 by 134 feet and, according to *Architecture* magazine, offered a "display of horticulture that would grace a botanical garden." Brick walkways surrounded the two bowl-shaped fountains. There were shrubs, yuccas, and flowers; vines hung from boxes placed in upper-story windows. All in all, the Apthorp exuded timelessness, with a mixture of classical styling, ostentation (private living on a public scale), and forward-looking development fever.

The West Side was a blighted area when Joe and Shirley settled there. A citywide housing shortage followed World War II; hastily, owners partitioned residence hotels and apartment buildings to squeeze more people into smaller spaces. The city passed a law encouraging this practice by making it quite lucrative, turning brownstones that had once hosted one or two families into overcrowded rooming houses, attracting hordes of real estate speculators, and driving out modest landlords who had overseen their properties with personal concern.

Many of the new tenants, back from the war and now facing horrid prospects, were in transit, troubled, isolated. At about the time Joe and Shirley moved into their apartment, Mayor Robert F. Wagner, disturbed by the deterioration of West Side housing, appointed the mayor's Slum Clearance Committee, headed by Robert Moses, to rebuild the area. In consequence, huge demolition projects displaced thousands of low-income families for years to come. Several tenements appropriated by redevelopers fell into greater ruin, but with higher rents and poorer care. The city's Welfare Department took over a number of crumbling furnished rooms in ratty hotels in order to stow away society's undesirables. Within a few years of Joe and Shirley's arrival at the Apthorp, West Side streets teemed with former mental patients still in need of treatment, single mothers with hungry children, prostitutes, petty thieves, and all manner of the destitute. Crime rates soared.

In spite of this steady decline, the West Side maintained a unique identity, formed by diversity and turbulence. Joe loved the atmosphere.

Chaos it was, but a *cohesive* chaos, able to bind people tightly. For example, the year before the completion of the Apthorp, a nearby charitable foundation built a 350-unit tenement for West Indian domestics. Over sixty years later, 650 people still lived in those rooms, most of them the children and grandchildren of the original tenants.

Simmering cultural tensions made the neighborhoods all the more exciting. Predominantly Protestant throughout the Civil War, the area became the province of Irish Catholics until around 1910, when Jewish immigrants from Russia, Poland, and Germany came crowding in. By the late 1930s, West Side neighborhoods felt European, dotted with bookshops, newspaper stands selling international publications, and sidewalk cafés. Throughout these demographic dances, vestiges of the area's former personalities clung to the streets and walls. To Joe Heller, in 1952, the area had a bit of the carnival, old and new, that he recognized from Coney Island.

Inside the Apthorp, a similar sensibility—continuity spiced with variety—rang out in hallway greetings. One of the first people Joe and Shirley learned about was Elizabeth Kirwin. For thirty-five years, she had operated elevators in the building's northern wing, after replacing her brother once he entered the army in World War I. She had thought her time in the building would be temporary, but her brother got another job after demobilization, so she stayed on. "She never had a cross word with a tenant or an employee. If a tenant fell ill, she paid a call and brought flowers. She did thousands of little services outside her job, always courteously and cheerfully. We found out later that her blood pressure rose to 280, but no one heard a word of complaint from her," said Mrs. William Byrne, one of Joe and Shirley's neighbors. After Kirwin collapsed in a locker room of a cerebral hemorrhage, most of the Apthorp's tenants—men and women of many faiths—gathered in Calvary Cemetery to pay their respects. The scene, a coming together of vastly different types, epitomized the Apthorp in those days. In the years ahead, growing differences would nudge aside communal gestures: In mid-February 1997, when a dead woman was discovered on the roof, no one in the building claimed to know her. Later identified as Gabriele Opferman, forty-one years old, she was apparently a German tourist. No illnesses or wounds. She was not intoxicated. An autopsy determined she had died of exposure. What she was doing at the

Apthorp and how she got on the roof without anyone knowing or seeing her remained a mystery, and spoke to some of what the Apthorp had become.

By this time, Joe had left the building, but Shirley stayed on. Rumors spread, like water damage, that management hoped to force everyone out so it could drive up rents or turn the apartments into condos. Asbestos leaked from the walls, toxins poured from the radiators, my god, we'll all die in a flood when the plumbing bursts. . . .

But in the beginning, Joe and Shirley loved their four small rooms, secured with financial help from Dottie and Barney. A daughter, Erica Jill, had joined them on February 1, 1952, right before they found a place at the Apthorp. Joe was in his last semester of teaching at Penn State. He made arrangements to be back in New York when Erica arrived. "I was born at French Hospital, a place with *nuns,* of all things," Erica says. The hospital, now gone, once stood on West Thirty-fourth Street, opposite what is now the Lincoln Tunnel exit. It had been built in 1904 by the French Benevolent Society, a nonsectarian organization determined, in its early days, to treat patients free of charge. William Carlos Williams interned there. It was Willa Cather's favorite infirmary.

"Erica, for Beethoven's Eroica Symphony, and Jill from Jack and Jill," Jerome Taub recalls learning from Dottie. "Joe named her."

By mid-summer 1952, father, mother, and daughter were ensconced in the Apthorp. Erica, blessed with her mother's fair coloring, was delighted by the flowers in the courtyard (where children were not allowed to play) and by the trembling glass pendants in the slow, gently swaying elevators.

"NOW HERE'S how it was . . . in the . . . fifties," wrote Shirley Polykoff, one of the most respected women in American advertising. "On T.V., women were having love affairs with refrigerators. . . . Bufferin . . . were racing Aspirin . . . from the stomach to the seat of the pain, while sinus cavities were being lit up and cleared out fast, fast, fast. The sell was hard, the voice-over was the voice of authority and the models mostly male because the research showed that, in the fifties, viewers were much too fine to watch a woman suffer." On the other hand, "magazine ads . . . were almost entirely peopled with high-fashion, overly made-up, overly groomed 'Park Avenue penthouse' types whose brilliant smiles reflected the sheer pleasure of mopping floors, baking cakes, and gentle laxative relief."

Joe would meet Polykoff at a cocktail party sometime in the late 1960s. By then, she knew him as one of the few former advertising copywriters to make a leap to literary success; certainly no one had pulled it off with as much panache as he had. In her memoir, *Does She . . . or Doesn't She?* Polykoff recalls her encounter with Joe. The exchange captures the easy sophistication men and women effected in that time and place (as well as Joe's rough charm):

> "Your name is familiar. . . ." [Joe said.] "You're in advertising."
>   "How do you know?"
>   "Because I once wrote you a letter asking for a job."
>   "You did?"
>   "But you didn't give me a job. Even though I'm Jewish."
>   "I can't go around giving everyone a job who's Jewish."
>   "But you could have given me one."
>   "No, I couldn't."
>   "Why?"
>   "Because you're a man. And I only hire women writers."
>   . . . Late in the evening he offered to take me home—to Park Avenue and 62nd Street.
>   "I don't live on Park and 62nd Street," I protested. "I live on Park and 82nd."
>   "I can only take you to Park and 62nd."
>   "How come?"
>   "That's where I'm meeting my wife."
>   . . . "So go meet your wife," I said. "Someone else will take me to Park and 82nd."
>   "That's not a nice attitude," he said. "First you don't give me a job. Now you don't let me take you home."

The "opportunity" in the "publishing field" on which Joe hung his leave from Penn State in the spring of 1952 never materialized. The position with the Army Air Force and Exchange Service was temporary. So one day, he purchased a "gray fedora with a dark band [and] . . . a new white-on-white shirt with French cuffs" and hit the streets, looking for jobs in advertising, where he felt he could unleash his creativity (and sparkling personality).

Briefly, he worked at the Merrill Anderson Company for sixty dollars a week; there, he drank his "first Gibsons with a copy chief named Gert Conroy and learned to love extra-dry martinis in a chilled glass with a twist of lemon peel"; he spent some time at Benton & Bowles, best known for its work with Proctor & Gamble in launching radio soap operas and the television show *As the World Turns* (at B & B, a fellow copywriter named Art Kramer recalled Joe's typewriter "going when I came into work and still going when I left in the evening. Everyone marveled at this non-stop output. As one writer joked, 'What, is that guy writing a novel or something?'"); he wrote copy for Remington Rand, the former arms manufacturer turned typewriter and then computer maker, alongside Mary Higgins Clark, who would later publish suspense novels.

In 1955, he became an advertising-promotion copywriter at *Time* magazine, where he received a starting salary of nine thousand dollars a year. For his steady and innovative work, he received one-thousand-dollar raises at the end of each of his first two years there. *Look* magazine offered him a thirteen-thousand-dollar annual salary beginning in 1958, and in 1959, he went to work for *McCall's* as an advertising and promotion manager.

Always, he said the men and women he met in advertising departments were far more creative and intelligent than the people he had worked with in academia. "All the copywriters were writing plays and novels and the people in the art department were interested in serious art," he recalled. To some degree, at the heart of the academic enterprise lies a conservative impulse, a desire to nurture and pass on traditions of learning, a valuable endeavor; on the other hand, the men and women in American advertising believed *they* were creating the future, and their shared excitement was palpable.

"Even before 1960, the agency world was glued to the new-wave movies by Visconti, Fellini, Antonioni, Truffaut, Godard, Orson Welles, Stanley Kubrick, to Mike Nichols and Elaine May, to the Group Theatre and Elia Kazan and Marlon Brando," Mary Wells, a prominent former ad executive, has written. "Advertising [was] always part of the [cultural] front line."

Moreover, as Shirley Polykoff insisted, for many kids, particularly the first-generation children of Eastern European immigrants, advertising was a key to successful assimilation. "[I]t was from the magazine advertisements that we really learned how to be truly American," she wrote. "How a home should look. How a table should be set. How to dress. How to be well groomed." Advertising "taught the immigrants that they could achieve a clean complexion by using the soap used by nine out of ten screen stars." Through advertising, "you could look right into the homes of real people," Polykoff said. "See how they act. Learn to do as they did."

These lessons were disseminated from a roughly four-block stretch of Madison Avenue, on Manhattan's East Side. Within a three-block span sat the headquarters of the nation's two largest radio and television networks, the main offices of "national reps" (over sixty of them) selling ad space to the country's newspapers, and the editorial and advertising offices of *Time, Look, Life, McCall's, Vogue, Redbook, Coronet, Esquire, Mademoiselle,* and *The New Yorker,* to name a few. As Martin Mayer wrote in *Madison Avenue, U.S.A.,* one of the first comprehensive studies of the ad world, "On the outside . . . the new buildings [were] mostly very much alike; on the inside, it [was] every man for himself."

Many of the city's finest restaurants and bars opened in this area, catering to high-paid executives and their clients, who prided themselves on discriminating taste (after all, they were the people *setting* America's tastes). "[I]t can truthfully be said that the great restaurants of New York are here quite simply to serve lunch to men in the advertising and communications fields," Mayer wrote. "The company will [always] pick up the tab."

Favorite spots for lengthy business meals included "21," with its collection of large wooden Negro jockeys, La Reine, dark and intimate, and Romeo Salta. Tom Messner, cofounder of the prominent ad agency Messner Vetere Berger Carey, recalls, "There was a steam table bar run by a World War II vet, Irving Bloom, called Kilroy's on Sixth Avenue between 42nd and 43rd Streets. Copywriters and Art Directors went there and often worked at the bar. The Tehran on 44th Street—a Persian restaurant and bar—was more upscale: free hors d'oeuvres between five and eight. Generally, account people did all the wining and dining [of clients]."

Mayer reported that "[s]urprsingly often . . . the business lunch really [was] for business purposes, part of a selling venture which may [have seemed] more certain of success after it [was] washed a few times in alcohol." (Some agencies installed in-house bars, open for cocktails each day at the close of business. A former employee at BBDO recalls the only client who ever showed up at *their* bar, Central Filing, was Pepsi's advertising director.)

Despite growing public perceptions, even in the immediate postwar period, that ad men caroused and drank more than they worked, the best people in the field spent brutal hours of hard concentration and constant pressure. According to *Advertising Age,* in 1956, the average age at which prominent people in the business died was 57.9, ten years under the national average for men.

Nor was the image of the man in the gray flannel suit ever really accurate—Sloan Wilson notwithstanding. In the fifties, many advertising executives lived in Westchester, Locust Valley, or other suburbs, and dressed modestly for their long subway rides into the city. "I thought it bizarre that people of such means should live where they did when they could easily have afforded to live where I did . . . and get to the office or back as quickly as I could," Joe wrote in *Now and Then.* He'd had enough subway rides as a kid shuttling to Times Square from Coney Island.

But many people thought the commute was worth it to jettison stress at the end of the day—the stress of handling multimillion dollar accounts (in 1956, seventy-three companies spent over ten million dollars each to advertise their products: soft drinks, cars, soaps, drugs, liquor, tobacco, and electrical supplies; Miles Laboratories spent nine million to push Alka-Seltzer; General Motors budgeted $162,499,248 to promote Cadillacs and Chevys; and Seagram's shelled out $31,547,043 to convince people their lives were poorer without Chivas Regal, Four Roses, and Wolfschmidt).

Stress also came from the hierarchical nature of most ad agencies. Someone was always fiercely watching your work. Mayer quotes a research company officer's account of a typical meeting: "The media people come first, usually about ten minutes early. Then about the time the meeting is supposed to start, the agency people show up and start kicking the media people around. The advertisers come about fifteen minutes late and for the rest of the meeting they kick the agency people around. Then everybody goes out for a drink."

The original Time-Life Building overlooked Rockefeller Center. From his office, Joe could watch ice-skaters in the rink below. In 1957, Marilyn Monroe detonated a block of dynamite to signal the construction-start of a new home for Henry Luce's empire, closer to the Avenue of the Americas. The new building would be distinguished by its column-free interior space and the brushed stainless-steel paneling of its elevator banks. Eames chairs graced many of the offices.

Time was a "man's world," according to Jane Maas, who worked there briefly around the time Joe was there. "The lines were clearly drawn" in the editorial department, she said: "[W]omen researched the stories, men wrote them." More than this, the organization was built around belief in the possibility of a "Great Man"—and the resident Great Man was Henry Luce (the Man of the Year, *every* year, to his employees). He had coined the phrase "The American Century," and he saw himself at the center of the era, shaping politics, minds, and culture. "[E]verybody was aware of the . . . biases that flowed from Luce," Maas said. "While I worked there, *Time* helped to defeat the candidacy of Adlai Stevenson when he ran for President in 1956."

One morning, in the old Time-Life Building, Maas accidentally rushed into Luce's private elevator and stood there staring at his "beetle brows" as he made his way to his thirty-second-floor penthouse. Luce was a devout Presbyterian, and he used his elevator time to pray. The sudden presence of a woman in the midst of his sacred ritual merely confirmed his greatness, for it is to the Great Man that the severest temptations appear.

In spite of hard work and stress, Joe recalled his stint at *Time* as one long party. Autumn's World Series hoopla gave way to Thanksgiving and holiday celebrations, and then to the rites of spring. Each fall, "during the World Series there were personal table radios brought in and installed for the duration" in most offices, he wrote. This enabled people "to go on listening to every game at work when they could no longer do so at the bars in the nearby restaurants in which they had spent their long lunches." Joie de vivre always "prevailed during business hours in [the] corridors in those days. The liquor would flow, the canapes would appear, the socializing would spill over after business hours into small groups in one nearby bar after another. Small wonder we were often reluctant to hurry home," Joe said. "The women at work there were lively, educated, and bright."

Meanwhile, Shirley was back at the Apthorp, tending two kids now: On May 11, 1956, at French Hospital, a son, Theodore Michael, had arrived. "We were pregnant together," Shirley's cousin Audrey Chestney said, "she with Teddy, me with my son Peter. We had lunch every day at Schrafft's, and then went to the same doctor on Park Avenue. Shirley was very kind and fun to be with," but the meetings at Schrafft's were among her few outings. Chestney felt sorry for her: "Joe didn't like to go to other people's houses—I guess it was boring for him."

He was often on the road. *Time* held sales conferences at deluxe resorts in Florida, Bermuda, and Nassau. In the hotels, Bloody Mary and brandy Alexander mixes were provided for the men's breakfasts. On the golf course, where most of the men spent their afternoons, barrels of ice filled with beer stood next to the ball washers and tee boxes at each hole. Joe did not enjoy golf. He spent his days reading and writing. Executives jockeyed for the honor of giving keynote speeches at these conventions; generally, Joe skipped the ceremonies.

During his tenure at *Time,* the company reached a paid circulation of two million. A few executive officers discovered they were alcoholic ("[There] was a rumor . . . that the company maintained an ongoing arrangement with the Payne Whitney Clinic at New York Hospital for the discreet admission and treatment of important employees," Joe wrote), and a few men, like Joe, kept getting promoted. He drew the attention of his competitors.

It was his job to provide a "platform" or "campaign theme" for a "purchase proposition." Magazine ad space—at *Time's* level—sold for approximately $24,000 for a black-and-white page, $30,000 for a two-color page, and $35,000 for a four-color page. One day, working with a colleague named Pete Haddon, Joe kicked off a sales presentation to a stubborn client by setting up an easel in a boardroom. On the easel, he placed an illustration of the Red Queen from an old edition of *Through the Looking-Glass.* The queen was dragging Alice on the ground, shouting, "Now, here, you see, it takes all the running you can do to keep in the same place!"

Word got around that Joe had thoroughly charmed his clients. Soon thereafter, a colleague asked to borrow the Red Queen. He was trying to persuade the Simmons mattress company to buy ad space in *Time* in order to reach motel and hotel owners (who subscribed to the magazine in large numbers). A second colleague wanted the Red Queen to help him sway the H. J. Heinz Company to purchase ads, thereby interesting coffee shop managers in its products. Joe got his first raise.

MEANWHILE, IN THE VILLAGE, George Mandel "slept little and gamboled much," he said, even though "seizures common to brain injury . . . harassed [his] every gesture." The Village, with its "distinctive taverns and cafeterias swarming with bogus artists and drug addicts," was "lucky" for him. In these environs, he found friendship and "romance," especially with a woman named Miki, who became his wife, and of whom Joe was terribly fond.

Mandel had grown disillusioned with comic-book work. He wanted to be a fine artist, but the exploitive nature of the business also wore him down. Before the war, he had done most of his work with Funnies, Inc., a "packager" operating out of a small office on West Forty-third Street, near Times Square. A packager created comics on demand for various publishers. Lloyd Jacquet, Funnies, Inc.'s founder, couldn't afford to be a publisher, so he hired writers and artists to sell the products to others. He made his first sale to Martin Goodman, a pulp magazine mogul: a spectacular package featuring the Human Torch and the Sub-Mariner. It was called *Marvel Comics #1*.

For Jacquet and a handful of companies—Better Publications, Timely Comics, Novelty, Hillman, and Fox—Mandel worked on "Doc Strange," "The Black Marvel," "The Woman in Red," "The Patriot," "Voodoo Man," "The Angel," and "Sons of the Gods." These were some of the projects Joe had seen him prepare for back at the Club Alteo.

Other gifted young men in Jacquet's stable included Mickey Spillane, Carl Burgos, and Bill Everett. Spillane said Jacquet, a Douglas MacArthur look-alike (right down to the corncob pipe), "never could understand artists and writers." He was a pure businessman; when Mandel, Spillane, and others went off to war, he replaced them with the cheapest labor he could find. "They had a bunch of creeps come in there . . . and they took over all our stuff," Spillane told an interviewer. "They'd formed a union, that's what the problem was, and we were going to kill that union. Because these guys, they didn't have the talent . . . we had, I'll tell you that!"

After the war, Mandel worked his way back into freelance drawing (at smaller wages than before), but he was itching to be "literary"—that is, *serious,* in comics, painting, or writing. Plus, he had discovered his injury made it harder for him to visualize, but easier to talk, write—torrents of language poured from him. Each time Joe visited him, he marveled at how much his friend had improved. He had come a long way from the days when restaurant noise unnerved him to the point that he'd slap at a waitress with his menu and shout that nothing pleased him, nothing, nothing.

Miki helped him. She typed the expanding manuscript of the novel he had told Joe about on his visit to Penn State. Initially, it was called "The Hook and the Tower," but it was retitled, at an editor's suggestion, *Flee the Angry Strangers.* Bobbs-Merrill brought out a hardcover edition of the book in 1952. The following year, with the appearance of a Bantam mass-market paperback edition (featuring a Harry Schaare cover, like that of a comic book: a woman shooting heroin), the novel got noticed by journals and prominent critics. "All [his friends] were ecstatically astonished when the paperback reprint rights . . . sold for a price of $25,000," Joe wrote. "His share of half that seemed a fortune. And . . . *was indeed* a fortune to someone living largely on disability payments for his war wound, and to someone like me . . . [working] as an advertising copywriter."

In time, critics saw *Flee the Angry Strangers* as a proto-Beat novel, capturing, before Kerouac, Ginsberg, Ferlinghetti, Burroughs, and others, what Thomas Newhouse called the cultural "transition between . . . [a] wail of hopelessness" after the war and a "freedom to choose dissolution" rather than middle-class life.

Mandel's protagonist, eighteen-year-old Diane Lattimer, a drug-hazed habitué of the jazz clubs on Bleecker and MacDougal streets, hustles by day and is, despite her self-destructiveness, a rare feminist heroine in the fiction of the time. Mandel's comic-book training showed in the larger-than-life appetites of his characters, in their heroic embrace of instantaneous pleasure (a kind of personalized justice for all) and their rejection of society's straight-and-narrow paths. These qualities would characterize all of Beat writing; the Beats' link to the comic-book ethos of the time—through figures like George Mandel—is not accidental.

Flee the Angry Strangers uncovered other crosscurrents swirling through American popular writing in the early 1950s—for, just as Mickey Spillane smuggled comic-book action into the hard-boiled detective genre, the values of proletarian fiction had stiffened comic heroes' spines.

Mandel's characters encompassed each of these strains; they were amalgams of the Human Torch, Mike Hammer, and Nelson Algren's Frankie Machine. The combination sowed a path for the Beats, who, in the late 1950s and early 1960s, would change America's popular vocabulary.

Mandel's people spoke "jive": jazz talk. They didn't *provide their partners with sexual delight*; they *sent* them. They didn't smoke *marijuana;* they indulged in *pod,* a term that degraded into *pot* after many "engorged [mis]pronunciations [by] its consumers," Mandel said. The novel's language was so strange, his publishers asked him to include a lexicon in the back of the book. Later, he regretted he didn't accede to this request, because soon, "Madison Avenue" began to "spoil" the "flavor" of jive's "perceptive music."

Other crosscurrents began to flow: Underground hip became a rich source for mainstream advertising.

Since the days of Charles Ward Apthorpe, and even before, America had been a scene of clashing images, but now the country was getting *really good* at producing these images, and presenting them in easy-to-get, inexpensive formats. The big books coming out of Manhattan's midtown publishers in handy paperback form—*The Naked and the Dead, From Here to Eternity*—showcased an America where values rooted in land still held sway over human destinies; the comic books, genre stories, and early Beat poetry—in throwaway tabloid formats—emerging from artists and writers, several of whom lived in the Village, pictured urban alleyways as free zones where the individual could be an outlaw hero; while the ads, many created by aspiring novelists and painters, packaged in East Side offices and sent to magazines and television stations, offered the accumulation of goods as the secret to bliss and America's world dominance.

From his perch above the skating rink at Rockefeller Center, Joe kept an eye on all this. The culture's variety impressed him, as well as the darker patterns he saw, like scratches in the ice below, in the city's (and perhaps the nation's) mood.

For example, he understood that, for a segment of middle-class American women who wanted to be valued for their "natural" looks, but to whom businessmen were banking on selling millions of dollars' worth of hair dye, the catch phrase "Does she . . . or doesn't she?" was irresistible because it was titillating without being *too* naughty. He also understood that a whole other group of American women whose lives had been junked by the war and its family upheavals had no truck with such cuteness. For them, the only thing that mattered was "Nembutal goofballs and pod." Sad, absurd, diverse—what American novelist had successfully gathered the country's currents, like a Coney Island hawker snagging all the cotton candy and wrapping it around a single cardboard stick? In his spare time, he reread Kafka and Céline, as well as Evelyn Waugh. He wrote no fiction.

"AN OLD LINE," Tom Messner says. "In the fifties, everyone wanted to write a novel; in the seventies, a screenplay; in the nineties, a business plan. Ad men—to wildly generalize—seek fame and fortune. And the novel [in the 1950s] they view[ed] as the quickest way. I don't think many reflect[ed] on the *art* of the novel." For one thing, it was too easy to be seduced by corporate perks—the long lunches, the bottles of scotch stashed in file drawers.

Messner recalls a book called *Advertising Man,* by Jack Dillon, and a review of the book by Israel Horowitz. In the review, Horowitz said copywriters were men who did things well that were not worth doing.

But this view undersold the business. The business "sought people who were funny, who could make things out of nothing when there was nothing unique to say, who understood TV, which the old guys didn't, who could find some notion or manner of expression that could guarantee rapid success," Messner says. The children of the well-to-do went into finance or medicine or law. Many ad writers prided themselves on the fact that they were the "sons and daughters of a lot of working-class people (Italians, Jews, Irish)," people "who could *think*."

"It took . . . the Jews with their great imaginations and dramatic writing skills and the powerhouse Italian artists to join up, take over, and make advertising the [country's] preferred entertainment," Mary Wells insists, unapologetic about her cultural generalizations.

Messner notes, "World War II vets were naturally the drivers of the business in that era. [In later years,] one that I worked for—Carl Ally— even imagined he was Yossarian."

Genuinely heroic figures: Joe Daly, Bill Bernbach, David Ogilvy.

So the ad people earned their perks. You couldn't blame them for straying into temptation. It wasn't unusual or surprising to find older men having dinner with younger women in Madison Avenue restaurants, especially on Thursday nights, says one old copywriter. He called Thursdays "Cheater's Night," figuring men were having dinner with their girlfriends prior to spending weekends locked away in the suburbs with children, pets, and wives.

In those days, there were no direct-dial phones in the offices. This aided and abetted nocturnal meanderings. At 5:30, when the company switchboard closed, a person could call out, but no one could call in. It was hard for a wife to check on her husband's whereabouts, or to be certain he was not working late.

In contrast to this, the sexual culture blocks away, at Columbia and Barnard, was characterized by frustration, ignorance, and tentative rebellion—true across much of the country, if the national reaction to the first Kinsey Report was any indication. In the early 1950s, police had to be summoned to Barnard to quell panty raids that had gotten out of hand. Mobs of boys, tanked up on testosterone and alcohol, moved up Broadway, stopping traffic, and planted themselves outside Barnard dormitories, shouting to see women's underwear. In his memoir *New York in the Fifties*, Dan Wakefield, who joined a mob one night, recalled that "girls came to the windows of the dorms, some of them tossing down tokens of intimate apparel, like morsels of meat to a pack of baying hounds." Compared to *these* desperate rituals—which spread across U.S. college campuses in 1952 and 1953—clandestine dinners seemed the height of civilization to the women and men of Madison Avenue.

The backlash against panty raids in newspapers and political speeches reflected the generally repressive national mood Joe McCarthy and others had been able to exploit. "Why aren't [the panty raiders] in the Army if they have so little to do?" asked *U.S. News & World Report*. College kids, unable to control their sexual urges, were blamed for giving the nation's enemies comfort and undermining U.S. efforts in Korea.

But students weren't the only ones challenging conventional attitudes. The January-February 1954 issue of *Partisan Review* featured a short story by Mary McCarthy entitled "Dottie Makes an Honest Woman of Herself." In it, the characters spoke openly about diaphragms, "female contraceptive[s], a plug." *Such words*, in pages that conveyed the deepest thinking of the day, from Lionel Trilling, William Phillips, and Irving Howe!

Then there was Trilling himself, discoursing on the Kinsey Report—again, in *Partisan Review*—calling its appearance "an event of great importance in our culture," a balm whose "permissive effect" might overcome the "sexual ignorance which exists among us" and create the possibility of a healthy "community of sexuality" in the country.

Mainstream magazines such as *Reader's Digest* weighed in on Kinsey and ran articles about abortion. The pieces were both reactionary and exploratory, but they indicated a surprising new openness about sexual subjects.

In this atmosphere, men and women Joe Heller's age, having married, as they thought they were supposed to do, now starting families and working their way into the heart of American success, naturally wondered if the social contract had changed just as they'd signed it. Were they *really* bound by their signatures? How bound were they?

Corporate culture encouraged *having it all*. Not only that, it provided multiple opportunities. Calvin Trillin, who worked at *Time* in the 1950s, recalled "there was lots of underground romantic stuff. . . . Working at *Time*, you had to be in close quarters with fifty people through the week. There were late closings, time spent with feet up on the desk. . . . You didn't know people were involved [with each other] until there was some awful scene in the hall or you got an invitation to a wedding."

In 1998, Joe admitted to British journalist Lynn Barber that he'd had "affairs" during his nearly ten years in the advertising business. "[T]here were not that many. . . . [I]t was part of the male culture," he said. "I was working in New York City in an atmosphere where men did that. We'd have parties and a couple would go into a room together. . . . I never had any wish to end my marriage." At the time, Shirley "never accurately detected" his affairs. She was too busy raising Erica and Ted.

Where sexual mores were concerned, the New York ad world (driven, as Tom Messner says, by World War II vets) was an extension of the army. The men reasoned that as long as they did their duty—this time, for wives, kids, extended families—they were entitled to R & R in the city, as they had been in Cairo, Rome, or Capri.

Joe enjoyed himself, but he insisted he was not a "womanizer." In 1975, he told *Playboy* interviewer Sam Merrill, "I would . . . say that my imagination . . . [kept] me from making foolish mistakes." Obviously, Shirley would not have agreed.

WQXR, the classical radio station Joe liked to listen to, started its broadcast days with Aaron Copland's *Fanfare for the Common Man*: a rousing send-off to work (with the children crying in another room).

In Joe's third year at *Time,* the company imposed a salary freeze, marshaling start-up funds for its new publication, *Sports Illustrated.* Employees grumbled; investors worried about company morale. At a sales convention, Joe was asked to set up projection equipment for slide shows to accompany various presentations, including one by Henry Luce. Sternly, the Great Man told his audience "publishing was the business" of the Time-Life Corporation, and he was not going to sacrifice *Sports Illustrated* just to ease investors' fears or soothe the ruffled feathers of his employees.

Piqued, Joe began to search for a higher-paying job. *Look* was delighted to take him in. "A friend from *Time,* Arky Gonzalez, who earlier had left for more money at *Reader's Digest,* cautioned me that things were very different in the rest of the business world from . . . *Time,* and that I might soon miss being there," Joe wrote.

Gonzalez was right. *Look* was not as festive, paternalistic, or forgiving of employees' foibles as *Time.* Its CEOs were obsessively poll-driven, constantly comparing subscription numbers and revenue forecasts. In *Madison Avenue, U.S.A.,* Martin Mayer called *Look* the "most intensely and destructively competitive of the magazines in its space-selling policy," and Joe did not last there more than a year.

In 1959, he moved to *McCall's* to work for a young and vigorous advertising manager named Gilbert Lea. Lea had schemed hard with his editorial department to establish a "feel" for the magazine, a core direction guiding the content of the articles as well as types of ads to accompany them. "Around 1900, it was not unusual for a woman to refer to her husband as The Governor," Lea told Mayer. "Somebody said that if you put men and women together around the turn of the century all you got was children. Today, there's a ninety per cent overlap, a man and his wife share the same life." This statement was questionable, coming from the center of a "male culture" condoning affairs. But Lea insisted Otis Wiese, *McCall's* editor and publisher, meant no irony when he hailed "Togetherness" as the magazine's philosophy. *McCall's* was aimed at a "woman with a family instead of . . . individual [women]."

"The Togetherness theme, implying the existence of children old enough to participate in family decisions (including buying decisions) gave the sales staff a 'feel' to sell, a 'feel' which matched exactly . . . the known audience characteristics of the magazine," Mayer explained. Polls showed women who bought *McCall's* were generally older than average, yet teenage girls also formed a large part of the readership— they saw the magazine in their mothers' houses.

Joe enjoyed exercising his imagination on considerations like these, but he remained frustrated that he had not found the confidence to do what George Mandel had done: finish a novel to satisfy his ambitions. Caught inside a seductive system, he firmly believed, with Mayer, that the "great bulk of advertising is culturally repulsive to anyone with any developed sensitivity. So, of course, are most movies and television shows, most popular music and a surprisingly high proportion of published books. When you come right down to it, there is not a hell of a lot to be said for most of what appears in the magazines."

Joe spent his creative energy spurring mass sales. This meant he could not rise far above the lowest common denominator. Still, like any good adman, he believed he had the ability to change public taste; after all, this is what he was asked to do: persuade, cajole, alter perceptions. "Advertising requires extreme simplification of complicated subjects, and the advertising writer must therefore stretch previously precise words to cover large areas," Mayer wrote: a principle that applied equally well to Joe's evolving concept of a new kind of American novel.

T HE NOVEL, you know," people whispered whenever Joe and
Shirley left a party early.

From the first, Joe had made no secret of his ambitions
beyond the world of advertising. At night, he indulged his literary side. But the novel was not the only experimental kite he flew. In
October 1952, at around the time George Mandel's *Flee the Angry
Strangers* appeared in hardback, Joe signed a contract with Mandel that
stated "the parties"—Joe and his friend—were "mutually desirous of
collaborating in the writing of a play provisionally entitled THE BIRD
IN THE FEVVERBLOOM SUIT—[they are] both member[s] in good
standing of the Dramatist's Guild of the Author's League of America."

A talent agent, Lucy Kroll, took the project on. A former story ana-
lyst for Warner Bros., and a cofounder of the Hollywood Theatre Alliance, Kroll had joined the Sam Jaffe Agency in New York in 1945, then
established her own agency two years later. Among the many distinguished playwrights, artists, actors, and writers she represented in her
career were Horton Foote, Lillian Gish, Martha Graham, James Earl
Jones, and Carl Sandburg.

The two old Coney Island pals drafted their play quickly, but work stalled on it at the revision stage. A throwback to the kinds of short stories Joe had abandoned, "The Bird in the Fevverbloom Suit" takes place in a tenement house "across the street from a railroad yard," among tough-talking children of European immigrants. Harry Karp, "a dour, balding man in his fifties," runs a tailor shop on the tenement's first floor (as did Irving Kaiser's dad in the building Joe lived in as a child). Harry's son-in-law, Mervyn, concocts one impossible business scheme after another. He is stuck with gambling debts. Of Mervyn's various plans, Karp says, "They fold like seersucker once he finds out he's gotta work."

Without exception, the play's women are harpies—"baby" and "doll" to each of the men. At the end, Mervyn appears to straighten up; he tells Kitty, his love, "With you sticking by me, I can only go one way. To the top. Doll, there's no stopping me. . . . You'll see, baby." The audience knows he still leads a secret life.

Joe had rejected such material for stories, and Mandel went nowhere near this sort of thing in his novel. Clearly, "The Bird in the Fevverbloom Suit" was a bid for quick commercial success—too much so. The play was bloated with clichés. Then Mandel received his check for the paperback rights to *Flee the Angry Strangers*. He believed he might be on the verge of serious literary success; his waning enthusiasm for the play departed altogether.

In later years, Joe floated various stories about the origins of his first novel. "There was a terrible sameness about books being published and I almost stopped reading as well as writing," he said. But then something happened. He told one British journalist that "conversations with two friends . . . influenced me. Each of them had been wounded in the war, one of them very seriously"—probably George Mandel. "The first one told some very funny stories about his war experiences, but the second one was unable to understand how any humor could be associated with the horror of war. They didn't know each other and I tried to explain the first one's point of view to the second. He recognized that traditionally there had been lots of graveyard humor, but he could not reconcile it with what he had seen of war. It was after that discussion that the opening of *Catch-22* and many incidents in it came to me."

The Czech writer Arnold Lustig claimed Joe told him at a New York party for Milos Forman in the late 1960s that he couldn't have written *Catch-22* without first reading Jaroslav Hasek's unfinished World War I satire, *The Good Soldier Schweik*. In Hasek's novel, a mad state bureaucracy traps a hapless man. Among other things, he stays in a hospital for malingerers and serves as an orderly for an army chaplain.

But the most common account Joe gave of the hatching of *Catch-22* varied little from what he said to *The Paris Review* in 1974: "I was lying in bed in my four-room apartment on the West Side when suddenly this line came to me: 'It was love at first sight. The first time he saw the chaplain, Someone fell madly in love with him.' I didn't have the name Yossarian. The chaplain wasn't necessarily an army chaplain—he could have been a *prison* chaplain. But as soon as the opening sentence was available, the book began to evolve clearly in my mind—even most of the particulars . . . the tone, the form, many of the characters, including some I eventually couldn't use. All of this took place within an hour and a half. It got me so excited that I did what the cliché says you're supposed to do: I jumped out of bed and paced the floor."

Likely, each of these scenarios is true; they don't contradict one another, and they probably occurred at some stage in the process of imagining the novel (along with rereading Kafka, Waugh, Nabokov, and, most particularly, Céline). But we also know from Whit Burnett's letter to Joe in California that, as early as 1946, he'd been considering a novel about "a flier facing the end of his missions." As a spur to return to fiction, Mandel's success with *Flee the Angry Strangers* can't be overstated. One imagines Joe thinking, If a man who's been shot in the head can write a novel, so can I.

The morning after the opening sentence took shape, he "arrived at work"—at the Merrill Anderson Company—"with my pastry and a container of coffee and a mind brimming with ideas, and immediately in longhand put down on a pad the first chapter of an intended novel," he wrote. The handwritten manuscript totaled about twenty pages. He titled it "Catch-18." The year was 1953.

Joe didn't send "Catch-18" to Lucy Kroll. Her interests lay more in the performing arts than in literature, and besides, Joe saw this new piece as more serious than the play. Back in his short story–writing days, he had corresponded with an editor at *The Atlantic Monthly* named Elizabeth McKee. She had offered to be his first agent. With Mavis McIntosh, McKee founded her own business; in 1953, her agency consisted of McIntosh, Jean Parker Waterbury, and a woman originally hired to do girl Friday work, Candida Donadio.

"The agents were not impressed" with "Catch-18"—in fact, they found the writing incomprehensible—"but [Donadio, the] young assistant there . . . was, and she secured permission to submit [the] chapter to a few publications that regularly published excerpts from 'novels in progress,'" Joe recalled in a 1994 preface to a new edition of *Catch-22*.

"While he was alive[,] Heller tried to suppress that his genius was not recognized instantly, but it was [only] after many, many submissions" that Donadio succeeded in placing the manuscript, says Neil Olson. He worked with Donadio in the 1980s. "She saw something in that wild and crazy, surrealistic, bent-headed humor. When she sent out the manuscript, she kept hearing the same replies over and over again—that this is not writing, this is foolishness."

Joe had known his literary models—especially Céline—were never popular. He began to fear his little experiment could not breathe in the marketplace. But then one day, Donadio received a phone call from Arabel Porter, the executive editor of the biannual literary anthology *New World Writing*, distributed by the New American Library's Mentor Books. She raved about Joe Heller. "Candida, this is completely wonderful, true genius," she said. "I'm buying it."

His confidence buoyed, Joe began to plan a second chapter. He had switched jobs. On five-by-eight-inch Kardex cards taken from the offices of Remington Rand, he scribbled character names and notes. The work went slowly. He turned to the novel mostly at night, and was frequently (often gladly) interrupted by his wife and kids. He did not have it in him to become an aesthetic monk. Despite Audrey Chestney's view that he never went anywhere, he and Shirley "socialized most agreeably," he said: "We mixed easily" with friends. The couple enjoyed their evenings out when baby-sitters were available.

They lived five blocks from Fred and Dolores Karl. Joe and Fred resumed the relationship they'd developed at Penn State. "Joe would call him and say, 'I could go to the library to look something or other up, but I know you know it off the top of your head,'" Dolores recalls. "Fred would be working and he'd say, 'It would do you good to go to the library. Leave me alone!' Joe would call right back and say, 'Come on, come have lunch with me and tell me about this stuff. I know you know it!'"

Often, Dolores and Shirley took walks together, or they'd meet at a store. "'For God's sake, Dolores, what have you got on? That's terrible!'

Shirley would say. And she'd help me," Dolores recalls. "She taught me how to dress."

Dolores's daughter Deborah says, "I grew up with the Heller kids. We were always together at holidays. Joe was fabulous with me and my sister, probably because we weren't his kids. We'd walk out the door after a visit. We weren't his responsibility. He was funny with us. Making jokes constantly. But Shirley was even funnier than he was sometimes. She was hilarious. Striking-looking, with bright red hair. Very smart. Quick Jewish humor. I loved her."

Children weren't supposed to play in the Apthorp courtyard, but "we'd always go over there, anyway, so the kids could be together," Dolores says. "We'd order lunch."

On some nights, the men would watch the kids while Dolores and Shirley went to a movie. Sometimes, the men went out while the women put the children to bed. When both couples could get a baby-sitter, they'd spend the evening together. "Fred didn't want to go to the movies with anyone except me or Joe," Dolores recalls. "He'd say that with anyone else, after the movie, there would always be a long discussion. But with Joe there was none of that. They'd just look at each other, knew whether they liked it or not, and that was it. And Fred liked that."

With the sale of "Catch-18" to *New World Writing,* Joe didn't change his work or social habits—not significantly at least. But occasionally, he'd leave a party early: "The novel, you know."

CANDIDA (pronounced *CAN-dida*) Donadio, Joe's new agent, was twenty-four years old, Brooklyn-born, from a family of Italian immigrants. She rarely spoke about what she implied was a grim Sicilian Catholic upbringing. Short and plump, her black hair in a tight bun, she'd fix her brown eyes on a person she'd just met and startle them with some bawdy remark, delivered in an unusually deep voice. "She had more synonyms for excrement than anyone you'd ever run across," says Cork Smith, Thomas Pynchon's first editor. "[S]he used to say all the time, 'That's caca,'" recalls Victoria Wilson, a senior editor at Knopf.

"People tell a lot of contradictory stories about Candida, and they're all true," Neil Olson told writer Karen Hudes. "I think [she] . . . really was a shy, self-doubting, very smart, very sharp person who was capable of having these operatic explosions. . . . [She'd become] this figure who carried on and pulled her hair and shouted other people down. . . . But these explosions were very seldom directed at anybody, they were just going on inside of her."

She liked to say the primary task of a literary agent was to "polish silver." She claimed she would have loved to have been a Carmelite nun. She smoked and drank heavily, indulged heartily in Italian meals, and disliked having her picture taken.

Perhaps her conflicting currents enabled her to be an intuitive appreciator (as she put it) of truly original writing. In time, her client roster came to include some of the most prominent names in American letters: John Cheever, Jessica Mitford, Philip Roth, Bruce Jay Friedman, Thomas Pynchon, William Gaddis, Robert Stone, Michael Herr, and Peter Matthiessen. "She really was the agent of her generation," Neil Olson said. And "Catch-18" started it all. "It is hard for us to realize now [how perceptive she was] when you look at what a Pynchon and what a Heller was doing," Olson said. "She was looking at these writers in the late fifties and early sixties. People were not writing that way."

Also, the business was tough. Soon after signing Joe, Donadio left McIntosh & McKee and joined Herb Jaffe Associates, a larger agency. Harriet Wasserman, who would one day become a successful agent, was working as a secretary for Jaffe. "Since a secretary was very important, I got paid ninety dollars a week," she recalled. "Candida, since she was only an agent, got . . . seventy-five dollars a week."

She spent most of her time promoting this fellow nobody had ever heard of, Joseph Heller.

ACCORDING TO HER BOSS, Victor Weybright, cofounder and editor in chief of New American Library, Arabel J. Porter was "a Bohemian Quakeress, with inspired eyes and ears which seem to see and hear all the significant manifestations of the literary, dramatic and graphic arts." Initially, she gained editorial experience with Lippincott and Dutton, before working with the Office of War Information. After the war, Weybright hired her to select content and work out royalties for the anthology series *New World Writing*.

New American Library, founded in 1948, had become (along with Pocket Books) one of the largest paperback publishers in the country. In 1951, Weybright proposed to his partners that NAL publish a regular anthology of new writing as a way of attracting fresh talent to the company, finding young writers who might be contracted to publish original books with them. His formal proposal for the series contained a hint of Cold War politics: "[Publishing] a literary and academic journal would naturally give us standing amongst critics, writers, teachers, at home and abroad; and it would, [I am] certain, make a most favorable impression upon the Department of State and other agencies concerned with projecting American culture abroad."

New World Writing would "provide a friendly medium for many of the young writers who have difficulty in finding a market for their work because, in some way or another, they 'break the rules,'" promised NAL. "Avant Garde Means You!" the journal proclaimed. "*Avant Garde* may sound stuffy—but it only means a reconnaissance party—adventurous people who willingly enter uncharted territory."

Weybright gave Arabel Porter free rein with the series; her literary tastes were varied, surprising, and bold. The first issue appeared in April 1952 and featured work by Christopher Isherwood, Flannery O'Connor, Tennessee Williams, Gore Vidal, William Gaddis, Thomas Merton, Shelby Foote, Wright Morris, Howard Nemerov, and James Laughlin. The second issue, on sale in November, offered pieces by James Jones, Norman Mailer, James Baldwin, Shirley Jackson, Dylan Thomas, W. H. Auden, Jean Genet, Theodore Roethke, and Pablo Picasso. Immediately, the series became the "cultural high-water mark for the paperback book during the 1950s," according to Kenneth C. Davis, author of *Two-Bit Culture: The Paperbacking of America. New World Writing* offered "the best and brightest in American letters ever published by a paperback house." Starting with the second issue, NAL established a print run of 150,700 copies every six months. Sales and critical responses were good. Britain's *Times Literary Supplement* observed that *New World Writing* exposed the "difference in quality" between new American and English literature. "The American stories are not only more skillful but in some indefinable way more 'alive,'" the paper said. "The life of a situation, the tang and feeling of it, is presented accurately and vividly."

The series ran until 1959, when competition from literary journals and other anthologies ate into its sales. "[T]he story begins to end," Weybright wrote in the final issue. "New 'little' and literary magazines, edited by young men and women who were still in blue jeans and ponytails

Joseph Heller, Coney Island, circa 1925. *(Courtesy Valerie Heller)*

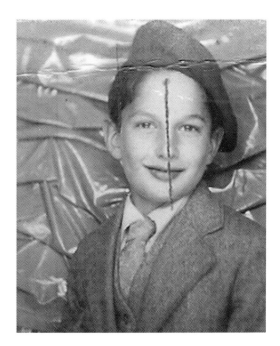

Joe, Coney Island, circa 1930. *(Courtesy Valerie Heller)*

Joe, Coney Island, circa 1930. *(Courtesy Valerie Heller)*

Dreamland at night.
(Photo by Walter G. Levison)

The Thunderbolt roller coaster, Coney Island. *(Photo by Phyllis Bobb)*

Devil, "Dante's Inferno," Coney Island. *(Photo by Phyllis Bobb)*

Joe (center, with hands in pockets) with bomber squadron buddies, Corsica, 1944. *(Photo by Captain Everett B. Thomas; courtesy Dan Setzer)*

Joe with tentmates, Corsica, December 1944. Joe sitting at right, Edward Ritter sitting highest, Bob Vortrees cutting the cake next to Hy Tribble and Emmit Hughes. *(Photo by Captain Everett B. Thomas; courtesy Dan Setzer)*

Tent city, American air base, Corsica, 1944. *(Courtesy Don Kaiser)*

(Courtesy Don Kaiser)

Bomber flying through enemy flak. *(Courtesy Don Kaiser)*

Pont-Saint-Martin, Italy, after being hit by American bombers, including Joe's plane, August 23, 1944. *(Courtesy Don Kaiser)*

Joe in Rome, summer 1966. *(Courtesy Erica Heller)*

Erica and Ted, Fire
Island, mid-1960s.
(Courtesy Erica Heller)

Robert Gottlieb, Joe's
editor on *Catch-22*, in 1973.
(Photo by Nancy Crampton)

Joe and Shirley Heller, early
1970s, in Amagansett.
(Photo by Jill Krementz)

back in 1951 and 1952, are . . . springing up all over the land." Besides, Weybright's interests were shifting to screenplays and bestselling books with potential tie-ins to Hollywood (a phenomenon made possible by the huge sales of cheap paperback editions).

For seven years, *New World Writing* had dazzled the American literary world. In terms of cultural impact, no single issue had been more dazzling—or remains so—than number 7, published in April 1955.

A subheading on the front cover said "A New Adventure in Modern Reading." The contents included work by Dylan Thomas, who had died in November 1953, poetry by A. Alvarez, Thomas Gunn, Donald Hall, and Carlos Drummond de Andrade, prose by Heinrich Böll, and two startling, unclassifiable pieces, one titled "Jazz of the Beat Generation," by a writer called Jean-Louis, and "Catch-18," by Joseph Heller.

Joe knew how valuable the exposure was in *New World Writing*. He wrote to Arabel Porter, "I should like to tell you at this time that it was with great delight and pride that I received news you were interested in publishing a section of *Catch-18*." In fact, it was the only section he had written so far. "[A]nd I should like to express my thanks for the recognition implicit in your decision and the encouragement I received from it."

As for Jean-Louis: This was the nom de plume of a writer long disgusted with his treatment by publishers. He felt *New World Writing* had done "him a great disservice" while editing his piece "by splitting an approximately five-hundred word sentence in two," according to biographer Ellis Amburn.

"Jazz of the Beat Generation" was part of a larger manuscript called *On the Road*. Jack Kerouac was "sick of well-meaning editors who championed his [manuscripts] but returned them with lame notes blaming lack of house support," Amburn wrote. "Then he would see the same editors at the San Remo [bar], and they would fawn on him, thrilled to be in the presence of a bona fide subterranean and pumping him for tips on how to be hip, slick, and cool. One editor . . . even asked him to write a nonfiction guide on how to be 'groovy.' 'You asshole,' Kerouac replied."

Though early versions of *On the Road* and *Catch-22* made their appearances in the same place at the same time, and were later linked in terms of aesthetic and cultural influence, they could not have sprouted from more different sources.

Kerouac's favorite hangout, the San Remo, located at 93 MacDougal Street, on the corner of Bleecker, was a self-proclaimed (self-conscious) den of bohemian, subversive, poetic intellectuals and wannabe Beatniks. Maxwell Bodenheim, a writer who all but lived in the bar, chanting poetry and cadging drinks, called the San Remo a "Coney Island of the soul."

Joe had worked his way out of the poverty of the real Coney Island to earn a spot in the Madison Avenue world and secure a place for his family in a well-appointed apartment building.

Kerouac considered himself literary. Joe projected confidence but worried he was not a natural writer. Kerouac groused about editors too dense to recognize his genius. Joe was grateful to receive encouragement. (As payment, Joe got $125 from NAL, Kerouac $120.)

In the Village, "the booze ran freely and the talk was always funny, sharp, knowing, dealing with what we cared about most—books, magazines and stories, the words and the people who wrote them," Dan Wakefield said. "Nobody talked of advances or royalties or how much money any book or writer made. That was the sort of thing business people talked about, the organization men, the ones in the gray flannel suits . . . [what we] called the Lamb Chop set."

Sitting up on the West Side, Joe Heller was an anomaly: a Beat in "Lamb Chop" clothing, one might say. But that wasn't quite right. More accurately, he was a unique individual, uniquely placed, his position within the Luce organization reminiscent of those of James Agee, Archibald MacLeish, and Dwight Macdonald. At the height of the Depression, these writers managed to fill the pages of *Fortune* with searching (often subversive) social commentary—before Luce purged "poetry" from his pages.

At first, in literary circles, Jean-Louis's "Jazz of the Beat Generation" sparked most of the chatter about *New World Writing* number 7. In San Francisco, Allen Ginsberg told people who Jean-Louis really was, and passed around copies of the journal. Kenneth Rexroth featured Kerouac's piece on a radio broadcast, and compared Kerouac to Jean Genet and Céline.

Meanwhile, Candida Donadio detonated several times because "Catch-18" had not received the traction she expected from its appearance. She talked up Joe to publishers, all of whom seemed baffled by the piece.

Still, the editors at New American Library remained convinced that when all was said and done, number 7's real gem was "Catch-18." "It is certainly the funniest thing we have ever had," Weybright told Arabel Porter. Endorsing the reader's report that first brought the story to her attention, Porter wrote, "Among all the recommended pieces lately, I think this stands out. It seems like part of a really exciting, amusing novel."

"CATCH-18"—only ten pages long in the journal's small print—introduces us to a World War II–era American soldier named Yossarian, in a military hospital "with a pain in his liver that fell just short of being jaundice. The doctors were puzzled by the fact that it wasn't quite jaundice. If it became jaundice they could treat it. If it didn't become jaundice and went away they could discharge him. But this just being short of jaundice all the time only confused them."

Yossarian is happy to be hospitalized, excused from flying bombing missions, and has not told the doctors his liver pain has gone away. He "had made up his mind to spend the rest of the war in the hospital," where the food was "almost palatable, and his meals were brought to him in bed."

Sharing the ward with him are his buddy Dunbar, a man "working hard at increasing his life span . . . by cultivating boredom" (so much so that Yossarian wonders if he is dead), a Texan so likable no one can stand him, and a "soldier in white," who is "encased from head to toe in plaster and gauze." A slim rubber hose attached to his groin conveys his urine to a jar on the floor; another pair of hoses appears to feed him by recycling the piss.

Outside, there is always the "monotonous, old drone of bombers returning from a mission."

One day, Yossarian receives a visit from a chaplain. A chaplain is something he has not seen before: Yossarian loves him "at first sight." "He had seen reverends and rabbis, ministers and mullahs, priests and pairs of nuns. He had seen ordnance officers and quartermaster officers and post exchange officers and other spooky military anomalies. Once he had even seen a justification, but that was a long time before and then it was such a fleeting glimpse that it might easily have been an hallucination."

Yossarian speaks to the chaplain—a slapstick and meaningless dialogue. Eventually, the Texan's friendliness drives his comrades batty. They clear out of the ward and return to duty. That's the story.

The charm and energy of the piece, its originality, lay in its playful language: There is a "vortex of specialists" swirling through the ward; a patient has "a urologist for his urine, a lymphologist for his lymph, an endocrinologist for his endocrines, a psychologist for his psyche, a dermatologist for his derma . . . [and] a pathologist for his pathos. . . ."

"Catch-18"—an arbitrary phrase—is a rule requiring officers who censor enlisted men's letters to sign their names to the pages. In the hospital, Yossarian, a low-level officer, spends his days editing letters and signing them, out of boredom and glee, "Washington Irving" or "Irving Washington." Instead of deleting sensitive information, he declares *"Death to all modifiers."* He scratches out adjectives and adverbs or, "reach[ing] a much higher plane of creativity," attacks everything but articles. *A, an,* and *the* remain on the page. Everything else, he tosses. At one point, the army sends an undercover man into the ward. He poses as a patient. His job is to suss out the prankster. In the end, he catches pneumonia, and is the only one left in the hospital when the others leave.

Readers who could not appreciate wordplay didn't cotton to the piece. What was the story's point? What did it say about war? Those who understood, from Yossarian's business with the letters, that instead of war, it was about the limitations and misuse of language (which foments disasters like medical malpractice and armed conflict) entered into the spirit of "Catch-18."

"I'm not that interested in the subject of war," Joe told the *New York Times*—somewhat coyly—in 1968. "I was [more] interested in personal relationships to bureaucratic authority." The second statement rings truer than the first. In any case, paramount to Joe in developing the material that became *Catch-22* was "seek[ing] a way of telling a story that [was] different from the mere narration of the events of history," something more like "an act of the imagination." In other words, he had shifted the emphasis in his writing from the story to the way the story was told. *The act of telling* became the point of the fiction.

He highlighted structure (music, rhythm, repetition), violated chronology, and played with language, making puns and setting up sophisticated verbal ironies (swift shifts in register from the comic to the tragic). Joe's first breakthrough of this sort had come in "Castle of Snow," with its retrospective narrator. The possibilities for tonal nuance were broad when placed in the voice of someone speaking through clashing emotions, repression, and misunderstandings.

In "Castle of Snow," the narrator recorded "history." In Joe's developing work, reporting gave way to performance—thus, the freer, longer sentences, the deliberate inconsistencies of tone, the indulgence in humor. Joe's weakness—his relative lack of detail—was no longer an issue. The energy came not from descriptions, but from gleeful mental leaps ("He had seen reverends and rabbis . . . Once he had even seen a justification . . .").

Joe's old fear that his war experiences were not enough meat for a novel—or that the moment for World War II fiction had passed—no longer mattered. War was not his primary subject. It was a pretext for verbal pyrotechnics and social critique (the extent of which would not be apparent until the novel appeared, years later).

He had been liberated by his evolving conviction that "literature, except for a brief period in recent history—and that was a really brief period—has never been realistic. Starting with the Greeks and moving through the Renaissance to the present, there seems to me only a period of twenty or thirty years in which realistic literature was strong. 'Realism' began in the nineteenth century . . . [and started] trailing off [around] World War II. . . . Apart from that time, literature has always been larger than life, romantic, imaginative. And this impulse of writers is, I think, essentially sound."

Furthermore, he insisted, "[A]ny writer who doesn't regard his work, his writing, as being a form of art, comparable, let's say, to architecture, painting, or sculpture, is probably not serious. There must be attention given to form. . . . The writer must figure out the form a specific work needs to take."

These beliefs, and their freeing effects, had resulted from the reading he had done. A reader of "Catch-18" who had known Joe's earlier stories could probably not identify his new influences. *The Good Soldier Schweik* was not well known in the United States; besides, the novel's deflationary humor ("Schweik . . . intervened in the World War in that pleasant, amiable manner which was so peculiarly his"—that is, by utter accident) was a staple now of the Jewish humor on nightly television shows. The echoes of Céline in Joe's prose would not be fully heard until *Catch-22*.

Joe was a better reader now, as well as being a better writer. He did not just imitate his new models. In a sense, his earlier stories were reflections on reading: what it meant to absorb Hemingway or William Saroyan. By contrast, "Catch-18" pulsed with antic high energy—the rhythms of Joe's metabolism, mental and physical. It had a tone all its own: not the grumbling misanthropy of Céline, but the lighthearted skepticism of Joe Heller. And beneath the wordplay, it had the gravity of lived experience. The kindly Texan who drove everyone crazy was every other pilot Joe had met at Goodfellow Field. The notion of writing about a chaplain (the freedom to do so) may have been suggested by the character of the military chaplain in *The Good Soldier Schweik*. But the boy in "Catch-18," with his "smooth tan hair and brown, uncomfortable eyes . . . [his] innocent nest of ancient pimple pricks . . . in the basin of each cheek," was clearly based on the shy, pimple-faced chaplain of the 340th Bombardment Group, James H. Cooper. Most importantly, the sense of being trapped in a system that could not withstand scrutiny, and the attempt to survive with a certain brand of verbal humor, was entirely Joe's—though, again, the idea of exploring it (the *permission* to do so, the examples that said, It's okay to write about this) came to him from Kafka, Waugh, and Nabokov.

Someone who had followed Joseph Heller's career from his first appearances in *Esquire* and *The Atlantic Monthly* to the appearance, now, of "Catch-18" would certainly have been baffled and surprised by the change in his work. The reasons for the change, and the paths to it—the intensive study, the confronting of doubts, the hard, slow work—would not be readily apparent. What *would* be obvious were Joe's rejection of straightforward narrative structure and the crimped, simple style of the previous decade's magazine fiction. Moreover, a discerning reader would see how shifts in structure and style indicated a more fundamental change, a radical new view of the subjects at hand: war, faith, heroism, and language. As the writer Pete Hamill would say many years later, "Joseph Heller . . . did more to debunk the Hemingway myth than any critic." Already, with "Catch-18," this movement toward a fresh American fiction was clear.

A YEAR WOULD PASS before Joe finished drafting a second chapter of his novel. He was working for *Time* now. At home and at work, the index cards piled up. Very early, Joe imagined most of the major characters in the novel, and devoted cards to them, with detailed notes about their backgrounds, characteristics, and fates. He outlined each potential chapter, and studiously cataloged each mission he had flown during the war, intending to use the missions as structural elements in the story.

"Joe started talking [to me] about [this] novel he was writing," Frederick Karl recalled. "It was hard to grasp what it was because he seemed more concerned with filing, sorting, indexing than with writing."

Dolores agreed. "We used to tease him that he was creating a filing system, not writing a novel. He had drawers and drawers full of file cards. He was very organized." In her various part-time clerical jobs downtown, Dolores encountered early versions of computers. Her descriptions of them fascinated Joe. He "wanted to discuss what she did and how it all worked," Frederick Karl said. "Somehow, this was connected to his novel, whatever that was."

In *Catch-22*, IBM punch cards are emblematic of a failed bureaucracy, in the messes they create (they are anachronistic, as well, signaling Joe's swerve from literary realism and adding to the story's absurdity).

"The novel began to assume primary importance" in Joe's life, Karl said. "Amidst all the . . . sorting and indexing [of the] file cards, something was emerging."

Ideas rejected. Structure shuffled. Small changes: eventually, a character named Aarky was re-christened Aarfy. Bigger changes: the entrepreneurial soldier, Milo Minderbinder, "exposed" as a ruthless, moneymaking crook in an early vision of the novel, developed into a more nuanced figure, amoral rather than simply villainous. Metaphysical considerations: "Yossarian is dying, true, but he has about 35 years to live." How thick to make the irony? "[Yossarian] really does have liver trouble. Condition is malignant & would have killed him if it had not been discovered"—a thought soon tossed.

"Big Brother has been watching Yossarian," said one card: a controlling idea that remains implicit, rather than explicit, in the final product. Joe axed a potential narrative thread in which Yossarian and Dunbar try to write a parody of a Hemingway war novel.

Joe always knew Snowden's death, on the mission to Avignon, would be the novel's central scene, and that it would be glimpsed in fragments until its full horror was finally revealed.

Also, early on, he developed the catch. In *New World Writing*, "Catch-18" is a regulation about censoring letters. With his index cards, Joe began to shade the idea into something grand enough to support a novel thematically. One card read, "Anyone who wants to be grounded can't be crazy."

In addition to honing themes, Joe polished his expressions of them. An early note had Yossarian "fight[ing] for [his] identity without sacrificing moral responsibility." Subsequent notes refined the wording, and thus the idea, complicating it: In the finished novel, Yossarian says, "I'm not running away from my responsibilities. I'm running to them."

"WE DISCUSSED his novel-in-the-making," said Frederick Karl, "until one day Joe pushed about seventy pages on me and wondered if I would read it. He didn't insist but I felt obliged." (Earlier, Joe had read the manuscript of a war novel Karl had drafted. It was called *The Quest*, and Joe told his friend honestly that he didn't think it was very good and that he should stick to literary criticism.) Joe's novel was "then called *Catch-18*. What I read was stream-of-consciousness, Joycean, [an] interrupted and free-associational narrative, if one could even find the narrative. It was arty, crafty, and difficult. In some ways, brilliant— inconceivable as a trade book, something that perhaps [the avant-garde publisher] New Directions might be interested in. It was almost incoherent, but the academic in me experienced a thrill. Joe's story line, such as it was, was [full of] experimentation with language. I saw something exciting there, told Joe, and also told him no one would read it."

Candida Donadio was getting similar reactions from editors and publishers. Joe packaged a thirty-nine page episode called "Hungry Joe," which she sent to Arabel Porter for another issue of *New World Writing*. Porter rejected it, though she asked, "Has he finished the novel, and if so, may we see it?"

Rust Hills, *Esquire*'s fiction editor, refused the same excerpt: "Too many loose ends," he said. However, he found parts of it "quite funny," and said, "If Heller wants to work any more on this, I guarantee him a sympathetic reading here; but, at this point, that is all I can guarantee him." The manuscript Donadio sent *Esquire* was terribly sloppy, which didn't help. It was shot through with scribbles and penciled changes in Joe's hand. The first line—typed—read, "Hungry Joe had fifty missions, but it did him no good at all." This was crossed out and replaced with a longhand sentence: "Hungry Joe had finished flying fifty combat missions and was waiting to go home, but that did him no good at all."

Lack of confidence and frequent loss of control screamed from every page. Donadio's dissemination of an unclean copy spoke of her blind loyalty to—and belief in—Joe, a trait she exhibited with all her clients.

Joe kept fiddling with the cards. "[Advertising work] helped me write *Catch-22,*" he told radio interviewer Don Swaim many years later. The novel was full of "[sudden] transitions and unexpected introductions [of material] . . . the unpredictable . . . [so] I felt there was a similarity between writing *Catch-22* and the work I was called upon to do in the daytime. What promotion and advertising is supposed to do, if it's done well—it should [have] some catchy, snappy, unexpected opening. I would bring as much imagination and intelligence . . . [to] my daily work . . . as I would to *Catch-22* in the evening."

He strove for greater precision, clarity, punch. The basics: more action verbs, no ambiguous pronouns, fewer adjectives and adverbs; drop the coyness: A "modest maiden" became a "prostitute in Rome."

ON SOME WEEKENDS, Joe took a break from the novel and went to Coney Island to visit his mother. Lena was not in good health. A strangulated hernia had led to emergency surgery. Doctors discovered she was diabetic. Severely weakened after the operation, she decided she could no longer live on her own. She left the old apartment and moved into the Hebrew Home for the Aged on West Twenty-ninth Street at the boardwalk. The home had once been the grand Half Moon Hotel, the construction of which Joe had watched as a kid.

Now, Lena whiled away her hours in the peeling old structure, which Joe found "somber . . . an apt symbol for the . . . faltering Island itself, which had certainly seen more vital days." He felt guilty for not asking her to move into the Apthorp with his family, but he didn't have room (or, truth to tell, time and patience to care for her). Sylvia and Lee also rented cramped apartments, and worked hard each day. Lena knew it wasn't possible to live with one of them, "didn't expect it to happen, and . . . didn't ask." Not for the first time, Joe regretted—but with some relief—that his "family . . . did not . . . talk about sad things."

LIKE HIS BROTHER AND SISTER, many of Joe's friends were beginning to make the move from Coney Island. Development in Levittown, on Long Island, on what had once been rolling farmland, drew young families with promises of cheap housing, modest down payments, and low-interest financing. Escape to the suburbs signaled a desire for betterment (or so the advertisers claimed). Lou Berkman had moved his plumbing business to Middletown, New York. Beansy Winkler had relocated to Ocean Parkway.

Certain areas of Brooklyn, particularly Brownsville, remained largely unchanged, at least for a while, but the toughness of that neighborhood— the poverty, gangs, and anti-Semitism (despite large Orthodox Jewish populations)—developed a resilience of character in some people that drove them toward "betterment" in wealthy, optimistic postwar America. Their drive was beginning to alter popular culture, and Joe would soon know many of the people responsible for the changes.

Daniel Kaminsky, later known as Danny Kaye, was a Brownsville product. He migrated to the Catskills, refined his showbiz chops in resort hotels, and took those talents to the new medium of television (where people like Norman Barasch, soon to be Joe's good friend, wrote for him). Mel Brooks, Zero Mostel, and Phil Silvers came from Brownsville. So did Jerry Lewis, Jerry Stiller, and Alfred Kazin.

In Brownsville, two teenaged friends, Eli Katz and Norman Podhoretz, drew a comic strip together called "Night Hawk." As an adult, Katz changed his name to Gil Kane and created the comic-book heroes the Atom and the Green Lantern. Podhoretz would edit *Commentary* and become a leading figure in the neoconservative political movement (over which he and Joe would have a severe falling-out). "America's junk culture can be found in superhero comic books, its high culture in magazines such as . . . *Commentary*," observes the writer Jeet Heer. Yet "comics and intellectual journals are often created by remarkably similar people." Podhoretz and Kane "were both following common patterns of their generation. Like so many other immigrant Jews, they were benefiting from the opening up of American culture that started in the 1920s and accelerated after the Second World War. . . . [In particular] the cultural industries . . . became open to outsiders, whether they were intellectuals or cartoonists. . . . Having made the difficult journey from Brooklyn to Manhattan, they were ready to enjoy the full blessings of American success."

In the 1960s and 1970s, the blurring of High and Low would characterize American art and entertainment—from the visual arts (Andy

Warhol, Robert Rauschenberg) to the movies (Mike Nichols, Francis Ford Coppola); from the comics (R. Crumb, Charles Schultz) to literature (exhibit A: *Catch-22*). Critics have attributed this development to many causes: the easy availability of paperbacks (Jane Austen consorting on bookshelves with Mickey Spillane), tabloids, and television programming; technological advances (silk screening, photographic manipulation); and advertising, with its hunger for co-opting original ideas to spur mass sales. But Heer is also right: Much of the energy behind this mixing of cultural products, aims, and ambitions came from the drive for integration by groups of people seizing opportunities formerly denied them.

Not surprisingly, individuals who held privileged social positions, and shaped *their* ideas of culture around them, fought change. On July 17, 1955—shortly after the appearance of "Catch-18" in *New World Writing*—Disneyland opened in Anaheim, California. If "Catch-18" was part of the trend toward *blurring,* bringing with it new ideas of art, literature, and entertainment, Disneyland (in spite of its technical dazzle and television promotions) was part of the resistance to change, a wistful attempt at preserving "old" culture.

Originally, Disney, a son of the rural Midwest, had intended to call Disneyland "Walt Disney's America." *His* America was not Joe Heller's. In fact, according to Raymond M. Weinstein, a scholar of modern culture, "Walt Disney had an intense dislike for Coney Island and what he thought it represented—dirty, disorganized . . . garish." It wasn't the amusement rides Disney objected to; his revulsion seemed tied to something deeper—perhaps the ethnic mix, the noisy clash of immigrant voices and styles?

"Disneyland [was] the embodiment of one man's prepossession toward America's most important beliefs, values, and symbols [rooted in] . . . his boyhood experiences in the . . . Midwest," Weinstein wrote. In its cleanliness, logical organization (its perfection of park administration), and old-fashioned Main Street atmosphere, it would be the anti–Coney Island. "Disney understood well the mood of the 1950s—with its bomb threats, Cold War, domestic paranoia, foreign conflicts," Weinstein said. "[H]is brand of amusement played into everyone's desire to go back to their childhood and the childhood of the nation."

Well, not everyone's—as the disruptive energy in the pages of *The Green Lantern, Commentary,* and *New World Writing* demonstrated.

JOE KNEW it was no exaggeration to say that in the pages of comic books, journals, and magazines, a war was being waged for America's soul. Superman had gone from fighting corporate greed to battling Nazis—now, in this era of atomic-bomb threats and rumors of UFOs, he fended off invaders from darkening skies. However ridiculous these scenarios seemed, they offered debates on threats to the nation and what to do about them.

Similar considerations filled *Commentary* and other journals. For example, as early as 1952, a prominent member of *Commentary*'s editorial staff, Irving Kristol, wrestled his conscience and broke with his fellow staffers' liberal views. He wrote that Joe McCarthy was certainly a threat to the nation's political integrity, but a bigger problem was the Left's refusal to disavow communism. The Left's dithering, he said, gave McCarthy ammunition. Kristol's colleagues fired back, accusing him in print of defending McCarthyism. The battle for the nation's soul—not to mention *Commentary*'s—intensified.

Meanwhile, inside Henry Luce's empire, where Joe was safely ensconced, the arguments centered on corporate culture, corporate responsibilities. *Fortune* and *Time,* reflecting Luce's belief that America must *own* the century, insisted corporate leaders had to do more than earn profits; they had to forge in America a "business civilization" in which financial values shaped everything from arts and entertainment to architecture to the nation's infrastructure to the behavior of families. Capitalism had to have a moral basis.

What did this mean? Luce summed it up in practical terms: "I am biased in favor of God, Eisenhower, and the stockholders of Time Inc." He promoted a certain image of American masculinity. *Time* and *Life* ran numerous articles on Billy Graham's increasingly popular Christian crusades, describing Graham as lean, blond, and handsome. Besides his physical attributes, a large part of what made Graham so attractive, said Luce, was the businesslike efficiency of his religious operation. When Graham went to New York City in the summer of 1957 for a series of rallies, he surrounded himself at news conferences with elite male business figures, including William Randolph Hearst, Jr., and Henry Luce. In Yankee Stadium, on July 20, Vice President Richard Nixon appeared at his rally. The stadium was an appropriate venue, not just for accommodating the crowd but also for stressing Graham's athleticism and love of sports, part of his all-American image. Sports metaphors leavened his sermons. "Christianity is not a religion for weaklings," he asserted. "We must be strong, virile, dynamic, if we are to stand."

What role did women play in this mix of bodybuilding, business, and faith? "I never talk alone with a woman," Graham told an interviewer. Fervently, he avoided "lovesick women [and] bobby soxers" (as the interviewer put it). The American soul demanded sexual vigilance. Luce, praying each morning in his private elevator, agreed.

Next to *Time* on the newsstands, competing views of masculinity waved their muscular pages, including the pulp version with postwar variations. "In wartime the Armed Services taught soldiers how to fight enemies, but [back home], working-class soldiers depended upon the mass-market magazines for their civilian life-lessons," wrote Adam Parfrey, editor of *It's a Man's World: Men's Adventure Magazines, the Postwar Pulps.* "All of them had, among the lures of woman flesh and vicious bad guys, a lot of warnings, how-to's, and comforting memories of wartime, when decisions were black and white, the villains darker and the victories sweeter."

Bruce Jay Friedman went to work for Martin Goodman's Magazine Management Company in 1954, after a stint in Korea. Racism, misogyny, and imperialism were "just the way things were" in titles such as *Male, Stag,* and *True Action*—known in the trade as "armpit" publications, he said. "We didn't think twice about it": This *was* blue-collar manhood.

The magazines printed the word *nympho* every chance they got. In addition to "girl pinching" pieces, a staple of the postwar pulps was "true" stories about battlefield heroism. Friedman would show Goodman a layout. "This one true?" Goodman asked. "Well, sort of," Friedman replied. His boss nodded happily.

One day, Friedman hired a young writer named Mario Puzo, a big man who loved a good drink and a fine cigar. Puzo "would create giant mythical armies, lock them in combat in Central Europe, and have casualties coming in by the hundreds of thousands," Friedman said. "Although our mail was heavy, I don't recall a single letter casting doubt on any of these epic conflicts." After work each day, Puzo pounded away on a novel, a "Mafia epic," he said.

Other regular features in the men's magazines included "Animal Nibbler" stories, "about people who had been nibbled half to death by ferocious little animals," Friedman explained. "The titles were terrifying cries of anguish. 'A Grysbok Sucked My Bones'; 'Give Me Back My Leg'; they seemed to have even more power when couched in the present . . . tense. 'A Boar Is Grabbing My Brain.'"

"Sintown" stories were a hit with readers. "I always thought [of them] as 'scratch the surface' yarns," Friedman said. "(Outwardly, Winkleton, Illinois, is a quiet, tree-lined little community. . . . But scratch the surface of this supposedly God-fearing little town and you will find that not since Sodom and Gomorrah and blah blah blah.) Any town with a bar and a hooker would do."

Even here, amid the puerility, soul struggles evolved. As Cold War dustups frayed the country's nerves, and cracks began to appear in suburbia's blissful pavement, previously suppressed fantasies crept into the men's magazines. They took the form of "Leg Shackler" stories: "Slaves of the Emperor of Agony," "Savage Rites of the Whip," "Tormented Love." As Parfrey noted, "Damsels [had] been distressed since the turn of the century in pulps, but nearly always the illustrations suggested that a hero was nearby, and his rescue pending." More and more, "heroes came to play an increasingly minor role in illustrations until [they were] completely phased out." Apparently, readers of these magazines came to believe that "saving women from torture was [no longer] on any level heroic." This growing trend would reach its peak in the mid-1960s, Parfrey said, at "the time of the Vietnam War's escalation and the emergence of feminism."

Skirmishes over manhood, politics, or corporate behavior might have been restricted to small pockets of readers here and there, given the specialized nature of magazines. But the tensions escaped their stapled spines. The term *culture war* would not achieve currency until decades later, but a culture war this was.

In 1954, Dr. Fredric Wertham published a book called *Seduction of the Innocent,* in which he claimed comic books and men's magazines were spreading an epidemic of juvenile delinquency and homosexuality among the nation's youth. His supporters boycotted newsstands and burned comic books. Writing in *Commentary,* Norbert Muhlen cursed the "dehumanized" and "repetitious" stories of "death and destruction" in comics, which were "helping to educate a whole generation for an authoritarian rather than a democratic society." With little change, his words could have served a leg-shackling Nazi, but the U.S. Congress became concerned enough (or alert enough to an issue worth exploiting politically—it was certainly easier to face this than Joe McCarthy) to threaten government censorship of comics. In response, William Gaines, publisher of Educational Comics, and his business manager, Lyle Stuart, created the Comics Magazines Association of America, a self-regulatory agency set up to administer a code—a stamp of approval guaranteeing "wholesome, entertaining and educational" contents. Any title that didn't comply would face distribution hurdles. This move was meant to stave off harsher regulation by the government.

Gaines's company published *Tales from the Crypt, Weird Fantasy, The Vault of Horror,* and a relatively new title (from October 1952), written and edited by a man named Harvey Kurtzman: *Tales Calculated to Drive You MAD: Humor in a Jugular Vein.*

"Of course, we had the big problem: could we ever live under the censorship of the Comics Code?" Kurtzman said. "We decided, absolutely *no.* We could not go on as a comic book." Thus, *Mad* was born. Technically, by shifting from hand lettering to set type, the publication became a magazine instead of a comic. It was not bound by the strict new code.

Restrictions on magazine content were lighter (not to say ambiguous and paradoxical). "[B]oys were allowed to purchase [men's] magazines that promoted wholesale violence against an entire gender, while *Playboy*-style girlie mags that revered women and their bodies were considered unfit material for underage [readers]," Adam Parfrey wrote. (*Playboy* debuted in December 1953.)

"In many ways *Mad* represented a group of alternative New York Jewish intellectuals," says critic David Abrams. "[M]any of *Mad*'s staff were Jewish, either native New Yorkers or émigrés from Europe, a high proportion of them survivors of Nazi Germany. Like the New York intellectual milieu, many of them had come to political awareness during the Depression."

Yiddish phrases stippled the magazine's pages. By 1967, theologian Vernard Eller could say, "Beneath the pile of garbage that is *Mad*, there beats, I suspect, the heart of a rabbi." Abrams contends that "*Mad*'s critique of America was far more effective and devastating than [its] better-known counterparts . . . such as *Commentary, Dissent, Partisan Review,* and *The New Leader.*" This was so, he says, because the intellectual journals were constrained by their sponsoring organizations (in

Commentary's case, the powerful American Jewish Committee) or editors' ideologies. "[W]e like to say that *Mad* has no politics and that we take no point of view," Gaines once said, but "the magazine is more liberal than not liberal."

Abrams may overstate *Mad*'s intellectual rigor, but he is right to call attention to its growing influence during the 1950s and 1960s. Its highly visible political satire, scored to Borscht Belt rhythms, perhaps eased the way for Mort Sahl, Lenny Bruce, and Joseph Heller, or helped them gain greater acceptance. Politics and punning, smarts and snappy play—the High and the Low—had embraced.

Mad carried no advertising (ironic, given the location of its offices on Madison Avenue). Among its favorite targets for satire were ad agencies—"the essence of *Mad*'s success is its nimble spoofing of promotions of all kinds," *Time* noted in 1958. The Disney Corporation came under fire (Mickey Mouse as a rat-faced thug). Joseph McCarthy didn't escape: "Is Your Bathroom Breeding Bolsheviks?" asked one of the magazine's fake ads.

Predictably, *Mad* spawned a backlash from the intellectual set. In *The New Yorker*, Dwight Macdonald wrote, "*Mad* expresses . . . teenagers' cynicism about the world of mass media that their elders have created—so full of hypocrisy and pretense governed by formulas. But *Mad* itself has a formula. It speaks the same language, aesthetically and morally, as the media it satirizes; it is as tasteless as they are, and more violent." *Mad*'s critiques took the form of their targets. Indecipherability, relativism, what critics would soon call "postmodernism" had crept into mass culture. What could Superman—or Lionel Trilling—do about *that*?

The truth is, the mixture of High and Low had already made enough mud to cause a landslide. Mike Hammer was Superman in a trench coat, with a couple of shots of whiskey under his belt. *Mad* was *Commentary* with its thumbs in its ears (and boy, did Alfred E. Neuman have ears!). Books were masquerading as comics. Publishers were no longer predictable: New American Library, disseminator of cutting-edge, avant-garde pieces in *New World Writing,* also gave us Mickey Spillane. To date, the country's biggest-selling paperback was Dr. Benjamin Spock's *The Pocket Book of Baby and Child Care* (it first appeared in June 1946). As Kenneth C. Davis wrote, "Paperback books and the baby boomers were made for each other": a "mass medium for a mass generation."

JOE KEPT TRACK of these trends: They were useful for his writing, in the daytime and at night. He roamed bookstores. Since *The Naked and the Dead* and *From Here to Eternity,* the American novel had taken a few intriguing twists. Norman Mailer had followed his war epic with a "political and ideological novel" that was a "dismal . . . failure," according to *Commentary. Barbary Shore,* published in 1951, attempted to transcend the naturalism that had made the earlier novel so old-fashioned. But Mailer's heart wasn't in the ideas or vaguely modernist style he'd adopted to try to please the intellectuals who'd dismissed him. Still, *Barbary Shore* gave "abundant indications of Mailer's talents . . . [and] stubborn integrity," *Commentary* averred. He remained a writer to watch.

Meanwhile, Saul Bellow had fashioned an expansive new style. While structurally familiar (a more or less straightforward first-person narrative), his latest novel leapt with the energies of American idioms more zestily than any writer's work since Mark Twain's. "One senses the joy with which Mr. Bellow breathes the freer air; he writes like a man set loose from prison," Norman Podhoretz said in a review of *The Adventures of Augie March* in October 1953. Whereas Twain had limned black dialects, Bellow drew upon Jewish-American rhythms and quirks, announcing major shifts in America's postwar cultural mix.

In 1955, William Gaddis published an immense novel called *The Recognitions,* all about plagiarism, forgeries, and counterfeiting, themes that made it, in Frederick Karl's view, "*the* novel of the fifties." As in the national discourse, disseminated through popular media, "[l]ayers of untruth" comprised the novel; beneath the lies, "somewhere, [lay] the real," Karl wrote. "[C]old war, pinkos, left-winger, Red China, McCarthyism, Hiss, Rosenbergs, liberal intellectual, egghead . . . labels [became] a kind of totem [in the fifties]. . . . We demeaned every experience and every response by means of a reductive vocabulary which transmitted only the artificial." In capturing this glutted, mediated atmosphere, *The Recognitions* became "our archetypal experience for the fifties, a model . . . for the way in which we saw and will continue to see ourselves," Karl said.

In conversations with Karl, Joe learned of other young writers to watch: James Baldwin, J. D. Salinger, Ralph Ellison, Grace Paley. American writers were stirring, trying to get their arms around this rough, slouching beast, the modern world.

Joe grew increasingly frustrated, although he tried to be patient, with his slow pace as a writer. His process—indexing, sorting, cross-referencing, reshuffling—was deliberate and fruitful, but it did not buzz with the excitement of the immediate dispatch. And the culture was shifting so fast!

Just as James Jones had surged ahead of him after their appearance in *The Atlantic Monthly,* now Jack Kerouac had jumped out of *New World Writing* with his novel. It was all the rage. *On the Road* appeared in 1957. Kerouac gave readings at the Vanguard, a popular jazz club in the Village, to the accompaniment of saxophone and drums. Dan Wakefield remembered going to see him one night: "[H]e was drunk by the time he appeared on stage, dropping the papers he was trying to read from, slurring his words, swaying back and forth not in time to the rhythm of the music but simply as a man does when he is trying not to fall down." Wakefield felt that "Kerouac was not only giving our generation a bad name . . . but by his antics he was also—a worse crime—giving writing and writers in general a bad name . . . playing right into the hands of the enemy—Time Inc.—giving them fodder for reams of copy decrying youth, writers, artists, iconoclasts, rebels."

Over in the enemy camp, Joe felt the same way. But he also had two kids to clothe and feed, clients to please, and many seductive perks it would be silly to ignore. His writing continued to crawl.

ONE EVENING in the winter of 1956, in a fourth-floor apartment in a brownstone on Fifty-eighth Street behind the Plaza Hotel, the Magazine Management staff threw a party. Present were Bruce Jay Friedman and his wife, Ginger, Mario Puzo, Martin Goodman, Stan Lee (in charge of the company's comic-book division), and a young man named David Markson, then working on his first novel, *The Ballad of Dingus Magee.* Also laughing and flitting about the rooms was Alice Denham, a young Floridian with literary ambitions who had come to New York to meet writers. She had hung around the San Remo with James Baldwin. She had flirted with Norman Mailer and had a fling with James Jones. While trying to write, she earned a living as a photographer's model (she was that year's "Playmate of the Year" in *Playboy* magazine).

A day or two before the party, she went to the "Mag Man" studios at 655 Madison Avenue for a photo shoot. One of the men's magazines planned a spread called "Girl Gun Runners of Saigon." A makeup artist gave her an Asian look. She posed in an open-necked shirt, showing plenty of cleavage, while cocking a rifle and gripping a pistol. She asked a young editor whether there *really* were girl gun runners in Saigon. "Please, Alice," he said, "this is *True Adventures*. We make it up."

In 2006, Denham published a memoir entitled *Sleeping with Bad Boys*. Despite its lurid title and steamy prose style, its fidelity to facts was confirmed by David Markson and Adele Mailer (Norman's wife in 1956), neither of whom came off particularly well in the book.

The night of the Mag Man party, Denham wrote, Joe Heller arrived with his "curvy" wife, Shirley. Joe was "everybody's buddy," Denham said. She was genuinely fond of him, but she perceived that his "wife did everything [for him]." According to her, he "didn't have to pick up a plate or his underwear. [Maybe] [o]ccasionally pat a child on the head."

Joe knew of Denham's literary ambitions. He said to her, "Let me introduce you to my agent, Candida." Donadio represented many of the fellows laboring as "editorial slaves" at Magazine Management. She was sitting on a sofa in the middle of the room. She "was dark, melancholic, haunted, and overweight," Denham wrote. "She did not move from the . . . sofa . . . where she received supplicants." Joe introduced Denham. "[Alice is] working on a novel you might take a look at," he suggested. According to Denham, the "dark lady . . . looked me over, glared at me . . . and refused to acknowledge my presence." Joe grabbed Denham's arm and pulled her away.

"What did I do?" she asked.

"She doesn't like good-looking women," Joe said. "I should've known."

Bruce Jay Friedman, who had witnessed the incident, assured Denham that Donadio wouldn't speak to his wife, Ginger, either.

Joe sighed. "Well, so much for the mother of us all," he said.

SUMMERS, Joe and Shirley rented a place on Fire Island. "I loved it there (no cars at all, fresh air, very walkable)," Ted Heller recalls. While the kids played on the beach, Joe worked on his novel. An outer landmass off Long Island's south shore, Fire Island provided a popular summer escape for New York City's middle-class and wealthy families, as well as for many artists. Truman Capote was rumored to have written *Breakfast at Tiffany's* there. Occasionally, W. H. Auden could be spotted beachside, along with Carson McCullers, Janet Flanner, and Jane Bowles. Earl Hamner, Jr., whose novel *Spencer's Mountain* would later serve as the basis for the long-running television series *The Waltons*, rented a house next to the Hellers'. Not far from them—but unknown to them at the time—the young TV writer Mel Brooks often took a place near his pal Carl Reiner.

Joe's job transitions—to *Look* and *McCall's*—played hell with his writing schedule. When he made the move to *McCall's*, he was required to take a series of psychological evaluations before his appointment could be confirmed (New York had *fallen* for European-style psycho-analysis).

At the company's request, he spent nearly two days in a midtown office submitting to questions on Rorschach and Thematic Appercep-tion tests administered by two Columbia University professors. In the TAT drawings, Joe saw only a mother holding her son. An overwhelm-ing sadness overcame him. In the color-card tests, he pictured blood and amputated limbs. "[I] was . . . catapulted into a state of startled confusion and silence," he recalled. In discussions with one of the pro-fessors, he mentioned he was working on a novel. Oh, what's it about? the man asked. "That question still makes me squirm," Joe wrote nearly forty years later. "[I]t was only then, in trying to talk about [the novel] coherently, that I realized . . . how extensively I was focusing on the grim details of human mortality, on disease, accidents, grotesque muti-lations," he wrote.

Earlier, he had applied for a life-insurance policy (his first) for his wife and kids. He was asked to list his father's cause of death on the application form. Joe paused, pen in hand. He didn't know. In all these years, he had never bothered to find out. He had not wanted to think about it. He called Sylvia to ask but didn't press for details.

"CRITICS AND PUBLISHERS . . . have . . . been calling for a new voice, a literary prophet capable of creating a meaningful form out of the con-flicting elements in the world we know," Arabel Porter had written in the publisher's note for the issue of *New World Writing* in which Joe's work appeared. "The editors . . . cannot now point to any one writer who has, so far, achieved the stature so urgently demanded. And yet, the writers themselves—or the best of them—continue to work with spirit, in their own ways, in their own idioms—quite aware of the world in which they live, and of the special demands now made upon them."

Jack Kerouac's crowd dismissed Joe as a Lamb Chop. His colleagues took him for just another adman. His literary agent couldn't make any headway with his work. His mother was probably dying.

These were the pressures Joe experienced while sitting at his kitchen table in the evenings. He felt not like a prophet, but a clown, a morbid jester. All he could do was shape one slow sentence at a time. They were good sentences. He believed that, but would anyone else? "Men went mad and were rewarded with medals. All over the world," he wrote. "There was no end in sight."

In another room, the children cried.

"The only end in sight was Yossarian's own."

11. 22

ROBERT GOTTLIEB was just a kid, really. And the company was his to play with.

"At that moment in the demented history of Simon & Schuster, there was no one in charge—which is often the case in publishing, but it was never acknowledged," he recalled.

In August 1957, at about the time Candida Donadio sent Gottlieb a roughly seventy-five-page manuscript entitled "Catch-18," Jack Goodman, Simon & Schuster's editorial director, had passed away unexpectedly. Poor health forced founder Dick Simon to retire later that year. According to Jonathan R. Eller, who has traced *Catch-22*'s publishing trail, six S & S executives died or moved to other firms in the mid-1950s, leaving the twenty-six-year-old Gottlieb and Nina Bourne, a young advertising manager with whom he worked, with remarkable editorial pull.

Dick Simon and Max Schuster had started the firm in 1924, publishing the first crossword puzzle book (Simon's aunt was a newspaper-puzzle aficionado). It became an immediate bestseller. In 1939, S & S, along with Robert Fair de Graff, created the country's first paperback publisher, Pocket Books. Gottlieb, a New York native, educated at

Columbia and Cambridge, where he studied with the literary critic F. R. Leavis, came aboard in 1955 as Jack Goodman's assistant.

In *Turning the Pages,* a history of the company, Peter Schwed said the personnel manager who first interviewed Gottlieb wondered "why this applicant, assuming he had the money, didn't seem to have the inclination to buy and use a comb." At the end of a lengthy interview session, Goodman told Gottlieb to "[g]o home and write me a letter telling me why you want to get into book publishing." According to Schwed, Gottlieb "brooded about this on his way home and exploded when telling his wife about it. 'What in heaven's name is Goodman telling me to do? The last time I had an idiot assignment like this was in the sixth grade when the teacher made us write a paper on 'What I did in my summer vacation'!" The following morning, he delivered a letter to Goodman. It read, in full, "Dear Mr. Goodman: The reason I want to get into book publishing is because it never occurred to me that I could work anywhere else. Sincerely, Robert Gottlieb." Goodman hired him on a six-month trial basis. At the end of the probationary period, Gottlieb walked into his boss's office and announced, "[My] six months are up and [I've] come to tell you that [I've] decided to stay."

Michael Korda, then another young S & S editor, recalled the publishing business as segregated, but changing, in those days. "Until the 1920s, book publishing in America was dominated by old, 'respectable' houses that for the most part, didn't hire Jews," he wrote in his memoir *Another Life.* "[Then], in the late twenties and thirties, there emerged houses that were owned by Jews who were willing to take risks, who knew how to promote and market books." Korda credited World War II with bringing "Jews and Gentiles together in large numbers for the first time, the common experience of war erasing many of the differences that had separated them."

Primarily, what characterized Simon & Schuster in 1958, when Korda "stumbled into [his] job" there, was its atmosphere of "thwarted ambition and intrigue"—largely a result of the recent deaths and defections. Additionally, the firm's list seemed moribund to Korda, stuck in the previous decade's celebration "of the suburban house, the six o'clock cocktail shaker, and the regulation suit, a world defined by [books such as] *The Organization Man* and *The Man in the Gray Flannel Suit*"—both S & S publications. The company needed to be "shaken by a revolution." A fresh vision was overdue. The big war novels of Mailer and

Jones had sent a "flurry of excitement" through the publishing industry for a while, and there had been a few "seismic tremor[s]" from *On the Road,* but "for the most part," Korda said, "publishing, like literature, slumbered on."

When he first arrived in his office at S & S, located in a building overlooking Rockefeller Center, he found on his desk a bronze plaque that read GIVE THE READER A BREAK. Designed by Dick Simon, the plaques, distributed among the staff, were the closest things the company had to an official editorial policy.

Others in the firm had described Bob Gottlieb to Korda as a "wunderkind." One morning, Korda wrote, "a tall young man, looking rather like one of those penniless perpetual students in Russian novels, squeezed his way into my office and sat down on the edge of my desk. He wore thick glasses with heavy black frames, and his lank, black hair was combed across his brow rather like the young Napoleon's." Gottlieb kept flipping his hair off his forehead with one hand; immediately, the hair resumed its old spot. His glasses were "so smeared with fingerprints . . . it was a wonder he could see through them." Korda said Gottlieb's eyes "were shrewd and intense, but with a certain kindly humorous sparkle that I had not so far seen at S & S."

After studying the room for a moment, Gottlieb told Korda, "You'll never meet anybody if your back is all they see." He pointed to the desk, which faced away from the door toward an outer window. He grasped one end of the desk and told Korda to take the other side. Together, they turned the desk around so it faced the door and the outer corridor. Gottlieb left, nodding with satisfaction. "Whatever I look at, whatever I encounter, I want it to be good—whether it's what you're wearing, or how the restaurant has laid the table, or what's going on on stage, or what the president said last night, or how two people are talking to each other at a bus stop," Gottlieb has said. "I don't want to interfere with it or control it, exactly—I want it to be happy. . . . I might have been, I think, a rabbi, if I'd been at all religious."

CANDIDA DONADIO was delighted by Gottlieb's enthusiasm for the "Catch-18" manuscript. Finally, someone got it! "I thought my navel would unscrew and my ass would fall off," she often said to describe her happiness when negotiations went well with an editor. She had also received a positive response from Tom Ginsberg at Viking. Both Gottlieb and Ginsberg offered options to draw up a contract when Joe had completed the novel. In late August 1957, Donadio met Joe in a West Side restaurant to ask him what he wanted to do.

Looking very much like "a creature from a Roman fresco" (as Robert Stone, one of her clients, once described her), she ordered a round of martinis. This pleased Joe. He was also tickled with the Yiddish in her speech, peppered among Italian phrases and bitter pearls such as "Trust is good. Not to trust is better." Most of all, he was gratified by her seriousness about literature, as well as with the level of personal attention she paid him. Once, describing her instinctual approach to working with writers, she said, "Language means the most to me. The way words are put together. . . . I want to see either a new insight or some kind of confirmation of what you already know. If I'm not sure, I look at a writer's eyes. They tell me a great deal. . . . When something is wrong in a story and a writer doesn't see it or doesn't know it—there is something in the writer's life he doesn't understand."

Joe sipped his martini and chewed a toothpick. He told Donadio he'd stopped smoking a few years earlier, when the price of a pack of cigarettes rose to twenty-six cents the same week the first lung-cancer reports appeared; the toothpick eased his oral cravings. He listened to her lay out the pros and cons of accepting or declining the offers on the table, of working with either Gottlieb or Ginsberg. Given the demands of Joe's day job, and his peripatetic working methods, she felt it best for him to complete more of the book and then ask for an immediate contract. He agreed. He was simply thrilled to be having this conversation. "I remember thinking that when I had the book one-third done and my agent was showing it to editors, that if they all had said 'No,' I would not have finished the book," Joe told George Plimpton in 1974. "I don't have that narcissistic drive, the megalomania involved in spending years working on a book that no one is really interested in publishing." The catch in this statement is that he never doubted someone would want Yossarian's story. ("He knew all along [the book] would change his life and make an impact on American fiction," Frederick Karl said. "I really can't emphasize that enough—his tremendous belief in this book from the beginning.")

Quietly, Donadio signaled for another martini. As for Robert Gott-lieb, she told Joe, he was untested but smart and ambitious. She liked what she knew of him.

The practice of submitting a promising manuscript to more than one publisher at a time was still relatively new, pioneered by agent Scott Meredith in 1952. Prior to that, literary agents had not traded much with book publishers, concentrating instead on magazine sales. The venerable agent Paul Reynolds once declined to represent Willa Cather because he did not want to bother checking periodic royalty statements from her publisher. Now, attitudes had changed: Hardback publication could lead to a paperback sale, a foreign publishing contract, serializa-tion in magazines, and perhaps a movie tie-in. Candida Donadio saw the possibilities early. She taught herself to be business savvy while serv-ing as a kind of den mother to her growing list of clients.

Joe went back to his kitchen table in the Apthorp. Most evenings, he'd write one to three pages in longhand on yellow legal pads. He'd compose the same scene many times, using the same opening and closing sentences, until some of the scenes swelled from three to over a hundred pages. He liked to fill in. In this laborious way, stories grew about the shrewd young soldier, Yossarian, determined to live forever or die trying.

WHILE JOE was scribbling in his kitchen, Norman Mailer made an-other bid to be the culture's most important and notorious bellwether. Depressed by his declining critical reputation since *The Naked and the Dead* (his third novel, *The Deer Park,* had fared just as poorly as *Bar-bary Shore*), he escaped to Mexico, where huge quantities of marijuana made him feel like a "psychic outlaw." "I liked it," he said later. "I liked it a good sight better than trying to be a gentleman."

He returned to the States, and in April 1957, he published a ram-bling manifesto for a cultural revolution based on personal liberation in Irving Howe's journal, *Dissent.* "Jazz is orgasm," he wrote. "Hip is an American existentialism" embedded in those who possess an "in-tense awareness of the present tense in life": ex-soldiers, druggies, gang-bangers, and, most particularly, blacks. The article was entitled "The White Negro: Superficial Reflections on the Hipster."

Superficial it certainly was, but as Fred Kaplan wrote in *1959: The Year Everything Changed,* Mailer's "frantic swings"—fueled by booze and pot—"matched those of the decade, [and he] managed to capture the spirit of the time, the rumblings of an undercurrent." Mailer's diagnosis of the moment was more insightful than his recommendations for surviving it. "Perhaps we will never be able to determine the psychic havoc of the concentration camps and the atom bomb upon the unconscious mind of almost everyone alive in these years," his essay began. "If the fate of twentieth-century man is to live with death from adolescence to premature senescence, [the] only life-giving answer is to live with death as immediate danger, to divorce oneself from society, to exist without roots, to set out on that uncharted journey into the rebellious imperatives of the self." This was the attitude prevalent in current movies such as *Blackboard Jungle* and *Rebel Without a Cause,* in Elvis's songs, in Kerouac's novel and Ginsberg's *Howl*: the recognition, as movie critic Pauline Kael put it, that the "image of instinctive rebellion expresses something in many people [at this time] that they don't dare express." The groundwork was being laid for mass expressions of rebellion, in both controlled and unlimited ways, from Madison Avenue to college campuses. The rebellions' weapons would not be guns and ammo or political orthodoxy, but, rather, weed, the transistor radio, the Pill, and the paperback book.

BY FEBRUARY 1958, Joe had completed seven handwritten chapters of "Catch-18" and typed them up into a 259-page manuscript. Donadio sent it to Gottlieb. "I . . . love this crazy book and very much want to do it," Gottlieb replied. Despite the firm's weakness at the top, he was not completely free to publish whatever he pleased. Henry Simon, the younger brother of the company's founder; Justin Kaplan, an executive assistant to Simon and Max Schuster; and Peter Schwed, an administrative editor, also read Joe's manuscript and discussed it with Gottlieb. Schwed and Kaplan expressed reservations about the novel's repetitiveness. Simon hated it altogether. Its view of the war was offensive, he said, and he recommended against publishing it.

Gottlieb strongly disagreed. "It is a very rare approach to the war—humor that slowly turns to horror," he wrote in his report to the company's editorial board. "The funny parts are wildly funny, the serious parts are excellent. The whole certainly suffers somewhat by the two attitudes, but this can be partly overcome by revisions. The central character,

Yossarian, must be strengthened somewhat—his single-minded drive to *survive* is both the comic and the serious center of the story." He conceded the book would probably not sell well, but he predicted it would be a prestigious title for S & S, "bound to find real admirers in certain literary sets." The board deferred to him. Simon & Schuster offered Joe a standard first-book agreement: $1,500—$750 as an advance and an additional $750 upon completion of the manuscript. The contract listed 1960 as the pub date.

Gottlieb worked well with Candida Donadio, though their business approaches were startlingly different. Donadio liked nothing better than negotiating over pasta and vodka. Gottlieb preferred to hunker down in his office. "[W]hen I had been at Simon & Schuster a year they said, You should have an expense account. I said, That's very nice but I don't know anybody to take out to lunch," he said. "[Anyway,] I had many, many lunches on my expense account . . . [but] I got to the point where having lunch with [people] all the time seemed to be yielding diminishing returns—you're out for two hours, two and a half hours, you overeat, you've wasted all that time, it's disgusting. So . . . I said, This is it. I won't do lunch anymore."

Right away, he hit it off with Joe Heller. "I suppose our convoluted, neurotic, New York Jewish minds work[ed] the same way," he said. He detected in Joe "two great qualities," and they appeared to exist "in such strange discord. First, there was anxiety. That, to me, [was] the subject of *Catch-22*. [That book] must have welled up from the most profound anxiety in him. And the other part was appetite and joy."

In retrospect, Gottlieb does not appear to be an obvious editor for Joe. In 1994, John le Carré, whom Gottlieb would edit, mused that Gottlieb was generally not comfortable with "battlefield sequences" in fiction. He "tends to go very quiet when he reads that stuff and turns over the pages very quickly. It's not a world he's ever had to venture into, thank God, and I think he just doesn't care for it very much. I would not see him as the best person to edit *The Naked and the Dead,* for example. Or James Jones." By the same token, literary agent Lynn Nesbit said, "I probably wouldn't send a postmodernist writer to Bob."

So what made him tumble to *Catch-22,* which has often been described as a postmodernist novel packed with battlefield scenes? At the time he met Joe, he had been reading Henry James. The master's lengthy, obsessive sentences may have prepared him for the complex rhythms in

Joe's prose. He had grown up—a sickly boy—listening to some of the same radio shows Joe had, "Your Hit Parade," "Fred Allen," "Inner Sanctum." He loved their comic timing and heightened sense of drama. He also saw that Joe's book was not fundamentally a novel about World War II, nor, despite its anachronisms and flirtations with implausibility, was it a fiction about fiction. It was, as he had written in his report to the editorial board, about one man's impossible wish: the desire to survive.

"I THINK I was [Bob's] first writer. Not his first published writer, however, because I worked so slowly," Joe told an interviewer in 1974. "It came so hard. I really thought it would be the only thing I ever wrote. Working on *Catch,* I'd become furious and despondent that I could only write a page [or so] a night. I'd say to myself, '*Christ,* I'm a mature adult with a master's degree in English, *why can't I work faster?*'"

The various stages of the novel, housed now in the Archives and Special Collections Department of the Brandeis University Libraries, reveal that, at one point, Joe was working with at least nine different drafts, both handwritten and typed, often cutting and pasting sections from one draft into another, leaving blank spaces in some of the handwritten drafts for typed paragraphs to be inserted later. A typed section was no closer to being finished, in Joe's mind, than a handwritten one; some of the typed paragraphs had been revised as many as three different times, in red ink, green ink, and pencil. Generally, the handwritten passages relished the intentional redundancy of expressions and images, which revisions tended to erase, largely by replacing proper nouns with pronouns. For example, the sentence "The two enlisted men who ran the medical tent for Doc Daneeka ran the medical tent so efficiently that Doc Daneeka . . ." became "The two enlisted men that ran the medical tent for Doc Daneeka ran it so efficiently that he . . ." There was a fine line, in the repetitions, between comic effect and clutter; in later drafts, Joe streamlined his descriptive passages. He retained the humor in situations, as well as in "Who's on first?"–style dialogues, straight out of old Borscht Belt routines.

He tried to temper the humor, as well. Comedy came easily to him. He didn't trust it. In an early passage labeled "Chapter XXIII: Dobbs," Joe originally wrote, "Yossarian lost his guts on the mission to Avignon because Snowden lost his guts on the mission to Avignon." Later, Joe decided the pun on "guts" lessened the horror of Snowden's fate; he was using the gunner's death to serve a cheap joke. He changed the passage to read, "That was the mission in which Yossarian lost his balls . . . because Snowden lost his guts. . . ."

From draft to draft, most of the major changes were structural. Joe shuffled chapters, finding more effective ways to introduce the large cast of characters. "I'm a chronic fiddler," he said. Left on his own, he'd "never finish *anything at all*" because "I don't understand the process of imagination. I am very much at its mercy. I feel that . . . ideas are floating around in the air and they pick me to settle upon. . . . I don't produce them at will." At the same time, the "limitations" inherent in writing ad copy—time constraints, clients' wishes, off-limits language—had taught him to "spur" his imagination under severe pressure. "There's an essay of T.S. Eliot's in which he . . . [claims] that if one is forced to write within a certain framework, the imagination is taxed to its utmost and will produce its richest ideas," Joe said. "Given total freedom, however, the chances are good that the work will sprawl."

He showed rough pages to George Mandel, who helped clarify scenes and intensify situational absurdities, and he depended on Frederick Karl's response. Karl had always felt Joe was one of the smartest people he knew. He was gratified to see Joe's intelligence reflected in the manuscript, notably in passages piercing institutional hypocrisies. Meanwhile, Candida Donadio sold the British publishing rights to Fredric Warburg of Secker & Warburg, who felt Joe was possessed of "true literary genius." The news gave Joe a boost.

Sometimes in the evenings, to clear his head before settling down to write, he'd take walks with his family: Shirley, elegant as ever in sleek black pumps, a black knee-length dress, and a simple pearl necklace, Erica in a double-breasted wool coat over a checkered dress, and Ted in a light pullover shirt and sweater. In a typical family photograph from this time, the children are clearly the center of Joe and Shirley's concern. Joe, his hair cut short and wearing a dark sport coat, appears anxious, herding the kids in a straight line down the sidewalk. He looks self-absorbed, possibly thinking about his book or his mother's continuing decline. Shirley holds back a little, watching the kids with relaxed and pleased attentiveness. Erica appears to enjoy her status as older sister; she is a head taller than her brother, and speaks to him with a knowing expression, nudging his shoulder with her arm. Ted seems happy, amazed by his surroundings, somewhat oblivious of the others in childhood's sweet way. Back in the apartment, Joe left Shirley to put the kids to bed and sequestered himself with his book.

"Catch-18" had doubled in length by the time Gottlieb saw any of it again. The original manuscript had expanded from seven to sixteen chapters, and Joe had added a whole new section consisting of twenty-eight more chapters. The pages were a mix of typescript and legal-size notebook paper covered in Joe's precise and rather crabbed handwriting.

He was taking so long to write the book, the literary world in which he'd conceived the novel no longer existed. Norman Mailer embodied most of the changes. Additionally, each new J. D. Salinger story in *The New Yorker* was cause now for literary buzz. The genteel comedies of suburban manners that had once characterized the magazine's fiction had given way to Salinger's Zen-like ambiguities. Already, Salinger had established himself as an enigmatic figure, "the Dead Okie of Fiction," present through absence.

Saul Bellow, Bernard Malamud, and a young hotshot named Philip Roth appeared to be establishing a Jewish beachhead in American fiction, bringing new brashness to American prose. As for the Beats, nothing signaled their mainstream acceptance more than Columbia University's invitation to Allen Ginsberg to read his poetry on campus in February 1959. Lionel Trilling refused to attend the reading, but his wife went. Despite her reservations about the Beats in general, Diana declared herself deeply moved by Ginsberg's seriousness and real lyrical gifts. A sea change had occurred.

Most importantly, by the end of the 1950s, World War II (and the cultural ferment immediately preceding and following it) could no longer be approached straightforwardly in fiction, at least not effectively. No one had topped—nor could they—*The Naked and the Dead* or *From Here to Eternity*. There was no need to repeat those novels' achievements, the vivid battlefield scenes and dissections of military hierarchies. And yet, night after night at his kitchen table, Joe Heller wrote a novel about the war.

But not really.

"It had upset many people when Mailer wrote the first war novel in which the troops swore the way they have always sworn in all armies since the beginning of warfare, but nobody in American publishing was prepared for a novel like *Catch-22* that made savage fun of war, had a hero who was proud to be a coward, and ridiculed both our side and the enemy's alike," Michael Korda wrote. "It was all very well for that kind of thing to have been done in a Czech book like *The Good Soldier Schweik,* but it was unthinkable in this country."

Looking back, he said, it was such a "strange period, the sunset of the Fifties, before rock and roll, Vietnam, the sexual revolution, and women's liberation changed all the rules we were living by." In the publishing houses, "carbon copies still reigned supreme, and everybody in the editorial department had black smudges on their fingers and shirt cuffs, the proud badge of the profession, like a coal miner's blackened skin."

He would pass by Bob Gottlieb's office and see parts of Joe's novel "endlessly retyped, look[ing] at every stage like a jigsaw puzzle as [Joe, Gottlieb, and Nina Bourne] labored over it, bits and pieces of it taped to every available surface in Gottlieb's cramped office. *That,* I thought, is editing, and I longed to do the same."

Joe prepared a 758-page typescript from this "jigsaw puzzle," deleting digressive episodes and expanding other chapters. He and Gottlieb plunged in again. Gottlieb inspected paragraphs for what he called "impoverished vocabulary," and asked Joe to stir things up with more active language. He caught places where Joe seemed to be "clearing his throat," dawdling, in Joe's characteristic way, and not getting directly to the point. "Some of Bob's suggestions . . . involved a lot of work," Joe recalled. "There was a chapter that came on page two hundred or three hundred of the manuscript—I believe it was the one with Colonel Cathcart; it was either that or the Major Major chapter—and he said he liked this chapter, and it was a shame we didn't get to it earlier. I agreed with him, and I cut about fifty or sixty pages from the opening just to get there more quickly."

The work was as exhilarating as it was difficult. "Joe . . . and I [were] on exactly the same wavelength editorially," Gottlieb said. "[We] never had a bad moment because he [was] perfectly detached. . . . [With Joe,] you [could] look at [a book] as though you were two surgeons examining a body stretched out upon a table. You just cut it open, deal with the offending organs, and stitch it up again. Joe [was] completely objective, he [had] that kind of mind."

In their concentrated hours together, the men grew close. Joe learned that Gottlieb was married to a former actress, Maria Tucci, loved theater and dance, and enjoyed collecting women's purses as a hobby. He didn't go in for "lit crit stuff"; for him, editing, like any kind of reading, was a matter of "common sense." Mostly, Joe came to appreciate Gottlieb's ability to surrender to a book. "If you do [that]," Gottlieb once explained, "when something in it seems to be going askew, you are wounded. The more you have surrendered to a book, the more jarring its errors appear."

Within the hallways of Simon & Schuster, an "aura of myth hovered around the book," said Michael Korda. It was a literary Manhattan Project. "[N]obody but Gottlieb and his acolytes had read it. He had shrewdly stage-managed a sense of expectation that grew with every delay." The occasional appearance in the office of Joe's "Sicilian Earth Mother" agent also increased the book's mystical status. Donadio "had a way of dismissing those she thought unimportant," Korda said, which included just about everyone but Bob Gottlieb and Joe Heller.

Eventually—the 1960 deadline had passed—Joe dropped 150 pages from the manuscript, and the remaining typescript, heavily line-edited, became the printer's copy. "We worked like dogs on *Catch* . . . and then just before it went to press I was reading it again, and I came to a chapter I'd always hated," Gottlieb said. "I thought it was pretentious and literary. I said to Joe, You know, I've always hated this chapter, and he said, Well take it out. And out it went. He printed it many years later in *Esquire* as the lost chapter of *Catch-22*. That [was] Joe Heller . . . [he was] a pragmatist."

Joe's work wasn't over once Gottlieb's job was done. Gottlieb sent the manuscript to a copyeditor "who misunderstood her instructions and rewrote whole paragraphs and changed the names, and made corrections," Joe said. "She missed the whole style. She'd edited—and very well—William Shirer's *The Rise and Fall of the Third Reich*. She was very good at that. Well, she took *Catch-22* [it was still called "Catch-18" at the time] and began making it historically correct; putting in dates where I didn't want dates." She also "apparently had an aversion to what I think might be called compound predicates. For example, if I wrote, 'He struck a match and lit a cigarette,' she would change it to 'He struck a match and *he* lit a cigarette.' It was even worse when she got to sentences like 'Get out, he said, foaming at the mouth.' This she would change to 'Get out, he said, *and he foamed* at the mouth.'" Joe spent six weeks in early 1961 correcting the copyeditor's changes, returning the book to the conversational idioms he desired, and underscoring deliberate anachronisms.

"The S & S house style called for a military rank to be capitalized, so in those cases 'the Major' or 'the Captain' or 'the General' were set that way," Peter Schwed recalled. "Not for long. Joe insisted, and he didn't want any rebuttals, that whenever he had written about a character using only his rank without his name, the word must be set in lower case, viz., 'the major,' 'the captain,' 'the general.' Joe got his way, [and] . . . the production department . . . suffered an unexpected sneak punch."

Meanwhile, Joe felt "lucky and glad" to be working with cover designer Paul Bacon. Bacon was Joe's age, a native of Ossining, New York, and a veteran of the war. In Newark, he had attended Arts High School. His career as a jacket artist got started after a publisher noticed covers he'd designed for a few small jazz periodicals, and for the Blue Note and Riverside record labels. In 1956, he set a new trend in jacket design. At the behest of Simon & Schuster's art director, Tom Bevins, Bacon designed the cover for a novel called *Compulsion,* by Meyer Levin. *Compulsion* told the story of two young men who carried out a well-planned, cold-blooded murder of a boy, along the lines of the famous Leopold and Loeb case. S & S figured the crime's similarity to the novel's plot might help sales, but the publisher didn't want to be seen as exploiting the case or resorting to lewdness. Bacon downplayed the cover's imagery, depicting two small jittery figures printed in red. He devoted most of the space to the title and the author's name. The novel became a bestseller; the design caught the eye of other publishers. The "big book look" was born.

"I'd always tell myself, 'You're not the star of the show. The author took three and a half years to write the goddamn thing, and the publisher is spending a fortune on it, so just back off,' " Bacon said. On the other hand, he felt writers often made cover suggestions that were too literal. These resulted in "dumb" illustrations. For Joe's book, he tried eleven different approaches. "I did a jacket that just [had the title] in very large lettering, and underneath, I can . . . remember . . . the [subtitle Heller wrote]: 'A novel wildly funny and dead serious about a . . . malingerer who recognized the odds.' Gottlieb liked it but didn't do it," Bacon said. "Then I did one that had Yossarian bull's-ass naked, but with his back to you, saluting as a flight of planes went over. I liked that one. Then I did the finger. Then I did a couple of modifications of those. Then, at some point, I came up with the little guy that I tore out of a piece of paper, representing Yossarian in full flight from everybody."

The image would soon become iconic: a cartoonlike red cutout of a soldier dancing, arms raised (or engaging in a grotesque parody of a march). It was Charlie Chaplin and Buster Keaton rolled into one. The new pub date was set for October 1961, in time for the Christmas marketing season.

The stress of writing the novel, as well as consuming "all that expense-account food and booze" while working for *Time* and *Mc-Call's,* Joe said, put fifty pounds on his once-thin frame. Some of his colleagues took to calling him "the Locust." "Whatever was there I'd eat it," he said. He still bit his nails.

His daughter believes that sometime in the summer of 1961, Shirley took the kids to a small motel in Pennsylvania, leaving Joe alone to attend to last-minute book business. "[I remember] my mother, brother, and I stayed at this motel . . . right on the highway, Uncle Morris' Motel (it was called that—he wasn't *our* uncle)," Erica says. "Dad . . . would come up there on the weekends and because my mother didn't know how to drive, we were pretty much stuck at this grim little place. There was a diner right across the highway. . . . 'Travelin' Man' by Ricky Nelson was always playing on the jukebox. . . . We'd have all our meals there and the rest of the time we'd just pretty much be in the motel pool. . . . I can't imagine . . . how on earth we ever found this place or why it was chosen."

While reading the *Catch* galley sheets, Joe had to write scripts for "dog and pony shows" at *McCall's*—national presentations to advertising agencies and prospective clients. Travel expenses associated with these presentations often went as high as ninety thousand dollars. Joe prepared flip charts and slide shows. He put together direct-mailing packets. His associates felt he had a "fantastic sense of the trends of the times and what was important to the people buying."

That year, at *McCall's* annual sales convention in Nassau, Joe's slide show, "The Pages That Sell," took center stage. His colleagues had taken a plane to the festivities. Joe still didn't fly. He'd booked passage on a boat. While his fellow conventioneers boozed it up in the bars, Joe sat on the beach, reading his galleys. One of his colleagues, Tom Buck, tried to talk him into flying back with the group. Buck, a big, gruff, friendly man with a passion for JFK, had been a barnstormer for a flying circus in the Depression years, and he spoke of the glories of flight. Joe took one look at his artificial leg—Buck had been injured in a plane crash in 1946, dropping two thousand feet into a field in Delaware—and said he'd stick with the boat. Buck laughed. "He was a self-made man and unable to hide it," Joe said of him.

Joe's advertising buddies saw him the same way. He was a great ad-man, but something else was on his mind. Some days he would walk into the office and announce he was "just going to brood and not work." One colleague said, "Joe worked [hard] on his . . . escape" from the "bureaucracy."

His escape seemed perpetually threatened. One day, he got a call from Gottlieb, who said the title "Catch-18" would have to go. Leon Uris was preparing to release a novel called *Mila 18,* all about the Nazi occupation of Poland (Uris's title was taken from the designation for the headquarters of a Jewish resistance fighters' bunker in Warsaw). Uris was a well-known writer—*Exodus* had been a huge bestseller; two novels with the number 18 in the title would clash in the marketplace, and Heller, the unknown, was bound to get the short end of the deal.

The number had always been arbitrary, part of the joke about military rules. Still, Joe, Gottlieb, and Nina Bourne had long thought of the book as "Catch-18," and it was difficult to conceive of calling it anything else. "[W]e were all in despair," Gottlieb said. In his office, he and Joe sat opposite each other, spitting out numbers like two spies speaking in code. Joe liked the sound of "Catch-11": hard consonants followed by vowels, opening up the mouth. Gottlieb thought there were too many syllables. Besides, it was too close to the new Frank Sinatra movie, *Oceans Eleven.* They agreed to sleep on the question of a title and try again later.

On January 29, 1961, Joe sent Gottlieb a note, bringing to bear all his adman persuasion: "The name of the book is now CATCH-14. (Forty-eight hours after you resign yourself to the change, you'll find yourself almost preferring this new number. It has the same bland and nondescript significance of the original. It is far enough away from Uris for the book to establish an identity of its own, I believe, yet close enough to the original title to still benefit from the word of mouth publicity we have been giving it.)"

Gottlieb wasn't sold.

In the meantime, Simon & Schuster's lawyers had been reviewing the galleys. They worried that Joe's old war buddies might recognize themselves in his descriptions and decide to seek damages. In part, this fear reflected changes in the publishing industry. In the past, books had been a luxury item. Most publishing firms had been owned by individuals or families, often with little capital invested up front. The business was as much about shaping culture as it was about making a profit. The audience for books was relatively small, but it was an educated and loyal one. Now, the mass-market paperback, distributed like magazines on newsstands, in bus stations, and drugstores, had created a whole new readership. Big profits were possible. Publishing was no longer a "gentleman's" venture, as the old-school owners liked to think of it. Michael Korda says that when "Bennett Cerf and Donald Klopfer took Random House public at $11.25 a share" in October 1959, they set off a "boom in publishing stocks that quickly drew other companies, including S & S, into the stock market." The Random House stock rose almost three dollars a share in a twenty-four-hour period, and it soon sold for forty-five dollars. Publishing became the "darling of Wall Street," and books would never be the same. The business was sharp, it was competitive, and it carried liabilities. The S & S lawyers asked Joe to detail how much of his book was based on fact.

Joe responded, accurately, that the people, places, and events in his novel were "extensions of the possible into the fantastic." For example, it is "fantastic" that an American would arrange, for business purposes, an attack on his own air base, as Milo Minderbinder does. But Joe was clearly recalling the surprise German air raid on Corsica just before he arrived at the base there. The raid had included "friendly" planes painted with British markings. The fantastic was one step away from the possible.

With regard to specific characters in the book, he said:

> My group commanding officer in Corsica was a colonel named Chapman who was similar in build to [the fictional] Colonel Cathcart and also smoked with a cigarette holder. Along with other group commanders in the Mediterranean, I'm sure, he kept inching up the number of missions the men in his unit had to fly, as the missions tended to grow less dangerous. It is in the last circumstance that the major dramatic conflict of the novel arises, although beyond these similarities I've listed, all resemblance ends.
>
> Every military unit of any size, I would guess, had a chaplain. . . . If memory serves me correctly, [our chaplain] was

of slight physique and light complexion. Other than that, I know not another thing about him; we did have a captain named Myers who was called by some men by the nickname Chief"; [o]ur flight surgeon was a man from Brooklyn named Marino, and he was as helpful and sympathetic as could be. Like [the fictional] Daneeka, he was a slight, dark man. Apart from the fact that people did go to him to complain about the increases in the number of missions—as the[y] did to all the flight surgeons in the group—he bears no additional resemblance to Doc Daneeka.

[With Milo Minderbinder] we may be a little close even for my comfort, both because of a slight similarity in names and because of the activities and opportunities common to all mess officers. The name of my mess officer was, believe it or not, Mauno Lindholm. Like other mess officers on Corsica, he had a certain amount of money at his disposal to purchase fresh provisions from local sources. He flew to other places regularly for fresh eggs, meat, and vegetables. Whether he used his position and resources to make money in the black market is his own secret; there was no reason to believe he did not, and much reason to believe he did.

[T]here was in my squadron a bombardier named Yohannon who was called by the nickname "Yo-Yo." In no other respects was he like Yossarian, whose actions are based more on my own attitudes and experiences than anybody else's.

Joe's experiences, barely fictionalized in the novel, included the encounter with Luciana in Rome and virtually every mission listed.
He concluded:

I should point out that the action of the book took place seventeen years ago, that I have no personal grievances against anyone involved in my military experiences, and that there is genuinely no attempt to embarrass or disparage any of the people I met in the army. I either liked them enormously or was indifferent to them. Keep in mind that . . . I made absolutely no impression on most of the people in my squadron, and none on any of the people at Group, and that, with a few exceptions, nobody was aware even at that time that a Joe Heller was serving among them, or would know it now.

He said he would prefer to "leave the book as it is." If changes were necessary to avoid possible legal actions, switching the location from Corsica to the "island of Pianosa" and "possibly . . . calling the B-25 planes B-22's, ought to be sufficient." The lawyers seemed satisfied (the B-25s would remain).

Candida Donadio took credit for retitling the book. "22 was chosen as a substitute because October 22 was [my] birthday," she said.

"Absolutely untrue," Gottlieb said later. "I remember it totally, because it was in the middle of the night. I remember Joe came up with some number and I said, 'No, it's not funny,' which is ridiculous, because no number is intrinsically funny. . . . And then I was lying in bed worrying about it one night, and I suddenly had this revelation. And I called him the next morning and said, 'I've got the perfect number. Twenty-two, it's funnier than eighteen.' I remember those words being spoken. . . . He said, 'Yes, it's great, it's great.' And we called Candida and told her."

Joe's suggestion that the bombers be called B-22s may have put the number in Gottlieb's mind. In any case, the number fit the story because of the novel's doubling structure: the constant linguistic repetitions, the instances of déjà vu, the repeated actions, the endless missions, and the concept of an inescapable loop.

The adman in Joe could not resist offering to the S & S marketing department "[s]uggested descriptive copy fragments for use on jacket, publicity releases, in conversation, etc." The "fragments" included the following lines: "[Catch-22 is] the story of a man who deserts from a society that will not allow him to live with safety and dignity"; "[it is a] modern allegory of immorality in which war is not merely horrible, but ridiculous, and brutality, vanity, and greed are not merely deplorable, but silly"; "[it is] a vivid, moving demonstration that man at his most virtuous is really not much better than man at his most immoral; that people at their most logical are no more intelligent than people at their most absurd"; "Packed with boisterous action and originality, Catch-22 takes an uninhibited look at all those principles and institutions we have been taught to revere—and finds each one laughable. And as a consequence, Catch-22 is perhaps as tragic a novel as has ever been written."

Finally, the revisions were done. The legal worries had been resolved. The fall book season had arrived. *Catch-22* was about to be launched.

ONE DAY IN MIDTOWN, a young man named Sam Vaughan agreed to share a cab with another man who was traveling in roughly the same direction. In the backseat of the cab, the men fell into conversation. Vaughan said he worked as an editor at a publishing house. The other man did, too. His name was Bob Gottlieb. After a moment's silence, Gottlieb turned to Vaughan and said, "Tell me about popular fiction. I really don't understand it."

> "That's some catch, that Catch-22," [Yossarian] observed.
> "It's the best there is," Doc Daneeka agreed. . . .
> Catch-22 . . . specified that a concern for one's own safety in the face of dangers that were real and immediate was the process of a rational mind. [A bombardier] was crazy and could be grounded. All he had to do was ask; and as soon as he did, he would no longer be crazy and would have to fly more missions. [A bombardier] would be crazy to fly more missions and sane if he didn't, but if he was sane he had to fly them. If he flew them he was crazy and didn't have to; but if he didn't want to he was sane and had to. Yossarian was moved very deeply by the absolute simplicity of . . . Catch-22.

Now in common usage, the term *catch-22*—an insoluble paradox, usually bureaucratic or legalistic in nature—has its roots in *yes* and *no,* and the recognition that there is often no difference between them. One is meaningless without the other, as *day* exists in opposition to *night.* That every *yes* has a *no* constituted Joe Heller's deepest knowledge and experience of the world: It was in the language he heard every day as a kid—the worrying complaint of "What, me worry?" at the core of so many Yiddishisms and Jewish jokes—and it was in his family story, when his brother became *not* his brother, his sister *not* his sister. It was in his immediate surroundings, the dirty and desperate "Funny Place" of his childhood. It was in his dreams of the future, when Lee brought him catalogs for schools he would never be able to attend. It was in his most primitive appetites—the conflict he felt in the social clubs between

wanting to protect girls from "fast" boys, or to be one of the boys pulling girls into dark back rooms. It was in his military service, when his
superiors (those with a "genius for ineptitude") told him the danger he
was exposed to was nothing personal, and therefore acceptable.

"They're trying to kill me," Yossarian [said].
    "No one's trying to kill you. . . ."
    "Then why are they shooting at me?"
    "They're shooting at everyone. . . . They're trying to kill ev-
eryone."
    "And what difference does that make?"

It was at the heart of identity, personal and national.

"Would you like to see your country lose?"
    . . . "We won't lose. We've got more men, more money and
more material. . . . Let somebody else get killed."
    "But suppose everybody on our side felt that way?"
    "Then I'd certainly be a damned fool to feel any other way.
Wouldn't I?"

It was in the rhythms of waking and sleeping; of being abandoned
in a place, and time, of healing. It was in the word *father;* in being told
the body was spirit, and we were all One.

There were bartenders, bricklayers and bus conductors all over
the world who wanted him dead, landlords and tenants, traitors
and patriots, lynchers, leeches and lackeys, and they were all out
to bump him off. That was the secret Snowden had spilled out to
him [along with his guts] on the mission to Avignon—they were
all out to get him; and Snowden had spilled it all over the back of
the plane.

But that was just the beginning.

There were lymph glands that might do him in. There were kid-
neys, nerve sheaths and corpuscles. There were tumors of the
brain. There was Hodgkin's disease, leukemia, amyotrophic lateral

sclerosis. There were fertile red meadows of epithelial tissue to catch and coddle a cancer cell. . . . There were billions of conscientious body cells oxidizing away day and night like dumb animals at their complicated job of keeping him alive and healthy, and every one was a potential traitor and foe.

A *yes* and a *no*.

The dying gunner's secret—"Snowden's insides slither[ing] down to the floor in a soggy pile"—leaves an "easy" message for Yossarian, whose attempts at ministrations, with morphine and sulfa powder, are grotesquely worthless. "Man was matter. . . . Drop him out a window and he'll fall. Set fire to him and he'll burn. Bury him and he'll rot like other kinds of garbage. The spirit gone, man is garbage. That was Snowden's secret. Ripeness was all."

This moment—Snowden's death in the back of the B-25—breaks the surface of the novel, near its end, like a grievous and stonily repressed memory: mortal flesh's negation of life's comedy, the book's harsh rebuke to its lighthearted entertainment. A paradox: From the book's first two sentences (essentially the same sentence, more or less repeated), language has been a useless and overdetermined loop. Finally, it reveals its power to shock; to kill. Joe had developed his narrative method—displacement, interruption—by reading Céline. The *subject* of his narrative he carried in his bones.

What eventually made *Catch-22* a cult favorite among young readers in the 1960s and 1970s was Joe's demonstration that all of language was a Jewish joke. Barblike "uh-uh's" were nestled inside each and every "sure." No official explanation, expression of patriotism, spiritual consolation, administrative rule, declaration of war, or pledge of assimilation could withstand such a withering exposé. The anachronisms—the McCarthyesque loyalty oaths, the computer glitches—felt absolutely right, though they were historically inaccurate. Chaos and nefarious methodologies have always predated their most efficient means of expression.

In Joe's novel, hypocrisy was revealed to be the DNA of rabid nationalism. According to Milo Minderbinder, one of America's "moral principles"—an ideal our country goes to war for, to protect—is that "it [is] never a sin to charge as much as the traffic [will] bear." The ultimate consequence of this philosophy is "war . . . without limits and without meaning," except blind profit, says Alfred Kazin, "a war that will only end when no one is alive to fight it."

It was this "next war" that *Catch-22* was about, which is why it came to be read, in the sixties, as a Vietnam book and why it seems to readers today prescient about the war on terror. "Frankly, I'd like to see government get out of war altogether and leave the whole field to private industry," Milo says—a wish virtually realized, after 9/11, with companies like the former Blackwater arming civilian contractors in Iraq.

If *Catch-22*'s skewering of national pieties made it a cult book, what made it "as tragic a novel as has ever been written" was its recognition of the ultimate hypocrisy: the death in life pumping through each and every organism, the body's betrayal of itself.

"How do you feel, Yossarian?"
"Fine. No, I'm very frightened."

The "rebels without a cause" in 1950s pop culture, and the tuned-in, dropped-out rebels of the 1960s, flattened into caricatures in *Time* magazine, did not share Yossarian's deep humanity, because, unlike the others, Yossarian, clear-eyed and scared to death, understood life's joke.

"I DIDN'T WANT to give him a Jewish name," Joe explained. "I didn't want to give him an Irish name, I didn't want to symbolize the white Protestant. . . . I wanted to get . . . somebody who could not be identified . . . geographically, or culturally, or sociologically—somebody as a person who has a capability of ultimately divorcing himself completely from all emotional and psychological ties."

The *yes* in this *no* is Yossarian's profound, *unstated* Judaism: his sense of worldly exile and intimation of connection to something ancient, even if that something survives only in an instinctual personal ritual.

While the chaplain—who quotes Psalm 137, about poor exiles weeping and hanging their harps in trees—conducts Snowden's funeral, Yossarian strips naked and crawls into a tree. He quips to Milo that he is sitting in the "tree of life." Critics have interpreted his actions as a return to innocence, a search for God-like perspective, a refusal of the military (the shucking of the uniform). His gesture embraces each of these motives, and is, as well, a shocked response to the unfathomable horror of

Snowden's death. But what gives the scene depth, beneath the comedy and superficial pleasure of Yossarian's rebellion, is its echo of the psalm.

"[T]hey that carried us away captive required of us a song; and they that wasted us *required of us* mirth," says the verse. "How shall we sing the LORD's song in a strange land?" Instead, the homeless Jews "hanged [their] harps among the willows" and "sat down, yea, we wept."

Yossarian has hanged himself like a harp in a tree. The potential indignity of his nakedness becomes its opposite, in his refusal of mirth, his denial of the "required song" of just another funeral oration. They that wasted Snowden have more in store for the others. Yossarian says no to them—while knowing he probably won't escape the final yes.

Early in the editorial process, Bob Gottlieb thought *Catch-22*'s comedy battled its tragic undertones. He feared it might be hard to reconcile the book's two registers. Instinctually, Joe knew the relentless rhythms of Borscht Belt jokes were like the incantatory prayers one finds in Psalms: The transition from one to the other was natural, almost unnoticeable.

The retrospective narrative mode Joe had discovered with "Castle of Snow" strengthened *Catch-22,* giving the novel an elegiac tone, despite the antic humor: *Everything is over, lost already.* Which is not to say the cycle won't start again—and again—as the book's repetitions made clear.

> "Haven't you got anything humorous [to offer as consolation] that stays away from waters and valleys and God?"[the colonel said].
> The chaplain was apologetic. "I'm sorry, sir, but just about all the prayers I know *are* rather somber in tone. . . ."

NINA BOURNE had worked hard on *Catch-22*. She saw herself as "the demented governess who believed the baby was her own." Her conviction that the novel was a work of literary genius led her to stand up in the book's first promotion meeting. With a tremor in her voice and tears in her eyes, she announced, "We have to print 7,500"—instead of the standard 5,000-copy first printing. "[I]f the book I feel this strongly about can't have 7,500 copies, what am I doing here?" No one argued. Bourne was not one to make a scene or issue demands. Since 1939, she had done her job quietly and efficiently. She said what she meant, and if she was willing to take a risk on this book, then the company would fall in behind her.

The truth was, following Jack Goodman's death and Dick Simon's retirement, Gottlieb and Bourne were nearly in a position to run their own operation within the walls of Simon & Schuster. "If we'd had anybody to ask [how to promote *Catch-22*], they'd never have let us," Bourne said.

She attached a quirky disclaimer to the cover of the prepublication proofs:

> A funny and tragic and tonic book that says what is on the tip of the tongue of our age to say.
>
> If a single word, thought, or overtone in the above sentence rubs you the wrong way, blame us, not the novel.

She wrote "crazed" cover letters to distinguished readers, she said, hoping to elicit comments from them for possible use in advertising. She mailed prepub copies of the novel to James Jones, Irwin Shaw, Art Buchwald, Graham Greene, S. J. Perelman, and Evelyn Waugh, among others. To each, Bourne wrote, "This is a book I'd get a critic out of the shower to read." According to Jonathan R. Eller, "One eminent critic avoided her for years after . . . that."

The "crazed" strategy seemed to backfire when, on September 6, 1961, Evelyn Waugh wrote:

> Dear Miss Bourne:
>
> Thank you for sending me *Catch-22*. I am sorry that the book fascinates you so much. It has many passages quite unsuitable to a lady's reading. . . .
>
> You are mistaken in calling it a novel. It is a collection of sketches—often repetitious—totally without structure.
>
> Much of the dialogue is funny.
>
> You may quote me as saying: "This exposure of corruption, cowardice and incivility of American officers will outrage all friends of your country (such as myself) and greatly comfort your enemies."

Bourne was relieved when a telegram arrived from Art Buchwald in Paris:

> PLEASE CONGRATULATE JOSEPH HELLER ON MASTERPIECE CATCH-22 STOP I THINK IT IS ONE OF THE GREATEST WAR-BOOKS STOP SO DO IRWIN SHAW AND JAMES JONES.

Just before the book's appearance in stores, Gottlieb and Bourne incited word of mouth with mysterious ads in the *New York Times* featuring Paul Bacon's cutout—nothing else. Then, in the September 11 issue of *Publishers Weekly,* a full-page ad appeared with a photo of Joe—casual, confident, handsome—and a picture of the book's cover. The copy, written by Gottlieb, read: "The growing ferment of interest in **Catch-22** confirms our faith that **Joseph Heller's** outrageously funny, powerful, totally original novel will be one of the major publishing events of the fall. Oct. 10. $5.95."

That autumn, Joe and Shirley, along with Frederick and Dolores Karl, "spent many an evening running from one bookstore in New York to another, putting [Joe's] novel on display when no one was looking, or moving copies of *Catch-22* from under the counter of numerous Doubledays and placing it on display while burying other bestselling books," Frederick Karl said. Joe's delight in holding the physical book, spotting copies of it in stores, was unbounded. The kid from Coney Island had pulled off something big.

Early reviews clashed—*Newsweek* favorable, *Time* tepid—but the promotional campaign had succeeded. The first printing sold out in ten days. Nina Bourne readied a second and third printing, all before Christmas.

Like Willa Cather saying the world broke in two at a particular point, Erica Heller recalled the excitement and confusion of that season. They had a "regular family life," she said. "Trips to Coney . . . Fudgsicles and two-cent pretzels. Lots of sports (well, it wasn't exactly a Jewish Hickory Hill). . . . Then, seemingly out of nowhere, this crazy war book with its red, white, and blue cover was suddenly everywhere."

She was only nine years old, but she noticed changes. "We used to go often on Sunday afternoons to Brooklyn to visit relatives. Before, we had taken the subway. Now we went in a cab," she says. "One day at school, a boy in my class told me that his parents thought my father was a 'great artist.' I went home and looked everywhere for an easel, for paints. I didn't even understand what that meant."

Home movie footage shows Erica and Ted, in a pink nightgown and dark cotton pajamas, respectively, trotting out copies of the book in front of a thick white curtain in the Heller apartment. As Erica holds up the novel, she smiles ruefully: a look of pride and pleased resentment at being forced to perform for Daddy, *about* Daddy. Ted peers shyly at his sister and at the camera over the top of his book. He rolls his eyes as he exits the scene, this *Catch* business, thank goodness, done for the evening.

On another occasion, while the family was renting a place on Fire Island, Ted, to Joe's delight, told strangers on the beach *he* had written the book. In a copy inscribed to "Erica Jill" on September 7, 1961, Joe wrote, "With the hope that when you read this book in ten or fifteen years, you will love it at least a little—and that you will love me too. Daddy."

High on momentum, Gottlieb and Bourne took Francis Brown, the editor of the *New York Times Book Review,* to lunch. They told Brown that *Catch-22* was unusual, as well as special, and that an older, conventional reviewer would be wrong for the book. Brown assured them he would think carefully about an appropriate reviewer. Gottlieb and Bourne left the meal excited, anticipating splendid treatment in the *Times.*

At work each day, Joe endured the ribbing of colleagues who said he must have found the manuscript under a rock or something. *He* couldn't have written it. Who was he kidding? Maybe you wrote a *few* of those jokes, but not the whole book. He said he'd treat people to lunch if they'd check the book's sales at nearby stores, and he chided friends who bought the novel on discount at places like Korvette.

Joe made regular trips to Coney Island's Hebrew Home for the Aged to sit with his mother. They exchanged few words. She was frail, moving in and out of lucidity. When she *did* try to speak, she would stutter or lose her train of thought, then smile at him apologetically, almost whimsically. Together, they listened to the waves on the beach below: regular sighs like openmouthed breaths. He helped her sip water from a plastic cup, fed her fragments of whitefish or soft pieces of sweet candy. He noticed stiff gray hairs sprouting from her cheeks and chin—her arthritic fingers were too twisted for tweezers now—and chastised himself for the revulsion he felt. Leaving was always a relief, but then on the subway he'd brood that he was an unfeeling, uncaring man—had he ever really cared for anyone? How could he be so cold? On the other hand, *wouldn't* it be better for everyone, including Lena, if she just slipped away quietly, quickly? How long could this go on?

Often at night, after these visits, he'd dream he was a boy and his mother was going away somewhere, leaving him behind, and he'd yell out to her with the most agonizing yearning. He'd wake with tears in his eyes. And then he'd be back at the home, feeding fish to his mother, resenting the cold, greasy texture of the food on his fingers, and the thick slipperiness of her saliva. He'd whisper, "There, there" and "Everything's okay," feeling just as silly as when he'd muttered these trifles to the kid in the plane over Avignon all those years ago.

In clear moments, Lena heard the no in his yeses just as well as he did; he understood this. Words had always been a barrier between them: her refusal to master English, his growing comprehension that meanings (*brother, sister*) were never really fixed. During these bedside vigils, he had been thinking it was a shame she could not appreciate or grasp his success with *Catch-22*, but she *did* understand. She was the source. Mother: insoluble paradox.

In years to come, Joe would grow fascinated with clinical definitions of schizophrenia, and theories tying it to family communication problems. According to one idea, schizophrenia results when there is: "1) Involvement in an intense relationship where accurate discrimination of the message has vital importance for the individual; 2) The other person expresses two orders and one of these denies the other; 3) The individual cannot react to the contradictory messages."

In developing themes for his second novel, Joe would work consciously with the concept of schizophrenia, but this first book had plenty of examples of it. Western culture seemed rooted in the pathology.

No. Lena didn't need to know about *Catch-22*. She had *lived* it as an immigrant, wife, and mother.

Besides, Joe wasn't sure how successful he was going to be—or what success even meant. There was a catch in Francis Brown's efforts to find a young, "with it" reviewer for Joe's book: The man he tapped, Richard Stern, thought himself an up-and-coming black humorist, for whom *Catch-22* was serious competition.

On October 22, 1961, Stern wrote, on page 50 of the *New York Times Book Review*, "[T]he book is no novel. . . . Its author, Joseph Heller, is like a brilliant painter who decides to throw all the ideas in his sketchbooks onto one canvas, relying on their charm and shock to compensate for the lack of design. . . . The book is an emotional hodgepodge."

Frederick Karl claimed Joe "was not dismayed" by this review, but Joe could quote it bitterly, word for word, three decades later. "I didn't think [my family and I] would ever smile again," he told David Strait-feld of *New York* magazine. Alice Denham recalled Joe as being exceed-ingly glum after the review. One day, he stopped by her apartment on West Fifty-fifth Street. She offered him a drink. "We thought we had the fix in," he told her. "A bad joke." He looked tired. He admitted, "I thought—now, don't laugh—I might be able to quit work and write full-time. That I'd make enough. . . ."

The better news was that more of the readers Bourne had courted popped up with favorable comments, including S. J. Perelman, who lauded the book's humor (and who would be instrumental in securing Joe a National Institute of Arts and Letters grant in 1963). Harper Lee said, "*Catch-22* is the only war novel I've ever read that makes any sense." Gott-lieb and Bourne bought ad space in the *Times* to trumpet this praise.

On November 4, Nelson Algren wrote in *The Nation*:

Below its hilarity, so wild that it hurts, *Catch-22* is the strongest repudiation of our civilization, in fiction, to come out of World War II. *The Naked and the Dead* and *From Here to Eternity* are lost within it. That the horror and the hypocrisy, the greed and the complacency, the endless cunning and the endless stupidity which now go to constitute what we term Christianity are dealt with here in absolutes, does not lessen the truth of its repudiation. . . . [T]his novel is not merely the best American novel to come out of World War II; it is the best American novel that has come out of anywhere in years.

Within twelve months, Norman Mailer, slow to acknowledge other novelists, would grudgingly admit, "*Catch-22* is the debut of a writer with merry gifts."

BY THANKSGIVING, nearly twelve thousand copies had sold—respectable, but not over the top. That fall, the bestsellers included Harper Lee's *To Kill a Mockingbird* (in its eighteenth printing, just one year after its release), J. D. Salinger's *Franny and Zooey*, John Stein-beck's *The Winter of Our Discontent*, Irving Stone's *The Agony and the Ecstasy*, Harold Robbins's *The Carpetbaggers*, and, predictably, Leon Uris's *Mila 18*.

Catch-22 was popular on the East Coast but did not gain national traction.

After the first of the year, S & S prepared a fourth printing. In March 1962 came the announcement of the thirteenth annual National Book Award finalists. Joe was named along with Salinger, Bernard Malamud for *A New Life,* Isaac Bashevis Singer for *The Spinoza of Market Street and Other Stories,* and another newcomer, Walker Percy, for a novel called *The Moviegoer.* Knopf, Percy's publisher, had done almost nothing to promote the book; despite positive reviews, the novel was all but forgotten by the time the finalists were assembled. *The Moviegoer* had sold fewer than five thousand copies. Readers and critics were stunned, and Knopf was somewhat embarrassed, when Percy walked away with the award.

In the following days, the news emerged that Knopf had not submitted *The Moviegoer* for NBA consideration. Jean Stafford was one of the fiction judges that year; her husband, A. J. Liebling, had read *The Moviegoer* and sung its praises to her. She recommended it to the other judges. She asked the NBA if it would be all right to add Percy's novel to the finalists, as it seemed the book had been unfairly overlooked.

Show magazine, interpreting the incident as more underhanded than it was, published an editorial denouncing Stafford and Liebling, and suggesting that "Joseph Heller's brilliant farce-tragedy" had been cheated out of the prize it deserved. Gottlieb and Bourne wasted no time in exploiting the controversy with a new barrage of ads for *Catch-22.* By April 1962, nineteen thousand copies had sold and a fifth printing was ordered.

"By conventional marketing standards, that should have been the end of it," Jonathan R. Eller wrote. "[T]he novel was selling moderately well, but Heller would clearly not reach bestseller status on the scale of John O'Hara or Harold Robbins, or in fact on any scale at all."

But the Bob and Nina Show was not bound by conventional marketing standards, and it was not done. Bourne sent special-order cards to bookstores all over the country, guaranteeing payment of transportation costs on any order for *Catch-22* placed on one of the cards; furthermore, S & S would pay return costs on any unsold special-order copies. The bookstores bit.

Next, Gottlieb purchased six columns of ad space in the April 29 issue of the *New York Times Book Review.* The ad's header read: "Report on *Catch-22,* a novel that is showing signs of living forever." Gottlieb quoted accolades from reviewers and writers, as well as excerpts from "the rush of wonderfully expressive letters that are coming in from readers everywhere." Bourne printed the ad on poster board and mailed copies of it to bookstores for counter displays.

Nelson Algren continued to champion the novel. On June 23, 1962, in the *Chicago Daily News,* he said, "'Catch' is a classic because it employs fantasy to depict truth too devastating to tell by factual narration. A classic because its burlesque of army brass is rooted soundly in the thinking of the businessman in uniform, and is told by a writer whose experience of Business at war is first-hand."

His article spurred interest in the novel throughout the Midwest. By the end of June, Joe had sold 25,000 copies.

"JOE'S CONTRIBUTION [to the promotion of the novel] was to stay calm and offer practical suggestions," Bob Gottlieb said. "He knew everything. He knew things that nobody could know. He would call up and say, 'Look, I'm not suggesting that you go back to press . . . but I think you should know, because I have a cousin [who told me], that the manufacturers of the paper in the plant you're using are probably going out on strike in two weeks, so if you need paper, you may want to order it now.' He was always right. We always did exactly as [we were] told. When things went wrong, he was cheerful. When things went right, he was thrilled and grateful."

This early in his career, Gottlieb didn't know how rare it was to find an author with such a refined combination of patience and pragmatism. "Many years later . . . I came upon [Joe] giving advice to Bob Caro, at the time we were preparing *The Power Broker* for publication," Gottlieb recalled. "He was explaining to . . . Caro that the most important thing he could do was to keep the publisher happy and calm because if we were happy and calm, we would do it right, but if he agitated us with complaints and constant questions, things could go wrong. This is a lesson I can say that Bob Caro didn't learn, because no one else has ever learned it. Joe is the only person [I've worked with] who ever grasped this essential fact about publishing."

IT WAS NOT EASY for Gottlieb to conduct the *Catch* campaign—or do *any* work. The world would not sit still for him. A young editor remembered getting a call from him one afternoon, suggesting lunch. This happened shortly after JFK's speech announcing the presence of Russian missiles in Cuba. "Things were pretty weird in Manhattan, all around," wrote Robert Nedelkoff, who heard this story from the young man.

Gottlieb's habit was to eat a sandwich at his desk. The young man stopped at an Italian deli, bought some antipasto, and headed for Simon & Schuster. Gottlieb's secretary insisted he hadn't left all day, but his office appeared to be empty. "That you?" came a voice from under the desk. "Yes," said the young editor. "I talked to my shrink this morning. He sounded kind of worried," Gottlieb explained from his crouch. "There's some space here. Sit down." The young man found a spot beneath the desk and opened his container of antipasto. "Just a second," Gottlieb said. He rose, went to the window, closed the blinds, and then resumed his position on the floor. The men ate and talked business, safe from "the Big One."

"THIS IS *THE NAKED and the Dead* scripted for the Marx Brothers, a kind of *From Here to Insanity*," Kenneth Allsop wrote in a prepublication review of *Catch-22* for Britain's *Daily Mail*. "What is especially intriguing is that [so much] excitement and enthusiasm should be a-boil in a nation so patriotically thin-skinned and fanatical about the flag. For *Catch-22* is anti-war, anti-militaristic, anti-organisation, anti-slogan, anti-chauvinism. It spoofs uniform, duty, and the Uncle-Sam-right-or-wrong outlook. It is a great demented belly-laugh at the concepts of unquestioning obedience and sanctioned killing."

That such a novel could come from Cold War America, with its nuclear bellicosity and lockstep thinking, was a delightful surprise to British readers, and the book became an immediate bestseller in England. The news was more than just pleasing to Joe; it was a palpable relief. On the eve of British publication, Secker & Warburg backed away from the novel, fearing Joe had made it far too long during final revisions and that the British public would not have patience for it. A young editor at Jonathan Cape, Tom Maschler, took it on. Following Nina Bourne's strategies, he whipped up tremendous publicity. He sent a copy to Philip Toynbee, who wrote in London's *Observer* on June 17, 1962:

> When I began reading *Catch-22*, I thought it was a farcical satire on life in the United States Army Air Force. Later I believed that Mr. Heller's target was modern war and all those who are responsible for waging it. Still later it seemed that he was attacking social organisation and anyone who derives power from it. By the end of the book, it had become plain to me that it is—no other phrase will do—the human condition itself which is the object of Mr. Heller's fury and disgust. . . . [A]t the risk of inflation, I cannot help writing that *Catch-22* is the greatest satirical work in English since *Erewhon*.

In July, Maschler sent Joe a note: "We sold just over 800 copies last week . . . and we have ordered yet another reprint. . . . I don't suppose we shall ever catch up with S & S but, to use an English understatement, we are not displeased."

On November 20, in the *Manchester Guardian,* W. J. Weatherby said:

> It is hard to imagine [Heller's] book being a best seller even five years ago, and we can only conjecture as to why it has proved so much in keeping with the general mood now when the Cold War is still with us. It may be that the only way we can live indefinitely in this state of tension, with this kind of reality, is to be coldly, even cynically, realistic about it. Just as the poor man must face reality every day whereas the rich man need not, so perhaps now we must face the reality of war whereas before the nuclear threat we could be fooled by the romance of it.

Writing in the *Evening Post,* Anthony Burgess was even blunter: Britain had no illusions about its ability to control the next war. "The thesis of 'Catch-22' can only be universally valid when the whole world has been absorbed into the American Empire," he said.

Gottlieb and Bourne rushed ads into the *New York Times,* saying, "Come on! Don't let the English beat us! Overnight, while America slept, Joseph Heller's **Catch-22** has become #1 bestseller in England.

Come on Yanks! To your booksellers! Help close the Catch-gap! On-
wards and upwards! Over the top! Let's go!"

In August 1962, when Candida Donadio sold the *Catch-22* film
rights to Columbia Pictures for $100,000, with a $25,000 option for a
treatment or first-draft screenplay, Joe took a leave of absence from
McCall's, ostensibly to prepare a chronology of events and narrative
time line for the movie studio. Few of his magazine colleagues expected
to see him return. One of his former bosses, Herbert Mayes, told a reporter, "Heller's a hell of a good publicist. Sorry we lost him. What I'd
like to know, though, is how he got the time on my time to write that
book."

Joe spent the rest of the summer and early fall drawing up a chart of
the novel's action for the movie people and making notes for a possible
dramatic adaptation to be performed on Broadway—the producer David
Merrick had suggested this idea. "I don't know yet whether I'll do the
play or turn it over to someone else, but I will probably do the film
script," he told the *New York Times.*

He also enjoyed himself. "It was wonderful for Joe," said Bob Gottlieb. "I've never known a writer who took a more innocent and marvelous, happy, wholesome joy in his success. He really appreciated it. It
had been a long time coming. And he loved it. He loved being the author of *Catch-22.*"

He was invited to parties where he met actors and writers, critics
and professors. He was so thrilled to be included in these gatherings, he
was slow to realize many people had come to meet him. Some of Gottlieb's colleagues felt embarrassed by Joe's frank delight in his good fortune, and they complained that his attitude was unseemly (especially
around other writers, comfortably miserable in their anonymous co-
coons). "They had an idea that I was supposed to look like Thomas
Wolfe, with this aura of suicidal melancholy," Joe quipped. Gottlieb
brushed away his colleagues' complaints. Let the man celebrate his success. He knew how to handle it.

"Both [success and failure] are difficult to endure," Joe reflected
years later. "Along with success come drugs, divorce, fornication, bully-
ing, travel, meditation, medication, depression, neurosis and suicide.
With failure comes failure. . . . Luckily, I was thirty-eight and pretty well
set in my ways when *Catch-22* came out. I had a good job and a nice
apartment. If I'd been, say, twenty-seven and living in a cold-water flat,

my marriage would have broken up, I would have bought an estate in East Hampton I couldn't afford and, to pay for it, I would have started a second novel too soon."

"*CATCH-22* is taking off!" Joe told Alice Denham. He had stopped by her apartment one afternoon.

"I'll drink to that," she said. She poured him a scotch and they toasted.

"Guess what?" Joe said. "I quit work. I'm writing a film script. For good money. I'm hot, hot!"

"Joe, that's fabulous." Denham's writing was going nowhere. She had begun to think the literary world was a "boy's club."

"Man, is Shirley relieved," Joe said. "Greenbacks, at last. I'm meeting writers I've always wanted to know. Like Algren."

"Wow, introduce me, bigshot."

For all his bluster, "Joe Heller was always a good guy," Denham wrote. "He didn't have an ounce of pomposity. He was macho, of course, but he was a buddy of sorts, bursting with high spirits and fun." Everybody liked him—"he was that sort of guy."

That day, he shocked her by admitting he'd been "celebrating life"— he'd "[s]pent too much time with a lady friend this afternoon." "So Joe played around, like so many others," Denham wrote. "Somehow I['d] thought he had a rockbound marriage."

And he *did,* according to the double standards he'd learned in the military and corporate offices.

She remembered he had once consoled her after she'd had an affair with David Markson, which ended badly. Joe asked her if she wanted children, if she really wanted to be faithful. She had to be honest with herself, he said. "You don't want to be married [now], Alice," he told her. "You want romance. That's different. . . . You're an adventuress. Don't knock it."

On that occasion, she wrote, he counseled her that "[w]hen people want to get married, *only then* do they look around for a permanent mate. It starts with wanting marriage."

"Is that what you did?" Denham asked him.

"Sure," he said. "You look at people differently. I'd been through the war. I wanted to settle down."

"A MATTER has been troubling me that I feel I should bring to your attention." So began a letter received by Simon & Schuster in mid-May 1962. "It has to do with the appearance of my name, Robert Oliver Shipman, in the novel *Catch-22*."

Mr. Shipman went on to say he was a member of the faculty at the Pennsylvania State College at the time Joseph Heller taught there. As "in the case of the chaplain in *Catch-22*, I was married and the father of three small children," he said; "in the United States Army [I held] the rank of captain, the same rank indicated as being held by the chaplain in *Catch-22*."

Given these similarities, the appearance of his name in the book embarrassed him, he said: "I find it difficult to believe that the use of the name . . . can be attributed to mere coincidence." He said he had no wish to humiliate Mr. Heller. He hoped the matter could be handled quietly and privately, but he wanted the name removed from all subsequent editions and reprints of *Catch-22*.

On May 18, Joe wrote a long and cordial letter to Mr. Shipman, assuring him the "matter was entirely coincidental." "I can no more explain why I used the name Robert Oliver Shipman than I can explain [my other choices] . . . except that in every case the basic intention was to *avoid* using the name of any person I had ever met or heard of. As a matter of fact, the name was originally R. C. Shipman (a fact you can verify in New World Writing 7, 1955, where the beginning of the book first appeared) and the 'c' became an 'o' as a result of an initial typing error that was allowed to stand, since the difference was of no consequence." Nevertheless, Joe said, he understood Mr. Shipman was troubled. "[W]ith a great deal of sadness" he would "accede to [his] request" if Mr. Shipman continued to insist. The problem was, "it will probably be impossible for me to find a seven-letter substitute that will have the same symbolic connotations that the name has as a word. For another, there is the feeling that Chaplain Shipman already has a literary identity for the many people who have already read the book and the many critics who have written about it. And for another, I like to think that the book will be read, discussed, and written about for several years to come, and I feel sorry for those graduate students who will read the book in one version and find themselves discussing it with professors who have read it in another."

Shipman remained politely unmoved.

For the sixth S & S printing, and all following editions of the novel, the name would be changed (though Shipman lives on in certain British paperback reprints). For the right new name, Joe returned to Penn State in his mind. He recalled the plucky young boxer, the perpetual underdog, Tapman (and, for good measure, added an extra *p* to the name).

On August 6, 1962, Paula Diamond, a literary agent, sent Joe a note: "Eek, I've just picked up the Dell [paperback] reprint. Who is that Tappman person and what have you done with R. O. Shipman? Are there *no* eternal verities?" Joe responded that, after wrestling with the problem "as Jacob wrestled with the angel," he had "capitulated" to Mr. Shipman like a "coward."

Mr. Shipman, who went on to serve as the assistant dean in Columbia University's Graduate School of Journalism, had a final exchange with Joe in April 1963. He wanted to say "how well I think you substituted for the name of the chaplain . . . particularly the effectiveness with which you retained the seven-letter symbolism of the surname." He had read with enjoyment in the *New York Times Book Review* that more than 800,000 copies of the paperback edition had sold since its release in September 1962. "Warm congratulations to you and this splendid success," Mr. Shipman said. "I am delighted to see a writer of your obvious competence and caliber being rightly recognized and rewarded."

Joe replied he was glad that "no permanent resentment exist[ed]" and thanked Mr. Shipman for his "kind feelings." He added, "To date, I have received but two queries regarding the change of name, which proves my fears that legions of Ph.D [*sic*] candidates would be thrown into confusion, were groundless."

"THE SUCCESS of [*Catch-22* in paperback] in the first few months was astonishing," said Don Fine, Dell's editor in chief. He had purchased rights to the novel from S & S and Pocket Books for $32,000. "This was a book lovingly and carefully prepared by Bob Gottlieb. But the book did not take off in hardcover. . . . I remember when I sent the contract information to Bill Callahan [Dell's vice president in charge of sales], he wrote to me saying, 'What the hell is a *Catch-22*?' I wrote back and said, 'It's a World War II novel.' We 'packaged' it so it could pass as a big important World War II [book]. . . . We had an aviator's head—not very good art—for the cover instead of [Paul Bacon's] dangling man, which was the trademark of the hardcover. It would have destroyed the paperback with that on the cover. And this was the magic of paperback publishing in those days. We didn't have any television spots. We probably didn't have much point-of-sale stuff. But people read it. Young people read it and war veterans read it and goddammit, it worked! The paperback public took over this book and made it a very big success. . . . This was the way books got talked about and became household words."

"[A] nation-wide sensation at $5.95[,] now complete and unabridged at 75¢," proclaimed the paperback cover. The *Catch* craze began.

"Not since the *Catcher in the Rye* and *Lord of the Flies* has a novel been taken up by such a fervid and heterogeneous claque of admirers," *Newsweek* announced in October 1962. "The book obviously inspires an evangelical fervor in those who admire it. . . . It has already swept the cocktail-party circuit where *Catch-22* is the hottest topic going and Joe Heller himself is the hottest catch."

Joe appeared on NBC's *Today* show with interim host John Chancellor, projecting congeniality, confidence, and an adman's smoothness. He talked about the universality of his characters and said, "Yossarian is alive somewhere and still on the run." After the show, "in a bar close by the studio in which I found myself drinking martinis at an earlier hour than ever in my life," Joe said, "[Chancellor] handed me a packet of stickers he'd had printed privately. They read: YOSSARIAN LIVES. And he confided he'd been pasting these stickers secretly on the walls of the corridors and in the executive rest rooms of the NBC building."

Eventually, similar stickers appeared on college campuses along with copies of the paperback. Professors assigned the book, using it to discuss not only literary modernism and World War II but also current American policy in Southeast Asia, which dominated the news more and more. "[T]he war that I [was] really dealing with was not World War II but turned out to be the Vietnam war," Joe told an interviewer.

"I don't think I'll ever recover [from reading this novel]," one university teacher wrote to S & S. "But before I die of *Catch-22*, I will do everything to keep it alive. . . . I'll write *Catch-22* on every surface I can find." Soon, Yossarian graffiti stamped campuses and cities, side by side with the stickers. The most popular slogan was "Better Yossarian than Rotarian." Yo-Yo went as many places as Kilroy ever had.

Publishers Weekly reported, "[At] the University of Chicago students [are] buying up second-hand Army field jackets and sewing on Yossarian name tags." In November 1962, *Esquire*'s editor, Arnold Gingrich, said, "The young people . . . tell me that the college students are still reading 'Catcher in the Rye' . . . [but] coming up fast is 'Catch-22.' . . . Call it, if you like, the resistance movement—their revolt against authority, against organizational conformity, against the materialistic, affluent society."

In his documentary film, *Stone Reader*, Mark Moskowitz captures the feel of the moment for an adolescent reader in the 1960s, as well as the joy of discovering *Catch-22*:

At some point, I outgrew the school library and found myself walking forty-five minutes to a paperback store—I think it was called Paperbacks Etcetera—in the next town. It was small, two aisles, but I could hang out there and just look at the covers, each cover with the promise of a wild story within. Tucked into a small, one-shelf section just a foot from the floor were books with World War II settings. . . . I looked for books in which heroes did things against all the odds. . . . I picked out James Jones. . . . A month later, having finished [his book], and therefore now feeling like an adult, I went back to get the book they compared it to on the back cover, *The Naked and the Dead*. The guy behind the counter, a tall, skinny older guy, was reluctant to sell it to me, so I took it out of the library instead: an old, falling-apart hardback, black cover, no dust jacket. They would say "Fug" in the book, and that seemed interesting. I couldn't figure out what that was—Fug. F-U-G. It couldn't mean "fuck." They wouldn't let someone put that much "fuck" in a book, would they? Fug. It made it fantasy, almost. Well, that was good, too, so I went back to the little store and perused what was left of the war section. I pulled out the last one: a bright blue one. *Catch-22*. Seventy-five cents. *That* was the book. It just appealed to my subversive self. . . . I had climbed onto the adult plateau of Jones and Mailer and looked around and couldn't find anything else, and then I came across *Catch-22*, way out there somewhere. . . . Everything else smacked of suburban grown-ups. . . . Yeah, right [I thought]. . . . And so I would go to the library and continue to take out books and search for articles on Heller. Anything. I couldn't believe people weren't just standing there and shaking *Catch-22* and talking about it. Why read anything else? Where *was* this guy? . . . They say one book can turn a kid on to be a reader for life. I was already a reader, but *Catch-22* excited me. It was the first book I read where the author's voice meant as much to me as the story or the characters. [Heller was] the first writer I wanted to know more about, because the voice behind the pages was a friend I thought I could never find in life.

Joe admitted, "When [the] book first came out in paper, I'd get into the subway or train and look at the books people were reading. If the paperback had blue edges, it was Dell. My book is in Dell, so then I'd have to try to see the cover. If the guy was reading my book, it was a good feeling."

With stunning swiftness, the term *catch-22* slipped into daily conversations nationwide—in corporate headquarters and on military bases, college campuses—to describe any bureaucratic paradox. Eventually, *The American Heritage Dictionary* sanctioned it, defining a *catch-22* as a "difficult situation or problem whose seemingly alternative solutions are logically invalid."

On October 15, 1962, Simon & Schuster, Dell, and Columbia Pictures bought a full-page ad in the *New York Times*. The ad announced, "Happy birthday CATCH-22." By April 1963, the paperback had sold 1,100,000 copies of the 1,250,000 in print. Hardback sales still averaged one hundred to two hundred copies a month. By the end of the decade, Dell had taken the book through thirty printings. In sales as well as critical acclaim, *Catch-22* had broken out of its literary trappings and East Coast box to become a perennial American classic.

"Without being aware of it, I was part of a near movement in fiction," Joe reflected in 1977. "While I was writing *Catch-22*, J. P. Donleavy was writing *The Ginger Man*, Kerouac was writing *On the Road*, Ken Kesey was writing *One Flew Over the Cuckoo's Nest*, Pynchon was writing *V*, and Vonnegut was writing *Cat's Cradle*. I don't think any one of us even knew the others. Certainly I didn't know them. Whatever forces were at work shaping a trend in art were affecting not just me, but all of us."

Apropos of Joe's remarks, it is worth noting that, according to critic

Anatole Broyard, the college professors he encountered in the 1950s, when these novels were being written, "did their best to make us feel like exiles in our own country." The professors remained shocked and appalled by World War II, the firebombings, Hiroshima, and the concentration camps; they were fascinated by psychoanalytic theories of the unconscious mind; and they worried about the Cold War. Thanks to the ongoing effects of the G.I. Bill, their classes were filled to capacity with the largest cross section of the American public ever to attend institutions of higher learning. "All the courses I took were about *what's wrong*," Broyard wrote in his memoir, *Kafka Was the Rage*. "[W]hat's wrong with the government, with the family, with interpersonal relations and intrapersonal relations—what's wrong with our dreams, our loves, our jobs, our perceptions and conceptions, our esthetics, the human condition itself. They were furious, the professors, at the ugly turn the world had taken."

It is also worth noting, as Jonathan R. Eller reminds us, that all the writers Joe cited "[came] to us almost entirely in paperback."

"FOR SIXTEEN YEARS I have been waiting for the great anti-war book which I knew WWII must produce," Stephen E. Ambrose, writer and historian, wrote to Joe in January 1962. "I rather doubted, however, that it would come out of America; I would have guessed Germany. I am happy to have been wrong. . . . Thank you."

In a letter written the following year, John Steinbeck said to Joe, "I would very much like to know which way you are going now. Your gargantuan approach [to literature] (and I use the term literally) can be of great value now, for peace has become almost as ridiculous as war."

PART FOUR **What Happened**

12. The Realist

AMERICA IN THE SIXTIES, ostensibly an effort by the editors of *Fortune* [magazine] to forecast the major social and economic trends of the 60's, reveals more about the Luce mind than about the [coming decade]." Thus began a review in the February 1961 issue of *Commentary.* "Written in the characteristic self-congratulatory and breathless style of *Fortune* . . . [the book] exhibits that willed commitment to a roseate view of the future which we have come to expect from Luce publications (though not, interestingly enough, from the ex-Luce men)," the reviewer said. The ex–Luce men now included Joseph Heller. "*Fortune* writes that soon the poor will no longer be with us. . . . This can be called the 'midtown' view of economic realities. Were *Fortune*'s writers to take an occasional trip some sixty blocks further downtown, they would learn that [most] people . . . hardly [try their luck] in the stock market. . . . But such realism would tend to spoil the picture so lovingly composed by *Fortune.*"

The "Luce men" *did* misperceive the sixties—badly. In retrospect, it seems they missed the mark not because they refused to speak of "drags on productivity" (on the grounds that this would be "a mark of disaffection, perhaps even of disloyalty"). No. *Fortune* correctly predicted the "miracles of rising income, rising productivity, [and] rising consumption" driving the decade. The federal government under Lyndon Johnson launched a war on poverty. The major indicators suggested everyone should have "afford[ed] a second divorce along with a second car and a second television set. Cheer up, boys!" Something happened. What was it?

If we tunnel through the years and glance back at the 1960s, from the point of view of a *Commentary* editor so rattled by the times that he reinvented himself, we confront the question once more: What happened? Writing in 2000, Norman Podhoretz, who once praised *Catch-22*'s author for his boldness as an artist, now condemned the novel as having done "moral, spiritual, and intellectual harm" to several generations of Americans.

Between *Fortune*'s "roseate" view, looking ahead in 1961, and Podhoretz's embittered summary in 2000 lay four decades of a culture at war with itself, during which *Catch-22* remained steadily in print, selling in vast numbers. What happened to make the novel a central document during this period, a touchstone—positive and negative—in our self-assessments? As early as 1962, before *Catch-22* sold so astonishingly, *Newsweek* was declaring a "Heller Cult," saying Joe was the man to write *the* novel of the American 1960s (without realizing that perhaps he already had). As for the new novel Joe would tackle, he had glimpsed it in his mind at the decade's outset, telling the *Newsweek* reporter he had begun to make notes on it in his rental house on Fire Island. It would be "about a married man who is working for a large company and who wants to work himself up to the point where he makes a speech at the company's annual convention in Bermuda."

He paused, as if to acknowledge how unpromising this material sounded.

"It has implications," he said.

That a thirty-nine-year-old World War II vet could be the literary spokesperson for a culture besotted with the Kennedys seems odd. Again in retrospect, we can see how many of the cultural skirmishes from the 1960s to the present orbited the World War II generation. Former television newscaster Tom Brokaw called this generation the "greatest" in a bestselling book in 1998. Born in the "fulcrum [years] of America in the twentieth century" and headed for a "rendezvous with destiny" (to quote FDR), this group represented our national peak, from which all subsequent generations—their artists, writers, and politicians—had fallen, Brokaw said. *Catch-22,* a book embraced both as a World War II novel and a novel about Vietnam, now seems an inevitable flashpoint.

In 1961, the Luce men were unprepared to envision Barnard College switching from the home of panty raids to the site of a major controversy over cohabitation before marriage. In 1968, Linda LeClair, a twenty-year-old sophomore at Barnard, would be punished for breaking school regulations by living off campus with her boyfriend, a junior at Columbia. The story was covered for weeks in national newspapers and sparked a dialogue about sexual mores. What had happened to our values? Our children? What would happen to marriage?

Eventually, LeClair dropped out of college and went to live in a commune with her boyfriend, who resisted induction into the army.

In 1961, the Luce men were unprepared to envision Catskills stages trading Borscht Belt shtick for the world's largest rock concert, a mud bath of collective property, free love, and drugs, serenaded by Jimi Hendrix's national anthem, whose "bombs bursting in air" became electric guitar riffs sounding like napalm falling from the sky. Many children of the Woodstock Nation wore army fatigues with Yossarian name tags on the breast pockets. What had happened to America's rendezvous with destiny? Was the mud at Woodstock a benign metaphor for Vietnam? Was destiny supposed to look like a quagmire?

What couldn't be seen in 1961 was the truth of Plato's dictum that "Forms and rhythms in [art] are never changed without producing changes in the most important political forms and ways." For years, the men on Madison Avenue had flirted with this concept in their attempts to manipulate the American consumer; soon, a man calling himself Dylan, men named John, Paul, George, and Ringo would seize the idea and plumb it to its core. Joe Heller had grabbed it when he'd changed the emphasis in his fiction from *the story* to *the way the story is told*.

What was true in 1961—the prevailing national temper that Joe would voice in his second novel, published in 1974, when sixties convulsions were settling (or subtler)—was this: "I know so many things I'm afraid to find out."

WHAT DID YIDDISH sound like with a Chinese accent?

Joe would soon find out via Irving "Speed" Vogel, who introduced him to Ngoot Lee and established an extended series of friendships that would comfort Joe for the rest of his days. Speed once said, "The "motivation of my entire life has been friends." Like Joe, he had a *gift* for friendship.

One day on Fire Island, in the summer of 1962, Joe, Shirley, and their children were walking on the beach. Speed Vogel had bought an oceanside house from Carl Reiner and was out, that afternoon, sunbathing. He noticed an attractive woman. He studied her face and recognized her as an old friend of his kid sister: Shirley Held. She told him she was married to the writer Joseph Heller. He gushed about *Catch-22*. She took him over to meet Joe and they hit it off. In no time, "Joe somehow managed to squeeze all [my] juicy gossip . . . out of [me]," Speed wrote.

Irving Vogel was the son of an Eastern European immigrant who became one of Manhattan's most prosperous building contractors. Julius Vogel built apartment houses in the Bronx, on the Upper West Side, and all along Broadway and Central Park. The family lived on Riverside Drive at Seventy-second Street. As a teenager, Speed referred to his dad's buildings as his father's "erections." The two did not get along. Dubbed "Speed" at the age of four by a wry camp counselor ribbing him for taking so long to tie his shoes, the young Vogel did not share his father's drive for achievement. He preferred a slower pace, a more bohemian life. He rebelled against the family and its riches (while continuing to accept his father's money). For a while, he worked as a herring taster at a Manhattan delicatessen, Zabar's, he started a textile business, he worked as an assistant to the architect Charles Gwathmey, and he tried his hand at sculpture, working with found metals.

One day in 1960, fleeing a failing marriage and seeking studio space for his art, he rented a place on West Twenty-eighth Street. Zero Mostel was one of his neighbors. A former Borscht Belt performer and an Off-Broadway actor, Mostel (who had tangled with the House Committee on Un-American Activities in the 1950s for giving "Red" speeches) was trying to be a painter, and he shared a studio with a sculptor named Herby Kallem, a friend of Speed. Recently, Speed had met at a party another downtrodden showbiz type, a loud little fellow named Mel Brooks. Born Melvin Kaminsky to a Russian-Ukranian Jewish family, and raised in a Brooklyn tenement, Brooks had been a tummler at Grossinger's, a writer for Sid Caesar's *Your Show of Shows,* and was now scrambling for money while trying to write a novel—or maybe it would be a play—tentatively titled "Springtime for Hitler." He was married to a woman named Florence, but the marriage was ending. Impulsively, Brooks asked Speed if he could move in with him. For three months, the men lived together uneasily, bickering over housekeeping and laundry, keeping alternate hours. "[Mel] had a blood-sugar problem that kept us a scintilla away from insanity, and his brushstroke of paranoia had me on the verge (more than once) of calling Bellevue to come and collect him," Speed wrote. For his part, Brooks did not appreciate Speed's sculptural talents. Once, while he was watching Speed—tall, wiry, deliberate in his movements—hammer metal, the phone rang. "Mr. Vogel can't speak to you now," Brooks said into the receiver. "He's working on his horsey and he cannot be disturbed."

Finally, tensions broke into the open. One day, while Speed was away, Brooks painted all over the walls "You snore, you son-of-a-bitch! Yes, that's what you do! All night! Snore! Snore! Snore! You fuck!" Speed called Brook's ex and asked her to take him back. "What do you want from me?" she said. "If you can't stand him anymore, throw him out." Throughout the ordeal, the men remained friends (Brooks referred to Speed affectionately as "Huck Finn on his raft in Manhattan"). Years later, Speed heard Neil Simon had based his play *The Odd Couple* on stories he'd heard about them.

Speed introduced Brooks to Joe. They became buddies. "Mel and Joe had tremendous similarities in their backgrounds," Speed said. "Their fathers died when they were young. Mel was two, Joe was five. They both lived in Brooklyn and were very poor. Neither expected to afford an education." In Brooks, Joe saw what he could not yet fathom in himself. "There's a side of Mel that will never be fulfilled, no matter how hard he drives himself," he told Kenneth Tynan for a *New Yorker* profile of Brooks in 1978, "and it all goes back to his father's death."

The men shared a wicked sense of humor. "Tragedy is if I cut my finger," Brooks once said. "Comedy is if you walk into an open sewer and die."

At about this time—early 1962—Zero Mostel smelled warm and grassy odors wafting down the stairwell from a second-floor loft late each afternoon. He walked up and introduced himself to the man in the apartment, a young Cantonese fellow named Ngoot. Mostel told Ngoot his cooking smelled marvelous, thereby earning an invitation to lunch. Speed wrote:

> Ngoot, a little guy, said Zero looked like a Japanese sumo wres-
> tler, so he prepared plenty to eat. As soon as Zero finished the
> food on his plate, without asking, Ngoot filled it again. Zero ate
> himself into a stupor. He could not rise from his chair. Acknowl-
> edging his guest's mumbled appreciation for the exquisite cui-
> sine, Ngoot thoughtfully removed Zero's plate so his head did
> not smash it as he fell asleep at the table.

Soon, Ngoot was feeding Mostel and his friends on a regular basis, and giving Speed lessons in Cantonese cooking: soy sauce chicken, bar-becued spare ribs, beef and spinach with oyster sauce, lobster, egg foo young, pork chops and onion in beer, shrimp in the shell, sautéed but-terfish. "If you don't have it, you don't need it," Ngoot would say, sur-veying his kitchen in the evenings. Speed asked if he could invite more friends to dinner. "No problem," Ngoot said.

Mel Brooks came by, bringing a pal, Julie Green, a diamond mer-chant he'd met. Joe came once, twice, twice more. He brought George Mandel. In time, George brought Mario Puzo. Joe Stein, a playwright who would one day write *Fiddler on the Roof,* showed up now and then. No one had any idea what Ngoot did for a living. They knew he had come from a Cantonese village run by his grandfather. They knew that as a kid he'd kept a pet water buffalo. Mostel taught him Yiddish, as well as curse words in English. According to Speed, no matter how hard he tried, Ngoot was unable to learn the phrase *Se schver tzu zein ah yid* ("It's hard to be a Jew").

The men called themselves "the Group of the Oblong Table" or "the Chinese Gourmet Club." Eventually, they shortened this to "the Gour-met Club." They met in Speed's studio, which had a fireplace, formerly walled off, and a cast-iron grate. "Mel was strangely attracted to fire so we put him in charge of providing us with heat," Speed wrote. "We picked up our fuel from the street—fruit crates, parts of cargo pallets, broken furniture—anything that would burn. Once Mel got started, there was no holding [him] back. . . . [T]he blaze was so tremendous it was coming out of the wall. We feared for the building and our lives."

The male camaraderie soothed them. They could just be themselves. They could confess their ambitions, career insecurities, and puzzlement over women. One night, Mario Puzo quipped, "The trouble with fucking is that it leads to kissing." On another occasion, George Mandel told the group the story of how he'd received his head wound. A silence fell; there was only the crackling of fruit crates in the fireplace. Then Brooks said, "I'm sure glad that happened to you and not to me." As Joe recalled, "He wasn't being cruel. [H]e was just being honest." That was the great thing about the Gourmet Club. "He just blurted out what we were all thinking but didn't dare to say."

JOE *NEEDED* FRIENDS NOW. It was fun to share his success, to be able to walk into a room, shout "I'm hot! I'm hot!" and give people bear hugs. More important, it was essential for folks who had long known him to keep him grounded. "Joe loved to move around Manhattan, being lionized," said Mell Lazarus, a cartoonist whose daily comic strip, "Miss Peach," Joe admired. Lazarus met Joe one day at the Café Renaissance, a place over in the East Forties, near the UN. Joe was sitting in the bar with Richard Condon, author of *The Manchurian Candidate*. Lazarus introduced himself, told Joe he had been "staggered" by *Catch-22*, and they got to talking. "We were both Jewish, both mother-stricken. We had so much in common," Lazarus said. "He was so much fun, so interesting to know. He seemed to get to know everybody very quickly. He was magnetic, charismatic." He was most at ease with men, but Lazarus learned how much Joe depended on his wife's "sweetness" and "typical middle-class" values to help him maintain a solid daily perspective. It was difficult to stay steady when reporters kept coming around asking him to expound upon literature, on the state of American politics. Little Joey from Coney Island! They wanted to know what *he* thought! He would say something—"The Kennedy Administration [is] like a bunch of spoiled fraternity brats celebrating after having bought a campus election . . . cavort[ing] around, pushing each other into swimming pools"—and reporters scribbled every word. Then Joe would go to a bar or restaurant with friends. "Women flock[ed] to him," said Barbara Gelb. It was "difficult to know whether this happen[ed] because of his curls, his fame, his hostility or a combination of all three." ("You can't be a female fan of [Heller's work] without feeling a bit daft," wrote the British journalist Sally Vincent years later. The writing, she believed, showed a "total disregard for [women]." Still, she was charmed by him.)

Joe had quit his advertising job, but among men in the pubs and eateries of Manhattan, success was still measured by the size of a paycheck and the number of affairs a man had—or the ability to brag, regardless of the truth. Joe insisted he wasn't all that invested in literature, writing, and reading; he admired *achievement*, no matter the field, and he had seized his opportunity. That it happened to be in novel writing was neither here nor there.

Shirley saw through this ruse. She had no patience with his posturing. Her insight was both reassuring and irritating. She never let him forget he had a family to support. But she also told him to guard his integrity. She knew he valued literature and art. She understood it mattered to him whether he had written a good, as opposed to a merely popular, novel. Sometimes, though, her support felt like pressure and he'd respond with anger or impatience. In truth, the pressure came from within: He'd gotten a few tentative ideas for his second novel; he'd written a few lines on index cards. But the fear that he might not be able to pull off another book never left him. It was all very well for Shirley to talk about integrity. She didn't have to do the work!

The apartment could seem stultifying when ideas weren't coming and the children ran from room to room, distracting him. "I think as soon as I was old enough to have my own opinions and challenge him things changed [between us]," Erica recalls. "As far as I was concerned, he pretty much always had to be right, and whenever I challenged that as a kid . . . I think he found it tiresome. George Mandel told me a story about a dinner party my parents gave when I was about three. Apparently, at some point they heard my father screaming and he was in my room, shouting and stabbing his finger at me for emphasis. No one knew what any of it was about, but I think George had to pull my father away from me. 'Joe!' he told Dad. 'She's *three* years old!'"

"[W]e were not an . . . affectionate family," Ted says. "Maybe this came from Joe not having a father . . . [but] I don't know if our relationship was that much different than any other one between fathers and sons back in those days. . . . I was always a very, very private person and still am and if our relationship was warier than others, I'll take the blame for it. . . . [I]t was a great thing to have a dad who didn't have to work all day long. We would often go to Riverside Park and play football or baseball or do it in the courtyard in the Apthorp. I loved sports (a lot more than he did) but when he could he was always ready to play."

In reflective moments, Joe understood it was confusing for his kids to watch him get so much attention from strangers. And he was sometimes confused about how to balance his responsibilities. "[I]t is never, or hardly ever, an entirely good thing [to be a celebrity presence in the household]," he wrote years later. "It would have been witless of me to attempt to ward off [people's] flattering acknowledgements, and hypocritical to pretend I did anything other than lap them up."

He would leave the apartment to relax with the Gourmet Club or he'd head down to P. J. Clarke's or some other place to sit and swap stories with buddies. "He was funnier, more incisive, more interesting than anybody else," said Norman Barasch. "He could be abrasive, but not if you made him laugh. I always made him laugh, so he didn't turn that abrasiveness on me. We always had a good time."

Joe's Swedish publisher, Per Gedin (a "very warm, open man," Erica recalls) became a close pal. "They loved each other and when Per would come to town, he would always take Dad to the Russian Tea Room, quite the place then, and I gather they would drink mass quantities of vodka and have a real blast," Erica says.

At parties with other couples, Joe was often the center of attention, sometimes to Shirley's embarrassment. "He was always complaining about the food," Barasch said. "'This is all you're serving?' he'd say. 'This is nothing!' He'd go around saying, 'Water! Water! I want more water!' He was like a camel." If in public his voice, stories, and gestures were getting grander, it was, Shirley knew, because he was swinging from the joy of being "lionized" to the terror of not being able to make another *Catch*.

He took screenplay assignments. Why not? People threw them his way. Easy money, he told himself. He could knock these things out in his sleep. The work was a merciful relief from brooding about his "serious" writing. On April 3, 1962, *Fred Astaire's Premiere Theatre* on ABC-TV aired an hour-long drama entitled "Seven against the Sea," starring Ernest Borgnine. Fred Astaire, dressed as if for a dinner party, introduced the story, walking along a set meant to evoke a war-wrecked beach. "This is the world of Stevenson, Conrad, and Gauguin," Astaire announced, "men who were inspired to great art by the beaches of the

South Sea Paradise. But even Paradise has its hell, and in the late spring of 1942, [the island of] Taratupa became an inferno." In the background, waving palm trees gave way to the flashes and sounds of big guns firing. The story concerned a U.S. Navy Commander named Quinton McHale—played by Borgnine—who was trapped on the island with a handful of men following a devastating Japanese attack. The script was attributed to veteran TV writer Albert Aley. Overwrought and melodramatic, the show received respectable ratings.

ABC ordered scripts for a series to be called *McHale's Navy*. The series producer, Edward J. Montagne, veered the material toward slapstick, as he had scored a previous TV success with a military comedy starring Phil Silvers. *McHale's Navy* evolved into a weekly half-hour situation comedy about a reprobate noncom officer and his motley PT boat crew: a forerunner of *M*A*S*H*, and both of them—*M*A*S*H* to a greater degree—descendants of *Catch-22*.

Montagne asked Joe to write a script for the show. At the time, John F. Kennedy was widely admired for having served on a PT boat; Joe may have relished the chance to lampoon him by representing PT crewmen as opportunistic, greedy, and none too bright.

Meanwhile, he was being courted by the literature crowd. The Cheltenham Literary Festival in London, in its thirteenth year in 1962, invited him to participate in a panel discussion on "Sex in Literature" (a topic designed to exploit the recent British publication of D. H. Lawrence's 1928 novel, *Lady Chatterley's Lover*). Without his family—the children were in school—Joe went to London. This was his first time in many years on a plane, and it took several drinks to calm him. He appeared on the panel with Carson McCullers and Kingsley Amis. McCullers had broken her left arm; she was drunk and nearly incoherent, waving her cast and slurring that "so long as a book is true and beautiful," it could never be pornographic. When it was his turn to speak, Joe observed that the makers of mink coats had corrupted more girls than any book had ever done. After the festival, Amis left his wife of fifteen years for the festival organizer, Elizabeth Jane Howard. Joe was surprised and bemused that literary types behaved like copywriters on Madison Avenue.

Following the festival, he rented a car and drove to Wales to meet the philosopher Bertrand Russell, who had praised *Catch-22* in print.

Russell was then in his nineties and somewhat hard of hearing. Joe came to the door and introduced himself. Russell waved his cane, shouting, "Go away, damn you! Never come back here again!" Perplexed, Joe started for his car, when Russell's manservant came after him. "I'm sorry, sir, but there's been a bit of a misunderstanding," the man said. "Mr. Russell thought you said 'Edward Teller.'" Confusion cleared, the men lunched together—Russell was quite hospitable—and though the exchange was uneventful, Joe described the afternoon as "thrilling."

On this same trip to Europe, he met James Jones for the first time. In Paris for a book signing, Joe ran into a fellow novelist, the son of John Marquand, who asked him, "What are you doing tonight?" Joe replied, "Nothing. I am alone in this city. I don't know anybody, and I'd like to meet someone like Marilyn Monroe." His companion took him for drinks with Jones and his wife. "[I] expressed my gratitude to Jim [for his book]," Joe said. Among the other guests at the table was a man named Mitchell Parish, who had written the lyrics to "Stardust" and "Deep Purple"—a "very fussy old man," Joe said. "[N]ot till six or seven o'clock the next morning did I find myself back at my hotel."

These activities—the screenwriting, the travel—were welcome distractions not just from anxieties about writing a second novel but also from daily life, with its occasional sorrows, which Shirley tried to keep as his center. His mother had finally died in the old Half Moon Hotel on Coney Island. The qualities he knew he shared with her—vanity, a deep cynicism, especially about institutions—became exaggerated in her speech and behaviors near the end. She worried about the way her hair looked, when there was not much hair to fret about. She accused the staff of mistreating her (increasing Joe's guilt that he had not invited her to live with him).

He remembered visiting Lena in the hospital years earlier, when she had broken her hip, and mistaking another woman for her. It occurred to him that this incident might have been the basis of the scene in *Catch-22* when a mother and father visit their dying son and mistake Yossarian for the boy: Well, why not? We're *all* dying.

Lena's biggest pleasure late in life was the taste of bacon—*trayf*! It pleased Joe to see her wolfing it down in the mornings. He remembered meals she had shared with his family before her incarceration in the old-age home, before Ted was born, when Erica was a baby and her every gesture seemed cute and charming, designed by nature to smooth the edges of an irascible old woman. Well, often it's best to shed even good things, Joe reflected. Especially when you have no choice. Youth— the past—has its limits. After one of his last visits to Lena, he wandered down the old block, past boarded-up taverns and cafés, the doorways filled with junkies and shivering runaways—kids not much older than his daughter. Despite the poverty, you never used to see that sort of thing before the war. We had character, Joe decided. Whatever else we lacked, we had that at least—in no small part, thanks to women like his mother.

He stopped to remember Irving Kaiser and his typewriter. He wished he saw more of Sylvia and Lee. Sylvia, now married to a man named Bernie Fields, still worked for Macy's, and Lee, the proud father of Joe's nephew, Paul, worked these days for a film-production company. Joe was sorry they had drifted apart. But that's what families did when they became successful.

ON NOVEMBER 1, 1962, *McHale's Navy* featured an episode entitled "PT 73, Where Are You?" written by Joe Heller. The program credits listed a man named Si Rose as "Script Consultant."

The plot concerned a group of hapless navy men who misplace their boat somewhere in the South Pacific. How this happened is never clear; it is simply the premise from which events ensue. In a bit of slapstick dialogue reminiscent of *Catch-22,* the skipper says, "I always felt it wasn't too easy to lose a boat." One of his men answers, straight-faced, "No, it wasn't easy at all. Why, the mosquitoes . . ." Everything works out in the end, paced by an annoying laugh track. The crew returns to its comic books and beer (cans of which have been stored in the torpedo tubes), and dreams of R & R, where everyone will "squeeze . . . red-head[s]" on shady spots in the sand.

Four months before the program's air date, Joe wrote producer Jay Sanford to complain about Si Rose. "Friends of mine in TV had warned me that there is usually a staff writer or story editor around on every show who will bend heaven and earth in order to get in on the script credit for the purpose of sharing in the residual earnings," Joe said. Worse, without consulting Joe, Rose had added material to the script that was "deplorably trite and singularly flat." Joe asked that his name be removed from the credits. "I am very serious about this because frankly, and unhappily, I think it is now a bomb. It is no longer a funny show but a show based on a funny situation, and that is something different entirely. . . . [T]he comic tensions have been removed and replaced by static intervals of dialogue that are not funny and do not advance the action." Finally, he insisted he receive full financial compensation for the work he had done.

On August 6, Edward J. Montagne wrote him: "I would like to assure you, Joe, that we didn't make the changes in the script purely for the sake of making changes. Nothing would please us more than to have a script come in that was perfect. Unfortunately, it is seldom the case—particularly so early in a series when characters are being formed." The producers stuck to this point—that the series was not yet properly established—to argue that Joe was not "contractually entitled" to the money promised him before Rose reworked the script. Joe's name remained in the credits. Seven years would elapse before the Writers Guild of America determined he had been wronged in the matter and was due a settlement of $2,375.

MEANWHILE, "[c]omedy [variety] shows were out of style," Mel Brooks said. "One day it's five thousand a week [to write skits], the next day it's zilch."

The Borscht Belt patter of *Your Show of Shows* had given way to the harder, jazzier, more political and absurd stand-up routines of Lenny Bruce, Mike Nichols and Elaine May, Mort Sahl, and Woody Allen. The accumulated dramas of McCarthyism, the bomb, the Cold War, and Camelot in the White House had relegated Catskills shtick to the past (on top of which, the routines had become overly familiar on TV).

The *New York Times* "generally ignored the satirical cabaret performers on the theory that such entertainment was not sufficiently highbrow," Arthur Gelb wrote in *City Room*, his memoir of working at the *Times*. Gelb would soon become one of Joe's close friends. "The best [of the comics] were well versed in literature, the Bible, psychology and current events," he said. "At times, I saw them as our new evangelists, using the cabaret stage as a pulpit to shock audiences into an awareness of hypocritical, repressive aspects of our culture."

Mort Sahl would carry a newspaper onto the stage: the source of

the new "black humor." In many ways, stand-up comedians and come-
dic actors in such clubs as Second City in Chicago (featuring a young
Alan Arkin), the hungry i in San Francisco, the Unicorn in Los Angeles,
the Crystal Palace in St. Louis, and New York's the Vanguard, the Bon
Soir, Basin Street East, and the Bitter End presaged the personal, social
nature of the coming cultural revolution—a trend with which *Catch-22*
was very much in step.

One of Sahl's jokes best embodied the moment: As he imagined responding to the badgering questions of an investigative committee, he
said, "I didn't mean to be subversive, but I was new in the community
and wanted to meet girls."

Lenny Bruce was the Catskills on weed (or something harder), with
a copy of *Howl* stuffed in its pocket. After a performance at the Jazz
Workshop in San Francisco in the fall of 1961, Bruce was arrested on
obscenity charges for having uttered onstage the word *cocksucker* as
well as the sexual term *to come*. He was acquitted after his lawyer,
Albert Bendich, argued that Bruce's humor was "in the great tradition
of social satire, related intimately to the kind of . . . satire found in the
works of such great authors as Aristophanes and Jonathan Swift." Bendich called literature professors and jazz critics to testify on Bruce's
behalf.

More arrests followed in cities across the country. Finally, Bruce
was brought to trial in New York after a performance in Greenwich
Village's Café Au Go Go, during which a former CIA agent named
Herbert Ruhe, now working as a license inspector for the city, noted
Bruce's use of the expressions "nice tits," "jack me off," and "go come
in a chicken."

Immediately, a petition circulated in the literary and entertainment
communities protesting the comedian's arrest. "Lenny Bruce . . . [is] in
the tradition of Swift, Rabelais, and Twain," the petition said. "Although Bruce makes use of the vernacular in his night-club performances, he does so within the context of his satirical intent and not to
arouse the prurient interests of his listeners." Joe signed the petition
along with hundreds of others, including Saul Bellow, James Jones, Susan Sontag, John Updike, Gore Vidal, Lionel Trilling, George Plimpton,
Norman Podhoretz, and Barney Rosset.

The trial, in the Criminal Courts Building downtown, was beyond
parody, with the former CIA man performing some of Bruce's routines

for the jury ("I'm going to be judged by *his* bad timing," Bruce groaned). A prosecutor asked a Presbyterian minister, "Would you say the phrase, and you'll excuse me, Reverend, for using this language, but the phrase 'motherfucker' is in accord with that Commandment, 'Honor thy father and thy mother?'" Following a thoughtful pause, the minister replied, "I don't think the term 'motherfucker' has any relationship to that Commandment."

Despite Bruce's pleas that the court not "lock . . . away [his] words," he was convicted of violating Penal Code 1140-A, prohibiting "obscene . . . entertainment . . . which would tend to the corruption of the morals of youth and others." Two years later, while still appealing the conviction, he died of a morphine overdose. One of his prosecutors, Assistant District Attorney Vincent Cuccia, admitted, "I feel terrible about Bruce. We drove him into poverty and bankruptcy and then murdered him. I watched him gradually fall apart. . . . We all knew what we were doing. We used the law to kill him."

In fact, as Arthur Gelb discovered while investigating for the *New York Times,* the NYPD regularly demanded graft from club owners and nightclub entertainers in exchange for not busting them or pulling club licenses. "[P]olice payoffs . . . were a fact of cabaret life," Gelb wrote. It was the New York literary community—sharing Bruce's concern that language could be outlawed—that led the charge against corrupt practices. At a meeting in George Plimpton's Seventy-second Street apartment, at which Random House's Jason Epstein and Robert Silvers, then of *Harper's,* were present, along with Barney Rosset, Norman Mailer, and Norman Podhoretz, Gelb got the go-ahead to write a story for the *Times* announcing the formation of a committee of intellectuals; this committee planned to petition Governor Nelson Rockefeller to investigate police corruption with regard to cabarets. The story appeared on page one. Eventually, cabaret supervision was transferred to City Hall, away from the police department. None of this helped Lenny Bruce, but a blow had been struck, loosening restrictions and allowing performers such as Woody Allen to carry comedy to further extremes of satire and absurdity—as in Allen's routine about a beatnik girl he wanted to seduce who liked to listen to Marcel Marceau LPs.

It was a transitional moment for the culture ("I feel the hints, the clues, the whisper of a new time coming," Norman Mailer had written) . . . and Joe Heller, the World War II vet who would soon be hailed for writing a Vietnam novel before Vietnam cracked the public consciousness, was an attractive transitional figure.

In addition to *Newsweek*, the first national magazine to conduct an in-depth interview with Joe was *The Realist*, founded by Paul Krassner. A former violin prodigy who had worked for a while as a stand-up comic and television comedy writer (he adored Lenny Bruce), Krassner identified himself as a lapsed, nonconforming Jew. In the late fifties, he was working in lower Manhattan, in the business office of Lyle Stuart, *Mad* magazine's business manager and publisher of the anticensorship magazine *The Independent*. Krassner wrote for *The Independent* and *Mad*, but felt these iconoclastic publications were becoming too tame in their appeal to more mainstream audiences. He penned a piece called "Guilt Without Sex: A Guide for Adolescents" and offered it to *Mad*. The editor, William Gaines, turned it down. Too racy, he said. Piqued by Gaines's ever-more-conservative editorial taste, Krassner said to him, "I guess you don't want to change horses in the middle of the stream." Gaines replied, "Not when the horse has a rocket up its ass." Krassner decided to start his own magazine. "I founded *The Realist* as a *Mad* for adults," he said.

He refused advertising. This freed him to throw rocks at America's prevailing mythologies. At first, he had only six hundred subscribers. He kept the magazine afloat with his own money, earned by freelancing. He spoofed religion, blacklisting, military expansionism, and nuclear fears ("Atoms for Peace," Ike called A-bombs, in a line that could have come from *Catch-22*).

Krassner printed a FUCK COMMUNISM poster, which outraged the Left *and* the Right (no one could tell where the satire was aimed). He interviewed Lenny Bruce as well as George Lincoln Rockwell, the leader of the American Nazi party. The Rockwell interview opened with a note to readers: "When canceling your subscription please include your zip code."

In time, Krassner's audience came to him. "What [our] readers had in common was an irreverence toward bullshit. Except their own, of course," he said. As the magazine found its footing, it combined satire with incisive investigative reporting. In 1972, with financial backing from John Lennon and Yoko Ono, *The Realist* would produce a special issue documenting the Nixon administration's improprieties in far more depth than the mainstream media had attempted.

One of Krassner's earliest "Impolite Interviews" was with Joseph Heller. Krassner recalled, "I had gone to my first literary cocktail party in my capacity as editor of *The Realist*," at about the time *Newsweek* ran its profile of Joe in 1962. "When I met Heller, he asked if I'd read his book. I said I was in the middle of it, but [later] admitted that I had lied to him and didn't have the book. As a result, he sent me a copy with a note: 'You don't have to read *Catch-22*, you write it every month.' So then I requested an interview and read the book very carefully to prepare my questions. I learned much from his answers about the structure and modus operandi of satire."

Whereas *Newsweek* had covered the novel's popularity and Joe's growing celebrity, Krassner focused on the novel's critique of society. In the interview, Joe insisted *Catch-22* was "quite an orthodox book in terms of its morality." He went on: "I think anything *critical* is subversive by nature in the sense that it does seek to change or reform something. . . . [T]he impetus toward progress of any kind has always been a sort of discontent with what existed. . . . But it doesn't necessarily follow from that, that people would take exception to [the book]." He affirmed his belief that "people, even the worst people, I think are basically good, are motivated by humane impulses," and he swore he was "more concerned with producing a work of fiction—of literary art, if you will—than of converting anybody or arousing controversy. I'm really afraid of getting involved in controversy."

"Are you serious?" Krassner asked.

"Oh, yes," Joe replied. "I'm a terrible coward. I'm just like Yossarian, you know. It's the easiest thing to fight—I learned that in the war—it *takes* a certain amount of courage to go to war, but not very much, not as much as to refuse to go to war."

In response to critics' charges that his characters were interchangeable, lacking real *selves*, Joe said, "People die and are forgotten. People are abused and forgotten. People suffer, people are exploited, *right now*; we don't dwell upon them twenty-four hours a day. Somehow they get lost in the swirl of things . . . so [I had] a definite technique [in mind], at the beginning of the book particularly, of treating people and incidents almost in terms of glimpses, and then showing as we progress that these things do have a meaning and they do come together."

Finally, he said, "I regard [*Catch-22*] essentially as a peacetime book. . . . [W]hen this wartime emergency ideology is transplanted to

262 / TRACY DAUGHERTY

peacetime, then you have . . . not only absurd situations, but . . . very tragic situations."

Following the interview, Joe "pretended he had taken the subway to our meeting," Krassner recalled. Later, he learned Joe had hailed a cab. "I thought [that] was revealing," Krassner said, "[but] I never thought that his identification with the counterculture and [his] desire for financial success were in the least mutually exclusive." The times they were a-changin'; everyone was trying to negotiate the seams.

"WE MOVED to [a] much larger apartment in the [Apthorp] building right before 1963," Ted Heller recalls. "I remember watching Oswald get shot in that apartment, live on TV. Most nights we ate in but we had a practice of going out on Sundays. We either went to a place called Tony's (Italian) on West 79th Street or a Chinese place called Eastern Gardens somewhere in the 80s or 90s on Broadway (neither place is still extant). Eastern Gardens was, as I remember, not on street level but on the second floor and was very old school: red checked tablecloths and silver metal serving dishes with the tops on them. The bartender and the maitre d' at Tony's knew my father and called him Giuseppe. The bartender's name was Flavio and he knew that my father liked a Beefeater martini straight up, extra dry, with a twist."

On weekdays, Shirley cooked at home. She was glad the new apartment came with a washer and dryer.

By 1963, among the biggest-selling Dell paperbacks were *Catch-22* and Betty Friedan's *The Feminine Mystique* (". . . the housewife-mother . . . [is] the model for all women; [this mystique] presupposes that history has reached a final and glorious end in the here and now, as far as women are concerned"). At the time, *Paperbound Books in Print* had no Women's Studies category. The "women's" line included books on beauty, cooking, and child care—though Benjamin Spock was still considered the national baby guru, and had the royalties to prove it. "Give up Dr. Spock? I'd rather give up my husband," said one woman in a UPI survey seeking to determine if Spock's growing political activism had eroded his readers' confidence.

Spock's political consciousness, like that of most men of his (and Joe's) generation had not yet widened to include feminism. "I think that when women are encouraged to be competitive too many of them become disagreeable," he was quoted as saying. *Newsweek* declared that menstruation was a "natural restriction" keeping women at home, and faulted American housewives for not accepting their destinies with "grace."

"Men went mad," Joe had written in one of the nation's bestselling books.

"[W]omen['s] . . . lives [are] confined," Betty Friedan claimed in another.

13. Bombs

BACK ON Corsica in 1966, on assignment for *Holiday* magazine, Joe realized the mission count was still being raised. As ten-year-old Ted hung out a car window, gazing with "sour . . . irritation" at his dad's wartime haunts, Joe understood *his* missions were over, but his son's "military service was still ahead": "I could have clasped him in my arms to protect him."

Joe predicted his narrator in *Something Happened*. "[My son's] terror . . . [is] more dreadful than any I have ever been able to imagine," says Bob Slocum, the narrator father. "I have to do something. I hug his face deeper into the crook of my shoulder. I hug him tightly with both my arms. I squeeze." He smothers his boy in his zeal to save him.

Nothing so dramatic happened on the return to Corsica, but Joe's impulse to shield his son, and its switch in the novel to murderous terror, suggests something crucial about his fiction-making process—a subject for later. For now, while Joe and his family walked the hills of Corsica, let's note: Joe didn't die as a child (surrounded by arcades simulating the noise of war); his father did. Joe didn't die in the war; army brothers did. In revisiting his past—and celebrating his continuing vitality—he felt something he would later imagine as hastening a child's death.

Sacrifice and honor, the liberated and the fallen: In a sense, these military tropes, which Joe first encountered as a boy reading the *Iliad,* defined his life view and mature fiction.

"Is this what we came to see?" Ted grumbled one day, gazing at gravel and dirt on a flat Corsican patch.

"The airfield was right here," Joe explained to his son. "The bombers used to come back from Italy and France and land right out that way."

"I'm thirsty," said Erica, fourteen.

"It's hot," Shirley said.

Ted said, "I want to go back."

Joe told him they weren't returning to the hotel. They were moving on to another spot.

"I mean back to New York!" Ted said. "I'm not interested in your stupid airfield! The only airfield I want to see is John F. Kennedy!"

From the first, the kids had been excited but wary about the trip. "Up until [this] time, we hadn't . . . really been anywhere and suddenly we were packing to go on the S. S. *Rafaello,* [one of its earliest] voyage[s], in first class, pretty heady stuff," Erica says. Before leaving the States, she had asked her father why the family couldn't go to Italy by car. At the time, Joe was paying to send her to the New Lincoln School, a progressive private school in Harlem, and he wondered if the money was worth it. "My brother and I played Ping Pong across the Atlantic," Erica recalls. "My always beautiful mother was now splendidly glamorous, dressed up for dinner and suddenly looking like some enchanting actress or a Tzarina. My father begrudgingly wore a tux to dinner every night and was the life of the party: sardonic, bored and faintly irritable, but still somehow a delight to all around him. The young Italian waiters in their spanking white jackets all giggled a bit when my mother spoke to them and I caught one, once, blushing while trying . . . to look down her celery-colored evening gown as he bent to serve her baked Alaska."

Holiday had assigned Joe to write about the old Alesan Air Field, to note the changes in people and places, and relive his experiences. The kids were bored by his talk of the past. "There [was] nothing [left]," Joe conceded. "It's almost . . . as though there had never been a war." The mountains were higher than he remembered, the landscape rougher, the dangers he had faced more intense than he had realized at the time. The cab rides, on steep, winding paths in reedy, dry hills spooked his wife.

At Ile Rousse, a summer resort where the army had built a rest camp in Joe's day, teenaged girls and boys from Paris, Marseille, and Nice lounged about or swam, listening to Nancy Sinatra, the Beatles, Bob Dylan, and the Rolling Stones on a jukebox. Up and down nearby beaches, fancy new cottages lined the shore: This could have been Fire Island. Only now and then did Joe catch a glimpse of something familiar: a bar on the road to Cervione, a mountain village, where pilots and bombardiers used to drink warm, bitter wine. Now the place, much brighter than it used to be, served Coca-Cola, and Joe's kids delighted in the *gelato allemagne,* the German ice cream he ordered for them there. "Don't drink the water," Shirley warned them. At one point, Joe wrote, a "shy, soft-spoken young man stepped toward us hesitantly," wishing to honor this American who had fought to liberate Italy. He "begged permission to give us a *cadeau,* a gift, a large, beautiful earthenware vase from the small pottery shop from which he gained his livelihood," Joe said. "It was touching, sobering; I was sorry I had nothing with which to reciprocate."

Joe was curious to see the town of Pietrasanta and to inspect its bridge. For years, he had not been certain he had hit it with his bombs. Recently, in New York, an acquaintance, the film producer Al Brodax, said he'd visited Pietrasanta. The villagers assured him the bridge had been ruined in the war.

Joe couldn't tell. The bridge had been small, sturdy, and smooth. Destroyed, it would have been easy to repair.

The family stayed at the Hotel Byron in Forte dei Marmi nearby, where the sculptor Henry Moore was also staying at the time. He went out in the mornings to Cararra, a white-marble quarry, to select pieces for his work. Erica recalls the Byron as a "little jewel of a hotel." She loved the "salty breezes" and the hotel chef's "salsa pomodoro, still the cleanest, freshest taste I know." On the beach, striped chairs stood in rows on the sand; every afternoon at three o'clock, a stooped, toothless man came around, wearing bright red sandals, selling "bambaloni balls of crisp, fried dough, dusted with sugar, hot in your hands, ambrosia in your mouth," Erica says.

In Florence, she and her mother bought earrings while Joe sat with his son in sidewalk cafés, scribbling, pondering, recalling his war. He remembered that, on his thirty-seventh mission—the one to Avignon—he'd learned the lead navigator had once been a history teacher. Flying over Europe, he'd recognized places he had read about. At one point, as the bombers made their way to France, he announced excitedly over the intercom, "On our right is the city of Orange, ancestral home of the kings of Holland and of William III." "And on our left," came the worried voice of a radio gunner, "is flak."

In Siena, Frederick Karl, Dolores, and their kids joined the Hellers for the Palio, a spectacular citywide horse race. In Rome, Joe perused the streets, recalling how American soldiers used to justify their visits to prostitutes here. Their money helped poor girls obtain the necessities of life, they said: For only thirty-five dollars (a couple of afternoon visits), a woman could get a nice pair of shoes. Frequenting brothels was a form of humanitarian aid.

As a young man on R & R, Joe had skipped the museums and architectural tours. Now, the city's art and history overwhelmed him. He was especially touched by Michelangelo's fresco of the Last Judgment in the Sistine Chapel. "It is the best motion picture ever made," he wrote. "There is perpetual movement in its violent rising and falling, and perpetual drama in its agony and wrath. To be with [it] is to be with Oedipus and King Lear. I want that wall." He dreamed of transporting and refashioning it in the Apthorp, turning his apartment into a Hall of the Great Dead.

HE HAD TAKEN the *Holiday* assignment for the same reason he accepted screenplay work. His portion of the *Catch-22* paperback sale to Dell—about thirteen thousand dollars—was gone now, and his royalties, though steady, were thinly stretched from month to month. "I started worrying about money," he told journalist Chet Flippo in 1981. "I had my savings in bonds—about $50,000, which was all I had in the world. . . . I had a few very bad nights . . . when I felt I might have to give up my apartment, have to take the children out of private school, have to tell my children that we're moving out to Queens or Brooklyn. It was not the poverty, but the *shame,* that worried me."

McHale's Navy had soured him on writing original screenplays, but he discovered he was very good at rewriting movie scripts quickly because of his facility for dialogue and humor. With George Mandel, he *did* form a production company, Scapegoat, to represent various projects they started together but never brought to fruition: "The Big Squeeze," a movie about the culture gap between 1960s teenagers and an older immigrant generation, featuring, Joe wrote, "much music . . . by many name entertainers—all of it good, loud, and fast," and ending with a "chase . . . that involves all the principals"; "Howe and Hummel," a musical about two shysters and lots of pretty girls; and an outline for a television series called "King Solomon's Smidjik," an international caper comedy swirling around a magical object with the power to impart wisdom but whose use inevitably leads to chaos and mischief.

In the summer of 1963, Joe was offered five thousand dollars a week to rework a script called *Sex and the Single Girl,* distantly based on the book by Helen Gurley Brown. Like Betty Friedan, Brown, a former copywriter for a California advertising agency, championed female independence. Rather than rejecting kittenish femininity, women should use sexual allure to get what they wanted from men, Brown said. Most nascent feminists did not consider her one of them, but her book, condoning casual affairs, sold briskly, and Brown became a regular on the television talk-show circuit. Warner Bros. optioned the book for $200,000. During development, a studio executive complained to producer Saul David that the book had no plot. "I told you that a hundred thousand dollars ago," David replied. The studio had bought a sexy title— that's all.

A veteran screenwriter, David R. Schwartz, took a shot at the script in February 1963. Joe inherited the project a few months later. Nudged by the studio, he based his script less on Brown's book than on Joseph Hoffman's *How to Make Love and Like It,* about a virgin anthropologist who writes a bestselling book on sex. He was told to "spice things up" with a car chase. The final product, starring Natalie Wood, Tony Curtis, Henry Fonda, and Lauren Bacall, was billed as "based on the book . . . by Helen Gurley Brown. Screenplay by David R. Schwartz and Joseph Heller. Story by Joseph Hoffman." Along the way, coherence vanished. The film's finest scene, said the *New York Times,* had the "two young, muddled protagonists yammering about love and Freud at a zoo, tiredly watched by monkeys and baboons." The script contained "some genuinely amusing, peppery dialogue and incidents," but the film reinforced stereotypes about strong women who secretly wanted a man, and unfaithful men who wanted a woman to keep them in line.

"We had never experienced anything like that [summer]," Erica recalls. "[W]e relinquished [our] summer house [on Fire Island] and got on a plane [to Hollywood] . . . We really didn't know we were going until about two days before; in fact, we had just gotten a puppy named Brillo and had to find a place for him to spend the summer. . . . Audrey Chestney's parents took him—and kept him, they were all so attached to each other. . . . Dad stretched out the script writing so it would take us through the summer until it was time to come back to school."

Erica's biggest thrill was meeting Eydie Gormé. "I just ran up to her like a lunatic, threw my arms around her and told her I loved her. She was probably very frightened," she says. "I learned two words [in L.A.] I was never able to forget: 'Charge it.' I remember tennis lessons and sitting at the pool with Ted and ordering hot fudge sundaes and charging it to 'the bungalow.'"

The flight to California was the kids' first experience on an airplane. "I remember thinking the boats and cars I was seeing after take-off were toys," Ted says. He recalls "swimming in Tony Curtis's pool, him getting me a Superman costume, being in a movie studio and seeing Bob Hope. . . . [M]y parents were astounded how expensive a room service hamburger was at the Beverly Hills Hotel."

Joe took Ted to a Hollywood studio to watch a TV show being filmed—*Arrest and Trial,* starring Ben Gazzara. "They were about to film a scene and my father told me not to make a noise. . . . I was so scared, I thought everyone could hear my heartbeat and hear me swallowing. I think I held my breath," Ted says.

Briefly, Joe met Natalie Wood. She hated the movie and agreed to act in it only because she was contractually obligated. Watching her on the set, Joe felt she "had a natural flair for comedy, something she dismissed" to be taken seriously as an actress. Tony Curtis signed on because he "needed the money to settle a divorce," Joe said. "That's what I like best about the movie industry: the art and idealism."

When producer Charles K. Feldman released *Casino Royale* in 1967, the film's publicity slogan was "*Casino Royale* is too much for one James Bond!"—a cover for chaos. David Niven, Peter Sellers, and Woody Allen all played Bond in what was supposed to be a spoof of the

343

spy genre. In fact, it was a grab bag of scenes directed by five different men, hired willy-nilly by Feldman, all working without communication, a clear budget, or a coherent script. Though Joe is not credited on the film, he worked on a draft of the screenplay (with George Mandel), as did a host of others, including Terry Southern, Ben Hecht, Billy Wilder, and Woody Allen. Allen "told me that he and I both did a version of the same scene," Joe said. Joe took the job because it "was tempting, and it came at a good time, as I was between novels, where I had been for five years, and where I would have liked to remain for at least four or five years more," he said. "[I figured the] work would be easy—there was no danger of failing, since somebody else had already done that."

During the filming, Sellers's marriage to Britt Ekland was crumbling. He behaved erratically, threw tantrums, and eventually walked off the set. Leo Jaffe, Columbia Picture's executive vice president, didn't seem to notice. One day, he mistook Allen for Sellers. "When you put glasses on them, they do sort of look alike," he explained. Nothing fazed Feldman. He was determined to make the biggest, most dazzling screen comedy in history, featuring the world's loveliest women. "No background dogs in my picture!" he told his crew. "Get only real beauties." The film showcased Ursula Andress, Joanna Pettet, and Jacqueline Bisset. Like many of the writers and directors, Joe wanted his name removed from the credits. In the end, the movie's anarchic silliness distilled some of 1967's psychedelic spirit; the film grossed $17.2 million dollars at the U.S. box office.

Dirty Dingus Magee, credited to Joseph Heller, along with Tom and Frank Waldman, released in 1970, and based on the novel *The Ballad of Dingus Magee,* by David Markson, is, according to one critic, "ninety minute[s] . . . of what appears to be Frank [Sinatra] having a mid-life crisis." Markson agreed, calling it the "worst movie you ever saw." He knew Joe. Both were friends of Alice Denham. Markson wrote the novel, a half-serious, half-satirical Western, "sort of on impulse," he said. "It's intricate and carefully plotted. . . . I had a bunch of rejections because everybody said there was no such thing as a satirical Western. Then a movie came out called *Cat Ballou* [starring Jane Fonda]. That suddenly made it interesting for the Hollywood types. So when *Dingus* was published, they jumped in and bought it. I got $100,000, and that was 1966." The lead was meant for a nineteen-year-old actor. Sinatra was fifty-five at the time. It was the last film role he would take for a decade.

Bret Wheadon, author of *Sinatra: The Complete Guide,* wrote that the movie conveyed "denigrating attitudes toward women, Native Americans, and anyone else . . . in [the] film's sights. . . . Truly a low point in the careers of Sinatra and writer Joseph Heller."

In a talk at the Poetry Center of the Ninety-second Street Y on December 7, 1970, Joe said, "I've had some experiences with motion pictures, all of which I have to apologize for. The latest one is something called *Dirty Dingus Magee.* I think I've gotten more [bad] notices . . . than Frank Sinatra. But that was just a youthful indiscretion, and we all commit those."

Shortly before his return to Corsica, Joe lunched with Al Brodax in Manhattan's Palm Restaurant. The men had met through Mel Brooks. Brodax told Joe, "You owe me."

"What for?" Joe asked.

"Pietrasanta."

"The bridge, the bridge!" Joe said.

He had once told Brodax about the Pietrasanta mission, and confessed he didn't know if he'd hit his target. Brodax said he had just visited the town—"I was in the neighborhood"—and nosed around.

According to Brodax, "Joe leaped to his feet" and asked, "And the bridge?"

"Direct hit . . . no question . . . gone . . . you blew that mother to smithereens."

"Joe dance[d] in small . . . circles and stomp[ed] his feet," Brodax said. "He howl[ed] in shameless joy. . . . 'No shit, Brodax . . . *I leveled the motherfucker!*'"

He had eased Joe's mind; in return, he wanted Joe to write a screen treatment for an animated Beatles film.

Many details in *Up Periscope Yellow,* Brodax's account of the making of *Yellow Submarine,* have been questioned by those involved in the film's production, and Brodax admits to stretching the truth when it suits him. But with the exception of overwriting, his anecdote about Joe rings true. "Time with Joe [was] always a joy," he wrote. "We share[d] lots of things . . . Brooklyn-born, Jewish-bred, war-torn slightly, but only slightly."

Brodax, working for King Features in New York, had produced a Saturday-morning Beatles cartoon show, which ran on American television beginning in 1964. The Beatles loathed it. They resisted his notion that an animated film could be built around their novelty tune, "Yellow Submarine." Still, Brodax pushed ahead, approaching several writers (the Beatles were legally bound to make one more film for United Artists after *A Hard Day's Night* and *Help!*).

Lee Minoff, a young playwright, claimed he wrote the first script. He recalled meeting Paul McCartney in London. "[A] little kid," Minoff said. At the time, McCartney was "twenty-one, twenty-three [at the] oldest. . . . We had some brief conversations [about the proposed movie] which Brodax sort of led. The only thing that seemed to come out of the meeting was Paul McCartney talked about a monster. He wanted a monster in it. Monsters are good."

Meanwhile, Brodax cast about for other writers. He told David Picker, a vice president in charge of production at United Artists, that he knew Joe Heller. "Heller's . . . very much the flavor of the sixties, a hell of a possibility if you can nail him," Picker said. Thus the meeting at the Palm.

In Brodax's account, Joe ordered a second brandy and considered the offer. "You're talking Lennon, McCartney . . . something with them . . . *The Beatles*?" Then he pulled out his credit card. "What the hell, the bridge is down, and the Beatles, they're up! . . . What a gift, dinner is on Heller. Sonofabitch, Brodax!" As he left the restaurant, he gave Brodax a "poignan[t]" bear hug.

"I [had] told [Joe] what he was desperate to hear," Brodax wrote. In fact, the people of Pietrasanta informed him the American bombs were "so far off" their targets, "they could hear [them] but . . . couldn't see them."

As for *Yellow Submarine*: "With Heller in [his] pocket," Brodax felt he had a hit on his hands. Once Joe finished the script, Brodax bound the "all-important Heller treatment" in a green cover and flew to London "with a stack of [other] scripts . . . each one with a different color cover." He presented the range of options to the Beatles' manager, Brian Epstein, certain he would "buy Heller." At the time, Epstein's behavior was increasingly bizarre—within a year, he would die of a drug overdose. At the meeting, Epstein "picked up the first treatment and said, 'I don't like this—it's purple,' and threw it on the floor," Brodax said. "The next one—'I don't like this, it's orange.' Then he gets to one in a green cover, which was written by Joseph Heller, and that one he throws away, too. So I said, 'Brian, that's by Joe Heller.' He said, 'I don't care who it's by, I don't like green.'" So ended Joe's flirtation with the Beatles.

In New York, Joe had told Brodax he saw a "connection between his Yossarian and [John] Lennon": "They share a dislike for bureaucratic institutions."

MANY WHO LIVED through the 1960s recall moments on which they believe the decade's movements hinged. One such instance, often cited by writers, occurred in August 1964, when Bob Dylan offered marijuana to the Beatles in their room at the Delmonico Hotel. John Lennon used one word to tap the evening's importance: "Surrealism." The awareness of growing cultural power shared by the five young men in that room; the willingness to play with mind-flexing "organics"; the spark of Dylan's influence on Lennon's songwriting, leading to more personal reflection as well as sharp political statements—and greater ambitiousness in rock music, generally; the meshing of music, poetry, politics, and celebrity to an unprecedented degree: It was, says writer Bob Spitz, a "cultural milestone . . . [and] nothing would ever be the same again."

Billy Graham knew it. This quintessential Luce hero—the hard-headed entrepreneur with an unshakable faith in the Christian God—warned that the Beatles and rock music were leading the children of the 1960s to perdition. When Lennon said the Beatles were more popular than Christ, the Ku Klux Klan rushed to Christ's defense. They burned Beatles records and showed, more than anything, that Lennon may have uttered an uncomfortable truth.

The ex–Luce man Joe Heller knew things had changed. "He loved Bob Dylan. . . . [He] had everything Dylan did on a reel-to-reel tape (he had a Tandberg tape deck—I *loved* playing with that thing)," Ted recalls. Joe tried wearing a string of love beads made by his daughter. "She told me that after about three days, I'd get used to them. This is the third day and, you know, she's right," he told an interviewer. (The beads clashed with the checkered blazer he often wore and the orange Stim-U-Dent toothpick perpetually hanging from his mouth.)

More seriously, he remained engaged with the underground press, even as mainstream publications courted him. In his blazers, Joe set "a new trend for the . . . 60s, along with the high-waisted dress and the overblouse," *Vogue* said. As often as not, he displayed his "trendiness" in *The Realist, Crawdaddy!* and other tabloid-style rock-music venues.

To a dismissal by Jean Shepherd of the "polemic[al]" satire of Lenny Bruce, Joe responded, in the pages of *The Realist,* "[I]t is [not] the function of satire to present all sides of a question; that is the function of . . . the *Sunday Times.* I'm not sure, even, that it is the *function* of satire to convey information, but, instead, to convey an *attitude* about information." He took Shepherd to task for suggesting that passion and intellect were mutually exclusive. "They are not at opposite ends of the pole, or even within the same circumference of definitions," he wrote. "One of the opposites of passion is indifference; and one of the opposites of intellect is stupidity."

In the May 1965 issue of *The Realist,* Joe attacked syndicated columnists Rowland Evans and Robert Novak for an "attempt to discredit the Student Non-Violent [*sic*] Coordinating Committee." Borrowing a page from Joseph McCarthy, Evans and Novak had claimed, without substantiation, that SNCC had been infiltrated by "known Communists." Joe called their charges "contemptible" and lauded the "hundreds of brave young men and women, white and colored, Northern and Southern," who had organized voter-registration drives in the South, at considerable physical risk, and "demonstrated virtues not often found anywhere else in this country of ours."

In more mainstream outlets—the *New York Times,* the *Harvard Crimson*—he criticized America's leaders. He insisted "[a]ny society that puts Cassius Clay and Benjamin Spock in jail and makes McGeorge Bundy head of the Ford Foundation is not one to which allegiance should be given lightly."

To Richard B. Sale, an editor of the academic journal *Studies in the Novel,* who asked him to talk about Yossarian, Joe offered this: "All I want to say is it ain't that hard. It ain't that hard to take a stand on something."

Increasingly, he was seen as—and accepted the role of—cultural spokesperson, as *Catch-22* came to be regarded as prophetic about the complexities of Vietnam (some war protesters even ragged Yossarian for not assassinating his commanding officer).

For all the talk in the "legitimate" press about a generation gap, hawks and doves, liberals and conservatives, one of the developments making possible the "American 1960s" was this: Figures such as Jack

Kennedy, John Lennon, Bob Dylan, Muhammad Ali, Joseph Heller, and John Yossarian moved fluidly from the mainstream to the underground and back again, from High Art to Pop Culture. The perfect icon of this blurring was the paperback book, the conveyor of classics and corn. With boundaries broken, nothing could resist change.

As early as 1960, Norman Mailer wrote in *Esquire* that a Kennedy presidency might give "unwilling charge" to forces now bottled up in the American underground. The underground could not be dismissed as marginal; now it existed on the fringe no more than *Time*'s latest cover. And because it could not be dismissed, it was, some believed, dangerous. In the mid-1960s, the FBI's COINTELPRO (counterintelligence program) switched its focus from investigating civil rights murders by the Ku Klux Klan to trying to block the rise of any "real Mau-Mau" who could unify black America. It tried to disrupt the "New Left movement['s] . . . propaganda activities," especially in its "anarchist-type" underground papers.

According to Abe Peck, "[T]he FBI . . . placed an ad in the L.A. *Free Press* designed to discredit the Communist Party." It asked the IRS to examine magazines' tax returns. It "use[d] its contacts to persuade Columbia Records to stop advertising in the underground press." The *Crawdaddy!* offices on Fifth Avenue in New York were burgled one night, in a way that would soon conjure the word *Watergate*. (Mark Felt, later famous as "Deep Throat," was a central figure in COINTEL-PRO operations.) John Lennon, whose FBI file gradually fattened as the U.S. government tried to deport him, told Paul Krassner that if anything happened to him and Yoko Ono, it would not be an accident.

Meanwhile, bombers roamed the skies above the heartland: the Strategic Air Command, keeping the United States safe from Soviet attack. Missile silos ticked among desert mirages in the American West. Watts burned. Assassins stalked leaders. Surrealism, indeed.

"If I wanted to destroy a nation, I would give it too much and I would have it on its knees, miserable, greedy, and sick," John Steinbeck wrote.

By mid-decade, the country's pace had quickened in a smoky, black-lighted whirl. In 1967, *Playboy* declared "the suburbs" were reeling from one college scandal after another, from sex to marijuana to "treated sugar cubes." Over ten years earlier, that magazine had broken ground, scandalously; now it was mainstream, almost respectable. The once-staid

New Yorker was upsetting longtime subscribers by printing the absurdist stories of Donald Barthelme.

Rolling Stone was another publication redefining cultural boundaries, straddling the fence between "alternative" and "general interest." One of its founders, Ralph J. Gleason, a jazz and pop-music critic, wrote, "I dare say that with the inspiration of the Beatles and Dylan we have more poetry being produced and more poets being made than ever before in the history of the world." He quoted Plato on the way music (broadly defined) alters politics: "The new style quietly insinuates itself into manners and customs and from there it issues a greater force . . . [it] goes on to attack laws and constitutions, displaying the utmost impudence, until it ends by overthrowing everything, both in public and in private." Gleason said, "That seems to me to be . . . the answer to the British rock singer Donovan's question, 'What goes on? I really want to know.'" In addition to the Beatles and Dylan, Gleason listed Joseph Heller as one of the purveyors of the "new style." "Heller . . . [has] hold of it," he wrote.

In the liner notes to an LP record of Lenny Bruce's performance in Berkeley on December 12, 1965, Gleason wrote, "Lenny Bruce was really, along with Bob Dylan and Miles Davis and a handful of others (maybe Joseph Heller, Terry Southern, and Allen Ginsberg in another way) the leader of the first wave of the American social and cultural revolution which is gradually changing the structure of our society and may effectively revise it, if the forces of reaction which are automatically brought into play by such a drive, do not declare military law and suppress it."

Always in the background were Vietnam and the Cold War.

That *Catch-22* was a Vietnam novel appeared to be confirmed with each new revelation of military strategies (or lack thereof), with buzzwords used by the country's leaders to obfuscate tactics and unintended consequences. Michael Herr produced some of the finest reporting on Vietnam. He collected the pieces in his book *Dispatches,* but they first appeared in a range of journals from the esoteric to the mainstream and in between—*New American Review, Rolling Stone,* and *Esquire.* Under editor Harold Hayes, *Esquire* recast journalism, stressing personal style and subjectivity over attempts at objective reporting. It was an approach perfectly suited to the merry, scary 1960s.

Herr, a Syracuse graduate, served for a time as the "unpaid film critic for a tiny, leftist magazine called *The New Leader,* but was fired after . . . [one] year for liking the wrong movies," wrote critic Keith Saliba. Candida Donadio tossed Herr his first break, negotiating a contract for a short-story collection that she converted to a book deal about Vietnam. *Esquire* issued him press credentials.

Dispatches opens with the following description:

> There was a map of Vietnam on the wall of my apartment in Saigon and some nights, coming back late to the city, I'd lie out on my bed and look at it, too tired to do anything more than just get my boots off. That map was a marvel, especially now that it wasn't real anymore. . . . [I]t was very old. . . . The paper had buckled in its frame after years in the wet Saigon heat, laying a kind of veil over the countries it depicted. Vietnam was divided into its older [no longer extant] territories. . . . [N]ow[adays], even the most detailed maps didn't reveal much anymore; reading them was like trying to read the faces of the Vietnamese, and that was like trying to read the wind. We [were learning] that the uses of most information were flexible. . . .

Herr went on to tell the story of an information officer who insists American troops controlled the ground once identified on maps as the Ho Bo Woods. The place had been pacified, "denying the enemy valuable resources and cover." The Ho Bo Woods had vanished. Maps now called the region something else. "And if in the months following . . . enemy activity in the . . . area . . . had increased 'significantly,' and American losses had doubled and then doubled again, none of it was happening in any damn Ho Bo Woods, you'd better believe it," Herr wrote.

Years earlier, another of Candida's boys had exposed the military's "flexible . . . uses of information." In chapter 12 of *Catch-22,* Yossarian moves the bomb line on the captain's map so the captain will think the Allies have captured more territory than they have, and thus won't force the men to fly a mission to Bologna. Throughout *Catch-22,* reality is never as powerful as perception and willed ignorance. If Doc Daneeka's paperwork says he's dead, then he's dead, even if he's in your face denying it. One can imagine a young GI crouched in the Ho Bo Woods, muttering, "That's some catch, that Catch-22."

AT PARTIES, Joe—the trendsetter, the cultural spokesperson—"was nothing if not a provocateur: perverse, paradoxical, consistently inconsistent," Erica Heller said. He would "casually let it slip that he'd [not] voted [for years], then sit back smiling, relishing the . . . whirlwind controversy as, one by one, people challenged him, asking quite reasonably how he could possibly criticize the government (as he often did), while not participating in the process of changing and electing its leaders. As soon as I was old enough to vote, I, too, got swept up in one of these . . . conversations with him, at a party I'd gone to with my parents. Midway through, just as I was beginning to get very worked up, my mother leaned over to me and quietly said, 'Don't even start. Don't you see? He loves this. He does it purposely.' "

In *Something Happened,* Bob Slocum wrestles emotionally with a strong-willed adolescent. "She would break my heart, if she were somebody else's [child]," he says, responding to his daughter's confusing combination of naïveté and maturity. "I realize now that I have not always given replies to her questions and comments that were appropriate. When she tells me she wishes she were dead, I tell her she will be, sooner or later. . . . My error, I think, is that I always speak to her as I would to a grown-up; and all she wants, probably, is for me to talk to her as a child."

Slocum's daughter *tries* to tell him how to speak to her, and they have this exchange:

"You always like to give short answers when we argue. You think it's a good trick."
"It is."
"You're so sarcastic."
"Be a sneak. I'm not being sarcastic now. . . . Sneak outside . . . when you want to smoke or burn that crappy incense or do something else you don't want us to know about. And close the door to your room when you're on the telephone so we won't have to listen to you complain about us to all of your friends or see those crappy sex novels you read instead of the books you're supposed to be reading for school. . . . Just don't let me find out. . . . Because if I do find out, I'm going to have to do something about it. I'm going to have to disapprove and get angry and punish you, and other things like that, and that will make you unhappy and me unhappy."

"Why will it make *you* unhappy?" she wants to know.

"Because you're my daughter. And I really don't enjoy seeing you unhappy."

"Really?"

"Yes."

"Ha!"

In many ways, Erica says, "*Something Happened* . . . was certainly [an] accurate" portrait of her family. When she argued with her father or tried to discuss a serious issue with him, "it wasn't really sparring or playing because we were not evenly matched. He was a brilliant grownup and I was a kid." To Barbara Gelb, Erica "acknowledg[ed] her resemblance to the daughter in *Something Happened,* commenting, 'That girl is out to make trouble every minute. As an adolescent, *I* was out to make it every five minutes."

Joe's relationship with Erica had *never* been easy—in part, because she was too young to understand his humor. Once, while Shirley was out shopping, he stuck little Erica on the upper shelf of a bedroom closet to see if Shirley would notice the child was missing. The experience frightened and puzzled Erica. When she was older, he told her he was going to lock her out of the apartment unless she came home with pizza every time she went out. To her, this was not a game, especially as, for days, the threat remained imminent.

And in part, Joe stayed masked in front of his children. Mario Puzo often remarked on how important it was to Joe to maintain control of his feelings—so much so, he couldn't have fun, even with his kids. If he caught himself feeling happy, he'd pull a sullen face.

In her teens, Erica tried to understand him indirectly through her mother. Often, he seemed "grumpy, disaffected and blasé, casual, seemingly bored by his own accomplishments," Erica said. But when she talked to Shirley, she glimpsed a different side of him. "When *Catch-22* came out, my mother told me, she and Dad would often jump into a cab late at night and ride around the city, just to look at all the bookstore windows filled with the red, white, and blue of his book jacket. He would giggle at the sight. There was a part of him, the poor boy from Coney Island, that had never stopped giggling. You just had to know how to read him."

As for her: "[I]t took many years for me to be able to properly decode him, learn the language . . . recognize the love he deeply felt, couched in gravelly growls and R's that often leaned into guttural V's. Like examining some complex pointillistic painting, standing too close was merely distorting."

Joe could not see Erica clearly, either. The happy baby who had charmed his mother, and given the old woman simple pleasures late in life, had become an individual with opinions, adult needs, and ambitions of her own. "[S]he is, I fear . . . dissolving into her surroundings right before my eyes," Slocum says of *his* daughter. "She wants to be like other people her age. I cannot stop her; I cannot save her. Something happened to her. . . . Her uniqueness is fading." The novel expresses every mother and father's lament: A child's growth augers prideful, painful losses for the parent.

Eventually, Erica learned to appreciate her father's nostalgia, fears of aging, and puzzlement. When *Something Happened* appeared in 1974, as she was about to graduate from NYU, she published her first piece, in *Harper's*. A response to the novel, it was entitled "It Sure Did." She wrote:

> What "happens" to Bob Slocum's children, that ineffable and awesome thing that he can neither explain nor undo, that change in his children that leaves him feeling so alone and so inept at human contact, is simply that his kids have grown up, have matured. . . . A terrible thing, this business of growing up, but it happens to the best of us. . . . [It] means adjusting yourself to the shortcomings of [your family], realizing their limitations and being glad that they are no more abundant than they are . . . and then going out into the world to transcend the disappointments.

This was hard-won wisdom. "Erica had a tough time with her father," says Norman Barasch. "One time she told me he said to her, 'You're not my daughter! You're not my daughter!' I was mad at him. I thought I couldn't be friends with someone who said something like that. And so we didn't talk for a while." Erica's *Harper's* piece drew little praise from Joe—her defensiveness, the hurt beneath the insight, was hard to miss. He told Erica all he wanted was for her to follow a path of steady work and money.

Meanwhile, like Slocum, Joe saw himself in his son: another form of misperceiving a child. For the time being, it made for a relatively smooth surface: perhaps too *much* parental concern. Ted responded to music and language. He admired his father's war medals in a dresser drawer. He watched television and played with his dad's tape deck. He enjoyed trips to Coney Island with his father.

"I always felt I was a disappointment to him but, to be honest, I've always felt that way with most people," Ted says. In part, he attributes this feeling to the family's noncommunicativeness. "He [n]ever mentioned his mother or father to me. And I felt strongly that I shouldn't ask," Ted says.

He remembers "the year *Sergeant Pepper* came out, I went to summer camp in the Berkshires (I was very homesick). When I returned to New York, everything was fine for a few days. My Aunt Sylvia was supposed to visit us and have dinner one night. Well, that night the doorbell rings and someone, I think my sister, goes to get it and *that* very second is when my parents told me Sylvia's husband, Bernie, had passed away. While the door was being opened to let her in! I didn't really care for him but was stunned by the timing. . . . I can't help but laugh [now]. . . . I can't explain why it's funny. It's just indicative of the family."

Ted loved the family's summers on Fire Island; his memories of the place suggest he was an unusually sensitive child. One day, Joe "warned me there was going to be something called an eclipse and told me not to look at the sun. I was so frightened that during the eclipse I hid under my bed," he says. On another occasion, "I was on the beach with a kite and Joe and I were flying it. All of a sudden the lifeguard (who seemed so old to me then but was probably sixteen) comes over and asks if he can hold the kite. I was reluctant. He kept asking nicely. Joe told me to hand the lifeguard the kite—everything would be okay. I was maybe six or seven but I *knew* something terrible would happen. I handed the lifeguard the kite and sure enough within six seconds the kite slipped out of his hands and was gone."

Shirley's cousins recall hearing from her mother that Ted struggled with school, experienced behavioral and discipline problems, but they never met him. When pressed for details, Dottie insisted Ted was working through his troubles and Joe and Shirley were "good parents."

"Teddy—that was a mystery," says Audrey Chestney. Ted confirms he didn't like school but prefers not to discuss that period of his life.

In *Now and Then,* Joe recalled taking Erica and Ted to Coney Island one day, along with George Mandel, Mario Puzo, and their kids. "The very qualities that had disappointed us in the past made Steeplechase now ideal for languid fathers in their forties," Joe wrote. "It was clean, it was orderly, it was safe. While the children chased [one another] . . . gawking . . . enjoy[ing] themselves . . . the three of us could rest calmly on a bench and talk quietly."

Before he left that day, Joe recognized the "passing of generations." He remembered running up to weary older people as a kid and asking if he could take their remaining ride tickets. Now he was one of those old dodderers who would have gladly relinquished the goods.

He often felt tired. He struggled with his weight. He was approaching two hundred pounds and did not feel comfortable in his body. "He went to a health club called Al Roon's on Broadway in the 70's (I think men only), before joining the Y," Ted recalls. "That Y is not around anymore . . . it was in the 60's on Broadway, I think. Lots of famous people went there [like the singer Paul Simon] and my father used to run around the small track. (It was something like five hundred times around to make a mile.) This was before there were dozens of gyms all over the place."

Joe noticed Shirley—still, as Erica said, a glamorous woman—fighting to adjust to middle age. She did not like to undress in front of him in the light. She felt self-conscious about the red marks her girdles left on her flesh. Sometimes she drank a little wine in the evenings—never too much, but if a day had been particularly tense, with chores, children, misunderstandings with Joe, it did not take much to make her irritable or, more rarely, sorry for herself. Dolores Karl saw she was discomfited by Joe's growing celebrity and the attention it brought him from women. In public, Joe always kidded about the adjustments necessary in a long marriage. "Neither one of us has ever had a divorce. We're beginning to think there's something wrong with us," he told one interviewer. To another, he said, "Maybe we just don't quit easily. I know many people whose marriages have ended for reasons I don't think are serious enough. If everyone were to end a marriage because of disappointments or dissatisfactions or moods or temporary attractions, almost no marriage would survive."

In *Something Happened*—certain sections of which Joe did not want to publish in magazines, fearing that, removed from the novel's context, they would embarrass Shirley—his narrator laments the loss of sexual novelty. Alternately, he cherishes and bemoans the infatuated tolerance that years of familiarity instill in a marriage. "I don't think my wife has learned how to lie to me yet. (My wife doesn't know how to flirt and doesn't know how to lie to me.) When she does have something she hopes to conceal, she remains silent about it and hopes I will not inquire," says Bob Slocum. "I try to keep away from whatever I think she is trying to hide. I suspect she does the same for me (I suspect she knows a great deal more about me than she discloses). Our conversations, therefore, are largely about nothing, and frequently restrained."

In another passage, Slocum recalls his wife "was always afraid" they'd be caught making love when they were young. "I didn't care," he says. "I was a pretty hot kid once. I didn't care whether she enjoyed it or not; just as long as I got *mine*." These days, "I often wish I were driven . . . by that same hectic mixture of blind ardor, haste, and tension," he says. "Maybe that's what's missing. . . . I have more control and maturity now . . . but it isn't nearly as much fun anymore as it used to be with her, and I miss her greatly and love us both very deeply when I remember how we used to be."

The family always found ways of displacing affection. Erica recalls "begging and nagging and driving my parents crazy about getting a puppy" when she was in high school. "One day Dad and Speed went to some pet shop on Queens Boulevard in Queens and Dad brought home a beagle named Lucy after 'Lucy in the Sky with Diamonds.'" For a while, the family lavished love on the dog, but that didn't last. "Lucy only lived [a short while]," Erica says. "She fell over in the park one day and sprained her back, and the next thing she was paralyzed and in agony, and it was only going to keep getting worse."

Work, though difficult, offered some consolation whenever Joe got to brooding about what was missing in his life. He fiddled with screenplays, writing with George Mandel; he filled cards with thematic possibilities for *Something Happened;* now and then, he spoke to movie people about the slow progress of turning *Catch-22* into a film. "[A]ctors ranging all the way from Wally Cox to Jack Lemmon, John Gielgud [and] Zero Mostel" contacted him, asking, "Don't you think I'm right for the part [of Yossarian]?" "Nobody else," Joe would tell them. "You're just the guy I had in mind when I wrote it."

"And I really believed it when I was saying it," he said. "I don't know whether it was because I genuinely felt that *Catch-22* as a novel was so adaptable that any good actor could play it, or whether I was corrupt, more corrupt than I understood myself to be."

During this period, Joe wrote, discarded, and rewrote drafts of a stage version of *Catch-22*, encouraged by Broadway producer David Merrick and actor Paul Newman, who urged him to work with the Actors Studio in New York. One of Joe's ideas was to have four actors and actresses speaking lines from the book and reciting passages from Shakespeare echoed in the novel. The more he pursued this thought, the more he entertained the possibility of staging *mis*readings of Shakespeare. Eventually, this tack led him to write an original play. He would call it *We Bombed in New Haven.*

He rented an office with a few other people, "purportedly for writing reasons, but I'm not so sure," Ted says. "[It] had an old-fashioned slot machine in it." Over time, Joe "had several studios," Ted recalls. "One was on 59th Street west of Broadway and Eighth Avenue. He also had one in the apartment complex west of Lincoln Center . . . rented from a man who taught French history at City College."

After spending a morning in his studio, he dropped in on friends. Regularly, he met with Joan Goodman, an old pal from his NYU days. He'd stop to see Alice Denham, who had moved to a small apartment west of Central Park. "Welcome to the Uppa West Side!" he'd bellow, coming through the door. "[C]lassy joint. Very uptown. You getting rich modeling?"

She'd talk about the novel she was trying to sell. She wanted to quit being a photographer's model. She asked Joe if his editor would look at her manuscript. "I'm not sure S & S is into female books," he told her, but he said he'd ask. Over drinks, he said it would be a "miracle" if Hollywood ever "stop[ped] diddling" and did *Catch-22*. But no matter. He'd gotten his money up front. "My charmed life is paved with green," he'd say unconvincingly.

One day, after a couple of scotches, "Joe strong-armed my head [and pulled me] toward him," Denham wrote. "I'm a young stud, baby," he said, half-joking. "How come we never made out?"

"You're hitched," she replied. She hated to admit he was too pudgy for her taste. She wrote, "I thought he deserved one good smack for fame," so she gave him a "movie-star" kiss.

In 1967, Bobbs-Merrill accepted Denham's explicitly feminist novel, *My Darling from the Lions.* She contacted her male literary pals, hoping they'd blurb the book. They all declined. "I honestly can't believe my name would sell a single copy. . . . I'll keep an eye out for reviews," William Gaddis wrote her. The most poignant passages in Denham's memoir concern her growing realization that her writer friends had never taken her seriously, had spent time with her because she was attractive and, for many of them, sexually available. "Why had I thought I was one of the gang . . . when I was the Second Sex?" she wrote.

Joe is the one man she forgives. For months, she left messages with him. He did not respond. In the spring of 1968, he dropped by and said he would have given her a blurb "for sure," but he'd been away in Hollywood, working on a screenplay. He had not received her messages. Joe was always honest, Denham said, and "good." "Probably he really would've given me a blurb for my novel, if I'd reached him."

THROUGHOUT THIS PERIOD—the mid- to late 1960s—the Gourmet Club weathered several changes. From time to time, the charter members suggested potential recruits. Guests came and went. For a while, the composer Hershy Kay (orchestrator of *Evita* and *A Chorus Line*) ate with the group, but Mel Brooks wanted him out. "Except for Joe, all of us are quite short," Brooks explained. "Some of us are very short. Hershy is *too* short." The truth is, Kay had broken one of the club's sacred rules: He had eaten from another man's plate.

One night, after years of preparing weekly feasts, Ngoot Lee turned to his companions and said, "Wassah matter with you fucking guys, you got no fucking class? I'm cooking my fucking ass off for you fucking guys, not once not any of you fucking guys got the brains to take me out to dinner? You schmucks! You guys ever hear about Mother's Day?"

Joe said, "Ngoot, you're right. Next week, we will take you to the best restaurant in Chinatown."

They did. Once the meal was over and the tab paid, the men pushed back their chairs. They asked Ngoot if he was happy. "No!" he said. "Not one of you fucking guys thought to bring me one *farshtunkener* flower for Mother's Day!" The men apologized and promised to do better the next year. On the way uptown, the car stalled at a traffic light. "Hey, Ngoot, get out and pull it!" Joe quipped, to everyone's delight.

Shortly afterward, Ngoot announced he had gotten a job as an advertising consultant for a department store and could no longer cook for this lousy bunch of "hot dog eaters." He agreed to recommend Chinatown restaurants as long as club members refused to tell other "round-eye[s]" about them. He did not want the restaurants spoiled by tourists. This arrangement worked fine, until one night Joe told the others that Ngoot had taken him to an establishment that served the best lobster in the world. Ngoot had sworn him to secrecy, even within their group, because this place was so small and special. Joe's friends did not believe him, so he led them to a joint called New Sun, which resembled a luncheonette. He asked the waiter to bring them the same meal Ngoot Lee had ordered the night they'd gone there. "The soup was superb, the braised crab perfect, the pork tender, crisp, and most delicious, and then . . . the lobster, steamed in lemon oil and other exquisite spices. Marvelous," said Speed Vogel. But Joe was frowning. This was not the lobster he had eaten before. He spoke to the waiter. Another pair of lobsters appeared on the table, served this time Cantonese-style, with egg, scallions, minced pork, and black-bean sauce. "Absolutely the best [lobster] we had ever had. We left nothing but the shells, and these were picked clean," Speed said. Joe said, "Just take it easy, guys. It's not the right dish." He spoke to the waiter once more. Speed groaned; he couldn't eat another bite. "Yeah, just wait till you taste this," Joe assured him. More lobsters arrived, prepared very simply this time, sautéed in chicken fat. "Oh boy, that's the one I meant," Joe said, and dug in. He was the only member of the Gourmet Club who did not use chopsticks, because they were "too slow."

The following morning, Joe got a call from Ngoot. "You Judas prick," Ngoot said. "I take pity on you, you animal. I take you this best place in Chinatown, you *gonif,* you swear you would not betray me. I'll never trust you again, you *dreck*!"

"Who told you?" Joe asked. "Was it Speed?"

"None of them fucking guys. You schmuck. [B]y now all fucking Chinatown knows about four crazy round-eyes . . . that ate up all the lobsters in town, you fuck. How fucking smart do you think I have to be?"

The Gourmet Club was not good at keeping rules, but the members were brilliant at setting them: no waiting for latecomers; no grabbing the best pieces of chicken and lobster without eating your rice; no eating from another man's plate; no women.

"Once—and only once—I managed to find out where the club was meeting, and I crashed the dinner," said Anne Bancroft, whom Brooks married in 1964. "As soon as I came in the restaurant, it was as if a blanket had descended on the gathering. Dead silence. Faces falling. I turned around and left without eating."

Guests were allowed as long as they were male, and as long as one of the members vouched for them in advance. Brooks's good friend Carl Reiner was welcome whenever he came to town. "The members [were] very polite," Reiner said. "Once, I had a seat facing the kitchen door and I looked through and saw a rat strolling across the floor. They immediately offered me a chair facing the other way."

Another rule: You were not allowed to complain about ordering too much food. This was known as "Heller's Law of Too Much Is Never Enough."

"I'd rather have a bad meal out than a good meal at home," Joe used to say. "When you're out, it's a party. Also, I like a big mediocre meal more than a small good one."

Success, he insisted, was never having to eat with anybody you didn't want to see.

Most nights, after Chinese food, the men walked to Little Italy for lemon ice in paper cups from their favorite place on Mulberry Street. Joe would keep them out all night if he could. "From the very start, we accepted Joe on Speed Vogel's word that he would behave, and Speed lied to us, because he did not behave," Brooks liked to say. "He took the best pieces of everything and laughed in our faces." One night, the men were amazed when Joe rose over a tureen of steaming soup on the table. He picked up a bowl and the ladle. "Here, I'll serve," he said. His friends had never seen Joe so generous at dinner. He filled the bowl, sat down, and handed the ladle to Reiner. "Now, *you* serve," he said, and began to slurp his soup.

IN THE SEPTEMBER 1966 issue of *Esquire,* a seven-page excerpt of *Something Happened* appeared, featuring a protagonist named Joe Slocum. Slocum believed he "deserved" punishment as a child, "although [he] did not know what for," and feared, as an adult, "that someone [was] going to find out something about [him]" that would mean "the end," though he couldn't imagine what. "Something happened to me somewhere that robbed me of courage and left me with a fear of discovery," he admitted. "[T]here are so many things I don't want to find out."

Dostoevsky's influence on Joe was confirmed by an epigraph from the Russian master: "It was then, while sipping my tea, that I formulated to myself in so many words the idea that I neither know nor feel what evil is." Joe was also reading Beckett for the first time, amazed by the long, mellifluous monologues in *Molloy, Malone Dies,* and *The Unnamable.*

Slocum is a World War II vet (formerly stationed in San Angelo, Texas), now working in the corporate world. He is doing well at his job despite the fact that there are many people in his office of whom he is afraid. He has an unhappy wife and unhappy children. He is unhappily aware that it is "almost impossible anymore to rebel and make any kind of impression. They'd simply fire and forget you as soon as you started. They would file you away." Individuals have sacrificed freedom for high salaries and lengthy vacations: "People in the company like to live well," he says. "We *are* those punched cards they pay us with."

Slocum is "very good with the techniques of deception," personally and professionally. His job depends on them. "[M]any people in the company . . . fall victim to their own propaganda," he says. "Every time we launch a new advertising campaign . . . people inside the company are the first ones to be taken in by it." He attempts to quell anxiety by starting affairs with girls he meets in the office. He is "experienced," he says, and "can control and direct things" sexually more than he could as a boy, but the thrills are perfunctory. Wistfully, he says his wife "used to be very pretty when she was young."

Such harsh honesty about middle age and the fate of many in the "greatest generation" ("I am one of those people . . . who are without ambition and have no hope") was surprising in 1966, coming from a man with a growing reputation, among idealistic young people, as a cultural spokesperson. The excerpt could be read as a cautionary tale. It could be read as a portrait of certain American realities. But it could not be read as satire in the antic mode of *Catch-22.*

Joe's words nestled among articles on "how our red-blooded campus heroes are dodging the draft," how Richard Farina was a "mystical child of darkness," how Marvel Comics had emerged as "twentieth century mythology." Bob Hope was described as an entertainer who would "play anywhere—even Vietnam, where he came in two laughs under par last Christmas." A cartoon showed a gruff present-day soldier speaking to an army chaplain who might have walked off the beaches at Normandy: "I don't give a damn what they said during World War II, Padre, this is my foxhole and I can be an atheist if I want to!" A reporter insisted Robert Kennedy was forming a "Shadow Cabinet" in a possible bid for the presidency. A fashion spread said white crew-necked sweaters were "in" on campus that fall; the photographs featured women squeezed helplessly between two well-groomed young men (not draft dodgers, but also not boys who had to worry about going to war).

Joe's excerpt served as bitter commentary on the rest of the magazine:

> I've got anxiety: I repress hysteria. I've got wars on my mind and summer riots, peace movements and L.S.D. I've got old age to face. My boy, though still an innocent and unsuspecting child, is going to have to spend from two to six years of his life in the Army or Navy, and probably at war. I've got the decline of American culture and the guilt and ineptitude of the whole Government of the United States to carry around on my poor shoulders. And I find I'm being groomed for a better job.
>
> And I find that I want it.

IN *WORLD OF OUR FATHERS,* Irving Howe wrote that the "first Yiddish stage production in New York was held on August 12, 1882, at Turn Hall on East Fourth Street between Second and Third avenues." Yiddish theater "betrayed a mixture of shrewdness and innocence . . . vivid trash and raw talent," and contained "hardly a glimmer of serious realism." It appealed to the audience's appetite for "spectacle, declamation, and high gesture"; it was born of Eastern European traditions in which "theatricality had long been suspect as a threat to social discipline"; it was a subversive art that "[crept] into culture" in "oblique ways."

On October 16, 1968, in Broadway's Ambassador Theater, Joseph Heller's play, *We Bombed in New Haven,* opened, meeting all of Howe's criteria for Yiddish theater—yet it was not talked about in terms of the deepest traditions from which it sprang. Instead, it was seen by audiences and critics as either an avant-garde production, in the vein of

Beckett, Pirandello, and the Theatre of the Absurd, or as antiwar agit-prop. Reviewers fought about it.

The play had premiered the previous year in New Haven. At a dinner party during a visit to Yale in December 1966, Joe mentioned to Robert Brustein, dean of the Yale Drama School, that he had been working on a stage adaptation of *Catch-22*, trying to distill from the book scenes about repression and death (the novel's central themes, as he saw them). One version of the play featured misreadings from Shakespeare interspersed among quotes from the book. Brustein expressed interest. A month later, Joe had written a sketchy draft of a farce called "Bomber in New Haven"—a completed first act and an outline for the rest of the play. He said it was a "manuscript to be read like a novel." Brustein encouraged Joe to flesh it out. Four months later, Joe sent him a full draft. Brustein was so excited by it—particularly by the second act, which turned the first act's comedy on its head, the way Snowden's death silenced *Catch-22*'s laughter—he called Philip Roth and read it to him over the phone. Encouraged by Roth's response, Brustein invited Joe to be Playwright-in-Residence at Yale in the fall of 1967, where he would teach classes and work with the Yale Drama School to produce his play. (With Roth's help, Joe also secured some teaching work during this period at the University of Pennsylvania.)

Some of the Yale students questioned Brustein's decision. In his talk at Yale's Calhoun College, the previous December, Joe, wearing a green blazer, a striped shirt, and a tie, said little about the craft of writing, presenting himself instead as a "born promotion man."

"He's incredible," one student said after the talk. "He comes on like a real Madison Avenue fat cat. . . . If I were the author of *Catch-22*, I'd bill myself as a born American author."

"Either that guy is wearing a mask or he didn't write that book," said another young undergrad. (When apprised of this comment, George Mandel said, "Of course he's masked. He'd be an open wound otherwise.")

Brustein had made the Yale Drama School a center for a theater of protest against the Vietnam War, staging, among others, Megan Terry's *Viet Rock*, Barbara Garson's *Macbird*, and the Living Theatre's *Paradise Now*. Joe's play, with its antiwar sentiments, fit the program beautifully. Besides, Brustein said, "Heller's script offers a perfect skeleton for using the improvisational and *commedia dell' arte* techniques we are interested in."

Each week, Joe rode the train from Manhattan to New Haven. He took seriously the classes he taught, and had a good time with the students. One day, walking down a gloomy hallway in the Drama School Annex, encountering a group of kids waiting to file into his classroom, he said, "Today's Rosh Hashanah, a religious holiday, right? No classes on Rosh Hashanah. So what're you doing here?" The students stared at him. He laughed and said, "All right, you convinced me. We'll have our class." He loosened his tie, unbuttoned the top two buttons of his shirt, and plunged into Aristotle's *Poetics*.

Unlike the kids he'd taught years ago at Penn State, these students wanted to be where they were and seemed generally well prepared. Joe liked hanging out with them, chatting. One day, he listened carefully to a student describe a talk given at the Law School by Jack Valenti. Valenti claimed to have killed ten thousand people in Italy during World War II by dropping bombs on them. He said, as a patriot, he was proud of his accomplishments. "If he said that, then he's a schmuck," Joe said. "First, I would suspect he's a liar because no one can keep such accurate count, especially from the air, of how many people are killed when a bomb explodes. Second, if he had indeed killed that many people, he's really something for boasting about it."

Joe felt most of the students, bright as they were, didn't know what they wanted in life. They only knew what they *didn't* want—to go to war.

In October, in the chilly old WNHC building on Chapel Street, drama students staged a reading of Joe's play. He was moved to tears by it. After that, rehearsals began in earnest for a full-scale production of the play, to open on December 4 at the Yale Repertory Theatre. Larry Arrick, a veteran of Chicago's Second City, would direct. The actors included Stacy Keach, Ron Leibman, and Estelle Parsons. The pun in the title suggests the conceit on which the drama unfolds, erasing distinctions between the reality of wartime bombing and showbiz fears of staging a play that might fizzle. Joe knew he was running a risk, daring critics to call the play a bomb—but that was part of the unsettling strategy.

The play concerns actors who believe they are impersonating members of a bomb squadron during an unspecified war. Intermittently, they dutifully act their parts, then stop to discuss the script, complain about the size of their roles, express puzzlement over their characters, and remember productions they—the actual actors—have been in. The curtain does not rise properly, a large wall clock keeps real time, and the actors treat the stage props as trinkets, never allowing illusions of realism to grip the audience. In the first act, amid much horseplay, the script calls for a character to die offstage during a bombing mission. Afterward, one of the performers, playing the role of Sergeant Henderson, wonders where the actor went. He seems to have vanished, though his bloody clothes remain. In act 2, a pair of wealthy sportsmen, one wielding a golf club and the other a hunting rifle, murder Henderson onstage. Captain Starkey, a father figure to Henderson, watches the young man die and does nothing—just like the audience.

Ruth, a Red Cross girl, accuses the audience of guilty passivity. We accept war as entertainment, lies as truth, she says. Here lay the difference between *We Bombed in New Haven* and the avant-garde plays against which it was measured. In Beckett's *Endgame,* Clov asks, "What is there to keep me here?" Hamm replies, "The dialogue." The effect is a blurring of the psychological and metaphysical—a burst of alienation. Joe had no interest in this. He had been reading Beckett ("I'd rather read him than see him staged"), but Joe used similar techniques for a different aim: social cohesion, rather than estrangement.

With *We Bombed in New Haven,* Joe intended to startle audience members into accepting personal responsibility for a war organized like a game, reviewed like a show, and managed largely offstage to hide mass killings. When Starkey asks an army major, "[L]et me in on the biggest military secret of all. Who's really in charge and who's really responsible," the answer is not some silent god in a meaningless universe; the answer is *us.*

Naturally, Joe opened himself to charges of didacticism, propaganda, and ham-handedness. He said he was extending theatrical principles. In Greek theater, endings were always inevitable: Audiences knew the myths behind the plays, he said. He was making a larger connection, not only between drama and ancient myths but between popular entertainments and the myths of society—patriotism, heroism, "surgical strikes." These myths allowed the killing of innocents, and let fellows like Jack Valenti sleep at night.

Moreover, in the tradition of Yiddish theater—forms of which Joe had encountered all his life, from neighborhood jokes to Marx Brothers movies, from Catskills skits to Lenny Bruce routines—he was engaging, obliquely and gleefully, in social disruption, forcing the audience to laugh at itself, to question its language and values. Sigmund Mogulesco, America's first great Yiddish comic, never made a distinction between "art and trash," according to Irving Howe. He'd do anything to get a reaction. Similarly, Mel Brooks said, "[I]f someone wants to call my movies art or crap, I don't mind."

When an interviewer asked Joe what he hoped to accomplish with *We Bombed in New Haven,* he said, "What else, I wanted to make a million dollars." "No, really," the interviewer said. "All right," Joe replied. "Right now I want to make every woman cry and every man feel guilty when he has to go home and face his sons. . . . You ask what did I mean to accomplish? I meant to write a very good play."

The rehearsals at Yale—the actors improvising, questioning, improving one day, backsliding the next, Joe rethinking, rewriting, learning the nuances of stagecraft—frazzled the playwright. Lines he'd thought were funny dragged when he heard them aloud. Some of the actors ignored his stage directions. Others seemed not to get his jokes. Shredded orange toothpicks lay at his feet. In the evenings, he'd go to his room at the Midtown Motor Inn and, tossing and turning, relive the rehearsals in his head. One night, he thought he heard maniacs in the room next door banging the walls and playing their radios loudly. At 5:00 A.M., he discovered his *own* bedside radio, built into the night table, had been on.

Arrick told students who came to watch rehearsals to slip quietly in and out of the building without disturbing the actors. Joe said the students could make as much noise as they wanted. "For god's sake, speak up if you have any criticism," he said. To streamline the first act, he cut Falstaff's speech on honor, as well as other Shakespearian echoes left over from the now defunct *Catch-22* adaptation. He increased Starkey's ineffectuality, and linked it more clearly to the audience's passivity. He added lines to the chorus of "idiots" who yammer behind the action ("They're not really idiots. They're no different from you or me, which is why they're idiots," he explained).

He asked that a different actor play the army major; the first actor spoke with a southern accent reminiscent of Lyndon Johnson's—a too-specific link to Vietnam. Joe didn't want that. On the other hand, he left in a reference to bombing Minnesota, because Hubert Humphrey had been born there, and Humphrey "told lies . . . believ[ing] they were true."

"I'm learning, I'm learning that I wrote a script, not a production," Joe said. "In novels, the writer defines and limits his characters, but not in plays. If an actor has any talent and is working with a good director, he will fill out bare words in the script." Still, the rehearsals racked his nerves. "It's not that I'm trying to dominate the director; it's just that I want the director to know what's in my mind and have the same thing in his mind so that he'll do what I want him to do without my trying to dominate him," he said.

Joe's agony surprised the students; they had expected an easygoing, round-the-clock funnyman. Worried about him—and more experienced with the tedium of rehearsals—the actors suggested he stay away from the final run-throughs. He agreed. "Listen, who's nervous?" he joked. "I've learned to suffer excruciating torture without making a sound while [you] blow my play."

"The real truth is that things have been going beautifully," he told *New York Times* reporter Elenore Lester. "Larry Arrick . . . and the actors have been a revelation to me—the way they've gotten hold of this thing. After the first week they understood the play better than I did. They've seen things in it, psychological meanings I never thought of. . . . The only thing is I'm not happy. It's my nature to be suspicious. I just don't trust people. I know it's not right, but that's the way I am. . . . I'm concerned about my literary personality. I don't want Joseph Heller distorted."

Uneasiness with the collaborative process signaled once and for all that Joe was a novelist, not a playwright. But he couldn't have been in better hands. Larry Arrick understood he was "close . . . to the Jewish sensibility of novelists like Mailer, Roth, Bellow, and Malamud who [had] a kind of self-loathing that [was] in itself a form of purification." Arrick said the Yale group was "the best company I've ever worked with anywhere. And the play is marvelous—its subject is war, but its theme is not. War is a metaphor here for [the] game . . . [w]e are all playing . . . in this country today, you know. We go to the theater or we look at Picasso's *Guernica* in the Museum of Modern Art and we say, 'Yes, war is terrible' and then we go and have some coffee. We aren't changed at all."

As opening night approached, the Drama School's publicist asked Joe if he could promote the play as a comedy in ads. Joe conceded that this might sell more tickets, but he didn't want the play hailed as a comedy. There were plenty of jokes. But at the beginning of the second act, a character announced, accurately, "There's nothing really funny about this, you know."

Joe got word that Walter Kerr, Barbara Harris, Mike Nichols, and Paul Newman planned to attend the premiere. "I thought we were going to have a good time putting on a play at Yale, but this way . . . you have all the stresses of a Broadway opening without its actually being Broadway," he groaned.

He lumbered to his classes in the shadow of Harkness Tower, feeling heavy and tired, carrying an overstuffed briefcase. To cheer himself up, he bought a sheepskin jacket. "It's not really very expensive and I hear they last forever," he told anyone who stopped to admire it.

On campus, rumors spread that the Yale Draft Refusal Committee, a student group, had bought a block of seats and planned to disrupt the play. "Heller's ending"—in which Starkey allows his son to go to war— "signified to them an acceptance of induction," Brustein said: a serious misreading of the drama. At the eleventh hour, Brustein dissuaded the protesters.

At the end of the first performance, the audience filed out of the theater, somber and quiet. "There's no remission at the end of my play," Joe said. "I felt the audience didn't deserve any consolation. The poor are suffering, the colored are suffering, the people with sons of eighteen and nineteen are suffering. I'm convinced that, if we remain accomplices of evil, we are not only guilty but deserve to be victims as well."

One student felt the performance had taught him the power of metaphor. "Most guys think they'll go into [the service], play the role of the soldier for two years, and then come back and pick up where they left off," he said. "They don't think: go in, play soldier, and be killed."

Generally, reviews were favorable. Roderick Nordell, writing in the *Christian Science Monitor,* said the play "cuts to the quick." He felt that most of the time "Mr. Heller's . . . comedy serves the ultimate purpose of his tragedy." And in *Newsweek,* Jack Kroll said that "the play is very likely the most powerful play about contemporary irrationality an American has written, with a natural cathartic jolt that comes from the genuineness of Heller as a moral comedian. . . . This is one of those rare productions that advance the whole notion of the theater."

On the other hand, Walter Kerr objected to Joe's premise. "The evening posits war as a glamorous game in which no one really expects to be killed. It supposes that we regard war in this way; in effect, it accuses us of [doing so]. But who now thinks of war in this way? . . . The accusation . . . is off-target." Heller, he said, "wants not to dramatize war in any way, shape or form, but to talk about it, shout about it, make proclamations about it—*now.*"

Tom F. Driver, writing in *The Saturday Review* two months before the play's New York opening, said the "imagination that created [*Catch-22*] is . . . totally verbal. . . . The humor of *Catch-22* depended on taking words with *absolute* seriousness, no bones about it, the same way you'd take the b.m. on the baby's diapers. I mean, there it is." Heller, he said, had failed to find a theatrical equivalent of this experience. "What we're after in the theater is energy. Not theory, and not fashion."

Sensitive to criticisms, Joe delayed the Broadway premiere by several months as he fine-tuned the play. "I have unlimited confidence in the stupidity of our government . . . I know that Congress and the President wouldn't let me down and do something intelligent like ending the war while I was revising," he said.

THE YALE PRODUCTION closed on December 23. Just over a month later, on January 31, 1968, in what came to be known as the Tet Offensive, 67,000 Vietcong troops attacked more than one hundred cities and towns in South Vietnam. U.S. military leaders were astounded by the enemy's organization and daring. The American public's faith in Lyndon Johnson, already badly frayed, unraveled almost completely. Thus began an extraordinarily turbulent year. As Joe tinkered with his play, as he made notes for *Something Happened*, public concerns swamped him; journalists would not stop pestering him for statements. Reflecting the anxiety of the moment, his pronouncements became increasingly extreme. "The American government is making war on the American people—not on Ho [Chi Minh]," he said. He applauded boys who burned their draft cards: "This could end the war. They can't put everybody in jail." He told the *New York Times,* "If it came to violence, I would not side with the Establishment, though my friendliest banker is there. . . . Reconciliation is not going to come from the Pope or Billy Graham or J. Edgar Hoover. . . . If it weren't for my basic optimism, I'd be packing up to leave the country. But I don't like packing."

He wasn't all talk. A few months earlier, having left New Haven to return to New York for the weekend, he had met Eugene McCarthy in Sardi's East. They'd had adjoining tables for dinner one night. A former Benedictine novice steeped in Thomistic theology, now a rather bored and iconoclastic U.S. senator, McCarthy impressed Joe with his charisma, honesty, and opposition to the war. He had decided to challenge LBJ for the Democratic party's presidential nomination (he announced his intentions on November 30, 1967). He asked Joe if he'd run in the New York state primary as a McCarthy delegate. Joe agreed.

"McCarthy [is] an easy man to defend," he told a reporter. "Maybe because we don't know as much about him as we do about Nixon and Humphrey." Joe felt the "issues were so stark that in good conscience I had to get involved." Stepping into the political arena, however, reminded him of a secret he had kept from most of his friends: In 1964, an acquaintance of his in the Democratic party asked Joe to draft a speech for LBJ in his campaign against Barry Goldwater, and "to [his] everlasting shame," Joe had done it. "It was good," he recalled, "because I was a good advertising copywriter. It was good enough considering the man it was written for."

From the late autumn of 1967 to the spring of 1968, Joe stumped for McCarthy. "Every place I went"—college campuses, mostly—"I ask[ed] if I would embarrass anybody if I wore a McCarthy button," he said.

Erica, now fifteen, was also "stung by the Gene McCarthy fever." She said later, "He provided for me (and for many others like me, I suppose) the perfect transition from adolescence to pre-adulthood. . . . We believed in him enough to cut school and go lick envelopes at his midtown headquarters, to wake up at four a.m. on a frosty February morning and pile all bleary-eyed onto buses to go to New Hampshire to canvas for him." She joined antiwar marches. "Whole classes at my high school would make the midnight run to Washington to protest the annihilation in Vietnam. And we'd return that night, exhausted, filthy, stinking of tear gas and feeling ever so virtuous," she said.

She didn't talk to her father about politics, though she hoped he would notice her engagement. "I guess he was proud, but who knows?" she says. "One time in D.C., there was some demonstration at the Justice Department and I looked around and saw him in a tree with Speed Vogel! I had no idea he'd be going."

Joe *did* notice her activism, but he was concerned why organizers did not ask him to make more rally appearances. "I'm not considered a first-stringer," he said. "They generally go for Norman Mailer first."

He noticed the gap in news coverage between mainstream and underground presses. Writing about protests, the *New York Times* tended to concentrate on beards, beads, and sandals—unlike, say, the *National Guardian,* which analyzed the politics and morality behind mass actions. There were many different ways to express ideology and bias.

On March 31, 1968, LBJ announced he would not seek another term as president. This followed Robert Kennedy's toss of his boater into the ring. McCarthy was turning out to be a lazy campaigner. Frequently, his speeches were uninspired. "All the candidates can use humor and they can all use better argumentation," Joe noted. "Even Senator McCarthy, the most intelligent of them all [could be doing] better." He sounded dispirited.

In early April, Joe met Kurt Vonnegut at a literary festival on the Notre Dame campus. Immediately, they bonded. They had in common World War II (famously, Vonnegut had survived the Dresden firebombing), corporate experience, humor. At the festival one night, they were scheduled to give back-to-back speeches. Vonnegut delivered his talk— "probably the best speech [about literature] I've ever heard," Joe recalled, "so casual and so funny." As Joe rose to approach the lectern, "some sort of academic, a professor, came up over the footlights," Vonnegut recalled. The man "shouldered Joe aside politely and said, 'I just want to announce that Martin Luther King has been shot.' And then this guy went back over the footlights and took his seat."

Joe stood immobile onstage, saying, "Oh, my god. Oh, my god. I wish I were with Shirley now. She's crying her eyes out."

On April 23, individuals under the direction of Students for a Democratic Society occupied Hamilton Hall at Columbia University, headquarters of the undergraduate college, to protest the university's contracts with the U.S. Defense Department. The group paralyzed the campus—a far cry from panty raids.

Two months later, Bobby Kennedy was killed in the hotel where Joe and Shirley had spent their honeymoon.

By the time Hubert Humphrey secured the Democratic party's nomination at the disastrous convention in Chicago, held in late August, Joe was immersed again in his play. It was scheduled to open on Broadway in October. About his involvement in the McCarthy campaign, he tried to sound casual. "He lost because of the nature of American politics," he said wearily. Then he joked, "I gave very good speeches. I don't think I was personally responsible."

On September 9, as Joe watched the first Broadway run-through of *We Bombed in New Haven*, a *New York Times* reporter approached him in the theater and asked what he thought of Eugene McCarthy now. Joe sighed. "[Politics is] not my thing," he said defensively. "I don't care enough about politicians to think it matters much who wins."

Sitting at home, Erica felt "utter political disillusionment." She said she realized her generation was "incapable of internalizing [its] irrelevancy to . . . 'Nam. . . . President Johnson finally did convince us, though. And of course President Nixon [would] reaffirm . . . it."

The nation's self-image had taken a pummeling. Arthur Schlesinger wrote in the *Washington Post,* "With the murder of Robert Kennedy, following on the murder of John Kennedy and the murder of Martin Luther King, we have killed the three great embodiments of our national idealism in this generation. Each murder has brought us one stage further on the downward spiral of moral degradation and social disintegration." One needn't have agreed with his politics or vision to share a massive gloom and worried apprehension.

Almost desperately, Joe turned his attention elsewhere. He took pleasure where he could. The Gourmet Club kept his spirits high—though he continued to worry about his weight. He *tried* not to sweat the play.

On Mott Street one evening, just days before opening night, the group gathered outside a new restaurant Ngoot had found. "Is it as good as our old one?" Joe asked.

"*New* one is as good as *old* one. I guarantee," Ngoot said.

"How do you know?"

"I know because *new* one steal chef from *old* one."

Carl Reiner was in town. He had joined the group for the evening. Every time Reiner ate with the club, he spotted rats in the kitchens. "Traditionally, honored guests, who aren't accustomed to seeing a rat scurry across a kitchen floor, don't . . . enjoy the evening as much as those of us who are accustomed to the intrusion," Joe told him. He said ritzy restaurants hid vermin by keeping their kitchen doors closed. "Which is dishonest! This is an honest restaurant with an open-door policy."

Scraps of conversation spun around the table like dishes on a lazy Susan. A typical sampling:

> GEORGE MANDEL: Everything here is salty. We're eating a lot of salt, like Pygmies.
>
> MEL BROOKS: Yes, but you know, Ngoot never ate a straight dish in his life. He sticks octopus eyes into a hamburger to make it taste good.
>
> JOE: [Mel,] if you were not a Jew, who would you be?
>
> BROOKS: I think I would go all the way, I think I would be, you know . . .
>
> JOE: No, you are you, it's not a choice. You are you. But when your ancestors came over on the Slovotnik, if instead of coming to New York, they went west and you wound up in Wisconsin, what would you be like? I know the answer already. You would be *Richard* Brooks.
>
> BROOKS: I'd be Richard Brooks. Of all the things we ordered, George, the truth, from the bottom of your heart, what is the best thing?
>
> MANDEL: The salt.
>
> BROOKS: Apart from the salt.
>
> MANDEL: Next to the salt is the lobster. I asked Ngoot how to eat it, and he said, "Watch Heller. He takes the best parts and leaves the worst for you."

After the meal that night, Joe asked Joe Stein, who was driving, if they could swing by *his* theater. "Hey, Joe, it's one a.m.!" Brooks said. "Let's go home!"

Joe persisted. As Carl Reiner recalled it, Joe directed Stein to stop the car about thirty feet from the Ambassador, which was on the other side of the street.

"Now what?" Stein asked.

"Now, I sit and look at the marquee," Joe said, rolling down his window.

WE BOMBED IN NEW HAVEN, A NEW PLAY BY JOSEPH HELLER.

"Just wanted to see my name up there," Joe said quietly. "I never thought I'd be on a Broadway theater marquee, and there I am! It's very exciting! Don't know how long the play will run or if I'll ever write another one so, if you guys don't mind—a couple more minutes?"

A rare reverential silence touched this usually boisterous group, and they all sat staring at the lights. After a while, Heller said, "Okay, Joe, drive."

IN THE DAYS AHEAD, Joe kept dropping by Forty-ninth and Broadway to look at his sign, but now it only worried him. A cartoon bomb adorned the marquee next to the title. Sometimes, the bomb looked thin and silly; on other days, it appeared too fat. (*Joe* was too fat, not feeling well, not himself.) All wrong. Everything was off.

Jason Robards had replaced Stacy Keach as Starkey, and Joe wasn't sure he had the proper intensity. The rehearsals had not been as exciting or fun as they'd been in New Haven (in retrospect, Joe could admit he'd had a ball at Yale). "I imagine every amateur production has been better than the New York production, where there [is] a great deal of self-consciousness on the part of the professionals," he said. The Theatre Development Fund had purchased sixty thousand dollars' worth of tickets to guarantee a six-week run, but would that ensure success?

At least Joe was pleased with Harold Leventhal, the play's New York producer. A legend, a staunch lefty, Leventhal had worked with Woody Guthrie, Pete Seeger, and Bob Dylan (having presented the latter at his first Town Hall concert, on April 12, 1963). More recently, he had produced a version of Bertolt Brecht's *Mother Courage,* featuring Yiddish star Ida Kaminska.

On October 17, the all-important *New York Times* review, written by Clive Barnes (who had also seen the Yale production), sounded a puzzled, ambivalent note about the play. "I am not at all certain what I felt, and even less certain what I think, about Joseph Heller's . . . 'We Bombed in New Haven,'" Barnes wrote. "If I was forced to a judgment I would call it a bad play any good playwright should be proud to have written, and any good audience fascinated to see."

Joe bit his nails.

"[A]lthough we know that all the world's a stage and all that jazz, the device is neither especially original nor meaningful," Barnes went on.

"[T]he [antiwar] message . . . becomes almost insupportable in its obviousness."

But Barnes loved the writing and the atmosphere. He applauded the play's ambition: "Mr. Heller is a writer to the tip of his keyboard. His dialogue flows out, natural, real, amusing, absorbing. Here [he] is . . . flying high." Additionally, Barnes said, he "has caught the anarchic mood of the present, the callousness, brutality, cynical jokiness, dissent and protest." Heller "demonstrates a profound moral concern for what is happening in our own theater of the world," Barnes wrote.

In sum, "Any way you look at it, this is a pretty remarkable theatrical debut for Mr. Heller," Barnes affirmed. "I hope he stays around our theater for a long, long time."

But Joe was telling friends already he never again wanted anything to do with the theater. The experience had wrung him out. Barnes's left-handed compliments embittered him.

Three weeks after opening night, Richard Nixon's landslide election seemed to confirm for Joe the hopelessness with which he'd ended his play. *Catch-22* reaches its climax with Yossarian asserting his freedom—vainly, perhaps, but trying. Capitulation concludes *We Bombed in New Haven*: a father sacrificing his son to the madness of wretched leaders.

The play had brought the spirit of Yiddish theater to the late twentieth century. Filtered through the Catskills, early television, and jazz club stand-up, it cross-pollinated with street theater, performance art, and Happenings such as the Bed-Ins for Peace staged by John Lennon and Yoko Ono in Amsterdam and Montreal. Now Joe wondered what all this had accomplished. Somewhat wistfully, he invited Eugene McCarthy to the New York opening. In the long run (the play closed after eleven weeks on Broadway), Joe pocketed the roughly $70,000 he would earn from various productions of the play, and the nearly $100,000 he had been paid by Knopf and Dell for rights to publish the script. He would not look back.

Except: *We Bombed in New Haven* solidified his literary vision. The play made it possible for this painfully slow writer to develop an important body of work. *Catch-22* stood on its own, and would remain his best-regarded work, but the play, in extending that novel's concerns about bureaucracy, linking them with broader views of social relationships—within families, corporate structures, and religious traditions—provided him with material for the rest of his career. *Something Happened*'s Bob

Slocum would be Captain Starkey in civilian clothes, sacrificing his son despite his mortal terror of losing him (at the end of the play, Starkey leaves the stage with a portfolio and a copy of the *New York Times,* a corporate man in the making). The hatred of war (expressed far more strongly in the play than in *Catch-22*) looks ahead to the scathing portraits of government flunkies animating Joe's third novel, *Good as Gold*. In assuring his son, "I will weep for you. I promise you that," Starkey echoes the biblical King David, a subject Joe would turn to in his fourth novel. "When King David was told his son had been killed . . . in a rebellion against him, he cried: 'O my son Absalom! . . . Would God I had died for thee!'" Starkey tells his boy. "I will weep for you. I will cry: 'My son . . . my son! Would God I had died for thee!'"

"But will you mean it?" his son asks.

Starkey replies "slowly, truthfully": "I won't know. I won't ever really know."

In what could only be heard, in 1968, as a rejection of U.S. culture and leadership, Starkey's son, bundled off to war, says, "Bastard."

THE 1960S, as a distinct cultural period in America, as opposed to a set of dates on a calendar, is hard to bracket. Did the era's immense social and political energies culminate in the *Eagle*'s landing in the Sea of Tranquillity in 1969? Abate (sanely or sadly, depending on one's view) in the rout of liberals in the elections of 1968? In the Kent State killings in 1970, or the announcement of the Beatles' breakup later that year? Or did they crumble, once and for all, in the rubble of the Nixon administration, following a minor break-in at the Watergate Hotel in the early morning hours of June 17, 1972? Historians, critics, and writers have suggested each of these moments, and more, as the period's capstone.

For Joe Heller, the closing of his play, spurring a wholehearted recommitment to fiction writing, was a watershed. Sixties fashions would pass; what remained for Joe were a love of literature and the discipline of writing. In a telling anecdote, journalist Tom Nolan reported that in 1969, in a corner booth of a restaurant on Hollywood Boulevard in L.A., "maybe a booth at which Dash Hammett once ate with Lilly Hellman—[I] had dinner with . . . Joseph Heller. Heller spoke of a recent meeting in San Francisco with the Jefferson Airplane, who were fans of his, and who tried to induce him to take LSD. 'But it'll make you want to write,' the Airplane crew told the author. 'I already want to write,' Heller said."

Another watershed for Joe was the destruction of Dustin Hoffman's apartment on West Eleventh Street on March 6, 1970. Joe had met the actor through Mel Brooks and Anne Bancroft, who lived on West Eleventh at the time (Bancroft had starred with Hoffman in Mike Nichols's movie *The Graduate*). "[Hoffman and I became] good friends [because] we have never been close," Joe wrote. "We have never worked together . . . leaving each of us with an unmarred respect for the judgment and consideration of the other that is probably unwarranted by both." The foundation of their friendship, he said, lay in the "ground rules": "he [didn't] have to read my novels, and I [didn't] have to see his movies."

Just past noon on that chilly March day in 1970, a woman named Marie-Thérèse Thiesselin, whom Hoffman and his wife had hired as a baby-sitter for their daughter, Karina, was standing in Hoffman's living room at number 16. Suddenly, the fireplace lurched at her, a violent blossoming of bricks. Shock made her strangely calm. She picked up Hoffman's pet terrier, O.J., walked into the kitchen, and phoned Hoffman (Karina was not at home). Then she walked out on the street, where she saw a gaping hole in the building next door, debris strewn across the pavement, flames licking the windows of number 18. Soon, the country would learn that members of the Weathermen had been manufacturing bombs in the basement of that building. By accident, one had gone off.

From the air, from his perch in a B-25 during World War II, Joe rarely knew if he had hit a little bridge. On the ground in Greenwich Village, the mayhem was impossible to miss and even harder to absorb. As Hoffman and his neighbors salvaged whatever they could from their apartments, they wondered if other blasts were imminent and might eliminate the street entirely.

In the aftermath, city officials discovered, buried in the waste, sixty sticks of live dynamite.

Some time later, speaking of the bombers on *The Dick Cavett Show,* Hoffman said he didn't feel anger, but fear—for all of us, our families, our nation. His words seemed a valediction for the decade. The dissidents at number 18 had benefited from the "rising income, rising productivity, [and] rising consumption" *Fortune* magazine, in 1961, had predicted would lead to contentment and glorious achievement. What could have steered them toward that basement? Disillusionment after years of racial strife, a questionable war, and a rash of political assassinations? Still, to most observers, the Weathermen's actions were unfathomable. The culture seemed to have come unhinged.

The old thrill rides at Coney Island were nothing compared to this.

In what seemed another eulogy for the sixties, a resident of West Eleventh Street expressed the mood of the neighbors in the days following the blast: "At first there was camaraderie, but then there was a general sense of helplessness, a kind of loneliness, [and finally] a sense of distance."

14. Where Is World War II?

I F IT HAD BEEN ACAPULCO, Joe would have beaten the film crew there. But the location scouts had staked out a patch of desert twenty miles northwest of Guaymas, in the Mexican state of Sonora. According to *Catch-22*'s screenwriter Buck Henry, the area offered a "breathtaking panorama of poverty, dust, [and] unidentified plant life"—not the ideal setting in which to ring out the old decade and, along with the roar of over half a dozen B-25s, ring in the new.

Originally, the film crew had hoped to shoot where Joe had fought the war. John Calley, the movie's producer, and Richard Sylbert, the production designer, flew to Corsica. Up and down the coast, they asked ("in our failing Italian," Sylbert said), "Where is World War II?" Joe could have told them. Nowhere. Oil refineries and highways had replaced the old American air base.

Besides a desire for accuracy, Mike Nichols, the film's director, wanted a setting that conveyed Yossarian's "how-do-I get-outta-here feeling." He found such a place near the Tetakawi mountain, known as "Goat's Teats," north of Guaymas. There, the crew built a $180,000 five-mile highway to haul necessary equipment to the location, and a $250,000 six-thousand-foot runway for the B-25s. The mayor of Guaymas welcomed these improvements to the infrastructure, particularly because he owned a local construction company.

In the years preceding production, Columbia, which had first optioned the book, sold the film property to Paramount/Filmways. At one point, Jack Lemmon wanted to make the movie (and play Yossarian). Later, Richard Brooks said he would do it, but he wound up making a version of Joseph Conrad's *Lord Jim* instead, exhausting his capacity for orchestrating war movies.

Columbia had financed *Dr. Strangelove* and purchased *Fail-Safe,* so the studio released two antiwar movies in the same year. "[T]he Pentagon didn't like it," Joe said. "Each of the studios has a man in Washington who talks to the generals and the admirals, and keeps them happy, and [the Columbia heads] didn't want to embark on another movie that they thought the Pentagon might not like. Then a stockholder's fight got in the way. All this time my reputation was suffering because the rumor was spreading that *Catch-22* was hard to adapt to the screen. And I was getting stigmatized. People in Hollywood and New York were saying, 'That's Heller over there—his books don't make good screenplays.' I stopped being invited to parties."

Joe was kidding when he made these remarks during a talk at the Ninety-second Street Y, but he wasn't exaggerating much.

Enter Mike Nichols. With two phenomenal successes, *Who's Afraid of Virginia Woolf?* and *The Graduate,* he had earned the right—in a shifting Hollywood climate—to make whatever he wanted. He had become the first American director since Orson Welles to gain creative control of his movie, including the right of final cut and the option of keeping studio executives from seeing daily rushes. Welles had wielded such power with *Citizen Kane* in 1941. Now, *Catch-22* was to be an important "auteur" film.

Throughout the early 1960s—in fact, since the end of World War II—the American film industry had floundered, losing its grip on an audience tired of the kinds of formulaic projects Joe had worked on (with certain exceptions, like *Casino Royale*). In 1968, Jack Valenti, a former insider in the LBJ administration, and now president of the Motion Picture Association of America, oversaw the creation of the movie rating system. It was established to assuage the fears of parents and politicians fussed about inappropriate material for children (much the way the comic-book industry had regulated itself in the 1950s). But the system was also designed to lure bigger audiences to "mature" movies, for which moviegoers were showing a predilection.

In his comprehensive *American Film: A History,* Jon Lewis says movies like *The Graduate,* explicit about sex and other "adult" behaviors, "moved the industry one step closer to a simple truth: the old guard running the studios were desperately out of touch, and a new breed of American filmmakers—young and audacious, with an understanding of and an interest in a more international film style and form—had a much better idea of what American audiences wanted than they did. The success of . . . *The Graduate* [which earned forty million dollars in its first run] made the auteur renaissance—the brief golden age . . . in Hollywood when directors finally seemed to be the ones to call the shots—not only necessary but inevitable."

In the 1950s François Truffaut was the first to use the term *auteur theory,* which refers to the notion that every movie had an author: the director. "A peculiarly American brand of auteurism was embraced by the studios only so long as the auteurs were able to satisfy the audience's tastes and make money," Lewis writes.

Nichols, a refugee from Hitler's Germany who spoke only two sentences in English when he first arrived in the United States—"I do not speak English" and "Please do not kiss me"—was thirty-seven years old when he was granted so much freedom with *Catch-22.* With Elaine May, in the 1950s, he had honed not just his English but his wit and comic timing. The couple took their comedy act from Chicago's Second City to Broadway. Nichols went on to produce and direct plays, then movies. *Catch-22* was his third feature-length film.

"Every time you get too much for what you've put in, you know it's going to come out of you later," he told Nora Ephron, who flew to Mexico to cover the filming for the *New York Times.* He said he kept thinking about the Beatles—in their early days, they wondered when "the Fall" would come: that inevitable moment when success dimmed, soured, or backfired. Nichols said he would almost welcome that moment. Perhaps it would dispel his feeling that he had been given more than he deserved. In the meantime, he would restage World War II.

One day in the Apthorp, Erica picked up the phone. "It's another one of your friends," she said to her father.

"Which friend?" Joe asked.

"I don't know, but he's giving me false names."

"I don't have friends like that, you do," Joe said.

"Well, he says he's Mike Nichols."

Like the students in the Yale Drama School, Nichols couldn't believe *this guy* had written *that book*. One of his associates said maybe Heller had found the manuscript of *Catch-22* on the body of a dead soldier. One night in Chinatown, Joe joined Nichols and Buck Henry over noodles and a movie script. The meal was awkward. Nichols wanted to know what Joe thought, but Joe did not want to criticize Henry's script in front of the man. The writing had been herculean: The first draft of the screenplay topped out at 385 pages (a typical script rarely exceeded 120). "[This] indicated to me that they had made an effort to include in the motion picture everything in the book that they themselves liked, and that was pretty much the whole book," Joe said. Touched but doubtful the film could succeed, he decided to stay out of the process. Buck Henry was working in good faith. Besides, Joe realized that when it came to movie scripts, he was probably too bound by conventional patterns. He understood that were he to have undertaken the adaptation of his novel, he would have made a mess of things by going for easy laughs and avoiding some of the book's darker moments. Whatever flaws stippled Henry's script, he was taking a mighty shot at doing the book justice.

Nichols said he'd "get back" to Joe. Over the course of many months, he would say this several times. Joe never saw him.

Nichols tapped Alan Arkin—a Brooklyn native and another Second City vet—to play Yossarian. "[It's] the only part I've ever worked on that didn't demand a conception," Arkin said. "[T]here isn't much difference between me and Yossarian."

The mayor of Guaymas dispatched seventy-five peones armed with machetes to clear a one-mile-square site of rattlesnakes, brush, and cactus, leaving only mesquite, which could pass for the small olive trees native to Corsica. Nichols issued a call for thirty-six bombers. Eventually, Frank Tallman, a stunt pilot, rounded up eighteen old B-25s, most of which had been destined for the scrap heap, repaired them, and readied them to fly, at a cost of ten thousand dollars each. One of the planes came from heiress Barbara Hutton, who had given it as a wedding present to a playboy pal of hers. It had been fitted with a bed, reclining seats, and a leather-lined toilet.

Tallman signed former fighter pilots to steer the planes. An additional plane, beyond repair, was shipped to the desert, burned to film a crash scene, and buried beside the runway, where it remains to this day.

The sight of Tallman's artificial leg unnerved all the actors scheduled to fly in the bombers.

A reporter from *Time* magazine, watching the filming, wrote, "Under Nichols' direction, the camera makes the air as palpable as blood. . . . [T]he sluggish bodies of the B-25s rise impossibly close to one another, great vulnerable chunks of aluminum shaking as they fight for altitude. Could the war truly have been fought in those preposterous crates? It could; it was."

The cockpits and the bombardiers' perches were so small, the crew had difficulty fitting actors, cameras, and cameramen in the planes. Nichols spent hours one day setting up a scene, arranging the camera the way he wanted it. The equipment filled the cockpit. "Uh—Mike—who's going to fly the plane?" Tallman asked.

John Jordan, a second-unit director, refused to wear a harness. While in the air one morning, in the tail gunner's spot, filming one plane from another, he sent a hand signal to a crew member in the other plane, lost his grip, and fell four thousand feet to his death, a late casualty of the war.

Painstakingly, Nichols staged the scene where Milo Minderbinder calls an air strike against the base; Yossarian watches in horror as building after building is destroyed. The crew set off tons of explosives. Afterward, Nichols told Arkin, "That was good terror, Alan." Arkin replied, "That was *real* terror, Mike."

The actor playing Snowden wore a flight suit packed with animal offal to simulate the spilling of his guts.

"I don't think of this as a film about World War II," Nichols told Nora Ephron. "I think of it as a picture about dying and a picture about where you get off and at what point you take control over your own life and say, 'No, I won't. *I* decide. *I* draw the line.' "

The *Time* reporter observed, "Nichols . . . was aware that laughter in *Catch-22* was, in the Freudian sense, a cry for help. It is the book's cold rage that he has nurtured."

"He caught its essence," Joe said of Nichols's approach to the book. "He understood."

The actors and crew revered the novel. On the wall of a portable men's room on the set, someone scrawled, "Help Save Joe Heller"—a reminder to everyone to preserve the book's integrity.

The novel's repetitive, retrospective structure did not translate easily to the screen. Nichols tried to give the film narrative coherence by folding the events into Yossarian's fever dream following a knife attack. A spirit of the absurd carried over from the novel in the actors' broad mugging (Borscht Belt–style) and in touches like the changing portrait on Major Major's wall—first it's FDR, then Winston Churchill, and finally Joseph Stalin.

"For the actors . . . making an Air Force film has turned out to be very much like being in the Air Force," Ephron reported.

"I'll tell you what we do around here in our free time," said Arkin. "We sit in the barracks out at the set with our muddy boots on and talk about women. That's what you do in the Army, isn't it? Sit around in your muddy boots and talk about women? I don't know why we do it."

Orson Welles had a small part in the movie. His arrival on the set discombobulated the crew: He went about criticizing performances, scene preparations, and camera setups, yet when it came time for him to deliver his lines, he nearly always flubbed them. Nichols sympathized with him. "I was very moved by Welles," he said. "I knew [he was] used to being in control—and I was sorry when people didn't see what that felt like. . . . I know that if I were acting in a movie, it would be very hard for me not to say, 'I wonder if you would be kind enough to consider putting the camera a little more there so that when I do this . . .' How do you kill that knowledge?"

On another occasion, John Wayne dropped by the set on his way to film a Western in Durango (and to look at some nearby land he wanted to purchase). He expected a welcoming party, but none of the younger actors knew who he was. Nichols and Henry were not informed of his arrival. Angry, convinced he had been snubbed for political reasons, he went to the Hotel Playa de Cortes in Guaymas, drank and smashed glassware in the bar, and wound up breaking two ribs in a nasty fall. "We're trying to make up [for not greeting him] by getting a print of *The Green Berets* and showing it to the crew," Buck Henry said. "In the meantime, we've just been sitting around here, watching the days go by, and waiting for him to come back and bomb us."

The Welles and Wayne incidents threatened crew morale. Nichols's energy kept everyone on task. Of being directed by Nichols, Dustin Hoffman once said, "He makes you feel kind of like a kite. He lets you go ahead, and do your thing [as an actor]. And then when you've finished he pulls you in by the string. But at least you've had the enjoyment of the wind."

During the shooting of a love scene between Arkin and Paula Prentiss, Nichols wanted a more passionate vocal reaction from the actress. He set the cameras rolling. While Arkin and Prentiss embraced, he sneaked up behind her and squeezed one of her breasts. "I let out this great hoot," Prentiss said. Nichols was pleased. "Then I was so overcome with emotion I had to go in a corner and be alone," Prentiss said. "Whenever someone touches me I'm in love with him for about eight hours."

The film crew spent nearly four months in the desert, having little contact with the outside world. The budget ballooned from eleven million to over thirteen million dollars. "I wonder if I could see something in a less expensive model?" the producer complained to Nichols.

Hollywood studio heads feared nothing more than an auteur film swelling out of control. One disaster—critically, financially—could spell the end of directorial independence and a return to tight studio control. (The nightmares finally occurred in 1979 and 1980, first with Francis Ford Coppola's *Apocalypse Now* and then with Michael Cimino's *Heaven's Gate*; in essence, the age of auterism ended, and Hollywood turned to churning out predictable special-effects blockbusters.)

Nichols's *Catch-22* came dangerously close to being an auteur disaster. The fall he feared appeared imminent. Though the film ended up eighth on the top earners' list in 1970 (after *Airport, M*A*S*H, Bob & Carol & Ted & Alice,* and *Woodstock,* among others), it struck critics and studio executives alike as a disappointment, given advance expectations. Jacob Brackman, writing in *Esquire,* said "it seemed . . . [like] two movies . . . intercut by some moon-struck studio editor. The one a dark, hysterical masterpiece, a Moby Dick of movies. The other a dumb, undergraduatey jackoff." The near-brilliant scenes, he said, played "as if Lewis Carroll had redone *The Inferno*—to make you laugh and steal the sound of your laughter." These scenes were undermined by the "fairly contemptible burlesque" of other scenes. Vestiges of Yiddish theater were not welcome on the silver screen; it was an irony (and an indicator of the novel's deepest tones) that comedy—Nichols's calling card—was the film's weakest aspect.

In *San Francisco* magazine, Grover Sales declared "Mike Nichols' *Catch-22* . . . an epic disaster." He blamed this on the "children's pop novel on which [the movie was] based." Sales had deeply resented social pressures to read the novel when it first appeared: "[O]ne could as soon avoid Warhol, Bob Dylan, *Blow-up,* or the zodiac. . . . The party-line of the middle-aged youth cult decreed that unless we dug *Catch-22* we couldn't relate to our kids," he wrote. He found the novel "harder going than *Critique of Pure Reason* and as fully devoid of wit." He was in no position, then, to evaluate the movie he was watching. Still, his disgruntlement echoed other critics' more measured responses.

Perhaps Nichols's biggest problem was the release, earlier that year, of Robert Altman's *M*A*S*H,* a similarly themed film made on a smaller budget, with a script that declared fidelity to the ordinary (overlapping conversations, situational humor). The actors (Elliott Gould, Donald Sutherland) were more conventionally antiestablishment—grizzled, irreverent, loose—than the tightly wound, highly spooked Alan Arkin.

In its spoof of *Catch-22, Mad* magazine showed the *M*A*S*H* doctors threatening "Shmoessarian" with scalpels. They declared, "WE did this 'Insane War Picture' bit FIRST . . . and BETTER!!"

For Joe, there was very little downside to all this. He had been paid; he didn't have to work on the movie; the critical failure was not his—in fact, the film's misfortunes were a boon to the book (lots of publicity). With a redesigned cover, touting the movie tie-in, paperback sales reached a million copies within six weeks. More than ever, the old ads, written by Robert Gottlieb, seemed true: *Catch-22*—the book—was showing signs of "living forever." After all these years, it made the bestseller list. "As soon as they told me that, I stopped working on my new novel, and I won't have to do any more work on that for a year," Joe said. Those who knew him understood how much fear his remark tried to hide. He said he took a "kind of sadistic" pleasure in knowing that many of the people who bought the new paperback edition "had never heard of the book before and . . . wouldn't be able to get past page six or eight. It's nice to get money from those people who make millionaires out of Harold Robbins and Jacqueline Susann."

To an audience at the Ninety-second Street Y, he joked, "[A]s I talk to you now, I'm kind of rich and famous and successful, but unchanged by success; I'm still as corruptible as [I used to be] . . . and God willing, I'll remain that way."

Before the movie's release nationwide, Joe, Shirley, and Erica attended a private screening of the film in an empty three-hundred seat theater near Times Square. Joe sat apart from his wife and daughter; he wanted to take in the movie alone. He "found it . . . overpowering," he said. (Erica says her mother was simply "relieved" the picture wasn't embarrassing.) Joe said, "When it was over, Nichols was kind of slipping away and I took him by the arm and pulled him aside and I said, 'Well, as far as I'm concerned, it may be one of the best movies I've ever seen.'" They went to the Russian Tea Room and toasted the movie.

Nichols's career would rise and fall, and rise and fall again, but his work on *Catch-22* remained crucially important to him. As soon as he had wrapped the film, he told a reporter, "*Catch-22* has made me feel differently about what I lay on the line. . . . [It] has helped me discover how I want to live—I'm going to get rid of myself in stages. . . . There are . . . so many things that we must do for one another to make sure that we continue to live on this earth." He stayed in touch with Joe.

Joe had preserved pieces of his war—the war that could not be found. One of the B-25s restored for the movie is now on permanent display in the Smithsonian's National Air and Space Museum. During filming, in the spring of 1969, when eighteen remade bombers rose into the air, they constituted the twelfth-largest air force in the world.

15. The Willies

I T WAS AFTER THE WAR, I think, that the struggle really began," says Bob Slocum in *Something Happened.*

Just as Joe had arrived many years late with his great war book, he straggled in the rear with his business novel. Sloan Wilson and Richard Yates had tackled corporate facelessness in the 1950s in *The Man in the Gray Flannel Suit* and *Revolutionary Road,* respectively. William Whyte had thoroughly analyzed the organization man. But when Joe finally addressed the matter—the "thousand-and-first version" of "this written-to-death situation," Kurt Vonnegut said in his ultimately ecstatic review of *Something Happened*—he made the subject his own, the way a great singer's cover version of a standard links that song to one voice. Joe stepped beyond Wilson's sentimentality and Yates's bitterness to eviscerate modern America's success ethic.

The subject screamed at him daily: middle-aged men, veterans of the war, muttering past one another on the sidewalks, indistinguishable in their suits, propelled, it seemed, by briefcases; frowning wives, wailing kids . . . the shouts of irritated drivers, convinced that if everyone else got out of the way, they would arrive at fulfillment, only to find, at their coveted destination, the parking lot full or the doors boarded up.

Joe witnessed all this in his walks around the West Side. It took him twenty-five minutes to get from the Apthorp to his studio. "There's no reason why I couldn't work at home," he said, "but I like some demarcation between my personal life and my work life. . . . [T]here's a certain renewal of the imagination that comes from getting out of the house and walking to the studio. Most of the time I'm walking I'm working. It's psychological, I suppose." Walking encouraged a "kind of free reverie within a very rigidly confined space."

There was a store at Amsterdam Avenue and Seventy-ninth Street called Osner Business Machines, which sold Olivetti typewriters, Royals, and Underwoods. It was operated by a man named Stanley Adelman, a Polish Holocaust survivor, dapper, well dressed, soft-spoken. Joe frequented the shop to buy ribbons for his Smith-Corona or to drop off the machine to Adelman whenever it needed repair. Philip Roth, Nora Ephron, Tom Wolfe, and Irving Howe were among many other writers who shopped at the store. They "stood around all day [and] talked [to Adelman's wife, Mary] like she was their bartender," Erica recalls.

On one trip to the store—or maybe it was a different afternoon when he went to Korvette or Brentano's with George Mandel (he couldn't remember)—Joe saw a commotion, people running toward the street, someone shouting, "Something happened!" A car wreck, a fallen pedestrian . . . whatever it was, the phrase stayed in Joe's mind.

As with *Catch-22*, he began *Something Happened* on what seemed like solid terrain, but by the time he finished the book, the tectonic plates had shifted in publishing. Of most immediate concern to Joe was the defection of his editor to Alfred A. Knopf. "As the sixties passed . . . Bob [Gottlieb's] reputation . . . had grown by leaps and bounds," Michael Korda wrote. "He seemed capable of anything, from securing . . . the U.S. rights to John Lennon's book *A Spaniard in the Works* to publishing a whole string of 'commercial' bestsellers. . . . [T]he news that he was leaving was a bombshell that rocked not only S & S but the industry."

In those days, it was rare for an editor not to stay with one firm until retirement. The move was one more indication—like Random House putting its stock on the open market—that publishing, once a genteel trade, had become just another American business.

"[A]gent after agent called to say that this author or that one wanted to go to Knopf with Bob," Korda recalled. "[It] was dispiriting and alarming." He felt the company had "nickel and dimed" Gottlieb, until he'd had enough. Knopf had offered him the position of editor in chief; he would be the "heir apparent" and "chosen successor to the Knopfs."

Joe tried to work without letting the news distract him. S & S insisted his contract did not give him the legal right to abandon the house just because his editor had left. He owed the firm a book and had to deliver it. He trusted Gottlieb and Candida Donadio to protect him.

One day, Korda met Donadio for a "stormy drink," probably in the Italian Pavilion, where she had a regular table. She wore "layers of black *schmatta*," he said, and her "enormous handbag [was] weighted . . . with the manuscripts of her clients." Almost everybody in the restaurant worked in publishing, and it occurred to Korda that they all knew why he was seeing her. She enjoyed watching him squirm. S & S had great plans for the future, he told her. He was certain they could make her clients happy. She smiled. She said she wished the company well but maintained that her clients had to go where they felt comfortable. Korda asked her to give S & S a chance. She insisted he expedite the release of her writers from their contracts. And if he didn't? Korda asked. "There isn't an agent in New York who will send S & S a manuscript," she said.

"All writers were like children, but her writers *were* her children," Korda wrote. "She felt about them as if she were their mother. If we forced the issue, she would fight . . . to defend them."

Joe went happily to Knopf.

Gottlieb had never worried about him—or the long-delayed second novel (in 1961, Joe had promised to deliver the book before men walked on the moon, but the Sea of Tranquility proved easier to achieve than his deadline): "When he finished *Catch-22*, he knew what the title of his next book would be, knew more or less what the book would say, and knew he didn't want to write it then, but he felt no pressure or neurotic agitation," Gottlieb said. "[I always knew] he'd turn it in—like all real writers—when he was ready."

Gottlieb could afford to be sanguine. According to *Esquire* magazine, he was, along with Donadio, at the "red hot center" of the New York publishing world. They were a formidable team. "We were of an age, and we had the same interests and the same tastes to a large extent," Gottlieb told Karen Hudes. "It was a real friendship." Donadio lived a block away from Gottlieb and his wife, at Fifty-third Street and Second Avenue. She would "pad over in her sneakers and babysit" their young daughter, Lizzie, he said. She longed to have her own children, but "I think she thought she wasn't attractive," Gottlieb explained. "There was a very big dark side. She was a hidden person . . . [and she] did more drinking than she should have done."

In 1965, she attempted marriage to a writer and academic named H. E. F. "Shag" Donohue. Gottlieb threw a dinner party in the couple's honor. The marriage lasted three months. Donadio's friend Harriet Wasserman claimed in a published interview with Karen Hudes that she once saw Donohue put Donadio in a headlock. "[S]he looked terrified," Wasserman said. Overall, "[s]he was a desperately lonely, unhappy person."

In public—combining business and pleasure—Donadio could be "a great pal, a great drinking buddy," said Herman Gollob, an editor at Little, Brown and then at Atheneum. When he first heard of her, he asked his colleagues if she was "screwing all the guys to get clients." When they met, she said, "You think I fuck to get clients, do you?" "I meant that as a compliment!" he insisted, and they became tight. When he worked at Little, Brown, he rejected only one manuscript she sent him. "It was about a guy screwing a gorilla," he said. He sent Donadio a note: "Dear Candida, Ape-fucking novels you're sending me?" She framed the letter and hung it on her office wall.

At home, she kept a macaw in a cage—if her bird gnawed on a manuscript, she said, it was probably good. Erica recalls having dinner once in Donadio's apartment and being startled by the macaw, which lived in the bathroom. "She had forgotten to mention [the bird]. I went in there at one point and almost had a coronary," Erica says. Donadio claimed her apartment was haunted, and visitors confirmed one spot was colder than others. She could be superstitious—a Sicilian weakness, she'd say. She'd consult the *I Ching* to make office decisions. Once, she told her colleague Neil Olson that she was taking Good Friday off. "Neil, we don't know, he may have *been* the son of God," she said.

About *her* sons, there was no doubt. She protected her boys, her writers—from editors, critics, often from one another. In 1969, when, according to reports, she negotiated a $250,000 advance for Philip Roth's *Portnoy's Complaint,* along with additional monies for a movie option and a paperback sale to Bantam, she refused to discuss the deal in public, fearing "sibling rivalry amongst her other charges."

Joe was especially sensitive about money. He always worried that he didn't have enough to take care of his family. In 1971, he returned to teaching, accepting a position—at the rank of full professor, specializing in creative writing—at New York's City College (though the previous year, he had earned eighty thousand dollars in royalties from *Catch-22*). At City College, he made $32,625 a year. Among his colleagues were Donald Barthelme and Kurt Vonnegut. The students (Oscar Hijuelos, for one) were talented, smart, and challenging. "Teaching takes a lot of my time, and I enjoy it . . . a lot," Joe said. His experience at Yale had erased the bad taste left by Penn State. When students were committed and ambitious, he discovered, universities could be a congenial place for a writer. "It's a job I would like to keep. It's interesting. It seems worthwhile," he said. "The hardest thing to teach these people is that writing is hard work—and hard work for everyone. I've got a doctor [in my class] who wants to give up medicine, a lawyer who wants to quit the law. They read the finished, published work and think that's exactly the way the writer dictated it. Well . . . they're wrong."

In the early 1970s, *his* novel writing still came hard—in part because of time in the classroom or reading student manuscripts, in part because he had been busy with short dramatic adaptations of *Catch-22*, and also because he remained intermittently active in politics, giving speeches for George McGovern. In East Hampton, he participated with other celebrities in a benefit softball game aimed at raising money for the Democratic party.

He spent many hours fretting about health. Toward the end of his time at Yale, he had caught a glimpse of himself in a mirror and was shocked by how bloated he looked. The double chins in his publicity pictures bothered him. A year or so later, an acquaintance of his, a man he often saw working out at the YMCA, died of a heart attack. This spurred Joe to action. "I was a really thin man who put on a lot of weight," he told writer Robert Alan Aurthur. He remembered the willpower he'd shown, years earlier, when he quit smoking; once more, he summoned that determination. For breakfast, he limited himself to coffee and grapefruit. He often skipped lunch. In the afternoons, he'd take Sweeney, the family's new Bedlington terrier, for long walks around the neighborhood (past the briefcase men) and think about his novel. On the small track at the Y, he ran three or four miles a day. From over 200, he dropped to 160. He looked ten years younger.

At the Y, he avoided meeting anyone's eyes. He pursued his running (nine sets of eight laps each) with grim seriousness. He worried about the slightest ache or twinge—in his lower back, bladder, calves, the tendons of his ankles, or the bottoms of his feet. Sometimes vertical pains shot through his chest and up through his collarbone. This was a hell of a way to try to feel better. He'd lift small weights in the often-empty exercise room near the sleep lounge, the television room, the showers, and the sauna.

"The Angel of Death is in the gym today," said the Y's patrons every so often: Not infrequently, ambulance crews showed up to cart away on a stretcher an elderly man in T-shirt and shorts who had collapsed while running or doing chin-ups on a bar.

In this melancholy spirit (stretching, rolling his arms to ease the needling pains), Joe squirreled away portions of *Something Happened* in a locker at the Y, in case fire raced through the Apthorp or his studio, or he keeled over one day.

In the spring of 1974—a fit fifty-one-year-old!—he completed the manuscript to his satisfaction and decided to copy it for Donadio. He took Erica with him to the photocopying shop. "I figured if a car hit me, if I got mugged, or if I dropped dead of a heart attack, the manuscript might still be saved," he said. "I asked him what would happen if he had a heart attack and *I* got run over," Erica recalls.

Joe said, "Then we're in trouble."

I think I'm in trouble. I think I've committed a crime. I've always felt so. The victims have always been children.

Oh my father—why have you done this to me?

I am in need of the nipple that succored me and whatever arms cuddled me. I didn't know names. I loved the food that fed me, the arms that touched and moved me and gave me to understand that I was not for that moment alone. Without them, I would be alone. I am afraid of the dark now. I have nightmares in strange beds, and in my own.

I was a boy when I met her and she was a girl, and now we are man and woman. We were shy once. . . .

. . . my children are parts of myself . . . in my wish to remain mute and dependent. All of us are projections of each other.

[There are] people everywhere of whom I am afraid.

These sentences, and hundreds of others, some typed, some written in red ink, black ink, or pencil, Joe kept on note cards or pieces of paper during the thirteen years he conceived, reconceived, shaped, and re-shaped *Something Happened*. Several sentences came with headers, such as "Boy," "Weird Experiences," "Torment," and "Wife (Sleep)." Many of the phrases made it into the final version of the novel, tucked into larger sections; others were dropped. Taken together, the poundage of rough drafts indicates that while Joe's concurrent projects—screenplays and dramas—were willed into shape by a craftsman conscious of their commercial appeal, *Something Happened* was a poetic meditation on the psyche of a disturbed middle-aged man, a series of excursions into waking dream states in which a lifetime of experiences, fears, and imaginative visions were distilled in fragments whose ultimate forms Joe could not predict, and did not try to force.

Despite the image he sometimes peddled of a man unmotivated by a strong desire to write, the obsessive nature of these meditations, the length of the process, and Joe's refusal to abandon it regardless of interruptions and the lure of more lucrative assignments reveal not only his ambition to be a serious artist but his inability to be anything else. No other activity besides novel writing challenged his mind or altered his perceptions so thoroughly—which is why he kept returning to *the novel*, agonies and all.

Ostensibly, *Something Happened* is about a businessman, but at the bottom of the pool of mind-material that surfaced and coalesced into the story lay the deaths of Joe's father and mother. Though it is impossible to date the composition of many of the rough-draft fragments, the repetitions of subjects and phrases, their revisions and eventual inclusion in larger segments support the notion that among the earliest scenes Joe established were those involving parental loss. The mother's death leads to devastation—unambiguously. "If I live to be a hundred and fifty, I will never hear any more [words] from [my mother]. If the world lasts three billion more, there will be no others," Slocum laments (though at this stage, there is only Joe's handwritten sentence on a note card; no character or narrative development is indicated).

Elsewhere, Slocum torments himself with the "last pleasant memory" he has of his mother, a dinner one day when, responding to a cute remark by his baby girl, the old woman "threw back her head and laughed." Joe circled this phrase.

On another card, he wrote clearly, carefully, "I think it was impossible for me to remain alone at night in my own room after my tonsillectomy. I think I remember being allowed to sleep in bed with my mother and father once, and I can't imagine why they would have let me unless I was ill and scared."

The tonsillectomy fills several cards. On one: "I woke up in the hospital without tonsils one thousand times and it was always dark, and I thought there would never be light again." In the finished novel, when Slocum's boy's tonsils are removed, Slocum recalls being left alone in the hospital as a child. He reexperiences old fears through his son's panic. "I nearly died the day my boy had his tonsils out, he looked so still lying there when they brought him back, smelling of ether," Joe wrote. "[W]hen he cried out suddenly, 'It hurts!' I could not stand the pain and shouted . . . 'Stop it! Stop it! You're scaring him!' "

From the cards, and the memories Joe would develop in his memoir, one thing is clear: Though his father died when Joe was a child, he felt *he* was the one who would pass away in the hospital. (The scene in *Catch-22* when a mother and father mistake Yossarian for their dying son also asks the question: Who is really dying—or should be?)

In *Something Happened*, Slocum's desire to protect his boy (childhood itself) becomes, by the end, a murderous impulse. Slocum smothers the child with a hug. Beyond Oedipal overtones, it seems obvious that for Joe, as he worked through these real and imagined experiences using the note cards, his father's death remained perplexing for a number of reasons, not the least of which was his obliviousness to it until after the fact. His ignorance was soon compounded by the confusion of learning other secrets about his family.

Something happened before Joe was born. Something else happened when he was little. In both cases, he missed the crucial facts: he thought he was living a life he was not really living. Perhaps, then, a version of him really *had* died (or hadn't been born). Maybe he had no choice but to devote himself to pinpointing what had happened. How had he missed it—and then, unbelievably, missed it again? The circlings and recirclings of this material on hundreds of note cards suggest the urgency of Joe's doubts and fears as he tried to fictionalize them and clarify the story of *Something Happened*.

Literary examples helped him find language and keep the material from becoming self-indulgent ("I don't think of myself as a naturally gifted writer when it comes to using language. I distrust myself," he once said). In one early draft, after Slocum has killed his boy and repressed his responsibility in the matter, Slocum says, "I miss my dead boy." Later, Joe crossed out the word *dead*. "I play golf with my betters . . . and now I have no freedom left. I am a cow."

This last sentence suggests Slocum's madness. But it is also an echo of two well-known literary passages, "My mother is a fish," from William Faulkner's *As I Lay Dying* (about, among other things, the death of a parent) and "The moocow came down the road" from James Joyce's *A Portrait of the Artist as a Young Man* (concerning, in part, the inability of some people to outgrow their childhoods).

Borrowings from great literature could be an evasion as well as an aid. Joe tried many other endings, moving increasingly toward straightforwardness—about subjects that could not be other than ambiguous. Over and over, he worked on the following short passage: "I want my little boy back. I don't want to lose him." Later, he changed this to "I don't want to lose him. I do." He struck through "I do." He added it once more. Then he preceded the passage with "Oh, my father . . . I want him back."

"I put everything I knew about the external world into *Catch-22* and everything I knew about the interior world into *Something Happened*," Joe said.

One evening, he admitted to his family that when they read the book, they might think it was about them. He told them the story. "What should I call the guy in . . . [the] book?" he asked. "Joe," said his son.

Around this time, the excerpt appeared in *Esquire*. "I was carrying the manuscript around with me, about forty pages, and I left it in a Horn and Hardart's," he recalled. "In total paranoia I pictured some guy finding the pages, rushing out and publishing it under his own name. So I told my agent to submit a carbon somewhere quick to establish my copyright. Rust Hills . . . [the] fiction editor [at *Esquire*] . . . bought it."

As the raw material crystallized, Joe distanced himself from his character by giving him thoughts, tics, traits, and stories (all exaggerated) from many other sources, chief among them George Mandel and Mel Brooks, by now a successful filmmaker. Before the movies, Brooks had made a series of comedy records with Carl Reiner. Among the characters he created was a WASP businessman named Warren Bland—a partial prototype for Bob Slocum. Beneath the humor ("[We] *have* children . . . [but] we send them to Hartford . . . to Jewish and Italian families, people who *like* children"), the character betrays a persistent melancholy. In one routine, Bland says, "We mock the thing we are to be. We make fun of the old, and then we become them." Slocum sounds just like this.

Before taking the manuscript to be photocopied, Joe changed Slocum's name from Joe to Bob and then to Bill. He downplayed Slocum's combat experiences and corporate duties, making him more of an Everyman. To sharpen Slocum's sense of loss, he expanded the man's memories of trysts he'd had as a youngster with a girl named Virginia in an insurance company file room (recalling his own experiences as an adolescent). He made sure Slocum would not be regarded as Jewish ("I may look a little bit Jewish to some people, and I think Jewish a great deal of the time, but it's proof I'm not," Slocum says).

Joe had to remind Candida Donadio she was reading fiction, not autobiography. More than once, she looked up from the manuscript and said, "Joe [,you] wouldn't do that!"

He hadn't spoken to Robert Gottlieb for a while. "Bob and I think of each other as close friends, but . . . years might go by before we talk to each other or drop each other a note," Joe once said. "In between my novels . . . we've barely communicated."

When Gottlieb *did* get hold of the 940-page manuscript, he saw there was "no book like it." It wasn't at all like *Catch-22*, "except in its power," he said. "It's very moving and very upsetting. It's the way we feel about ourselves."

Joe claimed not to know what the novel was *really* about. He said the "areas of combat" in it were "things like the wishes a person has, whether they are fulfilled or not, the close, intimate situations we have with our children when they're small and as they grow older, the memories we have of our relationship with parents as *they* grow older. . . . [T]hese areas are much more difficult to deal with than those in [wartime, when] we know what the dangers are."

Methodically, Gottlieb set about editing the manuscript. He trimmed it to eight hundred pages, then six hundred. He'd lie on the floor of his office in jeans and sneakers, with Joe's pages spread before him, munching a sandwich. He'd look for verbs to enrich, relative clauses to switch to participial phrases. He suggested making the first chapter the second chapter ("In the office in which I work there are five people of whom I am afraid") and opening the novel with "I get the willies when I see closed doors" (originally, Joe had written, "I get the willies whenever I think about my father.")

At one point, Gottlieb told Joe, "[T]his is going to sound crazy to you but this guy [Slocum] is not a Bill."

"Oh really, what do you think he is?" Joe replied.

"He's a Bob."

"He *was* a Bob, and I changed his name to Bill because I thought you would be offended if I made him a Bob," Joe said.

"Oh no, I don't think he's anything like me, it's just that this character is a Bob."

Okay, said Joe.

Now, Bob Slocum was ready to step out from behind closed doors.

"[I]T IS MIDSUMMER, 1974, and one begins to hear that Joseph Heller has another big one," Robert Alan Aurthur wrote in *Esquire*. "[He] will not be America's most celebrated one-book author since Michael Arlen." Or Henry Roth. Or Ralph Ellison. Responding to the buzz from the publishing world, Aurthur contacted Joe, hoping to write a profile. Joe suggested he start by interviewing the playwright Murray Schisgal—a notoriously tough critic—who was reading the book in galleys.

Aurthur met with Schisgal. Was it true he was halfway through the book? Aurthur asked.

Schisgal nodded. "I had dinner with Joe last night and the night before," he said.

Well, how's the book?

"I have never . . . not *ever* seen a man eat as much as Joe Heller." So much for the diet. Joe was celebrating.

But what about the book?

"Last night, we were put out of a restaurant when they had to close, and Heller was still on the first course."

The *book*?

"The book is brilliant. The man is a great writer. There are parts in here no other writer could approach; he gets right down to the bone . . . stunning."

Many early reviewers agreed, and Gottlieb and Nina Bourne, who had followed her old friend to Knopf from Simon & Schuster, wasted no time culling comments for magazine and newspaper ads. They touted the book as an immediate bestseller: "America's New #1" (the hardback sold for ten dollars). Right away, it went through three printings. In the ads, next to a darkly serious picture of Joe—one side of his face in shadow, furrowed brow, full lips about to break into a smile, the softness of his dimpled chin the only sign of middle-age—Larry Swindell of the *Philadelphia Inquirer* was quoted: "*Catch-22* became the novel of the 60s. Now Heller has provided the novel of and for the 70s . . . 50 years from now they'll be reading it and arguing it still." Walter Clemons, from *Newsweek*, said, "He has written an epic of the everyday." Then there was John W. Aldridge: "The most important novel to appear in this country in at least a decade."

In other ads, a dizzying pedigree appeared: "Tolstoyean," "Dickensian," "Joycean," "Faulknerian," "[Akin] to *Moby Dick*."

"No matter where you go or what you do, the scrawl on the wall will say: Heller was here," Milton Bass wrote in the *Berkshire Eagle*.

The major reviews—among them, Vonnegut's in the *New York Times Book Review* and Joseph Epstein's in the *Washington Post Book World*—did not agree; like *Catch-22*, *Something Happened* roiled critics at first and grew in stature over the years as writers considered it in more depth.

Epstein said the novel was static, repetitive, and dull, offering "no attempt to understand what is going on [with the main character], but only to describe what it feels like to live under [his] malaise." Awareness counts for nothing in a Joseph Heller novel, he complained: There were no realized *selves* in his fiction. "Nothing happens in *Something Happened*," he said. This would become the standard joke about the book, as Joe had anticipated (he had taken the same deliberate risk with the title of his play). Sweepingly, Epstein concluded, "[F]iction written under the assumptions of the post-Modernist sensibility cannot sustain itself over the length of a large novel. A Donald Barthelme can float a story or sketch under these same assumptions for eight or ten pages on sheer brilliance. But at greater length, things tend to flatten out." In *Something Happened*, he said, "the cargo ha[s] gone sour."

Vonnegut, though, felt the novel was "splendidly put together and hypnotic to read. It is as clear and hard-edged as a cut diamond." Joe was a "maker of myths":

> *Something Happened* . . . could become the dominant myth about the middle-class veterans who came home from the war to become heads of nuclear families. The proposed myth has it that those families were pathetically vulnerable and suffocating. It says that the heads of them commonly took jobs which were vaguely dishonorable or at least stultifying, in order to make as much money as they could for their little families, and they used that money in futile attempts to buy safety and happiness. The proposed myth says that they lost their dignity and their will to live in the process.
>
> It says they are hideously tired now.

He praised Joe's courage in stating "baldly" what other novels "only implied" or "tried with desperate sentimentality not to imply: That many lives, judged by the standards of the people who live them, are simply not worth living." (In literary circles, some wondered whether the *Book Review*'s editors should have assigned Vonnegut the novel, since he socialized with Joe.)

Despite the less-than-unanimous praise, and the obviously grim and challenging subject matter, *Something Happened* remained on the American bestseller lists for twenty-nine weeks, from October 1974 to May 1975. During this period, it earned Joe roughly $500,000. Gottlieb had succeeded in bringing to Knopf one of its biggest moneymakers ever.

"[This] is not a book for kids," Gottlieb said. "It's a book for everybody over thirty."

Delivering public readings from the novel, Joe realized he "must be reaching a wider, older audience than [with] *Catch-22*." At the University of Michigan, he "got a great response from the students with those passages dealing with Slocum's children," he said. "But during the parts about his office, his fearing old age, there was silence. The attention was there, but the magic was gone."

Still, what placed the book in the forefront of cultural awareness, and ensured its inclusion in any important discussion about the current state of American letters, was the way the country seemed to have caught up to it. In 1966, when the excerpt appeared in *Esquire,* Slocum's insistence that rebellion was no longer possible seemed out of place with profiles of draft dodgers and alternative lifestyles. In the September 1974 issue, which announced Joe's new "big one," the cover story was "Guess Who's Going to College?" The article began, "If there were a key word on campus these days, maybe it would be 'sensible.' No more grasping toward the infinite—right, kids? . . . Grades are real, school is earnest, and after that The Job." The piece discussed the end of the military draft—how the change had sent young people scurrying toward college programs or professional training guaranteed to secure them lucrative futures. Enrollments were slipping in humanities classes. Universities were developing sales-recruiting forces, based on corporate models, to "brand" themselves and lure students into business schools. "Zip code marketing," targeting potential students from desirable families, had proven especially successful. Now, more college recruiters than military representatives visited high schools, and students had developed a greater sense of personal responsibility: little Slocums on the make.

The tilt away from the excesses of the 1960s toward conservatism in the early to mid-1970s was not as straightforward or simplistic as it is sometimes painted. George McGovern's crushing electoral defeat, a few years after the deaths of Robert Kennedy and Martin Luther King, Jr., seemed to signal the end of the liberal political agenda. On the other hand, as Abe Peck points out, from "December, 1972, to April, 1975, alone, DDT was banned, abortions were legalized, the draft ended, U.S. troops finally left Vietnam, the American Psychiatric Association 'de-diseased' homosexuality, and draconian sentences for smoking plants were reduced. The safe-energy movement began . . . [and] Richard Nixon resigned."

By and large, the underground press, advocating for these changes, dissipated as much from a sense of mission accomplished as from persecution by the FBI. Many young people sought corporate positions, feeling not defeat or lack of choice, but glimmers of possibility: American business seemed to have become more enlightened.

Perhaps most important, Kurt Vonnegut's observation that the World War II generation was now "hideously tired" could be extended to cover most adults buffeted by cultural tumults. National emergencies had reached such a pitch, they threatened the U.S. presidency. With

Nixon gone and the gray-flanneled Mr. Ford at the helm, perhaps everyone could settle down now, especially with so much talk about an energy crisis.

Something Happened tapped into national exhaustion. Reaching back to 1966, it seemed as prophetic about post-Vietnam America as *Catch-22* had seemed about the rock-and-roll war years.

On publicity tours for the book, Joe projected seriousness and thoughtfulness. His demeanor suggested he sat "on top of the world"; his "whole manner gives the promise of further important books to come," said one journalist. For *The Paris Review,* Joe told George Plimpton, "If I thought I might never get another idea for a novel . . . I don't think it would distress me. I've got two books under my belt now. I would be content to consider that a lifetime's work, and I could just putter around and find other things to do. I've been very lucky. I've written two books that were unusual and unusually successful."

This sunniness was belied by confessions that he worried when too much time passed with no word from his publisher. He had dreamed up dozens of opening lines for another novel, but none of them was any good, and he feared the American public would soon grow too distracted by technological gadgetry to keep reading fiction.

Shirley was a silent presence during many of Joe's interviews, sitting beside him demurely as journalists pulled pencil and paper from briefcases or fiddled with tape recorders. In the middle of an interview at Harvard in October 1974, Joe listed fears he'd had about events—newspaper strikes, a new war—that might limit his public exposure. Shirley squirmed. Joe turned to her. "What? You're not worried about any of this?" he asked. She said she'd now like to see Harvard Yard. Dolores Karl says Shirley hated *Something Happened.* She felt it was too autobiographical. She was embarrassed and disconcerted by the portrait of a narcissistic, fretful man whose love for his wife and children is balanced by equal bouts of revulsion, and who engages in serial adultery to take the edge off his fears of failure.

Later, Mel Brooks would say to Joe, "If [your family] can live through [*Something Happened*], they can live through anything." Joe replied, "Oy, what we went through with that!"

Whenever an interviewer asked Shirley about the book, her face became a mask. "I . . . can't believe it's finally out," she'd say.

IN PLATO'S *Phaedrus,* Socrates says the purpose of language is "to put to test" our deepest beliefs. With words, we arrive at self-knowledge and "care of the soul." Socrates claims to know little; he challenges others, hoping to expose shallow values and to shame people into admitting ignorance. *Something Happened* submits the reader to a series of Socratic challenges regarding American ideals: love of country, family, material success.

Bob Slocum sees himself engaging in "brisk, Socratic dialogues" with his son. "I am Socrates, he is the pupil. (Or so it seems, until I review some of our conversations when I am alone, and then it often seems that *he* is Socrates)," Slocum says. In an essay on the rhetoric in *Something Happened,* Andre Furlani says Slocum does not hope to improve others with his questions: He seeks to draw them into paralysis. He is not genuinely interested in answers; his questions hide fears of results he does not want to face. Rather than a "test" serving "the soul," language, for Slocum, is a game in which the aim is to "outfox" everyone. It is meant to conceal his desires.

In fierce, painful exchanges, his daughter attempts to challenge him. But she is a child and cannot compete with his knowledge and ease with words. Smugly, Slocum watches as the "composure with which she entered [an argument with him] crumbles away into terrified misgivings and she is left, at last, standing mute and foolishly before me, shivering and exhausted, bereft of all her former confidence and determination. (I can outfox her every time.)"

Slocum knows he should take no pleasure in verbally abusing his child. "Why must I win this argument? . . . Why must I show off for her and myself and exult in my fine logic and more expert command of language and details—in a battle of wits with a fifteen-year-old?" he asks. "I could just as easily say, 'You're right. I'm sorry. Please forgive me.' Even though I'm right and not really sorry. I could say so anyway. But I can't. And I am winning . . . I am a shit. But at least I am a successful one."

Slocum cares more for his son than for his daughter. He sees himself in his boy, who does not rival him directly. The son is truly a Socrates figure, presenting an innocent face. At one point, Slocum sneaks behind the boy's back; he speaks to the physical education teacher at school, hoping to help the boy become more competitive at sports. Later, the son says to Slocum, "You didn't tell me that you went to see him." Slocum replies, "How did you find out? . . . Who told you?" His son says, "You told me. Just now. By answering me."

Ultimately, the boy's nonchallenges penetrate his father's psychic defenses. Caught in his own word traps, Slocum devolves into mild madness. The boy withdraws from him, disturbed by the ferocity with which Slocum attacks the daughter. Slocum recalls his father's disappearance when he was a child, and feels similarly betrayed by his boy. As Furlani says, the "son is a Socrates whom the father feels compelled to kill . . . [just like] the philosopher [was] fated to die, indeed condemned to death [by his society], because his presence ultimately [was] too sharp a goad."

The something that happened to Slocum was primal loss followed by conformity, as though the loss had never occurred. Now he witnesses this socialization process swamping his children. It is too late to save his daughter, but he believes he can rescue his boy by freezing him in time before the boy changes too much, inflicting on Slocum another irrecoverable loss. The mad logic of this is so pure, so embedded in life's yeses and noes, it becomes an emotional Catch-22: loss as the method of stopping further loss.

Slocum shows "signs that, I believe, are clinical symptoms of psychosis or schizophrenia," Joe said of his main character. "[H]e's saying, 'There's somebody inside me who wants to do these things I'm ashamed of. I'm too nice a guy to do this.' Then he has to create a third [personality], to supervise the other two. Then a fourth one that's watching everything. . . . What I'm trying to do is set up a process of alienation from oneself." Joe felt he had achieved alienation through point of view. "The first and third person are fused in a way I've never seen before, and time is compressed into almost a solid substance," he said. In the narration, there is a vast emotional distance between the observing and acting selves (conveyed by long, qualifying parenthetical asides), and yet there is very little temporal space between them:

My memory's failing, my bladder is weak, my arches are falling, my tonsils and adenoids are gone . . . and now my little boy wants to cast me away and leave me behind for reasons he won't give me. What else will I have? My job? When I am fifty-five, I will have nothing more to look forward to than . . . reaching sixty-five. When I am sixty-five, I will have nothing more to look forward to than reaching seventy-five, or dying before then. . . .

Oh, my father—why have you done this to me?
I want him back.

I want my little boy back too.
I don't want to lose him.
I do.
"Something happened!" a youth in his early teens calls excitedly to a friend and goes running ahead to look.
A crowd is collecting at the shopping center. . . . A plate glass window has been smashed. My boy is lying on the ground. . . . He is panic-stricken. So am I.
"Daddy!"
He is dying. . . . I can't stand it. He can't stand it. . . . I hug him tightly with both my arms. I squeeze.

Slocum is a "disorganized personality," Joe explained, "a personality that can't be integrated in a way that the healthiest of personalities should be. . . . [M]ore and more people I know about [are] having trouble [with this]. . . . It's becoming harder and harder for people to achieve in their work, to [hang on to] a personal sense of identity." But Slocum masks himself and pushes ahead. At the end, he is able to say, "Everyone seems pleased with the way I've taken command." He becomes a true American success story.

"AN UNPRECEDENTED COMBINATION of inflation and recession made 1974 a uniquely difficult year for the economy at home and abroad," said RCA's *Annual Report, 1974.* "Whipsawed by these forces, the company's net profit declined by 38 per cent to $113.3 million." In typically masked language, the writer of the report followed this gloomy news with a vague assertion that "hopeful signs" indicated "renewed strength and purpose ahead."

Among RCA's holdings in 1974 were the NBC television network, RCA Records, Banquet Frozen Foods, and Alfred A. Knopf (a division of Random House). In the report's glossy pages, along with a photograph of the singer John Denver sitting with the president of RCA Records and one of Freddie Prinze of the TV show *Chico and the Man,* is a picture of Joe with Random House president Robert L. Bernstein and

Bob Gottlieb. Bernstein stands tall over the other two, talking down to them. "Novelist Joseph Heller['s] . . . *Something Happened* is a major bestseller," reads the caption next to the photo. Largely on the back of Joe's novel, the publishing division (Random House, Pantheon, and Knopf) "increased its sales by 25 per cent to a new high," despite the adverse effects of "industry-wide inflationary costs." Unfortunately, the report says, a new accounting method will mean an overall "loss position" for the publishing division this year. Happily, these losses were offset by the successes of the "other products and services" lumped in with books, particularly the "inspiring performance" of "edible oils . . . [and the] Man Pleaser [frozen] Dinners, which offer larger portions of fried chicken, turkey, Salisbury steak, and meat loaf."

WILLIAM JAMES wrote, "[T]he exclusive worship of the bitch-goddess SUCCESS is our national disease." Joe had read this quote in a piece by Norman Podhoretz, the editor of *Commentary*. Podhoretz liked to cite James in order to dispute him. He believed America had a "dirty little secret": Ambition for affluence and fame had replaced "erotic lust" as the prime hunger of the "well-educated American soul." For Podhoretz, this was a perfectly fine state of affairs.

Certainly, the success of *Something Happened* suited Joe. He quit teaching at City College. He bought a summer house in the Amagansett dunes—"nothing special," Erica says. One day, Joe asked the architect Charles Gwathmey to look at the house. He had met the man through Speed Vogel, and he hoped Gwathmey might suggest ways "to make [the house] a bit more presentable." Gwathmey "shrugged his shoulders, squinting into the sun," Erica recalls. "'Gut it,' he said, got into his black car and drove away." (Some time later, Gwathmey visited the Hellers at the Apthorp; he strolled around the courtyard with Shirley, who asked him what changes he'd make to the building. "Gut it," he said.)

Joe loved the Amagansett place. He enjoyed tanning on the sundeck while drinking French-roast coffee, eating Jarlsberg cheese, and reading. He went for a daily run to try to get his weight back down. Sometimes in the evenings, a soft fog rose from the sea.

The small living room, painted white, was brightened by three Matisse lithographs Shirley had bought. Joe played Mozart or Wagner on the stereo system. Ted missed summering at Fair Harbor or Seaview, communities on Fire Island, cozier, calmer spots—but change, whether or not for the better, was the price of success.

In the city, "Elaine's had become the 'in' place . . . because of all the famous writers and . . . movie stars who frequented the place," said novelist Winston Groom. In fact, Joe had been a regular at the restaurant for years, but its glamour was growing along with the stature of its patrons. Groom recalled one evening in the mid-1970s when a reporter from a Kansas City newspaper showed up to do a piece on New York glitterati. Elaine would not let him approach her elite customers. She sat him in a corner—*they* could approach *him,* if they wished. Mailer was there, along with Joe, William Styron, Irwin Shaw, Woody Allen, and Diane Keaton. At one point, "Barbra Streisand swept through the door, wearing some kind of sequined gown that made her look like she had been set on fire," Groom said. No one spoke to the reporter.

Finally, at about 10:30, he called Elaine over. "If you won't let me talk to them, then can't you at least tell me what they are talking about?" he said. "What are they talking about?" Elaine replied. "Well, they're talking about what *all* writers talk about: baseball, money, and pussy."

Joe rented a new writing studio at 130 West 57th Street, a block from Carnegie Hall and the Russian Tea Room. It was in a quaint 1907 building where William Dean Howells had once lived, and where Woody Allen's film production company was headquartered. Joe's apartment had projecting bay windows set in ornamented cast-iron frames. Northern light flooded the room.

He often stayed late and sometimes slept in the studio. Making an excuse to Shirley, he would say he was trying to stay out of the way of Viola, the family's housekeeper, who was fiercely loyal to his wife. Shirley never asked about his comings and goings, though she speculated freely about friends whom she suspected of having affairs. Her circumspection and politeness (terror, exhaustion, boredom?) irritated Joe. He hated to say it, but shouldn't a successful man have a more thrilling marriage than this? The kids were young adults now, mostly on their own, both at NYU (Erica was finishing up there). The Apthorp apartment was empty and quiet. Excitement *zizzled* the rest of his life, although it's true that his favorite moments were at home with a book in his lap and Mozart on the stereo. "Right after he finishes [writing] a book he gets better; he's serene and sweet," Erica told Barbara Gelb.

Still, he didn't know what to do with his restlessness, his contradictory impulses. "I need . . . disturbances," he'd told Shirley once. "I draw inspiration from daily embarrassments." Many nights, he lay awake, worrying about how to stay interested in his life, while Shirley snored softly beside him.

To hide his anxieties, he told friends, "Thank goodness, we don't need love anymore. And without love, all we have to worry about is passion, bliss, and ecstasy."

What he really needed was a good first line for a novel. He'd thought of this: "The kid, they say, was born in a manger, but frankly I have my doubts." Not bad—better than most he'd imagined—but he didn't feel it would take him very far.

One day, to his great annoyance, Shirley announced she was going to throw a party for his sister. Sylvia told Shirley no one had ever made a birthday party for her. Joe didn't relish an apartment bursting with noisy people, silly family chatter, but Shirley made a lavish cake, put everyone at ease, and Sylvia wept with gratitude. Joe was moved to tears, especially when his sister (still missing her late husband) recalled job hunting as a girl, taking the subway into the city and being turned away because she was Jewish. It was good to see Sylvia and Lee again after so long a time (though the older they got, with their soft features, darker coloring, the less they looked like Joe and his mother). Shirley was a wonderful wife, always remembering family occasions, giving gifts at bar and bat mitzvahs—things Joe would never think of—and he felt fortunate, beyond measure, to be with her.

POLITICS BORED—NO, *enraged*—him. You could *not* say American leadership had been a success. The McGovern debacle, the Watergate disaster. . . . Joe could not stir himself from an almost paralyzing, cynical indolence. That goddamned moron, Nixon's young press secretary, Ronald Ziegler, had permanently damaged the language: "The President is fully aware of what is going on in Southeast Asia," he had said. "That is not to say that anything is going on in Southeast Asia." How could you respond to that? It was beyond ridicule.

And personally, now that the tear gas had cleared, who could deny it was easier to stay silent? Why not settle back on a comfy couch with pockets full of coins? (Recently, *Vogue* lingerie ads had announced,

"Every woman loves . . . pretty lingerie. And Scarlatti on the hi-fi. And Telly [Savalas] on the telly. And the new Joseph Heller . . . it's all part of the lure of life at home.")

Joe confessed to George Mandel, "I don't think I deserve all this money. It puts me into a class for which I have very little sympathy." But he couldn't kid himself: Politically, he was drifting toward the center. Maybe it was a hopeful sign that he didn't feel good about it. He consoled himself that he was not as out of step as his old acquaintance, and now sworn enemy, Norman Podhoretz, the "success" guru.

In 1961, in a review in *Show* magazine, Podhoretz had praised *Catch-22* as "one of the bravest and most . . . successful attempts we have yet had to describe and make credible the incredible reality of American life in the middle of the 20th century." Joe appreciated these comments. The men became "fairly friendly," Podhoretz recalled. They chatted now and then at literary parties. As the editor of *Commentary*, Podhoretz had "invigorat[ed] the magazine and steer[ed] it in a . . . more leftward direction," according to Ted Solotaroff, who began writing for *Commentary* in September 1960: "Norman made it clear that the magazine would hold its own as the suddenly prominent new voice of a new decade."

But it was also apparent that Podhoretz was hungry for social success. He "openly acted upon" his desire for money, publicity, and celebrity, Solotaroff said. In 1967, in a book called *Making It*, Podhoretz announced, "I [have] . . . experienced an astonishing revelation: it is better to be a success than a failure. . . . [I]t [is] better to be rich than to be poor. . . . Fame, I now [see] . . . [is] unqualifiedly delicious: it [is] better to be recognized than anonymous." He expressed his distaste for what the mainstream press called "the counterculture": The extreme Left wanted to destroy America, Podhoretz said. *He* wanted to bask in its luxuries.

In part, then, his rightward drift began as an ongoing and conscious act of integration. Like Joe, he was Jewish, Brooklyn-born, educated at Columbia under the tutelage of Lionel Trilling. He was strongly influenced by the anti-Communist liberal thinking of Trilling's immediate circle. Like Bob Gottlieb, he had gone to Cambridge to study with the literary critic F. R. Leavis. And now he was the editor of one of the leading intellectual journals of the day.

But intellectual pursuits did not bring him as much prestige as he wished. To get *inside* America—become indispensable to it—meant moving in the highest social spheres, meeting and influencing men and women of power. This was Podhoretz's aim. *Making It* was a paean to shameless social climbing. "Nothing, I believe, defines the spiritual character of American life more saliently than . . . [the] contradictory feelings our culture instills in us toward the ambition for success, and toward each of its various goals: money, power, fame, and social position," he wrote. "On the one hand, we are commanded to become successful . . . on the other hand, it is impressed upon us by means both direct and devious that if we obey the commandment, we shall find ourselves falling victim to . . . [a] radical corruption of spirit." He spelled out how the "gospel of success" reigned supreme in his Brooklyn childhood, at Columbia, and was reinforced by the "ethos of New York literary society." And he excoriated the hypocrisy of a culture that worshipped success but insisted the striver be modest, humble, and circumspect in chasing power. "I will no doubt be accused of self-inflation and therefore of tastelessness. So be it," he declared. He would embrace the free market, American materialism, and empire building abroad—because he could excel in these areas. If his fellow former lefties wanted anarchy or socialism, well . . . good luck and good riddance.

Making It was poorly received by the intellectual and literary communities; Podhoretz was arrogant, young, and untested, said reviewers. Some expressed their embarrassment that he exposed the "dirty little secret": American—and, in this case, specifically Jewish—greed for money and power.

Commentary began a "no-holds barred" campaign against the perceived counterculture, antiwar protesters, and liberal politics in general. In retrospect, Podhoretz's shifting attitudes had long been apparent. As early as 1963, in an essay entitled "My Negro Problem—and Ours," he had admitted to feelings of elitism and deep-seated racism. He said that "love is not the answer to hate—not in the world of politics, at any rate." As the 1960s wore on, this pragmatism (as he would have it) became bitter "revulsion" against the Left. He feared for the "health" of the nation after the "fevers and plagues" unleashed upon it by people whose politics did not fit his. In a very public manner, he lashed out at former leftie pals, including Norman Mailer, Hannah Arendt, and Lionel and Diana Trilling.

As for his friendship with Joe: "Heller . . . [is] far more politically Left than many of his readers ever realized," Podhoretz wrote in a book called *Ex-Friends*. "[T]o give credit where credit is due," Joe was "among the first to spot and denounce" Podhoretz's changing ideologies: He became "outraged by [what he saw as] the increasingly insupportable heresies to which I began giving vent."

"I never gave him the chance to dump me," Joe told Christopher Hitchens, who assessed matters this way:

> [A]s Podhoretz began to fawn more openly on Richard Nixon and the Israeli general staff (as if rehearsing for the [embrace] he would later [give] Ronald Reagan), Heller [withdrew from him] . . . what Heller saw coming is what we now term "neoconservatism." This is a protean and slippery definition, and very inexact as a category, but . . . if you take the version offered by its acolytes, you discover a group of New York Jewish intellectuals who decided that duty, honour, and country were superior, morally and mentally, to the bleeding heart allegiances of their boy- and-girlhoods. If you take the version offered by its critics, you stumble on an old Anglo-Saxon definition of the "upper crust": "A load of crumbs held together by dough."

Following the 1967 Yom Kippur War, Israel would become a serious dividing point between the evolving neoconservatives and their former friends on the Left. Defense of Israel at all costs, under all circumstances, became a foundational neoconservative tenant, and it would lead in the future to their support for aggressive, unilateral American military action worldwide. Joe felt ambivalent about Israel. To interviewer Sam Merrill, he admitted he felt a "strong attachment" to the country, though he had not visited it. Nevertheless, he considered unqualified support of the Jewish homeland, without regard to its sometimes contradictory motives, a "difficult, confusing question." He believed petroleum was the United States' only real interest in the Middle East, and he didn't think wars should be fought to enrich international oil companies. Beyond this, the notion that Jews could be at home *anywhere* in the world, land or no land, seemed to him too rosy a view of Jewish history, and of human life in general.

(In the early 1960s, Ted Solotaroff predicted Israel would split American Jewry between those, mostly of the older, immigrant generation, whose attachments were to Eastern Europe, and who had borne

Diaspora as a badge of dignity, and those, often younger, who viewed backing Israel as Judaism's burning issue.)

In any case, given Podhoretz's freshly militaristic views, this leading neocon had to distance himself from the praise he had once given Joe's antiwar novel. Eventually, he "reconsider[ed]" *Catch-22,* insisting it was "not as heroic as it seemed at first sight." Its inflated reputation, he said, was due to the fact that it had been "perfectly in tune" with the "radical movement" and with a "doctrine that was being preached by most of the major gurus of the era, including writers like Allen Ginsberg and Ken Kesey." It "justified draft evasion and even desertion." Heller's nefarious influence "lingers on," Podhoretz wrote, "in a gutted American military and in a culture that puts the avoidance of casualties above all other considerations." For the new Norman P., Joseph Heller lay at the heart of America's moral rot. *Catch-22* had spiritually crippled the country.

BUT WHAT A SUCCESS it had been! Podhoretz had to admire it on that account, Joe believed.

Now *everybody* wanted a piece of literary pie. Bags of money were waiting to be made in publishing. Once, writers hoped to grasp the golden ring of the Great American Novel; to achieve something in American letters, talent and integrity were thought to be necessary. But talent and integrity were rare. Rewards for hard effort couldn't be doled out widely enough. Now, with so much easy cash flowing, channels needed to be dug for everybody to take advantage of it. Profits shouldn't be left to the gifted and industrious. If you were rich and famous enough, why write your own book? Somebody would do it for you. Notoriety was the new coin of the realm. Movie stars, criminals, disgraced politicians—with a little moxie, anybody could buy their way into the literary big top. "Making it" was about finessing the angles; often, talent and integrity were impediments.

Such was Joe's view. His cynicism grew. Like Podhoretz, he had sometimes presented himself as just another comer looking to score. His success was sweeter for being unlikely: a Coney Island pug who had never expected to go to college, now a respected author! Delirious irony! And old Norm was not wrong about the pleasures of money and prestige.

But success hadn't jumped in Joe's lap. That was the thing. After

Catch-22, he didn't rush out a sequel or another antiwar novel to take advantage of his fame (never mind that he was temperamentally incapable of rushing out *anything*). He spent thirteen years working on a very different kind of book, risking everything for the sake of—what else?—talent and integrity.

Which didn't mean he didn't want success. But he was old-fashioned enough to equate it with effort. Apparently, this equation no longer counted in publishing, but that didn't change his mind. He could go two ways: be the starving artist or demand what he was worth. "I [am] getting very envious of seeing other writers get huge sums of money for not very good books," he admitted to the *Christian Science Monitor.* "It's now so profitable to get a book out of [one's time in] political office that few can resist. . . . [But] the controversies surrounding the publication often make more interesting reading than the books."

Before the 1970s limped to an end, Joe would write, in disgust, "John Ehrlichman, Spiro Agnew, and H. R. Haldeman had written books. Gerald Ford was writing a book. . . . If Gerald Ford could write a book, was there any reason [the racehorse] Secretariat could not? . . . Richard Nixon had written a book. . . . Even that fat little fuck Henry Kissinger was writing a book!"

For Joe, increasingly disaffected by American politics and the decline of public discourse, this was all a sign that cultural progress did not exist: Every change was for the worse. The American presidency had become a "public-relations enterprise," he said; "the world of finance dominat[ed] the world of government" (and literature).

As he would write in his new novel, "the most advanced and penultimate stage of civilization was attained when chaos masqueraded as order, and he knew we were already there."

JOE'S THIRD NOVEL, *Good as Gold*, published in 1979, began: "[He] had been asked many times to write about the Jewish experience in America. This was not strictly true. He'd been asked only twice, most recently by a woman in Wilmington, Delaware, where he had gone to read, for a fee, from his . . . books." This was an accurate account of the novel's origins. The cultural context in which it arrived became apparent in the last third of the book. Joe included a news clipping in the text:

To enhance the value of his memoirs in the marketplace, Secretary of State Henry Kissinger has retained a powerful literary agency to represent him. The agency is International Creative Management.

I.C.M.'s clients include Barbra Streisand, Steve McQueen, Isaac Stern, Peter Benchley, Arthur Miller, Tennessee Williams, Harry Reasoner, Joseph Heller, and Sir Laurence Olivier.

The novel follows the attempts of an academic named Bruce Gold to transcend his working-class Jewish background, earn recognition through his writing as an influential intellectual, and secure a powerful political post in Washington, D.C.

Since Joe was no longer teaching, he could devote every day to the project. He wrote the novel in record time for him: three years. "[I am] getting more efficient and may be prolific yet," he quipped to a journalist. More to the point, he said, "[W]hen I am close to finishing a book, *nothing* is more important to me. I might stop to save a life, but nothing less." And even more to the point: "When . . . James Jones died [in May 1977], leaving his last novel [*Whistle*] incomplete, I began to be afraid I might die before finishing *Good as Gold*." A year later, another friend, Robert Alan Aurthur, a screenwriter and magazine journalist, died of lung cancer, leaving an unfinished project, the screenplay for the movie *All That Jazz*. The Angel of Death wasn't confining itself to the gym. Joe was spooked.

Life got even grimmer when Mario Puzo's wife, Erika, died. Joe did his best to make things nicer for his friends—and to cheer *himself* up. He arranged a date with Puzo for Jones's widow, Gloria. "You're both Italian, he's a writer—what could be better?" he told her. He accompanied his friends to help break the ice. In her memoir, *Lies My Mother Never Told Me*, Gloria's daughter Kaylie writes:

I came home late . . . [one evening] and found the three of them in [our] living room [in Southampton]. My mother, sitting regally in a hard, tall-backed Spanish chair of carved, dark wood, was holding Mario Puzo's hand, who sat at the very edge of the couch, as if he were about to fall off. My mother was crying . . . and Joe Heller, their silent chaperon, sat at the other end of the room, sadly shaking his head.

"You're very sweet and charming," my mother said to Mario

Puzo, "but I still love my husband, you see. And he was a much better writer than you."

Puzo would soon find steady companionship with his wife's former nurse, Carol Gino. Joe remained depressed. His beloved dog, Sweeney, got cancer, and Joe and Shirley had to put him to sleep. Joe had been devoted to Sweeney, grooming, walking, cuddling him and waving his paw whenever guests dropped by the apartment or left. "Say hello. Say goodbye," he'd croon to the dog. Now he swore he'd never own another pet. The trauma was too hard to bear. One day, Shirley caught him hiding in a closet, crying about the dog.

He hurried to finish his novel before other calamities struck. More than ever, he felt his talents should earn him comfort and safety, a buffer against misfortunes.

An article entitled "Heller Takes the Money and Runs," in the March 19, 1979, issue of *New York* magazine, reported that Joe pitched his new novel to Simon & Schuster, abandoning Knopf and his trusted editor, Bob Gottlieb. Why? "For financial security," Joe said, "or for what I sometimes have to call greed. My agent, Candida Donadio, thought I could get a seven-figure guarantee for half of the first-draft manuscript."

He denied rumors that Gottlieb had rejected the manuscript on literary grounds. "Bob thought it was very funny, but he was a little concerned about overwriting and how critics and the public would receive a book so different from *Catch-22* and *Something Happened*. So he postponed the contract until he read the rest of the manuscript," Joe said.

In fact, Gottlieb *didn't* like the book. He thought it was "shticky—and I told Joe. I'd never be anything less than honest with Joe. He didn't take it personally. He told me later—and this was so typical of him—that when I said the book wasn't good, he figured he'd better get the big money up front and cash in while he could."

Given the dark angel's doings, "I might have gone into a depression that would have prevented me from finishing the book," Joe said. "I just didn't want to gamble. How did I know the rest would be any good? It takes me anywhere from four to fourteen years to write a novel, and I wanted to know that I had enough money to keep going on to the next one if *Gold* wasn't a success."

Gottlieb did not discuss the book publicly. He told a reporter he didn't "believe in guaranteeing such immense sums. [M]oney is what

Joe wanted this time." According to Herman Gollob, when Donadio first told Gottlieb that Simon & Schuster was making a bid for Joe's book, he refused to negotiate. "You mean you're not going to make an offer at all?" she asked. "You want an offer?" Gottlieb said. "Okay, here's my offer. Ten dollars."

"That's not exactly how I remember things," Gottlieb says. "It was all quite casual, really. I told Candida, 'Of course, we'll publish it,' but I didn't think it was so great. It wasn't really about the money."

"[Candida] would sort of start whimpering at you if you gave her a low offer for a book," recalled Victoria Wilson, whom Gottlieb hired at Knopf. "She would be operatic, but she would start with the snorkeling and snorfing. It was charming, I mean it was very disarming." But this time the charm did not work on Gottlieb, and Donadio was rattled. She walked around with a fierce expression, her eyes bulging, recalled Dan Simon, a young editor then. He met her one day in her Chelsea office. She was smoking, and he remarked that cigarettes could be bad for her health. "There are times when it's healthier to smoke," she snapped. "Jesus, God, she was intense," Simon said.

The deal for *Good as Gold* was a boon for Simon & Schuster, which had just acquired new offices in Rockefeller Center and was being touted by *New York* as the "showiest [publishing] house in town, with a kind of febrile energy . . . unmatched anywhere." "In a trade that clings to shabby gentility almost as passionately as an English squire treasures his twenty-year-old tweeds," S & S has not hesitated to step up and proclaim itself publishing's "Hot House," said the magazine.

Gottlieb's departure in 1968 had been a near disaster, but Richard Nixon's fall from grace salvaged the company's fortunes. In 1973, S & S purchased Bob Woodward and Carl Bernstein's Watergate expose, *All the President's Men,* for $55,000. Shortly afterward, Julie Nixon Eisenhower became an S & S author. Then Gulf & Western bought the company. It aligned the publisher with its Leisure Time Group (Paramount Pictures, Madison Square Garden, a string of Canadian movie houses). The corporate mandate said S & S should pursue "book publishing as show business." In 1975, the CEOs installed Richard E. Snyder as the publishing house's president. Snyder believed there was no such thing as a good book that didn't sell. He scoffed at the notion of literary fiction. "'Literary' may be chic," he said, "[but] it's not terrific for the author." It didn't earn any money. Snyder expanded the company's sales force. He monitored his editors' expense accounts—if the monthly total was low, it meant a "clear failure to be seen in the right places [around town], wooing the right agents of the right authors." He challenged young editors who were not spending enough to *make* enough: "You want to keep your job, don't you?" He greeted his staff gruffly each morning, asking, "How the fuck are you?" One of his coworkers called him a "terror of sorts . . . the [Mu'ammar] Qaddafi of publishing." Snyder's desk, in the new Rockefeller Center offices, was made of Carpathian elm. It glowed with a kind of golden light. Burnished brass knobs adorned the doors. The interior walls were fashioned of smoked glass. You tread carefully here.

Snyder made a deal for Marilyn French's novel *The Women's Room*: "By the time the book appeared, it had already been sold for a television mini-series," he said. Judith Rossner's rough-sex parable, *Looking for Mr. Goodbar,* was another example of the "synergy" Gulf & Western was after—a "product" that could take many forms and be sold and sold again: book, movie, sound-track album, and so on.

It was a coup for S & S to lure Joe Heller back. Joni Evans, by all accounts the most "aggressive" young editor in the firm, would edit *Good as Gold,* with help from Michael Korda, who had looked on, in the old days, as Gottlieb and Joe edited *Catch-22.* Korda said Evans had a "stick-shift personality . . . [a combination] of stand-up Jewish comedienne, [a] bundle of nerve-endings, [and] Daddy's little girl." Eventually, she would marry Dick Snyder and, in the words of one coworker, play the "good cop" to his "bad cop" in the S & S offices.

For all the energy and glee suffusing the slick new S & S, one observer felt the place was "haunted by the ghost of the departed Gottlieb and forever in search of the quality that left with him." Some agents steered clear of Snyder and company, feeling they didn't nurture young talent. For a while, in 1973, S & S employed former senator Eugene McCarthy as a senior editor. He took the work seriously and pursued it with the kind of integrity once common in publishing. According to *New York*:

> [McCarthy] put in prodigious amounts of time reading poetry and political manuscripts showered upon him by friends and admirers, while the executive staff [of S & S] sat around wondering how to tell this classy man, a former candidate for president no less, that he was supposed to be at the Four Seasons [on

the] expense account . . . hunting up new books. Everyone was a bit relieved when he left.

For *Good as Gold,* Joe received a nearly two-million-dollar advance, a "first for the publishing world," said *New York:* the "biggest advance for a novel in history." For years afterward, nothing would be the same in the "show biz" book world, and Joe was a key figure in the industry's transformation.

His character Bruce Gold writes an essay entitled "Nothing Succeeds as Planned"; in time, that sentiment would dog Joe and other novelists, as big-money publishing demanded more "synergy" and larger blockbusters, all but eliminating the cultural cachet of the small literary novel.

For now, Joe was pleased. He and Shirley bought a summerhouse in East Hampton and paid to put in a pool. "Shirley wanted to live it up a little," says Barbara Gelb.

The same article in *New York* that announced Joe's advance said, "[I]n the nonfiction area, it is rumored that Henry Kissinger's memoirs are being offered for around the same figure."

"[THE TROUBLE] about doing a comic novel with Henry Kissinger as the central [character is that] Kissinger will be forgotten and a man of almost no importance a very short time from now," Joe once said. "Right now he's a great joke, one of the genuinely funny characters in American life. But he won't last."

In *Good as Gold,* Kissinger appears as an animating spirit. Bruce Gold envies the former secretary of state; he is everything Gold wishes to be—a man revered as a public intellectual with almost unlimited political influence. But Gold also hates the man: In his view, Kissinger has sold his soul to get where he is, trading principles and political conscience for opportunism, cash, and lubricous shiksas. Kissinger is the ultimate assimiliationist; assimilation leads to spiritual death.

Gold considers writing an essay entitled "Invite a Jew to the White House (and You Make Him Your Slave)." Ralph Newsome, one of the president's toadies, tells Gold political appointments are one thing, but Washington revolves around the "social world . . . where competence doesn't count [and where] . . . Jews don't really make it. . . . They never did." Kissinger is "just another writer now scrounging around for royalties and publicity. I hope that doesn't sound snobbish, Bruce."

Gold keeps a file of newspaper items on Kissinger. For years, Joe did this, too (one example, from the *New York Times,* October 8, 1974: "Mr. Rockefeller gave Secretary of State Kissinger a $50,000 gift when Mr. Kissinger left his employ to join the Nixon administration." Underneath this, Joe scribbled, "Remember the Neediest!"; he seemed particularly interested in Kissinger's meddling in Iraq, the manipulations and abandonment of Kurdish leaders).

Like Joe, Gold contemplates writing a Kissinger book. On many levels, then, *Good as Gold* is a metafictional novel: a book about the writing of a book, which the reader now holds. But beyond this, *Good as Gold* was a metaevent. Its presence as an object in the world, mocking the kind of object it was—a cultural milestone notable for the money, gossip, and celebrity glitter attached to it—made it one of the oddest literary artifacts ever to appear in the United States.

Like many of the dialogues in *Something Happened,* the novel was a Socratic challenge. It offered reassessments of the categories of literature, commodity, cultural value, art, entertainment, hoax. Joe not only had his cake and ate it; he was selling the recipe at a hefty profit. It was up to the reader to decide what kind of taste it left in the mouth.

If the book succeeded aesthetically, it was because, behind the unattractive, celebrity-seeking hero (to whom the author invited comparisons), Joe also signaled: Reader, I'm in the same luxury liner you are, subject to the same tempests of rage, and I don't know how to feel about them, either.

Finally, as a companion to Kissinger's memoir (by virtue of being linked in the press to Kissinger's book), it was a fierce attack on America's self-image as crafted by a prominent government insider. In a review of the novel in *The New Republic,* Jack Beatty wrote, "*Good as Gold* is a cultural event. A major novelist has taken on our greatest celebrity with all the power of wit and language at his command. . . . [P]erhaps not since Tolstoy eviscerated Napoleon . . . has a central historical figure been so intimately castigated by the Word. Score one for literature."

More somberly, John W. Aldridge, reviewing the book for *Harper's,* remarked, "It is all about a society that is fast going insane, that is learning to accept chaos as order, and unreality as normal. The horror is that the time may soon come when the conditions Heller depicts will no longer seem either funny or the least bit odd."

GOOD AS GOLD was also about Jewish families from Coney Island. It marked a turn in Joe's writing toward straightforward, nostalgic auto-biography. This strain would grow and dominate his later work. Had he lived longer and abandoned the conviction that he *needed* to write the Great American Novel—a burden of his generation—it might have proved his greatest achievement.

The reviewers who did not cotton to *Good as Gold*—there were several—said its modalities did not mesh. Broad caricature distinguished the Washington scenes; the political flunkies spoke Ziegler-like non-sense: "[T]here is nothing in the world that can block your appointment, unless something gets in the way." By contrast, the family scenes—Gold's raucous dinners with his father, sisters, brother, and their spouses—are touchingly realistic, salted with Yiddishisms and noisy kvetching.

Finally, there are vivid and sensitive descriptions of Coney Island's decline since Gold's childhood, the crumbling infrastructure, abandon-ment of youth to joblessness, listlessness, and drugs—the neglect of the public good that comes from a bad government concerned only with per-petuating rituals, and individuals more interested in social climbing than caring for their families.

Joe established these tonal clashes to convey a clangorous culture into which it is finally impossible to integrate, for it is coming apart. From region to region, profession to profession, social class to social class, no one speaks the same language. Before writing the novel, Joe immersed himself in Charles Dickens to grasp the English master's sweep and whimsical satire. Joe was particularly impressed with *Bleak House*, which operates in two registers: the public voice ("London. Michelmas Term lately over, and the Lord Chancellor sitting in Lincoln's Inn Hall. Implacable November weather.") and Esther Summerson's private voice ("[S]omething happened when I was still quite a little thing."). Joe adopted *Bleak House*'s strategy, contrasting Gold's family dinners with his public experiences in Washington; the leap from literary realism to absurdity was too much for many readers. (On the other hand, Leonard Michaels, reviewing the novel for the *New York Times Book Review,* said it offered "an astounding vision of our leaders in Washington. As-tounding because, while fantastic, it doesn't seem incorrect.")

As with *Catch-22* and *Something Happened*, the events in *Good as Gold* resolve after a traumatic death. These deaths always occur in the books' penultimate sections, as if rising from the depths of repressed memory. In this case, Gold's older brother, Sid, passes away unexpectedly, forcing Gold to abandon his political ambitions and return to the family to care for his aging father and flailing sisters. Ambivalently, Gold embraces his Jewish heritage. At novel's end, as he is heading to his wife by way of Coney Island Avenue, he comes upon a "softball game in a schoolyard played by boys wearing *yarmulkes.*" He leaves his car to watch:

> Athletes in skullcaps? The school was a religious one, a *yeshiva.* Some of the teenagers had sidelocks, and some of the sidelocks were blond. Gold smiled. God was right [about the Jews]—a stiff-necked, contrary people. *Moisheh Kapoyer,* here it was winter and they were playing baseball, while everyone else played football and basketball.
>
> And a stubborn dispute was in progress. . . . The pitcher was sulking and refused to throw the ball. The batter was waiting in a squat with his elbows on his knees. . . . As Gold watched, the catcher, a muscular, redheaded youth with freckles and sidelocks and a face as Irish or Scottish or Polish as any Gold had ever laid eyes upon, moved wrathfully toward the pitcher with words Gold for a minute had trouble believing.
>
> "*Varf!*" shouted the catcher. "*Varf* it, already! *Varf* the fucking ball!"

This was as "vivid an anecdote of assimilation as I could find," Joe said.

WRITING IN *INQUIRY,* Murray N. Rothbard noted another crucial aspect of *Good as Gold*:

> [T]he most repellent character in Joseph Heller's hilarious novel . . . is one Maxwell Lieberman, the editor of a small, pretentious, once liberal now neoconservative monthly, a man who eats greedily with both hands, a New York Jewish intellectual whose sole literary output is a series of autobiographies celebrating his own life and thought. I have no way of knowing

what Norman Podhoretz's eating habits are. But Podhoretz is a New York Jewish intellectual, the longtime editor of the pretentious, once liberal now neoconservative monthly *Commentary,* and a man whose most visible literary output consists of autobiographical volumes celebrating his own career.

Podhoretz also noticed Joe's "savage caricature" of him. It "cement[ed] our new ex-friendship," he said.

Rothbard applauded Joe for satirizing Podhoretz's embrace of "the old question, 'Is it good for the Jews?'" Podhoretz believed foreign-policy initiatives should be grounded on "an all-out and unmitigated support for the state of Israel, which he identifies with the cause of Jewry." He had changed the "meaning of the word 'intellectual'"; to Podhoretz, an intellectual is a "man who push[es] and elbow[s] his way upward from the ranks to what passes for fame and fortune."

But Joe was not just being nasty about Podhoretz. *Good as Gold* mounts a full critique of neoconservative thought as it developed in the late 1960s and throughout the 1970s in the writings of Irving Kristol, Daniel Moynihan, and others. Specifically, Joe attacked the neocons' belief that the loss of faith in government, now widespread in the United States, was, in Peter Steinfels's words, "primarily a cultural crisis, a matter of values, morals, and manners," and not—as Joe saw it—a matter of abysmal leadership by self-serving scoundrels such as Nixon, Kissinger, and the neocons themselves. Neoconservatives espoused the "theory of unintended consequences," Steinfels said; the government was the "victim of 'overload.' Attempting too much, it has naturally failed," and so its "authority . . . should be shielded by dispersing responsibility for [its] failure as much as possible." This could be achieved by farming out government responsibilities to private enterprise, and forcing the free market to take the blame for screwups.

As Marshall Toman points out in *Studies in Contemporary Satire,* "When Bruce Gold, abandoning his former liberal beliefs and adopting neoconservative opinions for the power their [approval] will bring him, writes 'Nothing Succeeds as Planned,' he contributes precisely the intellectual support . . . the conservative government needs to justify its lack of social involvement."

Lieberman hopes to be appointed "broad gauge advisor on domestic policy," a position for which Irving Kristol was considered in 1972.

Lieberman misuses language the way Kristol often did, saying "literally" for "figuratively" ("Don't words mean anything to you?" Gold chastises him).

While writing the novel, Joe kept folders of newspaper stories on the neocons, as he did with Henry Kissinger. He told interviewer Charlie Reilly, "A phrase that really gets to me . . . would be one of those neoconservative references to Vietnam as a national tragedy, but only because we lost. That thought fills me with ire. To begin with, the person who says it is typically untouched by tragedy; like me, he has not lost a son or a job. In addition, the implication is that if we had won, the war would have been somehow less tragic. People with that mentality, I have to admit, impress me as being the scum of the earth."

"THE HONEYMOON is over for Joseph Heller," John Leonard declared in the *New York Times*. "He will be thumped . . . for having written this savage novel. . . . Those [who] have suggested that he might be more Jewish in his fiction are going to be sorry they asked."

Joe was courting trouble because *Good as Gold* entered (with fists aflutter) a Jewish family quarrel, not to mention a New York–Washington spat. It was, as well, a literary insider's joke. For these reasons, its appeal would be more limited than that of *Catch-22* and *Something Happened*. Despite this (and because, like *Catch,* it was a satire), it appeared on official bestseller lists, a paradox worthy of Ron Ziegler. An increasingly narrowing range of interests and reference points would plague the rest of Joe's career.

MOISHEH KAPOYER, a person who does everything in reverse: Mr. Backwards, Mr. Yes for No. Moisheh Kapoyer was also the name of a character in a cartoon feature in the *Jewish Daily Forward,* alongside letters in the "Bintel Brief." Like Socrates, his specialty was tossing off "upside down" remarks.

In *Good as Gold,* Joe used the expression to describe Jewish contrariness. He used it to deride Henry Kissinger: Here was a Jew seeking success in Christian Washington. In the deepest chill of the Watergate scandal, he fell on his knees to pray beside Richard Nixon, a man he considered anti-Semitic.

For Joe, *Moisheh kapoyer* captured the paradox of the integrated Jew—and, more broadly, of all Americans, living in a wealthy culture often inimical to moral principles. The phrase defined the style of humor propelling Joe's fiction. He could name it now, in his third novel, employing the language of his mother.

Good as Gold appeared at a transitional time, when many once-liberal Jews were turning "upside down," preparing to endorse Ronald Reagan. This alliance would give Norman Podhoretz and others like him the political influence they sought. The novel appeared at a time when Jewish humor, formerly marginalized in places like the Catskills, had reversed its fortunes to become perhaps the dominant mode of American entertainment, on television, in movies, comic books, satirical magazines (and some would say in the comic-strip worlds of good and evil displayed in certain intellectual journals).

By 1979, the Jewish-American novel, with its deflationary humor, could legitimately be called one of the most important literary developments in the second half of the twentieth century. Beside Joe's novel, in 1979, sat Philip Roth's *The Ghost Writer,* Bernard Malamud's *Dubin's Lives,* and William Styron's *Sophie's Choice,* meditations on writing, the legacy of World War II, and Judaism's place in the Western cultural imagination.

Earlier in the 1970s, Saul Bellow had secured his title of major American novelist with *Humboldt's Gift,* and even non-Jewish writers— Styron, Updike (in his Bech books)—were tackling Jewish themes, as if *they* were the ones trying to assimilate into mainstream culture.

The critic Leon Wieseltier observed:

America . . . was where Jewish humor fantastically flourished. It has become perhaps the most well-known product of American Jewish culture. But something happened to Jewish humor in America. It shrank in its scope. Its metaphysical commentary, its interest in the collective fate, the dimension of desperation that had made it an essential instrument of the healing heart, all disappeared. As the jokes have gone from Yiddish to English, they have gone from God to parents.

One could argue—as did biblical scholar Robert Alter—that Yiddish-based humor *always* had a tiny scope. In fact, this was its point: to whittle the metaphysical down to the daily ("If you want to forget all your troubles, put on a shoe that's too tight," said one Yiddish proverb).

In any case, *Good as Gold,* Joe's first openly Jewish novel, certainly trafficked in parent jokes, banal realities, and did so with gusto. Almost immediately, he decided his next effort would encompass *all* families—the generations of Jewish history. It would examine not only fathers but *the* Father. Joe Heller's next book would pose a direct challenge to God.

PART FIVE **Die Trying**

16. Hard to Swallow

WHEN IT WAS OVER and Joe could finally leave his hospital bed, emerge again into the world in a wheelchair, and visit a local restaurant, it was Jerry McQueen who, one night in April 1982, drove Joe to the Russian Tea Room, pulled the car onto the sidewalk, stopped within a few feet of the door, hugged Joe in his bearish arms, and carried him inside to be settled in his wheelchair at a cloth-covered table next to plush red leather seats. "I [had] never seen [Joe] so ebullient, so purely joyful," said Barbara Gelb, another dinner guest that evening, along with her husband, Arthur, a *New York Times* managing editor, and Joe's nurse-companion, Valerie Humphries. "That night, [Joe] was as close to euphoria as [he] had ever come."

A heavy rain was falling. "I was dry as a bone . . . when I was finally inside [the restaurant] in my wheelchair," Joe recalled. "[The] others were drenched and disheveled." During dinner, he felt "genuine happiness," though it remained difficult for him to swallow food; chewing awkwardly, his cheeks partially numb, he covered his mouth with his hand.

He had met Jerry McQueen through the Gelbs. Barbara had written a book called *On the Track of Murder,* all about McQueen, a homicide detective. A man "on good terms with himself and the world," he was nevertheless anxious about his health—a trait he shared with Joe (sometimes, said Gelb, McQueen would "develop mysterious muscle twitches . . . that vanished as inexplicably as they arose"). He was pugnacious, wary, and witty. He was not tall and could be, Gelb said, "self-conscious about his height. Perhaps in compensation, he often walked with a semi-swagger, suggesting latent menace—James Cagney playing a bad guy. His hands were blunt-fingered, not formed for eloquence."

He was patient, a good listener, quick to pick up body language from others, perhaps a consequence of being the son of deaf parents who had never learned to speak. As a young cop, McQueen took adult-education courses at John Jay College, developing an interest in the *Iliad* and Socrates. He earned a B+ on a paper denouncing Socrates for so blithely accepting his martyrdom.

But it was McQueen's knowledge of the city that attracted Joe—as though no harm could come to anyone close to a man who could smell danger. As a rookie policeman, McQueen had paced every filthy inch of his precincts, gotten to know the shopkeepers and street toughs, learned local lingoes, got to know the stink of each block's garbage. Like an animal marking territory, he had "peed on tenement rooftops," he said, in alleys all over Manhattan. In command of birth and death, he had delivered babies and examined corpses for the last stories they told. He could glance at a place—say, the Hudson View Hotel, located near Riverside Drive in the West Seventies—and tell in an instant that among its eccentric residents, any one of them was capable of murder. By the time he'd met Joe in the mid-1970s, he was tired of perpetual discouragement. Almost half the city's homicides went unsolved each year. Whenever a corpse appeared on a street, McQueen wanted to stick a "suicide note in his pocket, confessing to all our murders," he said.

But tonight was not about dying; it was, in fact, a resurrection. Within the warm, glowing green walls of the restaurant, among rows of round white tables arrayed along tomato-colored carpet, all of old New York seemed to have sprung to life to celebrate Joe's outing. He could almost hear the applause of prewar patrons, rising and saluting George Balanchine as he strolled across the room with a ballerina on each arm. The orange spice of tea, the tang of white chocolate, the wheaty steam rising from breads and blintzes made Joe's mouth water. Never mind that heavy renovations were occurring on either side of the restaurant, walls torn down, windows busted, towers raised (in New York, buildings, too, often became corpses overnight). This evening, this place, and all the people in it would live forever.

THE TROUBLE had started the morning of December 12, 1981, a Saturday. The previous evening, Joe had eaten dinner with his old friends Norman and Gloria Barasch. They lived in California now—Barasch had moved there to write for television—but they were visiting New York, and Barasch wanted to discuss *Good as Gold* with Joe. "I thought it was hysterically funny," he says. "I thought it could work as a movie. So I told Joe I'd like to try to get an option—chop off the first and last part of the novel, and turn that juicy middle into a crazy farce. Joe said, 'You can have the option for a dollar.' I said, 'Good!' In truth, I thought it was a little high." (Joe had been disappointed that Mike Nichols, who initially expressed interest in making a movie from the novel, had decided to pass on it.)

Later, Joe remembered how impressed the Barasches were that Friday night by his apparent health and good spirits. He had spent the summer and much of the fall in Aspen, Colorado, and Santa Fe, New Mexico (having returned to New York only ten days earlier). He had been working happily on a new novel about King David's estrangement from God. He was suntanned and lean, his hair a silver nimbus. A light snow fell after dinner. Joe felt chilled as he walked his friends back to their hotel, but this was not surprising. He was wearing only a trench coat with a light wool lining.

Then, on Saturday, Joe ate breakfast alone at the Red Flame on West Forty-fourth Street, an old-style diner with plastic menus in the windows and long Formica-topped tables. He thought about the breakfasts Shirley used to fix him in the Apthorp. He missed her cooking. Then he relished not being chastised by his wife for never helping her with chores. Suddenly, he found he couldn't swallow a forkful of hash brown potatoes he had brought to his mouth. He rolled the potatoes around on his tongue and finally spat them out. The rest of the meal— eggs, toast with butter, coffee—went down fine. He met Speed Vogel a few blocks away. Speed had agreed to go with him to look at the furniture of a man who was giving up his apartment and leaving Manhattan.

Joe was now subletting a place at 888 Eighth Avenue; he needed more tables and chairs (recently, he had wasted a morning, buying a lamp at Rosetta's Lighting and Supplies over on West Forty-fifth Street—his first domestic shopping spree solo—bringing the lamp home, setting it up near his writing desk, fiddling with it, sitting down to stare at the pages he'd written, deciding the lighting didn't suit him, fiddling some more, sitting down again, shuffling pages, getting back up, finally concluding that the lamp was just *wrong*, boxing it up, and taking it back to the store).

The day was quite chilly. Joe wore a heavy sweater over a velour shirt. He didn't like the furniture. He and Speed walked back to his apartment. Joe tugged the building's outer door; it didn't budge. Speed whisked it open. Inside the apartment, Joe could not pull his sweater off without Speed's help. Static electricity? Perspiration?

Speed baked a couple of sweet potatoes because Joe was hungry and Speed wanted to demonstrate how to use the toaster oven he had purchased for Joe: he knew his friend was helpless on his own, and he worried about the future (already, Joe had hired a once-a-week cleaning woman). Joe loved sweet potatoes. They reminded him of his mother. After a few bites, he could not swallow anything more.

He went with Speed to jog around the indoor track at the Y. Warming up, stretching, he lay on his back, bent his legs, and tried to touch his chin to his knees. He could not come close. "It struck me then that something was wrong," he recalled. He could ignore the signals no longer. "It was as though I had suffered a loss of communication between my wish and my capability to achieve it."

He ran a sluggish mile and a half on the track. Back at his locker, he struggled to remove his sweaty T-shirt.

That night, he and Speed ate dinner with a mutual friend, Cheryl McCall, a writer for *People* magazine, at a small West Side restaurant called Simon's. Joe enjoyed the fish he had ordered, but his martini tasted metallic. And then he began to have difficulty swallowing the vegetables. Speed's brows furrowed. "[Joe was] the most prodigious eater in the world," he said. "The very last thing to expect from him [was] trouble swallowing." With his fork, Joe waved away his friend's worry and kept his anxieties to himself. That night, alone in his apartment, he struggled once again while taking off his clothes, and he could barely hold the early edition of the Sunday *Times*.

The phone woke him the following morning. A young woman he had hired to type his novel in progress told him she had completed the most recent section and could deliver it whenever he wanted. Her name was Tedda Fenichel. She was brisk, attentive, efficient. She could tell she had awakened Joe from a very deep sleep. At first, he was disoriented, thinking it was late Saturday night. When she told him it was Sunday, he wondered if it was evening. When finally he came to himself, he told Tedda he would check his schedule and get back to her. As usual, he had slept in his underpants. Clumsily, he pulled on a loose pair of trousers and a sweatshirt. In the kitchen, he sliced a grapefruit. Another queer taste—that same metallic edge. His arms felt leaden.

He had agreed to meet the Barasches for brunch. When Norman phoned, Joe said he wasn't feeling so hot. They should go ahead without him—he recommended the scrambled eggs with imported ham at the Russian Tea Room. Speed called to see how he was doing. He admitted he was worried enough to phone one of the Baders, Richard or Mortimer, twin brothers who shared a medical practice and served his family as personal physicians.

Joe reached Morty by phone. He apologized for calling on a Sunday morning. When he described his symptoms—realizing, as he was talking, that he could not cross his right leg over his left—Bader muttered, "Guillain-Barré syndrome."

"Okay. Now what does it mean?" Joe asked.

"Can you get over here? To my apartment?"

Joe wasn't sure. "Sure."

FROM MID-DECEMBER 1981 to January 4, 1982, Joe stayed in the intensive care unit of Mount Sinai Hospital. At various times and in varying degrees, his limbs were paralyzed, his muscles useless; he was unable to defecate and pee on his own, unable to swallow ("dysphagia," nurses wrote in his daily reports). He was fed liquids through a nasogastric tube, medications through an intravenous tube attached to the back of his hand, and was cleared of phlegm and saliva through a third tube. Doctors debated cutting a hole in his throat and hooking him up to a respirator. They told Joe that Guillain-Barré syndrome caused an elevation in protein in spinal fluid. His body was manufacturing cells to destroy tissues. The malady is rare and mysterious, its origins unknown. Not a virus, its roots appear to be autoimmunological. "It's like a short circuit in the nerves," Speed Vogel took to telling folks. Frederick Karl informed Joe that the disease had been linked in the past to swine flu immunizations (such was the case in 1976). Respiratory failure and cardiovascular trouble were frequent results of the condition. It was sometimes fatal. Sometimes, people recovered.

As Mario Puzo muttered, "When they name a disease after two guys, it's got to be terrible."

As Joe lay in the ICU, wired to monitors, pale under the lights (despite his recent tan), his children and friends—among them, Joe Stein, Julius Green, and George Mandel—marveled at how calm he was. He asked someone to contact Tedda Fenichel and tell her to deliver the manuscript of his King David novel to the hospital. He asked for a dozen number-two pencils. "I was not [really] aware I faced any [lasting perils] until the most serious had been left behind," Joe admitted. Heartened by his fortitude, his friends joked that he was the immobile Soldier in White from *Catch-22*. "Did you hear what Joe said today?" they'd kid one another. "No, what'd he say?" "Nheh dehgrehda waddleta deh nahe nheh!"

Privately, they feared he might be dying.

One night, a nurse drew a curtain around his bed, shutting off his view. Joe heard a woman weeping nearby. Apologetically, the nurse whispered that the man in the bed next to him was about to expire. "That happens in here," she said.

THE BEGINNING of the 1980s should have been a glorious time for Joe and his family. *Good as Gold* earned him a record advance and had become a national bestseller. His brother, retired from the mail room at MCA–Universal Pictures, and his sister, retired from Macy's, lived comfortably in West Palm Beach, Florida (though Lee's wife, Perle, had died of cancer). Joe's children had graduated from college and appeared to be prospering. Erica was embarked upon a career in advertising, working with some of the best ad people in the city. She wrote copy for Doyle Dane Bernbach, and would soon handle multimillion dollar accounts from Seagram, Chanel, and Volkswagen. Ted, asked by Barbara Gelb if he had ambitions to be a writer, said, "No. But that's a lie." He worked in the clothing business, loading and unloading trucks, unpacking boxes, and shelving garments according to size and color; his literary talent showed in an uncanny ability to imitate the older Jewish fellows and young black men on the job. He would soon write a drama that merited a workshop production in L.A., "pleasantly shock[ing]" Joe, he recalled—his father had no idea he was writing seriously. "[He] was proud [but he] was merciless in his corrections of it," Ted says. "I remember a line in the play. It was sort of a malaprop: one character says that another character 'has the patience of Lot.' (I *know* that Job is the epitome of patience.) My father wrote in the margin something like, 'You mean Job. Lot was not known for his patience.' I think he was such a perfectionist that he missed the joke."

Joe was writing, and rather swiftly for him. He had come up with a good first line: "I've got the best story in the Bible," spoken by King David. Joe liked the comic possibilities, the opportunity to lampoon history and religion. He was physically fit, working out, keeping his weight down.

But in spite of good tidings, he was restless. On a large, impersonal scale, the election of Ronald Reagan disturbed him: The neoconservatives had gotten a foothold in the White House. He told interviewers the survival of America no longer mattered to him much. Capitalism was in its death throes. "I see hopelessness," he said to a reporter from *Rolling Stone*. The country's problems had grown so large, they were unsolvable. "An experienced businessman can't run his business, but the government can't either," Joe said. "So socialism won't work. I mean, we have a history of corrupt government. . . . [Incompetence is] our tradition. . . . It warmed my heart [recently], in the way that watching a Laurel and Hardy comedy might warm my heart, to read about the losses that General Motors and Ford posted. We just assume these companies are infallible and in expert hands, and everything's going to go beautifully. But not only was there incompetence, there was passive acceptance."

As for his career, Joe was beleaguered by the fact that, despite his successes, nothing matched *Catch-22* in the minds of most readers and critics. He groused that *Good as Gold* would not have been reviewed if it hadn't been for his first novel. Late in life, he responded to the comment "You've never written anything as good as *Catch-22*" by saying, "Who has?" But in the early 1980s, in his late fifties, he still fought to top himself. The critic Clancy Segal said of him, "Sheer, stark terror, however disguised as farce or satire, stalks the pages of Heller's writing. . . . [T]he temptation is to find the 'something happened' that helped cause Heller's deep, sad anger of life's hurtful illogic."

Especially in his personal life, Joe was whirling. Publicly, he spoke positively about the virtues of a long and comfortable marriage, but more and more frequently he had neglected Shirley. She found it increasingly galling to swallow the obvious but unspoken fact that he had led a double life throughout their marriage, seeing other women, privileging his own pursuits. "The Mogul," she called him in angry moments. "At one point, she got a feminist shrink who kept telling her to leave Joe—it's enough," said Barbara Gelb. For his part, Joe felt Shirley had not matured along with him and could no longer recognize his needs. In rough draft notes, written in the early 1980s, for what would eventually become a book about his illness, Joe wrote, "I began to feel the married life to which I had been accustomed for more than thirty years was falling apart irretrievably." Elsewhere, he said that one night when he and Shirley were returning from a party she turned to him quite suddenly and admitted she was jealous of his fame and success. "The problem," Joe said, "was that in all the years of my struggle to make it as a writer, she had never developed a career or life of her own."

So when, in the midst of all this, a rare illness with no known cause struck him unexpectedly, he said, "Stress? Maybe."

THE STRESS had built incrementally. While writing *Good as Gold,* Joe had seen a therapist, Dr. Robert Michaels of Payne Whitney. The writing, particularly the autobiographical sections of the novel, stirred Joe up, and he started to think of himself as a "fatherless Coney Island child." What had happened to him? He was in search of his real self, he said—poor abandoned Joey.

During this period, Lee made regular trips to New York from Florida, accompanying Perle as she received cancer treatments. Over coffee in diners, Joe nudged Lee to reminisce about their father. Lee was reluctant to talk, choked by the ambivalence the older man provoked in him. He admitted their father had beaten him on occasion. Then he'd express understanding and forgiveness—Isaac was only doing what he thought he must to raise a good kid. Joe stared at his brother in pity and wonderment.

In his memoir, he wrote, "The first time I met my father face-to-face to talk to him, so to speak, was in the office of a psychoanalyst some-time in 1979, when I was already fifty-six years old. My father had been dead for more than fifty of those years."

He had been having the old dream again: Once more, he was a child, trembling in bed. A faceless figure approached his bedroom door. After a few meetings with Dr. Michaels, Joe realized with a shock one day as he lay on the therapist's couch that the dream had not recurred since their sessions began. "You don't need that dream anymore," Michaels commented. "You have me here now."

So, with the doctor, Joe explored the patterns in his novels: threats to children, fathers betraying sons, deaths allowing the protagonists to live. Could the emotional confusion Joe had experienced in childhood be rooted in the feeling that his father had died *as a child;* that is, he was in his infancy *as an American,* unformed, unintegrated, whereas Joe had become the successful adult American male? Their roles had reversed.

Michaels warned Joe not to overintellectualize. The danger with a literary patient was, he read all the psychoanalytic literature. Joe knew Freud as well as the doctor. He batted around *repression, narcissism, Oedipal complex,* applying the terms to himself—"All that serious stuff was easy," Joe said. He would write in *Now and Then*, "My the-ory . . . about psychoanaly[sis] is that corrective therapy demands un-wavering concentration by a patient of intelligence with a clear and untroubled head who is not in need of it." Those who really need help won't be aided by the talk, however insightful it is.

Still, the sessions brought pragmatic results. Joe learned he "never really wanted to live in a house in Tuscany or the French Riviera or have Elizabeth Taylor and Marilyn Monroe in love with [him], and [he] didn't really covet . . . the bolder public life lived by Norman Mailer, although there was much there to envy. People with choices generally do what they want to do and have no real choice but to be what they already are."

At one point, he admitted to the doctor one of his reasons for seek-ing therapy was the "wish to have a psychiatric medical authority . . . to quote in comeback during domestic arguments—even to misquote, by attributing to [the shrink] statements that had not been made." Michaels laughed at this, but Joe did feel "enormously [helped] in the mat-ter of day-to-day embroilments at home."

The therapist examined Joe's and Shirley's actions dispassionately and rationally. "[H]e bound me to this," Joe said: "I was not to make fundamental changes in my life once we began—not in my marriage, my work, or other areas—without discussion with him." Michaels was prescient, making this warning: Within months, Joe, desperately angry and depressed for nonspecific reasons, would break his promise to the doctor and severely strain, if not shatter, every important relationship in his life.

Joe's marital miseries drove him from the Apthorp. In December 1980, he was living in his studio when he heard that John Lennon, whom he had often associated with Yossarian, had been shot to death just blocks away. Reporters described Lennon's murderer as a deranged fan. It was impossible not to contemplate the violence inherent in fantasy, fan identification, or disappointment with objects of adulation as one of the consequences of celebrity in America. Moreover, Joe believed Lennon, Yossarian, Lenny Bruce figures were similar to Socrates: questioners, provocateurs, flashing mirrors at the warped cultures that had spawned them. Inevitably, society found methods to eliminate them. Joe felt anxious and chilled as he walked the edges of Central Park.

In the months following, his life seemed to fragment. His movements became erratic. His path can be traced in bits and pieces.

In March 1981, he visited a literature class at Duke University, in Durham, North Carolina, at the invitation of Judith Ruderman, a literary critic and then director of continuing education at Duke. About his novels, Joe spoke graciously and patiently to students. Ruderman remembered him bringing an hors d'oeuvre—pickled herring—from Zabar's to the dinner she made in his honor. "How I came to know him is . . . Helleresque," she said. "[H]e developed a romantic relationship with my across-the-street neighbor after she wrote him a fan letter. When he got sick [later that year], that was the end of it."

In *Now and Then,* Joe admitted he flew off "intrepidly" for an "unlikely weekend rendezvous, a blind date with a woman I hadn't met or known about before (my most dangerous mission, marveled my friends) and whom nobody I knew had heard of either." When he arrived, he was "at first afflicted by an inability to function sexually." Upon his return to New York, he confessed his failure to his therapist. "[Y]ou didn't really want to do [it]," the doctor pronounced.

Two years later, the *New York Post* rehashed Joe's North Carolina contacts. Writing on October 19, 1983, the unidentified *Post* reporter said:

> Joseph Heller took the stand in Manhattan Supreme Court [at] his divorce trial. . . . He . . . took the Fifth when asked about his relationship with one Joanne Wood. Heller's estranged wife, Shirley, alleges that the author of *Catch-22* and *Something Happened* left her for Wood back in 1981. After questioning Heller . . . about Wood—and getting nothing but the Fifth Amendment as a response—Shirley's attorney, William Binderman, finally asked the author why he wasn't talking? Did he fear prosecution? "Yes," said Heller.

Speed Vogel named Joanne Wood in a rough draft of *No Laughing Matter,* a book he wrote with Joe about Joe's illness. In the published book, he said Joe's new "friend [had] once worked at Duke University Medical Center in the department of epidemiology."

Erica recalls long, tearful meetings with her father in diners, probably in the spring of 1981. He denied he had left her mother for anyone else.

Around that time, "I changed accountants," Joe said. "I changed lawyers and then changed lawyers again." He broke off with his therapist "abruptly."

On July 1, 1981, the *New York Times* reported that Joe and Simon & Schuster "have had a falling out that has ended up in arbitration." Joe said, "It's not a question of royalties but of interpretations of certain clauses in the *Gold* contract and in the contract for the new book, which may or may not result in more money." Then he said his "indignation" had to do with the publisher's "unacceptably low" royalty terms. "My complaints were brushed aside arbitrarily and I had no recourse but to institute legal action." Whatever the case's merits, Joe sounded hurt, inconsistent, perhaps unhappy with himself. He appeared to be looking for fights to pick.

Lashing out at everyone, he left Candida Donadio after nearly twenty-six years, accusing her of failing to support him in his tussle with S & S. She was devastated, particularly as she was on the verge of losing another cherished client, Thomas Pynchon. Melanie Jackson, Donadio's young assistant, had become romantically involved with Pynchon (later they would marry). The relationship rankled Donadio, who seems to have discovered their dalliance when her accountant pointed out an excessive number of Chinese take-out receipts among Jackson's expenses. In 1982, Jackson left the agency, taking Pynchon and several other authors with her. Pynchon sent Donadio an unusually chilly letter, severing their professional tie and telling her to please conduct any further business with him through Melanie Jackson.

At the time, Donadio was living unhappily with a screenwriter named Henry Bloomstein, whose work she was never able to place with publishers. Eventually, he moved to the West Coast, amid rumors he had only taken up with Donadio to advance his career. Donadio drank and smoked more than ever. You couldn't help but "agonize with her" during this terrible period, said Herman Gollob.

In the meantime, Joe had moved out of the Apthorp once and for all. He would never return to it as a home. He had rented the Eighth Avenue apartment. He and Shirley argued about who would spend the summer in their East Hampton house. Shirley won this round. Furious, Joe went to East Hampton, gathered a couple of pieces of furniture from the place on Skimhampton Road, and took them back to his apartment. He warned Shirley he would be "coming around" the Apthorp whenever he wanted.

He didn't have any idea how he would spend the summer—his apartment would be stifling. An opportunity presented itself when an old friend, Maia Wojciechowska, phoned to ask for his help in preparing a manuscript for publication. Wojciechowska, who wrote novels for young adults, had worked as a bullfighter before coming to the States— Hemingway once said she knew more about bulls than any woman he'd met. She had been married to the poet and art critic Selden Rodman. Now she lived in Santa Fe. She urged Joe to fly out and taste the freedom and independence of the West.

He asked his friend in North Carolina if she'd like to go with him. She said yes. With the impulsiveness that had spurred him the last several months, he agreed to help Wojciechowska with her novel; in return, she found him a place in Santa Fe. He wound up signing a year's lease for a one-bedroom apartment in the middle of town for two hundred dollars a month. For the rest of the summer and most of the fall of 1981, he sat in the sunshine with legal pads and pencils, writing his version of King David's story: the tale of an embittered old man in failing health who feels betrayed by his wife and children (while acknowledging his betrayals of them), wary of his closest associates, rueful about his achievements, uncertain about the meaning of history, and fearful about the future.

Fleetingly, the king realizes he may have believed too thoroughly in the myth of his royalty, and celebrated too much in public (his wife finds it disgusting that he has danced nearly naked in the streets of the Holy Land, showing off his genitals).

Mario Puzo once said Joe was "so concerned about controlling his life, he can't have fun. Actually, I can . . . see him changing into a wild man, but it would be in a very controlled sort of way." In 1981—Joe was fifty-eight years old—the "wild man" emerged.

The person sitting in the summer sunlight had estranged himself from his family and many of the people closest to him for decades. He had behaved recklessly in his professional affairs, impulsively and carelessly in his personal life. What, on its face, might be tagged a midlife crisis appeared to have several complex sources: a sense that nothing had turned out the way he wanted ("Nothing fails like success," his King David says); the knowledge that time was getting short and the feeling that he had *earned* a little fun; a conviction that his wife didn't love him enough, his children and publisher didn't love him enough—he couldn't *get enough love,* damn it. Therapy sessions had awakened anxieties as well as insights. Anxiety accompanied the mixed signals he received about his writing: complaints from critics, rumors that his talent had abated. And yet the sales were enormous. He had money, celebrity. Who was he, really? *What* was there to love?

"The older I get, the less interest I take in . . . everything. Who gives a damn?" says Joe's king. But then he admits that more than anything, "I would rather have my wife [right now]"—she "does not care about me and probably never did."

When Joe returned to New York for what he thought would be a brief interlude, he insisted to gossip columnists that he was not really part of the New York "party circuit," in spite of being one of the world's highest-paid novelists. "What would send me into incipient alcoholism is giving the impression that we're all enjoying ourselves tremendously," he said. "When I go out to give lectures, all these people look at me with envy because they see me photographed at parties talking with other writers or an actress or editor, and they imagine I'm having a great time when I'm not. Often, when my picture is taken, what I'm saying to someone is, 'What are we doing here?' I mean, the only reason I go to these literary parties is out of obligation."

His boasting sounded even more disingenuous when placed against items such as this from the *New York Post's* Page Six, printed October 1, 1981:

Joseph (*Catch-22*) Heller expressed a real writer's curiosity during the opening of Russell Chatham's show at the Central Falls Gallery in SoHo the other night, but it wasn't art that caught his fancy. Heller was taken with the black boots worn by an unidentified young lady. "They're vinyl, I can tell," he said as he bent to feel the girl's ankle. She insisted they were leather, but Heller's stroking persisted. "Leather has natural wrinkles. Where are the creases?" he asked. At this point, the young woman placed one foot on a table and Heller invited his friends to touch. Real thing, they decided. Earlier, Heller had a long discussion with Dr. Alan Marlis, who's hard at work on a book which he says will reveal Abraham Lincoln was a witch. The evidence: Lincoln's warty face, his love for cats and for Shakespeare's *Macbeth*.

Joe told another reporter he was eager to try new things, maybe even Plato's Retreat, a trendy Manhattan sex club. But then he backtracked and said he'd have to overcome a lifetime of inhibitions to go to Plato's Retreat.

In *No Laughing Matter,* published in 1986, Joe said he "earnestly believe[d]" neither he nor Shirley wanted a divorce, despite their tensions. He claimed he was forced to file a divorce motion only because he needed a place to live following his illness. Such a motion was his only hope of securing the East Hampton residence. He swore he did not seek the divorce until June 3, 1982. However, on November 1, 1981, the *New York Times* quoted him as saying, "I eat only in restaurants these days except on the days when I'm taking cooking lessons, learning to poach eggs. Why? I'm living alone because I'm getting a divorce. First my mother cared for me, then the Army cared for me, then my wife cared for me. I don't know how to cook."

This declaration followed a hearing, on October 27, in the family

court of the state of New York, presided over by the Honorable Jack Turret, in which Shirley's lawyer, Norman M. Sheresky, accused Joe of "raping" the East Hampton house. Sheresky told the court, "[Heller] announced
[to his estranged wife] . . . any time whether you like it or not . . . I will be
coming around. I won't tell you when I am coming to remove whatever it
is that I want to. . . . [In short] he . . . raped that place."

The parties had gathered in court to agree on terms of a marital
separation. As he walked into the courtroom, Joe noticed "interpreters" in the lobby speaking Spanish, Yiddish, Chinese, "assisting people
[in trouble who were] unable to understand English and even, perhaps,
to afford attorneys." He wondered how the hell he and Shirley had
ended up here. Wasn't family court for small claims? What had happened? He suspected Shirley's lawyer was trying to jack them both for
as much money as he could get.

His lawyer, Jeffrey Cohen, said Joe had taken only two pieces of
furniture out of over one hundred from the East Hampton house.
"Rape," he said, was a "mischaracterization." He described Joe as "a
decent man, and a sensitive man who wants to approach this in a civi-
lized way." Cohen's client was prepared to write a "maintenance check"
of three thousand dollars to his wife, to tide her over for a month until
matters could be settled. The court scheduled another hearing for December 16.

But then on Sunday, December 13, Morty Bader, convinced Joe was
exhibiting symptoms of Guillain-Barré syndrome, drove him to Mount
Sinai Hospital, along with a neurologist, Dr. Walter Sencer, who concurred with the diagnosis. As the men helped Joe toward the hospital's
emergency entrance, his knee buckled and he nearly fell to the sidewalk.
At the admissions desk, he forked over his Blue Cross card. A nurse
asked for his clothing and valuables. Who should the hospital contact
in case of an emergency? "My wife," Joe said.

PATIENT HELLER "[e]xpressed concern over ability to return to normal
life and ability to perform activities of daily life without assistance," according to a medical resident's notes dated 12/17/81.

12/19/81: "Inordinately depressed."

12/21/81: "Complained of feeling need to leave ICU. Having feelings of inability to cope with illness. Discussed seeing a psychiatrist. Has become agitated, depressed."

12/22/81: "Patient tries not to look at clock in ICU."

12/31/81: "Experienced anxiety re: falling asleep and therefore stopping breathing, hence dying. . . . Has had bad dreams related to 'not breathing.' "

1/3/82: "147.12 pounds."

These notes contradict the blithe and cheerful demeanor Joe later reported exhibiting at the time, though he did admit in *No Laughing Matter* that fears of not breathing led to the worst experiences of his life, even more frightening than the mission over Avignon. At one point, Jeffrey Cohen, Joe's divorce lawyer, said he thought Joe was "going crazy" in the hospital.

On December 17, 1981, the *New York Post* got wind of Joe's illness. On its gossipy Page Six, the paper said that, after what was first reported as a "sudden attack of something called polyneuritis," Joseph Heller was partially paralyzed and in serious but stable condition. "Jesus Christ! How am I going to make a deal with a publisher when this gets out?" Joe complained to Speed Vogel. His dispute with Simon & Schuster had not been resolved.

Day by day, Joe could see his "respiratory parameters . . . deteriorating," he said. "I had only to watch the needle on the gauge and hear the numbers spoken by the nurse each time I filled my lungs to my maximum and emptied them . . . with all the force I could muster from a tube whose opposite end had been stopped up by a thumb." The nurses gave him this test every three hours. "In the beginning I faced [it] with an attitude of competitive excitement," he wrote. "[I]t was a spirit that carried me back in memory to those trifling games of skill in the penny arcades of Coney Island." But when the numbers slipped from the thirties to the low twenties, and then to the teens, he ceased being "combative." His capacity to breathe had diminished by more than half. Doctors continued to consider a tracheotomy. Joe wasn't sure what they were talking about, but he trusted them to do the right thing. "I was agreeing to have my throat cut," he realized later.

His kids were "absolutely shocked" to see him incapacitated: "They thought I was immortal and invulnerable and ageless." As it turned out, Joe's father-in-law, Barney, had also been admitted to Mount Sinai

JUST ONE **CATCH** / 371

Hospital with a heart condition. He had undergone surgery. Joe's kids had a grim time of it, visiting their father and grandfather. Joe was aware that his "wife was . . . on the premises almost every day."

Bob Towbin, whom the Hellers had befriended in East Hampton, says, "I went to Shirley and I said, 'Listen, Joe is in the hospital. He's really sick. You gotta go see him.' It was out of place for me to say that, really, but I felt I had to. She said, 'Why should I go see him?' I said, 'Shirley, don't ask me why. I'm not the one who was married to him for however many years. I'm just telling you. For one thing, I know he'd love to see you.' None of their friends knew what to do when they broke up. It upset me for Shirley and it upset me for Joe."

Dutifully, Erica told Joe that Shirley would like to visit him. "What was she going to say?" Joe pondered. "She's sorry I was sick?" Prideful, humiliated, angry, he wouldn't let his wife come near—a stubbornness he knew would have "deep-felt emotional cost to both" of them. In truth, he said later, "I missed my mother and my brother and my sister, and I missed my wife and my mother-in-law and my father-in-law. I wished that I still had a home and a family life to which to return, and I knew that the wish was hopeless." He had blown out of his life, and would not now, even under these circumstances, show the weakness implied by an inclination to look back.

In his King David novel, he had written—in the voice of the king—that his wife really did love him, but "in the only way she knew how, with acrimony, injury, envy, and disdain. . . . We [had] kissed goodbye."

One night, alone with Speed in the ICU, Joe confessed that, like his embittered patriarch, wanting to speak to a silent God, he had prayed once or twice since his medical ordeal had begun. The prayers were not about recovery, writing, or lawsuits. Speed asked what they were about. "Someday in this life," Joe said, "I would like to eat another baked lobster, like the one at the old New Sun."

SPEED WAS LIVING now in Joe's Eighth Avenue apartment, paying Joe's bills (his artist's skills came in handy whenever he had to forge Joe's name on a check), tending to his correspondence (occasionally faking an autograph to a fan), and answering phone messages. "[T]he décor happened to be exactly to my taste, since I was the one who had been commissioned to design it," Speed said. He also took advantage of the Eddie Bauer coats Joe had ordered, since Joe was not able to wear them. "I had more or less assumed his identity," Speed said.

One day, he discovered on the phone machine a message from Joe's North Carolina friend. She still occupied the apartment in Santa Fe and expected Joe to return. "Joe, why haven't I heard from you? You dead or something?" she said. Speed called and told her what had happened. He urged her not to come to New York, as a visit might only upset Joe.

Nevertheless, one or two people reported seeing the woman standing silently in the ICU, sizing up the situation and slipping away. They never saw or heard about her again.

Joe's breathing improved and he avoided a tracheotomy. He survived a bout of pneumonia in the lower lobe of his left lung. Perhaps the Angel of Death wouldn't visit after all. At moments, his bedside was almost cheerful, with the appearance of old friends, among them Joe Stein, Julius Green, Barbara Gelb, Murray Schisgal, Joe's nephew Paul, Jerry McQueen, and George Mandel ("What're you doing here again?" Joe snapped amiably at Mandel one morning).

Unexpectedly, Mel Brooks showed up one day. Joe had not known he was in town. "Tell me honestly," Brooks said, "did it begin with numbness or tingling in your feet and work its way up along the peripheral nerves of the spine and into your cranial nerves to affect your pharynx and face?" He had memorized the entry for Guillain-Barré syndrome in the medical dictionary he kept at home, fearing that even hearing about the disease might make him susceptible to it.

He "tongue-lashed the resident on duty . . . when he learned I was unable to sleep," Joe said. Brooks told the young man to forget Valium. "Give him tryptophan. It's mother's milk to him. You can get it in any health food store. I'll send up a bottle of tablets tomorrow. Pulverize them in the blender and put them down his Levin tube. Do I have to tell you people everything? And give him a clean Yankaur tube. That one's filthy. I don't like the color of those secretions."

On another occasion, Mario Puzo dropped by, despite his horror of hospitals. With him was his longtime companion, Carol Gino, a former nurse. Joe kidded her: She was like "a hooker returning to the brothel," he said. "[A]ll [you] want . . . to do is schmooze with the nurses about the hottest news in intensive care." He saw how solicitous she was of Puzo—Gino was his private nurse—as he stood by the wall, pale and

Joe in his study with Sweeney, early 1970s. *(Photo by Nancy Crampton)*

Joe with his beloved Sweeney, early 1970s. *(Photo by Jill Krementz)*

Joe in Manhattan, 1976. *(Photos by Hans Namuth)*

Joe leaving the Apthorp, 1976. *(Photo by Hans Namuth)*

Joe arriving at his studio on 57th Street, 1976. *(Photo by Hans Namuth)*

Joe doing physical therapy with Don Shaw in Joe's East Hampton pool, summer 1982. *(Photo by Michael Abramson; courtesy Getty images)*

Joe with Valerie Humphries, East Hampton, 1984. *(Photo by Nancy Crampton)*

Joe and Speed Vogel, East Hampton, 1984. *(Photo by Nancy Crampton)*

Joe and Speed Vogel on the occasion of the publication of *No Laughing Matter*, 1986. *(Photo by Susan Wood Richardson)*

Joe at the time of the publication of *God Knows*, 1984. *(Photo by Nancy Crampton)*

Joe in his East Hampton study, early 1990s. *(Photo by Susan Wood Richardson)*

Joe in New York, mid-1990s. *(Photo by Jonathan Barth)*

unsteady on his feet. He had been asking friends if Joe was going to "croak." "If I was in his spot," he confessed to Speed, "you'd have to shoot me." To Joe, he said, "I gotta come clean with you. It may be a sacrilege to say so, but I really believe you've come back from the dead."

At Joe's request, Joe Stein read the rough pages of the King David novel. Joe feared he'd have to submit the pages to a publisher for quick money. Through friends, he tried a rapprochement with Candida Donadio, who was terrified and deeply concerned to hear about his illness. Stein cheered Joe by reporting the pages were "simply marvelous. A pure joy."

On New Year's Eve, one of the ICU nurses offered to pour a little champagne into Joe's tube. He didn't feel like celebrating.

On January 4, 1982, doctors moved Joe to a private room in the hospital's Klingenstein Pavilion. He was both grateful to leave the ICU and fearful any change would precipitate disaster.

"It's not bad here," Julie Green said, looking around. "We could do worse." From the window, Joe had a view of Central Park and the West Side skyline. George Mandel said the room's coziness reminded him of the old social & athletic clubs in Coney Island. "Did I tell you guys how we always used to kick Joe's ass out of our clubhouse because he was still just a kid?" Mandel asked Green and Speed. The question provoked laughter from someone behind them. They turned and saw Valerie Humphries, one of the three private-duty nurses who had been hired, at $2,100 a week, to tend Joe as long as he stayed in the hospital. She was slim and tall, with reddish brown hair—she "looked like she could easily eat apples off my head," Speed said.

All of Joe's nurses were attentive and cheerful, but Valerie seemed to find Joe and his pals especially amusing. "My first view of Nurse Humphries [had been] from the rear," Speed recalled. "She was bending over her patient, adjusting the pillow under his head, and making funny noises. It sounded like cooing. When she stood, I realized she was simply giggling. She was also blushing. I don't know what Joe said to make her laugh, but I surmised that it was either a probing, personal question or a lascivious remark. Or both."

For her part, Valerie admitted she knew little about Joe's literary accomplishments, except he "looked like Norman Mailer."

One of Joe's friends brought him a transistor radio so he could listen to classical music on WQXR. His weight had been dropping and his

muscles atrophying, so the nurses tried to bulk him up on carbohy-
drates, running ice cream, cookies, and chocolate milk through a blender
for his nasogastric tube. He had gotten movement back in his arms and
hands, some dexterity back in his fingers, and he could grip a paperback book. He took pleasure in brushing his parched lips with moist-
ened toothbrushes. Speed was happy to see him develop a new form of
oral gratification; he knew Joe missed chewing soft orange Stim-
U-Dents. Earlier, when Joe was still in the ICU, Dustin Hoffman had
read about his illness in the *New York Times,* and he dropped by, bringing a Sony Walkman (a gadget Joe had never seen) and an electric
toothbrush, with which he proceeded to brush Joe's teeth.

The private room was so much nicer than intensive care. Joe's
friends hesitated to leave after a visit. They enjoyed joking with one
another, trying to lift Joe's spirits—and it pleased them how easy it was
to tickle Nurse Humphries. Joe's kids came by. In *No Laughing Matter,*
Speed said that Ted "would phone and ask who was around before he
would commit to a visit that day. If Joe indicated he was either alone or
with people his son didn't find funny, Ted's response was, 'Nah, I think
I may go to a movie instead. Maybe tomorrow. Let me know who
shows up . . . is Dustin coming again?'"

One night, as Joe's visitors—Speed, George Mandel, Julie Green,
and Joe Stein—shuffled out the door, they expressed regret for abandoning him. He wasn't buying it. He knew they were eager to head to
Chinatown. The Gourmet Club was now "just a bunch of old guys
stuffing themselves and talking about girls," said Stein's son, Harry, but
they still had a good time together. It wasn't the same without Joe,
though. The latest restaurants they'd found didn't stack up to the old
ones, and their favorite all-night fruit stand for after-dinner treats had
been torn down, some time back, to make way for the World Trade
Center. You couldn't count on anything.

JOE WAS ATTRACTED to all of his nurses. His gratefulness approached
love, in the way a psychiatric patient will sometimes transfer familial or
erotic affections to a therapist. He got along particularly well with Valerie. She laughed easily and liked food as much as he did. He asked
about her likes and dislikes, favorite movies, books, and singers. One day,
she told him she was a fan of the country music singer Kinky Friedman.

Joe had heard of Friedman from Speed, a live-music aficionado. He had friends in the music business and knew Mort Cooperman, owner of the Lone Star Café, who introduced him to Friedman. Years earlier, Speed told Joe the name of the singer's group, the Texas Jewboys. Joe wanted to use it in *Good as Gold*. "Great. How much will he pay me?" Friedman asked Speed. "That I can tell you right now. Not a fucking nickel," Speed said.

Joe asked Speed if he would take Valerie to hear the Jewboys. "I . . . thought [she] was a bit tall for me, but she was good-looking," Speed wrote. It took a while for him to grasp that Joe was flirting with Valerie indirectly. The date was a hit. Prompted by Speed, Friedman announced from the stage of the Lone Star Café, "Here comes my good friend Speed Vogel, and with him is Joseph Heller's beautiful nurse, Valerie Humphries." He dedicated a song to her, "Ol' Ben Lucas," whose lyrics ran, "Ol' Ben Lucas had a lot of mucus / Comin' right out of his nose." She spent the next morning entertaining Joe with details of the evening. She said the song reminded her of him.

Later, when Friedman came to visit, he saw Joe had "taken a turn for the nurse."

Her official reports on his progress—"NG feedings of large quantity," "black phlegm," "four steps forward," "knees buckled"—indicate he was happier in her presence than with his other caretakers.

1/8: "Patient is in good spirits."

1/21: "In good spirits (still)."

Covert love notes.

"I court[ed] her with all my might," Joe said. He asked her to stay until 6:00 P.M. each working day, and bumped her pay for the added time. "She hung around for an extra hour or so [after that] most days anyway," he said. One night, Joe asked Speed to take her to dinner at Elaine's. She was dazzled by Joe's pals. Mario Puzo was there that night; Woody Allen and Diane Keaton sat at a nearby table. "I'm so glad I met you!" Valerie exclaimed to Joe later. "Otherwise, I would never have known how good borscht is, and I wouldn't be eating so much of it!" The only downside to her new life was the number of short men accompanying her. "If there were just two more of us," George Mandel said to her one day in Joe's room, "you could be Snow White."

On January 26, 1982, Joe was transferred from Mount Sinai to the Rusk Institute. Valerie agreed to stay on as his private nurse as he began physical therapy. Her cheerful presence was crucial to him. At Rusk, he was surrounded by victims of car accidents, people born with physical handicaps or permanently disabled. The staff had no patience with him when he responded, "I can't" to a request to lift an arm or leg. They knew he *could,* with effort. One doctor told him, "I think you're the only one [here] with a chance to recover enough to live a normal life."

In the novel he'd been writing before he got sick, bathing was an erotic bond between the king and his consort, Bathsheba. Now, Valerie sponged Joe clean. "There were wisecracks and verbal games between Valerie and me . . . when she was . . . in the shower room with me, none of them compromising," he said. "I could not extend my hands far enough to reach my knees, let alone her. . . . Valerie brought a shower cap from home. . . . She shampooed my hair and combed it too, and did not seem to mind doing that."

Her "technique" for bringing him to his feet from bed to sit him in a wheelchair was "[s]exually suggestive," he wrote. "In this stand-and-pivot maneuver, we [began] with our arms around each other and her skirt hiked over her knees, and we [came] to rest belly-to-belly and cheek-to-cheek, with her legs parted and her skirt still up, and with our arms still around each other."

He was not yet to the point where he could whisper sweet nothings in her ear. A speech-pathology report, prepared by the Institute of Rehabilitation Medicine of the NYU Medical Center, dated February 5, 1982, reports that "Mr. Heller presents mild symptoms of dysarthria . . . characterized by a mild distortion of articulation and a slight weakness in voice production (i.e. reduced loudness and breathiness). . . . [M]ost prone to distortion are [sounds] associated with lip rounding (r, w, o). There is also a mild distortion of sibilants (s, z) which patient reports predates his present illness. . . . Range of motion of tongue retraction and protrusion are affected."

In the meantime, Joe was trying to put on weight (the tube was still in his nose). "When my swallowing ability came back, it came back as an instinct, whole," he said. A salami sandwich, provided by one of his doctors, struck Joe as "more beautiful . . . [than the] Sistine Chapel." His lawyer, Jeffrey Cohen, brought him bagels. Julius Green arrived with cupcakes and Häagen-Dazs ice cream. The Gourmet Club brought him leftovers from Chinatown. Valerie ate almost as much of the food as he did, and he took great pleasure in watching her.

Mel Brooks came for another visit. For several minutes, he hovered over Joe in his wheelchair. Then he raised an arm and shouted, "For Jesus! Stand! Walk!"

When Joe couldn't do it, Brooks shrugged. "I thought I'd give it a shot," he said.

Finally, on March 18, the doctors removed Joe's tube. It "looked filthy when . . . [they] extracted it simply by pulling it out and dropped it in the wastebasket," Joe said. Valerie spread a red-checkered tablecloth across his bed for a celebratory picnic. Joe's friend Bob Towbin brought champagne from "21." Towbin, a former English major at Dartmouth, was now a Wall Street investment banker—"[the] only virtue of finance capitalism of which I have ever heard," Joe said.

"All that was missing [at the picnic] was a Dubonnet umbrella," he mused. He and his guests looked calmly out the window at the East River and at helicopters landing on a nearby helipad. "Knowing Valerie's esteem for the artist Manet . . . I suggested she undress and eat with us naked," Joe said. "She blushed . . . and declined."

Later, when the others had left, Valerie got Joe showered and helped him with a carbon dioxide suppository. Joe recalled, "[S]he had an extremely delicate technique [with the suppository] which I [soon] made known to the other nurses . . . who were not so instinctively gifted as she was in this area."

THE NIGHT in early April when Jerry McQueen pulled the car onto the sidewalk at the Russian Tea Room's door followed two occasions Joe considered his first official dates with Valerie. He was still paying her to be his nurse, but on St. Patrick's Day, she helped him shower and dressed him in a sports shirt and a V-necked sweater, combed his hair, and rolled him in his wheelchair into the elevator. Downstairs, a party ensued with Irish dancers, singers, and fiddlers. Joe sat next to a former policeman who had been shot in the spine while trying to prevent a holdup. A bagpipe group from the New York Police Department arrived to serenade the young man. Joe was deeply moved. Afterward, Valerie rolled him back to his room, removed his clothes, and helped him into bed. He told her he didn't believe in kissing on the first date. She smiled and pecked him on the forehead.

Ten days after jettisoning his tube, Joe received approval from the hospital to spend a weekend in his Eighth Avenue apartment. Valerie accompanied him. The place felt unfamiliar—Speed had added furnishings, including a "custom-built queen-sized platform bed with eiderdown pillows and a . . . down quilt in a smart Swedish quilt cover," Joe said. He and Valerie ate a modest Thai meal at a restaurant nearby, joined by Stanley Cohen, a friend of Joe. After dinner, Cohen helped Valerie get Joe inside the apartment and stayed long enough to make sure he was comfortably settled. "Then Valerie and I were in the apartment alone," Joe said. "She knew me intimately. The inevitable question was in the air." Valerie seemed to have answered it: "She had brought a nightgown."

The day was approaching when he would be released from Rusk. Technically, he would no longer need a private nurse. The thought terrified him. He did not know where to go. The weekend in the apartment had convinced him the place was inadequate for a man with mobility problems. To make matters worse, Speed and Julie Green had discovered, while paying Joe's bills, that in leaving the Apthorp and summering out west, Joe had inadvertently let an insurance policy lapse that would have covered 80 percent of his medical bills in excess of ten thousand dollars. Now where would the money come from? Two days at Rusk cost him more than a month's worth of book royalties (royalties reached approximately $830, depending on the month). In February alone, Speed had written checks on Joe's behalf totaling $17,097.32. Joe was paying for five residences, none of which he occupied (the Apthorp, the Eighth Avenue apartment, the East Hampton house, the Santa Fe apartment, and a co-op in Greenwich Village where Ted lived). On his own, Speed talked Joe's Santa Fe landlord into letting him out of his lease. To ship Joe's clothes and books, Speed forged Joe's name on a fifty-dollar check to Joanne Wood. At Joe's request, George Mandel notified Candida Donadio that, because of mounting expenses, Joe would like to forgo her commission, in the event he was able to finish and she was able to sell his King David novel.

On May 1, he was fifty-nine years old. He feared going broke, living alone, convalescing in a veteran's hospital somewhere.

To cheer him up, Jerry McQueen drove him to Coney Island. Valerie went with them, along with a physical therapist named Mary Kay Fish. Joe couldn't gaze long at the high-rise apartment buildings standing where the old walk-ups he had lived in as a child once stood. The Steeplechase was gone. He enjoyed watching fishermen on the piers dropping lines with colorful bobs and sinkers to catch crabs. Most of the men were Hispanic, another sign of change. There were no Italians, no Hasidic Jews davening on the boardwalk. Joe thought of his childhood pal Lou Berkman, who had died not long ago of Hodgkin's disease. He thought of his brother's wife, Perle, and his sister's husband, Bernie. Beansy Winkler was still alive and kicking, but he had moved to California and Joe never saw him.

He returned to Manhattan exhausted. A happy but wistful day.

"THAT'S NOT A GOOD thing to have," Bob Gottlieb said when he heard Joe had been felled by Guillain-Barré. A good editor, he got right to the point.

At the end of May, he read 325 pages of Joe's King David novel. He pronounced himself delighted and made a six-figure offer on the book. This was lower than Joe had hoped, but welcome during his financial crisis (his S & S lawsuit had gone nowhere). He figured he could live on the money for two years, whether he completed the manuscript or not.

To Gottlieb, King David was an unlikely subject, but the extended monologue, from the retrospective point of view of an embittered, shattered man, resembled that of *Something Happened*, Gottlieb's favorite Heller book.

Also in May—on the twenty-eighth—Joe regained public visibility, exhibiting a bit of King David's rage. Through legal counsel, he responded to Shirley's lawyer's contention that "Mr. Heller's [need for] the East Hampton home is out-and-out bull." Since leaving the hospital, Joe had assumed he would pay Shirley's rent on the Apthorp apartment; in return, she would let him stay in East Hampton, at least for the summer.

Heroically, his friends tried to suit the Eighth Avenue apartment to his needs. Valerie placed glasses and milk and juice containers at shoulder level so he could reach them; she made sure his wooden transfer board—for getting out of a chair and into bed—was handy. Lee came for a while and whittled down chair legs. Still, after only a few days, Joe felt nervous. The space was too cramped and ill-equipped for a man in a wheelchair.

It came as a complete surprise that Shirley would block his request for the East Hampton house. In a letter to Jeffrey Cohen, Shirley's law-yer, Norman Sheresky, said, "It is fortunate . . . in view of the tragedy [Mr. Heller] has recently suffered that he is not 'poor' . . . and that he is not like the tens of thousands of other human beings recovering from serious illnesses who cannot have the luxuries that Mr. Heller can." He chastised Cohen for "parad[ing] Mr. Heller in front of me with nurses and wheelchairs when, believe me, I do not need those props to feel sorry for Mr. Heller and to regret deeply his physical suffering." He stated that Mr. Heller could afford another house and that he should grant Shirley the marital apartment *and* the East Hampton property. Sheresky concluded, "What did Joseph Heller do with the millions upon millions of dollars that he has earned?"

Seething in his Eighth Avenue apartment, Joe stared at a $15,000 bill from the Rusk Institute and the latest bill from Mount Sinai for $4,500. He called friends—Mario Puzo, Bob Towbin—to ask for loans. He reached for a glass of milk and could barely lift his arm.

Painfully, he scribbled a few lines of his King David novel: "[O]ur inner lives ordain for us . . . terrors of loneliness. . . . The problem with the loneliness I suffer is that the company of others has never been a cure for it."

ON JUNE 3, 1982, he filed for divorce from his wife of thirty-seven years, charging her "with mental cruelty and abandonment" for refusing him the house. The motion was accompanied by an affidavit from one of his doctors attesting to the severity of his illness, his debilitated condition, and his needs. Another affidavit, this one from a physical therapist, de-tailed how the East Hampton residence would be optimal for a pro-gram of physical therapy.

Joe's lawyer submitted these materials to the court, along with a four-page affirmation deploring the fact that legal action had been nec-essary to obtain the use of the East Hampton house, Joe's only wish.

"I was not sure I had a case," Joe said. "Financially, in fact, I would gain if I lost. There would not be a division of property without a di-vorce and it was close to a sure thing that the support payments I'd been making monthly were not going to be increased by much over what they had been for the two years we had now been separated."

Shirley's lawyer contested the motion. His opposing affidavit re-

ferred snidely to the "famous Joseph Heller." He insisted that "[a]ll of
Mr. Heller's and Mr. Cohen's dirty tricks and legal maneuverings are
not erased and they cannot be erased by Mr. Heller's illness." The sudden request for a divorce was "without rhyme or reason." The "request
[for] exclusive possession of a house . . . in Easthampton [*sic*] . . . simply
ignore[d] the whole history of this case which preceded the request." As
Mr. Heller was "worth several million dollars," he could afford "thousands of better facilities," and to grant him the house would give him
nothing but a "senseless 'win'" over Mr. Sheresky's client.

Justice Hortense W. Gable heard the case on June 10 in New York
State Supreme Court. Joe did not attend the hearing. Jeffrey Cohen re-
iterated, "[I]t's tragic that I have had to make this application [for di-
vorce], because we have been willing to talk about some way to rectify
this situation that would give Mr. Heller the therapy he so desperately
needs and use of that home he so desperately needs, your Honor."

The judge did not discuss the marriage. She concentrated on the
request for the house. She remarked, "What [Mr. Heller] is suffering
from isn't funny, this condition. . . . He does need help, and from the
little I know of it he certainly needs not only the physical therapy . . .
but perhaps some kind of cushioning to cope with what has happened
to him." She decided Joe would get exclusive use of the house for
"June, July, and August and up through September 15th . . . condi-
tioned upon his payment . . . of the sum of $7,500 to Mrs. Heller so
that she may, if she so desires, use [it] towards the payment of a summer rental."

"THIS IS THE HAPPIEST SUMMER of my life," Joe told Cheryl McCall
for a *People* magazine profile. "This whole ordeal has deepened my friendships with a lot of people because of the solicitude they've showed—
and the love. Just as I avoided thinking I'd ever be seriously ill, I shied
away from the word love. . . . I realize now that love does exist between
me and a large number of people, and I'm glad." He added, "I've been
lucky most of my life. . . . [I]n World War II I thought I was safe. . . . I
was lucky there. I may be lucky with this illness."

He had talked Speed and Valerie into staying with him in the house.
His financial records for June, July, and August show he paid Valerie
three hundred dollars a week (prior to that, she had averaged close to

seven hundred). She tended him as needed, and typed the new pages of his novel.

Speed helped him dress (light cotton shirts, shorts, tennis shoes), cut his hair, and did most of the cooking. Don Shaw, a young physical therapist, came three times a week. He'd pull up to the lawn on a big Harley-Davidson. He worked with Joe in the backyard swimming pool, helping him stand in shallow water from a sitting position, make bicycle-riding motions with his legs, and push off from the sides of the pool while Shaw applied pressure from behind. Shaw would grip a wooden rod and tell Joe to push against him as he maneuvered away, forcing Joe to switch his angle of attack. "Each time he told me to change the direction, I was stunned for a second and did not know how to comply," Joe recalled. "I could understand the words. I could not comprehend the instruction. I had to reason it through, recall how to do what was expected of me."

He approached these exercises with eagerness and discipline. Each walk to the mailbox and each nightly emptying of the dishwasher was a victory. Most of the time, he managed to rise from bed without the transfer board and to bathe himself with the aid of a shower bench. He had a constant fear of falling. Valerie and Speed hovered near him. Sometimes, while he chewed food, his neck cramped.

In the mornings, he sat in the sun by the pool in an antique wheel-chair Speed had bought him, and wrote on yellow legal pads. His hospital experiences were showing up in the novel. On his deathbed, the king suffers weight loss and bedsores. He dreads days alone.

That summer, "Joe was an entirely different social being," Speed wrote. "That he was extending himself for others (Valerie and me) was remarkable":

I remember years back when I needed help hauling a refrigerator up the stairs to my studio, Julie Green and George Mandel immediately volunteered. Heller wouldn't lift a finger, despite my pleading. Without him we managed to get the damn thing half-way up but no further. Finally, he came toward us and offered advice: "Why don't you hire someone to do this?" We just yelled obscenities at him until he said, "Okay, I'll help." [But] he just stood there doing nothing until we yelled at him to get out of the way. We completed the job in spite of him. Later, while we were eating and our anger was gone, I asked Joe how come he behaved so uncooperatively. Predictably, his answer had the ring of a line out of a novel: "I would not do for others what I would not do for myself."

Now, Joe told Cheryl McCall, "I'll be grateful to Speed . . . Valerie Humphries, and other friends for the rest of my life. There's nothing that Speed or Valerie can ask me that I'd deny them, ever. I owe them both more than I can possibly repay—so I won't even try."

The three of them ate out often at a trendy new place called the Laundry or at the Lobster Roll, a popular roadside restaurant in Montauk. They accepted a number of social invitations. One night, they went to pick up some homemade ice cream at a shop in Bridgehampton. There they ran into Bruce Jay Friedman, a longtime area resident. He told Joe he was happy to see him on his feet. He said, "You guys gotta come over for dinner sometime." Speed was stunned when, instead of his usual answer (something like "Why? I've got my own food at home"), Joe said, "When?"

All was not bliss. "Every now and then, there's a little spat between Valerie and Speed . . . [and I have to] patch it up," Joe told Cheryl McCall. Speed was not happy with Valerie's attempts to help with the cooking. It offended him that "she [was] the kind of person who [would] buy canned peaches when fresh peaches [were] in season and use garlic salt when fresh garlic [was] at hand." She liked to leave bread wrapped in plastic ("It gets moldy that way"). He preferred to wrap it in paper ("Then it [just] gets stale"). In general, Speed thought Valerie's tastes were rather crude. She was not much of a reader. She "seemed no more in awe of Joe as a man of letters than Nora was of [James] Joyce," Speed said. Joe was amused by this, but her attitude "affronted" Speed. She talked too much for him. "[W]e were . . . like [an] old married threesome," he wrote. He could not believe Joe's patience with her, or how much he tolerated her chatter. He "was now the most . . . considerate of men. Nothing like the man he used to be," Speed said. "He strove to gratify Valerie's every wish. . . . I had never seen anyone *a zoi fahliebed* ('so much in love')."

One day, during one of McCall's interview sessions, Joe, McCall, Valerie, and Speed picnicked on the sand with a basket of bread, a cooler of drinks, and champagne in a bucket. Joe remarked, "It's expensive to be sick and a luxury to recuperate. . . . You see my nurse and my therapist. . . . I mean, they both get paid."

This was true. Nevertheless, Valerie no longer thought of herself as Joe's nurse. His comment angered her and she walked off. Later, she and Joe argued. He suggested she take a vacation for "seven or nine days and decide if she wanted to come back." She left. Joe asked Speed if they could manage without her. He feared she wouldn't return. A few days later, she phoned to remind Joe not to go into the pool unless someone was watching him. A few days after that, she moved back in.

OVER THE FOURTH OF JULY WEEKEND, Arthur and Barbara Gelb stayed over. On Saturday morning, by the pool, Arthur introduced himself to Speed. He was amazed at Speed's generosity. Speed said his friend's ordeal had been a boon for him: He'd gotten to stay in Joe's apartment, wear Joe's clothes, and forge Joe's name on checks. He was living the celebrity life without being a celebrity. The previous spring, Joe had arranged for Speed to travel with Bob Towbin on his yacht, the *Sumurun,* a ninety-four-foot Fife ketch built in 1914, on Towbin's annual trip to the Cannes Film Festival. Life couldn't get any better than that. Here he was, living for free in East Hampton.

Gelb laughed. He said Speed should write about his experiences for the *New York Times.* Speed wasn't sure he was serious.

As the deputy managing editor of the *Times,* Gelb rarely said things he didn't mean. He had developed a reputation for "encourage[ing] [positive] pieces about [his] friends," *Newsweek* reported. ("You can't blame the people who run the *Times* for thinking the paper belongs to them," Bob Gottlieb said. "[B]ut those of us who have grown up with it secretly believe it's ours. The *Times* is in the same position as the Jews: it's expected to behave better than everybody else.")

Gelb had been at the paper a long time. He trusted his instincts. He had seen the consequences of a powerful man's biases; as a youngster, he was appalled by the *Times'* scant mentions of Jewish suffering during World War II, even after stories of Buchenwald and other camps had broken. Subsequently, Gelb learned from "Jewish reporters on the staff that Arthur Hays Sulzberger [the *Times'* then owner] had serious conflicts about his Jewish roots, believing that Judaism was a religion and not a national or ethnic identity. . . . [He] determined that the *Times* must never be viewed as a 'Jewish paper,' which he believed would undermine its image as an objective source of news."

Gelb guarded the paper's objectivity, but he understood, from Sulzberger's example, that no man can escape personal obsessions. Sometimes you had to ignore them, on other occasions indulge them; learning the difference was part of being a good newsman. If some of his friends—say, Joe Heller—benefited in the process, so be it.

Speed mentioned to Joe what Gelb had said about writing a piece.

"What are you worried about?" Joe said, delighted. "Do it!"

"Seriously, do you really think I can?"

"It's easy. Of course you can."

"I already have an idea," Speed said. "It's 'How to Beat the High Cost of Living in the Hamptons . . . All You Need Is a Sick Friend with a House.' "

Joe loved it. So did Arthur Gelb. "I think it should go in the 'Living Section,' " he told Speed. "Do a thousand to fifteen hundred words. How about a two-week deadline?"

Within days, Speed had drafted a few pages. After cutting Joe's hair one afternoon, he asked Joe to critique them. "I thought the piece was to be about the high cost of living in the Hamptons, not 'The Speed Vogel Story,' " Joe said.

Speed redrafted the article. Several days later, he took it to Arthur Gelb's office. Gelb read it at his desk while Speed pretended to study the photographs on his walls. Finally, Gelb said, "It's funny." He hadn't laughed. "Needs some editing. . . . Thanks. . . . We'll get back to you. . . . Regards to Joe."

Speed left the building, certain he'd wasted his time.

On July 28, Joe shoved the morning paper at him. There he was, in the "Living" section: "Helping a Convalescent Friend (in Style)."

Speed boasted that he'd never known rejection as a writer. Joe warned him not to expect the Pulitzer Prize.

A month later, LuAnn Walther, a junior editor at Bantam, who'd met Speed through a mutual friend, the playwright Israel Horovitz, said to him (either by phone or during a stroll on Fire Island—their memories clashed), "I read your *Times* piece and the *People* story on Joe. Why don't you think about writing a book about it all?"

"Yes, do it," Joe said.

In *No Laughing Matter,* Speed said that a couple of days after urging him on, Joe said, "I've been thinking about your book, and I would like to be the co-author if you don't mind. Is that okay?" The truth is, Candida Donadio advised Joe the advance would be much larger with his name attached to the proposal.

Speed told Mario Puzo and George Mandel he might write a book. "[D]on't begin before you have a signed contract and an advance," Puzo counseled him. "Mario's got it wrong," Mandel said. "You don't write a word until you've *spent* the advance. Why should anybody write when he's got money?"

AS AUTUMN APPROACHED and Joe's summer idyll neared an end, he studied his financial records. He was on track to have spent, for the year, almost $80,000 in hospital costs, with $10,000 more for physicians' fees and over $23,000 for nursing care; physical therapy added nearly $4,000 to the total. Because of his lapsed insurance policy, he bore most of this sum personally. Additionally, he owed $35,248 in legal and accounting fees; he supported Shirley, paying rent and utilities; he gave incidental money to his children; and, in what he considered a moral obligation, he sent $250 a month to his in-laws: a gesture of support, given Barney's recent medical problems. The Helds took the money, but Dottie would not speak to him. To friends and relatives, she disparaged Joe's "interest in other women" and said, "How could he just discard my darling daughter like an old hat after all the years she cared for him?"

Joe got by on monthly royalties, loans from friends, the anticipation of his advance for the King David book, and an unexpected windfall: a royalty check of $21,890.07 from a special hardcover reprint of *Catch-22* by Simon & Schuster, in celebration of the novel's twentieth anniversary.

He was legally obligated to leave the house by September 15. His lawyer urged him to consider new arrangements, but Joe didn't want to think about the future. In late August, he, Speed, and Valerie attended an outdoor feast at the Long Island home of the *Times* food columnist, Craig Claiborne. It was Claiborne's birthday and he was celebrating the publication of a new cookbook.

The Gelbs had introduced Joe to Claiborne. According to Arthur, "Craig developed a crush on Heller, who had eyes only for attractive women and who often crankily rebuffed new acquaintances of both sexes. To my surprise, he good-naturedly tolerated Craig's flirting. After enough margaritas and wine, Craig was apt to launch into a routine about his sex life, past and present. He told us once that as a boy in Mississippi he had experimented with various barnyard stock, including chickens. 'Tell me, Craig,' Heller asked with a typically devilish grin, 'is there much foreplay with a chicken?' "

On that August evening, a chill tinged the air. Leaves were turning. Joe tried not to dwell on any of this or consider what it augured. With relish, he cut into a plate of grilled Cajun catfish. A man he didn't know approached him, limping. He said his name was Mike Alexander. He was a friend of Speed. He wished Joe continued luck with his recovery, and said he had also battled Guillain-Barré syndrome.

"How long ago?" Joe asked.

"I had it twice," said Alexander. "The first time—"

Joe cut him off. "I don't want to talk about it now. Really, I don't, not at a party."

No more missions. Please.

JOE RETURNED his rented wheelchair and commode. "I could get up from a toilet but not from a sofa," he said. He took walks along the relatively car-free road in front of the house. "[A]s I saw my time of privileged residence running out, I could envision no better place for me to be for the rest of that year than the one in which I was."

At Joe's urging, Jeffrey Cohen made application to the court to extend the occupancy order from September 15 until December 31. Shirley had procured a new lawyer, Diane Blank, from the firm of Gordon & Schechtman. Blank said her client would grant Mr. Heller occupancy of the East Hampton house until the end of the year if he agreed to relinquish claims to the house after that and to pay her client $2,500 a month.

Shortly after this, Ms. Blank would accuse Joe in court of being an active participant "on the East Hampton party circuit." She said he had been observed "carrying bags of groceries." Therefore, he was fully recovered and no longer needed the house for recuperation. Cohen argued that until the divorce proceedings came to trial, the status quo should be preserved, with Mr. Heller in East Hampton and Mrs. Heller in the marital apartment. Eventually, the judge agreed (Joe had already exceeded the deadline to move).

Two days before Joe was to leave the house, he wrote a check for $160 to cover Shirley's visit to a psychiatrist named Roberta Jaeger. Shirley would see Dr. Jaeger a few times that fall. On one of these occasions, Joe agreed to go with her, apparently at the doctor's request. He went to provide information to the doctor so she could treat Shirley more effectively. At least this was Joe's understanding at the time.

On October 2—while the court was still considering the occupancy issue—Speed went to his studio apartment in Manhattan for messages and mail. "One of the messages was from Jeffrey Cohen," he said. "[H]e explained that he had heard from Joe that his wife had unexpectedly shown up at the house in East Hampton. . . . Joe was, for the moment, alone in the house and frightened."

Speed rushed back to Skimhampton Road. By the time he got there, Valerie had arrived. "Joe was still upset, but he was trying to calm down," Speed wrote. "Valerie had been taking a riding lesson [at a nearby stable] and Joe was in his study, lying on the couch, going over some pages he had just written, when he heard someone at the door. He naturally thought it was Valerie and was astounded when he saw his wife. It must have been an awful moment and I felt sorry for them both. Joe and [Shirley] had not been on speaking terms. All I knew was that now she was in the guest cottage with her long-time housekeeper, Viola. [Joe] had no idea how long they intended to stay."

Speed talked Joe, Valerie, and a friend, Trudi Stretton, into going shopping with him. They bought a "good supply of shrimp, lobsters, pork, garlic, scallions, and ginger, as well as some vodka, gin, scotch, and appropriate wines." As therapy, Joe helped take the groceries into the house (presumably, this is the moment he was "observed" carrying bags).

Joe made martinis. Speed prepared lobster, rice, and Chinese barbecued shrimp. Viola, Joe's old housekeeper, loved his barbecued shrimp. "I could not conceive of a diplomatic way to invite her over [from the guesthouse]," Speed wrote.

"After dinner," he said, "Joe told me he'd been married exactly thirty-seven years [today]. This was his wedding anniversary. After everything that [had] happened . . . it was a bizarre announcement and we all fell silent for a moment, each with our private thoughts. None of us knew what to do until Trudi smiled and said, 'Open some champagne! Any anniversary, even this one, should be celebrated!' "

The following morning, Speed said, the guest house "seemed vacant."

"*CATCH-22* may have been the beginning of the end of the marriage of Joseph and Shirley Heller—but Mario (*Godfather*) Puzo didn't help matters any. So says Shirley in an affidavit filed in New York State Supreme Court, regarding the break-up of her 36-year [*sic*] marriage," wrote Susan Mulcahy in her syndicated gossip column, "Celebrity Corner," on March 12, 1983:

> The Hellers are about to give depositions and the divorce trial is expected to start in April. Shirley, who states that the phenomenal success of *Catch-22* started the "ruination of our marriage," also states that her husband shared a studio with "Mario Puzo, the famous writer, and unfortunately, the equally famous bon vivant and womanizer. After that, Joseph Heller was never the same." Joseph . . . scoffs at his estranged mate's charge: "Anybody with good vision and good sense cannot with a straight face describe Mr. Puzo as a bon vivant or womanizer, and he has never shared a studio with me."

On this last point, Joe was correct. As for "bon vivant," perhaps it was in the eye of the beholder. Puzo was a regular at Elaine's, the Cannes Film Festival, and the gaming tables in Monte Carlo. After his wife died, he maintained a long-term relationship with Carol Gino.

Mulcahy's column concluded: "In the court papers, Shirley says she is 'destitute' and asks for half of Heller's earnings, which she estimates as at least one million dollars. He calls her assessment of his financial situation 'fantasy.' "

Liz Smith's syndicated column said Shirley sought half the earnings from *Catch-22, Something Happened,* and *Good as Gold,* as well as moneys from "two unpublished novels"—"[o]ne of [which] . . . was not just unpublished but unwritten," Joe said.

For the next year and half, the battle got nastier. Shirley hired yet another lawyer, this one a minor celebrity in his own right, dubbed by newspapers the "Sultan of Splitsville": Raoul Lionel Felder, in his late forties, bearded, soft-spoken, the son of a poor Jewish immigrant from Brooklyn. He charged $450 an hour. He had represented Mrs. Martin Scorsese, Mrs. Carl Sagan, and Mrs. Frank Gifford, among others. The *Washington Post* once quoted him as saying, "A woman is like a Stradivarius violin. The humidity has to be right to play it. Otherwise, they'll throw in the towel." The *Post* said Felder's ability to "pluck" this "particular instrument, the grief-stricken wife" was unmatched among New York's high-profile lawyers.

Felder introduced himself to Joe by letter. He said he regretted Joe had not found "contentment and/or quietude of spirit."

On February 7, 1983, according to Joe's notes on the case, Felder declared publicly that Joe's illness was "ancient history"; he was "a highly visible figure on the party circuit [who] drives a car," and he was a "multimillionaire who can finance wearying and debilitating litigation."

In early March, during a bitter cold snap in Manhattan, William Binderman, another of Shirley's lawyers, deposed Joe in a small conference room in the legal firm's office. The deposition's sole purpose was the disclosure of financial information, and it dragged on for nearly two weeks, several hours each day. Shirley's legal team accused Joe of withholding financial documents. Joe told them to ask Shirley—most of what they wanted (tax returns, check stubs) was still in the Apthorp. One day, Binderman asked Joe where certain papers were. Joe pointed at him. "You're holding them in your hands!" he said. "You got them from the 'marital apartment'!"

Cohen and his team said the deposition resembled a "grand jury hearing [rather] than a disclosure proceeding." The time it took was completely "unreasonable"; Cohen charged Shirley's lawyers of stalling to pad their bills and deplete the "marital estate." (Joe declared that "not in [thirty-seven] years of marriage had I done anything as damaging to the aspirations of my wife as had been done to her by her attorneys.")

Cohen urged Supreme Court justice Marvin Evans to start the trial. A Miss Delbaum, representing Shirley's legal team, countered, "Mr. Heller is now saying . . . Let's go to trial. . . . Your Honor, this is not World War II. It's a simple matrimonial case."

During this period, Joe filled a notebook with observations of his medical progress: "Trouble with the letter 'l.'" "Trouble with 'w' and 'oo.' " "Bob Towbin commented that [the] right side [of my] upper lip seems immobile. . . . I still cannot suck in my cheeks and puff them out, although I am making a start." "Speed and Erica both commented on a habit they noticed of passing my finger to the side of my face. . . . [It is] not a habit, but a conscious means of cleaning food from between my teeth and cheek at the rear of my mouth."

It was his mental health that had become an issue in the divorce case. Back in September 1982, Dr. Roberta Jaeger, Shirley's psychiatrist, released a statement to the court that said Shirley "was eager to do whatever she could to save the marriage. . . . [T]hough she worked with unfailing determination toward that result, her efforts were futile. They were, in fact, doomed":

> They were doomed because of Joseph Heller's need to attribute all of his (chronic) unhappiness and personal lacks to his wife. If she was strong and supportive he resented her because she "made me feel inadequate." If she withdrew or was quiet, then he insisted that she needed him too much. It rapidly became apparent that Mr. Heller, who I had occasion to meet with in my office, could not be pleased by his wife. Indeed, he appeared intent on maintaining an imaginary picture of her which reality did not affect. During the meeting referred to above, Mr. Heller remarked, "I'm a celebrity. I'm rich. I'm famous. So how come I'm not happy?" This unprovoked rage toward Mrs. Heller was striking, even to him. It was, therefore, not surprising that he left the marital home after "attempts" to get along which were of an ilk worthy of a trash novel.

Dr. Jaeger accused Joe of depending on friends loyal to him because he was famous, and of using his illness to manipulate people, as well as to salve his guilty conscience: "Since I saw Mr. Heller as a man who was simultaneously dependent and enraged over that very need of his, his unfortunate illness appeared to be one affliction which would be extremely difficult to bear. . . . Mr. Heller seemed to be getting taken care of in a way he could tolerate (perhaps the only way)—by professional medical and nursing personnel."

Joe was outraged that the doctor would discuss his visit to her office. He had not been a patient of hers. (To make matters worse, he learned she had once been a physician resident where his father had died.) Naïvely, he had assumed his talk with her would remain confidential; he doubted he said the things she attributed to him, or if he did, he had done so in a context her account did not clarify: "The confession is not . . . [the] kind I would make," he said, "[especially] to a psychiatrist upon whom I was making a courtesy call."

Furthermore, he objected to her characterization of his attitude toward his children: "cavalier," she'd said. In a notebook, he scribbled, "[This was a] spectacular insight that even the psychiatrist I'd [seen] regularly . . . could have missed forever. But he, of course, unlike Dr. Jaeger, had the disadvantage of knowing me."

Jeffrey Cohen warned Joe to prepare for the worst. Things would deteriorate from here. Indeed they did: At one point, to establish background, Erica was forced to testify against her father.

Then, on July 19, William Binderman accused Joe of writing the "*Mein Kampf* of matrimonial warfare." He turned to Joe, who was on the witness stand, and said, "Are these the words of Joseph Heller, 'I want a divorce, I need a divorce, I crave a divorce, I pray for divorce, all my life I have wanted a divorce, even before I was married'? . . . You wrote these words in *Good as Gold,* didn't you, Mr. Heller?"

"No," Joe said.

Binderman had been quoting from *Something Happened.*

"And that was just about it for his foundation for my *Mein Kampf,*" Joe wrote in *No Laughing Matter* (besides which, the judge had stated, "If we were to say every author is guilty [of] all the sins of which he writes, Shakespeare would have been hung for murder fifteen times over in his earlier days and for rape and several other things. . . . [T]here is no adequate relationship between what may be written in a book and the actual action of the author outside of the book").

In his account of the court proceedings, Joe gloated over his cleverness in exchanges with Shirley's lawyers without addressing or mitigating the behaviors in question. Like Bob Slocum, he took perverse pleasure in winning each argument despite mounting emotional damage.

The clearest example of win at any cost occurred on October 19, 1983, shortly after the Hellers' thirty-eighth wedding anniversary. Once again, Joe took the witness stand. Binderman referenced the deposition Joe had given back in March: Under oath, he said he had never written a check to a woman named Joanne Wood. Convinced he had caught Joe commiting perjury, Binderman asked the court, rhetorically, "Is this man a liar or does he believe in the oath?"

He produced a photocopy of one of Joe's checkbooks. In it was a clear entry of a check for fifty dollars made out to J. A. Wood. He showed Joe the check. "Do you know what an oath is, Mr. Heller?" he asked.

The court transcript reads:

> A: I—
> Q: Do you recognize it, Mr. Heller?
> A: Do I recognize it as what?
> Q: Do you recognize this as being a check journal or check stubs for the checking account of the period indicated on the face of that document?
> A: I am trying to find a date. . . . Well . . . I recognize that as being from my book. I don't see my handwriting on it.
> Q: Is that the entry, J. A. Wood?
> A: Yes.

Joe kept denying he had written a check to J. A. Wood. Binderman was flabbergasted. But Joe was telling the truth. Speed had forged Joe's name on this particular check. When Binderman learned what had happened, he said it made no difference. The larger point remained: evidence of Joe's infidelity. Jeffrey Cohen counterpunched: "[Y]ou are trying to show credibility and you are asking . . . if he drew a check to J. A. Wood and he said he did not and there is a check registered in somebody else's handwriting."

"In *his* account!" Binderman protested.

"That was not the question," said Cohen.

The judge agreed. He sustained Cohen's objection. The absurd and irrefutable logic was worthy of *Catch-22*. "That is the way it is in life," said the judge.

IN THE FIRST WEEK of April 1984, the Hellers' long marriage was officially dissolved. Shirley was granted the divorce (she had countersued Joe). The terms of the settlement remained unclear. How much was Joe worth? The "value of copyrights [is] so amorphous," Liz Smith reported.

Shirley and Joe agreed to arbitration, to be conducted by an attorney and family friend named Sidney Elliott Cohn, the "most persuasive person I [have] ever met," Joe said. "If he did his work well, as I expected he would, I was sure that all sides would be at least a little disgruntled, and of course I was right."

As he anticipated, in the end his monthly support payments to Shirley amounted to roughly what he had been paying anyway. The cadre of lawyers on both sides made out well, amassing over $300,000 in aggregate. Shirley would remain in the Apthorp apartment, while Joe was granted exclusive occupancy of the East Hampton house. He would live there for the rest of his life.

Shirley's devoted friend Dolores Karl summed up what had happened: "Joe's public life was not good for him. My husband, Fred, used to tell him, 'Joe, cut out the celebrity stuff and do more work.' It did change Joe. There's no question about that, and it was his celebrity life that ended the marriage. Women . . . well, Shirley put up with it for a long time. It finally got to be too much for her and reached a breaking point."

Shirley's cousin, Audrey Chestney, said, "Joe went Hollywood in his own inane way. . . . [H]e was impatient and engrossed in his work, as all writers are, I guess. He was a controlling presence; he prevented Shirley from having the connection with her family she once had. That wasn't good for her."

Bob Towbin takes a broader view. "Shirley was very important to Joe," he says. "If Joe did one stupid thing in his life, it was when he split up with Shirley. But it wasn't just his fault. Shirley was pretty stupid about it, too"—when, for example, she opposed his move into the East Hampton house. "You know, they had typical fights between older husbands and wives," Towbin says. "I mean, you'd have separations, you know, fucking around, but when they really broke up . . . everyone who knew them was devastated."

Barbara Gelb agrees, adding, "Joe was very shaken by his divorce. He was a terrible philanderer, but he never wanted his marriage to end. He would never have left Shirley. He loved his wife. And she was never happy after he left. She was a sweet, nice woman, but a little bit helpless, with no career of her own. She kind of collapsed after he left."

At first, Shirley tried to put the best face on things. "Right after she was divorced from Joe, she came down to Florida to visit her mother,"

Chestney says. "I was living in Florida then, too. One day we went to the races, out at the track. We looked down the list of names and saw a horse called Time to Make a Change. We were hysterical with laughter. We bet on it and won." That day, Shirley must have recalled late afternoons watching the horses at Santa Anita with Joe, in the earliest weeks of their marriage.

As for Joe, settling into the East Hampton house, he mused on the emergence of what Mario Puzo had called his wild man during the explosive year of 1981. "I was alone for the first time in my life, rather nervous, hypochondriacal and desperately unhappy, though very active sexually," he told a London newspaper reporter. To his friend Cheryl McCall, he said, "I had been very unsettled and confused since the dissolution of my marriage. . . . I had no idea where I wanted to go or what I wanted to do . . . [I had] lots of choices. Guillain-Barré pinned me down, removed the choices"—just as World War II had done, when he graduated from high school—"and gave a strong organization to my life."

Before that, in truth, "I was a stranger to myself," he said.

He was now sixty-one years old. According to Barbara Gelb, he had one or two "girlfriends" during this period, but for the most part, he had begun a new, loving relationship with Valerie Humphries. ("The chemistry was plain dumb luck, I guess," he said. "Without [her], I would probably have been depressed for years.") He had recovered from his illness, though he still endured muscle weakness. He slurred some words and drooled a little at mealtimes. Apparently, he would not again be quite the vigorous man he once had been. This was not the end—far from it—but this phase of life had a penultimate feel to it.

By now, from close rereading and therapy sessions, Joe was aware of the patterns in his novels. In the penultimate chapters, someone crucial always died so the protagonist could survive: a comrade, a child, a brother.

Borrowing a page from Shirley's psychiatrist, or examining Joe's life the way a critic might read his work, we could say he had sacrificed his marriage in an attempt to shed unhappiness and move ahead: an act so awesome—in the oldest, truest sense of the word—he could not face what he had done, and so had slain himself. The man who emerged from the hospital was not the one who had gone in.

By nature, literary patterns are artificial. They can help illuminate life's sloppiness, dangers, and arbitrary byways but cannot ultimately account for them. Still, this was a time of life Joe approached with as much trepidation as relief. Artificial or not, the pattern had a strong pull on his imagination. Hence, perhaps, the repetition in his books: a desire to circle back, to hold the narative still. Joe would one day write in his memoir, "There is a reluctance to proceed," a sentiment applicable now as he contemplated his remaining years.

17. Go Figure

ONE NIGHT, during the second week of his stay in Mount Sinai's intensive care unit, Joe fell asleep under the influence of Benadryl. When he awoke, startled, he had "none of the customary feelings that tell us we have been asleep." Momentarily, he was disoriented, to the point of disembodiment. Nurses gave him a second dose of Benadryl. He slept and woke again later, he said, "without realizing I'd been gone." Eight or ten doctors and nurses huddled at the foot of his bed, discussing his condition "in voices raised to normal level," Joe recalled. "I was aghast: Why had I not had an inkling this was going on? And after that initial . . . moment of incomprehension and confusion, I felt humiliated and exposed, mocked, pathetic, vulnerable, and indignant. I was almost overcome by a powerful impulse to mourn."

It was not just the weakness, the pain of lying helplessly while others weighed his fate, that saddened him, but an even eerier sense of having passed on, of witnessing the immediate aftermath of his death. It was as though he had the long view: his whole life, condensed, and now the afterlife, beginning modestly, almost imperceptibly—hushed, dim, still.

A stark counterpoint to this experience occurred a couple of weeks later. In his private room, with nothing else to do for extended periods but watch television, he was "dismayed to discover that there is not even ten minutes' worth of authentic . . . news to be reported every twenty-four hours, and a good portion of that has to do with fires, record colds and snowfalls, gruesome homicides, and plane crashes that could have been excerpted from the newscasts of the week before."

The long view and the imperceptions of impatience; ignorance of what is before us and inability to see past substanceless shapes: These conditions—their paradoxes, ironies, absurdities, and tragic consequences—had been Joe's themes all along, but now, as he edited the final draft of his King David novel, the contrasts between longevity and shortsightedness, the tunnel of history and the boxy maze of the everyday, were visceral, sharp, almost as pungent as during his bombing missions.

They're not trying to kill *you;* they're trying to kill everybody.

What difference does that make?

There it was: the long view versus the short. And the hell of it was, the short view was nearly always celebrated as received wisdom. Nothing had changed over time. Received wisdom was the problem. By establishing it as the primary target of satire in the King David novel, Joe (granted, for now, a beyond-death perspective) hoped to better animate his perennial themes.

Through received wisdom, every generation learns that courage and purity of heart can overcome daunting odds—for example, David and Goliath. On that score, Joe's David proclaims, "If I'd known in my youth how I'd feel in old age, I think I might have given . . . Goliath a very wide berth that day, instead of killing the big bastard and embarking so airily on the high road to success that has carried me in the end to this low state of mind."

Obviously, Joe was not content to hurl javelins *straight* at the West's shibboleths. Maybe bravery *does* overcome long odds. But what the accepted knowledge doesn't tell us is how to cope with the emptiness that visits us once the odds are beaten and euphoria drifts away.

Nothing fails like success.

In his kvetching about the hollowness of grand achievement, it was hard not to hear, from Joe's elderly king, the ruefulness of the author of *Catch-22,* gazing back at his youthful exuberance . . . his reevaluation of what the real odds were, and what was worth beating.

GOD KNOWS was published with great anticipation on October 8, 1984. The print run was 150,000 copies. The advances from European publishers were ten times higher than Joe had ever gotten—Finland coughed up thirty thousand dollars. Dell snatched the paperback rights. The Book-of-the-Month Club planned to showcase the novel. Almost immediately, Joe could count on earning close to $500,000. Medically, he had overcome daunting odds (he made great newspaper copy). He was back with his old editor, Bob Gottlieb—the unbeatable team.

Shortly before the book appeared, Art Cooper, the big, garrulous new editor of *GQ*, had run an excerpt of *God Knows* in the magazine. "I had decided to put Joe on the cover . . . the first time a writer had been on the cover, and I was a little concerned," he recalled. "But Joe, who always reminded me that he was a handsomer version of Paul Newman, persuaded me that it would be a good idea. I did [it], and a couple years later I put Paul Newman on the cover. . . . [A]s always, Joe was right. [He] sold 150,000 more copies on the newsstand."

The *God Knows* book party, held at the Russian Tea Room, was a festive and moving affair, with survivors of Guillain-Barré syndrome whom Joe had met during his illness on hand to celebrate more than the launch of a novel. Speed, Valerie, and Joe toasted with flutes of champagne.

"Like cunnilingus, tending sheep is dark and lonely work," Joe's David says.

"Some Promised Land," he gripes. "To people in California, God gives a magnificent coastline, a movie industry, and Beverly Hills. To us He gives sand. To Cannes He gives a plush film festival. We get the PLO."

These lines were quoted as evidence of the novel's immature humor in the largely hostile reviews that appeared in the next few weeks. Reviewers compared the novel unfavorably to Mel Brooks's comic monologue "The 2,000-Year-Old Man" and decried the trouncing of biblical tradition. "Apparently written on the principle that shockingly bad taste is automatically funny, *God Knows* deliberately exploits Samuel 1 and 2 in the worst possible taste," said *Library Journal.* Christopher Lehmann-Haupt, writing in the *New York Times,* called the novel "very tired" and "shallow," while Richard Cohen, in the *Washington Post Book World,* found it "repetitious, often annoying . . . [and] at odds with itself." *Time* dismissed it as a "disappointing hodgepodge of repetition and irrelevancy" (a "slap in the face," Joe said of that review).

Most vitriolic was Leon Wieseltier's attack in *The New Republic*:

God Knows is junk. It is also a best seller. Thus historians will have employment. They will have the difficult task of explaining how it was that the arrested adolescence of a few Jewish men [i.e., Saul Bellow, Philip Roth, Bernard Malamud, and Joseph Heller] became the cherished currency of an entire chapter of American culture.

   God, and David, and the psalms, and all the strange and sublime things that Joseph Heller has . . . trivialized . . . have anyway survived worse.

The claw swipe at other Jewish novelists was telling: Wieseltier was not commenting on Joe's literary intentions, his success or failure on aesthetic grounds. Rather, he was morally offended by the nature of the project, the way earlier critics had fussed over Philip Roth's "defacing" of Jewish values in *Portnoy's Complaint* or Saul Bellow's depictions of indecorous Jewish behavior in *Herzog*. There was, in this criticism, an implicit charge of anti-Semitism, a concern that if we turn on ourselves, we give goyim the go-ahead to rush us full force.

   "Look, I've adjusted to this, that my books are not going to get unanimously good reviews. Though with this one I had the expectation," Joe said. "But all of my books deal in very rough, rude fashion with subjects about which there are great conflicts of opinion. And the average reader expects to be told in a few pages what the book is about, expecting the character to be fairly consistent in his personality."

   One of the few major reviewers to consider the book on its own terms was Mordecai Richler, writing in the *New York Times Book Review*:

The abundantly talented Joseph Heller has never accepted limits; neither has he repeated himself. He has yet to try to slip by with a "Catch-23" or a "Something Else Happened." Instead, each time out, he has begun afresh, discovering human folly for the first time: himself amazed, irreverent and charged with appetite. It couldn't have always been easy. The incredible success of his first novel . . . must, by this time . . . be maddening to him. . . . [I]f you are going to hit .400, don't be so reckless as to do it in your rookie season.

Following the uneven *Good as Gold,* Richler wrote, "Mr. Heller is dancing at the top of his form again." With *God Knows,* the "Jewish novel in America, which began by describing the immigrant experience and then sailed into the mainstream to excoriate Jewish mothers and deal with the ironies of assimilation, has . . . escalated to the highest rung of insolence, even [deliberate] sacrilege, addressing itself directly to God." Like "all [of] his work," this new novel was "informed by an uncommon generosity of spirit," Richler said. "He doesn't so much tell a story as peel it like an onion—returning to the same event again and again, only to strip a layer of meaning from it, saving the last skin for the moving [finale]." Readers, he said, were "unlikely . . . [to] see a more ambitious or enjoyable novel about God and man this season."

AS IN EACH OF JOE'S NOVELS, the conflicts in *God Knows* stem from a struggle between fathers and sons. In Joe's previous book, says David Seed, Bruce Gold "becomes the head of a family which is constantly denying its own structure"—a circumstance that vexes all of Joe's heroes. Yossarian's military superiors deny they are a threat to his life; Slocum denies the effects of his aloofness on his children; Gold's father denies the present, while the family's conversations ignore the group's warped dynamics.

King David also misses family stability. He yearns for a caring father, but each figure that might suffice—Jesse, Saul, God—disappoints him. Saul, especially, confounds David, hugging him to his breast, only to shove him away in jealous rage (it is easy to see Joe's brother in Saul's behavior: A father substitute for Joe, as Saul was to David, Lee vacillated between pride and envy as Joe went to college and achieved monumental success).

God retreats into silence. *David* must become the father, the responsible one, a development for which he is poorly prepared. Like Slocum, he overidentifies with his favorite son ("O my son Absalom! . . . Would God I had died for thee") and longs for childhood's pleasures. Guilt-ridden, he yearns to destroy himself, mentally hurling a javelin at his youthful face. In the end, under pressure from his estranged wife, David denies his family's structure. He appoints his youngest son, Solomon, his successor instead of Adonijah, his eldest surviving boy.

Joe presents David as an underappreciated author. He claims to have written most of the Western world's masterpieces; Shakespeare and Beethoven stole his best ideas, he says. He is a man devoted to, and fleeing, women: "I was always faithful to my wives and concubines." A relentless self-promoter, David reels off a monologue as slick as an ad-man's brochure.

Joe's favorite narrative method—the retrospective elegy—is firmly established here. On his deathbed, David considers his life's events, looking for the moment that made him the bitter husk he is. His accomplishments strike him as hollow; he is as politically successful, and corrupt, as Henry Kissinger in *Good as Gold*. He regrets the mess he has made of his marriage to Bathsheba. His children have foundered in various attempts to match his deeds.

His attendants have "perfumed [his] bed with aloes, cinnamon, and myrrh," but "I can still smell me," he says. "I stink of mortality and reek of mankind." We meet David as we met Yossarian: in bed, doted on by nurses. But Yossarian is bursting with life. David is riddled with death. No wound, like Snowden's, is necessary for the smell of his guts to come spilling into the open. He is rotting from the inside out.

Joe's use of biblical material energizes the retrospective view. David's story is both a look back, exploring the patterns of a life lived in full, and a prophecy, as the reader, familiar with biblical tales, knows what's coming. The import of David's actions for Western civilization is clear to us. As a key figure in Judaism and Christianity—two sides of a family that often deny *their* structural affinities—David is an all-encompassing father. His past remains our future. (On a personal level, Joe was aware of writing prophecy: David's predicament, he said, predicted his illness.)

The novel's structure demands a Socratic reevaluation of Judeo-Christian values. It does so by presenting *narrative* as *denial,* an elaborate cover-up justifying David's actions. For example, David claims he would do anything to save his children's lives, but, in fact, his adulterous behavior leads to the death of his infant, while his desire to hold power results in Absalom's slaughter. In the first instance, David blames God; in the second, his general Joab. "David, it's enough already," Joab tells him as David weeps for Absalom. "You're making a spectacle of yourself." But that's the point. The spectacle, the elaborate design, the boasts and drama of the narrative, hide David's complicity. As Joe depicts him, David is the West's first master of spin.

Traditional narratives often reveal private motivations behind public careers. For instance, "Shakespeare's method . . . [is] to show that what one is as a man determines what one is as king. In the plays of the Henry IV–Henry V cycle, Shakespeare chronicles ideal kingship, dramatizing that Hal succeeds as king precisely because he has previously succeeded as man," wrote David M. Craig. "Heller's method is exactly the opposite. Beginning with the record of kingship that the Bible supplies, he imagines what the man must be like who had done such deeds."

That the king archetype enabled Joe to create his most fully formed character is an irony rooted in Joe's wide reading. To begin with, he understood the difference between the Greeks' and the Hebrews' notions of character (two traditions that, not always easily, combine to form the heart of Western culture).

As Judith Ruderman says, "[I]t is the capacity for change, exhibited by biblical figures who are treated at length, that reveals the modernity of the ancient Jewish conception of character. As the writers and redactors of the Bible saw them, people were unpredictable—veritable centers of surprise." By contrast, characters in Greek drama and poetry are "labeled with Homeric epithets, fixed tags by which they are [consistently] identifiable." How is it, Joe wondered, that, during the course of Western history, Jewish characters in the Bible have come to be simplified (as heroes and villains) in the fixed manner of the Greeks? Go figure.

If, in his earlier novels, Joe's conceptions of character were largely fixed (Yossarian, heroic in his innocence; Slocum, paralyzed by the *something* that happened to him; Gold, emblematically Jewish in Protestant society), in *God Knows*, he rejected centuries of simplistic biblical commentary. He embraced the old Hebrew view of the self, presenting a flawed and fully human King David. Sacrilegious on the surface, perhaps, the project was consistent with—and respectful of—the tradition from which biblical stories sprang.

At one point in the novel, Samuel insists it was Saul's destiny to die in battle. David snaps, "That's bullshit, Samuel. . . . We're Jews, not Greeks. Tell us another flood is coming and we'll learn how to live under water." Far from traducing his Jewish heritage, Joe was engaging it more seriously than ever.

He often claimed he was not interested, one way or the other, in the existence of God: It is when an individual *turns away* from conceptions of the holy that the self, in its humble complexity, aware of its hungers and faults, starts to emerge. This point is illuminated by the retrospective view: An individual's actions are not as important as what the individual makes of them. Meanings and patterns belong to reflection and reconsideration. David's self-assessments contain both psychological and theological ramifications: On the one hand, we get a character study; on the other, a reexamination of Western culture's ethical, political, and spiritual foundations, embodied in David. In this sense, Joe partook of the rabbinic tradition of the midrash, adding commentary, in the form of stories, to the Bible in order to elucidate its meanings.

"To the Rabbis . . . the Torah was the perfect, immutable word of God," John Friedman and Judith Ruderman wrote. "Every letter, every word, every space between the words held strata of knowledge waiting to be revealed or interpreted. The superficial meanings of the words were merely that: the starting places for religio-literary excavation. A little digging, and an idea or story could even be found to mean the opposite of what one had thought at first glance."

Meaning after the fact: the ultimate anachronism.

With *God Knows,* it became obvious that "midrash" had been Joe's project all along—as, on some level, it was the task of many Jewish performers, writers, actors, and journalists of his generation: the comic routines of Lenny Bruce; the political analysis in *Commentary;* the book and motion picture parodies in *Mad* magazine.

If Western culture did not sparkle under the interpretive glare . . . well, don't shoot the man with the spotlight. In *God Knows,* Joe presents Solomon, the father of Western wisdom, as a blockhead (nicknamed "Schlomo"), someone who jots down and repeats knowledge without understanding its uses.

Many critics said Joe's portrait of Solomon had no basis in the Bible, but, in fact, for all his wisdom, the biblical Solomon lives carelessly, shortsightedly, far beyond his means. He winds up fatally weakening the kingdom he inherited. For the first time in Joe's work, a son outlives his father; through his profligacy, he undermines all that his father achieved.

Full of bitterness and regret, David understands one thing clearly: The short view will never suffice. Contemplating the beautiful young Shunammite Abishag, provided by his attendants to comfort him in his old age, he cries, "I want my God back; and they send me a girl."

With this fourth novel, Joe's prophecy skills improved. Just as

Catch-22 seemed to anticipate Vietnam, *Something Happened* the "Me Decade," and *Good as Gold* the neoconservatives' lock on political power, *God Knows* sketched the greedy, grab-what-you-can entrepreneur who would spark the United States' deepest economic crisis since the 1930s. He was there in the figure of Solomon—Western wisdom personified.

In the worst days of his illness, with the writing stalled on *God Knows,* Joe felt as paralyzed, physically and spiritually, as his beleaguered king. He was caught between events and the telling of them, preparing only for inevitable death. Now, largely recovered, with the novel behind him, he could take a longer, more sanguine view of his life. "There are such musical, soothing phrases in the King James translation [of the Bible], being 'full of years and full of days,'" he mused. "I think implicit in that was a resignation that if one *did* live to the point where he was full of days, it was time to go."

"I COULD DO without the city. It wouldn't bother me if I never set foot in Manhattan again. I've had enough of it," Joe told a *New York Times* reporter in the spring of 1987. He remembered his days in a wheelchair, when cabs wouldn't stop for him. Stairs and escalators still gave him trouble. It was better to sit on his back terrace in East Hampton, watching trees and shrubs start to bud, staring at brittle gold leaves in his swimming pool, emptied for the winter, the pool's aquamarine sides soothing to the eyes in the growing spring light.

But Joe also had in mind, in his disgust for the city, publishing in its "bulked-up" form. His hankering for the largest advances he could get and his enjoyment of celebrity had helped alter the business in the last three decades. But now, even those who benefited from the changes wondered what kind of monster sat among them. "As far as a literary scene, there is only one major place—and that is Manhattan," Joe said ruefully, repeating, "I've had enough of it." Describing the current "scene," journalist Henry Dasko wrote:

> Media and communication conglomerates [had] . . . [steadily] swallow[ed] independent companies from related fields, including magazine and book publishing. Cutthroat competition . . . replaced the leisurely, clubby atmosphere once prevalent in editorial

offices. Writers and artists, like movie stars in Hollywood's old studio system, became treasured business assets, and media and entertainment tycoons with unlimited resources—Charles Bluhdorn of Gulf & Western, Steve Ross of Time Warner, Si Newhouse of Condé Nast—reached out to ensure that their prized properties were treated accordingly, with Hollywood-grade perks and maximum exposure in publications they owned and TV programs they controlled or influenced. In the 1980s, publishing became a business so glamorous that even magazine and book editors—Tina Brown, Joni Evans, Sonny Mehta—became celebrities on their own.

Mort Janklow, a lawyer turned literary agent, liked to sit in his office, located appropriately between rows of art museums and the headquarters of American advertising, talking about the Hearst Corporation, which had bought William Morrow, with its extensive backlist and well-regarded children's book division, for $25 million in 1981. "Since that time," Janklow bragged, "I have made a few deals for individual authors in excess of that amount."

Janklow's new business partner, Lynn Nesbit, said, "It is the easiest thing in the world right now to make a great [book] deal. Look at the money being paid! You can take almost anything and oversell it."

This was true, Joni Evans explained, because as "we consolidate, there is a panic among the five or six megapublishers whenever a new brand name [author] comes on the market. It's like six countries and we each want to make sure we have the best strategic defenses, so we have . . . overinflated prices."

In time, the waste and excess on which publishing floated would sink large portions of the industry, as would happen in every sector of a national economy bingeing without forethought, but for now, many authors, agents, and editors seemed willing to trade quality for Solomon's curse: the rewards to be snatched from apparently limitless piles of money.

Joe had grabbed his share. He was a brand name. But he was battered. The reviews for *God Knows* had hurt him—not just the criticisms but also the *tone* of them, a loud cynicism unavoidable when people (in this case, reviewers) felt abashed to be part of a system everyone believed to be badly out of control.

It was a relief, then, to sit in East Hampton and hide behind Speed Vogel as they drafted the book about Joe's disease. "I wanted the book. I was trying to start a list—it would have been one of my first acquisitions," recalls LuAnn Walther, Speed's friend at Bantam. "I hadn't seen anything like the story of that illness and the way Speed became part of Joe's recovery. It struck me as an interesting idea for a nonfiction book. My editor in chief at the time, Linda Gray, was dubious about it. It may be that I wasn't able to bid on it. I don't quite remember. Maybe Candida didn't think a young editor at a mass-market publisher was right for it."

Clearly, in marketing terms, the book would be a risk. *God Knows* had become a bestseller, but Joe's critical reputation was shaky. Readers wanted another *Catch-22*. Nonfiction? A medical ordeal (not the happiest of topics)? A coauthor—a guy named *Speed*? Are you serious?

The book ended up at Putnam, with Faith Sale. Known as a literary editor, and a devoted writers' advocate, she had worked with Kurt Vonnegut, Thomas Pynchon, Amy Tan, and Donald Barthelme. She had gone to Putnam in 1979 at the behest of Phyllis Grann, the first female CEO in publishing, and a woman who "[made] books [like] Spielberg [made] movies," according to Tom Clancy, one of *her* brand-name authors. Grann modeled herself on the "mogul mode," and was famous in the book biz for her Thursday-morning breakfast meetings, the "only breakfast meeting where no food is served," said one of her colleagues. It was all business, all the time.

Sales, sales, and bigger sales were Grann's goal, but she had hired Faith to add prestige to the house. She left her alone to do her work. Speed and Joe liked Faith enormously. Her editing philosophy consisted of "back-and-forth exchange[s], in which both author and editor benefit from listening as well as speaking/writing," she said. She recalled that the "first time I was to edit [Joe], I could hardly bring myself to speak to him. . . . Who was I to presume to improve anything this world-class writer had put on paper? And [at first] he confirmed my worst fears by saying no to every suggestion I made. Little by little, however, in the course of two or three or four . . . phone sessions, during several days of each of many weeks, he went back and changed every spot I had pointed to. By the end of the process, he was deputizing me to do whatever I thought was necessary if I couldn't reach him. . . . [but] I didn't make the smallest change without consulting him."

Speed enjoyed not only Faith's editorial acumen but also Joe's, and the critiques of her assistant, Ben McCormick. The persona Speed projected in the book was perfectly in tune with his real-life demeanor, but initially he had difficulty finding the right ironic tone. On one page of an early draft, concerned with Speed's depiction of Joe's domestic helplessness, Faith scrawled in the margin, "You mustn't sound mean. Playful, yes." A few times, Joe winced at cruel-sounding passages meant as jokes about Joe's occasional grumpiness.

"I'm not that way, but if you want to write it like that, go ahead," he told Speed.

"Ask Valerie if you're like that," Speed replied.

A reporter, overhearing one of these exchanges at the East Hampton house, said Valerie, on the hot seat, responded, "I can't make a comment. I'm eating here and I'm sleeping here. I can't say a word."

"I don't think I snarl [as Speed wrote in the book]," Joe said.

Valerie said, "I don't want to jeopardize . . ."

"But I must concede this because my other friends have this impression of me," Joe said. "Valerie doesn't deny it. I can be impatient. I am not a good listener."

"I don't want to jeopardize my position," Valerie said. "No. . . ."

"With Valerie, with friends, if they're telling me something and I think they're digressing or taking too long to get to what they want to say, I will say, 'Get to the point,' or 'Why are you telling me this?'"

Sometimes, while drafting *No Laughing Matter,* Joe felt Speed was imitating his style. After one mild disagreement, Speed said, "How many times am I going to have to keep rewriting this?"

Joe gave his friend narrative openings, writing in the margin of a handwritten page, "Here's an entry for you into the Gourmet Club, if you want one" or "You can use this [passage], if you want to." Speed had landed in as fine a creative-writing course as anyone could imagine.

No Laughing Matter was jazzed by contrasts: Speed on the move (frequently on his bike), Joe paralyzed in bed; Speed capable, buoyant, a self-described *luftmensch* (literally "airman," according to Sanford Pinsker, "the sort of person who regards life as a roller coaster"), Joe helpless, bitterly melancholy, in spite of his unflagging humor.

The loyalty of Joe's pals makes for a moving primer on friendship. Today, medical narratives are common, a booming publishing trend, but in 1986, when the book appeared, they were not so plentiful. The book's mirth and restraint, as well as its remarkable lack of self-pity, remain refreshing. Joe's eye for situational ironies and institutional absurdities (in hospitals and courtrooms) was as sharp as ever.

In one review of the book, in the *East Hampton Star,* a medical doctor, Jay I. Meltzer, wrote that Joe unmasked himself as passive, unable to communicate with his doctors. In the ICU, Joe suffered "an altered mental state brought out by helplessness and withdrawal of the usual stimuli of life and its replacement by noise, constant activity, observation, and the feeling of being an object in an ambience of death." The book, Meltzer concluded, was a "picture of overwhelming denial."

As David Seed points out, the good doctor did not "consider how [much] artifice may be playing a part in *No Laughing Matter.* The role of passive victim was no doubt attractive to Heller [as a narrative device] because it opens up all sorts of possibilities of self-mockery and irony in his account."

Yet nothing Joe wrote failed to happen. The book's structure, with Speed as narrative buffer—comic relief, contradictory voice, at some points a silent presence stopping Joe from considering topics further—enacts repression.

As usual in a Joseph Heller book, a crucial death occurred in the penultimate section. Speed wrote: "With a peaceful smile, [Joe] turned his face toward mine and softly murmured, 'It's been such a wonderful year.' He looked up into my misty eyes and said, 'I'm going now. Thank you.' Slowly his eyes fell closed and he died in my arms."

A marvelous parody of sentimentality, which *No Laughing Matter* had resisted, the passage gave Joe a comic opening to the book's finale: "I did no such thing. What the hell's the matter with him?. . . . What I did do that evening was enjoy a hearty dinner of the pot roast he cooked."

But the passage repeated a pattern Joe knew was central to the vision of his novels: a sacrifice, ensuring the main character's survival. In this instance, Joe was main character *as well as* sacrifice. The moment occurred following harrowing depictions of disease and the dissolution of his marriage: further evidence that he saw his old life as finished (for it is almost certain Joe arranged the book's ending).

He had died and he had survived—as he had as a child when his tonsils were taken, as he had over Avignon. *Help him. I'm all right.*

And now: the fullness of days.

"[T]HIS IS AN INTOXICATING experience unlike any other I've ever had," Joe said. "I don't want to take it in stride. I want to revel in it."

He was speaking of his October 1986 visit to the Air Force Academy in Colorado Springs to celebrate the twenty-fifth anniversary of the publication of *Catch-22*. Flyers featuring a naked Yossarian in a tree overlooking the school were posted on campus, a sleek, modern facility at the base of Pikes Peak. Academic papers were presented on the cultural, social, and theological aspects of the novel. The movie was screened. A birthday cake with twenty-five candles was produced. And when Joe was introduced to the cadets in a cavernous auditorium, nearly "nine hundred future officers stood as one to applaud the white-haired author," said the *New York Times*.

Norman Podhoretz, Joe's neoconservative nemesis, publicly disparaged the fact that a military institution would honor a book he considered damaging to America's might, not to say the souls of the nation's youth. But Col. Jack Shuttleworth, head of the Academy's English Department, said, "We want these men and women to be a thinking part of a large military bureaucracy. We don't want them to be victims of the Colonel Cathcarts of the world. To put it bluntly, you don't want dumb officers out there protecting your country."

Joe was impressed with the officers in training. "We oversimplify our military," he observed. "We think they have one mind. But they are very educated today and they want their families and students to be well educated. The degree of acceptance here, maybe even love, for the book is very surprising, and gratifying."

He spoke to the cadets about the novel's continued relevance. "I don't understand the merger mania sweeping American business, but I'm sure Milo [Minderbinder] would," he said. As for the catch: "It doesn't exist. That's the catch. If it existed in writing or something, we could change it."

Not all students were admiring. "I'd like to know what your book should make those of us at the Air Force Academy think of our duty to defend our country," demanded one freshman, with a grim and angry look on his face.

Calmly, Joe said, "Well now, there's nothing in the book that says you shouldn't defend your country. It's been called an anti-war book, but it's certainly not an anti–World War II book. There is never an objection raised in the book to the legitimacy of our participation in World War

Two. The conflict . . . had to do with individuals, individuals being under an authority that has no concern for those individuals and their needs as human beings. The whole sensibility of the book is not about fighting in World War II but about the war between individuals and this inhuman, bureaucratic authority."

The young man sat back down, although his combative demeanor did not abate.

Students offered Joe an example of an Air Force Academy catch-22: Before repairing a uniform, it had to be freshly cleaned. But the cleaning staff had orders not to clean any uniform needing repairs.

While the celebration unwound, newspapers and magazines worldwide noted *Catch-22*'s birthday and debated its legacy. Writing in the *New York Times,* John W. Aldridge said the novel was a "monumental artifact of contemporary American literature, almost as assured of longevity as the statues on Easter Island. Yet . . . we [are still learning] how to read this curious book and, as is the case with those statues, to understand how and why it got here and became what it is instead of what we may once have believed it to be."

On its arrival, he said, the book "seemed anomalous and more than a trifle ominous," but it appeared to answer Philip Roth's complaint in his essay "Writing American Fiction," printed the same year, that American experience "stupefies . . . sickens . . . infuriates," and makes any attempt to write about it feeble. Heller answered Roth by creating a novel that "remind[ed] us . . . of all that we have taken for granted in the world and should not, the madness we try not to bother to notice, the deceptions and falsehoods we lack the will to try to distinguish for truth."

Aldridge concluded, "Twenty-five years later, we can see that the situation Mr. Heller describes has, during those years, if anything grown more complicated, deranging and perilous than it was in 1944 or 1961. The comic fable that ends in horror has become more and more clearly a reflection of the altogether uncomic and horrifying realities of the world in which we live and hope to survive."

Other critics named cultural icons stemming directly or indirectly from *Catch-22: Dr. Strangelove, McHale's Navy, M*A*S*H* (television's Hawkeye, a domesticated Yossarian). "[T]he novel's first and greatest sequel was to be the war in Vietnam," J. Hoberman wrote a few years later in *ArtForum:* "Scarcely a week goes by when the phrase [catch-22] is not invoked by someone" in print to describe "government regulations, hospital procedures ... war ... [or] matters of housing, ranging from mortgages and rent laws to co-op boards and homelessness."

Back at the Air Force Academy, Joe, addressing the largest audience he had ever faced ("Sir, could you autograph your book for me, please sir?"), said, "I'm as happy as a lark. All my fantasies have been fulfilled. The sad part to me is that now I'll have to wait another twenty-five years to come back."

WE THINK the world will be very interested in what Joe Heller has to say on the subject after all this time, Phyllis Grann announced in April 1987.

Joe was not so sure.

Grann was referring to the meat of the two-book contract Joe had just signed with Putnam Berkley—reportedly a four-million-dollar deal for an unnamed novel and a sequel to *Catch-22*.

Most certainly the idea for a sequel did not come from Joe. For years, he had assiduously avoided the thought (though perhaps his experience at the Air Force Academy made the possibility of a sequel more palatable). Grann told everyone, "Joe is one of the greatest writers of my generation." This acquisition, she said, was "one of the most exciting" Putnam had ever made. Eventually, Joe himself was persuaded. Grann would not disclose specifics of the deal, which only fueled publicity. "If all the rumors of what we are said to have paid authors were true, they would never have to work again," she said. The old adman in Joe enjoyed this game, even as the novelist in him shied away from it. "I will only confirm that I got less than I asked for and more than I deserve," he told a *New York Times* reporter.

Who wouldn't want the money? If you wanted it, you had to give people what they demanded. This time, the top-dollar opportunity had come about because Bob Gottlieb had left Knopf to edit *The New Yorker*. Publishers, thinking Joe must be a free agent now, wooed him. His pleasant experience with Faith Sale on *No Laughing Matter* gave Putnam the edge—but on Phyllis Grann's terms. The money was there. People wanted another *Catch-22*. How about it?

What Joe wanted was to "write good novels." That's "[a]ll I'm trying to do," he told Charlie Ruas. He believed even a recluse like Samuel

Beckett wanted to be wildly successful. Any American novelist, if he's honest, Joe said, would like to be as brilliant as Beckett and fiscally solvent as a writer of potboilers. In the end, Joe's only "objective [was] to be successful in writing what I and other people would consider a serious work," he said. Money had nothing to do with this ambition. It was partly a matter of character—like "my characters [I] may not be decent, but [I] do know what decency is"—and partly temperament. "I can be a fairly prolific writer if I don't have distractions, because there is very little else that I want to do. . . . If I retired, I would live exactly the way I live now, assuming my health was good. Sleep as late as I want to, which is about eight in the morning, have a leisurely breakfast, and begin writing fiction. That's what I want to do."

Money *enabled* him to do it. As for the mind-boggling *amount* of cash—well, it was a crazy culture, and there was no escaping the looniness. Joe had long associated money with life, and poverty with death. At least he could conduct his negotiations from a distance now, without traveling to Manhattan. He didn't miss Manhattan—really, he didn't. Editorial offices were awful—too much frenzy in the air. It was so much saner to sit on the back terrace, listening to classical music, reading Thucydides, Aristotle, and Plato, to whom he had returned with deep pleasure. He would soon be sixty-four years old. He had earned a little sanity. If only his children would visit from time to time . . . not long, mind you, just enough to stay in touch. . . .

Reportedly, Valerie had the impression he was estranged from his children, but this wasn't exactly the case. They'd show up if needed. But they were frankly suspicious of their father's liaison with this woman. It was obvious to them what he had done. In the grip of illness and marriage woes, he had reached out for the first caretaker he could find, an enabler. The children were hurt on their mother's behalf, confused, dismayed by his behavior. Sensing this—hurt and angry himself over the perceived loss of loyalty—Joe spoke to Erica and Ted "badly about the other," Erica says. "My mother tried very hard to undo the damage"—to encourage affection and mutual engagement—"but couldn't, and the result is that [nowadays] Ted and I barely know each other."

ON APRIL 11, 1987, Joe consented to set foot in Manhattan, where he would marry Valerie in the lavish East Side apartment of his friend

Stanley Cohen, a lawyer whose legal affairs frequently took him to the south of France, and his wife, Toby Molenaar, a writer, photographer, and documentary filmmaker.

In the days before the wedding, Joe was voluble and excited. "I was helpless. [Valerie] took care of me," he told a *Boston Globe* reporter, recounting, to his own amazement, how he'd gotten to this point. "There were no secrets between us, absolutely no pretensions. I discovered she was the most cheerful person I had ever known. She had fun listening to me, and I had fun listening to her. I guess it all boils down to her positive attitude. . . . I'm going to marry Valerie because there's no one in the world I love more. We learned to live successfully with each other when she was taking care of me. She made my life entertaining when it wasn't entertaining. . . . [In time, friends] invited me to parties. Valerie knew exactly how to push the wheelchair in front of the corridor and maneuver me inside. So she came with me to parties and we became social creatures. This was our 'dating.' My life became 'our' life."

Speed told Joe he didn't have to *marry* Valerie. The "engagement came about because I didn't know what to give [her] for Christmas," Joe said. "She had never been engaged or married so I gave her an engagement ring. I said, 'Is this a serious engagement?' She said, 'Yes.' "

He mused, "I do know I like the idea of marriage. . . . I never thought I'd marry again because I never thought I'd take time to look. This was one of the great benefits of my illness. I met Valerie under the most trying circumstances and the trials brought us together. Marriage will put my life in context again. I really like being attached to somebody."

The wedding was small. Joe's kids did not attend. Valerie, with her hair cut short, wore a traditional white lace dress and pearl earrings. Her reddish hair, red cheeks, and red lips glowed warmly against the apartment's pale blue walls, parquet floors, and richly colored paintings in elaborate gold frames. Joe wore a simple blue suit with a plain red tie. He was trim and fit, his white hair swept away from his forehead. All day, he infected his friends with loud, sincere, and hearty laughter.

THE LONG VIEW, the tunnel of history, Thucydides, Plato, and Aristotle—Joe had been contemplating these things, reading and researching, since his illness. He was in the mood for summing up, for Big Picture thinking.

He felt he had to move fast. "I'm in the twilight of my career," he told friends matter-of-factly. In an astonishingly short time for any author, but especially for Joe, he had, since his recovery, completed *God Knows, No Laughing Matter,* occasional pieces (on illness and food) for *McCall's* magazine and the *New York Times'* "Sophisticated Traveler" column, and completed preparatory reading for a novel "about money and war."

In Plato's *Phaedrus,* Socrates says, "[W]riting . . . has this strange quality about it, which makes it . . . like painting: the painter's products stand before us quite as though they were alive; but if you question them, they maintain a solemn silence." The quote intrigued Joe. It affirmed his aesthetic approach, and renewed his energy for attempting another "new" kind of novel.

He had once said, "I like to think of the books I write as being interesting in themselves, rather than in just what they say. It's like a painting. A Renoir nude is not telling you about the nude; the painting itself has an existence. Not because of what's in it. It's like what I try to do with my books. The book itself is what it's about." If his novel's *ostensible* subjects were "money and war," its style—the experience of it— would be painterly, whatever that meant.

When friends asked what he was working on, he muttered *art, philosophy*: "There's no evidence that Socrates even lived. . . . And Plato never says anything about himself. Aah, the more I talk about it, the less interesting it sounds."

Fortuitously, Joe was reading—in addition to the Greeks—three books that crystalized the method he was groping toward: Julian Barnes's novel, *Flaubert's Parrot*; Gary Schwartz's 1985 biography, *Rembrandt: His Life, His Paintings*; and Simon Schama's 1987 study of Dutch commerce, trade, and culture, *The Embarrassment of Riches.*

Flaubert's Parrot was a meditation on the French writer's art. It read less like a novel than a series of philosophical disquisitions on the creative process. Joe admired it enormously, not least because it made a distinction between art and artist, the one an ideal, the other a flawed reality, a needy individual scrabbling in a deeply unsatisfactory world.

Gary Schwartz's portrait of Rembrandt supported this view. Schwartz emphasized the gap between the artist's exquisite paintings and his squalid life. Rembrandt's days and nights had all been about money. To Joe, he was part Milo Minderbinder, hustling and dealing, and part Bob

Slocum, manipulating his poor son, Titus, whose trust fund Rembrandt tried to control.

The Embarrassment of Riches traced links between seventeenth-century Dutch art and business. Schama showed how Rembrandt's paintings were tied to social prestige; how art, as a commodity, promoted Dutch sovereignty and legitimized its cultural codes; how art and politics were the tools of a particular social class whose passion—no, sole purpose—was to generate money from money, and did so by rigging markets and going to war.

All of this sounded quite contemporary to Joe. It dovetailed with his experience as an artist caught in a commodity culture out of control (to his benefit *and* harm). His pal Mario Puzo often spoke of the choice he'd made to stop writing "literary" novels and do everything he could to capitalize on *The Godfather*'s success. "If you're a guy who has a wife and children, and you continue to write small classics, you're committing murder. You're murdering your family," Puzo would say.

Joe wanted to earn serious money *from* serious art, and he labored hard at it, though he remained doubtful it was possible. "[T]here's . . . something contradictory in what I say," he admitted. "I'm one of the people who profit from the profit motive. I deal with money as a phenomenon and an inducement and portray this directly in my books. . . . I'm very conscious of money. I don't sell my books to publishers for a small amount. . . . Negotiations are very intense. I know the value. [At the same time,] I . . . know when I have enough. But I also know I'd rather write the books I want to than leave writing and go speculate and double or triple my money."

As his recent studies reminded him, material reality tends to shape (or corrupt) ideals. In the novel, he offered a vivid example of this dynamic, formulating the core theme of the book, binding the various topics (money, art, war).

Writing about seventeenth-century Holland, Joe said, "To a country whose economic health depended on sea voyages, the telescope, like cartography and all other navigational devices, was of primary importance, and even a man of great mind like the Dutch Jew Spinoza earned a respectable living grinding lenses. . . . Spinoza died at forty-four, from lungs ruined, it is conjectured, by particles of glass inhaled in the performance of his honest duties as a lens grinder." With ideals and ethics, Spinoza had hoped to unlock the secrets of the universe. In the end, the materials with which men probed the cosmos undid him.

Just so with an artist or a writer. The art, the ideal, was also a commodity (complete with price tag). Could the two be reconciled? Did they destroy each other? In *Good as Gold,* Joe had tackled this conundrum, calling into question the legitimacy of his novel by reminding the reader of its productness—its similarity to Henry Kissinger's book, with which it competed in the marketplace.

Now again, thinking of the Greeks, of Rembrandt, of commerce and trade, Joe raised the paradox: In 1961, he wrote, Rembrandt's painting, *Aristotle Contemplating the Bust of Homer*—made at a time when Rembrandt's "reputation had dimmed" because he pursued his art rather than the portraits the public wanted from him—sold to New York's Metropolitan Museum of Art at a record-breaking price of $2.3 million. That was the year Joe—who would earn record-breaking advances for novels he hoped were ambitious works of art—published *Catch-22,* the book that made him a brand-name author (people spoke of a Heller, as they did of a Rembrandt).

Through this ingenuous combination—a meditation on Rembrandt creating Aristotle on a canvas that lands in contemporary New York—Joe achieved the long view in his novel. The setup enabled him to discuss Greek ideals of art and democracy, the beginnings of modern trade and economic manipulation, and ongoing worldly debacles. In Joe's hands, Fifth Avenue in Manhattan was an extension of a grubby back alley in old Amsterdam.

History unraveled as a blur of folly: "From Athens to Syracuse by oar and sail was just about equivalent to the journey by troopship today from California to Vietnam or from Washington, D.C. to . . . the Persian Gulf," Joe wrote. The consequences of these travels—and the sense that nothing would ever change—went without saying.

In Joe's conception, as Aristotle's figure emerges on Rembrandt's canvas, he observes his surroundings, including present-day New York:

"A man cannot expect to make money out of the community and to receive honor as well," [Aristotle] had written in Athens in his *Nicomachean Ethics.*

In Sicily [where the painting of Aristotle first got shipped] he was no longer positive.

In London and Paris he began to have doubts.

In New York he knew he was wrong, because all the people who had contributed to the acquisition of his painting by the Metropolitan Museum of Art were making much money out of the community and were held in very great honor, especially after the purchase, for on the brass wall label in the museum the names [of the donors] . . . appear[ed] alongside the masterpiece with the names of Aristotle, Homer, and Rembrandt.

Homer begged and Rembrandt went bankrupt. Aristotle, who had money for books, his school, and his museum, could not have bought this painting of himself.

Rembrandt could not afford a Rembrandt.

When most of a nation's money sits in the vaults of an exclusive social club whose existence is predicated on the adventurism of war, waged to pry open global markets, justice cannot flourish, Joe argued. The public good will not be served, and the most terrible suffering will fall on children.

This view had animated all of Joe's novels—never more explicitly than this one, which at first he called *Poetics,* after the Aristotle book he had first read as a graduate student at Columbia. Later, he taught *Poetics* at the Yale Drama School. When published, the novel's title became *Picture This.*

Joe had crafted a painterly verbal style by flattening his prose, deleting adjectives and adverbs, muting anything distinctive in the voice. Individual sentences have the quick, sometimes tentative, investigative quality of a brushstroke. There are few transitions, mooting the whole question of anachronisms (for there is no single setting, in time or place). As much as possible, given the nature of writing, the reader is forced to confront the entire novel at once, as one might a painting on a wall.

Socrates (the provocateur) dies—indeed, *accepts* his death—in the penultimate chapter, a Heller scapegoat: "[T]here was [no] tolerance . . . for the satirical dissent for which Socrates was notable." Today, the world knows only an idealized version of Socrates through Plato's writing. The sacrifice of material reality (the philosopher's body) makes possible the ideal of artistic portraiture.

And the *uses* of art? On this subject, Joe, the old antiwar playwright, was grumpier than ever: "Aristophanes," he said, "was writing [satirically] about an autocratic wartime leader who was at the height of his popularity. / Athens voted first prize to both these plays. / And voted . . . to continue the war."

"IN WHAT I HOPE is an amusing way, it's really an extremely pessimistic book," Joe conceded in a conversation with Bill Moyers for Public Television's *World of Ideas. Picture This,* Joe said, does not flinch from the fact that "the United States is . . . founded solely on the philosophy of business . . . [and] is the only society in which virtue has become synonymous with money." The word *democracy* does not appear in the Constitution, he said. "Democracy was always a threat that [the Founding Fathers] wished very much to avoid. . . . They felt that the mob—that's a word they used—would not know how to vote, would not know where their interests lay. The other fear was that the mob indeed *would* know where their interests lay, and . . . would vote [accordingly]."

Beyond all this, Greek history teaches that a pure "democratic ideal is [not] even possible," Joe said. "[T]here can be [no] such thing as participatory democracy. One of our illusions—and it's a very comforting illusion—is that by voting, we are participating in government. Voting is a ritualistic routine. The right to vote is indispensable to our contentment, but in application it's absolutely useless . . . [because] the candidates are supported by people who are from the same financial and social status."

When Moyers accused Joe of fatalism, Joe said, in effect, Read your history. "I went back to ancient Greece because I was interested in writing about American life and Western civilization," he said. "In ancient Greece I found striking—and grim—parallels. . . . Extremely grim. In the war between Sparta and Athens, the Peloponnesian War, I could see a prototype for the Cold War between this country and Russia."

"Our popular notion of Greece is of a wise, humane, intelligent, moderate society. Is that what you found?" Moyers asked.

"I didn't find that at all," Joe said. "I found that as democracy was instituted, Athens became more chaotic, more corrupt. . . . [C]ommerce was important to Athens, so business leaders . . . obtained control of the political machinery, and Athens became more and more warlike." There you have the genesis of present-day American democracy. "I'm trying to say that the . . . people in a democratic society are no more rational than they are in any other type of society," Joe ventured. "They are manipulated. It is the function of a leader in a democracy, if he wishes to be a leader, to manipulate the emotions and the ideas of the population. . . . [M]oney and conquest and commerce [are] the constants in human history."

In his curmudgeonly tirade, he seemed to confirm one reviewer's observation that the author of *Catch-22* had become like the embittered, sassy Mark Twain who had tired of life and begun to think of himself as a philosopher rather than a humorist.

In general, reviewers of *Picture This,* which was released on September 6, 1988, expressed perplexity, impatience, and irritation. Richard Raynor, in *The Times* of London, praised Joe's "most endearing quality," his refusal to "take institutions seriously; or rather . . . he takes them so seriously they become hilarious." Other writers hated the book or fumbled to offer a coherent response. "[I]t represents very spaced-out writing," said Robert M. Adams in the *New York Times Book Review.* "It may be funky as well, and for all I know it's awesome." The New York *Daily News* proclaimed the novel to be "[t]hought-provoking," but then gave up: "It is as difficult to write *about* as it probably was to write."

In the *Washington Post Book World,* Jonathan Yardley pulled no punches. "It's true, as Dr. Johnson put it, that 'no man but a blockhead ever wrote except for money,' " he said, "but it's also true that writing done primarily for money often lacks both inspiration and authority—in both of which 'Picture This' is notably deficient. . . . 'Picture This' may do wonders for Joseph Heller's bank account, but what it is likely to do for his literary reputation is another matter altogether." Clearly, Joe had not "tossed off [the book]," Yardley said. "[H]e seems to have worked diligently at it." But "[m]ore's the pity"—the novel was "random," "unoriginal," and "ill-digested."

Yardley's view found support in most major review outlets. Walter Goodman of the *New York Times* sneered, "We have picked up a word from the Greeks for this sort of thing. Sophomoric."

Goodman's words "had a devastating effect on me," Joe confessed. He endured the worst reviews of his career; in many cases, it was hard not to believe the confluence of money and art had not shaded the responses, making for disturbingly personal remarks. " 'Picture This' . . . is devoid of energy, bite, wit, imagination—of just about everything save a dogged determination to plow through to the final page and fulfill the contract's demands," Yardley wrote. "At its conclusion, one can only cringe at the prospect of what the 'sequel' to 'Catch-22' may bring."

Not surprisingly, *Picture This* sold dismally.

"Very few complex good books are popular to a mass audience," Joe said.

Apparently, readers wanted *Mad* magazine. Joe was giving them the old *Commentary*—which most of them wouldn't have known about anyway. Late in life, the trouble with the long view was this: Few were left to share it.

18. The New World

ON THE LATE-EVENING sea, just along the shore, boats beat against the current. Joe didn't much care for boats, and he rarely went to the beach—too many noisy children. On this day, he walked and ran a little on the sand, not to go anywhere, but to move his muscles, still weak, still heavy at unexpected moments. He didn't get far. He had neither the will nor the stamina to complete a rigorous workout. Forward motion felt like backward sliding, especially where the sand was softest and wettest. Perhaps he would come back tomorrow, and then, tomorrow, run a little faster, stretch his arms past the rim of the island.

Most days, he exercised at the Omni Health and Racquet Club in Southampton, a modest gym whose unassuming facade would have fit any strip mall in America. The spa, pool, and rowing machines were too downscale to draw wealthy tourists; most of the patrons were locals, there to do their business and go home. Joe fast-walked on a treadmill, wearing street clothes, sometimes reading handwritten pages he had labored over that morning. Then he'd swim a few laps. Sometimes, the writer Sidney Offit saw him at the club. "Is [the spa] sanitary?" Joe asked him once. "I don't even shower here. None of that Charles Atlas stuff for me. A muscleman kicks sand in my eye, I go to the ophthalmologist." The staff and other club members seemed clueless about Joe. Good, Joe told Offit: "I prefer to sweat unobserved." One day, when a young woman behind the front desk heard Joe and Offit discussing books, she said to Joe, "I didn't know you're a writer. What do you write?"

LIGHTLY PERSPIRING, hair damp from the pool, he would slide into his Volvo and drive the short distance to his house, a two-story clapboard tucked into a pinewood glade not far from the beach. He'd park in slanted shade from the eaves of the shingled roof, walk slowly past balustrades and ornamental pillars, unlock the door, and drop onto the floral-patterned couch at the edge of the dining room. Usually, the house would be empty except for Phillipe, a small and somewhat aggressive bichon frise, who got so excited when people came through the door, he'd frequently hump the legs of the guests. In the past, Joe had sworn he would never own another pet—he had been so devastated by the death of his old dog, Sweeney. But Valerie wanted Phillipe, and Joe had gotten attached to him, too.

Valerie played golf and tennis and went horseback riding. She had taken bridge lessons, figure-skating lessons, country line-dancing lessons. She started knitting. She radiated enough stamina for her *and* her husband. When her enthusiasms wore Joe down, he turned testy, inclined to see her this way: "She [is] a person who, unfortunately, to my way of thinking, [is] interested in just about everything, with equal and nondiscriminating curiosity and enthusiasm." On days when Joe felt strong, absorbing a little of Valerie's energy and endearing capacity for enjoyment, his judgment, though still ironic, softened: "Like Browning's 'Last Duchess,' she tends to like whatever she looks upon." For about ten years prior to becoming a nurse, she had worked as a secretary in Manhattan real estate offices and for Union Carbide. In East Hampton, she had landed in a dream, and savored it.

Joe hated it when she left, even for a short time, to visit her sister in Pleasant Valley or to see friends in the city. Whenever she traveled, she'd leave him prepreared meals to heat in the oven, but "I still use fifty dishes and bring chaos to the kitchen," he admitted. If an appliance malfunctioned (or if he couldn't figure out how to use it), he'd throw it away and go into town to buy another one.

Valerie had a "good mouth," Joe said—that is, she liked to eat as much as he did. Eating together was one of their great pleasures. After dinner, which they often had out, Joe would graze in the kitchen, standing in front of the open fridge and spooning chocolate ice cream out of the frosty container, or snatching a bagel from the sideboard, or finishing a half-eaten banana he'd left lying around that morning. Sometimes, he drooled a little when he ate—the numbness in his face had never entirely vanished—and sometimes the exertion of raising hand to mouth hardly seemed worth the effort. But it was one of the blessings of his life that his digestive system remained robust and steady. He'd scold Valerie playfully for not helping him bring more discipline to his snacking. "Hide the cookies," he'd say. He had, he lamented, a "kind of nervous appetite."

The couple went to bed, turning off lamps one by one in rooms still decorated, simply and tastefully, the way Shirley had left them. Phillipe padded closely up the stairs behind Joe. Purple night filled the windows. Valerie liked to read British thrillers in bed. Joe reread F. Scott Fitzgerald ("I became aware of the old island here that flowered once for Dutch sailors' eyes . . .").

At dawn, Phillipe would leave his place on the floor, sneak into bed, and find a tight, warm spot between Valerie and Joe.

On the best of mornings, sunlight glimmered through the dining room windows onto a smooth, flat table, pale vases on the living room mantel, and creamy white lamp shades. Valerie liked to sleep late. Just past eight or so, after coffee, cereal, and a grapefruit, Joe slipped on his trifocals and slipped out back, passing through the sliding glass door to reach his studio in the guesthouse. On the shelves, dozens of copies of his books, translated into various languages. Once, the child of a guest who had stayed in the low wooden house said, "Boy, this guy really likes to read books by Joseph Heller!"

Joe sat in a swivel chair at the desk and turned on the new computer he'd bought. Word processing was certainly more convenient than clacking away on an old manual or electric typewriter—and easier on his arms and hands—but he still preferred to write with pen or pencil on note cards or yellow legal pads. Depending on the season, he'd pull a cardigan sweater over his cotton shirt and sit with his pads by the backyard pool for two or three hours, listening to classical music on the radio and the soft calls of terns in the blue-white sky.

Like the staff members at the health club, many local bookstore clerks did not recognize Joe as an author—but this was par for the course on Long Island, where writers were as common as sand dunes. Besides, the stores—Bookhampton, Encore, Canio's—were filling up with celebrity tell-alls, ghostwritten tracts by disgraced politicians and TV personalities. To be an author meant you were really a talk-show host, or something of the sort. Once, Regis Philbin, later famous for emceeing the television game show *Who Wants to Be a Millionaire?* walked into Encore Books. He wanted to see his book display. Later, he joked on a TV program that the cheeky desk clerk didn't know him. "I acted like I didn't know who he was because that's how most authors in the Hamptons like to be treated," Wendy Rhodes, the young employee, protested when she heard this. "Stephen King has been in here three times this summer and we ignored him," said Deborah Schall, the store manager.

"Writers out here are like earthworms in a bottle, trying to suck nourishment from each other," James Jones once observed of the Hamptons. "It's weakening to weak writers, and it's not strengthening to strong writers."

"I don't see it," Joe said when asked by a magazine reporter if East Hampton had become a literary town. Novelists are temperamentally antisocial, he insisted. They don't like to hang out with one another. John Knowles agreed. "This isn't an art colony," he said. "This is [just] a rural potato-growing place."

Of course, Long Island had a history of attracting artists and writers, as well as the wealthy. As early as 1849, James Fenimore Cooper, who went to Sag Harbor to begin a whaling enterprise, decried the changes occurring on the island, the way the "rustic virtues" he so dearly loved were "rudely thrown aside by the intrusion of what are termed improvements." These days, students still made pilgrimages to see the painting studios of Jackson Pollock and Willem de Kooning. Each summer, a Bridgehampton art gallery hosted a John Steinbeck Book Fair, held in honor of the distinguished former resident.

Writers had certainly swarmed the area in recent years. They gathered in gravel-lined gardens behind boxy hedgerows to drink white wine. They strolled the beaches in the summer's afternoon mist, searching for seashells, literary subjects, love. George Plimpton, Irwin Shaw, Truman Capote, Jean Stafford, Willie Morris, Kurt Vonnegut, Gail Sheehy, John Knowles. . . .

When neighboring novelists *did* get together, there was "very little bitchiness," Joe noted. "If I were to speak *critically,* I would eliminate most of the writers [here]," he said. "But the social situation transcends that."

More darkly, it could lead to cronyism and mutual favors in book reviews and articles in critical journals.

"Very few people have done major work here," Jason Epstein groused. "There's too much social life. It's too pleasant."

Or as Barbara Howar put it: "If you have writers in to dinner, you set the food on the table early, because pretty soon they're going to be *bombed.*"

Joe called these affairs "Gatsby parties." Cynical, rueful, bemused by his compatriots' self-indulgence, he nevertheless enjoyed the romantic atmosphere of lavish gatherings. "[E]very summer, I think Great Gatsbys are giving big parties out [here] right out of the novel," he said.

Truth be told, most nights he'd just as soon stay home and *read* Fitzgerald's novel. This author impressed him more than ever. Dipping into *Gatsby,* Joe marveled at the older writer's faultless control of language, a gift Joe didn't feel he'd ever fully developed. Fitzgerald's combination of romance and realism, philosophy and poetry was stunning. Joe was also moved by the man's example. He was "a successful writer, and then . . . a writer who saw himself go into decline," Joe said.

BRUCE JAY FRIEDMAN grew fonder and fonder of Joe once Joe settled permanently in East Hampton. Friedman saw the physical toll exacted by the "bumps he had taken in his life," but he also observed that Joe was capable of "arriv[ing] at what appeared to be a totally and almost disreputably happy state."

Friedman had lived for a decade on the South Fork. The day after Joe showed up, Joe "told me not to worry, he could get me invited to lots of parties," Friedman said. They lunched regularly, usually with Julie Green and Speed (now married to the writer Lou Ann Walker), occasionally Mario Puzo. Once, they considered inviting James Salter to join their group, but Joe said nah, he was too good a writer.

Joe didn't want to talk books or writing. He said he "didn't really enjoy light reading because it was too heavy." He was suspicious of decaf coffee. He thought it had more caffeine in it than regular coffee. He and Puzo talked about resurrecting a board game they'd invented years ago with George Mandel—all about horse racing—and making a million overnight.

One day, a young man approached the table and asked Joe what he thought about future generations. Joe looked at the kid, astonished. "Why on God's earth should I care about future generations?" he said.

"Well, he did care, but he preferred not to be caught at it," Friedman said. "He loved family, friends, his achievements, pretty girls." Though they were contemporaries, Friedman considered Joe "authentic American royalty."

Joe took to eating lunch downtown about four days a week, often in a restaurant called Barrister's. He liked its casual atmosphere. He worried about the weight he was gaining, in spite of workouts at the Omni, but decided "people my age are either portly or dying." He knew all the waitresses' names: Kehau, from Hawaii; Lori ("He likes coffee, water, and extra pickles"); Robin ("He's my favorite—people don't go 'ooh' when they see him. For Christie Brinkley, they [go] 'ooh,' but Mr. Heller doesn't have to wear sunglasses when he comes in here").

Typically, Joe ordered oysters, mock-turtle soup, or a grilled chicken sandwich on rye, followed by a brownie covered in chocolate sauce and topped with whipped cream. Only rarely did he sip a martini at lunch. He got too sleepy if he drank. Alcohol he saved for the Gatsby parties.

Valerie was glad Joe found something to do in the afternoons instead of sitting around the house. At night, she liked to step out with him to parties, dress up and mingle, her tall, slender figure unmistakable in a crowd, her red cheeks and her eyes (the "color of lobelia," one acquaintance described them) drawing stares, her cheerfulness a source of energy and delight ("She'd be happy even if she was a Kurd," Kurt Vonnegut said). Depending on his mood, Joe enjoyed being swept along by her giddiness, or he'd sulk, prevented from grandstanding by her movement and talk.

Mostly, he went for the food. One night, he asked Vonnegut's wife, Jill Krementz, for the recipe of the chicken salad she'd brought to a party. She wouldn't give it to him. He kept needling her. Finally, she admitted she'd bought it in the city somewhere, but she wouldn't reveal the name of the store. Later, when she went to the powder room, Joe sidled up to Vonnegut and pumped him for information. Vonnegut protested he'd get in too much trouble with his wife. He wouldn't say a word.

Special events were common (therefore not really special) in the Hamptons. Regularly, Joe's and Valerie's names popped up in newspaper gossip columns, among the names of celebrities attending this or that soiree. There they were at the new Bobby Van's; someone had spotted them at the Blue Parrot, eating killer enchiladas (and was that Paul McCartney slipping in the back?).

Joe cheered at the annual Artists and Writers Softball Game, held every August on the second Saturday of the month in a field in the center of East Hampton. The annual event had begun in 1948. That year, it featured Harold Rosenberg, Franz Kline, Pollock, and de Kooning. Eugene McCarthy had played second base for the Writers in 1968; Joe had been his teammate then, back when politics seemed to matter.

In September 1990, Hamptons notables, including Valerie and Joe, took the party on the road. They attended an international feast arranged by Craig Claiborne in Saint-Jean-Cap-Ferrat, France. Chefs from all parts of the globe—Jean-Louis Palladin of Washington's Watergate Hotel, Pierre Wynants from Comme Chez Soi in Brussels, Eckart Witzigmann from Munich's Aubergine—served regional dishes, along with more than one hundred cheeses from Cannes, at a garden party at the Villa Ephrussi de Rothschild. One guest described the affair as "downright Byzantine." Joe was eager to try the white asparagus prepared by Jimmy Schmidt of Detroit's Rattlesnake Club, but most of it had wilted in transit.

Joe had only so much tolerance for gala shindigs. "Yeah, he lived the celebrity life, but he wasn't really part of it," said his friend Bob Towbin. "Some piece of him was always holding back."

At his most sanguine, Joe told himself either he'd gotten everything he wanted or he'd stopped wanting it.

One night, at a billionaire's party on Staten Island, Vonnegut approached Joe and pointed to their host. He asked his pal how it made him feel to know that just yesterday, this young man had made more money than *Catch-22* has earned in nearly thirty years? I have something he doesn't have, Joe said: The knowledge that I've got enough.

He preferred lunches with his cronies or quiet dinner parties with pals. Through Craig Claiborne, he had met Warner LeRoy, one of Manhattan's most prominent restauranteurs, and Sam Aaron, former chair of Sherry-Lehmann, the jewel of New York wine merchants. Joe had gone to high school with Aaron's wife, Florence, though they had not known each other. Joe enjoyed the Aarons immensely. With Florence, he could reminisce about Coney Island—hot dogs and hucksters. He spoke to Sam of "worldly" matters Valerie found boring: business, international trade. "Valerie was a bit of a dipsy-doodle," Florence thought. "Sometimes, Joe got impatient with her chatter. We'd be at a dinner and he'd tell my husband to come over and sit by him because he didn't want to sit next to her any longer. 'Let her talk to your wife,' he'd say."

Most of all, Joe enjoyed staying home, puttering around the kitchen with Phillipe at his heels, making himself a sandwich with a day-old bagel and some leftover turkey. He'd put Count Basie on the CD player. With his sandwich on a plate, he'd flop on the couch and open *The Great Gatsby*: ". . . for a transitory enchanted moment man must have held his breath in the presence of this continent . . . face to face for the last time in history with something commensurate to his capacity for wonder."

19. Closing Time

THIS IS NO WAY for any writer to cap a career."

This was the judgment of David Straitfeld, writing in *New York* magazine in September 1994. "If it were Philip Roth, no one would mind his getting creamed, just to see the smirk wiped off his face. But Heller is a nice guy, at least for a writer. . . . His career has been an honorable one. He has never, at least until now, directly or egregiously exploited the fact that he wrote such a popular and influential book. His biggest mistake was writing his best novel first."

Straitfeld was relating the miserable saga of the sequel to *Catch-22*, a story that had taken a nasty turn when negative reviews of *Picture This* spread like coffee stains in newspapers. In retrospect, Joe admitted he'd hoped *Picture This* would "be another *Catch* . . . captur[ing] the intellectual imagination." The critical drubbing shook him. "Even at my advanced age, with the money for the book guaranteed, it was an awful situation," Joe said. "It does not make anyone happy to have something he's worked on, and for which he has high hopes, be dismissed or attacked publicly."

Over at Putnam, Phyllis Grann was not happy, either. The four-million-dollar package she had arranged in 1987 for *Picture This* and the *Catch* follow-up appeared foolhardy in the wake of the novel's failure. For the first time, Joe had not earned back his advance (though whose fault this was, given publishing's inflated prices, can be argued). Grann scrambled to contain the damage to Putnam's account ledgers and her reputation for picking winners.

In 1989, Putnam announced that "by mutual agreement" with Joseph Heller, the contract for the *Catch-22* sequel had been canceled. Grann insisted sales for *Picture This* had nothing to do with the decision. Joe did not feel prepared to begin writing the sequel at this time, she said. Putnam still had the utmost faith in his talent—he would write a nonfiction book for them in the near future, perhaps with Speed Vogel (no evidence suggests any such agreement existed formally). Joe told a reporter the contract was "an oppressive obligation. I had outlined [the sequel] and written a few chapters, but I sensed it was not the book they hoped to get. I did not want to put myself in the position of laboring to do a book which was not one I wanted to write."

He admitted he was daunted by the prospect of tackling another novel after *Picture This,* but he reread *Catch-22* for the first time in years, and found himself tickled, amazed he'd once commanded such an extensive literary vocabulary. "[M]y reaction was, 'My god, what talent I had,'" he said. Buoyed, he asked Candida Donadio to pitch the sequel to another publisher.

"I was told you can have this [book] for $1.2 million," said one publishing insider. "A few days later, it was down to $800,000. The price was going south in a hurry."

At Simon & Schuster, Dick Snyder said no. "Heller's talent [is] exhausted," he stated.

Reportedly, Donadio got two decent offers, which Joe refused. The money was insulting, he felt. Donadio was not in good shape. At the beginning of her career, she had been "maternal and nurturing to [all these] young guys, then many of them didn't want that anymore," Bob Gottlieb said. "They became stars and they didn't want a 'mamma mia' any longer. And then she would be distressed." Gottlieb had stopped working with her in the early 1980s because she became increasingly untrustworthy. "Well, she lied [to me], and then she was caught," he said. "I mean she knew she had done something terrible. She was finally forced to acknowledge it, and I never spoke to her again. . . . [W]e just don't lie to each other. . . . [I]t was a serious matter, and dealing with a well-known author and a great deal of money, and the whole thing was just a disgrace."

She was often inebriated and forgetful, and she had not maintained her contacts in the television and movie industries. Her negotiations with editors smacked of desperation, a need to prove she could still pull off a big score. She would not speak of Thomas Pynchon or other writers who had left her. "She seemed so grief-stricken," said one observer.

When she failed to get Joe the money he wanted for the sequel, he "dealt with her kindly but firmly," Gottlieb says. "Joe was too clearheaded for her extreme psychic needs." Joe turned to Amanda "Binky" Urban of International Creative Management, whom Straitfeld described as a "younger, more aggressive, less devotedly arty" agent.

At Simon & Schuster, Michael Korda told his colleagues that *Catch-22* had sparked a "major moment in S & S's postwar history"— therefore, the sequel should bear the S & S imprint. He overcame Dick Snyder's resistance.

That's one story. Another version says Urban demanded payback from Simon & Schuster for canceling publication of Bret Easton Ellis's *American Psycho* at the last minute. Urban had represented the novel; the publisher decided it was too obscene. Many publishing folk thought the *Catch-22* sequel was her compensation for the Ellis debacle.

In any case, Joe received $750,000 for the novel—still a shoddy amount, as far as he was concerned, but by now he had resigned himself to taking what he could get. Publicly, he declared, "The advance was very modest. I felt much better that way."

(Soon afterward, Dick Snyder was forced out at Simon & Schuster, after thirty-three years, replaced by a young man named Jonathan Newcomb, who believed literacy's future lay in digital publishing.)

". . . IN THE HOSPITAL, Yossarian dreamed of his mother, and he knew again that he was going to die," Joe wrote on a note card. He had dreamed of his mother for the first time in years.

This sentence (in *Closing Time*, it opens the third chapter) marked the beginning of his sequel to *Catch-22*. Once these words came to him, he knew he could write the book. He scrawled another sentence: "When people our age speak of the war it is not of Vietnam but of the one that broke out more than half a century ago and swept in almost all the world." The first statement committed Joe to some of the high jinks of the previous novel; the second ensured a deeper register in the new book, a straightforward, serious, crepuscular tone, one that would encompass all of Joe's learning and experience. His ambition was to write one more fiction the likes of which no other American had tried.

In *Catch-22*, he had devised a carnival ride of a novel. He would do so again—more deliberately this time—alternating realistic chapters with chapters as wild as fun-house mirrors, distorting reality. The two worlds— *step inside, be amazed; now step aside, let others through*—showed what had happened in half a century to fictional heroes (Yossarian, Dr. Strangelove) and actual World War II veterans (Kurt Vonnegut, Mel Brooks, Joey Heller).

If Coney Island had been the world, as barkers once claimed, then New York would be Coney Island. As Joe imagined it, a hellish amusement park stretched beneath the grim carneylike atmosphere of the Port Authority Bus Terminal, with tentacles reaching planet-wide. He hired a researcher, Ken Miller, a freelancer who had worked for *Time* magazine, to hang around Port Authority. Miller took notes on activities in and around the buses, and recorded anecdotes about the people who boarded them. He drew maps of the area and wrote numerous descriptions of it. (Joe had last caught a bus there years ago, to visit his pal Lou Berkman, who was dying of Hodgkin's disease.)

"At 4:30 I stood contemplating the place from across Tenth Avenue, trying to achieve some communion with it before venturing inside," Miller wrote on November 2, 1989. "[A] dark flood of people. . . . [It] smell[s] powerfully of piss. . . . [A] bony, scared-looking white woman in her fifties—she wears a kerchief over her hair, a clean, cheap raincoat and glasses. . . . [She] smells wonderfully of chocolate and mint. . . ." Joe underlined details he thought he could use, augmenting them with a list of images from Dante's *Inferno*: "[C]ircular staircases; terraces; a dark wood; flaming eyes; heads reversed on bodies and forced to walk backwards; twinkling with little flames; frozen lake; cold rain; walled city; sinners walking in both directions." Port Authority didn't need much refurbishing to resemble a tidy little hell.

To refresh his memory, he typed up a list of characters from *Catch-22*. As he typed, he jotted outlines of possible scenes and lines of dialogue associated with the updated characters. At one point, he ripped out pages from a paperback copy of *Catch* and wrote notes about who these people might have become, given their personalities. The chaplain, still hapless, would bumble into trouble, posing an international security threat; Milo Minderbinder would employ everybody on the planet.

Line by line, Michael Korda's editing hand was light, but he helped Joe shape and clarify portions of the book, particularly the autobiographical sections. He trimmed the manuscript from eleven hundred pages to just over six hundred. In the summer of 1994, four months after Joe had completed final revisions and was awaiting the novel's release in the fall, he told reporters, "I'm keeping my distance from the publisher. . . . I'm in a state of curiosity [about how the book will be received,] but I'm not going to let it become acute." Touchingly, somewhat defensively, he added, "There's no indication of any hostility toward it [in publishing circles], or any dissatisfaction. I'm . . . secure."

Still, he knew the book would disappoint readers who wanted *Catch-22* again. "[W]e don't live in that type of world any more," he said. "The spirit of this novel is kind of moody. . . . [I]t is pessimistic. . . . We don't have heroes. We don't even know who our enemy is. The enemy is death—death!"

Then denial kicked in. He veered from the topic of the book. "I look good. I'm tan," he said unconvincingly. "I have my hair. I don't have many wrinkles for my age. Well, I do have a wart here. . . ." He worried his thumb.

With Joe out of earshot, Valerie wept one day when a reporter from England asked about the book. "I hate that title, *Closing Time*," she said. "It's as if he's saying everything's finished, and it isn't."

AS THE LATE-SUMMER leaves began to redden, Joe sat on his back terrace with a portable phone at his side, anxiously anticipating the first reactions to his novel. He reflected that, on balance, the last few years had been worthy of celebration, in spite of setbacks, restlessness, and pessimism. His father-in-law, Barney, had died of cancer in 1987. Joe missed the man's gentleness, and regretted his estrangement from Barney and Dottie (she was now living in Florida). Joe consoled himself with the fact that Barney had lived a long and enriching life. In 1990, Erica had frightened the family with an occurrence of breast cancer. But she had recovered and published a novel, *Splinters*. It included a wry portrait of her father in the guise of a roguish and untrustworthy young man (upon receiving a Nobel Prize, he lights out for Sweden). During her illness, her father was "around," Erica says, "[though] not especially helpful, as I recall. But he was still dealing with me at that point as an extension of my mother because she and I were very close, and he was still in a rage at her."

Joe met his children fairly often in the city. They'd have lunch or dinner, and he looked forward to seeing them. He pressed Erica for her mother's secret pot roast recipe, one of his favorite meals and one he missed terribly; under strict orders from her mother, she would not give it to him. She still worked in advertising. Ted had joined *Nickelodeon* magazine as a writer and photographer. If he or Erica needed to know how "to punctuate a sentence at work, or . . . needed a fact, anything about anything," they'd phone their dad, Erica says. "He was like Google pre-Google. He always knew about everything. He met my various boyfriends over the years at dinners and I generally spent at least one weekend a summer at his house." She preferred to see him in the city, though, because she did not feel comfortable around Valerie. Her father's apparent impatience with his wife's talk and endless puttering unnerved her.

On his patio, Joe considered recent changes in the world, possibly worth celebrating—most notably, the fact that on November 9, 1989, the Berlin Wall had fallen. The Cold War had shaped most of Joe's life, in its effects on American politics, culture, and economics. His novels had been Cold War novels, right down to the smell of the ink on the page. The period had given him his subjects, and influenced the scope and nature of his fame. The Cold War: peace without peace, Orwell called it. Was it really over? Well, human nature wouldn't change (already, neo-Nazis were building hives inside the new, unified Germany), nor would the blunders of world leaders. Witness the Gulf War, Joe told friends. "[A]n atrocity," he'd say. "Bush . . . didn't [even] know why he was making war in Iraq."

Joe celebrated travel. Often, he was asked to read or speak at universities, arts festivals, and conferences. "I'm a narcissist and an exhibitionist," he admitted. "It's good being the center of attention, having people make a fuss over me. And I love the good food, the good hotels."

Invitations came from literary symposia, military commemorations, and—more and more frequently—Jewish Festschrifts. "It was always easy to accept who I was," Joe told members of the Beth Shalom and Sinai Temple in West Los Angeles. "As I enter my senior years it's something

I'm very proud of and most comfortable with. I believe I'd rather be Jewish than anything else. And I've always felt that way."

In the spring of 1992, he spent several weeks in Italy at the Rockefeller Foundation's Bellagio Study and Conference Center at Lake Como. There, he worked on *Closing Time* with "more [ambitions] than any one human could realistically hope to accomplish," he said. In Rome, at a restaurant called Colline Emiliane, dining with Valerie and actors Mickey Knox and Martin Balsam, old acquaintances of Joe, he ran into Federico Fellini. Forty-five years had passed since Fellini had drawn a caricature of Joe in a side-street storefront. The men had little to say to each other. They sat praising the restaurant's mushrooms. "The evening ended quietly with the restaurant emptied of all patrons but [us], with Balsam and I consuming one good grappa after another while Valerie and Mickey Knox waited with helpless impatience to steer us back to our respective hotels," Joe recalled. "Finally, the owner poured the two of us another large glass, this one complimentary, on condition we go the hell home when we finished." For one pleasant evening, Joe had scuttled back in time. He was on R & R again during the war, in the night world of Rome, enveloped in a wistful nostalgia appropriate to the valedictory musings of *Closing Time*.

He could have rested on his laurels, reading from *Catch-22* wherever he went, but—here was the miracle most worth celebrating in his seventy-first year—he still wanted to write, and to send ripples through American literature.

JOE PAID A BRIEF VISIT to Coney Island in the company of a European television crew just before the first advance reviews of *Closing Time* were scheduled to appear. The film crew was making a documentary on the old amusement parks. The British producers had carried across the sea images of a place that no longer existed. Joe witnessed their disappointment at the rusting reality. His melancholy did not match theirs; it was personal, attached to faces blown on the wind. His brother Lee had died. Joe hadn't seen him much in recent years, and felt bad about that. Hillel. Elias. Lee.

Over here, a patch of sand where Joe and Beansy Winkler had once hawked sodas to tourists; over there, the site of a triumphant joke-telling round by Lou Berkman.

Joe ordered a hot dog and fried potatoes with extra salt at Nathan's. He perked up. The Brits became excited when they spotted the red skeleton of the Parachute Jump. The old Luna Park was now a row of apartment projects, but the filmmakers, reciting the history they'd learned, were beginning to see past the bleakness. They strolled through a ghost Coney. Their mood improved, and so did Joe's. A school bus pulled into a parking lot, disgorging a group of Asian, black, and white children. They ran screaming toward the Wonder Wheel, one of the few rides remaining. On the boardwalk, Joe watched a huddle of Orthodox Jewish kids contemplating the foaming surf. The film crew turned a camera on him. The director asked about his past. He spoke of immense changes; the breeze took most of his words. Out of the corner of his eye, he noticed the Wonder Wheel turn and turn again.

"THEY COULD POSSIBLY SHIT on it," said Candida Donadio. She had not sold *Closing Time,* but she took a proprietary interest in it. As the critics sharpened their pencils, she fretted on Joe's behalf: "If the reviews [are] bad, I suppose he may not choose to write again."

"There's no question, Joe is running a risk," Bob Gottlieb said. "If you have a lifelong love affair with a book, you're likely to want a sequel to be, in essence, the same book. But *Closing Time* couldn't possibly be the same—the events are 50 years later. Joe is an older man, writing about a different time. He isn't capable of writing the same book." Would he have counseled Joe not to attempt a sequel? "Serious writers should do what they feel they should do. You can't prescribe for them," Gottlieb said.

"We've positioned it as a bestseller, but we will see and react," Bob Wietrak, a director of marketing for the Barnes & Noble book chain, announced. "If the reviews aren't good, that will affect [the way we try to sell it]."

In September 1994, as 170,000 copies of the book were readied for shipment, the Book-of-the-Month Club declared it would pass on *Closing Time*: Female readers—the club's bread and butter—were not likely to be engaged by a novel about elderly war veterans. *Vanity Fair* canceled a planned profile of Joe, offering no explanation.

Penny Kaganoff, editor in chief of *Kirkus,* fired the first shot: "There comes a time when an author just can't write anymore. That's the time to close the chapter down. . . . If someone wanted to do [Heller] a favor, they would have stopped him."

In London's *Times,* Ben Macintyre spoke for most reviewers: "[I]n *Catch-22,* Heller chose his targets carefully. In *Closing Time,* the effect is more that of napalm, an angry old man settling accounts and preparing for The End."

A dissenting view came from William H. Pritchard, writing in the *New York Times Book Review.* He praised the novel's "richness of narrative tone and human feeling," its "poetic quality." Heller had "more than got away" with the sequel, he said; the book was "an independent creation in whose best parts the seriousness and the joking are inseparable, as they should be in art."

"Score one for Joseph Heller," said Carlin Romano in the *Philadelphia Inquirer.* He described the book as having a "fictional architecture (complicated by multiple narrative voices) that's nervy for a writer facing serious chain-store expectations for the fall season. *Closing Time* is a gutsy feat. For a writer co-opted years ago by various critics and politicos, it's a declaration of independence."

Many reviewers suggested the sequel dimmed the reputation of *Catch-22* and tarnished Joe's career. "What I sense in most of these reviews is a personal rebuke," Bob Gottlieb said sadly. People were mad at Joe for messing with their memories of *Catch-22.* As for the author, he was, as David Craig said, making a bid for literary immortality.

MAN IS MATTER.

Yossarian learns this lesson in *Catch-22* when he plunges his hands into Snowden's torn body in the back of the B-25. In *Closing Time,* Yo-Yo, elderly, working like Bob Slocum in corporate offices, living like Bruce Gold in an America run by nincompoops, railing like King David against a hellish world, questioning like Socrates society's narrow choices, experiences the material breakdown of bodies, including his own, at every turn.

The novel begins by revealing the backstage machinery behind the comic pageantry. "In . . . twenty more years, we will all look pretty bad in . . . newspaper pictures and television clips, kind of strange, like people in a different world, ancient and doddering, balding, seeming perhaps a bit idiotic, shrunken, with toothless smiles in collapsed, wrinkled cheeks," says Sammy Singer, an old Coney Island boy who served with Yossarian on the mission to Avignon. He was, the reader learns, the unnamed crewman who fainted as Yossarian tried in vain to save Snowden's life.

"People I know are already dying and others I've known are already dead," Singer says. "We don't look that beautiful now. We wear glasses and are growing hard of hearing, we sometimes talk too much, repeat ourselves, things grow on us, even the most minor bruises take longer to heal and leave telltale traces. And soon . . . there will be no more of us left."

This is the gruesome reality propping up the fiction. Yossarian flies through the world of *Catch-22* free of gravity. He breathes anachronisms and absurdity. In *Closing Time*, he remains a fictional character inhabiting a comic-book planet (as opposed to Sammy Singer and Lew Rabinowitiz, who operate in a realistic milieu), but he is specifically identified with the World War II generation. At the end of the novel, he survives—indeed, he believes he is immortal, living happily ever after in good fictional style—but he has not escaped time's depredations. In his previous incarnation, he has decided to live forever or die trying. Now, he says the best way to live is to prepare to die.

The Yossarian chapters are packed with comic invention—mad sexual escapades; surreal worlds (Dante's *Inferno* as Steeplechase, in tunnels beneath Port Authority); apocalyptic moments; satirical set pieces lampooning the jet set; literary, musical, and cultural allusions (Thomas Mann, Richard Wagner): Here is the novel as roller coaster. In these sections, readers encounter distorted images of themselves, just as the old Steeplechase offered visitors opportunities to laugh at their follies.

But then, in the Singer-Rabinowitz chapters, Joe dropped the garish curtains, killed the blinking lights. He exposed the show's cogs: old age, divorce, illness, death. By yo-yoing the reader from whimsy to severity, Joe hoped to achieve what critic Robert Polhemus called the height of comic art: to "combin[e] the intensity of the [humorous] moment—the mood of laughter and release—with the promise of some form of enduring life in which we have a part."

The fulcrum from fantasy to reality and back again was the moment Joe returned to in memory and writing all his life: the wounded gunner in the back of the plane over Avignon.

In *Catch-22*, Snowden's death turns comedy into tragedy. In *Closing Time*, it binds the literary (Yossarian) to the real (Singer). It demonstrates how events inform literary art. Man is matter, but the imagination soars above it. We inhabit two realms, body and mind, even if they are really only one. Sammy Singer *is* Yossarian—and Joey Heller, among many others. (Storytelling is a matter of organizing experience and fantasizing, indulging in a conscious extension of the imagination, Joe once said. A schizophrenic exercise, it is both denial and confession).

At novel's end, the world appears to be hurtling toward its doom. Nevertheless, with the insouciance of a hero in a fiction, Yossarian feels "stimulated . . . by . . . optimism." He believes "that nothing harmful could happen to him, that nothing bad could happen to a just man. This was nonsense, he knew; but he also knew, in his gut, he'd be . . . safe."

On the other hand, Sammy Singer holds "no illusions." His theater of operations is the real. Widowed, aging, he is last seen (fittingly enough) in an airplane, listening to "mournful . . . Jewish" music, reading the death-haunted stories of Thomas Mann. "Mostly of late in [art] he preferred the melancholy to the heroic," the narrator says of this quiet, elderly man. There is only one place Sammy Singer can end up. It will not be an imaginary Sweden, and it will not be in Yossarian's immortal embrace.

"IT'S MY MASTERPIECE," Joe told Jerry McQueen, speaking of *Closing Time*. The reviewers did not agree, but Joe felt the novel would survive them. It would fly through the darkness long after the newspapers had wrapped old fish.

For the first time in his career, he had created rounded characters, not just the comic figures that had been his signature. He had written movingly and honestly about women, marriage, fatherhood, and companionship. He had lovingly evoked Coney Island and the ethnic atmospheres of his childhood neighborhoods. The novel would not replace *Catch-22* as his bestloved book, but it was, Joe believed, a better, richer book, and the finest one he was capable of writing.

The reviews' bitterness was offset by personal responses he received from readers and people he had known. One day, he got a phone call from Meredith Berkman, niece of Lou the junkman. Lou had died in 1981. Joe based the character Lew Rabinowoitz on him. Meredith wanted to meet and talk about her uncle. Saturday afternoon at the Plaza? Fine, Joe said.

"[I had heard that Heller] . . . had the reputation of being a gruff, arrogant man with little patience [for others]," Berkman said, "but he [was] warm and open throughout our conversation."

Her eyes welled up. Joe clasped her hands across the table. "Don't start to cry," he said nervously. She told him her family loved the Coney Island sections of *Closing Time*. Joe professed his affection for her uncle. The only reason he hadn't gone to Lou's funeral was because "I don't like rituals," he said. He cautioned her not to mix fiction with facts. "This is *not* your [family's] life [in the novel]. I think you may or may not be projecting onto me a love or a nostalgia . . . that's much more romantic than it actually was," he said. He pulled a Stim-U-Dent from the pocket of his tweed jacket. "I must tell you something else. Even when I'm writing about subjects that are real and intimate, I don't feel that intimacy while I'm writing it. I doubt I'm different from other authors. When an author's in an emotional state, he can't write. There's something cool and calculating and objective about the act of writing fiction." They ordered coffee. "For me, most of the act of writing now consists of two emotions," Joe said. "One is strength. The other is apprehension, the stress of . . . deciding what to do and doing it. [I feel] almost triumphant relief when it's done."

Berkman thanked him for his honesty—and for stimulating the first frank talk her family had ever had about sex. When her sister was reading the novel, she said, she came across a reference to "Coney Island whitefish." Their father, Charlie, had to explain they were condoms.

Who knew what services novels could perform?

JOE SAT IN HIS STUDY, staring at a framed invitation to a 1987 luncheon in honor of his marriage to Valerie, hosted by Craig Claiborne. He stared at his smiling face on magazine covers (*Esquire, Connoisseur*), framed and hanging on the wall. He stared at the spines of his books and the titles in multiple translations. Unsuccessfully, he tried to ignore the latest reviews.

In the October 10, 1994, issue of *The New Yorker*, Christopher Buckley, critic, novelist, and magazine editor (*Forbes FYI*), wrote a perceptive, if mixed, review of *Closing Time*. "How would you like to be a seventy-one-year-old certified American literary heavyweight, only to have your latest work [victimized by] the piling on that has been under way for over a month [by reviewers who seem] . . . annoyed with [Heller] for messing with characters they've come to regard over the years as their own[?]" Buckely wrote. "What praise there was for 'Closing Time'—from Robert Gottlieb, the editor of 'Catch-22'—was rather faint. So, Joe—glad you wrote 'The Sequel to 'Catch-22'?' To such inquiries, Heller has patiently replied that birds gotta sing, girls gotta dance, and writers gotta write."

Buckley ended his review by saying, "There's much in 'Closing Time' that can't have come easily. As the critics sharpen their knives . . . it seems we can afford to celebrate 'Catch-22s' thirty-third anniversary by welcoming Yossarian, Sammy, Milo, Lew, Wintergreen, and Chaplain Tappman, even as we take leave of them, and give credit to their creator, who has given us such consequential imperfections, and has dared not to leave well enough alone."

Joe sent Buckley a note: "I think you know me, and my novel, better than I do myself, and I was touched in more ways than you might expect by the time I came to your concluding paragraph. Valerie, my wife, was also moved nearly to tears of gratitude. Thank you from both of us."

So began a series of letters, faxes, and notes, and perhaps the warmest friendship of Joe's final years. Almost immediately, Buckley tried to talk Joe into writing articles for *Forbes FYI*. "A magazine editor is a hunter/gatherer, and when a lion appears on the savannah, one gives chase," he said.

"Christopher: Have you taken leave of your senses?" Joe wrote on December 1, 1994. "I can't write good prose—that's why I do novels that don't really require much. If I could, I would have found happiness forty years ago writing anonymous columns for [*The New Yorker*'s] 'The Talk of the Town.'"

Joe traveled to promote *Closing Time,* giving interviews on radio and television, readings at universities ("I think I will have a [good] audience at Yale, and a . . . respectable one, for I am, as we tend to forget, a senior citizen. . . . [A]n advantage I tend to bring with me is that I myself am usually at least half drunk before I step out to face an audience," he wrote Buckley). The younger man nudged him, again, for a magazine piece.

"I hate writing, as you know," Joe told him. "[A]nd I have felt for a long time now that it is never a good idea for a novelist to get on friendly terms with a book reviewer." But he was warming to the idea of a satire, or perhaps an article on his love of food. First, he had to swing through Western Europe for a series of press junkets.

Finally, in mid-December 1994, Joe, Valerie, and Buckley enjoyed a brief meeting in an Italian restaurant in the city. "I knew [Joe] was a gourmand. My bait: risotto with white truffles," Buckley said. Shortly afterward, Joe wrote him to say, "[Okay,] let's go ahead [with an article]. I will have some fun and you will too, and if the check comes and clears, I might make most of an alimony payment. . . . Valerie love[s] the idea . . . and why shouldn't she, since she does not have to do the work."

Buckley suggested he do a humorous piece on famous meals in history—the first seder in the Garden of Eden, the role of indigestion in Napoleon's defeat at Waterloo.

He hoped Joe would travel to Washington, D.C., to meet the *Forbes* staff. Joe said it was "too far" to go, "too many" people would expect him to talk to them, and he was feeling too "fragile and faint-hearted" to step back out in public right then.

ON A CHILLY MID-DECEMBER morning, when locals expected only deer to appear on the runways at the East Hampton airport (as opposed to summertime, when the private jets of the rich and famous swarmed the skies), a low roar cut through rising strings of mist. Bernie Comfort, a former World War II fighter pilot, out for an early walk, paused at the edge of a runway, pulled his leather jacket tight around his chest, and stared in wonder at a bulky olive-colored object. "I can't believe it," he muttered. Soon, a small crowd gathered at the airfield.

A bomber had landed on Long Island.

The onlookers watched a film crew set up equipment and lights. The star of the show, Joseph Heller, in a bright red blazer, his shocking white hair lifting erratically in the breeze, strolled up to the B-25. "Oh boy, oh boy," he said. "I haven't stood next to one of these since 1945." He touched the fuselage. "I had forgotten how small it was. I've ridden in stretch limousines bigger than this." He stepped beneath the Plexiglas nose cone. "I always wondered why they couldn't have made an escape hatch up here," he said softly. "We flew across the ocean on [a plane like this]. First Brazil, then to Ascension Island, then eight hours to Africa."

This particular plane, one of thirty B-25s still in existence, had flown to East Hampton from the Mid-Atlantic Air Museum in Reading, Pennsylvania, at a cost of $2,500. It had been featured in the movie of *Catch-22*. Now it provided dramatic backdrop for an interview with

Joe. The Discovery television channel was filming a series called *Great Books*. The show's producers, including Walter Cronkite, had asked the Center for the Book, at the Library of Congress, to select the finest books ever written. These included volumes by Plato, Machiavelli, Freud, Twain, Hawthorne, Melville . . . and Joe Heller. He was the only living author in the group. In addition to the television program, a celebratory festival was planned for autumn 1996 at the Library of Congress. "I will be reading from my book, Plato will be reading from his, Melville will be reading from *Moby Dick,*" Joe said.

While Bernie Comfort and others looked on from beyond the runway, cameramen centered Joe beneath the bombardier's perch. The film crew had to work quickly, as museum officials wanted the plane back in Pennsylvania before nightfall. The B-25 had no heater and would be too cold for a pilot after dark.

Gently, Joe ran his hand along the plane's glass curvature. His arm trembled. Honestly, he said, the war "was the most memorable and best period of my life. Because we were young. It was an adventure, and we were considered heroes when we came back."

"The B-25 is a wonderful prop," said Dale Minor, a senior producer, watching Joe quietly. "But the magic is in Joe Heller."

"Most of the time I have nothing to do," Joe said, as if speaking to himself. "Most of the parties [around here] I'm not invited to. They either don't want me or they know I won't come. . . . Writing and thinking about writing and taking part in things connected with writing is pretty much my major recreation. . . . Unlike many people I know out here, I'm not interested in tennis, I'm not interested in golf, I'm not interested in sailing, and I don't really enjoy cocktail parties anymore. . . . I read and I write. . . . And I drink and I eat. . . . There's really nothing else I'd rather do. I no longer experience any pressure. . . . As I look back," he said, staring straight into the bombardier's glass bowl, "it has been a wonderful life."

CLOSING TIME had been a major summing up, but Joe wouldn't believe it was his swan song as a novelist. If he didn't write, he didn't know what to do with himself. In early April 1995, he wrote Christopher Buckley, "I've got one more VE Day just ahead, and then I'll have nothing to do . . . but [start] another novel. Some fun."

Valerie, in the back garden with a watering can and shears, could tell when he'd had a poor or productive morning, depending on how quickly he emerged from his lair.

He'd go to lunch with Speed and B. J. Friedman. Sometimes, eavesdropping on silly conversations at nearby tables, he wished Shirley were sitting beside him so the two of them could make fun of people's talk, the way they used to.

Back pains plagued him and his walk had slowed.

He welcomed opportunities to mentor Chris Buckley. "You spread yourself too thin," he advised. "[Y]ou have a good heart—keep it in good shape. . . . [B]efore you know it, in only thirty years, you're going to be as old as I am now. . . . You will be surprised at how much you will want a [pension plan] and how quickly the day will rush to you when you're entitled to it. I talk from experience."

He told Buckley to wrangle "a corporate furnished apartment in Manhattan for your . . . business and pleasure, or do you prefer hotels?"

When Buckley asked Joe to critique a piece intended for *The New Yorker,* Joe shot back, "Why in heaven's name are you sending [this] to . . . me who never could earn more than a dismissive one-sentence rejection slip from anyone there?"

Meanwhile, his daughter quietly informed him her mother was ill.

What's the matter? Joe asked.

Lung cancer.

Erica had moved back into the Apthorp from her Upper East Side studio to care for Shirley. Norman and Gloria Barasch arrived in the city to treat Erica to lunch and dinner every day and drive her home at night. "[We're] not about to let you go through all this yourself," Norman said.

In swift succession, Shirley braved lung surgery, brain surgery, chemotherapy, and radiation at Sloan-Kettering.

Joe called Erica every evening, his voice gravelly and shaken. What were the doctors saying? Was Shirley eating anything? Getting fresh air? He couldn't bring himself to talk to his former wife.

Was she taking her medications?

Wearily, patiently, night after night, Erica answered his questions. She heard the hurt bewilderment in his voice.

He sat on his back patio, watching the moon rise, recalling times he had spent with Shirley in this house, remembering the taste of meatballs wrapped in cabbage she'd cook every summer for East Hampton lawn parties, the trips they'd taken together to Stuart's Fish Market over in Amagansett. . . .

"It is painful for me to recall how my wife was, to know the kind of person she used to be and would have liked to remain, and to see what is happening to her now, as it is painful for me to witness the deterioration of any human being who has ever been dear (or even near) to me," he had written, presciently, in *Something Happened*.

But of course, he *wasn't* witnessing what was happening.

Late one evening, exhausted and sad, impatient with the terror conveyed by her father's silences on the phone, Erica raised her voice: he'd never forgive himself if he didn't make an attempt to communicate with Shirley before she died. "Call her. Write to her. Send flowers, but do *something*," she said. "There isn't much time left and if you don't, I just feel that you will always be sorry."

For what felt like several minutes, a sound like ocean surf washed across the phone line. Finally, Joe said, "I don't need you to tell me what to do," and hung up.

The next day—it was late spring 1995—an orderly knocked on the door of Shirley's room at Sloan-Kettering. He delivered a spray of flowers. A "sumptuous truckload," Erica said, "the most exquisite flowers I had ever seen." Their stems curled elegantly from a cut crystal vase. Erica placed the bouquet on a table next to her mother's bed. She opened the card and read aloud: "My darling Shirley. I am so sorry. Joe."

Shirley, frail, hands resting lightly on the sheets, said, "Joe who?"

"Joe Heller," Erica said softly.

"Well, he *is* a sorry soul."

"But he sent you flowers. They're from Dad."

Shirley asked what she wanted her to do—hire jugglers? It was the kind of wit Joe had heard, over and over, in imaginary conversations with her. Jugglers indeed: bused in, perhaps, from the old, defunct Grossinger's. Shirley turned her head, closed her eyes, and went to sleep.

THAT NIGHT on the phone, Joe asked Erica, "Well, what did she say?" He asked it so often, so urgently, she had no chance to answer.

SHIRLEY HELD HELLER died on June 18, 1995. Shortly afterward, family and friends arranged a memorial service in the Apthorp apartment. Joe was reluctant to attend, but Valerie insisted he be with his children. According to Erica, "[H]e showed up the night before with his sister Sylvia—who had come up from Florida—and then they came the next day for the service. He was very sad and seemed very fragile to me. . . . [T]he rabbi . . . came up to my father after the service. I think they had met in East Hampton at some point, and he asked how Dad was and how his wife was. 'Shirley was my wife,' he said."

JOE'S BACK pains worsened. "Into each soup a little rain must fall. . . . I have a herniated disc . . . and something called spinal stenosis . . . crippling, painful," he wrote Chris Buckley. "For something like four weeks now I have been reminding myself of those two characters in that . . . play by Beckett whose names I won't look up, but one is unable to sit, and the other is unable to stand. I bob up and down as I type these amusing words. The neurosurgeon I saw in New York this week was optimistic as hell. . . . The pain treatment involves a series of injections called epidural cortisone blocks, and I've just had the first of these."

Buckley responded, "Valerie would be the best of company at the best of times, but at times like this I bet she really comes into her glory. Do everything she tells you to do. Without complaint."

In mid-October, doctors scheduled Joe for surgery. His recovery was painful and slow. "[D]isabled, weak, despondent, uncomfortable," he reported to Buckley. "[M]y hands shake—from codeine," but without the pills he would "dissolve in a puddle of tears." He looked forward to the day he could celebrate normalcy with an extra-dry martini.

Finally, in early November, he felt better. "Valerie is at least as good a nurse this time a[s] she was last time. She improves with practice," he said. "The left side of my ass is starting to hurt again. . . . [O]ne of the very good things to emerge is the [doctor's] order that I am not to exercise for the next two months. . . . This, of course, leaves me free to start a new novel."

When he was back on his feet, he admitted the ordeal had been more serious and frightening than he had wished to acknowledge.

He still wouldn't admit how much he missed Shirley.

Several months later, in mid-September 1996, he and Valerie went to Washington, D.C., so Joe could be feted as the author of a Great Book at the Library of Congress. They dined with Chris Buckley and Christopher Hitchens at Buckley's house. (Later, Joe wrote Buckley, "Valerie loves, loves your house. . . . [T]he martinis were stimulating, and the . . . salmon was as good as any we've eaten.") At the Ritz-Carlton bar, Joe drank with Walter Cronkite. Dressed more casually than the rest of the patrons, in a blue button-down shirt, khaki pants, a sport coat, glasses suspended across his chest on a blue cord wrapped around his neck, he enjoyed surveying the room, trying to spot political hacks and staffers. He talked loudly, so no one could miss it, about the disgrace of government kickbacks. He recited a passage from *Catch-22* about farmers getting rich off the federal dole for *failing* to grow alfalfa. He drew stares and smiled into his drink.

At the Great Books ceremony at the Library of Congress, Ruth Bader Ginsburg read a passage from *Moby-Dick*. Joe went to the podium and read a section of *Catch-22*. In front of lobbyists, lawyers, and legislative assistants, he recited, "Some men are born mediocre, and some achieve mediocrity, and some have mediocrity thrust upon them."

Afterward, tired, a bit unsteady on his feet, he said, "It feels wonderfully strange to be both alive and immortal. I'm somewhat in awe of myself."

20. When They Speak of the War

I N THE 1990S, Joe was just as likely to attend dinners or cocktail affairs in England, Sweden, Denmark, or Italy as he was to appear at
lawn parties on Long Island. In general, his critical reputation declined. *Catch-22* grew in stature. It no longer belonged to a particular moment or to Joe or to a publisher's marketing department, but to
American literature. By and large, even its detractors no longer questioned this. Love the novel or hate it, it was here to stay and deserved to
be. Discussions of war as depicted in art could not be conducted without Yossarian. He might die someday, his creator said, but it wouldn't
be by Joe's hand.

As Joe got older, he was seen less as a celebrity author than as a
grand man of letters. The slur in his voice had worsened as age further
weakened his muscles, but he was a much sought-after speaker in the
United States and abroad.

At the annual Cheltenham Festival for the Book in London, he de-
bated feminist criticism with Ariel Dorfman, Dava Sobel, Germaine
Greer, W. G. Sebald, and Seamus Heaney; at the Key West Literary
Seminars in Florida, he discussed the "romance" of war novels with
Philip Caputo and Robert Stone—typically, a novel's concentration on

individual names and characters misrepresents the chaos and anonymity of combat, he said; at a symposium in honor of James Jones on the Southampton Campus of Long Island University, he praised Jones as America's greatest war novelist.

He was made a fellow at Oxford, and returned to St. Catherine's College, where he and Shirley had spent his Fulbright year so long ago. Flying didn't bother him now the way it had just after the war, but he irritated Valerie by insisting they arrive at airports hours in advance, as if *extreme* control of the itinerary could avert any possible disaster.

Inspired by the nostalgia and travel pieces he had written for *Forbes FYI*, he penned an autobiography entitled *Now and Then: From Coney Island to Here*. By letter, he collected family anecdotes from his sister in Florida. He asked Bob Gottlieb to edit the manuscript. He had written it with little hesitation or revision, using a ballpoint pen and yellow notepads. The only passages that made his hand shake were those about Shirley, which often trailed off altogether. Uncharacteristically, what revisions he did make *heightened* sentimentality, as, for example, when writing of adolescence, he replaced the sentence "We worked at what we could because we never doubted we had to" with "We did not want what we could not hope to have, and we were not . . . bitter."

While waiting to proof the galleys in the summer of 1997, he booked a flight to the Pritikin Institute in California "to lose about ten of the pounds I've been putting on," he wrote Chris Buckley. "Valerie refuses to believe I will be going there as though to a retreat. She suspects, I suspect, I will be going there to tryst, and thus far she insists on going to California too and seeing me for dinner every night."

Alfred A. Knopf published *Now and Then* in February 1998. Most reviewers found it thin. It obfuscated more than it revealed about the author's life, and demonstrated a remarkable lack of self-awareness, they said. "I have a feeling . . . there's a part of me I've never been in touch with," Joe admitted freely. "I know underneath there's anxiety, a tendency toward despondency, a feeling of loneliness. I don't know if that's me or whether every human has it." Reviews demanding soul-baring confessions did not bother Joe. In writing of intensely personal matters, he felt he had protected the people he loved. Rather than evading incidents, he believed he had shown dignity and restraint.

Letters from Coney Island acquaintances and people he had not known there, thanking him for jogging their childhood memories, gratified him. The book's appearance occasioned a publicity tour through Europe and readings up and down the eastern seaboard of the United States. Joe loved the attention but wore down quickly. "Knopf finds it difficult to believe that I truly would prefer *not* to sit in a Barnes and Noble bookstore in New York for an hour and sign books," he wrote Buckley. At a reading and book signing in Brooklyn's Prospect Park in early August 1998, his hand shook and his voice, soupy and soft, kept breaking. "I've become a dyspeptic recluse," he told one young fan waiting in line with a book. He stammered on the word *dyspeptic*. He sold as many copies of *Catch-22* as he did of *Now and Then,* and noted, ruefully, that an illustration of a Ferris wheel on the title page of his autobiography obscured his signature.

Back in East Hampton, he kept to himself, reading (Don DeLillo, Upton Sinclair, John Barth), listening to music (Mahler, Count Basie). He resisted Valerie's attempts to get him to go to movies (despite himself, he enjoyed *Thelma and Louise* one night), to go skiing in upstate Vermont, or to take another restaurant tour of Paris. He walked a little on the grounds around the house and napped each afternoon. He skittered in and out of his study. He joked with friends that he was semiretired, but he was desperate for a new idea for a novel. He toyed with the notion of another updated Bible story, or a sex book written from the point of view of a woman. He embarrassed Valerie, pestering her with questions about her sexual history and her attitudes toward the men she had been with.

She struggled with his curmudgeonly outlook on politics, children, television (there's no *news* on the News—why do you watch it all the time? he asked her). In turn, Joe showed little patience for her interest in movies, pets, Britain's royal family, and pop-culture trends. There were those who worried he'd begun to feel trapped with a woman who didn't share his passions. He'd quip that divorce was no longer cost-effective at his age, so he supposed he would just stay put.

One night, at a dinner party with another couple, he banged a spoon on his glass and asked everyone to stop and listen to his wife pontificate on a subject she knew nothing about.

Friends thought Valerie seemed jealous of Speed and his wife, Lou Ann Walker, once they had a baby together. From the first, tensions had simmered between Valerie and Speed, but "the *fact* of Speed [in my father's life] was non-negotiable," Erica says.

At the end of an evening, after dinner with friends, Joe might take a spoonful of three-flavored ice cream topped with chocolate sauce and mutter, "Life is pretty good, even though it is completely shitty."

"I'm gripped by the somber realization that I have nothing to do I . . . enjoy doing," he said. "Not much merry going on. Sleep a lot. Have the blues."

"I don't think he knows himself," Erica said. "At any given point during a day," she thought, he probably veered from satisfaction to deep despair.

Constantly, he worried that in the middle of the night he was going to have a stroke.

HIS BAD MOOD did not stay locked away at home. "I feel like the malevolent witch at the party, because the title and topic I've chosen for my speech do not seem appropriate for an occasion on which so many people are in good spirits," he told an audience at the University of South Carolina on November 12, 1997. Readers had gathered to celebrate the work of F. Scott Fitzgerald. Professor Matthew J. Bruccoli had expanded the school's Fitzgerald archive, working with Fitzgerald's daughter, Scottie. Several writers, among them Frederick Busch, Richard Bausch, and Budd Schulberg were on hand to offer tributes to the author of *The Great Gatsby*.

Joe had decided to speak on "The Literature of Despair."

"I'd known about Fitzgerald, of course, about his drinking, his decline in reputation," Joe said. "[But] the more I thought, the more impressed I was with the fact that so many writers do have at least some serious emotional trouble in their lives." He rattled off a list of novelists whose lives "took sad turns before they were over," among them Charles Dickens, Henry James, Joseph Conrad, Jack London, Edgar Allan Poe, William Faulkner, Sinclair Lewis, Eugene O'Neill, and John Cheever. "Of course, the question to be answered is *why*? What is there about the literary occupation that causes, or is the concomitant of, so much wretchedness among so many people who are successful? And the answer I give you tonight is: I don't know," Joe said:

What are some of the factors that might cause or contribute to these predilections toward unhappiness? Well, in a general—a most general—way, I can try to guess:

1. There could be something in the nature of the work, the uncertainty of success, the greater uncertainty of maintaining a peak of success and income, over a working lifetime. After all, a writer can be discovered only once, and after that, the scrutiny of critics grows more exacting.

2. Or there could be something in the nature of the individual and the early family setting that influenced the person toward fantasizing, fictionalizing—a tendency toward daydreaming extravagant scenarios of accomplishment. These imply a wish to excel and, with those who turn to writing fiction, plays, or poems, an ambition to excel as a writer.

3. Most likely, there is an indefinable mix of both, and maybe half a dozen other factors I haven't mentioned.

Then add to these the Freudian discovery that the conflicts, feelings of loneliness, and disappointments we possessed that at the beginning led us toward fictionalizing are not entirely satisfied by the success but instead remain. There has been no miraculous transformation, and in many ways the sensitive parts of us remain exactly the same.

Let me throw in one more element, the factor that feelings of failure are almost certain to enter into the life of the published author, even with works that appear to be triumphs. . . . [I]nstead of rejoicing, [the writer is likely to be] enraged by those literary critics who [find the work] deficient in quality.

Warmly welcomed by the audience, Joe finished by insisting that "after . . . tonight, I think I'm going to be in a very good mood for a good long time," but he continued to brood on the issues he had raised. The talk was the closest he'd come to examining the "parts of himself" he'd refused to explore. Over the next couple of years, he refined his thoughts; a variation of them would appear in the novel he started and worked on until his death. The book would be called *Portrait of an Artist, as an Old Man.*

"[T]HE GAME IS OVER," wrote the critic D. T. Max in *Salon* magazine in 1997, referring to Saul Bellow, Norman Mailer, and Philip Roth, whom he identified as the "grizzled Jewish peers" of Joseph Heller. "They're all past retirement age, they've been thoroughly trashed by feminists and the (many) women in their lives, [and] they seem sadly out of touch with the multicultural literary fashions of the day." The article was entitled "The Twilight of the Old Goats."

A few months later, a bibliophile named Lewis Pollock wrote a letter to the London *Times,* asking if readers could account for the "amazing similarity of characters, personality traits, eccentricities, physical descriptions, personnel injuries and incidents" in *Catch-22* and a 1950 novel by Louis Falstein called *The Sky Is a Lonely Place* (in the United States, it was published as *Face of a Hero*). The *Washington Post* ran a front-page story investigating the possibility of plagiarism.

Joe did not know Falstein's book. Falstein died in 1995; he could not have missed *Catch-22,* but he never mentioned Joe's book to any member of his family. The rituals and monotonies of war could easily account for the novels' similarities. Joe pointed out "how much war fiction depends on the same elementary variations on themes and characters." Bob Gottlieb defended him vigorously. "I've never seen, heard, or felt Joe Heller doing anything remotely less than honest during our forty-year relationship," he said. "It is inconceivable that he used any other writer's work."

Mel Gussow wrote a persuasive account of the novels in the *New York Times*, exonerating Joe. The "books are widely disparate in approach, ambition, style and content," he concluded. Still, the flap, coming so soon after assertions by critics that *Closing Time* had taken the shine off *Catch-22,* was another blow.

"What a *nothing* story!" Chris Buckley wrote Joe. "Honestly: do not lose *one* minute's sleep . . . on this." Joe responded, "Chris: Stop grieving . . . [though] absurdly, I find myself in a rage against a man I never knew who died a few years [ago] and was the author of a novel I never heard of!"

IF ANYTHING, the controversy—which blew over quickly—upped the sales of *Catch-22.* More than ever, the book seemed impervious to critical assaults, literary fashion, and time.

Meanwhile, multiculturalism had become a vital publishing trend. "Ethnic" books flooded the market, promoting diversity while, sadly, seeming much the same. Still, genuine talents emerged. Finally, U.S.

fiction began to reflect the mix of blood, belief, and outlook that had blessed the nation—but not many of its books—from the first. Voices readers had not been privileged to listen to before, from ethnic enclaves, from deep within the nation's midst, told of change and the harvests we were likely to reap from it. The names suggested the varied roads these young writers had taken: Julia Alvarez, Chang-rae Lee, Gish Jen, Junot Díaz.

Many times, Joe had worked in, and through, changing literary climates. Could he do it once more? He resisted Buckley's requests for new magazine articles. "I'd rather not think about another piece for *FYI* or anywhere else," he said. "I feel it's time now to begin thinking about another book, and since in my lifetime I've never been able to come up with more than one idea at a time, I'd like the idea I do come up with to be for that one."

Shortly afterward, he told Buckley he feared "my next and final novel will be about a spent novelist who spends . . . his [last] years writing travel articles read by few people he knows for a younger novelist like you, in a kind of odd Faustian bargain in which Mephistopholes himself is also prey to the capitalist cool he serves."

Valerie said *she* would write an article for *FYI*. "Here's how my piece about taking [Joe to Europe] will begin. 'He didn't want to go. I did. I won.' "

JOURNALISTS, many discovering *Catch-22* for the first time, came regularly to East Hampton. Joe never ceased to enjoy the attention, but the interviews became ordeals. He didn't handle them as smoothly as he had in the past. For one thing, he was physically uncomfortable sitting in one place for extended periods. He squinted, hunched his shoulders, shifted his haunches. He'd flutter his fingers under a now-flabby chin. He pursed his lips, cleared his throat, bit his nails. Often, he felt frustrated by his slow speech, his inability to articulate crisply what he wanted to say. He had always spoken off the cuff; his apparent nonchalance used to be more calculating than it was now. He was no longer so quick on his feet. Cavalierly, he told interviewers to clean up his grammar when quoting him. They rarely did.

In a pair of late-life interviews with female journalists, he flirted openly, talked freely of the many affairs he'd had, professed his faith in "old-fashioned ideas" about men and women—"strong women have a tendency to create weak men," he said—and admitted his desire to be "fed [and] . . . coddled, [as well as to have] things fixed up for [me]."

He seemed to be baiting the women to admit he remained attractive. One day, Erica came across some of his comments in a London paper. She called and said he should be more discreet when speaking of his affairs. The words were hurtful to family and friends. Even if they appeared in foreign publications, the U.S. press was bound to pick them up. He agreed to be more careful.

Valerie talked openly to reporters. In an interview with Lynn Barber in March 1998—the longest and most candid (not to say careless) interview Joe gave in his final years—Valerie and Joe exhibited "strange turbulent undercurrents." "I'm never sure if they're joking or [arguing]," Barber admitted. "The effect of the Hellers together is : . . unhingeing [*sic*]." They sniped at each other over travel plans, food, their lives together, his children. "She's as bossy as can be," Joe said.

"[He used to be] different," Valerie said. "He was a very happy person, very agreeable. Even though he was almost paralyzed, he was very happy and he really did not realize that he might not recover. The doctors said, 'You'll be fine,' and he believed it. A lot of times, when people are sick, there is a different personality to when they are well."

"When I met her in the hospital, I was flirting," Joe said.

"And now he flirts with everybody else!" Valerie added.

"You have noticed that she talks more rapidly than I do. . . ."

"Have you ever heard his daughter speak?" Valerie asked. "She speaks in entirely slow motion. I've never heard anyone speak like that in my life. Never. It's very strange to me. Real . . . slow."

"What she's saying is that she talks rapidly, and I get irritated by people who talk rapidly," Joe snapped.

Getting back to flirting, Barber asked Joe if he regretted the affairs he'd had. "[They] were just individual sexual encounters," he said. "It was a delightful phase. It mostly started after *Catch-22,* and I felt very good about myself. Looking back, I don't feel so good about it because the effect on my wife was devastating. I regret much of the outcome. On the other hand, I enjoyed very much the experiences and if I had to do it all over again, I don't know which I would do."

Speaking of daughters, there were "some truly harrowing scenes between father and daughter in *Something Happened,*" Barber ventured. "I don't relate to children particularly, or even young people anymore—there's no basis for conversation," Joe replied.

What did he make of the fact that his children had never married? "They don't relate as openly to people as I do." Was that because he set a bad example? "Not me!" Joe protested. "They had a mother, too, and they had a grandmother [Dottie] who was a tyrant!"

"But he agrees that he was probably an 'oppressive' parent and . . . fatherhood was not his thing," Barber wrote.

What drew him to Valerie? "Well . . . she's attractive. She was my day nurse, she was single, and it developed. One thing I say which is amusing but true is that we were intimate before we were friendly."

When the interview was over, Joe drove Barber to a bus stop so she could catch her plane. He "burbled fondly about Valerie as if they hadn't just been verbally beating each other to a pulp—maybe it's their normal form of conversation," Barber wrote. He gazed out the window at local landmarks—the boat docks, the bagel store, the tackle shop, and a pig shed with the name Elvis painted in huge letters on its side. He said he felt lonely here. Most of his neighbors were people with whom he had nothing in common, egocentric businessmen. "Really?" Barber said. "Some people might say *you* were a bit egotistical."

"Do you mean egotistical or self-satisfied?" Joe said. He turned the steering wheel. "I'm well into my seventies. I'm in good health. I have a nice personality. I can live comfortably. It doesn't mean I don't go into periods of depression or anxiety like now . . . wondering . . . what you're going to write about me, but I'm no longer anxious about things like money, and I'm no longer really anxious about sexual activity—that's in the past. I wish I was younger. I wish I was as virile as I was, and I wish I was ambitious. I wish I had as much energy." They had arrived at the bus stop. Barber opened her door. "But all those things"—Joe waved his hand—"waned with age."

HE COULDN'T HELP it: He stared at women's butts more than he used to. It wasn't a sexual gaze. It was idle curiosity, flavored with a residue of prurience, like a faint vanilla smell. It gave the experience a sweet, nostalgic spice. It was instinctual, like something barely remembered. When he looked at young people's faces, he couldn't help but imagine their features wrinkled, slack, dry.

His major activity was observing himself observing the world.

IT WAS THE SEASON of Bill Clinton and Monica Lewinsky. People joked, "Hear about the new game they're playing in the White House? 'Swallow the Leader.'"

JOE SPOKE FREELY about missing his father, though he'd never known the man. He could not talk about his mother without a sting of tears.

"YOU'VE GOT A DAUGHTER and a son and you may find yourself . . . touched very deeply [by *Something Happened*]," Joe wrote Chris Buckley. Buckley was reading the novel for the first time. Joe continued to give him writerly advice: "The life of a novelist is almost inevitably destined for anguish, humiliation, and disappointment."

As if to underscore the point, he said, "My new novel was not a great hit with Bob Gottlieb and [it was] a puzzlement to Binky [Urban] too, both of whom seem to prefer a different approach to the subject matter and a different novel than the one I have written." He went on to say, "So I'll be finding a different publisher for this one and a different agent. . . . Binky and I are still on the friendliest of terms, but you'll appreciate the irony: The book is mainly about a well-known novelist . . . my . . . age struggling to come up with a subject for a new novel that will be welcomed with enthusiasm by his editor and his agent. Don't grieve for me: I've been through this many times before, almost every time, in fact."

Buckley replied, "[M]y heart goes out to you. I know this kind of thing hurts. . . . Hold on to the fact that you wrote one of the most amazing novels of all time."

Meanwhile, Joe's son had written a novel, a satirical look at the inner workings of New York's magazine world, in which he'd had considerable experience. While still in the garment business, Ted delivered clothes one day to the *Vogue* offices. He was too scruffy for the snobbish reception staff. When he asked if he could use a bathroom, a secretary told him, "No. We don't have one." Soon afterward, he worked at *Spy* and *Vanity Fair.* His first assignment, in the late 1980s, was to help organize *Spy*'s index for *The Andy Warhol Diaries.* "Every time [Warhol mentioned] a famous name, [I had to] say why," Ted said. "I would write things like, 'Halston, cocaine use of.' "

Then he went to work for *Nickelodeon.*

Simon & Schuster was interested in Ted's novel. Joe figured he was "going to have a better year as a writer than I'm having." Buckley cautioned him, "[T]ell Ted—from me—expect the absolute worst. Every interview will begin with, 'What is it like to grow up the son of the author of *Catch-22*?' [Buckley, the son of conservative commentator William F. Buckley, spoke from experience.] Tell him the only solution to this intractable situation is . . . roll with it."

Buckley's comments turned out to be prophetic. "[Ted's] great joy has been diminished already by an item in a . . . paper insinuating nepotistic preference," Joe reported. (Ted said, "I sort of have a reputation but it's not my reputation.")

"[He should] ignore shit like this," Buckley said. "Writing is the most bottom-line profession there is. Either you can or you can't, and the truth becomes apparent in seconds. . . . So tell him to kick back and enjoy. He is a novelist."

In *his* work, Buckley was struggling with the "old dilemma": Is "serious" writing more significant than satire? "[K]eep in mind it is possible to be both humorous and mordantly serious," Joe told him. "Have you read the novels of Joseph Heller? If you've not read *God Knows,* do so right now."

Literary faxing with a colleague was one thing, but because of his recent rejection, and the nastiness Ted was facing, Joe had no desire to go into the city. "What does someone like you or I do at a lavish book party in which crowds of people there seem more important to us than we know they are?" he asked Buckley.

Valerie went to parties without him. "So I walk into the Norman Mailer book party last night and someone pinches my bottom and it's—Valerie! She looked great," Buckley said. "We had a good catchup, then she went over and pinched Muhammad Ali's bottom and left with him. She sure gets around."

Joe shot back, "Valerie has long experience at grabbing attractive men by the crotch . . . but she won't have sex with black men or Jews."

On another occasion, Buckley mentioned he'd run into Joe's "old pal" Henry Kissinger. Kissinger "cornered" him at a gathering to "defend his [old] Vietnam policies. I was drunk as a skunk. Amazing twin sensations."

Joe replied, "The picture of being both drunk and in conversation with Kissinger is appalling." It was Buckley's birthday. "Steadily . . . you grow wiser," Joe said. "But, by the time you figure out what to do with your life, much of it may be over. Happy 46th."

"SO WE WERE SITTING by Joe's pool one day and he asked me to be the agent for his novel *Portrait of an Artist, as an Old Man*," says Deborah Karl. "I said sure. He was very easy to work with. He was who he was, and the book wasn't that hard to sell. He liked me and I loved him almost as a parent."

In her forties, Karl had built an impressive client list as a literary agent, but Joe turned to her as a friend. She had grown up with his kids. Despite his public professions of impatience with children, he loved her son, Christopher, and her baby daughter, Sofia. His backyard pool was a favorite gathering spot for Karl's family. She knew Erica and Ted had a hard time with Valerie, but she enjoyed spending summer days with the couple. "Valerie was a good wife to Joe," she says.

Karl appreciated the way Joe stayed loyal to her mother and father despite Fred's disapproval of Joe's "celebrity" life. Fred had been diagnosed with kidney disease. "He was determined not to let illness be a topic of conversation," Deborah says. Her mother recalls, "People would phone and say casually, 'Hi, how are you?' and Fred would get furious at me. He'd say, 'You've been telling people I'm sick,' and I'd say no. He'd say, 'People keep saying "How are you?"'" It was just a normal greeting!"

Joe "broke through" to her father, says Deborah. He got him to talk about his fears. He was the only person who could. In turn, Fred was the only one who could tell Joe he was wasting time on "being famous" and should get back to work. Joe knew it wasn't so easy.

"Joe was a disappointed man—disappointed with himself. I do think that," Dolores says. "One night, he and Valerie came to dinner. We were having a conversation about people like Gaddis and Pynchon who avoided publicity. And Valerie said something about, 'Oh well, they're crazy. Why do they do that?' She went on and on about it. And Joe looked at us and said, 'She doesn't understand.' He enjoyed the celebrity. But he knew."

IN FEBRUARY 1999, Joe and Valerie took a two-week cruise to Norway's Arctic region. Joe was paid to give a reading and a talk—he had done a similar cruise the year before.

To her delight, Diane Armstrong, a fellow passenger, found that "instead of shying away from inquisitive strangers, [Joe] had a friendly word for everyone on board, and [chatted] with them whether they [spoke] English or not. But then . . . [he'd profess] he [didn't] like meeting people. 'They usually end up boring me,' [he'd say]."

One day on deck, Armstrong's husband, Michael, started to tell a joke. "Don't bother," Joe said. "I've heard them all. They're all variations of each other. Why don't you save time and tell me the punch line? Or just tell me the beginning and I'll know if I've heard it already."

"There was this guy—"

"I've heard that one!"

Later, Armstrong overheard Joe muttering to Valerie, "Why are you telling me this? I don't want to know about that."

Valerie rolled her eyes. "He's not interested in anything," she said.

One chilly afternoon, Armstrong came upon Joe leaning against the ship's railing. He watched the boat's prow nudge the ice barrier. A brisk and gusty North Pole breeze ruffled his still-thick hair. She made small talk. "I've heard that already!" Joe snapped. "Time to get off the ship."

By now, she'd witnessed this routine often enough to know it was pose as much as truth. She asked what he *did* like to speak about. What did he enjoy in life?

"Little," he replied. "I feel passionately about nothing anymore." Back home, he still went to lunch with old friends, but they didn't talk much these days, he admitted. "We've said it all. There's nothing new to say."

The wind reddened his cheeks. Ice walls rose around the ship. "I'd like to be in love again," Joe confessed. "Women seem more beautiful to me now than they ever were, or else I'm noticing them more than ever now that I can't make use of them. I love sex and I miss it."

Gingerly, Armstrong mentioned Viagra.

Joe shook his head. "There's a big difference between desire and arousal. First, you have to find someone exciting enough to want to use it. Sex starts in the head. I need some sense of romance. Men have one fatal flaw." He watched a seabird tilt against cloud light. "It's the yearning for love and romance. And that longing for love outlasts the capacity for sex. It persists to old age."

Armstrong was silent. Joe shrugged. Despite the cold, he suggested they go below for ice cream. Ever since childhood, he said, ice cream had been his favorite comfort food.

They joined Valerie and Michael. Later, on deck, Joe continued to be in a ruminative mood. "I'm realistic and resigned about life, but there's one thing I regret," he said. "I wish I'd been more adventurous, more confrontational. I'm a bit of a moral coward, really. Maybe it's because I want people to like me. I've never had the courage to live like Norman Mailer, have four wives and stab one." Armstrong couldn't tell if he was joking. "I'm too conventional." Joe sighed.

Valerie shook her head. "He's lying," she said. "He's not at all conventional."

"I don't like arguments," Joe insisted. "I withdraw and stop talking. I do anything to avoid confrontation. Maybe that's because at home my family never talked about deep feelings." The light was fading. The ship had eased into a narrow fjord. Joe stepped away from the group. Intently, he gazed at the jagged line of granitic mountains on the yellow-and-blue horizon.

FAITH SALE HAD CANCER.

Frederick Karl was on dialysis.

Mario Puzo's legs pained him.

Speed Vogel was susceptible to respiratory infections.

Sister Sylvia took Coumadin for blood clots.

Candida Donadio was deteriorating.

Shirley was gone. Perlie was gone. Lee was gone. So was Lou Berkman.

What was it Willa Cather once said? When you reach a certain age, life rains death all around you.

The good news: Ted's book had moved closer to publication. Michael Korda at Simon & Schuster had bought *Portrait of an Artist, as an old Man.* "What next, then?" Joe's alter ego in the novel, the aging scribbler Eugene Pota, asks himself. "The artificer who lives long enough, particularly the writer of fictions . . . may come to a time in his life when he feels he has nothing new to write about but wishes to continue anyway." It isn't a choice, even though the "singular fact about the creation of fiction is that it . . . turn[s] more, not less, difficult with seasoning and accomplishment."

On most days, Joe still had interest and—knock wood—time. Nothing forced him more deeply into himself than the writing of novels.

And then Erica announced she was getting married.

She had met the Dutch artist Ronald van den Boogaard. He owned an advertising agency in Amsterdam called Brains-in-the-Box. He shared Erica's wry sense of humor and was "incredibly expressive about his feelings," an honesty that, in her experience, had been "verboten on this side of the Atlantic."

The couple planned a small wedding at the Brant Point Lighthouse on Nantucket Island in November. Joe met them one day at a diner in Manhattan. He said he was pleased to see them looking so happy and hoped they would have a long life together. Marriages were made to last a lifetime, he told Erica with tears in his eyes, just like mine and your mom's.

If you need money, we'll talk, he said. Don't fax anything to the house.

At Thanksgiving, he dropped in on Deborah Karl and her husband, Bob Massie. Sofia, their eighteen-month-old, had eaten a Popsicle and smeared chocolate all over her face. Joe was so amused by her surprised and messy expression, he took Valerie back the next day to watch Sofia eat another Popsicle.

At the end of November—now a proud father-in-law—he underwent a complete physical exam. The doctor pronounced him fit. He said it wouldn't be a bad idea for Joe to consult a cardiologist, but there was no hurry. It just made good sense for a man of his age and weight (he was back up to 185 pounds) to take precautions.

During the first week of December, Arthur Gelb saw Joe at a dinner party in East Hampton. "That evening he was sweet-tempered and subdued," Gelb recalled. "I asked him if he was feeling well. He said he regretted to report that age seemed to be mellowing him, and that people would have to stop referring to him as curmudgeonly."

Walking to lunch a day or so later with George Mandel, Joe "expressed horror of the exceptionally broad avenue we were crossing, but strode right on to the safer side . . . short of breath," Mandel said. "I think that disturbing symptom . . . escaped me because of his unfailing nerve."

On the evening of December 10, 1999, a Friday, "Joe was on the phone, trying to get a friend to get him off the hook . . . so he wouldn't have to go to the movies [with me]," Valerie said. "But no one answered, so Joe and I went to see James Bond. And *did* have a good time. He was laughing out loud, grabbing my arm, slapping my knee. So much laughing. Thrilling at the special effects. It was a wonderful date."

The movie was *The World Is Not Enough*, starring Pierce Brosnan. Perhaps the film's finest moment was the line "If you can't trust a Swiss banker, what's the world come to?" Joe could have delivered something better—*had* topped it, in fact, with greater wit and timing in his part of the screenplay for *Casino Royale* so many years ago.

The next day, he sent Chris Buckley a fax: "We both may have reason to be [smug] for backing what thus far looks like a winner of sorts with Ted's novel. As a . . . proud father, I'm taking the liberty of sending you a couple of good pre-pub reviews." Afterward, he and Valerie drove to a restaurant called the Palm, in the Hunting Inn on Main Street in East Hampton, for steaks and Nova Scotian lobster.

The following morning, clear skies ushered unusual winter light and warmth into the backyard. Joe and Valerie talked of the trips they'd take in the coming year—a new century, a new millennium—Italy, Ireland at the end of the summer. The publication of his novel would bring a fresh round of travel and events—enjoyable if planned well in advance and not scheduled too close together. "He was looking forward to so much," Valerie said. A copy of the galleys for Ted's book, *Slab Rat,* lay open on a living room table. Joe smiled each time his glance fell on the pages.

After dinner that evening, he said the house felt stuffy. He wanted to take a walk on the beach. The stars were as clear as the sunshine earlier. Later, Valerie couldn't remember how long he'd been gone. When he returned, he was sweating and pale. He went to bed early (Phillipe following quietly at his heels) with what he thought was indigestion. "That night . . . he became my patient again," Valerie said.

"VALERIE CALLED us at about five A.M.," Dolores Karl recalled. "I heard the phone ring. Fred was already awake, and I got up. Who would call that early? Fred came out of his study and said, 'Dolores, sit down. Joe is dead.' I could see how shaken he was. Right away, I phoned Valerie and asked if she needed help, and she said she would appreciate it if I came over. When I told Fred, he said, 'Don't leave me alone.' Well, if you knew Fred—'Don't leave me alone' was not one of his statements. Usually, he was happy to be left alone to work. I knew something was wrong. So I called the doctor and immediately the doctor hospitalized him. He was suffering a severe heart attack."

Much later, once Fred was resting comfortably and Dolores knew he would be all right, she learned from Valerie that *Joe's* heart attack had probably started during his walk on the beach. Back in the house, in bed, he took some medication for indigestion. It didn't help. Soon, he slipped into unconsciousness, breathing shallowly. Valerie tried to resuscitate him. By the time she got the ambulance there, he was dead.

She spent the morning of December 13 phoning East Hampton friends and friends in the city. Finally, she called Joe's kids.

"Oh God, this is a calamity for American literature," Kurt Vonnegut said when he got the news.

John Updike was more restrained: "[As a novelist,] he wasn't top of the chart, [but] he was a sweet man. And *Catch-22* is an important book."

Taken together, the comments traced Joe's critical reputation during his lifetime.

Elie Wiesel said, "I will miss reading the books he didn't write."

On the afternoon of the thirteenth, Chris Buckley faxed Valerie: "Sweetheart, he *loved* you so deeply. He talked about you at every lunch and dinner we had, always with pride. . . . [Years ago,] if someone had told 2nd Lieutenant Joey Heller, as he was about to set off on one of those harrowing sixty missions in his B-25 that he would survive the war and die peacefully more than half a century later, one of the most celebrated writers in American history, a proud father, in the arms of the woman he loved, surely he would have said, 'What's the catch?'"

THE RABBI at Joe's funeral service did not know Joe's son and daughter would appear, and so he did not mention them in his remarks. He had understood from Valerie that Joe's kids were estranged from him. Joe's nephew, Paul, who now ran a Chinese restaurant in Los Angeles, managed to plug the restaurant in his eulogy for his uncle.

Joe had wanted to be cremated, but he was placed in a casket draped with an American flag. "I could hardly believe my eyes," Erica said. Someone told her that because her father was a war veteran, the costs of the funeral would be mitigated if it were conducted military-style. Erica's weeping appeared to unnerve Valerie.

Joe was interred in the Cedar Lawn Cemetery in East Hampton. Jerry McQueen was one of the pallbearers. He remembered hefting Joe into the Russian Tea Room years ago when Joe—as Mario Puzo put it—had come back from the dead.

"When we left the grave site, Mel Brooks was reading some of the names on the tombstones—McCarthy, Smith, Vitale," McQueen recalled. "Brooks said, 'Joe, they buried you in a goy cemetery.' We all laughed"—the day's last sound.

Epilogue : Cleaning House

TWO WEEKS [after my father died], a messenger came to me at work and delivered [my] book to me. . . . This was the biggest moment in my life, and I couldn't tell him about it," Ted said. Subsequently, Ted married and had a daughter, whom he dearly wishes his father could have met. He published his second novel, *Funnymen,* in 2002.

Erica continues to live in the Apthorp. It remains a haunted house of sorts, under constant renovation (often without heat or electricity), new ownership, and with byzantine alterations to its occupancy policies. She has written a memoir of her mother and father.

Valerie sold the house she shared with Joe, but she still lives nearby.

The reception of Joe's posthumously published *Portrait of an Artist, as an old Man* was tepid. Joe's profile of an elderly fiction writer prone to frequent naps, lustful urges with no chance of fulfillment, discouraging talks with his editor, and false starts on novels (Tom Sawyer as a Wall Streeter, Hera as a harpie, *A Sexual Biography of My Wife*), met its toughest resistance from the *New York Times*' Michiko Kakutani. She called the novel "embarrassing" and expressed "regret" that it would harm a "distinguished," "inspired," and "sometimes brilliant" career. Heller's old skills—"bravura satire . . . zany, improvisational humor . . . ferocity and swagger"—were "sorely lacking" in *Portrait,* she said.

On the other hand, *The Observer*'s Tim Adams called the novel a "sardonic little abdication address, a posthumous piece of self-parody . . . [and] one last muted hurrah from a writer who [knew] his place in the authorial Hall of Fame was never really in doubt." Listing the book as one of the best American novels of 2000, David Gates, writing in *Newsweek,* said it was Heller's "slightest but scariest [production]: it amounts to a literary suicide note. . . . Heller must have known this book would chill every writer, and many readers, to the heart, while offering not a bit of comfort. For having that much nerve, you've got to admire him." And *The New Yorker,* which never published Joe, even when Bob Gottlieb edited the magazine, said, "There is something bleakly bracing in [the old writer's] obsession with his own literary desiccation."

A DECADE AFTER JOE'S DEATH, *We Bombed in New Haven* was staged regularly in regional theaters (in Fullerton, California, Valparaiso, Indiana, and Portland, Oregon), its antiwar theme perpetually timely. *God Knows* had been adapted for the stage in Israel. A new Hebrew translation of *Catch-22* had become an immediate bestseller in that country. *Something Happened* served as one of the templates for cable television's hottest new show, *Mad Men,* and Joe's novels, particularly *Something Happened* and *Closing Time,* were receiving renewed scholarly attention.

In the summer of 2010, the journalist John Grant wrote that Heller's "vision" was "tragically in synch" with the "highly privatized" way the U.S. military was prosecuting its war in Afghanistan—that is, paying its enemies to run convoys delivering food and supplies to U.S. troops. "Milo Minderbinder [is alive] in Afghanistan," Grant declared. At the same time, said the *New Statesman,* Milo oversaw British Petroleum's massive oil spill in the Gulf of Mexico. "Even when it's fouling its own nest and screwing everything in sight, [Milo's] syndicate"—in which "everybody has a share," making it too big to fail—"is good for the country. Similar logic is being used by . . . BP," wrote William Wiles on the magazine's blog site.

As these references suggest, Joe's reputation and importance to American literature rests—as he always knew it would—with *Catch-22,* which has sold over ten million copies to date, is a mainstay in college courses ranging from English to history to political science, and currently averages annual sales (according to Nielson BookScan) of around 85,000 copies.

On that basis alone, Thomas Edwards was right when he asserted in *The New York Review of Books* that "Heller is among the novelists of the last [few] decades who matter."

"[*Catch-22*] still blows me away," says Carl Hiassen. "[It] is one of the most phenomenal novels in the English language because of Heller's ability to make you laugh literally on every page while writing about the darkest of all human conditions, wartime."

Recently, Adam Mars-Jones, grousing in *The Observer* about what he felt was an overpraised new war novel, said, "Joseph Heller found . . . [that] a pose of heartlessness twists the knife more than any amount of earnest pain: thanks to this discovery, a book written about the second world war, published in 1961 (the year Hemingway died), belongs to the future rather than the past."

IN RECENT YEARS, with the deaths of Norman Mailer, John Updike, and J. D. Salinger, following the earlier losses of Saul Bellow, John Cheever, Donald Barthelme, Grace Paley, Bernard Malamud, William Gaddis, Susan Sontag, and Joe, among others, readers, critics, and observers of American culture have noted the passing of an astonishingly fertile era of U.S. literature.

It has coincided with the disappearance of the World War II generation. "Veterans of the Second World War dominated American public life for decades, but [John Paul] Stevens is practically the last one still holding a position of prominence. He is the only veteran of any kind on the [Supreme] Court," Jeffrey Toobin wrote in the March 22, 2010, issue of *The New Yorker*. "The war helped shape his jurisprudence, and even today shapes his frame of reference."

Weeks later, Stevens announced his retirement.

With the advent of the e-book, publishing, as understood by Joe's generation (one that still believed in the possibility of the Great American Novel and an underground press), may also have reached the finish line—or at least found a tipping point, with ramifications for authors, editors, booksellers, and readers still unclear.

Exactly ten years after the night Joe died, the *New York Times*, whose print version, like that of most newspapers and magazines, was struggling to remain afloat financially, reported that a legal battle had commenced for the digital rights to *Catch-22*. "[E]xactly who owns the rights to such [a title] is in dispute" among authors' heirs, traditional print publishers, and purveyors of new electronic formats, "making it a rising source of conflict in one of the publishing industry's last remaining areas of growth," Mokoto Rich wrote.

If he were here, Joe might ask if digital money was the same as printed money. In any case, his response to the information revolution, and the turmoil into which it has plunged publishing, would likely be a laugh and a shrug. Writing is just a form of procrastination, he used to say. What's all the fuss?

ON THE TENTH ANNIVERSARY of Joe's death, Christopher Buckley published a piece on the op-ed page of the *New York Times*. He yearned to know what Joe would have thought about America's absurd and terrifying entry into the twenty-first century, including incidents such as "9/11 . . . Saddam Hussein's hanging, available on cellphone and You-Tube, Dick Cheney shooting his lawyer . . . John Kerry, war hero, being depicted as a Swift-boating wimp . . . A.I.G. bonuses . . . [and] President Obama's accepting the Nobel Peace Prize shortly after ordering 30,000 more Americans to war."

But the world, propelled or pulled by events, ignores us—as Joe recognized in his most intimate writings. Perhaps the purest measure of a woman or man is not in the moments we manage to catch and consider publicly, but in the instants, minute to minute, we nearly miss.

Like this: "In the early 1980s, I was cleaning houses with my friend Mary in East Hampton and we had Joseph Heller's house on our schedule. I'd been there a few times and I remember it as very simply done inside. It seemed exactly the kind of house a man who was focused on other things would keep: it had only the essentials. It wasn't homey. It didn't show any personality. It was just pleasant and practical. That made it really easy to clean," says Margaret Dawe, now an associate professor of English at Wichita State University. "One day, Mary and I were simultaneously having family/love crises. On the way to Joseph

Heller's we stopped and bought lottery tickets because we were desperate for something good to happen.

"We went into his kitchen to start and by then we were in tears. Usually, Mr. Heller left for the day when we came and we didn't know he was there. We were standing at the sink filling a bucket of water and we'd already sprinkled the Spic and Span and we were both crying as the water ran, when Mr. Heller walked into the kitchen. I knew him from pictures in the paper. He was one of the writers who turned me upside down. I was fifteen when I read *Catch-22*, and I was laughing so hard reading it, the tears ran down my face.

"When he walked in the kitchen, we were all surprised to see one another and he saw us just sobbing and everyone kind of stopped. I was so embarrassed. And he looked from one of our faces to the other and he said, 'Is there anything I can do except leave?' Everything dire and dreadful inside us melted and Mary and I threw our heads back laughing. So, you know, we *did* win the lottery."

Joe hesitated only a moment between the freezer full of ice cream and the bucket of warm cleanser, in the presence of laughing women in tears, in sunlight promising good work hours ahead, and slipped quietly out of the kitchen.

ACKNOWLEDGMENTS

MICHAEL HOMLER of St. Martin's Press asked me one day if anyone had written a full-length biography of Joseph Heller, and this project was born. I am grateful to Michael for his suggestion and pitch-perfect editorial guidance. It has been a pleasure to work once more with Michael, George Witte, and the St. Martin's team. My thanks to Henry R. Kaufman for his legal counsel, Carol Edwards for the copyediting, and John Morrone for overseeing editorial production.

Kit Ward's enthusiasm and wisdom were essential to the book.

Kerry Ahearn, Chair of the English Department at Oregon State University, arranged for a sabbatical leave which enabled me to research and write. To Kerry, Ann Leen, and my colleagues in the College of Liberal Arts at OSU, I am grateful for years of friendship and support.

Ted Leeson is the best prose-doctor in the country. He coaxed several of my sentences to life.

Ryan Wepler at Brandeis University proved to be an efficient and discerning research assistant. Thanks to Rebecca Olson for putting me in touch with Ryan. At the University of South Carolina's Thomas Cooper Library, Patrick Scott, Jeffrey Malkala, and Elizabeth Sudduth offered me warmth, hospitality, and help. Sandra Stelts at Penn State University was gracious in gathering Helleriana for me.

Daniel Setzer's and Don Kaiser's military knowledge is matched by their generosity. Their research and resources are invaluable to all students of World War II. At Goodfellow Field, the base historian, Chad Dull, treated my father and me to a wonderful day while providing fascinating information about the base during Heller's time there. Betty Whitely, Archives Technician at the Military Personnel Records Facility of the National Personnel Records Center in St. Louis ably assisted Erica Heller and me in our search for Joseph Heller's military discharge records.

Phyllis Bobb, Tammy Carter at the University of Arizona, Nancy Crampton, Jill Krementz, Jonathan Barth, and Susan Wood Richardson were very kind in helping me secure photographs and permissions.

At the Jewish Theological Seminary, Ellen Kastel offered patient aid and kindness.

For their expert guidance through the world of 1950s American advertising, I am indebted to Bob Levenson, Tom Messner, and Curvin O'Reilly.

I am grateful to Robert Gottlieb for walking me through some of the ins and outs of publishing, particularly with reference to *Good as Gold*.

Joseph Heller was blessed with a capacity for friendship, as evidenced by the eagerness of so many of his family, friends, and colleagues to speak of him openly and with tremendous warmth. In particular, Erica Heller has gone out of her way to help me and her father's readers know his life as well as it can be known. Our many exchanges have been as delightful as they were fruitful, and her tour of the Apthorp was lovely. Ted Heller has been exceptionally generous. I am more grateful than I can say for his help and good humor.

My sincere thanks to Valerie Heller, George Mandel, and Luann Walker for sharing glimpses of their lives with Joe and Speed Vogel. Valerie was most helpful in providing encouragement, contact information, and rare photographs.

Joseph Stein spoke movingly and eloquently about his old friend with me. I am blessed to have had the chance to speak with him.

For their help, patience, forbearance, and kindness I am also indebted to the following people. In some instances, their willingness to return my calls or answer e-mails gave the book a necessary boost. Any errors of fact or interpretation in the narrative are mine, not theirs or anyone else's I spoke to for this project:

Florence Aaron, Norman Barasch, Skip Blumberg, Mel Brooks, Christopher Buckley, Audrey Chestney, Margaret Dawes, Bruce Jay Friedman, Per Gedin, Barbara Gelb, Charles Gwathmey and his staff, Herman Gollob, Ronnie Heller, Christopher Hitchens, Deborah Karl, Dolores Karl, Paul Krassner, Mell Lazarus, Amy Lubelski, David Markson, Bob and Abby Mason, Gerald McQueen, Judith Ruderman, Kirkpatrick Sale, Edith Seligson, Liz Smith, Jerome Taub, A. Robert Towbin, Amanda Urban, David Wood, and Lou Ann Walther.

I cannot claim Joseph Heller's gift for friendship, but I am graced with marvelous friends who make all work possible and worthwhile. I gratefully acknowledge each of them for their patience with me, particularly Michelle Boisseau, Glenn Blake, Elizabeth Campbell, Tom Cobb and Randy Mott, Karen Holmberg, Sue Rodgers, and Keith Scribner.

Kathie Lang, Keith Gregory, and George Ann Ratchford, late of SMU Press, are three reasons I was here to write this book, as is Ehud Havazelet who, in our weekly meetings, enhanced my literary education and enthusiasm.

Marjorie Sandor and Hannah Crum: there are not enough words for our human geography. They are all yours. I wish for more.

PROLOGUE: YO-YO

pages

1 *In his maturity, he will concede that most of us are never more conscious*: In several late-in-life interviews and in his 1998 memoir, *Now and Then,* Heller discussed his tendency to repress certain experiences, like war trauma and the death of his father, that might otherwise be self-revealing. See, for example, Lynn Barber, "Bloody Heller," *The Observer,* March 1, 1998, posted at guardian.co.uk/books1998/mar/01/fiction. josephheller; Joseph Heller, *Now and Then: From Coney Island to Here* (New York: Alfred A. Knopf, 1998), pp. 73, 178, 226, 234.

2 *"[h]eavy, intense and accurate"*: Daniel Setzer, "Historical Sources for the Events in Joseph Heller's Novel, *Catch-22,*" p. 21; posted at home.comcast.net/~dhsetzer.

2 *"I was in the leading flight"*: Heller, *Now and Then,* pp. 181–82.

3 *"I believed with all my heart and quaking soul"*: ibid., pp. 179–80.

3 *"The bombardier doesn't answer"*: ibid., p. 180.

3 *"Be nice to daddy"; "I [have] come to the wrong place"*: Joseph Heller, "Catch-22 Revisited," *Holiday,* April 1967, p. 53.

4 *"You will find out"*: This and subsequent conversation regarding this incident in ibid., p. 145.

5 *"How they landed the plane safely"*: War Diary report posted at warwingsart .com/12thAirforce/8u8p.html.

5 *"2nd Lt. J. Heller"; "2nd Lt. F. Yohannan"*: orders for the 488th Bombardment Squadron, 340th Bombardment Group, posted at usmilitariaforum.com/forums/index.php?act =attach&type=post&id=91891.

5 *"His self-insight comes and goes"*: Phillip Lopate, "Back to the Boardwalk," *New York Times,* February 15, 1998.

5 *"I . . . don't understand what's meant by"*: Ramona Koval, "Books and Writing," ABC

Radio National, 1998; transcript posted at abc.net.au/rn/bookshow/stories/2008/2266926 .htm.

6 *"I'm the bombardier"*: This and subsequent conversation taken from Heller, *Now and Then,* pp. 179–80.

1. DOMESTIC ENGAGEMENTS

pages

9 *"help women who on occasion feel nervous"*: This and details about San Angelo, Texas, in the 1940s are taken from Mark Kneubuhl, "Boomtown San Angelo," posted at san angelolive.com/node/2205.

10 *"were quite dubious whether or not we were capable of flying"*: John V. Garrett, *A Brief History of Goodfellow Air Force Base* (San Angelo, Texas: 17th Training Wing History Office, 2008), p. 34.

11 *"scant, inacc[urate] flak"*: Daniel Setzer, "Historical Sources for the Events in Joseph Heller's Novel, *Catch-22,*" p. 67; posted at home.comcast.net/~dhsetzer.

11 *Transportation home could be delayed for many reasons*: Daniel Setzer in an e-mail to the author, July 9, 2009.

11 *"I pretty much enjoyed [Texas]"*: Joseph Heller, *Now and Then: From Coney Island to Here* (New York: Alfred A. Knopf, 1998), p. 194.

11 *"his large nose and his eyes"*: Susan Braudy, "A Few of the Jokes, Maybe Yes, But Not the Whole Book," *The New Journal* 26 (1967): 7.

12 *"almost nothing to do"*: Heller, *Now and Then,* p. 194.

12 *"I was so terrified on my last few missions"*: Sam Merrill, "*Playboy* Interview: Joseph Heller," *Playboy,* June 1975, pp. 64–66.

12 *"turned out to be true"*: Heller, *Now and Then,* p. 172.

12 *the number of training accidents*: History of the 2533rd AAF Base Unit (Pilot School, Prim-Basic) at Goodfellow Field, San Angelo, Texas, p. 46. For further information on domestic accidents involving military aircraft, see "USAAF Stateside Accident Reports," posted at aviationarchaeology.com/src/AARmonthly.

13 *"hard-nosed, sexist attitudes"*: Heller, *Now and Then,* pp. 186–87.

13 *"He turned over on his back"*: Joseph Heller, "I Don't Love You Any More," in *Catch as Catch Can: The Collected Stories and Other Writings,* ed. Matthew J. Bruccoli and Park Bucker (New York: Simon & Schuster, 2003), p. 5.

13 *"boyish and ravenous satyr"*: Heller, *Now and Then,* p. 170.

14 *"I married you because it was part of the dream"*: Heller, *Catch as Catch Can,* p. 3.

14 *"I don't want to sit in a room filled with people"*: ibid.

16 *"mountains had everything"*: Joey Adams, with Henry Tobias, "Comics, Singers, and Tummlers," in *In the Catskills: A Century of the Jewish Experience in "The Mountains,"* ed. by Phil Brown (New York: Columbia University Press, 2002), p. 233.

16 *"This is what it was like"*: Joyce Wadler, "The Fine Art of Mountain *Tummling,*" in *In the Catskills,* ed. Brown, 248.

18 *"air was redolent"*: Brown, ed., *In the Catskills,* p. 269.

18 *"I learned to spot a single woman"*: Tania Grossinger, *Growing Up at Grossinger's* (New York: Skyhorse Publishing, 2008), p. 14.

18 *"[G]oods and entertainment that were previously unavailable"*: Phil Brown, *Catskill Culture: A Mountain Rat's Memories of the Great Jewish Resort Area* (Philadelphia: Temple University Press, 1998), p. 182.

19 *"There was not time for subtle flirtations"*: Grossinger, *Growing Up at Grossinger's,* p. 19.

19 *"I met the girl"*: Heller, *Now and Then,* p. 197.

19 *"At a dance contest one night"*: Erica Heller in an e-mail to the author, August 26, 2009.

19 *"They had each grown up very poor"*: Erica Heller in an e-mail to the author, July 11, 2009.

20 *"He was very handsome"*: ibid.

20   *"derived from tumult-maker"*: Adams "Comics, Singers, and Tummlers," p. 228.
20   *"included a whole variety of ethnic caricatures"*: Ellen Schiff, "Shylock's Mishpocheh: Anti-Semitism on the American Stage," in *Anti-Semitism in American History,* ed. David Gerber (Urbana: University of Illinois Press, 1986), p. 84.
21   *"I returned to the city"*: Heller, *Now and Then,* p. 197.
21   *"sugar and tinsel dream of life"*: Heller, *Catch as Catch Can,* p. 3.
22   *"A pitcher of beer"*: ibid., p. 5.
22   *In 1942, for both economic and patriotic reasons*: See "Combatting Advertising Decline in Magazines During WWII: Image Ads Promoting Wartime Themes and the War Loan Drives," *WJMCR* 1, no. 1 (1997), posted at scripps.ohiou.edu/wjmcr/vol01/1-1a-B .htm.

2. A CONEY ISLAND OF THE MIND

pages

25   *"At Coney Island"*: Alex Marshall, "Coney Island: The Train Is the Thing," posted at alexmarshall.org/index.php?pageId=96.
25   *"One must go to Coney Island"*: Michael Immerso, *Coney Island: The People's Playground* (New Brunswick, NJ: Rutgers University Press, 2002), p. 127.
26   *"vomiting multitudes"*: ibid.
26   *"If France is Paris"*: ibid., p. 50.
26   *"race up and down the hard sand"*: ibid., p. 14.
26   *George Tilyou*: For details regarding Tilyou's hucksterism and the founding of Steeplechase Park, see Jeffrey Stanton, "Coney Island—First Steeplechase," posted at westland .net/coneyisland/articles/steeplechase1.htm.
27   *"glorified city of flame"*: Immerso, *Coney Island,* p. 79.
27   *"moving like [the] compositions of Michelangelo and Rubens"*: Richard Cox, "Coney Island: Urban Symbol in American Art," in *Brooklyn USA: The Fourth Largest City in America,* ed. Rita Seiden Miller (New York: Brooklyn College Press, 1979), p. 145.
27   *"The only thing about America that interests me"*: Immerso, *Coney Island,* p. 3.
27   *"Centrifugal force never fails"*: ibid., p. 55.
27   *"scarier than flying"*: "The Riegelmann Boardwalk Is Built," *The American Experience,* Public Broadcasting Service (WGBH), 1999–2000; posted at pbs.org/wgbh/amex/coney/ peopleevents/pande10.html.
27   *"succeeded because they combined socially acceptable thrills"*: Marshall, "Coney Island."
27   *"barnfires"; "mickeys"*: Joseph Heller, *Now and Then: From Coney Island to Here* (New York: Alfred A. Knopf, 1998), p. 79.
28   *"It brent a fire in street"*: Joseph Heller, *Good as Gold* (New York: Simon & Schuster, 1979), p. 323. Heller spoke openly about the autobiographical nature of the Coney Island sections in *Good as Gold.* See, for example, Adam J. Sorkin, ed., *Conversations with Joseph Heller* (Jackson: University Press of Mississippi, 1993), p. 195.
28   *"I was not aware of coldness or warmth"*: ibid., p. 194.
28   *"I . . . never grappled much with the idea"*: Heller, *Now and Then,* pp. 233–34.
28   *"from somewhere in western Russia"*: ibid., p. 38.
28   *Ambiguity clouds the family name*: Details and surmises about Heller family history are taken from various sources. See "The Heller Surname," posted at ancestry.com/facts/ Heller-places-origin.ashx, as well as discussions on the Heller Family Genealogy Forum, posted at genforum.genealogy.com/heller. For information about Yom-Tov Lipmann, see Joseph Davis, *Yom-Tov Lipmann Heller* (Oxford: Littman Library, 2004) and *The Jewish Encyclopedia* (New York: Funk and Wagnalls, 1900–1906). See also C. U. Lipschitz and Neil Rosenstein, *The Feast and the Fast* (New York: Maznaim, 1984). I am grateful to Sheila Heller, who shared information with me in an e-mail on July 14, 2009.
29   *fourteenth census of the United States*: 1920 United States Federal Census, posted at ancestry.com.
29   *ship manifest*: "New York Passenger Lists, 1820–1957," posted at ancestry.com.

29 *The likely possibilities*: A useful online database for locating alternate names and spellings of Eastern European cities, past and present, can be found in ShtetlSeeker database at jewishgen.org/wconnect/wc.dll?jg~jgsys~shtetlexp5.

29 *"redistributing [America's] wealth"*: "Roosevelt's Super-Socialism," *New York Times*, September 30, 1913.

29 *"Not to take [the] paper"*: Irving Howe, *World of Our Fathers: The Journey of the East European Jews to America and the Life They Found and Made* (New York: Shocken, 1989), p. 518.

30 *"where the doctors eat"*: Various publications have reported versions of Handwerker's story. See, for example, Bee Wilson, "Dog's Dinner," *The New Statesman*, January 21, 2002, p. 47.

30 *"People often need the opportunity"*: Isaac Metzger, ed., *A Bintel Brief: Sixty Years of Letters from the Lower East Side to the Jewish Daily Forward* (New York: Shocken, 1971), p. 13.

30 *"I am a girl from Galicia"*: letter cited in "The Bintel Brief" at pbskids.org/bigapple history/life/topic6.html. See also Sarah Weiss, "'A Bintel Brief': A Journey to America," *The Concord Review* 9, no. 4 (1999): 220. Weiss's essay provides useful background information on the *Jewish Daily Forward*'s advice column.

31 *"strangers to [your] own neighbors"*: Weiss, "'A Bintel Brief,'" p. 218.

31 *"If you got money, come down and buy"*: Charles T. Powers, "Joe Heller, Author on Top of the World," *Los Angeles Times*, March 30, 1975; reprinted in Sorkin, ed., *Conversations with Joseph Heller*, pp. 142–43.

31 *"He used to wet my carriage"*: Sorkin, ed., *Conversations with Joseph Heller*, p. 195.

32 *"There were lots of Jewish criminals around"*: Heller, *Now and Then*, p. 233.

33 *"When you come from California"*: ibid., p. 231.

34 *The 1930 census*: 1930 United States Federal Census, posted at ancestry.com.

35 *"I was told [by my playmates] to lie on the ground"*: letter from Lee Heller to Joseph Heller, undated, Joseph Heller Archive, Department of Rare Books and Special Collections, Thomas Cooper Library, University of South Carolina, Columbia, South Carolina.

36 *he began to bite his nails*: Heller, *Now and Then*, p. 14.

36 *"I approached [the Chaser]"*: Joseph Heller, "Coney Island: The Fun Is Over," *Show*, July 1962, p. 50.

37 *"[Eventually,] I could anticipate"*: Heller, *Now and Then*, p. 50.

37 *"chozzer mart"*: ibid., p. 37.

38 *"real impression"*: Dale Gold, "Portrait of a Man Reading," *Washington Post Book World*, July 20, 1969; reprinted in Sorkin, ed., *Conversations with Joseph Heller*, p. 57.

39 *"Joe brought home a note"*: Sorkin, ed., *Conversations with Joseph Heller*, pp. 195–96.

39 *"He was brighter than all of us"*: ibid., p. 195.

40 *"emotional surge"*: Mervyn Rothstein, "Morris Lapidus, an Architect Who Built Flamboyance into Hotels, Is Dead at 98," *New York Times*, January 19, 2001.

40 *"morbid[ity]" and "comedy" in his writing*: Joseph Heller, remarks made at Michigan State University, March 9, 1992; audio recording available at matrix.msu.edu/cls/view celebrity?first=Joseph&last=Heller.

40 *"when the ticket booths close[d]"*: Heller, *Now and Then*, pp. 100–01.

40 *"My world was small and horrible"*: Isaac Babel, "The Story of My Dovecot," in *Collected Stories*, trans. David McDuff (New York: Penguin, 1994), pp. 38–39.

41 *"I didn't realize then how traumatized I was"*: Sorkin, ed., *Conversations with Joseph Heller*, p. 195.

41 *"As always, when talking of his parents"*: ibid., p. 196.

41 *"Joe was a nervous wreck"*: ibid.

41 *"I do recall"*: George Mandel in an e-mail to the author, July 20, 2009.

41 *"suffering headaches"*: Heller, *Now and Then*, p. 14.

42 *"I was in heaven"*: ibid., p. 10.

42 *"[F]ew pleasures are so thoroughly reinforcing"*: ibid.

42 *"I associate money with life"*: ibid., p. 118.

42 *"Extra! Hitler dies"*: ibid., p. 10.
42 *"First this was Coney Island"*: Heller, *Good as Gold,* p. 319.
43 *"repeal unemployment"*: "Third Parties: Repeal Unemployment," *Time,* August 8, 1932; posted at time.com/time/magazine/article/0,9171,744111,00.html.
43 *"Hoover, Hoover, rah, rah, rah!"*: Heller, *Now and Then,* p. 25.
44 *"haunted imagination"*: ibid., p. 72.
45 *"You've got a twisted brain"; "Ma, can I have a glass of milk"*: ibid., p. 75.
45 *"At once I saw with terror"*: ibid.
45 *"How long have you been doing that?"*: ibid., pp. 138–39.
46 *he married a sweet woman named Perle*: Perle Ingber, who came from Brooklyn, went to work for the President Novelty and Jewelry Company in Manhattan.
46 *though he was not her biological son*: Heller, *Now and Then,* pp. 5–6. See also Sorkin, ed., *Conversations with Joseph Heller,* pp. 196–97.

3. FEAR OF FILING

pages
48 *"I felt victimized, disgraced"; "I [fell] silent"*: Joseph Heller, *Now and Then: From Coney Island to Here* (New York: Alfred A. Knopf, 1998), p. 6.
48 *"to stifle painful emotion"; "walking proof"*: ibid., p. 73.
48 *"Our stepmother raised us"*: Adam J. Sorkin, ed. *Conversations with Joseph Heller* (Jackson: University Press of Mississippi, 1993), p. 197.
48 *The* Lapland's *manifest*: "New York Passenger Lists, 1820–1957," posted at ancestry .com. Sylvia's stepson, Charles Gurian, has discovered that Isaac Heller's first wife was named Pauline Yellin. Born in Russia, she died in the United States on March 14, 1918.
48 *"just mom and me"*: letter from Lee Heller to Joseph Heller, undated, Joseph Heller Archive, Department of Rare Books and Special Collections, Thomas Cooper Library, University of South Carolina, Columbia, South Carolina.
49 *"I still am unable to decide"*: Heller, *Now and Then,* p. 15.
49 *"coming to [his listeners] from the city of New York"*: Joseph Heller, *Closing Time* (New York: Simon & Schuster, 1994), p. 207.
49–50 *"Coney Island whitefish"*: ibid., p. 131.
50 *though the teachers were mostly second-generation Jewish college graduates*: Deborah Dash Moore, *At Home in America: Second Generation New York Jews* (New York: Columbia University Press, 1981), p. 98.
50 *"Okay, youse guys, quiet down"*: letter from Lillian Morgenstern to Joseph Heller, undated, Joseph Heller Archive.
50 *"Titty Bottles"*: Heller, *Now and Then,* p. 86.
51 *"I didn't even know what Protestant was"*: Heller, *Good as Gold,* p. 115.
51 *"Where does a Jew come to a horse?"* ibid.
52 *"We all hated [it]"*: letter from Sylvia Heller Gurion to Joseph Heller, February 14, 1976, Joseph Heller Archive.
52 *"I taught you how to hustle, so listen to me"*: Richard Lehan and Jerry Patch, "Catch-22: The Making of a Novel," in *Critical Essays on Catch-22,* ed. by James Nagel (Encino, CA: Dickenson, 1974), pp. 39–40.
52 *"When I [finally] came in contact with good literature"*: Joseph Heller, interviewed by Don Swaim, "Wired for Books," CBS Radio, September 19, 1984; audio recording available at wiredforbooks.org/josephheller.
53 *"secret and serious, nonsexual crush[es]"*: Heller, *Now and Then,* p. 94.
53 *"prowl[ed] about the kitchen"*: ibid., p. 75.
53 *"[One evening] I learned"*: ibid., p. 82.
55 *"perceptive enough to be wary of [people]"*: George Mandel, remarks made at "Joseph Heller: A Celebration," a memorial service held at the New York Society for Ethical Culture on June 13, 2000. Transcribed by the author from a video recording (courtesy of Erica Heller).

55   *the comic-book industry was beginning to burgeon*: For an overview of the comic-book industry, see Bradford W. Wright, *Comic Book Nation: The Transformation of Youth Culture in America* (Baltimore: Johns Hopkins University Press, 2001), pp. 1–29.

56   *"Pepsi Cola hits the spot"; "If there's a gleam in her eye"*: Heller, *Closing Time*, pp. 205, 208.

58   *"This is the voice of"*: letter from the *Jewish Daily Forward* in Isaac Metzger, ed., *A Bintel Brief: Sixty Years of Letters from the Lower East Side to the Jewish Daily Forward* (New York: Shocken, 1971), p. 107.

58   *"[w]e were prudent with money"*: Heller, *Now and Then*, p. 17.

60   *"Miss Peck or Miss Beck"; "dark, buxom, married, mature"*: ibid., p. 131.

61   *College was out of reach for them financially*: In *Now and Then* (page 22), Heller wrote that as a "concession to respectable conformity," he applied to night school at Brooklyn College when he was eighteen, though this was not financially feasible and he "much preferred [his] nighttime social life" to the idea of going to night classes.

61   *"[You] have been reading about the bad break I got"*: Lou Gehrig, speech at Yankee Stadium, July 4, 1939; posted at lougehrig.com/about/speech.htm.

61   *"fragrances of olive oil"*: Heller, *Now and Then*, p. 136.

65   *"Circumcised"*: ibid., p. 156.

66   *"[At the time,] we did not know about the concentration camps"*: "World War II Writers Symposium" at the University of South Carolina, April 12–14, 1995," in *Dictionary of Literary Biography Yearbook 1995*, ed. Matthew Bruccoli (Farmington Hills, MI: Thomson Gale, 1996), p. 157.

66   *"[B]y the end of 1942"*: ibid., p. 139.

66   *"The day I enlisted"*: ibid., p. 153.

66   *In the hours following the invasion at Pearl Harbor*: LeRoy Ashby, *With Amusement for All: A History of American Popular Culture Since 1830* (Lexington: University Press of Kentucky, 2006), pp. 263–64.

67   *"[T]he feeling after Pearl Harbor was nationwide"*: "World War II Writers Symposium," p. 156.

67   *"[S]ociety in America"*: ibid., p. 143.

67   *"'moratorium' that emerges in the lives"*: Heller, *Now and Then*, pp. 166–67.

4. A COLD WAR

pages

69   *aviation cadet training*: According to Susan Braudy, "First Heller went to armorers' school. Then he transferred to cadet school when rumors began to circulate that armorers became gunners. Gunners didn't last long in combat." See Susan Braudy, "A Few of the Jokes, Maybe Yes, But Not the Whole Book," *The New Journal* 26 (1967): 9–10.

70   *"You have a twisted brain"*: Joseph Heller, *Now and Then: From Coney Island to Here* (New York: Alfred A. Knopf, 1998), p. 151.

71   *Years later, Heller recalled doing the lindy hop*: See Joseph Heller, *Closing Time* (New York: Simon & Schuster, 1994), pp. 221–22. The character of Sammy Singer in the novel shares almost identical biographical experiences with Heller. According to journalist Philip Marchand, "[Heller] admits that *Closing Time*'s Singer is based on himself." See Philip Marchand, "Joseph Heller Looks Back with Fondness," *Toronto Star,* April 7, 1998.

72   *"I loved Denver"*: Joseph Heller, "I Am the Bombardier!" *New York Times Magazine,* May 7, 1995, p. 61.

73   *"They put us in dark rooms"*: "World War II Writers Symposium" at the University of South Carolina, April 12–14, 1995, in *Dictionary of Literary Biography Yearbook 1995,* ed. Matthew Bruccoli (Farmington Hills, MI: Thompson Gale, 1996), p. 162.

73   *"The most surprising thing about preflight school"*: Samuel Hynes, *Flights of Passage: Recollections of a World War II Aviator* (New York: Penguin, 1988), p. 37.

74   *"weird, twisted pieces of metal"; "The Norden bombsight"*: "World War II Writers Symposium," pp. 159–60.

74   *"Mindful of the secret trust"*: The Bombardier's Oath is posted on numerous Web sites. See, for example, centennialofflight.gov/essay/Dictionary/NORDEN_BOMBSIGHT/DI145.htm.

74   *"not all that it should be to obtain the maximum efficiency"*: See 389thbombgroup.com/timeline01.php.

75   *"the President ha[d] appointed and commissioned [him]"*: The standard appointment letter can be seen at reddog1944.com/charles_cook_air_corps_bio001.htm.

75   *By the end of the following month*: Joseph Heller, individual flight record, March 1944, Joseph Heller Archive, Department of Rare Books and Special Collections, Thomas Cooper Library, University of South Carolina, Columbia, South Carolina.

75   *"entertainment [in Columbia] was limited"*: See "History: Activation and Training Period Before Departure, Sept. 11, 1942 to Feb. 14, 1943," posted at reddog1944.com/487th_Squadron_Album_History%20of%20the%20340th.htm.

75   *logged over 230 hours in the air*: Joseph Heller, individual flight record, April 25, 1944, Joseph Heller Archive.

75   *The B-25s on which he trained*: For details on bomber training, I have drawn upon Samuel Hynes's *Flights of Passage*, reddog1944.com, and Harry D. George and Harry D. George, Jr., *Georgio Italiano: An American Pilot's Unlikely Tuscan Adventure* (Victoria, BC: Trafford, 2000).

77–78   *"jackassing around"; "It is an unwritten law"*: Captain Everett B. Thomas, *Round the World with the 488th Bombardment Squadron, Aug. 20, 1942–Nov. 7, 1945* (privately printed yearbook, 1946), pp. 11, 15. A rare copy of this yearbook is kept in the Joseph Heller Archives.

78   *"[T]hey weren't entirely at home with its raucous splendor"*: Heller, *Now and Then*, p. 136.

78   *"in transit overseas"*: Joseph Heller, individual flight record, April 27, 1944, Joseph Heller Archive.

79   *Once airborne over the ocean*: For details of the overseas journey, I have drawn upon George and George, *Georgio Italiano*.

79   *"[In Algeria], I shared a tent with a medical assistant"*: Heller, *Closing Time*, p. 224. Philip Marchand cites Heller's admission that the character of Singer in *Closing Time* is based on him in "Joseph Heller Looks Back with Fondness," *Toronto Star*, April 7, 1998.

80   *a sign on the outskirts of the field*: For a photograph of this sign, see "The 489th Bombardment Group in Corsica," posted at warwingsart.com/12thAir Force/page.html.

80   *"Capt. Winebrenner"*: Daniel Setzer, "Historical Sources for the Events in Joseph Heller's Novel, *Catch-22*," p. 27; posted at home.comcast.net/~dhsetzer.

80   *"[T]he sound of a .45 discharging"*: Dominique Taddei, *U.S.S. Corsica, L'ile porte-avions* (Ajaccio, Corsica: Albiana, 2003), p. 95.

81   *"A few practice shots"*: Setzer, "Historical Sources for the Events in Joseph Heller's Novel, *Catch-22*," p. 18.

82   *"something of a tireless wonder"*: Heller, *Now and Then*, p. 174.

82   *"symptoms of fear"*: ibid., p. 175.

83   *"Word is going around"*: Setzer, "Historical Sources for the Events in Joseph Heller's Novel, *Catch-22*," p. 55.

84   ibid., p. 56.

84   *"I wanted to see what was happening"*: "World War II Writers Symposium," p. 161.

84   *"[The] smell of romance"*: ibid., p. 179.

84   *"I saw it as a war of necessity"*: ibid., p. 186.

85   *"Medium level bombing of bridges"*: This and all subsequent quotes taken from the "History [of the] 488th Bombardment Squadron, 340th Bombardment Group" are from a copy of the document sent to the author by Daniel Setzer.

87   *"People think it's a joke"*: "World War II Writers Symposium," p. 150.

87   *"had dysentery all the time"*: ibid., p. 146.

87   *"[H]alf the squadron was inundated"*: Setzer, "Historical Sources for the Events in Joseph Heller's Novel, *Catch-22*," p. 32.

87   *"Seven planes [were holed]"; "Vandermuelen died"*: ibid., p. 45.

87   *"I'm cold"*: Heller, *Now and Then*, p. 178.

88   *"sickly attempts"*: ibid.

88   *"Ferrara . . . had [already] assumed in my memory"; "They were trying to kill me"*: ibid., pp. 178, 181.

88   *"This period was one of ordinary activity"*: Daniel Setzer, "Raid on the Settimo Road Bridges," p. 22. Setzer's article is based on Roger Juglair and Silvana Miniotti, *Ponte San Martino: Martirio di un paese valdostano.* Setzer's translation of Juglair and Miniotti's account, along with his additional research and commentary, is the most detailed English-language version of what happened at Pont-Saint-Martin. It is posted online at http://home.comcast.net/~dhsetzer/Settimo.pdf.

89   *"I'm not aware of any of our consciences ever being bothered"*: "World War II Writers Symposium," p. 162.

89   *"bombing a totally undefended village"; "Dunbar . . . dropped his bombs"*: Joseph Heller, *Catch-22* (New York: Simon & Schuster, 1961), pp. 325, 330.

89   *"men [were] . . . apprehensive"*: Setzer, "Historical Sources for the Events in Joseph Heller's Novel, *Catch-22*," pp. 48–49.

89   *"The first American soldiers [marched into] Rome"*: Heller, *Now and Then*, p. 176.

90   *"[F]ellow fliers were coming back from Rome"*: Joseph Heller, rough draft of "Innocents Abroad," p. 16, Joseph Heller Archive.

90   *"most valuable phrase"*: ibid.

90   *"[We] had horse-drawn cabs"*: ibid.

90   *"On the second day of my first leave there"*: Heller, *Closing Time*, pp. 229–30.

91   *"Killing time between meals"*: This and all subsequent quotes about Rome are taken from Heller, rough draft of "Innocents Abroad," pp. 16–21.

92   *"Once upon a time"*: For this and other details about the legend of the Lucky Little Bell of San Michele, see "The 57th Fighter Group: The Lucky Little Bell of San Michele," posted at warwingsart.com/12thAirForce/luckybell.html.

92   *"Because we carried no bombs"; "It's okay,"*: Heller, *Now and Then*, pp. 184–85.

93   *"I have not been able to get an answer"*: Daniel Setzer in an e-mail to the author, July 9, 2009.

93   *"Many of the crews"*: This and subsequent War Diary entries cited in Setzer, "Historical Sources for the Events in Joseph Heller's Novel, *Catch-22*," p. 58.

93–94   *"two chaste beginners"; "huge and invisible divide"*: Heller, *Now and Then*, pp. 169, 185.

94   *"There were flies in inflamed eyes"*: This and all subsequent quotes about Cairo, Naples, and shipboard experiences are taken from Heller, rough draft of "Innocents Abroad," pp. 24–25, 30–31.

5. "I DON'T LOVE YOU ANY MORE"

pages

96   *"[T[here were[n't] many young men who came out of World War II"*: "World War II Writers Symposium" at the University of South Carolina, April 12–14, 1995, in *Dictionary of Literary Biography Yearbook 1995*, ed. Matthew Bruccoli (Farmington Hills, MI: Thompson Gale, 1996), p. 180.

97   *His flight record for March 1945*: Joseph Heller, individual flight record, March 1945: Joseph Heller Archive, Department of Rare Books and Special Collections, Thomas Cooper Library, University of South Carolina, Columbia, South Carolina.

97   *"great number"*: This and subsequent quotes about the returnees are from History of the 2533rd AAF Base Unit (Pilot School, Prim-Basic) at Goodfellow Field, San Angelo, Texas, p. 46.

98   *"name band"*: Flight Time 3, no. 46 (1945): 2.

98   *"courtesy patrols"*; *"military discipline of personnel at this station"*: ibid., 63.

98   *"My mother got cold feet"*: This and subsequent comments about her parents are from Erica Heller in an e-mail to the author, May 31, 2009.

99   *"Trains that made stops at most every small town"*: David Wood in an e-mail to the author, June 3, 2009.

99   *"It was Shirley's mother who [really] took the initiative"*: Joseph Heller, *Now and Then: From Coney Island to Here* (New York: Alfred A. Knopf, 1998), p. 197.

99   *"V-E Day"*: Michael Dorman and DeQuendre Neeley, "New Yorkers Remember V-E Day," posted at chicagotribune.com/topic/ny-history-ww2ved2,0,1025579.story.

100   *"without foundation"*: Flight Time 3, no. 28 (1945): 2.

100   *"The State Department has made public"*: Flight Time 3, no. 46 (1945): 2.

100   *Later, he claimed he left Texas in mid-May*: Heller, *Now and Then,* pp. 55–56; "World War II Writers Symposium," p. 153.

100   *Chad Dull*: Dull's opinion expressed in conversation with the author, Goodfellow Field, August 10, 2009.

101   *"[One] weekend . . . an order arrived"*: Heller, *Now and Then,* pp. 55–56.

101   *His individual flight record confirms*: Joseph Heller, individual flight record, May 14, 1945, Joseph Heller Archive.

101   *"a spell of beautiful weather"*; *"passed away of attrition"*: Heller, *Now and Then,* pp. 55, 56.

101–02 *"When we went on the Parachute Jump"*; *"felt with sadness"*: ibid., p. 57.

102   *"Overnight, I was"*: ibid., p. 189.

102   *"I cannot recall a single expression of outrage"*: "World War II Writers Symposium," p. 168.

102   *"I really honestly believe"*: ibid., p. 169.

102   *"I was a very happy civilian"*; *"[O]nce we were in formation"*: ibid. pp. 161, 162.

103   *"purposely" cruel*: This and all other quotes from "I Don't Love You Any More," as well as Heller's comment in the contributor's notes from *Story* magazine, are in Heller, *Catch as Catch Can: The Collected Stories and Other Writings,* ed. Matthew J. Bruccoli and Park Bucker (New York: Simon & Schuster, 2003), pp. 1–8.

103   *"[I]t [was] based on things I knew nothing about"*; *"malign and histrionic"*; *"convention"*: Heller, *Now and Then,* p. 189.

104   *"most appreciative audience"*: This and all other quotes from Barbara Gelb are taken from Adam Sorkin, ed., *Conversations with Joseph Heller* (Jackson: University Press of Mississippi, 1993), pp. 189, 193, 198.

104   *"very elegant, though understated"*: Dolores Karl in conversation with the author, April 24, 2009.

104   *"privileged"*: Heller, *Now and Then,* p. 192.

104   *"Dottie and Barney were an interesting couple"*: Jerome Taub in an e-mail to the author, January 8, 2010.

104   *"knew the difference between sirloin steak and top sirloin"*: Heller, *Now and Then,* p. 205.

105   *There was at all times a degree of competition"*: Israel Goldstein, *My World as a Jew,* vol. I (New York: Herzl Press, 1984), p. 261.

105   *"initial step toward the definitive solution"*; *"sufferance ha[d] been the badge"*: ibid., pp. 170, 171.

106   *"was a lot of drinking"*; *"one of Joe's relatives"*: Jerome Taub in an e-mail to the author, January 4, 2010.

106   *"The motives for my decision"*: Heller, *Now and Then,* p. 193.

6. WORDS IN A BOX

pages

110   *"We feel compelled to say no to it"*: Ben Yagoda, *About Town: The New Yorker and the World It Made* (New York: Scribner, 2000), p. 235.

111   *"He had been kept close to home while his father was alive"*: Joseph Heller, "World

Full of Great Cities," in *Catch as Catch Can: The Collected Stories and Other Writings,* ed. Matthew J. Bruccoli and Park Bucker (New York: Simon & Schuster, 2003), p. 63.

112 *David Seed notes the many direct echoes*: David Seed, *The Fiction of Joseph Heller: Against the Grain* (New York: St. Martin's Press, 1989), p. 14.

112 *a "distaste for everything that had happened to him in the war"; "isn't fun any more"*: Ernest Hemingway, "Soldier's Home" and "The End of Something," in *The Fifth Column and the First Forty-Nine Stories* (New York: P. F. Collier and Son, 1938), pp. 243, 208.

114 *"wanted to do something for the United States"; "If your mother dies"*: Carey McWilliams, "Watts: The Forgotten Slum," *The Nation,* August 30, 1965; posted at thenation.com/doc/19650830/mcwilliams.

114 *"neon-lighted slum"*: This and subsequent quotes by Raymond Chandler are from David Wyatt, *Five Fires: Race, Catastrophe, and the Shaping of California* (New York: Oxford University Press, 1997), pp. 161–62.

115 *"I wanted to find [things] out"*: Joseph Heller, *Now and Then: From Coney Island to Here* (New York: Alfred A. Knopf, 1998), p. 194.

115 *"I am embarrassed to confess"*: ibid., p. 200.

116 *"And thus a new weapon, the pure science method"*: Joseph Heller, "Bookies, Beware," in *Catch as Catch Can,* ed. Bruccoli and Bucker, p. 11.

116 *"fiction is not merely a diversion"*: letter from Joseph Heller to Whit Burnett, November 22, 1962, Archives of *Story* Magazine and *Story* Press, 1931–1999, Princeton University Manuscripts Division, Princeton University Library.

116 *"I am wondering, too, if the treatment of a flier"*: letter from Whit Burnett to Joseph Heller, August 22, 1946, Archives of *Story* Magazine and *Story* Press.

117 *"I [then] had thoughts of becoming a playwright"*: Heller, *Now and Then,* p. 202.

117 *"held as sacred"*: ibid.

118 *"I couldn't deny to myself that I really had an imagination"*: Charles Ruas, *Conversations with American Writers* (New York: Alfred A. Knopf, 1985), pp. 147–48.

118 *"[H]e pointed out my faults to me"*: Heller, *Now and Then,* p. 208.

119 *"wrote perfect short stories"*: ibid.

119 *"a meager, short fellow"*: ibid.

119 *"[H]e would sit down at his typewriter"*: ibid.

119 *"[I]t's a pity . . . we [didn't] meet then"*: Joseph Heller, remarks made at the "1999 James Jones Literary Society Symposium," Long Island University (Southampton campus), June 1999; posted at jamesjonesliterarysociety.org/jheller.htm.

120 *"That should have steeled me against unkind critiques"*: Heller, *Now and Then,* p. 212.

121 *"long[s] for people who were real"; "Darling, something terrible has happened"*: Joseph Heller, "The Death of a Dying Swan," in *Catch as Catch Can,* ed. Bruccoli and Bucker, pp. 213, 214.

121 *"I was [always] taking too long to begin"*: Heller, *Now and Then,* p. 209.

121 *"thinking and writing in terms of peace"*: *The Atlantic Monthly,* March 1948, p. 52.

121 *In later years, he would claim his best work was generated*: See, for example, Ruas, *Conversations with American Writers,* p. 155.

122 *"My Uncle David was a sober man"*: This and all other quotes from "Castle of Snow" are from *The Atlantic Monthly,* March 1948, pp. 52–55.

123 *"vanguard of the much-heralded and long awaited 'post-war generation' "*: Martha Foley, foreword, *Best American Short Stories 1949 and the Yearbook of the American Short Story* (Boston: Houghton Mifflin, 1949), p. vii.

7. NAKED

pages
125 *"inept and immature"; "[a] tome, [a] masterwork"; "book with tremendous brea1dth"*: Charles Ruas, *Conversations with American Writers* (New York: Alfred A. Knopf, 1985), p. 150.

125 *"We were about the same age"*: George Plimpton, "Joseph Heller," *The Paris Review* 15

(1974); reprinted in Adam J. Sorkin, ed., *Conversations with Joseph Heller* (Jackson: University Press of Mississippi, 1993), p. 116.

125   *"War novels were coming into vogue"*: Ruas, *Conversations with American Writers*, p. 150.

125   *"Mailer was very good as an illusionist"*: ibid.

126   *He took a course taught by Lionel Trilling*: The course was titled American Literature Since 1870.

126   *Trilling had become the first Jew to get tenure*: Several faculty members opposed Trilling's appointment on the grounds that his Jewish upbringing would hamper his ability to understand fully English literature's Anglo-Saxon roots. See Norman Podhoretz, *Breaking Ranks: A Political Memoir* (New York: Harper & Row, 1979), p. 11.

126   *"literature is the human activity"*: Louis Menand, "Regrets Only: Lionel Trilling and His Discontents," posted at newyorker.com/arts/critics/atlarge/2008/09/80929crat_atlarge_menand?

127   *"in large part . . . Jewish middle-class"*: ibid.

127   *"never possible for a Jew"*: ibid.

127   *a "horror"; "[T]here was just nobody there"*: Adam Kirsch, "Lionel Trilling and Allen Ginsberg: Liberal Father, Radical Son," posted at vqronline.org/articles/2009/summer/kirsch-trilling-ginsberg.

128   *"panic-stricken kids in blue jeans"*: ibid.

129   *"Most of the students were veterans"*: Untitled article, *The Owl: The Alumni Newsletter of the School of General Studies* (Columbia University), Fall/Winter 2006, p. 24.

129   *"acquire . . . standards"*: Joseph Heller, *Now and Then: From Coney Island to Here* (New York: Alfred A. Knopf, 1998), p. 211.

129   *"We can scarcely understand postwar fiction"*: Morris Dickstein, *Leopards in the Temple: The Transformation of American Fiction, 1945–1970* (Cambridge: Harvard University Press, 2002) p. 25.

130   *"were the diminished heirs"*: ibid., p. 26.

130–31   *"[F]rom the fate of a people"; "civilization rent asunder"*: Joseph Freeman, introduction, *Proletarian Literature in the United States* (New York: International Publishers, 1935), p. 8.

131   *"something that has never been done before in this country"*: John Tebbel and Mary Ellen Zuckerman, *The Magazine in America, 1741–1990* (New York: Oxford University Press, 1991), p. 343.

131   *"Running parallel to many combat/war novels"*: Frederick R. Karl, *American Fictions, 1940–1980* (New York: Harper & Row, 1983), p. 95.

132   *"[I]n the 1930s . . . the pulp fiction world"*: "World War II Writers Symposium" at the University of South Carolina, April 12–14, 1995, in *Dictionary of Literary Biography Yearbook 1995*, ed. Matthew Bruccoli (Farmington Hills, MI: Thompson Gale, 1996), p. 189.

132   *"that type of writing was going to go out of style"*: Sorkin, ed., *Conversations with Joseph Heller*, p. 160.

132   *"popular novelist of today"*: This and all subsequent Evans quotes are from Bergen Evans, "This Thing Called Love," *The Atlantic Monthly*, February 1948, pp. 26–29.

133   *"[Americans] have [now] been told"*: Tebbel and Zuckerman, *The Magazine in America, 1741–1990*, p. 252.

134   *"[I]f Rockwell drew cliché situations"*: ibid., p. 175.

134   *"It was fortunate . . . [he] did not live"*: ibid., p. 176.

134   *"transact our necessary business"*: "The Atlantic Report on the World Today," *The Atlantic Monthly*, February 1948, p. 20.

135   *"Not for one hundred years"*: Martha Foley, foreword, *Best American Short Stories 1948 and the Yearbook of the American Short Story* (Boston: Houghton Mifflin, 1948), p. vii.

135   *"an original contribution of nothing new"*: Joseph Heller, manuscript of *Catch-22*, chapter 8; unpaginated: Joseph Heller Collection, Brandeis University Libraries, Robert D. Farber University Archives and Special Collections Department, Waltham, Massachusetts.

135   *"I'm surprised [it] was approved"*: Chet Flippo, "Checking in with Joseph Heller," in *Rolling Stone,* April 16, 1981; reprinted in Sorkin, ed., *Conversations with Joseph Heller,* p. 234.

135   *"I'm not sure that my motivations"*: ibid., p. 234.

135   *"[H]er parents found delight in watching me eat"*: Heller, *Now and Then,* p. 205.

136   *"gushed in praise"*: ibid., p. 204.

136   *"Superheroes allowed adolescents"; "It had been a long, nerve-wearing run"*: Gerard Jones, *Men of Tomorrow: Geeks, Gangsters and the Birth of the Comic Book* (New York: Basic Books, 2004), p. 232.

137   *"All the guys think I'll make a million dollars"*: George Mandel's story is recounted in Mario Puzo, *The Godfather Papers and Other Confessions* (Greenwich, CT: Fawcett, 1972), pp. 30–31.

137   *"You're not going to England"*: Heller, *Now and Then,* p. 192.

137   *"I didn't even wait to see if my master's thesis"*: Jonathan Sale, "Passed/Failed: Joseph Heller," *The Independent,* March 11, 1999; posted at independent.co.uk/news/people/profiles/passedfailed_joseph_heller_1079745.html.

137   *"cut corners"*: Heller, *Now and Then,* p. 192.

137–38   *"When I had the Fulbright"; "war mentality"*: Sorkin, ed., *Conversations with Joseph Heller,* pp. 56–57.

138   *"very good progress"; "was impressed by the place"*: David Seed, *The Fiction of Joseph Heller: Against the Grain* (New York: St. Martin's Press, 1989), p. 12.

138   *"I [always] had a distinct sense of the strength of this guy"*: Sorkin, ed., *Conversations with Joseph Heller,* p. 190.

138   *"I have had no previous teaching experience"*: letter from Joseph Heller to Theodore J. Gates, January 31, 1950, Special Collections Library, University Libraries, Pennsylvania State University, College Park, Pennsylvania.

138   *"I believe I should not encourage you to apply"*: letter from Theodore J. Gates to Joseph Heller, February 17, 1950, Special Collections Library, University Libraries, Pennsylvania State University.

138   *"Although I should prefer to finish the year at Oxford"*: letter from Joseph Heller to Theodore J. Gates, March 4, 1950, Special Collections Library, University Libraries, Pennsylvania State University.

139   *"detailed information on his personality"*: letter from Theodore J. Gates to the Director of Placement, Columbia University, March 14, 1950, Special Collections Library, University Libraries, Pennsylvania State University.

139   *"a very fine appearing young man"*: letter from Margaret Morgan to Theodore J. Gates, March 24, 1950, Special Collections Library, University Libraries, Pennsylvania State University.

139   *Follow-up letters of recommendation*: All quotes excerpted by the Columbia University Placement Bureau and included in Joseph Heller's confidential placement file, Special Collections Library, University Libraries, Pennsylvania State University.

139   *"I am twenty-seven years old and married"*: letter from Joseph Heller to Theodore J. Gates, January 31, 1950, Special Collections Library, University Libraries, Pennsylvania State University.

140   *"scheduled to arrive in New York"*: letter from Joseph Heller to Theodore J. Gates, May 9, 1950, Special Collections Library, University Libraries, Pennsylvania State University.

140   *"In other words"*: letter from Theodore J. Gates to Joseph Heller, May 16, 1950, Special Collections Library, University Libraries, Pennsylvania State University.

140   *"I am not in the reserves"*: letter from Joseph Heller to Theodore J. Gates, July 31, 1950, Special Collections Library, University Libraries, Pennsylvania State University.

8. TEA AND SYMPATHY

pages

142   *"In those days, [Penn State] was more of an agricultural school"*: Unless otherwise indicated, this and subsequent comments by Frederick Karl are taken from his remarks

made at "Joseph Heller: A Celebration," a memorial service held at the New York Society for Ethical Culture on June 13, 2000. Transcribed by the author from a video recording (courtesy of Erica Heller).

142   *"Come have lunch"*: Dolores Karl in conversation with the author, April 24, 2009.

143   *"walking on the street"*: Erica Heller in an e-mail to the author, May 13, 2009.

143   *"malfeasance"*; *"compelled . . . to show mercy"*: Joseph Heller, *Now and Then: From Coney Island to Here* (New York: Alfred A. Knopf, 1998), pp. 162–163.

144   *"What happened on* this *spot?"*: This anecdote was related to the author by Bob Mason in a conversation on November 3, 2009.

144   *a World War II drama that never went anywhere*: According to David Seed, Twentieth Century–Fox asked Heller if he would like to work on movie scripts; at the time, he was teaching at Penn State. Heller worked with Bernard Oldsey on a script entitled *The Trieste Manuscripts,* described by Oldsey as a "hundred-page stripped-down novel functioning as an adaptation script for a movie." The project came to a halt when *Night Train to Trieste* and *Diplomatic Courier* were released; both movies dealt with spies in Trieste near the end of World War II, the subject of Heller and Oldsey's script in progress. See David Seed, *The Fiction of Joseph Heller: Against the Grain* (New York: St. Martin's Press, 1989), p. 91.

144   *"wanted to be honest"*; *"When you needed him"*: Bob and Abby Mason in conversation with the author, November 3, 2009.

145   *"Top [Nittany] Lion Boxer"*: "Al Tapman Receives Goodman Trophy as Year's Top Lion Boxer," *Penn State Collegian,* May 5, 1939.

145   *"plucky"*; *"gentlemanly"*; *"magnificent physical condition"*: "Boxing Intercollegiates' Last Weekend," *Penn State Collegian,* March 12, 1939.

145   The *"old lion in [him]*: Charlie O' Connor, letter in *Penn State Collegian,* March 17, 1939.

145   *"You look at the number of Jewish comedy writers"*: Norman Barasch in conversation with the author, April 29, 2009.

146   *"the idea of being charged with something"*: Dale Gold, "Portrait of a Man Reading," *Washington Post Book World,* July 20, 1969, p. 2.

146   *"persons who are disloyal to the United States"*: "Communists in Government Service, McCarthy Says," posted at senate.gov/artandhistory/history/minute/Communists_In_Government_Service.htm. See also Robert Griffith, *The Politics of Fear: Joseph R. McCarthy and the Senate* (Amherst: University of Massachusetts Press, 1970), p. 49.

147   *"structure"*; *epic feeling*: Gold, "Potrait of a Man Reading," p. 2.

147   *"slangy use of prose"*; *"flippant approach to situations"*: "The Heller Cult," *Newsweek,* October 1, 1962, pp. 82–83.

147   *"blending of the comic and tragic"*: W. J. Weatherby, "The Joy Catcher," *The Guardian,* November 20, 1962.

147   *"restores our theater to an art again"*: Bruce Weber, "Robert Anderson, Author of 'Tea and Sympathy,' Dies at 91," *New York Times,* February 10, 2009; posted at nytimes .com/2009/02/10/theater/10anderson.html.

147   *"Joe said that, in New York"*: This and subsequent comments by Bob Mason are from a conversation with the author, November 3, 2009.

148   *"That play is a fraud"*: Weber, "Robert Anderson, Author of 'Tea and Sympathy,' Dies at 91."

149   *"State Department is infested with Communists"*: Griffith, *The Politics of Fear,* p. 49.

149   *"conspiracy so immense"*: Joseph McCarthy, *Major Speeches and Debates of Senator Joe McCarthy Delivered in the United States Senate, 1950–1951* (Washington D.C.: U.S. Government Printing Office 1953), p. 215.

149   *"career destruction"*: Unless otherwise indicated, this and subsequent quotes from George Mandel are taken from his remarks at "Joseph Heller: A Celebration."

149   *"Jewish hang-ups"*: Seed, *The Fiction of Joseph Heller,* p. 8.

149   *"only one of my contemporaries"*: Morris Dickstein, *Leopards in the Temple: The Transformation of American Fiction, 1945–1970* (Cambridge: Harvard University Press, 2002), p. 32.

150 *"[At the time,] I could not see myself spending more than two years"*: Joseph Heller, remarks made at the James Jones Literary Society Symposium, June 1999; posted at james jonesliterarysociety.org/jheller.htm.

151 *Joe "calculated" that his life was half over*: Barbara Gelb, in conversation with the author, August 2, 2010.

151 *"I have the opportunity at this time"*: letter from Joseph Heller to Theodore J. Gates, May 27, 1952, Special Collections Library, University Libraries, Pennsylvania State University, College Park, Pennsylvania.

151 *"Mr. Heller is an accomplished writer"*: letter from Theodore J. Gates to Ben Euwema, June 2, 1952, Special Collections Library, University Libraries, Pennsylvania State University.

151 *"I don't hate anybody here"*: Nadine Kofman, "Novelist Taught Composition at Penn State in Early 1950s," *Penn State Collegian*, October 21, 1974.

151 *"It is now certain"*: letter from Joseph Heller to Theodore J. Gates, March 20, 1953, Special Collections Library, University Libraries, Pennsylvania State University.

151 *"ability to get along with others"*: letter from Lillian M. Farkas to Penn State University, September 1, 1953, Special Collections Library, University Libraries, Pennsylvania State University.

152 *"honest, dependable, and loyal"*: letter from Theodore J. Gates to the Personnel Department at the Army and Air Force Exchange Service, undated, Special Collections Library, University Libraries, Pennsylvania State University.

152 *"He declined"*: Stanley Weintraub in an e-mail to Sandra Stelts of the Special Collections Library, Pennsylvania State University, April 23, 2009; e-mail provided to the author by Sandra Stelts on behalf of Mr. Weintraub.

9. CAUGHT INSIDE

pages
155 *"Isn't this the building where they found dead people on the roof?"*: Comment posted at ny.therealdeal.com/articles/mann-slated-to-settle-apthorp-lawsuit.

155 *"This is like the House of Usher"*: Frank Bruni, "Dispute at Ritzy Address Is Emblem of NYC Rent Control Debate," *New York Times*, April 13, 1997; posted at www.tenant.net/Alerts/Guide/press/nyt/fb041397.html.

155 *"pigeon feathers"*: Michael Idov, "Apoplectic at the Apthorp" posted at www.printthis.clickability.com/pt/cpt?action=cpt&title=Apoplectic+at+the+Apthorp.

156 *The house, finished in 1764*: For details on the design of Elmwood Manor, see Ellen Susan Bulfinch, ed., *The Life and Letters of Charles Bulfinch, Architect* (Boston: Houghton Mifflin, 1896), pp. 83–84; Kenneth Hafertepe and James F. O'Gorman, *American Architects and Their Books to 1848* (Amherst: University of Massachusetts Press, 2001), p. 7.

156 *"doughty royalist Charles Ward Apthorp"*: "End 100-Year Fight Over Apthorp Land," *New York Times*, July 24, 1910; posted at query.nytimes.com/mem/archive-free/pdf?_r=1&res=9501E6DB1239E433A2575C2A9619C946196D6CF.

157 *a "display of horticulture"*: Christopher Gray, "The Not-So-Secret Garden in the Apthorp's Courtyard," *New York Times,* July 22, 2007; posted at www.nytimes.com/2007/07/22/realestate/22scap.html.

158 *"She never had a cross word"*: "Tenants Mourn Elevator Woman Who in 35 Years Was Never Cross," *New York Times*, October 15, 1953; posted at spiderbites.nytimes.com/pay_1953/articles_1953_10_00003.html.

159 *"I was born at French Hospital"*: Erica Heller in an e-mail to the author, April 21, 2009.

159 *"Erica, for Beethoven's Eroica Symphony"*: Jerome Taub in an e-mail to the author, January 5, 2010.

159 *"Now here's how it was"*: Shirley Polykoff, *Does She . . . or Doesn't She? And How She Did It* (Garden City, NY: Doubleday, 1975), p. 30.

160 *"Your name is familiar"*: ibid., p. 108.

160 *"gray fedora with a dark band"*: Joseph Heller, *Now and Then: From Coney Island to Here* (New York: Alfred A. Knopf, 1998), p. 113.

161 *"first Gibsons"*: ibid., p. 167.

161 *"going when I came into work"*: Art Kramer, "Art Kramer's WWII Stories: The Birth of the Catches," posted at www.coastcomp.com/artkramer/catches.html.

161 *"All the copywriters were writing plays"*: Ann Waldron, "Writing Technique Can Be Taught, Says Joseph Heller," *Houston Chronicle,* March 2, 1975.

161 *"Even before 1960"*: Mary Wells, "The Truth About 'Mad Men' Told by a Real-Life 'Mad' Woman," posted at www.wowowow.com/print/612.

162 *"[I]t was from the magazine advertisements"*: Polykoff, *Does She . . . or Doesn't She?,* p. 10.

162 *"On the outside"*: Martin Mayer, *Madison Avenue, U.S.A.* (New York: Harper & Brothers, 1958), p. 7.

162 *"[I]t can truthfully be said"*: ibid., p. 8.

162 *"There was a steam table bar"*: Tom Messner in an e-mail to the author, September 2, 2009.

162 *"[s]urprisingly often"*: Mayer, *Madison Avenue, U.S.A.,* p. 9.

163 *A former employee at BBDO recalls*: This information was provided to the author in an e-mail on September 8, 2009, by a person who wishes to remain anonymous.

163 *According to* Advertising Age: Mayer, *Madison Avenue, U.S.A.,* p. 11.

163 *"I thought it bizarre"*: Heller, *Now and Then,* p. 109.

163 *"The media people come first"*: Mayer, *Madison Avenue, U.S.A.,* p. 15.

164 *"man's world"*: Jane Maas, *Adventures of an Advertising Woman* (New York: St. Martin's Press, 1986), pp. 21–22.

164 *"beetle brows"*: ibid., p. 22.

164 *"during the World Series"*; *"prevailed during business hours"*: Heller, *Now and Then,* pp. 110–11.

165 *"We were pregnant together"*: Audrey Chestney in conversation with the author, January 5, 2010.

165 *"[There] was a rumor"*: Heller, *Now and Then,* p. 111.

165 *"Now, here, you see"*: ibid., p. 112.

166 *"slept little and gamboled much"*; *"distinctive taverns"*; *"lucky"*: George Mandel, *Flee the Angry Strangers* (1952; reprint, New York: Thunder's Mouth Press, 2003), pp. x, xiii.

166 *"never could understand artists and writers"*; *"They had a bunch of creeps come in there"*: Roy Thomas, "'Comics Were Great!': A Colorful Conversation with Mickey Spillane," posted at twomorrows.com/alterego/articles/11spillane.html.

167 *"All [his friends] were ecstatically astonished"*: Heller, *Now and Then,* p. 252.

167 *"transition between . . . [a] wail of hopelessness"*: Thomas Newhouse, *The Beat Generation and the Pop Novel in the United States, 1945–1970* (Jefferson, NC: McFarland, 2000), p. 105.

168 *degraded into* pot; *"Madison Avenue"*: Mandel, *Flee the Angry Strangers,* p. xiv.

169 *"Nembutal goofballs and pod"*: ibid., p. 164.

169 *"An old line"*: Tom Messner in an e-mail to the author, September 2, 2009.

169 *"sought people who were funny"*: ibid.

169 *"It took . . . the Jews"*: Wells, "The Truth About 'Mad Men' Told by a Real-Life 'Mad' Woman," posted at www.wowowow.com/print/612.

169 *"World War II vets"*: Tom Messner in an e-mail to the author.

170 *"Cheater's Night"*: Noted in an e-mail to the author on September 8, 2009, by a person who wishes to remain anonymous.

170 *"girls came to the windows of the dorms"*: Dan Wakefield, *New York in the Fifties* (Boston: Houghton Mifflin, 1992), pp. 206–07.

170 *"Why aren't [the panty raiders] in the Army"*: ibid., p. 207.

170 *"female contraceptive[s], a plug"*: ibid., p. 233.

171 *"an event of great importance in our culture"*: ibid., p. 204.

171 *"there was lots of underground romantic stuff"*: ibid., p. 231.

171 *"affairs"*: Lynn Barber, "Bloody Heller," *The Observer,* March 1, 1998; posted at guardian.co.uk/books1998/mar/01/fiction.josephheller.

171 *"womanizer"*: ibid.

171 *"I would ... say that my imagination"*: Adam J. Sorkin, ed., *Conversations with Joseph Heller* (Jackson: University Press of Mississippi, 1993), p. 174.

172 *"A friend from* Time": Heller, *Now and Then,* p. 113.

172 *"most intensely and destructively competitive"*: Mayer, *Madison Avenue, U.S.A.,* p. 187.

172 *"feel"*: This and subsequent Gilbert Lea quotes are taken from ibid., p. 180.

172 *"The Togetherness theme"*: ibid., p. 179.

173 *"great bulk of advertising"*: ibid., p. 315.

173 *"Advertising requires extreme simplification"*: ibid., p. 316.

10. 18

pages

174 *"The novel, you know"*: Susan Braudy, "A Few of the Jokes, Maybe Yes, But Not the Whole Book": *The New Journal* 26 (1967): 7.

174 *"the parties"*: Joseph Heller and George Mandel, Dramatist's Guild Collaboration Contract, October 17, 1952, Joseph Heller Archive, Department of Rare Books and Special Collections, Thomas Cooper Library, University of South Carolina, Columbia, South Carolina.

175 *"across the street from a railroad yard"*: This and subsequent quotes from Joseph Heller and George Mandel, "The Bird in the Flevverbloom Suit," are taken from the draft of the play, Joseph Heller Archive.

175 *"There was a terrible sameness"; "conversations with two friends"*: W. J. Weatherby, "The Joy Catcher," *The Guardian,* November 20, 1962.

175 *The Czech writer Arnold Lustig*: Arnold Lustig, with Frantisek Cinger, *3 X 18: Portraits and Insights* (Prague: Nakladatelstvi Andrej Stastny, 2003), p. 271.

176 *"I was lying in bed"*: Adam J. Sorkin, ed., *Conversations with Joseph Heller* (Jackson: University Press of Mississippi, 1993), pp. 106–107.

176 *"a flier facing the end of his missions"*: letter from Whit Burnett to Joseph Heller, August 22, 1946, Archives of *Story* magazine and Story Press, 1981–1989, Princeton University Manuscripts Division, Princeton University Library.

176 *"arrived at work"*: Joseph Heller, *Now and Then: From Coney Island to Here* (New York: Alfred A. Knopf, 1998), p. 167.

177 *"The agents were not impressed"*: Joseph Heller, "Preface to *Catch-22*," in *Catch-22* (1961; reprint with a preface by Heller, London: Vintage, 1994), unpaginated.

177 *"While he was alive"; "She saw something"*: Karen Hudes, "Epic Agent: The Great Candida Donadio," *Tin House* 6, no. 4 (2005): 153.

177 *"Candida, this is completely wonderful"*: Jonathan R. Eller, "Catching a Market: The Publishing History of *Catch-22*," *Prospects: An Annual Journal of American Cultural Studies* 17 (1992): 478.

177 *"socialized most agreeably"*: Heller, *Now and Then,* p. 249.

177 *"Joe would call him"*: This and all other comments by Dolores Karl are from a conversation with the author, April 24, 2009.

178 *"I grew up with the Heller kids"*: Deborah Karl in conversation with the author, April 18, 2009.

178 *"She had more synonyms for excrement"; [S]he used to say all the time"*: Hudes, "Epic Agent," p. 152.

178 *"People tell a lot of contradictory stories"*: ibid., p. 155.

179 *"polish silver"; Carmelite nun*: Daniel Simon, "Literature's Candida," posted at www .thnation.com/doc/20010528/simon.

179 *"She really was the agent of her generation"*: Lawrence Van Gelder, "Candida Donadio, 71, Agent Who Handled 'Catch-22,' Dies," *New York Times,* January 25, 2001; posted at www .nytimes.com/2001/01/25/arts/candida-donadio-71-agent-who-handled-Catch-22.

179 *"Since a secretary was very important"*: ibid.

179 *"a Bohemian Quakeress"*: letter from Victor Weybright to Mrs. Carleton Palmer, May

25, 1953, *New World Writing* Collection, Beinecke Rare Book and Manuscript Library, Yale University, New Haven, Connecticut.

180   *"[Publishing] a literary and academic journal"*: letter from Victor Weybright to Rudolf M. Littauer, *New World Writing* Collection.

180   *"provide a friendly medium"; "Avant Garde Means You!"*: Thomas L. Bonn, "Among the Eminent, the Aspiring, and the Young: A Short History of *New World Writing*," *Publishing Research Quarterly* (1993): 6, 17.

180   *"cultural high-water mark"*: Kenneth C. Davis, *Two-Bit Culture: The Paperbacking of America* (Boston: Houghton Mifflin, 1984), pp. 191–92.

180   *"difference in quality"*: Bonn, "Among the Eminent, the Aspiring, and the Young," p. 9.

180   *"[T]he story begins to end"*: Victor Weybright, "To the Reader," *New World Writing 15* (1959): unpaginated.

181   *"I should like to tell you"*: Davis, *Two-Bit Culture*, p. 200.

181   *"him a great disservice"*: Ellis Amburn, *Subterranean Kerouac: The Hidden Life of Jack Kerouac* (New York: St. Martin's Press, 1999), p. 209.

181   *"sick of well-meaning editors"*: ibid.

182   *"Coney Island of the soul"*: Bill Morgan, *The Lost Generation in New York: A Walking Tour of Jack Kerouac's City* (San Francisco: City Lights Books, 1997), p. 89.

182   *"the booze ran freely"*: Dan Wakefield, *New York in the Fifties* (Boston: Houghton Mifflin, 1992), p. 283.

183   *"It is certainly the funniest thing"*: letter from Victor Weybright to Arabel Porter, June 28, 1954, *New World Writing* Collection, Beinecke Rare Book and Manuscript Library, Yale University.

183   *"Among all the recommended pieces"*: comments by Arabel Porter to Walter Freeman, June 14, 1954, *New World Writing* Collection.

183   *"with a pain in his liver"*: This and subsequent quotes from "Catch-18" are taken from Joseph Heller, "Catch-18," *New World Writing*, no. 7 (1955): 204–14.

184   *"I'm not that interested in the subject of war"*: Israel Shenker, "Did Heller Bomb on Broadway?" *New York Times*, December 29, 1968.

184   *"seek[ing] a way of telling a story"; "an act of the imagination"*: Richard B. Sale, "An Interview in New York with Joseph Heller," *Studies in the Novel* 4 (1972); reprinted in Sorkin, ed., *Conversations with Joseph Heller*, pp. 79–80.

185   *"literature, except for a brief period in recent history"*: Sorkin, ed., *Conversations with Joseph Heller*, p. 79.

185   *"[A]ny writer who doesn't regard his work"*: ibid., p. 80.

185   *"Schweik . . . intervened"*: Jaroslav Hasek, *The Good Soldier Schweik*, translated by Paul Selver (1930; reprint, New York: Frederick Ungar, 1962), p. 12.

186   *"Joseph Heller . . . did more to debunk the Hemingway myth"*: Pete Hamill, "The Bearing of a Green: Some Thought[s] on Being Irish-American," posted at petehamill.com/bearinggreen.html.

187   *"Joe started talking [to me] about [this] novel"*: This and subsequent remarks by Frederick Karl were made at "Joseph Heller: A Celebration," a memorial service held at the New York Society for Ethical Culture on June 13, 2000. Transcribed by the author from a video recording (courtesy of Erica Heller).

187   *"We used to tease him"*: Dolores Karl in conversation with the author, April 24, 2009.

187   *Ideas rejected*: Notes Heller made on index cards are cited in James Nagel, "The *Catch-22* Note Cards," *Studies in the Novel* 8 (1976): 394–405. In the early 1970s, Heller gave Nagel permission to study the cards.

187   *a character named Aarky was rechristened Aarfy*: This happened late in the process; in an undated note to his editor Robert Gottlieb, Heller explained that "[s]ince beginning [the] book, I have become associated in business with a man named Arky"—Arky Gonzalez, a colleague at *Time*—"[and it] would be embarrassing to him and me to use the name Aarky." This note is part of the Joseph Heller Collection, Brandeis University Libraries, Robert D. Farber University Archives and Special Collections Department, Waltham, Massachusetts.

188   *"I'm not running away from my responsibilities"*: Joseph Heller, *Catch-22* (1961; reprint, New York: Dell, 1971), p. 461.

188   *"Has he finished the novel"*: Davis, *Two-Bit Culture,* p. 200.

188   *"Too many loose ends"*: letter from Rust Hills to Candida Donadio, March 11, 1959, Joseph Heller Collection, Brandeis University.

188   *"Hungry Joe"*: Joseph Heller, draft of "Hungry Joe (from the Novel 'Catch-18')": Joseph Heller Collection, Brandeis University.

189   *"[Advertising work] helped me write* Catch-22*"*: Joseph Heller, interviewed by Don Swaim, "Wired for Books," CBS Radio, September 19, 1984; audio recording posted at wiredforbooks.org/josephheller.

189   *"modest maiden"*: Joseph Heller, notes for *Catch-22,* Joseph Heller Collection, Brandeis University.

189   *"somber"; "didn't expect it to happen"; "family . . . did not talk"*: Heller, *Now and Then,* pp. 46–47.

190   *"America's junk culture"*: Jeet Heer, "Gil Kane and Norman Podhoretz," *National Post,* January 8, 2004; posted at www.jeetheer.com/comics/kanepodhoretz.htm.

191   *"Walt Disney had an intense dislike for Coney Island"*: Raymond M. Weinstein, "Disneyland and Coney Island: Reflections on the Evolution of the Modern Amusement Park," *Journal of Popular Culture* 26, no. 1 (1992): 131.

191   *"Disney understood well the mood"*: ibid., p. 52

192   *The Left's dithering*: See Norman Podhoretz, *Ex-Friends: Falling Out with Allen Ginsberg, Lionel and Diana Trilling, Lillian Hellman, Hannah Arendt, and Norman Mailer* (San Francisco: Encounter Books, 2000), pp. 10–11.

192   *"business civilization"*: Judith Smith, "Writing the Intellectual History of *Fortune* Magazine's Corporate Modernism," *Reviews in American History* 33, no. 3 (2005): 419. For more background on Henry Luce's corporate philosophy, see Michael Augspurger, *An Economy of Abundant Beauty: Fortune Magazine and Depression America* (Ithaca, NY: Cornell University Press, 2004).

192   *"I am biased in favor of God"*: James L. Baughman, *Henry R. Luce and the Rise of the American News Media* (Boston: Twayne, 1987), p. 173.

192   *"Christianity is not a religion for weaklings"*: James Gilbert, *Men in the Middle: Searching for Masculinity in the 1950s* (Chicago: University of Chicago Press, 2005), p. 127.

193   *"I never talk alone with a woman"; "lovesick women [and] bobby soxers"*: ibid., p. 125.

193   *"In wartime the Armed Services"*: Adam Parfrey, *It's a Man's World: Men's Adventure Magazines, the Postwar Pulps* (Los Angeles: Feral House, 2003), p. 5.

193   *"just the way things were"*: This and subsequent quotes from Bruce Jay Friedman are taken from ibid., pp. 15–17.

194   *"Damsels [had] been distressed"*: Parfrey, *It's a Man's World,* p. 178.

194–195   *"dehumanized" and "repetitious"; "wholesome, entertaining and educational"*: Nathan Abrams, "From Madness to Dysentery: *Mad*'s Other New York Intellectuals," *Journal of American Studies* 37, no. 3 (2003): 437.

195   *"Of course, we had the big problem"*: ibid., p. 438.

195   *"[B]oys were allowed to purchase [men's] magazines"*: Parfrey, *It's a Man's World,* p. 178.

195   *"In many ways* Mad *represented"*: Abrams, "From Madness to Dysentery," p. 439.

195   *"Beneath the pile of garbage"*: ibid., p. 440.

196   *"[W]e like to say that* Mad*"*: ibid., p. 441.

196   *"the essence of* Mad's *success"; "Is Your Bathroom Breeding Bolsheviks?"*: ibid., pp. 443, 447.

196   *"Mad expresses . . . the teenagers' cynicism"*: ibid., p. 449.

196   *"Paperback books and the baby boomers"*: Davis, *Two-Bit Culture,* p. 1.

197   *"political and ideological novel"*: William Barrett, "Lapse of a Novelist," posted at commentarymagazine.com.

197   *"One senses the joy"*: Norman Podhoretz, "The Language of Life," posted at commentarymagazine.com.

197 *"the novel of the fifties"*: This and subsequent Karl quotes are taken from Frederick Karl, *American Fictions 1940–1980* (New York: Harper & Row, 1983), pp. 179–80.

198 *"[H]e was drunk by the time he appeared on stage"; "Kerouac was not only giving our generation a bad name"*: Wakefield, *New York in the Fifties*, pp. 167–68.

199 *"Please, Alice"*: This and all other quotes regarding Denham are taken from Alice Denham, *Sleeping with Bad Boys: A Juicy Tell-All of Literary New York in the 1950s and 1960s* (New York: Book Republic Press, 2006), pp. 96–98.

199 *"I loved it there"*: Ted Heller in an e-mail to the author, October 7, 2009.

200 *"[I] . . . was catapulted"; "That question still makes me squirm"; "[I]t was only then"*: Heller, *Now and Then*, pp. 227–29.

200 *"Critics and publishers"*: publishers' note, *New World Writing*, no. 7 (1955).

201 *"Men went mad and were rewarded with medals"*: Heller, *Catch-22*, p. 16.

11. 22

pages
202 *"At that moment in the demented history of Simon & Schuster"*: Robert Gottlieb, remarks made at "Joseph Heller: A Celebration," a memorial service held at the New York Society for Ethical Culture on June 13, 2000. Transcribed by the author from a video recording (courtesy of Erica Heller).

203 *"why this applicant"; "[g]o home and write me a letter"; "brooded about this"; "Dear Mr. Goodman"*: Peter Schwed, *Turning the Pages: An Insider's Story of Simon & Schuster 1924–1984* (New York: Macmillan, 1984), pp. 235–36.

203 *"Until the 1920s"*: This and subsequent Korda quotes are taken from Michael Korda, *Another Life* (New York: Dell, 2000), pp. 46–48, 41–42, 52, 53–55.

204 *"Whatever I look at"*: Larissa MacFarquhar, "Robert Gottlieb: The Art of Editing I," *The Paris Review* 36, no. 132 (1994): 222.

204 *"I thought my navel would unscrew"*: Karen Hudes, "Epic Agent: The Great Candida Donadio," *Tin House* 6, no. 4 (2005): 152.

204 *"a creature from a Roman fresco"*: ibid.

205 *"Language means the most to me"*: "The Agents: Writing with a $ Sign," posted at www .time.com/time/printout/ 0,8816,900028,00.html.

205 *"I remember thinking"*: Adam J. Sorkin, ed., *Conversations with Joseph Heller* (Jackson: University Press of Mississippi, 1993), p. 115.

205 *"He knew all along"*: Frederick Karl, remarks made at "Joseph Heller: A Celebration."

206 *"I liked it"*: Fred Kaplan, *1959: The Year Everything Changed* (Hoboken, NJ: Wiley, 2009), p. 17.

206 *"Jazz is orgasm"*: This and subsequent quotes from the essay are taken from Norman Mailer, "The White Negro: Superficial Reflections on the Hipster," *Dissent* 4 (1957): 276–93; reprinted in Norman Mailer, *Advertisements for Myself* (New York: G. P. Putnam, 1959), pp. 337–58.

206 *"frantic swings"*: Kaplan, *1959*, p. 21.

207 *"I . . . love this crazy book"*: Robert Gottlieb, reader's report on *Catch-22*, dated February 12, 1958, cited in Jonathan R. Eller, "Catching a Market: The Publishing History of *Catch-22*," *Prospects: An Annual Journal of American Cultural Studies* 17 (1992): 480.

207 *"It is a very rare approach to the war"*: ibid.

208 *"[W]hen I had been at Simon & Schuster a year"*: MacFarquhar, "Robert Gottlieb," p. 208.

208 *"I suppose our convoluted, neurotic"*: ibid., p. 187.

208 *"two great qualities"*: Gottlieb, remarks made at "Joseph Heller: A Celebration."

208 *"battlefield sequences"*: MacFarquhar, "Robert Gottlieb," p. 213.

208 *"I probably wouldn't send"*: ibid.

209 *"I think I was [Bob's] first writer"; "It came so hard"*: Robert Alan Aurthur, "Hanging Out," *Esquire*, September 1974, pp. 54, 64.

209 *"The two enlisted men"*: This and subsequent quotes are from the rough drafts of *Catch-22*,

Joseph Heller Collection, Brandeis University Libraries, Robert D. Farber University Archives and Special Collections Department, Waltham, Massachusetts.

210 *"I'm a chronic fiddler"; "I don't understand the process of imagination"*: Sorkin, ed., *Conversations with Joseph Heller*, pp. 161, 107.

210 *"true literary genius"*: Eller, "Catching a Market," p. 481.

211 *"It had upset many people"*: Korda, *Another Life*, p. 53.

212 *"strange period"*: ibid., p. 94.

212 *"endlessly retyped"*: ibid., p. 77.

212 *"impoverished vocabulary"*: This and other quotes from Robert Gottlieb on the following pages are taken from MacFarquhar, "Robert Gottlieb," pp. 186–87, 197–98, 199, 200.

212 *"Some of Bob's suggestions"*: MacFarquhar, "Robert Gottlieb," p. 205.

213 *"aura of myth"*: Korda, *Another Life*, p. 53.

213 *"Sicilian Earth Mother"; "had a way of dismissing those"*: ibid., pp. 236–37.

213 *"who misunderstood her instructions"*: Seth Kupferberg and Greg Lawless, "Joseph Heller: 13 Years from *Catch-22* to *Something Happened*," *Harvard Crimson*, October 11, 1974.

214 *"The S & S house style"*: Schwed, *Turning the Pages*, p. 156.

214 *"lucky and glad"*: Steven Heller, *Design Literary* (New York: Allworth Press, 2004), p. 241.

214 *"I'd always tell myself"; "I did a jacket"*: ibid., pp. 238, 240.

215 *"all that expense-account food;" "the Locust"; "Whatever was there"*: Sorkin, ed., *Conversations with Joseph Heller,* pp. 103–04.

215 *"[I remember] my mother, brother, and I stayed at this motel"*: Erica Heller in an e-mail to the author, December 30, 2009. Ms. Heller is not certain about the timing of this motel stay. Initially, she thought it was the summer of 1961, but later she believed it could have been the summer of 1962. Her descriptions of her father's work at the time inclined me to place the incident in 1961.

215 *"fantastic sense of the trends of the times"*: Susan Braudy, "A Few of the Jokes, Maybe Yes, But Not the Whole Book," *The New Journal* 26 (1967): 39, 40.

216 *"He was a self-made man"*: Rinker Buck, *Flight of Passage* (New York: Hyperion, 1997), p. 5.

216 *"just going to brood and not work"; "Joe worked [hard]"*: Braudy, "A Few of the Jokes . . . ," p. 40.

216 *"[W]e were all in despair"*: Hudes, "Epic Agent," p. 153.

216 *"The name of the book is now CATCH-14"*: note from Joseph Heller to Robert Gottlieb, January 29, 1961, Joseph Heller Collection, Brandeis University.

217 *"Bennett Cerf and Donald Klopfer took Random House public"*: Korda, *Another Life,* p. 102.

217 *"extensions of the possible into the fantastic"*: This and all subsequent quotes regarding the novel and its relationship to real-life events are taken from Joseph Heller's notes to Robert Gottlieb, analysis of characters in *Catch-22*, Joseph Heller Collection, Brandeis University.

219 *"22 was chosen"*; Hudes, "Epic Agent," pp. 153–54.

219 *"Absolutely untrue"*: ibid.

219 *"[s]uggested descriptive copy fragments"*: Joseph Heller, notes on *Catch-22*, Joseph Heller Collection, Brandeis University.

220 *"Tell me about popular fiction"*: Katherine McNamara, "A Conversation about Publishing with Samuel S. Vaughan," *Archipelago*, 3, no. 2 (1999): 39.

220 *"That's some catch"*: This and other quotes from *Catch-22* on the following pages are taken from Joseph Heller, *Catch-22* (1961; reprint, New York: Dell, 1971), pp. 47, 17, 107, 177, 449–50, 266, 463, 269, 197.

222 *"war . . . without limits"*: Alfred Kazin, *Bright Book of Life: American Novelists and Storytellers from Hemingway to Mailer* (Boston: Little, Brown, 1973), p. 83.

223 *"I didn't want to give him a Jewish name"*: Paul Krassner, "An Impolite Interview with Joseph Heller," *The Realist,* November 1962; reprinted in Sorkin, ed., *Conversations with Joseph Heller,* p. 18.

224 *"the demented governess"*: Gottlieb, remarks made at "Joseph Heller: A Celebration."

224 *"We have to print 7,500"*: Eller, "Catching a Market," p. 486.

225 *"If we'd had anybody to ask"*: ibid.

225 *"A funny and tragic and tonic book"*: ibid.

225 *"crazed"; "This is a book I'd get a critic"*: ibid.

225 *"One eminent critic"*: ibid.

225 *"Dear Miss Bourne"*: letter from Evelyn Waugh to Nina Bourne, September 6, 1961, Joseph Heller Collection, Brandeis University.

225 *"PLEASE CONGRATULATE JOSEPH HELLER"*: Eller, "Catching a Market," p. 489.

226 *"The growing ferment of interest in* **Catch-22***"*: Eller, "Catching a Market," p. 488.

226 *"spent many an evening"*: Frederick Karl, remarks made at "Joseph Heller: A Celebration."

226 *"regular family life"*: Erica Heller, remarks made at "Joseph Heller: A Celebration."

226 *"We used to go often on Sunday afternoons"*: Erica Heller in an e-mail to the author, December 5, 2009.

227 *"With the hope that when you read this book"*: ibid.

227 *he chided friends who bought the novel on discount*: Melvin J. Grayson, who worked for a time with Heller in the promotion department at *Look* magazine, recalled that he bumped into Heller on Fifth Avenue right after *Catch-22* was published. "Have you seen the reviews of *Catch-22?*" Heller asked him. "I'll bet you wish you could write like that." Grayson was apparently not one of Heller's favorite people, or vice versa. Grayson recalls two other unpleasant encounters with Heller, one in Heller's office, when Heller told Grayson to "go away" because he was busy, and one in which, as the men passed casually in the hallway, Heller told Grayson, "You have dandruff." See the letters page of *New York* magazine, October 10, 1994.

228 *"Involvement in an intense relationship"*: Michael Moore, "Pathological Communication Patterns in Heller's *Catch-22,*" posted at www.thefreelibrary.com/_/print/Print Article.aspx?id=17838029.

228 *"[T]he book is no novel"*: Richard G. Stern, "Bombers Away," *New York Times Book Review,* October 22, 1961, p. 50.

228 *"was not dismayed"*: Frederick Karl, remarks made at "Joseph Heller: A Celebration."

228–29 *"I didn't think [my family and I] would ever smile again"*: Harold Bloom, ed., *Bloom's Guides: Joseph Heller's Catch-22* (New York: Infobase Publishing, 2009), p. 10.

229 *"We thought we had the fix in"*: Alice Denham, *Sleeping with Bad Boys: A Juicy Tell-All of Literary New York in the 1950s and 1960s* (New York: Book Republic Press, 2006), p. 198–99.

229 *"Below its hilarity"*: Nelson Algren, "The Catch," *The Nation,* November 4, 1961, p. 358.

229 *"Catch-22 is the debut of a writer with merry gifts"*: Norman Mailer, "Some Children of the Goddess: Norman Mailer vs. Nine Writers," *Esquire,* July 1963, p. 63.

230 *"Joseph Heller's brilliant farce-tragedy"*: "Editorial: Who Gets the Awards and Why Not Everybody?" *Show,* June 1962, p. 14B.

230 *"By conventional marketing standards"*: Eller, "Catching a Market," p. 494.

231 *"Report on* Catch-22*"*: ibid., p. 495.

231 *" 'Catch' is a classic"*: Van Allen Bradley, "Bookman's Week: Novelist Nelson Algren Campaigns for Neglected Book," *Chicago Daily News,* June 23, 1962; cited in Eller, "Catching a Market," p. 496.

231 *"Joe's contribution"*: Gottlieb, remarks made at "Joseph Heller: A Celebration."

231 *"Many years later"*: ibid.

232 *"Things were pretty weird in Manhattan"*: This quote and the following anecdote are taken from Robert Nedelkoff, "Catch-2008," posted at thenewnixon.org/author/Robert-Nedelkoff.

232 *"This is* The Naked and the Dead *scripted for the Marx Brothers"*: Eller, "Catching a Market," p. 501.

232 *"When I began reading* Catch-22*"*: Philip Toynbee, "Here's Greatness—In Satire," *The Observer,* June 17, 1962; reprinted in Frederick Kiley and Walter McDonald, eds., *A "Catch-22" Casebook* (New York: Thomas Y. Crowell, 1973), p. 12.

233 *"We sold just over 800 copies"*: Eller, "Catching a Market," p. 499.

233 *"It is hard to imagine [Heller's] book"*: W. J. Weatherby, "The Joy Catcher," *The Guardian*, November 20, 1962.

233 *"The thesis of 'Catch-22'"*: Anthony Burgess, "Review of *Catch-22*," *Yorkshire Evening Post*, June 28, 1962; cited in Eller, "Catching a Market," p. 503.

233 *"Come on! Don't let the English beat us!"*: Eller, "Catching a Market," pp. 504–05.

234 *"Heller's a hell of a good publicist"*: Braudy, "A Few of the Jokes . . . ," p. 39.

234 *I don't know yet whether I'll do the play"*: Eugene Arthur, "'Catch-22' Movie Set by Columbia," *New York Times*, August 22, 1962.

234 *"It was wonderful for Joe"*: Hudes, "Epic Agent," p. 154.

234 *"They had an idea I was supposed to look like Thomas Wolfe"*: Sorkin, ed., *Conversations with Joseph Heller*, p. 123.

234 *"Both [success and failure] are difficult to endure"*: ibid., p. 164.

235 "Catch-22 *is taking off!"* The quote and the ensuing conversation are taken from Denham, *Sleeping with Bad Boys*, p. 201.

236 *"A matter has been troubling me"*: letter from Robert O. Shipman to Simon & Schuster, May 14, 1962, Joseph Heller Collection, Brandeis University.

236 *"matter was entirely coincidental"*: letter from Joseph Heller to Robert O. Shipman, May 18, 1962, Joseph Heller Collection, Brandeis University.

237 *"Eek"*: note from Paula Diamond to Joseph Heller, August 6, 1962, Joseph Heller Collection, Brandeis University.

237 *"as Jacob wrestled with the angel"*: letter from Joseph Heller to Paula Diamond, October 30, 1962, Joseph Heller Collection, Brandeis University.

237 *"how well I think you substituted for the name"*: letter from Robert O. Shipman to Joseph Heller, April 18, 1963, Joseph Heller Collection, Brandeis University.

237 *"no permanent resentment exist[ed]"*: letter from Joseph Heller to Robert O. Shipman, June 10, 1963, Joseph Heller Collection, Brandeis University.

237 *"The success of [*Catch-22 *in paperback]"*: Kenneth C. Davis, *Two-Bit Culture: The Paperbacking of America* (Boston: Houghton Mifflin, 1984), pp. 298–300.

238 *"[A] nation-wide sensation"*: ibid., p. 299.

238 *"Not since* The Catcher in the Rye*"*: "The Heller Cult," *Newsweek*, October 1, 1962, pp. 82–83.

238 *Joe appeared on NBC's* Today *show*: Heller recounts this anecdote in "Preface to *Catch-22*," written in 1994 for a new edition of the novel (London: Vintage, 1995).

238 *"[T]he war that I [was] really dealing with"*: Creath Thorne, "Joseph Heller: An Interview," *The Chicago Literary Review: Book Supplement to the Chicago Maroon*, December 3, 1974, p. 8.

238 *"I don't think I'll ever recover"*: Eller, "Catching a Market," p. 514.

239 *"[A]t the University of Chicago"*: ibid., p. 515.

239 *"The young people"*: ibid.

239 *"At some point, I outgrew the school library"*: Mark Moskowitz; *Stone Reader* (Jet Films LLC, 2002); transcribed by the author.

240 *"When [the] book first came out in paper"*: Braudy, "A Few of the Jokes . . . ," p. 45.

240 *a "difficult situation"*: Davis, *Two-Bit Culture*, p. 300.

240 *"Happy birthday CATCH-22"*: Eller, "Catching a Market," p. 513.

240 *"Without being aware of it"*: Joseph Heller, "Reeling in *Catch-22*," in *The Sixties*, ed. Lynda Rosen Obst (New York: Rolling Stone Press/Random House, 1977), pp. 50–52.

241 *"did their best to make us feel like exiles"*: Anatole Broyard, *Kafka Was the Rage: A Greenwich Village Memoir* (New York: Vintage Books, 1993), p. 15.

241 *"[came] to us almost entirely in paperback"*: Eller, "Catching a Market," p. 519.

241 *"For sixteen years"*: letter from Stephen E. Ambrose to Joseph Heller, January 23, 1962, Joseph Heller Collection, Brandeis University.

241 *"I would very much like to know"*: letter from John Steinbeck to Joseph Heller, July 1, 1963, Joseph Heller Collection, Brandeis University.

12. THE REALIST

pages

245   "America in the Sixties": Lewis A. Coser, "Faith, Hope, and the Facts," *Commentary* 31, no. 2 (1961): 181.

245–46   *"drags on productivity"; "miracles of rising income"*: ibid.

246   *"moral, spiritual, and intellectual harm"*: Norman Podhoretz, "Looking Back at *Catch-22*"; reprinted as "Norman Podhoretz on Rethinking *Catch-22*," in *Bloom's Guides: Joseph Heller's Catch-22*, ed. Harold Bloom (New York: Infobase Publishing, 2009), p. 120.

246   *"about a married man"*: "The Heller Cult," *Newsweek,* October 1, 1962, pp. 82–83.

246   *"fulcrum [years] of America"; "rendezvous with destiny"*: Tom Brokaw, *The Greatest Generation* (New York: Random House, 1998), p. 3.

247   *"Forms and rhythms in [art]"*: quoted in Ralph Gleason, "Like a Rolling Stone," posted at jannswenner.com/Press/Like_A_Rolling_Stone.aspx.

247   *"I know so many things I'm afraid to find out"*: Joseph Heller, *Something Happened* (1974; reprint, New York: Ballantine Books, 1975), p. 154.

247   *"motivation of my entire life"*: Bruce Weber, "Speed Vogel, Author's Aide, Dies at 90," *New York Times,* April 18, 2008; posted at nytimes.com/2008/04/18/books/18vogel.html.

248   *"Joe somehow managed"*: Joseph Heller and Speed Vogel, *No Laughing Matter* (New York: Simon & Schuster, 1986), p. 99.

248   *"erections"*: Speed Vogel, "The Gourmet Club," *The Southampton Review 2,* no. 1 (2008): 214.

249   *"[Mel] had a blood sugar problem"; "Mr. Vogel can't speak to you now"*: Heller and Vogel, *No Laughing Matter,* p. 98.

249   *"You snore"; "What do you want from me?"*: ibid.

249   *"Huck Finn on his raft in Manhattan"*: Jane Ayer, "Speed Vogel Obituary," posted at reuters.com/article/pressRelease/idUS16311+18+-Apr-2008+PRN20080418.

249   *"Mel and Joe had tremendous similarities"*: Vogel, "The Gourmet Club," p. 210.

249   *"There's a side of Mel"*: Kenneth Tynan, "Frolics and Detours of a Short Hebrew Man," *The New Yorker,* October 30, 1978, p. 68.

249   *"Tragedy is if I cut my finger"*: ibid., p. 94.

250   *"Ngoot, a little guy"*: Vogel, "The Gourmet Club," p. 208.

250   *"If you don't have it"*: ibid., p. 209.

250   *"It's hard to be a Jew"*: Heller and Vogel, *No Laughing Matter,* p. 105.

250   *"Mel was strangely attracted to fire"*: Vogel, "The Gourmet Club," p. 209.

251   *"The trouble with fucking"*: Mario Puzo, *The Godfather Papers and Other Confessions* (Greenwich, CT: Fawcett, 1972), p. 226.

251   *"I'm sure glad that happened to you"; "He wasn't being cruel"*: Tynan, "Frolics and Detours of a Short Hebrew Man," p. 101.

251   *"Joe loved to move around Manhattan"*: This and other comments by Mell Lazarus are from a conversation with the author, May 20, 2009.

251   *"The Kennedy Administration"*: Sam Merrill, "*Playboy* Interview: Joseph Heller," *Playboy,* June 1975, pp. 66–68.

251   *"Women flock[ed] to him"*: Adam J. Sorkin, ed., *Conversations with Joseph Heller* (Jackson: University Press of Mississippi, 1993), p. 193.

251   *"You can't be a female fan"*: Sally Vincent, "Portrait: Catch-94," *The Guardian*, September 24, 1994.

252   *"I think as soon as I was old enough"*: Erica Heller in an e-mail to the author, October 21, 2009.

253   *"[W]e were not an . . . affectionate family"*: Ted Heller in an e-mail to the author, January 15, 2010.

253   *"[I]t is never, or hardly ever, an entirely good thing"*: Joseph Heller, *Now and Then: From Coney Island to Here* (New York: Alfred A. Knopf, 1998), p. 214.

253   *"He was funnier"*: Norman Barasch in conversation with the author, April 29, 2009.

253   *a "very warm, open man"*: Erica Heller, in conversation with the author, February 18, 2010.

253   *"He was always complaining about the food"*: Norman Barasch in conversation with the author, April 29, 2009.

253   *"This is the world of Stevenson, Conrad, and Gauguin"*: Albert Aley, "Seven Against the Sea," Universal City Studios LLLP, 1962. The drama is available for viewing at the Paley Center for Media in Los Angeles. See also the listing at at imdb.com.

254   *"so long as a book is true and beautiful"*: D. J. Taylor, "Culture, Commerce, Clinton," *The Guardian,* May 25, 2002; posted at guardian.co.uk/books/2002/May/25/hay festival2002.guardianhayfestival.

255   *"Go away, damn you!"*: Heller's account of his meeting with Bertrand Russell is related in Kinky Friedman, *'Scuse Me While I Whip This Out: Reflections on Country Singers, Presidents, and Other Troublemakers* (New York: William Morrow, 2004), p. 141.

255   *"thrilling"*: Joseph Heller, "Joseph Heller Talks about *Catch-22*," in Heller, *Catch as Catch Can: The Collected Stories and Other Writings,* ed. Matthew J. Bruccoli and Park Bucker (New York: Simon & Schuster 2003), p. 299.

255   *"What are you doing tonight?"*: Heller told the story of meeting James Jones at the James Jones Literary Society Symposium in June 1999; posted at jamesjonesliterarysociety.org/jheller.htm.

256   *"I always felt it wasn't too easy to lose a boat"*: Joseph Heller, "PT 73, Where Are You?" Universal City Studios LLLP, 1962.

256   *"Friends of mine in TV"*: letter from Joseph Heller to Jay Sanford, July 20, 1962, Joseph Heller Collection, Robert D. Farber University Archives and Special Collections, Brandeis University, Waltham, Massachusetts.

257   *"I would like to assure you, Joe"*: letter from Edward J. Montagne to Joseph Heller, August 6, 1962, Joseph Heller Collection, Brandeis University.

257   *Comedy [variety] shows were out of style"*: Tynan, "Frolics and Detours of a Short Hebrew Man," p. 49.

257   *"generally ignored the satirical cabaret performers"*: Arthur Gelb, *City Room* (New York: Berkley Books, 2003), p. 304.

258   *"I didn't mean to be subversive"*: ibid., p. 306.

258   *Lenny Bruce*: All quotes by and about Lenny Bruce, including a link to the "Petition Protesting the Arrest of Lenny Bruce, June 13, 1964," are taken from Doug Linder, "The Trials of Lenny Bruce," posted at law.umkc.edu/faculty/projects/ ftrials/bruce/bruceaccount .html.

259   *"[P]olice payoffs"*: Gelb, *City Room,* p. 310.

259   *"I feel the hints, the clues"*: Abe Peck, *Uncovering the Sixties: The Life and Times of the Underground Press* (New York: Pantheon, 1985), p. 9.

260   The Realist: For details about Paul Krassner, William Gaines, and *The Realist,* see ibid., pp. 10–13.

261   *"I had gone to my first literary cocktail party"*: Paul Krassner in an e-mail to the author, July 5, 2009.

261   *"quote an orthodox book"*: This and subsequent quotes from the interview are taken from Paul Krassner, "An Impolite Interview with Joseph Heller," *The Realist,* November 1962; reprinted in Sorkin, ed., *Conversations with Joseph Heller,* pp. 6–7, 8–9, 10, 22.

261   *"pretended he had taken the subway"*: Paul Krassner in an e-mail to the author, July 5, 2009.

262   *"We moved to [a] much larger apartment"*: Ted Heller in an e-mail to the author, October 22, 2009. The apartment was 10C.

262   *"the housewife-mother"*: Kenneth C. Davis, *Two-Bit Culture: The Paperbacking of America* (Boston, Houghton Mifflin, 1984), p. 304.

262   *"Give up Dr. Spock?"*: ibid., p. 9.

262   *"I think that when women are encouraged"*: Gail Collins, *When Everything Changed: The Amazing Journey of American Women from 1960 to the Present* (New York: Little, Brown, 2009), p. 11.

263   *"natural restriction"*; *"grace"*: ibid.
263   *"Men went mad"*: Joseph Heller, *Catch-22* (1961; reprint, New York: Dell, 1971), p. 16.
263   *"[W]omen's . . . lives [are] confined"*: Davis, *Two-Bit Culture,* p. 304.

13. BOMBS

pages
264   *"sour . . . irritation"*: Unless otherwise noted, this and subsequent quotes regarding the
         visit to Corsica are taken from: Joseph Heller, "Catch-22 Revisited," *Holiday,* April 1967,
         pp. 45–60, 120, 141–42, 145.
264   *"[My son's] terror"*: Joseph Heller, *Something Happened* (New York: Ballantine Books,
         1974), p. 524.
265   *"Up until [this] time"*: Erica Heller, reader comment, "The View Remains the Same . . .
         Thankfully," posted at wowowow.com/post/the-view-from-my-horizon.
266   *"little jewel of a hotel"*: ibid.
267   *"I started worrying about money"*: Chet Flippo, "Checking in with Joseph Heller," *Roll-
         ing Stone,* April 16, 1981, reprinted in Adam J. Sorkin, ed., *Conversations with Joseph
         Heller* (Jackson: University Press of Mississippi, 1993), p. 229.
268   *various projects they started together*: These projects included a screenplay based on
         Mandel's novel *The Breakwater.*
268   *"much music"*: Joseph Heller and George Mandel, "The Big Squeeze," rough draft, Jo-
         seph Heller Archive, Department of Rare Books and Special Collections, Thomas Cooper
         Library, University of South Carolina, Columbia, South Carolina.
268   *Rather than rejecting kittenish femininity*: See Jennifer Scanlon, *Bad Girls Go Everywhere:
         The Life of Helen Gurley Brown* (New York: Oxford University Press, 2009), p. 69.
268   *"I told you that a hundred thousand dollars ago"*: ibid., p. 113.
268   *"spice things up"*: ibid.
268   *"two young, muddled protagonists"*: A. H. Weiler, "Screen: Promoting Those Castles in
         Spain: 'The Pleasure Seekers' and Other Films Bow, 'Sex and Single Girl,' Tenor's Biogra-
         phy," *New York Times,* December 26, 1964; posted at movies.nytimes.com/movie/
         review?_r=l&res=9501E7DD143BE53ABC4E51DFB4.
269   *"We had never experienced anything like that [summer]"*: Erica Heller in an e-mail to the
         author, January 4, 2010.
269   *"I just ran up to her like a lunatic"*: ibid.
269   *"I remember thinking the boats and cars I was seeing"*: Ted Heller in an e-mail to the
         author, January 19, 2010.
269   *"had a natural flair for comedy"*: Suzanne Finstad, *Natasha: The Biography of Natalie
         Wood* (New York: Random House, 2009), p. 252.
269   *"needed the money to settle a divorce"*: Sorkin, ed., *Conversations with Joseph Heller,*
         p. 166.
270   *"told me that he and I both did a version of the same scene"*: Sam Merrill, *"Playboy* In-
         terview: Joseph Heller," *Playboy,* June 1975, pp. 66–68.
270   *"was tempting"*: Joseph Heller, "How I Found James Bond, Lost My Self-Respect and
         Almost Made $150,270 in My Spare Time," *Holiday,* June 1967, p. 123.
270   *"When you put glasses on them"*; *"No background dogs in my picture!"*: "General Infor-
         mation, Casino Royale, 1967," posted at 007museum.com/casino_royale-1967.htm.
270   *"ninety minute[s] . . . of what appears to be Frank [Sinatra]"*: See sinatraguide.com/
         filmedsinatra.
270   *"worst movie you ever saw"*; *"sort of on impulse"*: Tayt Harlin, "Inteview with David
         Markson," posted at conjunctions.com/webcon/harlinmarkson07.htm.
271   *"denigrating attitudes toward women"*: See sinatraguide.com/filmedsinatra.
271   *"I've had some experiences with motion pictures"*: Joseph Heller, remarks made at the
         Poetry Center of the 92nd Street Y, December 7, 1970; audio recording available at ny
         times.com/books/98/02/15/home/heller.html#hear.

271 *"You owe me"*: This and all other quotes and details regarding Heller's meeting with Brodax are taken from Al Brodax, *Up Periscope Yellow: The Making of the Beatles' Yellow Submarine* (Pompton Plains, NJ: Limelight Editions, 2004), pp. 53–56.

272 *"[A] little kid"*: Bob Hieronimus, "Transcript of Interview with Lee Minoff, 12/15/97, Originator of the Story 'Yellow Submarine' and Author of the First Script and Screenplay for the Film," posted at 21scentury radio.com/articles/0523005.html.

272 *"With Heller in [his] pocket"*: Brodax, *Up Periscope Yellow,* p. 56.

273 *"connection between his Yossarian"*: ibid.

273 *"Surrealism"; "cultural milestone"*: Bob Spitz, *The Beatles: The Biography* (New York: Little, Brown, 2005), p. 536.

273 *"He loved Bob Dylan"*: Ted Heller in an e-mail to the author, October 23, 2009.

273 *"She told me that after about three days"*: Ken Barnard, "Interview with Joseph Heller," *Detroit News,* September 13, 1970.

273 *"a new trend for the . . . 60s"*: cited in Susan Braudy, "Laughing All the Way to the Truth," *New York,* October 14, 1968, p. 41.

274 *"polemic[al]"*: Jean Shepherd, "Radio Free America," *The Realist,* May 1964, p. 27.

274 *"[It] is [not] the function of satire"*: "Joseph Heller Replies," *The Realist,* May 1964, p. 30.

274 *"attempt to discredit the Student Non-Violent [sic] Coordinating Committee"*: Joseph Heller, "A Letter from Joseph Heller," *The Realist,* May 1965, p. 9.

274 *"[a]ny society that puts Cassius Clay and Benjamin Spock in jail"*: Israel Shenker, "Did Heller Bomb on Broadway?" *New York Times,* December 29, 1968.

274 *"All I want to say is it ain't that hard"*: Richard B. Sale, "An Interview in New York with Joseph Heller," *Studies in the Novel* 4 (1972): 14. This interview was conducted in 1970.

275 *"real Mau-Mau"; "New Left movement['s] . . . propaganda activities"*: Abe Peck, *Uncovering the Sixties: The Life and Times of the Underground Press* (New York: Pantheon, 1985), pp. 139–41.

275 *"[T]he FBI . . . placed an ad"*: ibid., pp. 174–75.

275 *"If I wanted to destroy a nation"*: Allen J. Matusow, *The Unraveling of America: A History of Liberalism in the 1960s* (New York: Harper & Row, 1984), p. 12.

275 *"the suburbs"*: Jacob Brackman, "The Underground Press," posted at trussel.com/lyman/brackman.htm.

276 *"I dare say that with the inspiration of the Beatles"*: Ralph J. Gleason, "Like a Rolling Stone," posted at jannswenner.com/Press/Like_A _Rolling_Stone.aspx.

276 *"Lenny Bruce was really"*: Ralph J. Gleason, "The Berkeley Concert," posted at golbalia.net/donlope/fz/related/Berkeley_Concert.html.

276 *"unpaid film critic"*: Keith Saliba, "Hayes, Herr and Sack: *Esquire* Goes to Vietnam," *Journal of Magazine and New Media Research* 9, no. 2 (2007): 12–13.

277 *"There was a map of Vietnam"*: This and subsequent Herr quotes are taken from Michael Herr, *Dispatches* (New York: Alfred A. Knopf, 1977), pp. 3–4.

278 *"nothing if not a provocateur"*: Erica Heller, "Joseph Heller's Daughter Remembers Her Prickly Pa," *New York Observer,* January 10, 2000; draft copy provided to the author by Erica Heller.

278 *"She would break my heart"*: Heller, *Something Happened,* p. 120.

278 *"You always like to give short answers"*: ibid., p. 32.

279 Something Happened . . . *was certainly [an] accurate*: Erica Heller in an e-mail to the author, October 21, 2009.

279 *"acknowledge[d] her resemblance to the daughter"*: Sorkin, ed. *Conversations with Joseph Heller,* p. 198.

279 Mario Puzo often remarked: See ibid., p. 189.

279 *"grumpy, disaffected, and blasé"*: Erica Heller, "Joseph Heller's Daughter Remembers Her Prickly Pa."

280 *"[S]he is, I fear"*: Heller, *Something Happened,* p. 66.

280 *"What 'happens' to Bob Slocum's children"*: Erica Heller, "It Sure Did," *Harper's,* May 1975, p. 4.

280 *"Erica had a tough time with her father"*: Norman Barasch in conversation with the author, April 29, 2009.

281 *"I always felt I was a disappointment"*: Ted Heller in an e-mail to the author, January 19, 2010.

281 *"the year* Sergeant Pepper *came out"*: ibid.

281 *One day, Joe ". . . warned me"*: ibid.

282 *"Teddy—that was a mystery"*: Audrey Chestney, in conversation with the author, January 5, 2010.

282 *"The very qualities that had disappointed us in the past"*: Joseph Heller, *Now and Then: From Coney Island to Here* (New York: Alfred A. Knopf, 1998), p. 59.

282 *"passing of generations"*: ibid.

282 *"He went to a health club called Al Roon's"*: Ted Heller in an e-mail to the author, October 23, 2009.

282 *"Neither one of us has ever had a divorce"*: Barnard, "Interview with Joseph Heller."

282 *"Maybe we just don't quit easily"*: Merrill, "*Playboy* Interview: Joseph Heller," pp. 66–68.

283 *"I don't think my wife has learned how to lie to me yet"*: Heller, *Something Happened*, p. 92.

283 *"was always afraid"; "I didn't care"*: ibid., p. 110.

283 *"begging and nagging and driving my parents crazy"*: Erica Heller in an e-mail to the author, March 21, 2010.

283 *"[A]ctors ranging"*: Joseph Heller, "On Translating *Catch-22* into a Movie," in *A "Catch-22" Casebook,* ed. Frederick Kiley and Walter McDonald (New York: Thomas Y. Crowell, 1973), p. 348.

284 *write an original play*: Heller told journalist Beatrice Berg that he was about 250 pages into writing *Something Happened,* and he wrote a scene where Slocum's son asks him, "Do I have to go into the army?" The chapter started him thinking, he said. He set the novel aside and began writing ideas that eventually became *We Bombed in New Haven.* See Beatrice Berg, "Heller of *Catch-22,*" *St. Louis Post-Dispatch,* November 17, 1968.

284 *"purportedly for writing reasons"*: Ted Heller in an e-mail to the author, October 23, 2009.

284 *"Welcome to the Uppa West Side!"*: This and subsequent quotes regarding Heller and Denham are taken from Alice Denham, *Sleeping with Bad Boys: A Juicy Tell-All of New York in the 1950s and 1960s* (New York: Book Republic Press, 2006), pp. 225–27, 283.

285 *"Except for Joe, all of us are quite short"*: Kenneth Tynan, "Frolics and Detours of a Short Hebrew Man,": *The New Yorker,* October 30, 1978, p. 102.

285 *"Wassah matter with you fucking guys"*: Unless otherwise noted, this and subsequent quotes and details regarding the Gourmet Club are taken from Joseph Heller and Speed Vogel, *No Laughing Matter* (New York: Simon & Schuster, 1986), pp. 106–10.

286 *"Once—and only once"*: Tynan, "Frolics and Detours of a Short Hebrew Man," pp. 101–02.

287 *"The members [were] very polite"*: ibid., p. 102.

287 *"I'd rather have a bad meal out"*: ibid.

287 *"From the very start"*: ibid., p. 106.

287 *"Here, I'll serve"*: There are several versions of this story, related by different members of the Gourmet Club. See, for example, Speed Vogel, "The Gourmet Club," *The Southampton Review* 2, no. 1 (2008), p. 211; Carl Reiner, *My Anecdotal Life: A Memoir* (New York: St. Martin's Press, 2003), p. 180.

287 *"deserved"*: This and all other quotes from the excerpt of *"Something Happened"* are taken from Joseph Heller, "Something Happened," *Esquire,* September 1966, pp. 136–41, 212–13.

288 *"how our red-blooded campus heroes"*: This and other quotes from articles in this issue of *Esquire* are from ibid., pp. 115, 121, 128–29.

289 *"first Yiddish stage production"*: Irving Howe, *World of Our Fathers: The Journey of East European Jews to America and the Life They Found and Made* (New York: Harcourt Brace Jovanovich, 1976), pp. 461–62.

290   *Joe mentioned to Robert Brustein*: Heller first met Brustein in 1961, when they attended a party at the home of a *Village Voice* art critic.

290   *"manuscript to be read like a novel"*: David Seed, *The Fiction of Joseph Heller: Against the Grain* (New York: St. Martin's Press, 1989), p. 72.

290   *"born promotion man"*: This and subsequent quotes regarding Heller's talk at Calhoun College are taken from Susan Braudy, "A Few of the Jokes, Maybe Yes, But Not the Whole Book," *The New Journal* 26 (1967): 7.

290   *Brustein had made the Yale Drama School a center*: Seed, *The Fiction of Joseph Heller*, p. 73.

290   *"Heller's script offers a perfect skeleton"*: Elenore Lester, "Playwright-in-Anguish," *New York Times*, December 3, 1967.

291   *"Today's Rosh Hashanah"*: Braudy, "A Few of the Jokes . . . ," pp. 9–10.

291   *"If he said that, then he's a schmuck"*: Braudy, "A Few of the Jokes . . . ," pp. 9–10.

292   *"What is there to keep me here?"*: Samuel Beckett, *Endgame* (New York: Grove Press, 1958), p. 58.

292   *"I'd rather read him than see him staged"*: Lester, "Playwright-in-Anguish."

292   *"[L]et me in on the biggest military secret of all"*: Joseph Heller, *We Bombed in New Haven* (New York: Dell, 1967), p. 14.

293   *"art and trash"*: Howe, *World of Our Fathers*, p. 477.

293   *"[I]f someone wants to call my movies art or crap"*: Tynan, "Frolics and Detours of a Short Hebrew Man," p. 56.

293   *"What else, I wanted to make a million dollars"*: Braudy, "A Few of the Jokes . . . ," pp. 9–10.

293   *heard maniacs in the room*: ibid.

293   *"For god's sake, speak up"*: ibid.

293   *"They're not really idiots"*: Israel Shenker, "Did Heller Bomb on Broadway?" *New York Times*, December 29, 1968.

293   *"told lies"*: ibid.

294   *"I'm learning"*: Braudy, "A Few of the Jokes . . . ," p. 10.

294   *"It's not that I'm trying to dominate the director"*: Lester, "Playwright-in-Anguish."

294   *"Listen, who's nervous?"*: Braudy, "A Few of the Jokes . . . ," p. 10.

294   *"The real truth"*: Lester, "Playwright-in-Anguish."

294   *"close . . . to the Jewish sensibility"*: ibid.

295   *"There's nothing really funny about this"*: Heller, *We Bombed in New Haven*, p. 122.

295   *"I thought we were going to have a good time"*: Lester, "Playwright-in-Anguish."

295   *"He lumbered to his classes"*: In addition to the stress of rehearsals and anticipating the play's opening, Heller missed the amenities of New York. Susan Braudy, a young journalist who audited Heller's playwriting course, wrote: "I was dying to learn how to be a writer. But all Heller wanted to talk about was Zabar's. Actually, he bragged about his proximity to the greatest delicatessen in the world. He was unseemly in his pride. He wagged [a] finger . . . 'This orange drink here at Yale is terrible.' He raised his voice. 'Zabar's fresh orange juice is the best in the world, and it's only a few blocks from my apartment.' When he wasn't talking about the wonders of, say, Zabar's cheeses, he bragged about New York. "Everybody's a little Irish, a little Jewish, and more than a little black.' See "Susan Braudy's Manhattan Diary: An Introduction to Zabar's from Joseph Heller," posted at www.dnainfo.com.

295   *"It's not really very expensive"*: Lester, "Playwright-in-Anguish."

295   *"Heller's ending"*: Seed, *The Fiction of Joseph Heller*, p. 73.

295   *"There's no remission at the end of my play"*: Shenker, "Did Heller Bomb on Broadway?"

295   *"Most guys think they'll go into [the service]"*: Braudy, "A Few of the Jokes . . . ," p. 9.

295   *"cuts to the quick"*: Roderick Nordell, "Premiere of *We Bombed in New Haven*," *Christian Science Monitor*, December 8, 1967.

295   *"the play is very likely the most powerful play about contemporary irrationality"*: Jack Kroll, "War Games," *Newsweek*, December 18, 1967, p. 96.

295   *"The evening posits war as a glamorous game"*: Walter Kerr, "Walter Kerr VS. Joseph Heller," *New York Times*, October 27, 1968.

296 *"imagination that created"*: Tom F. Driver, "Curtains in Connecticut," *The Saturday Review*, August 31, 1968, pp. 22–24.

296 *"I have unlimited confidence"*: Braudy, "A Few of the Jokes . . . ," p. 9.

296 *"The American government is making war"*: Seed, *The Fiction of Joseph Heller*, p. 85.

296 *"This could end the war"*: Braudy, "A Few of the Jokes . . . ," p. 7.

296 *"If it came to violence"*: Shenker, "Did Heller Bomb on Broadway?"

297 *"McCarthy [is] an easy man to defend"; the "issues were so stark"; "to [his] everlasting shame"*: Israel Shenker, "Joseph Heller Draws Dead Bead on the Politics of Gloom," *New York Times*, September 10, 1968; posted at nytimes.com/books/98/02/15/home/heller-politics.html?_r=1.

297 *"Every place I went"*: ibid.

297 *"stung by the Gene McCarthy fever"*: Erica Heller, "I Don't Want to Be in That Number When the 'Saints' Go Marching In," *New York Times*, September 30, 1990; posted at nytimes.com/1990/09/30/opinion/personal-i-don-t-want-to-be-in-that-number.

297 *"I guess he was proud"*: Erica Heller in an e-mail to the author, May 7, 2009.

298 *"I'm not considered a first-stringer"*: Brother Alexis Gonzales, "Notes on the Next Novel: An Interview with Joseph Heller," *The New Orleans Review* 2 (1971): 218.

298 *"All the candidates can use humor"*: Shenker, "Joseph Heller Draws Dead Bead on the Politics of Gloom."

298 *Joe met Kurt Vonnegut*: All quotes and details regarding Heller and Vonnegut at Notre Dame are taken from Carole Mallory, "The Joe and Kurt Show," *Playboy*, May 1992; posted at vonnegutweb.com/vonnegutia/interviews/int_heller.html.

298 *"He lost because of the nature of American politics"*: Shenker, "Joseph Heller Draws Dead Bead on the Politics of Gloom."

299 *"[Politics] is not my thing"*: ibid.

299 *"utter political disillusionment"*: Erica Heller, "I Don't Want to Be in that Number When the 'Saints' Go Marching In."

299 *"With the murder of Robert Kennedy"*: Jules Witcover, *The Year the Dream Died: Revisiting 1968 in America* (New York: Warner Books, 1997), p. 263. For another insightful view about the atmosphere of the late 1960s in the United States, see Charles Kaiser, *1968 in America* (New York: Grove Press, 1988).

299 *"Is it as good as our old one?"*: Unless otherwise noted, this and subsequent comments regarding Gourmet Club get-togethers are taken from Reiner, *My Anecdotal Life*, pp. 177–82.

300 *A typical sampling*: This exchange is reported in "Eating with Their Mouths Open," *New York Times*, November 3, 1985; posted at select.nytimes.com/search/restricted/article?res=FAOB1EFC3.

301 *"I imagine every amateur production"*: Robert Merrill, *Joseph Heller* (Boston: Twayne, 1987), p. 57.

301 *"I am not at all certain what I felt"*: Clive Barnes, "Heller's *We Bombed in New Haven* Opens," *New York Times*, October 17, 1968, p. 51.

302 *he never again wanted anything to do with the theater*: Heller did, in fact, complete two other stage plays, both adaptations from *Catch-22*. *Catch-22: A Dramatization* was first performed on July 13, 1971, in the John Drew Theater in East Hampton, New York. Heller finished the play at the urging of Larry Arrick; in it, the chaplain comments on war scenes in letters he writes to his wife, and Wintergreen serves as a dispenser and censor of military information. *Clevinger's Trial* (1973) adapts chapter 8 of the novel. Samuel French published Acting Editions of both plays in 1971 and 1973, respectively, and in 1973, Delacorte Press published a trade edition of *Catch-22: A Dramatization*. In a foreword to that edition, Heller railed against the "bloody enterprise" of Vietnam, whose tragedy had been made all the more plain, he wrote, by revelations in the Pentagon Papers in 1971.

303 *"I will weep for you"*: This and subsequent quotes from the play are taken from Heller, *We Bombed in New Haven*, pp. 216–17.

303 *the Eagle's landing in the Sea of Tranquility*: Sylvan Fox, a *New York Times* editor, called

Heller at the time of the *Apollo 11* moon landing and asked him to write an article of about eight hundred words on the event's historical and cultural importance. Heller was interested but said he could not write eight hundred words in the two- or three-day time period the paper's deadline required. He said he would need several weeks, and Fox did not have that much time.

303 *"maybe a booth at which Dash Hammett once ate with Lilly Hellman"*: Tom Nolan, "Martinis and Mythology," *Los Angeles Times Magazine,* February 6, 2000; posted at articles.latimes.com/2000/feb/06/magazine/tom_61592?pg=3.

304 *[Hoffman and I became] good friends"*: Heller and Vogel, *No Laughing Matter,* p. 77.

305 *"At first there was camaraderie"*: Mel Gussow, "The Day Dustin Hoffman's House Blew Up," posted at mrbellersneighborhood.com/story.php?storyid=524.

14. WHERE IS WORLD WAR II?

pages
306 *location scouts had staked out*: Unless otherwise noted, this and all other details and quotes in this chapter regarding the filming of *Catch-22* are taken from four invaluable sources: "Some Are More Yossarian than Others," *Time,* June 15, 1970, pp. 66–74; Buck Henry, "A Diary of Planes, Pilots, and Pitfalls," *Life,* June 12, 1970, pp. 46, 48; Nora Ephron, "Yossarian Is Alive and Well in the Mexican Desert," *New York Times,* March 16, 1969, posted at nytimes.com/books/98/02/15/home/heller-yossarian,html?_r=1; and Joseph Heller, "On Translating *Catch-22* into a Movie," in *A "Catch-22" Casebook,* ed. Frederick Kiley and Walter McDonald (New York: Thomas Y. Crowell, 1973), pp. 346–55.

308 *"moved the industry one step closer"*: Jon Lewis, *American Film: A History* (New York: W. W. Norton, 2008), pp. 278–79.

308 *"A peculiarly American brand of auteurism"*: ibid., p. 282.

311 *incidents threatened crew morale*: In his memoir, *Halfway through the Door* (New York: Harper & Row, 1979), Alan Arkin wrote that "the film took a direction I could not understand, and this became a source of great pain for me.... [I was] isolated and on edge ... in emotional limbo" (p. 13). Art Garfunkel, who had a small role in the movie, was apparently at odds with his singing partner, Paul Simon, over the movie's shooting schedule. Simon wanted Garfunkel back in New York to work on the *Bridge Over Troubled Water* album (initially, Simon also had a part in *Catch-22,* but his role was written out—possibly another source of Simon's irritation). The song "The Only Living Boy in New York" was reportedly written to chide Garfunkel. It refers to getting a plane on time and flying to Mexico. The song is addressed to "Tom," a name Simon sometimes used for Garfunkel, as the duo billed itself as Tom and Jerry when they first started singing together.

312 *"it seemed ... [like] two movies"*: Jacob Brackman, "Review of *Catch-22,*" *Esquire,* September 1970, pp. 12, 14.

313 *"Mike Nichols'* Catch-22": Grover Sales, "Catch-$22," *San Francisco,* October 1970, pp. 9–10.

313 *"WE did this 'Insane War Picture' bit FIRST"*: Mort Drucker and Stan Hart, "Catch-All-22," *MAD,* March 1971, p. 10.

15. THE WILLIES

pages
315 *"It was after the war,"*: Joseph Heller, *Something Happened* (New York: Alfred A. Knopf, 1974), p. 78.

315 *"thousand-and-first version"*; *"this written-to-death situation"*: Kurt Vonnegut, "Something Happened," *New York Times Book Review,* October 6, 1974, pp. 1–2.

315 *"There's no reason why I couldn't work at home"*: Alden Whitman, "Something Always Happens on the Way to the Office: An Interview with Joseph Heller," in *Pages: The World of Books, Writers, and Writing,* ed. Matthew J. Bruccoli and C. E. Frazer Clark, Jr. (Detroit: Gale, 1976), p. 78.

316 *"stood around all day"*: Erica Heller in an e-mail to the author, December 3, 2009.

316 *"As the sixties passed"*: This and subsequent quotes regarding Heller's move to Knopf are taken from Michael Korda, *Another Life* (New York: Dell, 2000), pp. 229–30, 236–38.

317 *"When he finished* Catch-22*"; "[I always knew] he'd turn it in"*: Israel Shenker, "Second Heller Book Due 13 Years After First," *New York Times,* February 18, 1974; posted at nytimes.com/books/98/02/15/home/heller-due.html.

317 *"We were of an age"*: Unless otherwise noted, this and subsequent quotes regarding Candida Donadio are taken from Karen Hudes, "Epic Agent: The Great Candida Donadio," *Tin House* 6, no. 4 (2005): 154, 161, 163.

318 *"She had forgotten to mention [the bird]"*: Erica Heller in an e-mail to the author, June 8, 2009.

318 *"sibling rivalry amongst her other charges"*: Howard Junker, "Will This Finally Be Philip Roth's Year?" *New York,* January 13, 1969, p. 46.

319 *"Teaching takes a lot of my time"; "It's a job I would like to keep"*: Robert Alan Aurthur, "Hanging Out," *Esquire,* September 1974, p. 64; Creath Thorne, "Joseph Heller: An Interview," *Chicago Literary Review,* December 1974, pp. 1, 8.

319 *"I was a really thin man"*: Aurthur, "Hanging Out," p. 54.

320 *"The Angel of Death is in the gym today"*: Joseph Heller, *Good as Gold* (New York: Simon & Schuster, 1979), p. 200.

320 *"I figured if a car hit me"*: Edwin McDowell, "Often Lost, Sometimes Found, Authors Tell about Manuscripts," *Ocala Star Banner,* September 23, 1983.

320 *"I asked him what would happen"*: Erica Heller in an e-mail to the author, May 29, 2009.

320 *"I think I'm in trouble"*: This and other rough-draft sentences are from the *Something Happened* note cards, Joseph Heller Archive, Department of Rare Books and Special Collections, Thomas Cooper Library, University of South Carolina, Columbia, South Carolina.

321 *"If I live to be a hundred and fifty"*: This and subsequent quotes are from the *Something Happened* note cards.

323 *"I don't think of myself as a naturally gifted writer"*: Adam J. Sorkin, ed., *Conversations with Joseph Heller* (Jackson: University Press of Mississippi, 1993), p. 111.

323 *"I miss my dead boy"*: This and subsequent quotes are from the rough draft of *Something Happened,* Joseph Heller Archive.

323 *"My mother is a fish"*: William Faulkner, *As I Lay Dying* (New York: Random House, 1990), p. 84.

323 *"The moocow came down the road"*: James Joyce, *A Portrait of the Artist as a Young Man* (New York: Penguin Books, 1977), p. 7.

323 *"I put everything I knew"*: Sam Merrill, "*Playboy* Interview: Joseph Heller," *Playboy,* June 1975, pp. 66–68.

323 *"What should I call the guy"*: Aurthur, "Hanging Out," p. 54.

323 *"I was carrying the manuscript"*: ibid.

324 *"[We] have children"*: Kenneth Tynan, "Frolics and Detours of a Short Hebrew Man," *The New Yorker,* October 30, 1978, p. 92.

324 *"I may look a little bit Jewish"*: Heller, *Something Happened,* pp. 349–50.

324 *"Joe [, you] wouldn't do that!"*: Sorkin, ed., *Conversations with Joseph Heller,* pp. 173–74.

324 *"Bob and I think of each other as close friends"*: Larissa MacFarquhar, "Robert Gottlieb: The Art of Editing I," *The Paris Review* 36, no. 132 (1994): 218.

324 *"no book like it"*: Israel Shenker, "Joseph Heller Draws Dead Bead on the Politics of Gloom," *New York Times,* September 10, 1968.

324 *"areas of combat"*: Sorkin, ed., *Conversations with Joseph Heller,* pp. 113–14.

325 *"In the office in which I work"; "I get the willies"*: Heller, *Something Happened,* pp. 9, 1.

325 *"[T]his is going to sound crazy to you"*: This and the subsequent dialogue between Heller and Gottlieb is from MacFarquhar, "Robert Gottlieb," p. 87.

325 *"[I]t is midsummer, 1974"*: This quote and the subsequent dialogue with Murray Schisgal are from Aurthur, "Hanging Out," p. 50.

326 *magazine and newspaper ads*: Ads for *Something Happened* and review blurbs from various sources can be found in the Joseph Heller Archive.

326 *"no attempt to understand what is going on"*: Joseph Epstein, "Joseph Heller's Milk Train: Nothing More to Express," *Washington Post Book World,* October 6, 1974, pp. 1–3.

327 *"splendidly put together"*: "Something Happened . . . *could become the dominant myth"*; *"baldly"*: Vonnegut, "Something Happened" pp. 1–2.

327 *"[This] is not a book for kids"*: Robert Gottlieb quoted in *Stone Reader,* a documentary film by Mark Moskowitz, 1999.

327 *"must be reaching a wider, older audience"*: Merrill, *"Playboy* Interview: Joe Heller," pp. 66–68.

328 *"If there were a key word"; "Zip code marketing"*: *Esquire,* September 1974, pp. 89, 94.

328 from *"December, 1972, to April, 1975*: Abe Peck, *Uncovering the Sixties: The Life and Times of the Underground Press* (New York: Pantheon, 1985), p. 291.

329 *"on top of the world"; "whole manner gives the promise"*: Charles T. Powers, "Joe Heller, Author on Top of the World," *Los Angeles Times,* March 30, 1975.

329 *If I thought I might never get another idea for a novel"*: Sorkin, ed., *Conversations with Joseph Heller,* p. 116.

329 *"What? You're not worried about any of this?"*: Seth Kupferberg and Greg Lawless, "Joseph Heller: 13 Years from Catch-22 to Something Happened," *Harvard Crimson,* October 11, 1974.

329 *"If [your family] can live through"*: Mel Brooks, "Mel Brooks Meets Joseph Heller," *Washington Post Book World,* March 11, 1979, p. 4.

329 *". . . can't believe it's finally out"*: Kupferberg and Lawless, "Joseph Heller."

330 *"to put to test"*: Andre Furlani, "Brisk Socratic Dialogues: Elenctic Rhetoric in Joseph Heller's Something Happened," *Narrative* 3, no. 3 (1995): 253.

330 *"brisk, Socratic dialogues"*: This and subsequent quotes from the novel are in Heller, *Something Happened,* pp. 268, 185, 236, 128.

331 *"son is a Socrates"*: Furlani, "Brisk Socratic Dialogues,": p. 259.

331 *"signs that, I believe, are clinical symptoms of psychosis"*: Kupferberg and Lawless, "Joseph Heller."

331 *"My memory's failing"*: Heller, *Something Happened,* pp. 523–24.

332 *"disorganized personality"*: Kupferberg and Lawless, "Joseph Heller."

332 *"An unprecedented combination of inflation and recession"*: Robert W. Sarnoff, *RCA's Annual Report,* 1974, pp. 2–3.

333 *"Novelist Joseph Heller['s]"*: ibid., p. 17.

333 *"[T]he exclusive worship of the bitch-goddess SUCCESS"*: William James cited in Norman Podhoretz, *Making It* (New York: Random House, 1967), p. xiii.

333 *"nothing special"*: This and the subsequent quotes about Gwathmey are by Erica Heller, posted at artsbeat.blogs.mytimes.com/2009/08/04/charles-gwathmey-architect-of-the-modernist-school-is-dead-at-71.

334 *"Elaine's had become the 'in' place"*: A. E. Hotchner, *Everyone Comes to Elaine's* (New York: Harper Entertainment, 2004), pp. 125–27. Heller had been going to Elaine's since the early 1960s. Steve Coates reported that in 1963, George Plimpton, after attending that year's Venice Film Festival, gathered a number of literary friends at Elaine's to discuss the possibility of forming a Film Writers International Group. Present were Norman Mailer, Terry Southern, and Heller, among others. The idea was to formalize their already-regular meetings so they could "[drink] and talk . . . about wanting to get their novels and plays made into movies." Heller, with some experience writing screenplays, was "wary" of the idea. (see Steve Coates, "Plimpton's Party," posted at papercuts.blogs.nytimes.com/2008/12/11/plimptons-party/?pagemode=print). Steve Katz reported that in 1968, Plimpton tried again to formalize his drinkfests with friends. He "arranged a gathering at Elaine's with a sappy name like Convergence of Genius, or the Genius Club." Heller was among those included, along with Robert Rauschenberg, Truman Capote, Susan Sontag, Merce Cunningham, John Cage, Yvonne Rainer, and Norman Mailer. The gathering was "meant to create an artistic, literary think tank," Katz wrote. Again, the idea went nowhere. (See Steve Katz, "Three Memoirrhoids," posted at Keyholemagazine.com/Steve-Katz/three-Memoirrhoids.)

334 *"Right after he finishes [writing] a book"*: Sorkin, ed., *Conversations with Joseph Heller,* p. 198.

335 *"I . . . need disturbances"*: ibid.

335 *"Thank goodness, we don't need love anymore"*: ibid., p. 193.

335 *"The kid, they say, was born in a manger"*: Joseph Heller, unpublished jottings, Joseph Heller Archive.

335 *"The President is fully aware"*: Todd S. Purdum, "The Nation: The Nondenial Denier," *New York Times,* February 16, 2003; posted at nytimes.com/2003/02/16/weekinreview/ thenation-the-nondenial-denier.html.

336 *"Every woman loves"*: This and lines from various ads are from the Joseph Heller Archive.

336 *"I don't think I deserve all this money"*: George Mandel, in conversation with the author, July 20, 2009.

336 *Politically, he was drifting toward the center:* On November 24, 1975, in the *New York Times* editorial section, Heller published a short satirical piece entitled "This Is Called 'National Defense,' " in which he lampooned FBI agents engaged in domestic spying and said he wished they would "stop interfering with such decent people as Socrates, Martin Luther King, Eugene V. Debs, Galileo, and me." The piece felt rather dated, not what one expected from the prophetic writer of *Catch-22* and *Something Happened.* It would soon be clear that he was saving his satirical strength for a long exposé of American political chicanery, *Good as Gold.* The full text is posted at gonzomuckraker.blogspot .com/2007/11/this-is-called-national-defense.html.

336 *"one of the bravest"*: Norman Podhoretz, "The Best Catch There Is," reprinted in Podhoretz, *The Bloody Crossroads: Where Literature and Politics Meet* (New York: Simon & Schuster, 1986), p. 229.

336 *"invigorat[ed] the magazine"*: Ted Solotaroff, "Adventures in Editing: Ted Solotaroff's 'Commentary' Days," posted at thenation.com/doc/20090209/solotaroff.

336 *"I [have] . . . experienced an astonishing revelation"*: Podhoretz, *Making It,* p. xi.

337 *"Nothing, I believe, defines the spiritual character of American life"*: ibid., pp. xiii–xvii.

337 *"no-holds barred"*: Joseph Epstein, "Remaking It," *New York Times,* October 21, 1979; posted at nytimes.com/books/99/02/21/specials/podhoretz-breaking.html.

337 *"love is not the answer to hate"*: Norman Podhoretz, "My Negro Problem—and Ours," reprinted in Podhoretz, *The Bloody Crossroads,* p. 369.

337 *"revulsion"; "health"; "fevers and plagues"*: Norman Podhoretz, *Breaking Ranks: A Political Memoir* (New York: Harper & Row, 1979), pp. 16–17.

337 *"Heller . . . [is] far more politically Left"*: Norman Podhoretz, *Ex-Friends: Falling Out with Lionel and Diana Trilling, Lillian Hellman, Hannah Arendt, and Norman Mailer* (San Francisco: Encounter Books, 2000), p. 50.

338 *"I never gave him the chance to dump me"*: Christopher Hitchens, *Unacknowledged Legislation: Writers in the Public Sphere* (New York: Verso, 2001), p. 325.

338 *"strong attachment"; "difficult, confusing question"*: Merrill, "*Playboy* Interview: Joseph Heller," pp. 66–68.

339 *"reconsider[ed]" Catch-22:* Norman Podhoretz, "Looking Back at *Catch-22*"; reprinted as "Norman Podhoretz on Rethinking *Catch-22,*" in *Bloom's Guides: Joseph Heller's Catch-22,* ed. Harold Bloom (New York: Infobase Publishing, 2009), pp. 118–20.

Periodically, *Catch-22* has been subject to censorship in the United States. For example, in 1972, the Strongsville, Ohio, Board of Education disapproved purchase of the novel despite faculty recommendations. The board called *Catch-22* "completely sick" and "garbage." In 1974, parents in Dallas, Texas, insisted the book be removed from all high school libraries because it contained the word *whore.* The parents' challenge, heard in meetings of the Dallas Independent School District, was unsuccessful. A similar failed challenge was mounted in the Snoqualmie Valley (Washington) School District in 1979. See Dawn B. Sova, *Banned Books: Literature Suppressed on Social Grounds,* rev. ed. (New York: Infobase Publishing, 2006), pp. 82–84.

340 *I [am] getting very envious"*: Maria Lenhart, "Wielding Humor's Two-Edged Sword," *Christian Science Monitor,* April 9, 1979.

340   *"John Ehrlichman, Spiro Agnew, and H. R. Haldeman"*: This and subsequent quotes from the novel are taken from Heller, *Good as Gold*, pp. 359, 355, 3, 360.

340   *"public-relations enterprise"*: Merrill, *"Playboy* Interview: Joseph Heller," pp. 66–68.

341   *"I [am] getting more efficient"*: Lenhart, "Wielding Humor's Two-Edged Sword."

341   *"[W]hen I am close to finishing a book"*; *"When . . . James Jones died"*: Sorkin, ed., *Conversations with Joseph Heller*, p. 199.

341–42   *"You're both Italian"*; *"I came home late . . . [one evening]"*: Kaylie Jones, *Lies My Mother Never Told Me* (New York: William Morrow, 2009), p. 234. According to Erica Heller (e-mail to the author, September 8, 2009), most people found Gloria Jones "obnoxious" and her father "tolerated" her because he had liked her husband.

342   *Joe remained depressed*: For a glimpse of his state of mind during this period, see "Joseph Heller on America's 'Inhuman Callousness,'" *U.S. News & World Report*, April 9, 1979, p. 73.

342   *"For financial security"*: "Heller Takes the Money and Runs," *New York*, March 19, 1979, p. 54.

342   *"shticky"*: Robert Gottlieb in conversation with the author, August 29, 2010.

342   *"believe in guaranteeing such immense sums"*: "Heller Moves Back to Simon and Schuster for Third Novel," *Publishers Weekly*, February 7, 1977, p. 37.

343   *"You mean you're not going to make an offer at all"?*: Herman Gollob in an e-mail to the author, June 5, 2009.

343   *"That's not exactly how I remember things"*: Gottlieb in conversation with the author.

343   *"[Candida] would sort of start whimpering"*; *"There are times when it's healthier"*: Hudes, *"Epic Agent,"* pp. 155, 162.

343   *"showiest [publishing house]"*: This and subsequent quotes about Simon & Schuster, unless otherwise noted, are from Helen Duder, "Why 'Literary' Is a Dirty Word at Simon & Schuster," *New York*, January 16, 1978, pp. 36–40.

344   *"terror of sorts"*: Dinah Prince, "The Book on Joni Evans," *New York*, March 10, 1986, p. 32.

344   *"aggressive"*; *"stick-shift personality"*: ibid., pp. 33–34.

345   *"first for the publishing world"*: "Stellar Sum for Heller Novel," *New York*, February 7, 1977, p. 60.

345   *"Shirley wanted to live it up a little"*: Barbara Gelb in conversation with the author, August 3, 2010.

345   *"[I]n the nonfiction area"*: "Stellar Sum for Heller Novel," p. 60.

345   *"[The trouble] about doing a comic novel with Henry Kissinger"*: Powers, "Joe Heller on Top of the World."

345   *In Good as Gold, Kissinger appears*: The book's working title was "Moths at a Dark Bulb." On May 24, 1976, Heller published an excerpt from his novel in progress, under the title "Moths at a Dark Bulb," on the *New York Times* editorial page. The excerpt was a mock presidential news conference. Presumably, the "dark bulb" was American government; the "moths" were members of the press and, by extension, American citizens.

345–46   *"social world . . . where competence doesn't count"*; *"just another writer now"*: Heller, *Good as Gold*, p. 462.

346   *"Mr. Rockefeller gave Secretary of State Kissinger a $50,000 gift"*: clipping from Joseph Heller Archive.

346   *"Good as Gold is a cultural event"*: Jack Beatty, review of *Good as Gold*, *The New Republic*, March 10, 1979, pp. 42–44.

346   *"It is all about a society that is fast going insane"*: John W. Aldridge, "The Deceits of Black Humor," *Harper's*, March 1979, pp. 115–18.

347   *"[T]here is nothing in the world that can block your appointment"*: Heller, *Good as Gold*, p. 461.

347   *"London. Michelmas term lately over"*; *"[S]omething happened"*: Charles Dickens, *Bleak House* (New York: Heritage House, 1942), pp. 15, 28–29.

347   *"an astounding vision of our leaders in Washington"*: Leonard Michaels, "Bruce Gold's American Experience," *New York Times Book Review*, March 11, 1979, p. 1.

348 *"softball game in a schoolyard"; "Athletes in skullcaps?"*: Heller, *Good as Gold*, pp. 487–88.

348 *"vivid an anecdote of assimilation as I could find"*: "Baseball's Jewish Accent," *The Economist,* January 8, 1994.

348 *"[T]he most repellent character"*: Murray N. Rothbard, "The Evil of Banality," *Inquiry,* December 10, 1979, pp. 26–28.

349 *"savage caricature"*: Podhoretz, *Ex-Friends,* p. 50.

349 *"primarily a cultural crisis"*: Peter Steinfels, *The Neoconservatives: The Men Who Are Changing America's Politics* (New York: Simon & Schuster, 1979), pp. 55, 58, 64–65.

349 *"When Bruce Gold"*: Marshall Toman, "The Political Satire in Joseph Heller's *Good as Gold,*" *Studies in Contemporary Satire* 17 (1990): 6–14.

349 *"broad gauge advisor on domestic policy"; "Don't words mean anything to you?"*: Heller, *Good as Gold,* p. 164.

350 *"A phrase that really gets to me"*: Charlie Reilly, "An Interview with Joseph Heller," *Inquiry,* May 1, 1979, pp. 25–26.

350 *"The honeymoon is over for Joseph Heller"*: John Leonard, "Good as Gold," *New York Times,* March 5, 1979; posted at nytimes.com/books/98/02/15/home/heller-gold.html.

351 *"America . . . was where Jewish humor fantastically flourished"*: Leon Wieseltier, "Shlock of Recognition," *The New Republic,* October 29, 1984, p. 31.

352 *"If you want to forget all your troubles"*: Robert Alter, *Defenses of the Imagination: Jewish Writers and Modern Historical Crisis* (Philadelphia: The Jewish Publication Society of America, 1977), p. 156.

In a piece on contemporary American literature, Alter accuses a number of American writers, including Heller, of exhibiting an "apocalyptic" temperament "reworked" from the "Christian tradition" and exaggerated for absurd and picaresque effects. For a writer like Heller, with a Jewish background, such an attitude is a turning away from "Judaism's concern with 'the factual character of human existence,' " Alter says. "There is no room for real people in apocalypses." See Robert Alter, "The Apocalyptic Temper," *Commentary,* June 1966, pp. 61–66.

16. HARD TO SWALLOW

pages
355 *"I [had] never seen [Joe] so ebullient"*: Barbara Gelb, "Catch-22 Plus: A Conversation with Joseph Heller," *New York Times,* August 28, 1994; posted at nytimes.com/books/98/02/15/home/heller-conversation.html?_r=1.

355 *"I was dry as a bone"*: Joseph Heller and Speed Vogel, *No Laughing Matter* (New York: Simon & Schuster, 1986), p. 244.

356 *"on good terms with himself"*: This and subsequent quotes regarding Jerry McQueen are taken from Barbara Gelb, *On the Track of Murder: Behind the Scenes with a Homicide Commando Squad* (New York: William Morrow, 1975), pp. 15, 40, 128.

357 *"I thought it was hysterically funny"*: Norman Barasch in conversation with the author, April 29, 2009.

357 *recently, he had wasted a morning*: This anecdote was related by LuAnn Walther in a conversation with the author, January 26, 2010.

358 *The day was quite chilly*: This and subsequent details and quotes regarding the onset of Heller's condition and his hospital admission are from Heller and Vogel, *No Laughing Matter,* pp. 14, 18–19, 22, 23, 26, 44.

360 *"No. But that's a lie"*: Adam J. Sorkin, ed., *Conversations with Joseph Heller* (Jackson: University Press of Mississippi, 1993), p. 198.

361 *"pleasantly shock[ing]"; "[He] was proud"*: Ted Heller in an e-mail to the author, January 15, 2010. Details about Ted's work in the garment industry are from his interview with Terry Gross for National Public Radio's "Fresh Air" (WHYY-FM), March 23, 2361.

361 *"I've got the best story in the Bible"*: Joseph Heller, *God Knows* (New York: Alfred A. Knopf, 1984), p. 5.

361 *"I see hopelessness"*: Chet Flippo, "Checking in with Joseph Heller," *Rolling Stone,* April 16, 1981, pp. 57, 59–60.

361 *"You've never written anything as good as* Catch-22*"*: Erica Heller, in conversation with the author, June 25, 2009.

361 *"Sheer, stark terror"*: John Cornwell, "What's the Catch?" in *Sunday Times* [London], September 18, 1994.

362 *"The Mogul"*: Dolores Karl in conversation with the author, April 18, 2009.

362 *"At one point, she got a feminist shrink"*: Barbara Gelb in conversation with the author, August 2, 2010.

362 *"I began to feel the married life"*: Joseph Heller, rough draft of *No Laughing Matter,* Joseph Heller Archive, Department of Rare Books and Special Collections, Thomas Cooper Library, University of South Carolina, Columbia, South Carolina.

362 *"The problem"*: Cornwell, "What's the Catch?"

362 *"Stress? Maybe"*: Joseph Heller, *Now and Then: From Coney Island to Here* (New York: Alfred A. Knopf, 1998), p. 221.

362 *"fatherless Coney Island child"*: ibid., p. 216.

362 *"The first time I met my father"*: ibid., pp. 217–18.

363 *"You don't need that dream anymore"*: ibid., p. 219.

363 *"All that serious stuff was easy"*: ibid., p. 221.

363 *"My theory . . . about psychoanalysis"*: ibid., p. 222.

363 *"never really wanted to live"*: Heller, rough draft of *No Laughing Matter.*

363 *"wish to have a psychiatric medical authority"*: Heller, *Now and Then,* p. 220.

364 *"[H]e bound me to this"*: ibid., p. 222.

364 *"How I came to know him"*: Judith Ruderman in an e-mail to the author, January 10, 2010.

364 *"intrepidly"*; *"[Y]ou didn't really want to do [it]"*: Heller, *Now and Then,* pp. 223–24.

365 *"Joseph Heller took the stand"*: "Joe Heller Takes, and Takes the Fifth," *New York Post,* October 19, 1983.

365 *Speed Vogel named*: Heller, rough draft of *No Laughing Matter,* Joseph Heller Archive.

365 *"friend [had] once worked at Duke University"*: Heller and Vogel, *No Laughing Matter,* p. 40.

365 *Erica recalls long, tearful meetings*: Erica Heller in conversation with the author, June 25, 2009.

365 *"I changed accountants"*: Heller, *Now and Then,* p. 221.

365 *"have had a falling out"*: Edwin McDowell, "Joseph Heller in Dispute with Simon and Schuster," *New York Times,* July 1, 1981.

366 *please conduct any further business*: Karen Hudes, "Epic Agent: The Great Candida Donadio," *Tin House* 6, no. 4 (2005): 158.

366 *"agonize with her"*: ibid., p. 166.

366 *"coming around"*: Heller and Vogel, *No Laughing Matter,* p. 265.

367 *"so concerned about controlling his life"*: Sorkin, ed., *Conversations with Joseph Heller,* p. 189.

367 *"Nothing fails like success"*: Joseph Heller, rough-draft notes for *God Knows,* Joseph Heller Archive. See also *God Knows,* page 187, where King David says, "Succeeding is more satisfying than success."

367 *"The older I get"*; *"I would rather have my wife"*: Heller, *God Knows,* p. 3.

368 *"party circuit"*; *"What would send me into incipient alcoholism"*: Marie Brenner, "Social Studies," *New York,* June 22, 1981, p. 27.

368 *"Joseph* (Catch-22) *Heller"*: "Joseph Heller's Boot-Black," *New York Post,* October 1, 1981.

368 *"earnestly believe[d]"*: Heller and Vogel, *No Laughing Matter,* p. 323.

368 *"I eat only in restaurants these days"*: Fred Ferretti, "Eating Out: Their Way of Life," *New York Times,* November 20, 1981.

369 *"raping"*; *"[Heller] announced [to his estranged wife]"*: Heller and Vogel, *No Laughing Matter,* p. 265.

369 *"interpreters"*: ibid., p. 266.

369 *"Rape"*; *"mischaracterization"*: ibid., p. 266.

369   *"[e]xpressed concern over ability"*: This and other medical notes are from the Joseph Heller Archive.

370   *"going crazy"*: Heller, rough draft of *No Laughing Matter,* Joseph Heller Archive.

370   *"sudden attack"*: "Heller Ill," *New York Post,* December 17, 1981.

370   *"Jesus Christ!"*: Heller, rough draft of *No Laughing Matter,* Joseph Heller Archive.

370   *"respiratory parameters . . . were deteriorating"*; *"I was agreeing to have my throat cut"*: Heller and Vogel, *No Laughing Matter,* pp. 87, 89.

371   *"wife was . . . on the premises"*: ibid., p. 81.

370   *"absolutely shocked"*: Cheryl McCall, "Something Happened," *People,* August 23, 1982, p. 29.

371   *"I went to Shirley"*: Robert A. Towbin in conversation with the author, April 26, 2009.

371   *"What was she going to say"*; *"I missed my mother"*: Heller and Vogel, *No Laughing Matter,* pp. 76, 81.

371   *"in the only way she knew how"*: Heller, *God Knows,* p. 161.

371   *"Someday in this life"*: Heller and Vogel, "*No Laughing Matter,* p. 113.

371–72   *"The décor"*; *"I had more or less assumed his identity"*: ibid., pp. 40–41.

       Speed had decorated Joe's living space before. Many years earlier, when Joe first moved his family into the Apthorp apartment, he hung a large painting of Speed's on the wall. Most of Joe's family, and most visitors to the apartment, did not particularly care for the painting, which seemed out of place with the rest of the décor, but Joe liked it for that very reason.

372   *"Joe, why haven't I heard from you?"*: ibid., p. 72.

372   *"What're you doing here again?"*: ibid., p. 39.

372   *"Tell me honestly"*: ibid., pp. 60–61.

372–73   *"a hooker returning to the brothel"*; *"croak"*; *"If I was in his spot"*; *"I gotta come clean with you"*: Heller and Vogel, rough drafts of *No Laughing Matter,* Joseph Heller Archive; Heller and Vogel, *No Laughing Matter,* p. 57.

       Mario Puzo was not the only one with a horror of hospitals: Joe hated them, too (recall his traumatic tonsil experience). Norman Barasch, in conversation with the author on April 29, 2009, recounted the following anecdote: "[My] daughter was being treated for leukemia at MD Anderson in Houston. Joe was on a book tour in Dallas— this may have been around 1975. Joe had a friend in Houston, Jerry Argovitz, a dentist, and his wife, Elaine. They'd met at a resort or something. He put us in touch with them and they were very helpful to us. Joe made a detour and came to Houston just to see us. Now, Joe Heller was not an overly sentimental man. But Jerry told me later that he sat downstairs at MD Anderson for half an hour to compose himself to come into the room. When he did, Emily gave him a big smile. It was wonderful. He inscribed a book to us, 'To the bravest family I know.' "

373   *"simply marvelous"*: Heller and Vogel, *No Laughing Matter,* p. 75.

373   *"It's not bad here"*: This and subsequent quotes regarding Joe's move to a private room and his friends' comments are from ibid., pp. 105, 125, 136–41.

375   *"Great. How much will he pay me?"*: Kinky Friedman, *'Scuse Me While I Whip This Out: Reflections on Country Singers, Presidents, and Other Troublemakers* (New York: William Morrow, 2004), p. 139.

375   *"I . . . thought [she] was a bit tall for me"*; *"Here comes my good friend"*; *"Ol' Ben Lucas"*: Heller and Vogel, *No Laughing Matter,* pp. 137–38, 152.

375   *"taken a turn for the nurse"*: Friedman, *'Scuse Me While I Whip This Out,* p. 138.

375   *"NG feedings"*: This and other medical notes are in the Joseph Heller Archive.

375   *"I court[ed] her with all my might"*; *"I'm so glad I met you"*; *"If there were just two more of us"*: Heller and Vogel, *No Laughing Matter,* pp. 151, 230–31; Joseph Heller, rough draft of *No Laughing Matter,* Joseph Heller Archive.

376   *"I can't"*: This and the ensuing quotes concerning Valerie's care of Joe are from ibid., pp. 187, 203, 208.

376   *"Mr. Heller presents mild symptoms of dysarthria"*: speech pathology report, Joseph Heller Archive.

376 *"When my swallowing ability came back"*: This and subsequent quotes regarding his condition and the removal of the tube are from Heller and Vogel, *No Laughing Matter*, p. 210.

377 *Joe's friend Bob Towbin*: Active in Democratic Party politics, Towbin was close to Ted Kennedy. In a book called *Trader's Tales*, Ron Insana recorded the following anecdote about him: "A few years after Chappaquiddick, Kennedy visited the trading floor at Unterberg, Towbin. First, Towbin spoke to his traders and then asked the senator to say a few words and mingle with the group. After they finished, and Towbin was ushering his good friend to the exit, Bobby Anotolini [who worked for Towbin] asked the group, 'Hey girls, the senator's leaving. Anyone need a ride?'" See Ron Insana, *Trader's Tales: A Chronicle of Wall Street Myths, Legends, and Outright Lies* (New York: Wiley, 1997), p. 54.

377 *"All that was missing"; "Knowing Valerie's esteem for the artist Manet"*: Heller and Vogel, *No Laughing Matter*, p. 188.

377 *"[S]he had an extremely delicate technique"*: ibid., p. 210.

378 *"custom-built queen-sized platform bed"; "Then Valerie and I were in the apartment alone"*: ibid., p. 213.

379 *"That's not a good thing to have"*: ibid., p. 248.

379 *"Mr. Heller's [need for] the East Hampton home"*: ibid., p. 267.

379 *"Joe felt nervous"*: As a joke, Speed had hung a life-size photograph of himself above Joe's bed in the apartment. It *was* funny, but unnerving. Later, when Joe moved full-time into the house in East Hampton, he hung the picture of Speed in his guesthouse out back.

380 *"It is fortunate"*: Heller and Vogel, *No Laughing Matter*, pp. 268–69.

380 *"[O]ur inner lives ordain for us"*: Heller, *God Knows*, p. 61.

380 *"with mental cruelty and abandonment"*: "Joe Heller Takes, and Takes the Fifth."

380 *"I was not sure I had a case"*: This quote and the subsequent quotes concerning the affidavit and the June 10 hearing are from Heller and Vogel, *No Laughing Matter*, pp. 268–73.

381 *"This is the happiest summer of my life"; "I've been lucky most of my life"*: McCall, "Something Happened," pp. 28–29.

382 *"Each time he told me to change the direction"*: Heller and Vogel, *No Laughing Matter*, p. 294.

382 *"Joe was an entirely different social being"*: ibid., pp. 282–83.

383 *"I'll be grateful to Speed"*: McCall, "Something Happened," p. 28.

383 *"You guys gotta come over for dinner sometime"; "When?"*: Heller and Vogel, *No Laughing Matter*, pp. 282–83.

383 *"Every now and then"*: McCall, "Something Happened," p. 28.

383 *"she [was] the kind of person"*: This and subsequent Speed Vogel quotes are from Heller and Vogel, *No Laughing Matter*, pp. 259, 278–79.

383–84 *"It's expensive to be sick"*: ibid., pp. 287–88.

384 *"Seven or nine days"*: ibid., p. 330.

384 *"encourag[ing] [positive pieces]"; "You can't blame the people who run the* Times*"*: Charles Kaiser, "Friends at the Top of the Times," posted at charleskaiser.com/kosinski.html. Similarly, Edwin Diamond wrote, "Complaints of cronyism . . . and backscratching hounded . . . [Arthur] Gelb. . . . The *Times*' solicitous treatment of cultural figures as disparate as Jerzy Kosinski, Joseph Heller, and Betty Friedan became a running joke among the [Russian] Tea Room crowd." See Edwin Diamond, *Behind the Times* (Chicago: University of Chicago Press, 1995), p. 324.

384 *"Jewish reporters on the staff"*: Arthur Gelb, *City Room* (New York: Berkley 2003), p. 82.

385 *"What are you worried about?"*: This quote and subsequent quotes and details regarding Speed Vogel's writing are from Heller and Vogel, *No Laughing Matter*, pp. 284–86, 306.

385 *during a stroll on Fire Island*: LuAnn Walther in conversation with the author, January 26, 2010.

386 *"interest in other women"*: Jerome Taub in an e-mail to the author, January 4, 2010.

386 *"Craig developed a crush on Heller"*: Gelb, *City Room*, pp. 622–23.

387   *"How long ago?"*: Heller and Vogel, *No Laughing Matter,* p. 301.

387   *"I could get up from a toilet"; "[A]s I saw my time of privileged residence"*: ibid., pp. 312–13.

387   *"on the East Hampton party circuit"; "carrying bags"*: ibid., p. 314.

388   *he wrote a check for $160*: financial records in the Joseph Heller Archive.

388   *"One of the messages"*: This and subsequent quotes regarding the incident at the East Hampton house are from Vogel, rough draft of *No Laughing Matter,* Joseph Heller Archive.

389   *"seemed vacant"*: Shortly after this incident, Heller—against the wishes of his lawyer and his accountants—took much of his King David advance money and spent it on a late fall–early winter vacation to St. Croix, accompanied by Valerie and Speed. The weather had turned cold in East Hampton. The house seemed haunted, and Heller wanted to prolong the feelings of intimacy, contentment, and celebration he had experienced during the summer. For an account of the St. Croix trip, see Heller and Vogel, *No Laughing Matter,* pp. 326–28, 330.

389   *"Catch-22 may have been the beginning of the end"*: This and subsequent Mulcahy quotes are from Susan Mulcahy, "Celebrity Corner," *St. Petersburg Evening Independent,* March 12, 1983.

389   *"two unpublished novels"*: J. Heller, rough draft of *No Laughing Matter,* Joseph Heller Archive.

390   *"Sultan of Splitsville"; "A woman is like a Stradivarius violin"; "pluck"*: Howard Kurtz, "'The Sultan of Splitsville': Lawyer Raoul Lionel, Making Headlines of Heartache," *Washington Post,* November 21, 1988.

390   *"Contentment and/or quietude of spirit"*: This and subsequent quotes related to the divorce proceedings, unless otherwise noted, are from Heller and Vogel, *No Laughing Matter,* pp. 317–18.

390   *"Mr. Heller is now saying"*: Joseph Heller, rough draft for *No Laughing Matter,* Joseph Heller Archive.

390   *"Trouble with the letter 'l'"*: Joseph Heller, personal medical journal, Joseph Heller Archive.

391   *"was eager to do whatever she could"*: This and subsequent quotes by or about Dr. Roberta Jaeger are from documents in the Joseph Heller Archive.

392   *"Mein Kampf of matrimonial warfare"*: This and subsequent quotes from or about William Binderman's exchanges with Joseph Heller in court, unless otherwise noted, are from Heller and Vogel, *No Laughing Matter,* pp. 318–22.

393   *The court transcript reads*: transcript in the Joseph Heller Archive.

393   *"value of copyrights [is] so amorphous"*: Liz Smith, "Battle Royal" *Toledo Blade,* April 6, 1984.

394   *"most persuasive person I [have] ever met"*: Heller and Vogel, *No Laughing Matter,* p. 322.

394   *"Joe's public life was not good for him"*: Dolores Karl in conversation with the author, April 23, 2009.

394   *"Joe went Hollywood in his own inane way"*: Audrey Chestney in conversation with the author, January 5, 2010.

394   *"Shirley was very important to Joe"*: Robert A. Towbin in conversation with the author, April 26, 2009.

394   *"Joe was very shaken by his divorce"*: Barbara Gelb in conversation with the author, August 2, 2010.

394   *"Right after she was divorced from Joe"*: Audrey Chestney in conversation with the author, January 5, 2010.

395   *"I was alone for the first time in my life"*: Graham Bridgstock, "Happiness Is My Catch Number 2," *Evening Standard* (London), February 7, 1995.

395   *"I had been very unsettled"*: McCall, "Something Happened," p. 28.

395   *"girlfriends"*: Barbara Gelb in conversation with the author, August 2, 2010.

395   *"The chemistry was plain dumb luck"*: McCall, "Something Happened," p. 29.

396   *"There is a reluctance to proceed"*: Heller, *Now and Then,* p. 226.

17. GO FIGURE

pages
397 *"none of the customary feelings"*: Joseph Heller and Speed Vogel, *No Laughing Matter* (New York: Simon & Schuster, 1986), p. 120.
398 *"dismayed to discover"*: ibid., p. 155.
398 *"If I'd known in my youth"*: Joseph Heller, *God Knows* (New York: Alfred A. Knopf, 1984), p. 56.
399 *"I had decided to put Joe on the cover"*: Art Cooper, remarks made at "Joseph Heller: A Celebration," a memorial service held at the New York Society for Ethical Culture on June 13, 2000. Transcribed by the author from a video recording (courtesy of Erica Heller).
399 *"Like cunnilingus"*: Heller, *God Knows*, p. 65.
399 *"Some Promised Land"*: Heller, ibid., p. 40.
399 *"Apparently written on the principle"*: Earl Rovit, review in *Library Journal*, September 15, 1984, p. 1772.
399 *"very tired"; "shallow"*: Christopher Lehmann-Haupt, "God Knows," *New York Times*, September 19, 1984.
399 *"repetitious, often annoying"*: Richard Cohen, "Old Testament Time Warp," *Washington Post Book World*, September 30, p. 1.
399 *"disappointing hodgepodge"*: Paul Gray, "The 3,000-Year-Old Man," *Time*, September 24, 1984, pp. 74–75.
399 *"slap in the face"*: Curt Suplee, "Catching Up with Joseph Heller," *Washington Post*, October 8, 1984.
400 *"God Knows is junk"*: Leon Wieseltier, "Schlock of Recognition," *The New Republic*, October 29, 1984, pp. 31–33.
400 *"Look, I've adjusted to this"*: Suplee, "Catching Up with Joseph Heller."
400 *"The abundantly talented Joseph Heller"*: Mordecai Richler, "He Who Laughs Last," *New York Times Book Review*, September 23, 1984, p. 1.
401 *"becomes the head of a family"*: David Seed, *The Fiction of Joseph Heller: Against the Grain* (New York: St. Martin's Press, 1989), p. 160.
401 *"O my son Absalom!"* Heller, *God Knows*, p. 327.
402 *"I was always faithful"*: ibid., p. 104.
          Apparently, at one point, Heller had planned to write an erotic romp along the lines of Philip Roth's *Portnoy's Complaint* or John Updike's *Couples*, but wound up folding the erotic material into *God Knows*.
402 *"perfumed [his] bed with aloes"*: ibid., p. 107.
402 *"David, it's enough already"*: ibid., p. 327.
403 *"Shakespeare's method"*: David M. Craig, *Tilting at Mortality: Narrative Strategies in Joseph Heller's Fiction* (Detroit: Wayne State University Press, 1997), p. 147.
403 *"[I]t is the capacity for change"*: Judith Ruderman, *Joseph Heller* (New York: Continuum, 1991), p. 107.
403 *"That's bullshit, Samuel"*: ibid., p. 56.
404 *"To the Rabbis"*: John Friedman and Judith Ruderman, "Joseph Heller and the 'Real' King David," *Judaism* 36, no. 3 (1987): 298.
404 *"I want my God back"*: Heller, *God Knows*, p. 353.
405 *"There are such musical, soothing phrases"*: Seed, *The Fiction of Joseph Heller*, p. 171.
405 *"I could do without the city"*: Shirley Horner, "About Books," *New York Times*, March 1, 1987; posted at nytimes.com/1987/03/01/nyregion/about-books.html?pagewanted=all.
405 *"bulked-up"*; Henry Dasko, "Kosínski's Afterlife," posted at xtract.art.pl/daskografia/x/2004-Afterlife.html.
405 *"As far as a literary scene"*: Horner, "About Books."
405 *"Media and communications conglomerates"*: Dasko, "Kosínski's Afterlife."
406 *"Since that time"*: Trip Gabriel, "Call My Agent!" *New York Times Magazine*, February 19, 1989; posted at nytimes.com/1989/02/19/magazine/call-my-agent.html?pagewanted=all.

406   *"It is the easiest thing"*: ibid.

407   *"I wanted the book"*: LuAnn Walther in conversation with the author, January 26, 2010.

407   *"[made] books" [like] "Spielberg [made] movies"; "mogul mode"; "only breakfast meeting where no food is served"*: Marion Maneker, "Now for the Grann Finale," posted at nymag.com/nymetro/news/media/features/5618/.

407   *"back-and-forth exchange[s]"; "first time I was to edit [Joe]"*: Gerald C. Gross, *Editors on Editing* (New York: Grove Press, 1994), p. 271.

408   *"You mustn't sound mean"*: Faith Sale's note on rough-draft page of *No Laughing Matter,* Joseph Heller Archive, Department of Rare Books and Special Collections, Thomas Cooper Library, University of South Carolina, Columbia, South Carolina.

408   *"I'm not that way"*: This quote and the following exchange with Speed and Valerie is from Henry Kisor, "Joseph Heller's Pen Pal: Author and Crony Tell Two Humorous Views of Road to Recovery," *Chicago Sun-Times,* February 23, 1986; posted at highbeam.com.

408   *"Here's an entry for you"; "You can use this"*: Joseph Heller's notes on rough-draft pages of *No Laughing Matter,* Joseph Heller Archive.

408   *"the sort of person who regards life as a roller coaster"*: Sanford Pinsker, *Understanding Joseph Heller* (Columbia: University of South Carolina Press, 1991), p. 135.

409   *"an altered mental state"*: Jay I. Meltzer, "Long Island Book," *East Hampton Star,* July 3, 1986.

409   *"Consider how much [artifice]"*: Seed, *The Fiction of Joseph Heller,* pp. 182–83.

409   *"With a peaceful smile"*: Heller and Vogel, *No Laughing Matter,* pp. 333–34.

409   *"I did no such thing"*: ibid., p. 334.

410   *"[T]his is an intoxicating experience"*: This and subsequent quotes regarding Heller's visit to the Air Force Academy are from Andrew H. Malcolm, " 'Catch-22': Cadets Hail a Chronicler of the Absurd," *New York Times,* October 6, 1986.

411   *"monumental artifact of contemporary American literature"*: John W. Aldridge, "The Loony Horror of It All: 'Catch-22' Turns 25," *New York Times,* October 26, 1986.

411   *"stupefies . . . sickens . . . infuriates"*: Philip Roth quoted in ibid.

411   *"[T]he novel's first and greatest sequel"*: J. Hoberman, "Only One Catch—Social Influence of the Book *Catch-22,*" posted at findarticles.com/p/articles/mi_m0268/is_n2_v33/ai_16315374/.

412   *"Joe is one of the greatest writers of my generation"; "If all the rumors"; "I will only confirm"*: Edwin McDowell, " 'Catch-22' Sequel by Heller," *New York Times,* April 8, 1987; posted at nytimes.com/1987/04/08/books/catch-22-sequel-by-heller.html?pagewanted=1. See also David Straitfeld, "Catch-23," *New York,* September 12, 1994, p. 103.

412   *"write good novels"*: This and subsequent quotes from the interview with Heller are from Charles Ruas, *Conversations with American Writers* (New York: Alfred A. Knopf, 1985), pp. 172, 179.

413   *"badly about the other"*: Erica Heller in an e-mail to the author, March 28, 2010.

414   *"Stanley Cohen and Toby Molenaar"*: On Heller's first outing with Valerie Humphries, when doctors at the Rusk Institute allowed him to stay in his own apartment, Cohen was the friend with whom the couple dined. In France's Loire Valley, Cohen and Molenaar owned a fifteenth-century mill that had once belonged to the sculptor Alexander Calder. They also owned a house in Sag Harbor, at which Molenaar created a spectacular garden.

414   *"I was helpless"*: This and Heller's subsequent remarks about his courtship of Valerie are from Marian Christy, "Joseph Heller: Getting Back to Wellness," *Boston Globe,* February 4, 1987; posted at, highbeam.com.

415   *"I'm in the twilight of my career"*: Kevin Haynes, "Contemplating Joseph Heller," *W,* September19–26, 1988.

415   *"[W]riting . . . has this strange quality"*: Plato, *Phaedrus,* trans. W. C. Helmbold and W. G. Rabinowitz (New York: Bobbs-Merrill, 1956), p. 69.

415   *"I like to think of the books I write as being interesting in themselves"*: Charles T. Powers, "Joe Heller, Author on Top of the World," *Los Angeles Times,* March 30, 1975.

416   *"If you're a guy who has a wife and children"*: Jeffrey Goldberg, "Puzo Knows," *New York,* July 29, 1996, p. 40.

416   *"[T]here's . . . something contradictory in what I say"*: Betty Sue Flowers, ed., *Bill Moyers: A World of Ideas* (New York: Doubleday, 1989), p. 37.

416   *"To a country whose economic health depended on sea voyages"*: Joseph Heller, *Picture This* (New York: G. P. Putnam's Sons, 1988), p. 116.

417   *"reputation had dimmed"*: ibid., p. 17.

417   *"From Athens to Syracuse"*: ibid., p. 208.

417   *"A man cannot expect to make money out of the community"*: ibid., pp. 70–71.

418   *"[T]here was [no] tolerance"*: ibid., p. 26.

418–19   *"Aristophanes was writing [satirically]"*: ibid., p. 176.

419   *"In what I hope is an amusing way"*: This and subsequent quotes from the Moyers interview are from Flowers, ed.: *Bill Moyers*, pp. 28–37.

420   embittered, sassy Mark Twain: Robert M. Adams, "History Is a Bust," *New York Times Book Review,* September 11, 1988, p. 9.

420   *"most endearing quality"*: Richard Raynor, "Another Mission Flown; Author of *Catch-22,* Joseph Heller," *The Times* (London), October 19, 1998.

420   *"[I]t represents very spaced out writing"*: Robert M. Adams, "History Is a Bust," p. 9.

420   *"[t]hought-provoking"*: cited in the ad copy of the paperback edition of *Picture This* (New York: Ballantine Books, 1988).

420   *"It's true, as Dr. Johnson put it"*: Jonathan Yardley, "Musings Minus the Muse; From Joseph Heller, Flat Philosophizing," *Washington Post Book World,* August 31, 1988.

420   *"We have picked up a word from the Greeks"*: Walter Goodman, "Heller Contemplating Rembrandt," *New York Times,* September 1, 1988; posted at nytimes.com/1988/09/01/books/books-of-the-times-heller-contemplating-rembrandt.html.

420   *"had a devastating effect on me"*: Straitfeld, "Catch 23," p. 102.

421   *"Very few complex good books"*: ibid., p. 103.

18. THE NEW WORLD

pages

422–23   *"Is [the spa] sanitary?"; "I didn't know you're a writer"*: Sidney Offit, *Friends, Writers, and Other Countrymen* (New York: St. Martin's Press, 2008), pp. 240–41.

423   *"She [is] a person"; "Like Browning's 'Last Duchess' "*: Heller and Vogel, *No Laughing Matter,* p. 148.

423   *"I still use fifty dishes"*: This and subsequent remarks about Heller's eating habits at home are from Graham Bridgstock, "Happiness Is My Catch Number 2," *Evening Standard* (London), February 7, 1995.

424   *"I became aware of the old island here"*: F. Scott Fitzgerald, *The Great Gatsby* (New York: Charles Scribner's Sons, 1925), p. 182.

424   *"Boy, this guy really likes to read books by Joseph Heller!"*: Skip Blumberg in an e-mail to the author, May 9, 2009.

425   *Regis Philbin; "I acted like I didn't know who he was"; "Stephen King has been in here three times"*: Diane Ketcham, "About Long Island: Hamptons Bookstores Take Extra Steps for Hometown Writers," *New York Times,* September 10, 1995; posted at nytimes.com/1995/09/10/nyregion/about-long-island-hamptons-bookstores-take-extra-steps-for-hometownwriters.html.

425   *"Writers out here are like earthworms"*: This and subsequent quotes about the Hamptons, unless otherwise noted, are from Anthony Haden-Guest, "Out Here in the Hamptons: Snapshots of a Literary Life," *New York,* September 1, 1975, pp. 43–47.

425   *Of course, Long Island had a history*: For a detailed summary of Long Island's attraction for writers, see Constance Ayers Denne, "Writers of the East End: Responses to a Special Place," transcript of a lecture delivered at the East Hampton Library, August 1998; posted at easthamptonlibrary.org/history/lecture/19980828.pdf.

426   *"[E]very summer, I think Great Gatsbys are giving big parties"*: Joseph Heller speaking on the program "Great Scott," PBS *NewsHour,* September 27, 1996; transcript posted at pbs.org/newshour/bb/entertainment.october96/fitz_9-27.html.

426 *"a successful writer"*: ibid.

426 *"bumps he had taken in his life"*: This and subsequent remarks by Bruce Jay Friedman were made at "Joseph Heller: A Celebration," a memorial service held at the New York Society for Ethical Culture on June 13, 2000. Transcribed by the author from a video recording (courtesy of Erica Heller).

427 *"people my age are either portly or dying"; "He likes coffee"; "He's my favorite"*: Diane Ketcham, "Meeting with a Group of Cronies to Chew the Fat, but There's a Catch," *New York Times,* May 18, 1997; posted at nytimes.com/1997/05/18/nyregion/meeting-with-a-group-of-cronies-to-chew-the-fat-but-theres-a-catch.html.

427 *"color of lobelia"; "She'd be happy even if she was a Kurd"*: Sally Vincent, "Portrait: Catch-94," *The Guardian,* September 24, 1994; Carole Mallory, "The Joe and Kurt Show," *Playboy,* May 1992, posted at vonnegutweb.com/vonnegutia/interviews/int_heller.html.

427 *Mostly, he went for the food*: A source who wishes to remain anonymous related this anecdote to the author in an email, April 1, 2010.

428 *Artists and Writers Softball Game*: For a lively description of this annual event, and many other Hamptons people, places, and incidents, see Dan Rattiner, *In the Hamptons* (New York: Harmony Books, 2008), pp. 332–44.

428 *"downright Byzantine"*: Florence Fabricant, "At a Gathering of Top Chefs, the Food Gets Star Billing," *New York Times,* September 5, 1990; posted at nytimes.com/1990/09/05/garden/at-a-gathering-of-top-chefs-the-food-gets-star-billing.html.

428 *"Yeah, he lived the celebrity life"*: Robert A. Towbin in conversation with the author, April 26, 2009.

428 *One night, at a billionaire's party*: Famously, Vonnegut commemorated this event in a poem published in the May 16, 2005, issue of *The New Yorker.*

429 *"Valerie was a bit of a dipsy-doodle"*: Florence Aaron in conversation with the author, May 29, 2009.

429 *"for a transitory enchanted moment"*: Fitzgerald, *The Great Gatsby,* p. 182.

19. CLOSING TIME

pages

430 *"This is no way for any writer to cap a career"*: This and all other quotes regarding the publication of *Closing Time,* unless otherwise noted, are from David Straitfeld, "Catch-23," *New York,* September 12, 1994, pp. 102–05.

431 *he would write a nonfiction book for them*: See Edwin McDowell, "Book Notes: A '93 Sequel to Catch-22," *New York Times,* February 27, 1991; posted at nytimes.com/1991/02/27/books/book-notes-768091.html.

431 *"maternal and nurturing"; "Well, she lied [to me]"*: Karen Hudes, "Epic Agent: The Great Candida Donadio," *Tin House* 6, no. 4 (2005): 163.

432 *She was often inebriated; "She seemed so grief-stricken"*: ibid., pp. 166–68.

432 *"dealt with her kindly but firmly"*: Robert Gottlieb in conversation with the author, August 29, 2010.

432 *". . . in the hospital, Yossarian dreamed of his mother"*: Joseph Heller, *Closing Time* (New York: Simon & Schuster, 1994), p. 19.

432 *"When people our age speak of the war"*: ibid., p. 11.

433 *"At 4:30 I stood contemplating the place"*: Ken Miller's research notes for *Closing Time,* Joseph Heller Archive, Department of Rare Books and Special Collections, Thomas Cooper Library, University of South Carolina, Columbia, South Carolina.

434 *"I'm keeping my distance from the publisher"*: Straitfeld, "Catch-23," p. 104.

434 *"I look good"*: Margarita Fichtner, "Heller Takes a Chance and Resurrects Yossarian," *Albany Times,* October 2, 1984.

434 *"I hate that title"*: Mark Lawson, "Joey Heller's Happy Ending," *The Independent,* September 25, 1994; posted at independent.co.uk/arts-entertainment/joey-hellers-happy-ending.html.

435 *her father was "around"*: Erica Heller in an e-mail to the author, February 11, 2010.

435   *"to punctuate a sentence at work"*: ibid.

435   *"[A]n atrocity"*: Carole Mallory, "The Joe and Kurt Show," *Playboy,* May 1992; posted at vonnegutweb.com/vonnegutia/ interviews/int_heller.html.

435   *"I'm a narcissist"*: Straitfeld, "Catch-23," p. 104.

435   *"It was always easy to accept who I was"*: Itabari Njeri, "Joseph Heller: The Jewish Novelist Explains Just Why It Wasn't Easy to Become a Jewish Novelist," *Los Angeles Times,* January 13, 1988; posted at articles.latimes.com/1988–01–13/news/vw-23881_1_joseph-heller.

436   *"more [ambitions] than any one human"*: Heller's remark published in *Voices and Visions* (promotional catalog for the Rockefeller Foundation's Bellagio Study Center), posted at rockefellerfoundation.org/uploads/files/o.

436   *"The evening ended quietly"*: Heller's rough-draft notes for a 1992 article in *Forbes FYI,* Joseph Heller Archive.

436   *His brother Lee had died*: Lee Heller died in West Palm Beach, Florida, on November 28, 1992.

437   *"They could possibly shit on it"*: Straitfeld, "Catch-23," p. 104.

437   *"There's no question"*: ibid., p. 105.

437   *"We've positioned it as a bestseller"*: ibid.

437   *"There comes a time"*: ibid., p. 104.

438   *"In Catch-22, Heller chose his targets carefully"*: Ben Macintyre, "The Perkiest of Pessimists," *The Times* (London), October 21, 1994.

438   *"richness of narrative tone"*: William H. Pritchard, "Yossarian Redux," *New York Times Book Review,* September 25, 1994; posted at nytimes.com/books/98/02/15/home/heller-closing.html.

438   *"Score one for Joseph Heller"*: Carlin Romano, "Catching Up with 'Catch-22' in 'Closing Time,'" *Philadelphia Inquirer,* October 2, 1994.

438   *"What I sense in most of these reviews"*: Straitfeld, "Catch-23," p. 105.

438   *"In . . . twenty more years"*: Heller, *Closing Time,* p. 13.

439   *"combin[e] the intensity of the [humorous] moment"*: Robert Polhemus, *Comic Faith* (Chicago: University of Chicago Press, 1980), pp. 18–19.

440   *"stimulated . . . by . . . optimism"*: Heller, *Closing Time,* p. 461.

440   *"no illusions"*: ibid., p. 462.

440   *"It's my masterpiece"*: Jerry McQueen in an e-mail to the author, July 29, 2009.

440   *"[I had heard that Heller] . . . had the reputation"*: This and subsequent quotes from the conversation between Berkman and Heller are from Meredith Berkman, "A Family Gets Together After Closing Time," *Newsday,* October 5, 1994.

441   *"How would you like to be a seventy-one-year-old certified American literary heavyweight"*: Christopher Buckley, "Gotterdammerung-22," *The New Yorker,* October 10, 1994, pp. 104, 109.

442   *"I think you know me"*: This quote and subsequent exchanges between Heller and Buckley are from their correspondence, Joseph Heller Archive.

443   *"I can't believe it"*: This and subsequent quotes and details regarding the landing of the B-25 on Long Island are from Diane Ketcham, "Long Island Journal: Writer Outgrows His B-25," *New York Times,* January 1, 1995, posted at nytimes.com/1995/01/01/nyregion/long-island-journal-488095.html; Ellen Kaiser, "It's Official," *Dan's Papers,* September 13, 1996; Irene Keller, "Catch '94," *Dan's Papers,* December 16, 1994; Renee Schilhab, "Memories of a Wartime Friend," *Southampton Press,* December 15, 1994.

445   *"[We're] not about to let you go through all this yourself"*: Erica Heller in an e-mail to the author, February 21, 2010.

446   *"It is painful for me to recall how my wife was"*: Joseph Heller, *Something Happened* (New York: Alfred A. Knopf, 1974), p. 103.

446   *"Call her"*: This and subsequent quotes and details regarding Shirley Heller's last days are from Erica Heller, draft of a memoir, *Yossarian Slept Here,* provided to the author on February 11, 2010.

447   *"[H]e showed up the night before with his sister Sylvia"*: Erica Heller in an e-mail to the author, February 11, 2010.

448   *"It feels wonderfully strange"*: David Zurawik, "Heller Impressed with TV's 'Catch-22,'" *Baltimore Sun,* September 14, 1996.

20. WHEN THEY SPEAK OF THE WAR

pages

450   *"We worked at what we could"*: Joseph Heller, rough draft of *Now and Then,* Joseph Heller Archive, Department of Rare Books and Special Collections, Thomas Cooper Library, University of South Carolina, Columbia, South Carolina.

450   *"to lose about ten of the pounds"*: This quote and subsequent exchanges between Heller and Buckley in this chapter are from their correspondence, Joseph Heller Archive.

450   *"I have a feeling"*: Heller's remarks were made during an interview on *The Charlie Rose Show,* October 24, 1994; see charlierose.com/guest/view/3857.

451   *"I've become a dyspeptic recluse"*: Michael Hirsch, "Brooklyn People," *Bay News,* August 3, 1998.

451   *There were those who*: anecdote provided to the author by an anonymous source in February 2010.

451   *One night, at a dinner party*: ibid.

451   *Friends thought Valerie seemed jealous*: ibid.

451   *"the fact of Speed"*: Erica Heller in an e-mail to the author, February 19, 2010.

452   *"Life is pretty good"*: John Cornwall, "What's the Catch?" *The Sunday Times* (London), September 18, 1994.

452   *"I'm gripped by the somber realization"*: Sylvia Rothchild, "In a New Book, Joseph Heller Remembers Where He Comes From: Despite Oxford Fellowship, Accent on Brooklyn," *Jewish Advocate,* April 23, 1998; posted at highbeam.com.

452   *"I don't think he knows himself"*: Paula Span, "Catch-23; For Joseph Heller, A Late-Life Summing Up," *Washington Post,* September 29, 1994.

452   *"I feel like the malevolent witch at the party"*: This and subsequent remarks from Heller's talk, "The Literature of Despair," were delivered at "The F. Scott Fitzgerald Centenary Celebration," September 24–26, 1996, University of South Carolina; text posted at sc .edu/fitzgerald/centenary.proceedings.html.

453   *"[T]he game is over"*: D. T. Max, "The Twilight of the Old Goats," *Salon,* May 1997; posted at salon.com/may97/goats970516.html.

454   *"amazing similarity of characters"*: This quote and Heller's and Gottlieb's comments regarding the controversy over the Falstein novel are from Michael Mewshaw, "New Questions Dog 'Catch-22'; Joseph Heller Defends Originality of '61 Classic": *Washington Post,* April 27, 1998.
      In a follow-up article on the matter, after Heller's death, Michael Mewhaw concluded that "there are indeed fundamental similarities between Catch-22 and The Sky is a Lonely Place. . . . While they don't rise to the level of plagiarism, they do suggest that Heller might have been aware of Falstein's work. . . . [He may have] written an oblique homage to Falstein. . . . Of course, in a universe of pure contingency where chaos reigns . . . it's perhaps perfectly possible that two men . . . would write hauntingly similar novels. . . . Talk about Catch-22!" See Mike Mewshaw, "Too Easy to Catch Heller Out?" *Jerusalem Post,* December 31, 1999.

454   *"books are widely disparate"*: Mel Gussow, "Critic's Notebook: Questioning the Provenance of the Iconic 'Catch-22,'" *New York Times,* April 29, 1998; posted at nytimes .com/1998/04/29/books/critic-s-notebook-questioning-the-provenance-of-the-iconic -catch-22.html.

455   *"capitalist cool"*: This was an FYI slogan.

456   *"old-fashioned ideas"*: Sally Vincent, "Portrait: Catch-94," *The Guardian,* September 24, 1994.

456   *"strange turbulent undercurrents"*: This and subsequent quotes from the interview are in Lynn Barber, "Bloody Heller," *The Observer,* March 1, 1998; posted at guardian.co.uk/books/1998/mar/01/fiction.josephheller.

459   *"No. We don't have one"*: Molly Watson, "Releasing a Rat into the New York Jet Set: Ted Heller, Son of Joseph," *Evening Standard* (London), February 9, 2000; posted at high beam.com.

459   *"Every time [Warhol mentioned] a famous name"*: Ted Heller's comment was made during an interview with Terry Gross for National Public Radio's "Fresh Air" (WHYY-FM), March 23, 2000.

459   *"I sort of have a reputation"*: ibid.

460   *"So we were sitting by Joe's pool one day"*: Deborah Karl in conversation with the author, April 18, 2009.

460   *"People would phone"*: Dolores Karl in conversation with the author, April 24, 2009.

461   *"instead of shying away"*: This and subsequent quotes and details regarding the 1999 cruise to Norway's Arctic region are from Diane Armstrong, "Heller Frozen Over," *The Guardian,* March 27, 1999; posted at guardian.co.uk/theguardian/1999/mar/27/week end7.weekend3.

463   *"What next, then?"; "The artificer who lives long enough"*: Joseph Heller, *Portrait of an Artist, as an Old Man* (New York: Simon & Schuster, 2000), pp. 19, 20–21.

463   *"incredibly expressive"*: Lois Smith Brady, "Weddings: Vows; Erica Heller, Ronald van den Boogaard," *New York Times,* November 28, 1999; posted at nytimes.com/gst/fullpage .html?res= 9B01EEDF143FF93BA15752C1A96F958260.

463   *"That evening he was sweet-tempered and subdued"*: Arthur Gelb quoted in *Salon,* text posted at salon.com/people/obit/1999/12/13/Heller.

463   *"expressed horror"*: George Mandel's remarks were made at "Joseph Heller: A Celebration," a memorial service held at the New York Society for Ethical Culture on June 13, 2000. Transcribed by the author from a video recording (courtesy of Erica Heller).

464   *"Joe was on the phone"*: Valerie Heller's remarks were written for "Joseph Heller: A Celebration."

464   *"That night . . . he became my patient again"*: ibid.

464   *"Valerie called us at about five a.m."*: Dolores Karl in conversation with the author, April 24, 2009.

465   *"Oh God, this is a calamity"*: Duncan Campbell, "Joseph Heller Is Dead at the Age of 76," *The Guardian,* December 14, 1999; posted at guardian.co.uk/books/1999/dec/14/ josephheller.

465   *"[As a novelist,] he wasn't top of the chart"*: Nicholas Roe, "Indiscreet Charm of the Bourgeoisie; Nicholas Roe Discovers That the Prolonged and Amazing Creative Life of John Updike Is Alive and Well," *Canberra Times* (Australia), January 29, 2000.

465   *"I will miss reading the books he didn't write"*: Rosemary Herbert, "Heller Remembered for His Philosophical Dimension," *Boston Herald,* December 14, 1999.

466   *"I could hardly believe my eyes"*: Erica Heller in an e-mail to the author, February 19, 2010.

466   *"When we left the grave site"*: Jerry McQueen in an e-mail to the author, July 29, 2009.

EPILOGUE: CLEANING HOUSE

pages
467   *"Two weeks [after my father died]"*: Ted Heller's comments were made during an interview with Terry Gross for National Public Radio's "Fresh Air" (WHYY-FM), March 23, 2000.

467   called the novel *"embarrassing"*: Michiko Kakutani, "Joseph Heller's Valedictory Holds a Mirror to Himself," *New York Times,* May 30, 2000.

468   *"sardonic little abdication address"*: Tim Adams, "What's the Catch?" *The Observer,* July 30, 2000; posted at guardian.co.uk/books/2000/jul/30/fiction.josephheller.

468   *"slightest but scariest"*: David Gates et al., "*Newsweek*'s Best Novels of 2000," *News-*

week, December 28, 2000; posted at newsweek.com/2000/12/27/newsweeks-best
-novels-of-2000.html.

468 *"There is something bleakly bracing"*: "Briefly Noted," *The New Yorker,* July 17, 2000, p.
81.

468 *Heller's "vision" was "tragically in synch"*: John Grant, "Gangs with Guns: Milo Mind-
bender in Afghanistan," *Counterpunch,* June 11–12, 2010; posted at www.counterpunch
.org/grant06112010.html.

468 *"Even when it's fouling its own nest"*: William Wiles, "What *Catch-22* Tells Us about the
BP Spill," posted at www.newstatesman.com/blogs/cultural-capital/2010/06/syndicate
-milo-share-pension.

469 *"Heller is among the novelists of the last [few] decades who matter"*: Thomas Edwards,
The New York Review of Books, April 5, 1979, p. 20.

469 *"[Catch-22] still blows me away"*: Keith Staskiewicz, "Carl Hiaasen on Movie Adaptations, Dostoevsky, and Buying Historical Novels," posted at shelf-life.ew/com/2010/08/12/
carl-hiaasen-star-siland.

469 *"Joseph Heller found"*: Adam Mars-Jones, review of *Matterhorn,* by Karl Marlantes, in
The Observer, August 15, 2010; posted at guardian.co.uk/books/2010/aug/15/
matterhorn-karl-marlantes-vietnam-war.

469 *"Veterans of the Second World War"*: Jeffrey Toobin, "After Stevens," *The New Yorker,*
March 22, 2010, p. 43.

470 *"[E]xactly who owns the rights"*: Mokoto Rich, "Legal Battles Over E-Book Rights to
Older Books," *The New York Times,* December 13, 2009; posted at nytimes
.com/2009/12/13/business/media/13ebooks.html.

470 *"9/11 . . . Saddam Hussein's hanging"*: Christopher Buckley, "Catch-2009," *New York
Times,* December 12, 2009; posted at nytimes.com/2009/12/12/opinion/12buckley.html.

470 *"In the early 1980s, I was cleaning houses"*: Margaret Dawe in an e-mail to the author,
July 10, 2009.

BIBLIOGRAPHY

FICTION BY JOSEPH HELLER

Catch-22. New York: Simon & Schuster, 1961.
Something Happened. New York: Alfred A. Knopf, 1974.
Good as Gold. New York: Simon & Schuster, 1979.
God Knows. New York: Alfred A. Knopf, 1984.
Picture This. New York: G. P. Putnam's Sons, 1988.
Closing Time. New York: Simon & Schuster, 1994.
Portrait of an Artist, as an Old Man. New York: Simon & Schuster, 2000.
Catch as Catch Can: The Collected Stories and Other Writings. Edited by Matthew J. Bruccoli and Park Bucker. New York: Simon & Schuster, 2003.

MEMOIRS BY JOSEPH HELLER

No Laughing Matter, coauthored with Speed Vogel. New York: Simon & Schuster, 1986.
Now and Then: From Coney Island to Here. New York: Alfred A. Knopf, 1998.

PLAYS BY JOSEPH HELLER

We Bombed in New Haven. New York: Alfred A. Knopf, 1968.
Catch-22: A Dramatization. New York: Samuel French, 1971.
Clevinger's Trial. New York: Samuel French, 1973.

MOTION PICTURE SCREENPLAYS BY JOSEPH HELLER

Sex and the Single Girl, with David R. Schwartz. Warner Bros., 1964.
Casino Royale (uncredited). Columbia Pictures, 1967.
Dirty Dingus Magee, with Tom Waldman and Frank Waldman. Metro-Goldwyn-Mayer, 1970.

INTERVIEWS WITH JOSEPH HELLER

Sorkin, Adam J., ed. *Conversations with Joseph Heller.* Jackson: University Press of Mississippi, 1993.

UNCOLLECTED PROSE BY JOSEPH HELLER

"Too Timid to Damn, Too Stingy to Applaud." *New Republic,* July 1962, 23–24, 36.
"How I Found James Bond." *Holiday,* June 1967, 123–25.

BOOKS ABOUT JOSEPH HELLER

Bloom, Harold, ed. *Joseph Heller's Catch-22.* Philadelphia: Chelsea House, 2001.
Craig, David M. *Tilting at Mortality: Narrative Strategies in Joseph Heller's Fiction.* Detroit: Wayne State University Press, 1997.
Kiley, Frederick, and Walter McDonald, eds. *A "Catch-22" Casebook.* New York: Thomas Y. Crowell, 1973.
Merrill, Robert. *Joseph Heller.* Boston: Twayne, 1987.
Nagel, James, ed. *Critical Essays on 'Catch-22.'* Encino, California: Dickenson, 1974.
————, ed. *Critical Essays on Joseph Heller.* Boston: G. K. Hall, 1984.
Pinsker, Sanford. *Understanding Joseph Heller.* Columbia: University of South Carolina Press, 1991.
Potts, Stephen W. *From Here to Absurdity: The Moral Battlefields of Joseph Heller.* San Bernardino, California: Borgo Press, 1995.
Ruderman, Judith. *Joseph Heller.* New York: Continuum, 1991.
Scotto, Robert M., ed. *Joseph Heller's Catch-22: A Critical Edition.* New York: Delta, 1973.
Seed, David. *The Fiction of Joseph Heller: Against the Grain.* New York: St. Martin's Press, 1989.
Woodson, Jon. *A Study of Catch-22: Going Around Twice.* New York: Peter Lang, 2001.

ONLINE

Setzer, Daniel. "Historical Sources for the Events in Joseph Heller's Novel, *Catch-22.* home.com cast.net/~dhsetzer.

BIBLIOGRAPHIES AND BIBLIOGRAPHICAL ARTICLES

Bruccoli, Matthew J., and Park Bucker, eds. *Joseph Heller: A Descriptive Bibliography.* New Castle, Delaware: Oak Knoll Press, 2002.
Eller, Jonathan R. "Catching a Market: The Publishing History of *Catch-22.*" *Prospects* 17 (1992): 475–525.
Keegan, Brenda M. *Joseph Heller: A Reference Guide.* Boston: G. K. Hall, 1978.
Scotto, Robert M. *Three Contemporary Novelists: An Annotated Bibliography of Works by and about John Hawkes, Joseph Heller, and Thomas Pynchon.* New York: Garland, 1977.
Weixmann, Joseph. "A Bibliography of Joseph Heller's *Catch-22.*" *Bulletins of Bibliography* 31 (1974): 32–37.

SELECTED CRITICAL BOOKS WITH SECTIONS OR CHAPTERS ON JOSEPH HELLER

Aichinger, Peter. *The American Soldier in Fiction, 1880–1963.* Des Moines: Iowa State University Press, 1975.
Bier, Jesse. *The Rise and Fall of American Humor.* New York: Henry Holt, 1968.
Bryant, Jerry H. *The Open Decision: The Contemporary American Novel and Its Intellectual Background.* New York: Free Press, 1970.
Burgess, Anthony. *The Novel Now: A Guide to Contemporary Fiction.* New York: W. W. Norton, 1967.

Dickstein, Morris. *Leopards in the Temple: The Transformation of American Fiction, 1945–1970*. Cambridge: Harvard University Press, 2002.

Harris, Charles B. *Contemporary American Novelists of the Absurd*. New Haven: College and University Press, 1971.

Hauck, Richard Boyd. *A Cheerful Nihilism: Confidence and the Absurd in American Humorous Fiction*. Bloomington: Indiana University Press, 1971.

Karl, Frederick. *American Fictions 1940–1980*. New York: Harper & Row, 1983.

Kazin, Alfred. *Bright Book of Life: American Novelists and Storytellers from Hemingway to Mailer*. Boston: Little, Brown, 1973.

Kostelanetz, Richard, ed. *On Contemporary Literature*. New York: Avon, 1964.

Miller, Wayne Charles. *An Armed America, Its Face in Fiction: A History of the American Military Novel*. New York: New York University Press, 1970.

Moore, Harry T., ed. *Contemporary American Novelists*. Carbondale: Southern Illinois University Press, 1965.

Olderman, Raymond M. *Beyond the Waste Land: The American Novel in the 1960's*. New Haven: Yale University Press, 1972.

Podhoretz, Norman. *Doings and Undoings: The Fifties and After in American Writing*. New York: Farrar, Straus, 1964.

Richter, D. H. *Fable's End: Completeness and Closure in Rhetorical Fiction*. Chicago: University of Chicago Press, 1974.

Scott, Nathan A., ed. *Adversity and Grace: Studies in Recent American Literature*. Chicago: University of Chicago Press, 1968.

Tanner, Tony. *City of Words: American Fiction, 1950–1970*. New York: Harper & Row, 1971.

SELECTED CRITICAL ARTICLES ON JOSEPH HELLER

Aldridge, John W. "The Deceits of Black Humor." *Harpers*, March 1979, 115–18.

Aubrey, James R. "Heller's 'Parody on Hemingway' in *Catch-22*." *Studies in Contemporary Satire* 17 (1990): 1–5.

———. "Major –de Coverly's Name in *Catch-22*." *Notes on Contemporary Literature* 18, no. 1 (1988): 2–3.

Beidler, Philip. "Mr. Roberts and American Remembering; or, Why Major Major Major Major Looks Like Henry Fonda." *Journal of American Studies* 30, no. 1 (1996): 47.

Bertonneau, Thomas F. "The Mind Bound Round: Language and Reality in Heller's *Catch-22*." *Studies in American Jewish Literature* 15 (1996): 29–41.

Blues, Thomas. "The Moral Structure of *Catch-22*." *Studies in the Novel* 3 (Spring 1971): 64–97.

Bradbury, Malcolm. Introduction to *Catch-22*. New York: Alfred A. Knopf, 1995.

Burhans, Clinton S., Jr. "Spindrift and the Sea: Structural Patterns and Unifying Elements in *Catch-22*." *Twentieth Century Literature* 19 (1973): 239–50.

Caciedo, Alberto. "You Must Remember This: Trauma and Memory in *Catch-22* and *Slaughterhouse-Five*." *Critique: Studies in Contemporary Fiction* 46, no. 4 (2005): 357–68.

Cheuse, Alan. "Laughing on the Outside." *Studies on the Left* 3 (1963): 81–87.

Costa, Richard Howard. "Notes from a Dark Heller: Bob Slocum and the Underground Man." *Texas Studies in Literature and Language* 23, no. 2 (1981): 159–82.

Craig, David. "Rewriting a Classic and Thinking about a Life: Joseph Heller's *Closing Time*." *CEA Critic* 58, no. 3 (1996): 15–30.

Davis, Gary W. "*Catch-22* and the Language of Discontinuity." *Novel* 12, no. 1 (1978): 66–77.

Day, Douglas. "*Catch-22*: A Manifesto for Anarchists." *Carolina Quarterly* 15, no. 3 (1963): 86–92.

Doskow, Minna. "The Night Journey in *Catch-22*." *Twentieth Century Literature* 12 (1967): 186–93.

Frank, Mike. "Eros and Thanatos in *Catch-22*." *Canadian Review of American Studies* 7 (1976): 77–87.

Friedman, John, and Judith Ruderman. "Joseph Heller and the 'Real' King David." *Judaism* 36, no. 3 (1987): 296–301.

Furlani, Andre. "'Brisk Socratic Dialogues': Elenctic Rhetoric in Joseph Heller's *Something Happened.*" *Narrative* 3, no. 3 (1995): 252–70.

Galloway, David. "Clown and Saint: The Hero in Current American Fiction." *Critique* 7, no. 3 (1965): 46–65.

Gaukroger, Doug. "Time Structure in *Catch-22.*" *Studies in Modern Fiction* 12, no. 2 (1970): 70–85.

Granger, Jamie. "Love During Wartime: Adam and Eve in *Catch-22.*" *Pleiades* 14, no. 2 (1994): 79–85.

Green, Daniel. "A World Worth Laughing At: *Catch-22* and the Humor of Black Humor." *Studies in the Novel* 27, no. 2 (1995): 186–96.

Greenfield, Josh. "22 Was Funnier Than 14." *New York Times Book Review,* March 3, 1968, 1, 49–51, 53.

Henry, G. B. McK. "Significant Corn: *Catch-22.*" *Melbourne Critical Review* 9 (1966): 133–44.

Hewes, Henry. "A Game for Our Sons." *The Saturday Review,* November 2, 1968, 53.

Hidalgo-Dowling, Laura. "Negation as a Stylistic Feature in *Catch-22*: A Corpus Study." *Style* 37, no. 3 (2003): 318–41.

Kazin, Alfred. "The War Novel from Mailer to Vonnegut." *The Saturday Review,* February 6, 1971, 13–15, 36.

Kennard, Jean E. "Joseph Heller: At War with Absurdity." *Mosaic* 4, no. 3 (1971): 75–87.

Klemptner, Susan S. "A Permanent Game of Excuses: Determinism in Heller's *Something Happened.*" *Modern Fiction Studies* 24 (1978–1979): 550–56.

LeClair, Thomas. "Death and Black Humor." *Critique* 17, no. 1 (1975): 5–40.

———. "Joseph Heller, *Something Happened,* and the Art of Excess." *Studies in American Fiction* 9, no. 2 (1981): 245–60.

Lowin, Joseph. "The Jewish Art of Joseph Heller." *Jewish Book Annual* 43 (1985–1986): 141–53.

McDonald, James L. "I See Everything Twice: The Structure of Joseph Heller's *Catch-22.*" *University Review* 34 (1968): 175–80.

Mellard, James M. "*Catch-22*: Déjà Vu and the Labyrinth of Memory." *Bucknell Review* 16 (1968): 29–44.

Merrill, Robert. "The Structure and Meaning of *Catch-22.*" *Studies in American Fiction* 14, no. 2 (1986): 139–52.

Merrill, Robert, and John L. Simons. "Snowden's Ghost: The Waking Nightmare of Mike Nichols's *Catch-22.*" *New Orleans Review* 15, no. 2 (1988): 96–104.

Miller, Wayne C. "Ethnic Identity as Moral Focus: A Reading of Joseph Heller's *Good as Gold.*" *MELUS* 6, no. 3 (1979): 3–17.

Monk, Donald. "An Experiment in Therapy: A Study of *Catch-22.*" *London Review* 2 (1967): 12–19.

Moore, Michael. "Pathological Communication Patterns in Heller's 'Catch-22.'" *ETC: A Review of General Semantics,* December 22, 1995. Posted online at freelibrary.com.

Muste, John M. "Better to Die Laughing: The War Novels of Joseph Heller and John Ashmead." *Critique* 5, no. 2 (1962): 16–27.

Nagel, James. "The *Catch-22* Note Cards." *Studies in the Novel* 8 (1976): 394–405.

———. "Joseph Heller and the University." *College Literature* 10, no. 1 (1983): 16–27.

Nelson, Thomas Allen. "Theme and Structure in *Catch-22.*" *Renascence* 23, no. 4 (1971): 173–82.

Nolan, Charles J., Jr. "Heller's Small Debt to Hemingway." *The Hemingway Review* 9, no. 1 (1989): 77–81.

Pinsker, Sanford. "Once More into the Breach: Joseph Heller Gives *Catch-22* a Second Act." *Topic: A Journal of the Liberal Arts* 50 (2000): 28–39.

Pearson, Carol. "*Catch-22* and the Debasement of Language." *CEA Critic* 38, no. 4 (1976): 30–35.

Percy, Walker. "The State of the Novel: Dying Art or New Science?" *Michigan Quarterly Review* 16 (1977): 359–73.

Pletcher, Robert. "Overcoming the 'Catch-22' of Institutional Satire: Joseph Heller's 'Surrealistic' Characters." *Studies in Contemporary Satire* 15 (1988): 220–27.

Protherough, Robert. "The Sanity of *Catch-22*." *Human World* 3 (1971): 59–70.

Raeburn, John. "*Catch-22* and the Culture of the 1950s." *American Studies in Scandinavia* 25, no. 2 (1993): 119–28.

Robertson, Joan. "They're After Everyone: Heller's 'Catch-22' and the Cold War." *CLIO* 19, no. 1 (1989): 41–50.

Ruderman, Judith. "Upside-Down in *Good as Gold*: Moishe Kapoyer as Muse." *Yiddish* 4 (1984): 55–63.

Savu, Laura Elena. "'This Book of Ours': The Crisis of Authorship and Joseph Heller's *Portrait of an Artist, as an Old Man.*" *Intertexts* 7, no. 1 (2003): 71–89.

Scoggins, Michael C. "Joseph Heller's Combat Experiences in *Catch-22*." *War, Literature, and the Arts* 15, nos. 1 and 2 (2003): 213–37.

Searles, George J. "*Something Happened*: A New Direction for Joseph Heller." *Critique* 18, no. 3 (1977): 74–82.

Seltzer, Leon F. "Milo's Culpable Innocence: Absurdity as Moral Insanity in *Catch-22*." *Papers on Language and Literature* 15, no. 3 (1979): 290–310.

Sniderman, Stephen L. "It Was All Yossarian's Fault: Power and Responsibility in *Catch-22*." *Twentieth Century Literature* 19, no. 4 (1973): 251–58.

Solomon, Eric. "From Christ in Flanders to *Catch-22*: An Approach to War Fiction." *Texas Studies in Language and Literature* 11 (1969): 851–66.

Solomon, Jan. "The Structure of Joseph Heller's *Catch-22*." *Critique* 9, no. 2 (1967): 46–67.

Stern, Frederick C. "Heller's Hell: Heller's Later Fiction, Jewishness, and the Liberal Imagination." *MELUS* 15, no. 4 (1988): 15–37.

Strehle, Susan. "Slocum's Parenthetical Tic: Style as Metaphor in *Something Happened*." *Notes on Contemporary Literature* 7, no. 5 (1977): 9–10.

———. "'A Permanent Game of Excuses': Determinism in Heller's *Something Happened*." *Modern Fiction Studies* 24, no. 4 (1978–1979): 550–56.

Toman, Marshall. "The Political Satire in Joseph Heller's *Good as Gold*." *Studies in Contemporary Satire* 17 (1990): 6–14.

———. "*Good as Gold* and Heller's Family Ethic." *Studies in American Jewish Literature* 10, no. 2 (1991): 211–24.

Tucker, Lindsey. "Entropy and Information Theory in Heller's *Something Happened*." *Contemporary Literature* (1984): 323–40.

Tyson, Lois. "Joseph Heller's *Something Happened*: The Commodification of Consciousness and the Postmodern Flight from Inwardness." *CEA Critic* 54, no. 2 (1992): 37–51.

Wain, John. "A New Novel about Old Troubles." *Critical Quarterly* 5, no. 2 (1963): 168–173.

Way, Brian. "Formal Experiment and Social Discontent: Joseph Heller's *Catch-22*." *Journal of American Studies* 2 (1968): 253–70.

JH stands for Joseph Heller. Books and stories are by JH unless otherwise noted.

Orthodox Jews, 437
Orvieto, 85
Osner Business Machines, 316
Oxford University, 137–38, 450

Paddy Shea's saloon, Coney Island, 56
The Pages That Sell (slide show), 215
Palestine, 105
Paley, Grace, 197, 469
Pantheon, 333
panty raids, 170
paperback books, 131–32
Parachute Jump, Coney Island, 101–2,
    437
Paramount/Filmways, 307
Paramount Pictures, 343
Parfrey, Adam, 195
    *It's a Man's World: Men's Adventure
    Magazines, the Postwar Pulps,* 193
Paris, France, 137
Parish, Mitchell, 255
Parker, Jimmie, 10
Parsons, Estelle, 291
Partini, Dolly, 53
Partisan Review, 170–71, 195
Pastrudi's, Cairo, 94
Payne Whitney Psychiatric Clinic, New York
    Hospital, 165, 362
Peck, Abe, 275, 328
Peck or Beck, Miss, 60, 62
Peloponnesian War, 419
Pennsylvania State College, 138–52, 160,
    236–37, 319
Pentagon, 307
Pentagon Papers, 505n302
People, 381
Pepsi-Cola, 56
Percy, Walker, *The Moviegoer,* 230
Perelman, S. J., 225, 229
Philbin, Regis, 425
Phillipe (pet dog), 423, 424, 429, 464
Phillips, William, 170
Picasso, Pablo, 180
    Guernica, 294
Picker, David, 272
Picture This (novel), 415–21, 430
    reviews of, 420–21
Pietrasanta, 86, 266, 271–72
Pinsker, Sanford, 408
Pirandello, Luigi, 290
P. J. Clarke's, 253
Plato, 247, 276, 330, 413, 414–15, 444
    Phaedrus, 415
Plato's Retreat (sex club), 368
Playboy, 195, 275–76
Plimpton, George, 205, 258, 259, 329, 425,
    508n334
PM, 58
Pocket Books, 202
Podhoretz, Norman, 190, 246, 258, 259, 333,
    336–39, 349, 351, 410
    Ex-Friends, 338
    Making It, 336–37
    "My Negro Problem—and Ours," 337

Poe, Edgar Allan, 135, 452
Poggibonsi, 4, 85
Pointe des Issambres, 1
Polhemus, Robert, 439
politics
    JH's insight into, 43
    post-World War II, 128–29
Pollock, Jackson, 425, 428
Pollock, Lewis, 454
Polykoff, Shirley, 159–60
    Does She . . . or Doesn't She? 160, 161–62
Pompeii, Italy, 81
Pont-Saint-Martin, 88–89
Port Authority Bus Terminal, 433, 439
Porter, Arabel J., 177, 179–83, 188, 200
Portrait of an Artist, as an Old Man (novel), 453,
    458, 460, 462–63, 467–68
    conception and writing of, 453, 458
    publication planned, 462–63
    reviews, 467–68
Port Said, 94
postmodernism, 196
poverty, threat of, 58
Preminger, Otto, 148
Prentiss, Paula, 312
presidential election of 1968, 297–99, 302
Presley, Elvis, 207
Pritchard, William H., 438
Pritikin Institute, 450
proletarian fiction, 130–31, 167
prostitutes, 14
Provenzano, Tony, 36, 44
Provenzano family, 34, 44
PS 188, Coney Island, 38–39
Psalms, 224
"PT 73, Where Are You?" 256–57
Publishers Weekly, 239
publishing business, 203–4, 212, 217, 231, 316,
    339, 405–6, 469–70
pulp fiction, 131–32
Putnam, 407
Putnam Berkley, 412, 430–31
Puzo, Erika, 341
Puzo, Mario, 120, 193, 198, 250–51, 279, 282,
    341–42, 360, 367, 372–73, 375, 380, 386,
    389, 395, 416, 426–27, 462
    The Godfather, 416
Pynchon, Thomas, 179, 365–66, 432, 460
    V, 240

Rabinowitz, Murray, 36
Rafaello, S.S., 265
Rainer, Yvonne, 508n334
Random House, 217, 332–33
rationing, wartime, 22
Rauschenberg, Robert, 191, 508n334
Raynor, Richard, 420
RCA, 332–33
Reader's Digest, 14, 133, 171, 172
Reagan, Ronald, 338, 351, 361
The Realist, 260–62, 274
rebellion, spirit of, 207, 328
Rebel Without a Cause (film), 207
Redbook, 162

Sellers, Peter, 270
Sencer, Walter, 369
September 11, 2001, terrorist event, 223
Setzer, Daniel, 84, 89, 93
"Seven against the Sea" (TV drama), 253–54
Seventies, 328–29
Sex and the Single Girl (film), 268–69
"Sex in Literature" (panel discussion), 254
sexual morality, 133, 170–71, 247
shadchans (marriage brokers), 20
Shakespeare, William, 137–38, 284, 290, 293, 392, 402, 403
Shaw, Don, 382
Shaw, Irwin, 13, 52, 103, 115, 225, 334, 425
Sheehy, Gail, 425
Shepherd, Jean, 274
Sheresky, Norman M., 369, 380–81
Shipman, Robert Oliver, 144, 236–37
Shirer, William, *The Rise and Fall of the Third Reich,* 213
Shorter, Mr. (worked for Western Union), 58
Show, 230, 336
Shuttleworth, Jack, 410
Siegel, Nat, 35, 38
Siena, Italy, 267
Silvers, Robert, 259
Simon, Dan, 343
Simon, Dick, 202, 204, 224
Simon, Gladys, 54
Simon, Henry, 207
Simon, Neil, 38, 145
  The Odd Couple, 249
Simon, Paul, 506n311
Simon & Schuster, 202–6, 212–20, 224–25, 230–34, 236–40, 316–17, 342–45, 365, 370, 379, 386, 431–32, 459, 462
Sinatra, Frank, 87, 216, 270
Sinclair, Upton, 451
Singer, Isaac Bashevis, 20, 230
Singer, Israel, 20
sitting shivah, 33
Sixties, 190–91, 245–47, 273–77, 303–4
S. Klein's, 59
Sloan, Tom, 14, 94
Sloan-Kettering, 445–46
Slocum, Bob (character), 264, 288, 330–32
Slum Clearance Committee, 157
Smith, Cork, 178
Smith, Gordon, 144
Smith, Liz, 389, 393
Snoqualmie Valley (Washington) School District, 509n339
Snowden (character), 187, 222, 223–24, 439
Snyder, Richard E., 343–44, 431–32
Sobel, Dava, 449
socialism, 29, 43
Socrates, 330–31, 364, 415, 418
"Sodom by the Sea," 26
Solotaroff, Ted, 336, 338–39
Something Happened (novel), 246, 264, 278–83, 287–89, 302–3, 315–33, 350, 379, 389, 392, 405, 457, 458, 468
  conception and writing of, 245, 252, 264, 321–23

critical assessment of, 327
  early published extracts, 287–89, 323
  editing and revisions, 324–25
  JH's assessment of, 331
  publication and sales, 327
  publicity for, 326
  reviews of, 326–27
"something happened" (shout), 316
Sontag, Susan, 258, 469, 508n334
Southern, Terry, 270, 276, 508n334
South Figueroa Street, Los Angeles, 112–13
Special Committee on Un-American Activities, 146
Spillane, Mickey, 131, 132, 166
Spinoza, 416–17
Spitz, Bob, 273
Spock, Benjamin, 262–63, 274
  The Pocket Book of Baby and Child Care, 196
Sports Illustrated, 172
Spy, 459
Stafford, Jean, 123, 230, 425
Stan Kenton's Orchestra, 98
Staten Island, 428
Steeplechase Park, Coney Island, 27, 36, 37, 65, 67, 282, 378, 439
Stein, Gertrude, 130
Stein, Harry, 374
Stein, Joe, 250, 300–301, 360, 372, 373, 374
Steinbeck, John, 130, 241, 275, 425
  The Grapes of Wrath, 114, 130
  In Dubious Battle, 130
  The Winter of Our Discontent, 229
Steinfels, Peter, 349
Stern, Richard, 228
Stevens, John Paul, 469
Stevenson, Adlai, 164
Stimson, Henry L., 100
Stohl, Phyllis, 147–48
Stone, Irving, *The Agony and the Ecstasy,* 229
Stone, Robert, 179, 205, 449
Story, 22, 102, 104, 116, 139
Straitfeld, David, 229, 430
Stretton, Trudi, 388
Strongsville, Ohio, Board of Education, 509n339
Stuart, Lyle, 195, 260
Student Non-Violent Coordinating Committee (SNCC), 274
Students for a Democratic Society, 298
Styron, William, 84, 96, 102, 334, 351
  Sophie's Choice, 351
suburbanization, 190
success, gospel of, 333, 336–40
Sullivan, Miss, 62
Sulzberger, Arthur Hays, 384–85
Superman, 55
Surprise Lake camp, 38
Susann, Jacqueline, 313
Swaim, Don, 189
Sweeney (pet dog), 342, 423
Swift, Jonathan, 138, 258
Swindell, Larry, 326
Sylbert, Richard, 306

Warhol, Andy, 191, 459
Warner, Time, 406
Warner Bros., 268
war novels, 125–32, 150, 185, 211, 237–38, 449
Warshow, Robert, 127
Washington Post, 454
Washington Square Park, 109
Wasserman, Harriet, 179, 318
Waterbury, Jean Parker, 176
Watergate affair, 343, 350
Watts district, Los Angeles, 113–14
Waugh, Evelyn, 129, 169, 176, 186, 225
Wayne, John, 311
Weatherby, W. J., 233
Weathermen, 304
We Bombed in New Haven (play), 284, 289–96, 299–303, 468, 503n284
  Broadway production, 300–302
  rehearsals, 293–94
  reviews, 295–96, 301–2
Weidman, Jerome, *I Can Get It for You Wholesale,* 117
Weinstein, Raymond M., 191
Weintraub, Stanley, 152
Welles, Orson, 307, 311
Wells, Mary, 161
Wertham, Fredric, *Seduction of the Innocents,* 194
West, Jessamyn, 123
West, Nathanael, 117, 130, 147
  The Day of the Locust, 114
West 11th Street, New York, bombing, 304–5
West 76th Street apartment, 110–11, 135–36
West End Bar, New York, 128
"Western Craze," 9
Western Union, 57, 58–61
West Side, New York City, 157–59
Weybright, Victor, 179–83
Whitman, Walt, 26, 52
Who's Afraid of Virginia Woolf?, 307
Whyte, William, *The Organization Man,* 315
Wiese, Otis, 172
Wiesel, Elie, 465
Wieseltier, Leon, 351, 400
Wietrak, Bob, 437
Wilder, Billy, 270
Wiles, William, 468
William Morrow, 406
Williams, Tennessee, 180
Willkie, Wendell, 60
Wilson, Sloan, 163
  The Man in the Gray Flannel Suit, 315
Wilson, Victoria, 178, 343
Winkler, Marvin "Beansy," 31, 36, 39, 48, 65, 136, 190, 379, 436
Winkler family, 31
Wiswell, George, 124

WNYC, 49
Wodehouse, P. G., 52
Wojciechowska, Maia, 366
Wolfe, Thomas (1920s writer), 116, 234
Wolfe, Tom, 316
Woman's Home Companion, 118
women, seducing, 90
Women Airforce Service Pilots (WASPs), 10–11
women's magazine fiction, 132–33
Women's Studies, 262
Wonder Wheel, Coney Island, 437
Wood, David, 99
Wood, Joanne, 365, 366, 372, 378, 393
Wood, Natalie, 269
Wood, Paul S., 139
Woodstock Nation, 247
Woodward, Bob, 343
  and Carl Bernstein, *All the President's Men,* 343
Woolf, Virginia, 130
The World Is Not Enough (film), 464
World War II, 57–58, 84, 128–29, 203, 241, 291, 298, 351, 384, 410–11
  end of, 102
  end stage of, 84
  generation, 469
  rationing, 22
  U.S. enters, 66–67
  veterans, 9–10, 110–11, 246–47, 315
WQXR, 64, 172, 373
Wright, Richard, *Black Boy,* 130
writers, common in Long Island, 425–26
Writers Guild of America, 257

Yale Draft Refusal Committee, 295
Yale Drama School, 290–91, 295, 319, 418
Yale Repertory Theatre, 291–96, 301
Yardley, Jonathan, 420–21
Yates, Richard, *Revolutionary Road,* 315
Yeats, W. B., 52
Yellin, Pauline, 481n48
Yellow Submarine, 271–73
Yiddish humor, 220, 222, 224, 351–52
Yiddish language, 28, 37, 56, 195, 247
Yiddish theater, 20, 146, 289, 292–93, 302, 312
YMCA, Westside, New York, 282, 319–20, 358
Yohannan, Francis "Yo-Yo," 5, 77, 82, 88, 218
Yom Kippur War, 338
Yossarian (character), 183, 187, 221, 223, 238, 438
"Your Hit Parade," 35
Your Show of Shows, 145, 249, 257

Zabar's, 364, 504n295
Ziegler, Ronald, 335, 350
Zionism, 105